The Practice
of Writing

FIFTH EDITION

The Practice of Writing

Robert Scholes
Brown University

Nancy R. Comley
Queens College, CUNY

Janice Peritz
Queens College, CUNY

BEDFORD/ST. MARTIN'S   Boston ◆ New York

For Bedford/St. Martin's

Developmental Editors: Simon Glick, Mark Gallaher
Production Editor: Harold Chester
Senior Production Supervisor: Cheryl Mamaril
Marketing Manager: Brian Wheel
Art Direction and Cover Design: Lucy Krikorian
Cover Art: Saul Steinberg, *Self Portrait*, 1945. Ink and graphite on paper. 12 ¾″ ×
    9 ¼″ (32.4 × 23.5 cm). Private collection. Photography by Ellen Page Wilson,
    courtesy of Pace Wildenstein. ©2001 Saul Steinberg, ©2000 Estate of Saul
    Steinberg / Artists Rights Society (ARS), New York.
Text Design: Wanda Kossak
Photo Research: Inge King
Composition: Pine Tree Composition, Inc.
Printing and Binding: RR Donnelley & Sons Company

President: Charles H. Christensen
Editorial Director: Joan E. Feinberg
Editor in Chief: Nancy Perry
Director of Marketing: Karen R. Melton
Director of Editing, Design, and Production: Marcia Cohen
Managing Editor: Erica T. Appel

Library of Congress Control Number: 00–104678

Manufactured in the United States of America.

6 5 4 3 2 1
f e d c b a

For information, write: Bedford/St. Martin's, 75 Arlington Street, Boston, MA 02116
(617–399–4000)

ISBN: 0–312–20105–2

Acknowledgments

To our students, who have taught us so much

Practice, practice. Put your hope in that.
                                        W. S. MERWIN

Preface

This book is devoted to the practice of writing. It presents more opportunities for writing—"practices," as we call them—than anything else. The book also contains numerous "readings." This is so because we believe that, just as talking involves listening, and drawing involves looking, writing involves reading. The readings in this book are not meant to be put upon pedestals and admired, however admirable they may be. They are there to be worked with and responded to—in writing. They are there to be transformed, imitated, analyzed, argued with, and incorporated into new writing by the students who use this book.

Actually, there is more material here then anyone could possibly use in a single quarter or semester. The reason for this abundance is to provide instructors with options, choices, flexibility. After the first chapter, which is introductory, the writing opportunities move from the personal to the more impersonal and academic. The weight of the book, however, falls upon the more academic or critical kinds of writings, the forms and processes required for college courses. Thus, the last four chapters emphasize the kinds of analysis, argumentation, and synthesis required in research papers.

Obviously, we think that work in all the forms of writing is useful, or we would not have included them all in the book. But we understand also that there are many reasons why an instructor may wish to touch only lightly on the materials in Parts One and Two, in order to concentrate heavily on Parts Three and Four. The book is designed to allow for this emphasis. There is, in fact, more material in every part than would be needed if all the parts were emphasized equally. The instructor will find that this text will support any emphasis that he or she chooses to make, though we have anticipated an emphasis on analysis, argument, and synthesis, providing the greatest depth in those chapters.

Within each chapter we present a particular form of writing, beginning with the most basic kinds of practice and moving toward more extended and demanding assignments. Using the chapter introduction, the first reading/practice set, and one further set will allow an instructor to treat a particular chapter without lingering over it for too long; there is enough variety so that the second assignment can be chosen to suit the interests and capabilities of a given class.

However, this book also lends itself to a portfolio approach to the teaching of writing. After doing a number of different practices in a chapter or unit, the student writer might choose one to develop, revise, and edit as a paper for public presentation and evaluation.

Although we think the order in which we present the forms of writing in this book makes sense, we have tried not to be dogmatic. The forms of writing may in fact be introduced in any order, so long as the arrangement leads to synthesis at the end. In the chapter on synthesis, we have provided sufficient material so that library research is not necessary, but many of the suggested assignments there can be expanded and enriched by library work if the instructor desires it.

NEW TO THIS EDITION

Users of previous editions may be interested in knowing the rationale for what we retained and what we changed in the present edition. As the table of contents indicates, we have continued to use a framework that differentiates writing practices by discursive orientation and form. Chapters 3–10 cover the forms of writing that students will use in all of their college courses—reflection, expression, narration, description, classification, analysis, direction and persuasion, and argumentation—while Chapter 11, on synthesis, encourages them to apply these forms to larger topics.

As pragmatists whose primary commitment is to further the practice of writing, we took seriously what instructors in the field had to say about our framework; since most of them reported it worked well, we were inclined to retain it. That inclination was reinforced by our own experiences as composition teachers. Our only change was to merge the chapters on direction and persuasion, thus moving persuasion closer to argument, as many reviewers suggested.

Although we support the recent turn to cultural studies, it is our experience that students need a practical way to work through questions of identity, knowledge, and power. And so, we decided to retain the arrangement by forms of writing, while revising the titles and subtitles in Parts Two, Three, Four, and Five that signal this cultural emphasis. In addition we have provided short essays on self, knowledge, and power at the beginning of each of these parts to further clarify and emphasize the cultural emphasis.

New topics, fresh voices

Similar principles guided our review of each of the readings. When instructors in the field agreed that an assignment worked well in their classrooms, we were inclined to retain it. Such was the case with "The Job Letter and Résumé" and "Analyzing Images of Women in Advertising."

Yet half of the readings in this edition are new. Based on reviewer responses, less successful or little-used material was either dropped or replaced with readings and practices that are likely to be more effective and appealing. So, for example, we dropped "Indirection," and Gabriel García Márquez's magic realism was replaced with "Half a Day," a Naguib Mahfouz story that manipulates time. Other new readings include selections from writers such as Julia Child and Craig Claiborne, Paul Auster, Patricia Nelson Limerick, Brent Staples, Gary Wills, Sherry Turkle, and Sharon Olds.

Finally, the chapter on argumentation was almost completely revised, so as to better represent various strategies and current issues, such as school choice. In choosing new material, we have striven to preserve the balance between high and low culture, the academic and the everyday, that has distinguished *The Practice of Writing*.

Enhanced use of visual images

To strengthen critical reading of visual texts, we have included two new essays on analyzing advertising images and interpreting video texts. We have also added new images throughout the text including contemporary photographs, advertisements, film stills, and computer screen shots.

Increased coverage of the writing process

To support our commitment to practice, we have followed instructors' responses by adding increased coverage of the writing process in a new chapter on "Writing as a Process" (Chapter 2). At the same time, we have kept short the chapter introductions to each form of writing, saying just enough to get students started on the readings, questions, and practices that follow. In working through this material, both teachers and students will find numerous opportunities to clarify, complicate, and challenge our introductory remarks about a specific form of writing. As in prior editions, our general principle has been to begin with a reading and practice that clarify, to move through a set of assignments that complicate, and to end with a reading and practice that challenge.

Longer readings and assignments

New to this edition are three sets of *projects*. You will find the terms *practice* and *project* used throughout the text. The term practice designates shorter assignments that can be used as ways to get started, as exercises in the use of a particular form of writing, or as shorter, self-contained essays. Practices frequently work toward a pair of longer projects; Parts Two, Three, and Four are each followed by such a pair. The two projects always take the same form—a "Getting It Together" project followed by a "Taking It Further" project.

For example, the chapter on reflection contains four short practices, which can be combined for the "Getting It Together" project "Aspects of My Self: A Collage" found at the end of Part Two. This project encourages students to pull together the ways of thinking they've just practiced. The "Taking it Further" project following Part Two invites students to take a further step, applying their reflections on the self to the issue of "Cyber-Chat Selves."

In the chapter on analysis, the five practices exercise different strategies of analysis, while the first project that follows, based on Toni Cade Bambara's "Education of a Storyteller," makes use of one or more of the practices from analysis and three other chapters. The second project, "Reading On and Off Line: Comparing Text and Hypertext," asks students to take a further step, and of course is another signal of this edition's acknowledgment of the digital age. The projects in Argumentation examine TV talk shows, public debate, and online politics.

Expanded treatment of synthesis

The expanded concluding chapter, "Putting It Together: Synthesis," contains two significantly revised and updated projects—on reading photographs, the American West and American Culture—and an entirely new project on Virtual Relationships. Students use the wide array of materials in each project to make sense of a complex topic. While there is enough material in each of these projects for a substantial paper, suggestions are also given for further research.

ACKNOWLEDGMENTS

We would like to thank our reviewers and other users of *Practice* for their helpful suggestions, in particular: N. Bradley Christie, Erskine College; Kay Halasek, Ohio State University; Stephen Phillip Policoff, New York University; Peggy L. Richards, University of Akron; David Sharpe, Ohio University; and Douglas M. Tedards, University of the Pacific.

Our thanks goes also to the Bedford St. Martin's team: to Chuck Christensen, President, who inspired us into a substantial revision; to Joan Feinberg, Editorial Director, for her good sense and good humor; to Nancy Perry, New York Editor in Chief, who assisted at the birth of *Practice*, for her enthusiasm and wisdom; to the Developmental Editors: Mark Gallaher, for another year of superb work, and to Simon Glick, for good ideas and good cheer; to Harold Chester, the Project Editor, and Cheryl Mamaril, Senior Production Supervisor, whose hard work transformed *Practice*, Fifth Edition from virtual to reality.

As always, special thanks go to our colleagues and students at Brown University and Queens College of the City University of New York. Our experiences with them over four editions have taught us a lot about what our strengths and weaknesses are, which encouraged us to make changes that, we trust, will further enhance the pleasure and usefulness of the text.

Nancy R. Comley
Janice Peritz
Robert Scholes

Brief Contents

Contents

PART FOUR

Writing and Power   215

The Practice
of Writing

PART ONE

Practicing Writing

*First question: Who is speaking? Who, among the totality of speaking in-
dividuals, is accorded the right to use this sort of language? Who is qualified to do so? Who derives from it his own special quality, his prestige, and
from whom, in return, does he receive if not the assurance, at least the
presumption that what he says is true?*

— *Michel Foucault*, The Archaeology of Knowledge

*In our society, and probably in all others, capacity to bring off an activity
as one wants to — ordinarily defined as the possession of skills — is very
often developed through a kind of utilitarian make-believe . . . [in which]
muffing or failure can occur both economically and instructively. What
one has here are dry runs, trial sessions, run-throughs — in short, "practicings."*

— *Erving Goffman*, The Presentation of Self in Everyday Life

In a society that encourages self-development and economic mobility,
the skills of language—and foremost among them, writing—are a
major path to advancement, whether personal, professional, or social.
Michel Foucault recognized this reality and that is one reason why he
insists that so much is at stake in the way we use language. According
to Foucault, what's at stake is not just an individual's "prestige," but
also a society's conceptions of the "right" and the "true"—of power
and knowledge. With so much at stake, is it any wonder that so many
people want to become better writers?

Key to becoming a better writer is play—or what Goffman calls
"utilitarian make-believe." While some things can be learned through
instruction, the actual doing of anything always involves practice.
Writing classes give students the opportunity to engage in "dry runs,
trial sessions, run-throughs—in short, practicings." And they do so
because we know that the way to write better is to write more—but

1

not alone, not aimlessly, and not without encouragement as well as guidance.

The motto of this text comes from the writer W. S. Merwin: "Practice, practice. Put your hope in that." To promote an emphasis on practice, we have tried to keep our talk about writing to a minimum. However, we believe that all writers need some way to scope out and respond to various writing situations as well as some terms to use when discussing their works in progress. In the following two chapters, we address these needs, first by describing writing as a cultural and rhetorical act of communication and second by representing writing as a process of composing.

1

Writing as a Human Act
Situations and Strategies

Hand most human beings a baby and they will make faces at it. Why do they do that? Why do human beings talk to cats and dogs and even to babies in language far more complicated than an animal or a human infant could possibly understand? The answer is simple: human beings need to communicate, and they will speak to any creature that appears to listen. To communicate with a baby, an adult will often make a face that imitates the face the baby is making. Baby sticks tongue out—adult sticks tongue out. Adults mimic babies all the time. In this way (and others), babies learn to mimic adults. And from the first simple sentences children hear, they develop a grammar—they acquire a language.

Language is an extraordinary thing, yet every human being can learn one. In learning a language, we learn not only the language itself but also two ways of using it. One way is public, and we call it "discourse" or "speech." The other way is private, and we call it "thought." With language we give shape and meaning to our world. Words let us name the things we experience, as well as describe these things in relation to each other and to ourselves. Words also help us remember things we no longer have before us, and even to think of things we have never seen: unicorns, the universe, God, woman, man. We see men and women of course, and this particular man and that particular woman, but we do not see "man" or "woman." Those words name classes or categories, what the philosophers call *universals*. Language gives them to us, and we use them to help us think. "All humans are mortal," we think, along with other things that do not trouble the minds of cats, dogs, or babies.

SITUATING WRITING

Learning a language gives us the power to think and to express our thoughts in speech. But human development does not end there. At some point, speaking is inevitably extended to include writing. Anthropologists have found isolated tribes that seem to be on the other side of that great linguistic divide, yet even these groups use signs of all sorts to make and maintain their culture. Tools, clothes, and pictures: people have invented countless ways of leaving their mark on the world. Writing is just such an invention.

But writing is not a uniform thing, invented once and for all. It is a complex human practice that emerges in specific places, assumes a variety of forms, and changes in many ways over time. In the West, it took the development of numerous writing systems over a period of 2,500 years to set the scene for the Greek "invention" of alphabetic writing between 650 and 550 B.C. And then, it took another 2,500 years—as well as the "invention" of the printing press, democracy, public education, and electronic media—for writing and reading to become the commonplace activities they now are for many of us. These days, a person might compose a must-do list for the day, check the headlines in the newspaper, and write replies to those e-mail messages that can't be left until later—all before finishing the first cup of morning coffee. And that person is not alone. Others wrote those headlines and e-mail messages.

We are surrounded by writing, so much so that it's often hard to make sense of it all. What does this or that piece of writing mean? Where is it coming from? Who wrote it and why? Is it a means to some end? To answer these and other questions, you might begin by situating the specific piece in relation to three key tasks that writing performs in our culture: representing the self, reporting knowledge, and exerting power over people's actions or beliefs. Self, knowledge, and power—every piece of writing tends to make one of these issues the primary one. And yet, no piece of writing is without some connection to all three issues. To understand why this is so, consider writing as an act of communication.

Every act of communication involves someone who sends a message and someone who receives it: an adult making faces and a baby watching, a speaker telling a story and a listener paying attention, a writer explaining communication and a reader deciphering signs on a page. On occasion, the sign to be deciphered may even be a diagram:

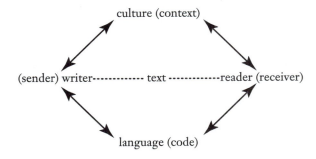

The central level of this simple diagram (writer—text—reader) describes the basic process of written communication. The writer produces a written message (the *text*) and the reader receives it, interprets it, and understands it, thus completing the communication process. By necessity, written communication involves self, knowledge, and power: some self who writes, an inscribed message to be known, and the power to reach, if not to grab and hold on to, a reader.

But, as the saying goes, necessity is also the mother of invention. In our culture, we recognize that writing invents or composes what it communicates, including the self, knowledge, and power. When the task at hand is self-composition, the writing will probably foreground the writer's feelings and reflections. But when the main task is documenting knowledge, the emphasis is more likely to be on the topic and message, not on the writer. Finally, when the goal is power over the beliefs and actions of others, the writing usually emphasizes the reader—or what is assumed to appeal to the reader. Understanding the main purpose of a piece of writing means knowing something about the kinds of work that writing does—or is expected to do—in our culture.

PRACTICE 1.1

Purposeful Pieces

Get a newspaper—on- or offline—and find one or two pieces that seem primarily designed to accomplish each of the following three tasks: to represent a self, to document knowledge, and to influence your beliefs or actions. Does the newspaper contain any pieces of writing primarily designed to accomplish some task other than one of these three? If so, what is this task? Bring copies of the relevant pieces to class, compare what you found with what others found, and discuss how readers can identify the general purpose or task of a piece of writing.

For a directory to newspapers available online, visit **<http://ajr .newslink.org/searchn.html>** or **<http://www.Newsdirectory.com>**. If you want to use a well-known national newspaper, try one of the following: the *Washington Post* (**<http://www.washingtonpost.com>**) or the *Los Angeles Times* (**<http://www.latimes.com>**) or the *New York Times* (**<http://www.nytimes.com>**).

LANGUAGE AND CULTURE

To fulfill its purpose and complete its task, a piece of writing needs to be read; but this can only happen if readers and writers share two things. In the diagram of written communication on page 4, these two things are labeled language and culture. Notice that both terms are connected to the writer and reader by double-ended arrows, indicating that language and culture must be shared for communication to occur. At one level, this means that reader and writer must be literate in the same language. If we write in English, you must read English to understand us. But suppose that you have never been on-line and that the topic we've written about is designing an instructional MOO—a multi-user, object-oriented computer program. How likely are you to understand what we've written? Clearly, the less you know about a particular cultural context—be it the world of cyberspace, football, or science fiction—the less you will know about its topics of discussion, topics that partly define what the cultural context is all about. And, of course, the less the reader knows about a cultural context, the more care the writer must take to ensure that shared understanding or communication occurs.

Instead of taking communication for granted, writers and readers should see shared understanding as something that must be created again and again. Imagine a document written hundreds of years ago and carefully preserved because its message was felt to be of great importance. Imagine as well an important story being passed down from parent to child over many generations. Most scholars would agree about the fate of these two messages as they moved through the generations to the present. The written document would remain the same in its linguistic form, but because language and culture changes over the years, the document would become more and more difficult to understand. It would require interpretation, commentary—perhaps even translation, such as texts in Old English now receive. The oral text—the story transmitted from parent to child—would probably be thought of as the same story: "My mother told me this when I was little, and now, my child, I am telling you the same story." But in fact, with every telling, big and small differences would have crept into the story. There are two reasons for this. First, differences always occur because language changes, and a storyteller must use the language as it exists at a given moment. Second, since speakers want to be understood, they make any changes that are necessary to ensure that their listener understands.

In face-to-face communication, we have the luxury of a present audience, a listener who encourages us to make our message immediately understandable. But written communication doesn't offer us this luxury. Every writer writes for a reader who is some distance away in space and time. For the writer there are no friendly smiles, nods, "uh-huhs"— nor any helpful comments like, "Hey, wait a minute, I don't get that." Writers must always imagine their audience and try to predict how readers will respond to the words being set down on a page. As for readers, they need to know something more than basic English to understand a piece of writing. A simple report of a football game would be incomprehensible to someone who has had absolutely no experience of football, who has never heard of a quarterback or a tackle or a scrimmage. In short, some familiarity with the cultural context of a topic is essential if writer and reader are to complete the communication process.

PRACTICE 1.2

Imagining Your Reader

Write directions for getting from your college library or dorm to a specific place, such as your home or a restaurant near the college. First, write the directions for a classmate familiar with the college campus but not with the location of your home or the restaurant. Next, write directions to the same place for a stranger who is not familiar with your college or with the surrounding area.

Compare the two sets of directions: What did you have to change to make the directions understandable to a stranger? Was one set of directions easier to write than the other? What would you have to change if the directions were meant for a reader from another country—a reader visiting the United States for the first time who had learned English in school?

READING AND WRITING

To communicate well through texts, you have to be able to "read" the writing situation. We are thinking here of the way a quarterback reads the opposing defense, or how a doctor reads a patient's symptoms. Reading in this way is a means of diagnosing what is required and figuring out the course your writing should take to accomplish its task. What are the topic and context of your specific writing assignment? As a writer, what do you want to say about the topic and how do you want to affect your readers? Who are your readers and what do they already know and feel about the topic and context? Given your purpose, what strategies are likely to work best? Reading the writing situation means finding answers to questions like these.

As these questions suggest, reading your writing situation usually requires other kinds of reading as well. For example, it is often a good idea to research *what* has already been written about the topic; obviously, you cannot write well on a subject you know nothing about. Just as important, though, is reading to become familiar with *how* other writers have written about the topic. Are there typical ways of dealing with the topic? Is the topic associated with a certain kind of writing task? In the talk about this or that topic, what's conventional and therefore expected?

Writing is like entering a conversation that is already going on before you start to speak. If you want readers to appreciate what you have to say, then you must demonstrate your understanding of the relevant conventions. The conventions may include many matters, from ending a sentence with a period, to documenting sources properly, to choosing a stance that suits a specific situation, task, and topic. How do you learn these conventions? Babies learn the conventions of speech by observing and imitating the activities of adults; speakers learn the conventions of writing by reading and understanding how others have successfully handled a task.

Think for a moment about the many conventions of writing you already know. Even something as simple as a note to a friend involves a fairly complicated set of conventions. These conventions are probably easy for you to follow because you have read and written many personal notes. But imagine being faced with writing a different kind of note: it's your first day in a new job and your boss asks you to compose a memo to be circulated among the staff—a task that will be part of your job responsibilities. Even if you've been given the topic and told fairly specifically what should be said, the task will pose significant problems until you have a sense of the conventions you are expected to follow. The obvious solution to these problems is to check the files for examples of memos written in the past. Then, with the benefit of reading, imitation, and practice, writing memos will begin to come as naturally to you as writing an informal note, so much so that you may soon find yourself modifying the established form, trying to discover more effective ways of communicating.

In any field, we learn the conventions of writing by reading and practicing. This does not mean that all writing is nothing more than imitation. But, to achieve originality, we must read the work of our predecessors. Originality begins as imitation and moves on to recombination, finally emerging as something new and different enough to be called original. Those who do not read and practice are condemned to repeat the work of those they have not read, to reinvent the wheel when what is needed is the invention of the axle, the bearing, or the differential gear.

■ **PRACTICE 1.3**

Recognizing Conventions

As you know, articles in periodicals usually have titles. Here are twenty such titles—half from daily newspapers and half from a very different kind of periodical: scholarly journals.

**Beyond the Bounce
In Bond Yields**

*"Federalism and Urban Revolt
in France in 1793"*

Mayor Pushes
Voucher Plan

Community Members Honored

"Taking Economic Power Seriously in
a Time of Sectoral Change"

Sprewell Goes From a Misfit to a Nice Fit

*"Epistemological Crises, Dramatic Narrative,
and the Philosophy of Science"*

**Video Legacies
Are Preserved**

"The Antecedents of Beethoven's *Liederkreis*"

Orphans Who Weren't
Recall Care That Wasn't

TRUSTEES PICK SITE FOR NEW LIBRARY

**Objection to Nude Statue
Prompts Bus Stop Change**

*"Medusa's Head: Male Hysteria
under Political Pressure"*

**Salvadoran Ruling Party
Gains Early Edge**

"Shadow-Hunting: Romantic Irony,
Sartor Resartus, and Victorian Romanticism"

"Changes in prison culture: Prison gangs
and the case of the 'Pepsi Generation'"

"Coping with Post-Colonialism"

"The Scientific Status of Causality"

Deeper Look Into the Tale
Of a Daughter and an Ax

"Lechtin Release by Soybean Seeds"

Putting like with like, make two lists—one of newspaper headlines and the other of titles of scholarly articles. Then, figure out how you know which title goes in which list:

- Examine the items in each list, noting similarities in length, diction (word choice), syntax, punctuation, mechanics, and graphics. Remember to note what's *not* there as well as what is.
- Write a set of rules—or conventions—for composing newspaper headlines, titles of scholarly articles, or both.
- Compare your lists as well as your set of conventions with those of your classmates. Did all of you come up with the same lists? Did you all notice the same features of headlines and scholarly titles?

WRITING: ISSUES AND STRATEGIES

Every writing task is done within a framework of expectations about the kind of words that will be used, the kinds of sentence structures that are appropriate, and the sort of organization that will make communication most effective. In other words, given a specific relationship between a writer and the intended reader as well as a particular topic with a history that the participants know something about, the text that results is likely to make use of typical strategies and therefore to have certain features in common with other texts composed in similar circumstances. This principle helps explain why, say, a letter from a seller to a prospective buyer sounds so unlike a funeral oration or an opinion of the Supreme Court, while a news article differs greatly from all three. It also helps explain why we are able to make predictions about how advertisements, elegies, legal opinions, and news articles will sound before we have read them.

Understanding the requirements of a writing situation can help us choose the strategies that are most appropriate for particular writing tasks. In this book, we will focus on three major tasks that writing performs in our culture: representing the self, reporting knowledge, and exerting power over people's actions or beliefs. Self, knowledge, and power: each of these issues has a current context as well as a long history, aspects of which you will explore as you work through the readings in this book.

The readings in this book not only exemplify *what* others have thought and said about the self, knowledge, and power, but also show *how* other writers have handled the tasks of representing the self, reporting knowledge, and exerting power over actions and beliefs. To talk about the *how* of writing, we use the terms *strategies* and *tactics*. A **strategy** is like a game plan—a multidimensional way of dealing with the demands of a specific situation. For example, you want to win Saturday's football game, so you decide on an overall strategy: a "passing game." A **tactic** is like one move or play in an overall strategy or game plan; it's third and ten, so you decide to try a "play-action pass."

Like the game of football, the tasks of representing the self, reporting knowledge, and exerting power are each associated with a number of conventional writing strategies. And those writing strategies are associated, in turn, with a number of typical tactics or features such as creating a mood or defining a term. By practicing writing strategies in a tactical manner, you can learn something more about the self, knowledge, and power. But you can also do something else: you can gain the understanding and confidence you'll need in order to perform well as a writer both in and after college.

Writing and the Self: Expression and Reflection

In self-writing, the writer is usually the center of attention, even when the topic appears to be something else, like a favorite teacher, a family photograph, or a trip to Niagara Falls. Since the emphasis is on the writer's response to some individual, thing, or event, self-writing tends to be identified with personal writing and, as such, opposed to academic writing. But the personal and the academic need not be seen as absolutely opposite. In and out of academia, writing is a way of thinking and learning, and one of the things it can be used to think and learn about is the self. Of course, many academic writing tasks demand impersonality—the restraint, if not the suppression, of personal feelings and values. Such a demand will be easier to negotiate if you know what counts as personal writing and if you understand your feelings, ideas, and values—in short, your self. We can readily recognize two common strategies that are key to writing the self: expression and reflection.

EXPRESSION.   Expression is a way of giving voice to feelings, images, and ideas. By writing expressively, we try to move from a basic feeling like rage or joy to some elaboration, some articulation of it in words. On a personal level, putting things into words can make us feel better and help us to understand ourselves. Practice in expressive writing can also help us learn how to show as well as tell—how to dramatize whatever we have to say. When we dramatize our thoughts, we give them a chance to move and grow and change; for this reason, writers often find that expression is a key strategy in the early stages of all their writing projects.

REFLECTION.   Reflection is not the same thing as expression. If you stand in front of a mirror, your image will be doubled. You will be present in the flesh and your reflected image will be present also. In reflective writing, the writer's self is doubled. We don't simply write *from* ourselves; we also write *about* ourselves. To do this we must get some distance from ourselves, some perspective. One way to do this is to look back—that is, our present, writing self looks back upon some previous self and gauges, in some way, the distance between *then* and *now*. Reflection allows us to discover significance in the events of our own lives and is key to critical as well as creative thinking.

Writing and Knowledge: Narration, Description, Classification, and Analysis

Most academic situations call for writing in which the personality of the writer is not a key issue. Instead of exploring the self, the key issue is reporting knowledge for a reader's information and consideration. The careful recording of actions and observations, the thoughtful connection and organization of data, and the logical examination of how the parts of something are related: these intellectual strategies are expected in the work of all educated writers, whether they are writing for professional or popular audiences. In this book, we take up four common strategies for reporting knowledge: narration, description, classification, and analysis.

NARRATION.   A narrative reports an event, a happening that unfolds in time. Narration is a writing strategy used by reporters and researchers who seek to record some actual sequence of events. These may be actions that happened once, like the development of the first camera, or processes that happen again and again, like the development of a roll of film.

DESCRIPTION.   In description, we take a scene or an object and capture it in language. That is, we organize the details of an object or scene in a way that effectively conveys a sensual image. Just as narration organizes time in writing, description organizes space, whether the subject be a room, a street, or a person's face.

CLASSIFICATION.   In classification, we organize our material not by time or space, but by a principle of logic. We put items with different key features into separate categories and treat those categories as subdivisions of a larger class. We may classify things as different as tools, rock performers, and computer programs.

ANALYSIS.   Like classification, analysis involves making distinctions and connections. In particular, it involves taking something apart and seeing how its parts are related, so as to understand how the object of analysis works. This taking apart, of course, is done mentally, not physically. Literature, social trends, paintings, and a television sitcom: all could be the subject of analysis.

Writing and Power: Direction, Persuasion, and Argument

Like sticks and stones, words have the power to hurt. But they also have other, less violent powers, including the power to influence our actions and beliefs. In democratic and capitalist societies, we count on the power of writing rather than brute force to move people to act in specific ways—say, to count calories, to buy this product, or to vote for that candidate. But we also count on the power of writing to provoke thinking. Besides emotion, written arguments may appeal to logic and values, thereby encouraging us to reason together about issues of public concern, including the issue of how the power of writing is best used. In this book, we focus on three uses or strategies of writing with power: direction, persuasion, and argument.

DIRECTION.   We are all familiar with directions. We find them in cookbooks, textbooks, exercise manuals, and all sorts of do-it-yourself pamphlets and self-help books. Directions make the reader central, first by purporting to offer information that the reader both wants and needs, and then by presenting that information in a clear and practical way. Ideally, the reader should be able to follow directions with a minimum of confusion and complaint.

PERSUASION.   In persuasion, too, moving the reader is the prime consideration. But instead of giving readers directions for something they already want, persuasion works by creating a want readers didn't know they had. Advertisers and politicians use persuasion a lot, often relying on numerous tactics that appeal to emotion, including vivid imagery, a pattern of connotations, repetition, rhythm, and rhyme. As a strategy, persuasion is so prevalent in our society that every citizen should understand how it works.

ARGUMENT.   Argument is often differentiated from persuasion, but it too exerts power over readers — especially over those readers who value reasoning. In academia, most readers and writers like to think of themselves as reasonable — as people whose minds are open and therefore responsive to the judicious formulation of a thesis, the clear presentation of supporting evidence, and the thoughtful use of logical principles such as non-contradiction. To such people, arguments matter. They are a thoughtful way of figuring out where one stands on a debatable issue as well as a powerful way of convincing others to stand there too.

Writing with Personality, Knowledge, and Power: Synthesis

Since academic papers usually work in more than one way, college writers need to learn a number of different writing strategies. For purposes of practice, it helps to focus on one strategy at a time and to consider how a strategy relates to such tasks as representing the self, reporting knowledge, and exerting power. However, it is also important for writers to put things together — to synthesize what they've learned by writing with personality, knowledge, and power. The last part of this book offers you the opportunity to use a variety of strategies and tactics to compose a synthesis.

A **synthesis** is a text that uses many strategies in order to make sense of a complex set of materials—a set usually produced by research. The different academic subjects are concerned with the study of different kinds of material, but the goal of most academic research projects is the production of a synthesis. In a synthesis, the writer may weave together reflection, description, analysis, and argument—whatever it takes to present, explain, and support some hypothesis about the material. A hypothesis is key to a synthesis because this type of writing is designed to help readers understand something significant about a body of data, not to present everything that is known about a topic. In short, a synthesis makes sense, and the sense it makes should be personally meaningful, intellectually informed, and thoughtfully provocative.

PRACTICE AND CONFIDENCE

In this book we help you understand what is required in different writing situations, provide examples of various types of writing for you to read, and, most important, give you a chance to practice some moves of your own. But you must remember that practicing writing is not like football practice, where everybody goes out together with a lot of group support and encouragement. It is more like practicing tennis, where you bang a ball against a wall for hours, or practicing the piano, where you make no progress from one lesson to the next if you don't put in time alone playing the instrument. Only you can do it.

You should also remember that in your writing class, all the work you do is a form of practice. You are trying things out, seeing where your strengths are, finding out what you need to work on so that in time you can gain confidence in yourself as a writer. Such confidence can come from thinking of your work as practice: first, from using your writing class as an opportunity to practice different kinds of writing tasks, and second, from realizing that the act of writing always allows you to practice what you have to say before you present it to an audience of strangers.

But there is another aspect of writing that especially pertains to confidence: the notion of the writer as an actor. The existentialist philosopher Jean-Paul Sartre once observed that a waiter in a cafe was handling the most difficult part of his job—the strain of being shouted at, hurried, always referred to as *garçon* ("boy")—by a simple but beautiful trick. He was *imagining* that he was a waiter in a cafe. Instead of presenting his real, vulnerable self to the abuse of customers and his boss, he was acting out the role of waiter. He put the *role* of waiter between his actual self and his function as waiter. This enabled him to perform the job with a high degree of skill, without the anxiety of feeling that his real self was always on display.

Writers can learn a lesson from this. Even in writing tasks that involve our real selves—such as composing an application for a job we really desire—we may function better, may represent ourselves better, if we accept the task as a role to play. You don't need any special training for role playing because you do it all the time. In a single day, you may play the role of attentive student in the classroom, irate driver in a traffic jam, affectionate child at home, and romantic lover with a special friend. You move in and out of these roles almost unconsciously, and this ability that you have in everyday social situations can also be used in most writing situations. When the idea of the writer as role player is combined with the idea that the reader must be imagined by the writer, the stage is set for a certain kind of practice. By imagining yourself in a variety of situations, addressing a variety of readers, you can in fact become a better writer—an actor who enjoys working through the writing process.

2

Writing as a Process
Experimenting, Planning and Drafting, Revising, Editing

Confronted with a blank piece of paper and the prospect of setting down your thoughts for others to read—and judge—you are bound to feel at least a bit nervous. This is the same kind of nervousness that every performer feels: the actress before going on stage, the football player before the kickoff, the politician before a speech. Even the best performers feel nervous, and most of them say that they need and use that feeling. With the confidence that comes from understanding and practice, writers, like performers, can convert their nervousness into excellence in the performance itself.

However, nervousness can also cause writers to freeze up, to lose concentration and go blank, particularly when the audience is made up of strangers. This kind of anxiety is really a fear of what comes at the end of writing—a fear of being read and evaluated—but it creeps back to inhibit the beginning. Inexperienced writers sometimes assume that writing works like this: first you have an idea; then you put it down on paper; then you are finished writing. But this is not the case at all. Writing is indeed a tool for communication, for transmitting ideas or transcribing what has been thought, but it is also in and of itself a way of thinking— of developing ideas, trying them out, arranging them, and testing them. It is a way of separating your thoughts from your self—making them take a visible form outside your mind so that you can think about them and develop them. Writing is, in fact, always practice, and realizing this can make you a stronger, more confident writer.

Remember that there is no one way to write, no magic process guaranteed to produce a perfect piece of writing if followed step-by-step. Not all writers work in the same way; even an individual writer approaches different tasks in different ways, depending on his or her writing habits and on the writing situation. However, experienced writers can point to particular moves that generally occur in the act of writing, even though these moves can be combined in different ways. In addition to the basic psychomotor act of writing—the way the hand, eye, and brain work so that we can put words on paper—we can distinguish four moves in the practice of writing: experimenting, planning and drafting, revising, and, finally, editing. The first three moves don't need to occur in a strict sequence; this is because writing is a complex, interwoven process like a hooked rug, rather than a set of distinct compartments like a freight train. But each of these moves does represent a particular kind of work that writers do.

EXPERIMENTING

Your most productive way of beginning almost any writing task will be to try out and test your thoughts on paper without the pressure of structuring your expression into its final form. (Even a thank-you note to Aunt Martha can be less difficult if you simply jot down various things you might say *before* you write "Dear Aunt Martha.") If you consider your first words on paper as something tentative, as a way of starting to think rather than as a monument to perfected thought, you will be able to explore whatever subject you approach more deeply and fully, and you will go a long way toward taking the initial nervousness out of writing. Such experimenting is your chance to practice what you have to say before you begin to worry about how your audience will judge the eventual form of your work.

The following sections discuss some methods writers use to get started in the process of finding a subject to write about, narrowing that subject to a manageable topic, and generating ideas about that topic. These methods are illustrated with examples from the writing process of Therese Ludwig, a student in a first-year composition course.

Listing

Listing is a form of brainstorming in which you jot down as many possible ideas as you can think of. Give yourself a time limit of five to ten minutes, and write down on a piece of paper—or type into your word processor—whatever pops into your head. Listing is often a good way to find a broad subject area that you can later narrow into a more focused topic suitable to the length of your assignment. Lists generally consist of words or phrases rather than complete sentences.

Therese Ludwig's assignment was to write a paper about images related to the American West, a theme her instructor was emphasizing throughout the semester. Based both on discussions that had taken place in class and on her own interest in the West, Therese used listing to come up with possible subjects to write about. Here is part of that list:

```
The image of the cowboy in fiction and film

Fictional images of women in the old West

Changing images of Native Americans

Images of the Western landscape ("Big Sky" country)

Advertising images of the West

Images of California as a land of plenty

Representations of the West as frontier

The idea of the hero conquering the West

The wagon train as a symbol of Western settlement

The West today: urban sprawl into the desert
```

Freewriting

Freewriting (also called open-ended writing) is another technique writers may use as a way of experimenting with ideas. The point is simply to write without stopping for a set period of time—generally, five to ten minutes provides a good limit. When freewriting, you write down on paper—or key into your word processor—whatever comes into your head without regard to the quality of your thoughts or the correctness of your expression. You may use words, phrases, or complete sentences. (For more on this technique, see the section "What's on Your Mind?" in chapter 3.)

Once you have reached your time limit, stop and read over what you have written. Underline or box any passages that seem fruitful or worth further exploration. At this point, you may use one of these ideas as the basis for another round of freewriting. (Freewriting based on such an opening idea is called focused freewriting because it is not so open-ended; here you try to focus your ideas on a more specific subject.) Freewriting can be used throughout the early stages of the writing process to find a subject, discover a narrower topic, or generate ideas for a draft.

Because she had been impressed by a slide show of Western landscape art, which her instructor had presented to the class, Therese Ludwig chose from her list "Images of the Western landscape" as the basis for focused freewriting. She hoped she could use this freewriting to help her find a narrower topic for her paper. Here is part of that freewriting:

```
Big sky country. Craggy mountains dropping off into
steep valleys. The paintings are all so monumental.
There was that one of a storm in the mountains. I
can still remember the way the mountains were almost
obliterated by the ominous dark thunderclouds. Yet
the sky above them was a luminous blue lit by the
rays of the sun. It was almost as if the scene had
been painted by the hand of God. Or at least that
the artist wanted his painting to have a sense of
almost religious majesty. Which artist was that any-
way? I'll have to check. It might be interesting to
look at other works by him. I wonder if he used the
same kind of imagery in other paintings.
```

Therese's focused freewriting led her to ask her instructor for the names of both the artist (Albert Bierstadt) and the storm scene painting she remembered (*A Storm in the Rockies*). She found a book in her library and several Web sites that gave her access to other Western landscapes by Bierstadt, as well as some information about the nineteenth-century Hudson River School of painters, of which he was a member. She chose several of these paintings as the basis for more focused freewriting and decided on Bierstadt's Western landscapes as the topic for her paper.

Brainstorming and Clustering

Unlike straightforward listing, brainstorming allows a writer to explore ideas graphically, in order to suggest connections and relationships among them. Here, words and phrases may appear anywhere on the page, and arrows can help show how ideas are related. (Brainstorming is often a productive way for groups to generate ideas.)

Based on her analysis of and freewriting about several of Bierstadt's paintings, Therese brainstormed to see what ideas for her paper she could come up with. Her brainstorming notes are reproduced on page 20.

Clustering is another kind of graphic representation, but it is more orderly than brainstorming. Here writers begin to organize their ideas around a main idea, centered and circled on a sheet of paper. Radiating out from this center are clusters of related ideas, also circled and connected by lines. Based on her brainstorming notes, Therese produced the clustering notes reproduced on page 21.

Experimenting, then, is essential to the practice of writing. Much of it will take place before drafting; but even as you write your first draft, you may find yourself jotting down ideas to use later or stopping to explore ways of working through a difficult section. And, of course, some experi-

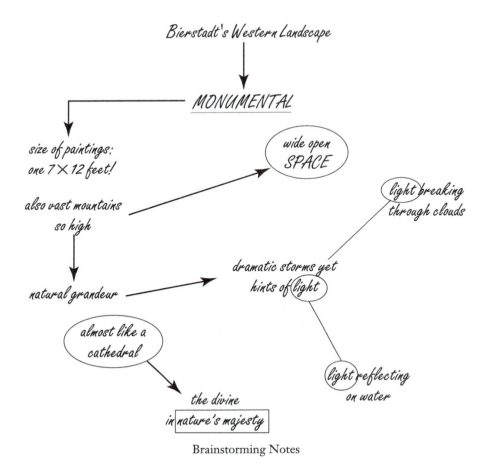

Brainstorming Notes

menting may be done in your head. However, capturing those experiments on paper gives you a way of working through—rather than worrying about—the problem of getting started. It is natural to want to put off the work of drafting; experimenting lets you do so productively.

■ PRACTICE 2.1

Experimenting in Writing

You have been asked to write an article for a group of high school seniors about what they should expect during their first few weeks at college. Practice using several of the techniques described in the previous section to generate ideas and to find a focused topic for such an article.

Clustering Notes

PLANNING AND DRAFTING

As you can see, Therese generated a lot of materials as she experimented with different ideas for her paper. Based on these, she felt she was ready to develop a plan for her first draft.

Defining Your Purpose and Considering Writing Strategies

Before beginning a draft, it is a good idea to define a clear purpose for whatever you are writing. For example, you might decide that your goal in writing is to explore your own personal thoughts and feelings, using the strategies of expression and reflection. Or you might decide that your purpose is to share your knowledge of what you are writing about—that is, to inform readers about something you have learned or discovered. To this end, you might want to tell about something that happened (narration), communicate what you have seen (description), connect ideas and observations (classification), or show how the parts of something function and relate to each other and to the whole (analysis). Another possible purpose is to exert influence upon your readers, either moving them to action through direction or persuasion or getting them to examine and perhaps change their opinions through reasoned argumentation. (These strategies will be discussed in detail in the chapters that follow.)

In some cases, you may have more than one purpose in writing. For example, in order to influence your readers through argumentation, you may decide that you also need to inform them about the topic of your argument. Still, you'll need to determine a primary purpose because this central purpose will govern the type of thesis you develop.

Therese decided that while her purpose was, in part, to explore her own responses to Bierstadt's paintings, her primary purpose was to inform readers about her discoveries as she analyzed the works. She also realized that the main strategies she would use to do so would be description (to communicate what the paintings look like) and analysis (to show how the various elements of the paintings contribute to a larger impression).

Developing a Thesis

A **thesis** is the controlling idea that governs a piece of writing. It is usually expressed as a statement that makes a focused assertion about a topic. A thesis should be neither a statement of fact nor a statement of purpose nor a question. Rather, it should be a claim that can be developed or supported with more specific details.

As suggested earlier, one's purpose for writing will determine the kind of thesis one develops. If a writer's purpose were to communicate his or her own personal thoughts about, for example, on-line relationships, the following thesis would be appropriate:

> I find that I am more open when I communicate on-line than when I do so face to face.

If the purpose were to share knowledge and observations, the thesis might be something like the following:

> People find communicating on-line satisfying because it allows them to connect with one another and to meet others with similar interests.

If the purpose were to influence readers' opinions through reasoned argument, a writer might develop the following thesis:

> As online communication becomes more and more a central part of people's lives, our whole idea of human relationships, and even self-identity, will be transformed.

Not every piece of writing has an explicitly stated thesis, but such a statement is generally expected in most academic writing. Thesis statements are conventionally included at the end of the first or second paragraph—or at the point at which the introduction concludes—although they may occasionally come elsewhere, even at the end of a paper.

Knowing that her purpose was to inform, Therese developed the following statement to summarize the points she wished to make:

> Particularly in his landscapes of the American West, Bierstadt conveyed an awesome sense of space and nature's majesty.

Keep in mind that at this stage of the process a thesis is only tentative. It may change considerably over the course of drafting and revising.

Considering Audience

At some point in the planning of your essay, you need to think about your eventual readers. There will be times in your life—many, perhaps—when you will be writing for nonacademic audiences: friends and relatives, of course, but also current or prospective employers, coworkers, clients, professional groups, and even the broad readership of newspapers and magazines through letters to the editor. But for academic writing, your primary audience will be your instructor and, in some cases, your classmates. Most instructors do not expect you to write specifically for them but rather for a general academic audience, a group of learners interested in your particular insights about a topic.

Thinking about your audience will govern many of your choices as a writer, especially about the following issues:

- What level of detail to include. The less your readers know about a topic, the more detail you'll probably need to provide.
- How to organize your ideas. Readers need to get crucial background information early on so that they can follow the points you are making.
- What tone to assume. You might write sarcastically when complaining to a coworker about an annoying company policy, but a neutral tone

might be a better choice when making similar complaints to a supervisor.

■ What level of diction to use. You can assume that experts in a specific
area are familiar with technical terms and concepts, but when writing
for readers with less expertise, your better choice is to use simpler,
more widely recognized words.

Assuming that her instructor and other readers would not be familiar
with all the paintings she planned to discuss, Therese realized that she
would need to describe them in enough detail to illustrate her thesis. She
also knew that she would need to organize her information in such a way
that she could use particular paintings to illustrate the specific points she
wished to make. Therese knew that a fairly formal academic tone would
be expected, and that her chosen words should not be too technical (an
easy decision since she herself—not an art major—didn't feel comfortable using too technical a vocabulary).

Outlining

Before she began drafting, Therese made an informal outline to help her
remember the ideas she wanted to use in developing her thesis. Such an
outline is usually quite rough and may be frequently rearranged and
amended during the drafting process. Here is Therese's outline, based on
the clustering she had done during her experimenting stage:

```
Intro: sense of space and nature's majesty
Size of paintings
    one as large as 6 × 10
    another 7 × 12
Use of mountains
    high and vast
    God-like heavenly peaks
Use of storm clouds
    ominous but hints of light
    natural wonder
Water and light
    reflections
    light opposite of darkness
Conclusion: Western landscape = natural treasure
            Like cathedrals of Europe
```

Making an extensive formal outline before drafting is difficult because
you are bound to discover much of what you will say during the act of
writing and not beforehand. Some writers even prefer to draft first and
outline later, after they see what they've said. Then they can check if any-

thing has been left out or repeated. For long papers, however, it may be helpful to use a formal outline, roman numerals, capital letters, standard numbers, and lowercase letters to indicate heading levels.

Drafting

The process of putting words on paper is a process of thinking, and that is why most writers frequently look back at what they have written to see if what they are about to write follows logically. Pausing and rereading at intervals will not cause you to forget the point you wanted to make; such pauses can actually spark new ideas for developing your point more effectively. If these ideas do not relate to the section you are working on, jot them down in the margin or on your outline, and return to them at the appropriate time. Remember that the first draft is still an experiment and new discoveries can be made.

Continue writing until you have reached your proposed destination. When you think you have finished your first draft, stop. Then give yourself some time before you begin revising.

Here is Therese's first draft.

```
Albert Bierstadt was a nineteenth-century painter
who, along with other members of the Hudson River
School, used landscapes to depict divine themes. His
early works included landscapes of New England scenes,
but he is best known for his monumental landscapes of
the American West. Particularly in these landscapes
of the American West, Bierstadt conveyed an awesome
sense of space and of nature's majesty.
    In analyzing Bierstadt's paintings, the first
thing one notices is that a great many of his works
are enormous in size. The Rocky Mountains, painted in
1863, measures close to six by ten feet, while Storm
in the Rocky Mountains measures close to seven by
twelve feet. One cannot ignore the message Bierstadt
attempts to communicate. Through the sheer size of
his tableaux, he alludes to the grand majesty of na-
ture.
    Another majestic element in Bierstadt's paintings
is his use of mountains as subjects. The height and
mass of mountains is a marvel to people even today.
In Bierstadt's paintings, the peaks reached so high,
he surely must be posing the question, "What does
rest upon those peaks?"
    The use of natural phenomena like storms, for ex-
ample, was another way to express this theme. In Storm
```

in the Rocky Mountains, the colors and areas of light and shade help to create the dramatic and powerful storm scene before the viewer's eye. The underside of the impending storm cloud is such a dark black-blue, it shadows the land beneath it. Though the painting is primarily in dark shadows, there are a few areas of light. To the right of the storm, the light still touches the green mountain valley. The dramatic contrast of light and shadow is a natural wonder.

Bierstadt also uses the elements of water and light in his landscapes. For example, in *Among the Sierra Nevada Mountains,* Bierstadt uses water as a means of reflecting the sky, particularly the light from the sky. The sky itself opens up to let rays of sunshine touch the water, mountains, and surrounding trees. Another beautiful example of light breaking through clouds is *Passing Storm over the Sierra Nevada.* Most of the composition is left in shadow, while a few beams of light pierce the darkness.

America in the nineteenth century was a young and vibrant country that yearned for a heritage, something that could be held as a national treasure. The Western frontier was the only thing America had at that time to compare to the cathedrals and churches built in the formative years of Europe. Thus, Bierstadt educated a nation unfamiliar with its heritage.

▓ PRACTICE 2.2

Planning and Drafting

Go back to the material you generated through experimenting in Practice 2.1. Now, complete the planning stage for your article addressed to high school seniors, up through outlining. Your instructor may ask you to write a first draft of your article as well.

REVISING

As Joan Swift shows in her three drafts of the poem "The Line-Up" (pp. 70–73), a professional writer's secret is *revision and revision and revision.* Imagine a speaker halfway through a political talk stopping and saying, "Actually, I've begun this all wrong. Now I see what I really want to say. Forget what you've just heard. I'm going to start over." Ridiculous, is it not? Or imagine a football team watching movies of their last game and one of them saying, "I missed a block on that last play; run it again and I'll do it right this time." Impossible! But in writing this is exactly what we do all the time. We run the instant replay and correct our mistakes—not only the mistakes in execution, such as spelling or punctuation, but also the mistakes in conception. That is, if we see that one play isn't working, we can call another play entirely. Think what a tremendous advantage that would give a quarterback. It is an advantage we can all have if we *revise and rewrite*. If you are the sort of writer who never revises, who never writes a second draft, who thinks of every word as a finished product, you may be doomed to remain at a superficial level of understanding about your subject. To refuse revision is to refuse thought itself.

What guides you in revising? How can you tell when changes are necessary and what sort of changes must be made? This requires *critical perspective*. You must try to get outside yourself and see things from another perspective, as you would in writing a reflective essay. Imagining what an audience needs to know is also helpful. You must try to see your writing in terms of your purpose and the writing strategy you are employing. Think about what you are trying to accomplish, and the strategies you are using. If you are writing an argument, check the clarity of your thesis and the logic of your supporting reasons. Do you need more evidence? Should you concede something or change your thesis? If you are describing, have you emphasized the right things, found the right words for them, put them in the right order?

In a writing class, you may very well have an opportunity to engage in peer review: to critique the drafts of other writers, as well as to consider revisions of your own drafts based on the comments you receive from your peers. The purpose of peer review is to help you get critical distance, not to tell you what to do. You can learn a great deal from such opportunities. First, as a reader, you must articulate why you do or do not find certain aspects of someone else's draft effective; if you take your role as a reader/critic seriously, you can develop critical powers that you can then transfer to your own work. In addition, the feedback you receive from other readers of your drafts can make you more aware of the needs of an audience of strangers. This awareness can lead you to imagine more clearly how those strangers—your readers—will react to a particular piece of writing. What will they find confusing or distracting in this work? If you can find the problems, you can fix them.

Therese Ludwig had input from both her instructor and a peer reader in evaluating the preliminary draft of her paper on Albert Bierstadt's Western landscape paintings. Her instructor pointed out that the thesis for her essay seemed a little vague and that she brought up an interesting point in her opening sentence—that the landscapes of painters like

Bierstadt often depicted "divine themes"—that wasn't explored in the body of her paper. A classmate suggested that a point she made in her closing comparing the American Western frontier to the cathedrals and churches of Europe might be developed more fully. Therese herself realized that she needed to more clearly tie together the pattern of images she found in the paintings.

Picking up on her instructor's suggestion, Therese decided to do some research that would help her explore the idea of "the divine" in Bierstadt's work. One book she found in her school's library, *Nature and Culture: American Landscape and Painting* by Barbara Novak, provided the supporting idea that much American landscape painting in the nineteenth century was firmly grounded in a view of "divine nature." Looking over her earlier notes, Therese realized that she herself had sensed this notion of divinity in Bierstadt's work in her earlier freewritings about particular paintings. So in going back to revise her essay, Therese decided to explore the ways in which Bierstadt used the imagery in his paintings to "communicate a vision of divine wonder." In doing so, she realized she would need to revise her thesis and expand her discussion of each painting to include an interpretation of its divine characteristics.

Also based on her research, Therese realized that her point about Bierstadt's effect on nineteenth-century Americans' views of their country was an important one that deserved greater attention. She decided to weave this idea into her introduction and to expand on it in her conclusion.

As the final version of Therese's essay (page 29) suggests, revision often involves considerable redrafting and the development of additional supporting information.

▦ PRACTICE 2.3

Revising

If you drafted an article aimed at high school seniors for Practice 2.2, read it carefully from the kind of critical perspective described in the previous section. Your instructor may also give you advice and/or have you solicit comments from a peer reader. Based on these, map out a revision plan and revise your article.

EDITING

The last act of writing is editing, which involves checking for style, grammar, and mechanical errors. When editing, look for problems with sentence clarity, subject-verb agreement, punctuation, and spelling, and when needed, consult a handbook. Your reader can accept last-minute corrections better than outright errors and will be grateful to you for taking the trouble to correct the errors.

THERESE LUDWIG'S FINAL PAPER

Therese's instructor considered the final draft of her paper on Albert Bierstadt effective for a number of reasons. First of all, Therese had made sense of a complex topic. As a writer, she had ordered her material well in the process of supporting her thesis; she had used several reputable sources and cited them properly; stylistically, her writing was fluent and free of all save minor errors. Finally, her interest in her topic was evident: Therese had worked hard on this paper and had enjoyed the work.

Albert Bierstadt and the Divine Landscape

During the middle to late nineteenth century, Americans in the eastern part of the country were very curious about the West, a frontierland few of them had ever seen. Albert Bierstadt, one of the Hudson River painters, helped satisfy this curiosity. His monumental depictions of the Western landscape communicate a vision of divine wonder characteristic of the Hudson River Valley School.

Like his peers, Bierstadt was preoccupied with divine themes. The period during which Bierstadt painted was characterized by an obsession with anything divine. As art historian Barbara Novak has noted, every discipline, including art and science, aspired to decipher the mysteries of God: "Nature's truths, as revealed by art, could be further validated by the disclosures of science, which revealed God's purposes and aided the reading of His natural text. At mid-century, landscape attitudes were firmly based on this unity of faith, art, and science" (47). The detail Bierstadt implemented in his paintings conveyed an awesome sense of space and of nature's divine majesty.

In analyzing Bierstadt's paintings, the first thing one notices is that a great many of his works are enormous in size. The Rocky Mountains, painted in 1863, measures close to six by ten feet, while A Storm in the Rocky Mountains measures close to seven by twelve feet. One cannot ignore the message

Bierstadt attempts to communicate. Through the sheer size of his tableaux, he alludes to the grand majesty of nature and the omnipotence of God.

Another majestic element in Bierstadt's paintings is his use of mountains as subjects. The height and mass of mountains are a marvel to people even today. In Bierstadt's day, they were viewed as a wondrous creation of God. Imagine the privilege of the artist who could create them in his own fashion. In Bierstadt's paintings, the peaks reached so high he surely must be posing the question, "What does rest upon those peaks?"

The use of natural phenomena like storms, for example, was another way to express the theme of divinity. In *A Storm in the Rocky Mountains,* the colors and areas of light and shade help to create the dramatic and powerful storm scene before the viewer's eyes. The underside of the impending storm cloud is such a dark black-blue it shadows the land beneath it. Though the painting is primarily in dark shadows, there are a few areas of light. To the right of the storm, the light still touches the green mountainous valley. The dramatic contrast of light and shadow provokes "intimations of infinity" (38). On closer observation, one notices that the mountain peak breaks the storm clouds and is bathed in light. Was this Bierstadt's way of saying that God, in his tranquillity and majesty, oversees the travails of man?

Bierstadt also uses the elements of water and light to elaborate on themes of divinity. For example, in *Among the Sierra Nevada Mountains,* Bierstadt uses water as a means of reflecting the sky, particularly the light from the sky. The sky itself opens up to let rays of sunshine touch the water, mountains, and surrounding trees. The sun shining through the clouds onto the land symbolizes God's blessing unto America. The water, because it reflects this light that symbolically stands for God, emphasizes this theme. Another beautiful example of light breaking through clouds is *Passing Storm over the Sierra Nevada.* Most of the composition is left in shadow, while a few beams of light pierce the darkness. This is yet another symbol for God, who pierces darkness or evil and gives us his blessing. The water in both works captures the tranquil light from the sky, which may symbolize God.

In *Bridal Veil Falls,* tranquillity is communicated

once again. By now tranquillity is understood to be associated with what God offers us. The majestic waterfall, a creation of God, is breathtaking by itself, but with closer examination more can be deciphered. The water creates an atmospheric effect in this picture. The spray at the waterfall's base looks like clouds. Clouds are associated with heaven and in turn this landscape may be seen as heaven on earth.

The divinity and sublimity of the Western landscape that Albert Bierstadt expressed through his paintings helped stimulate the belief that the West was land given by God for the young American nation to settle and tame. As Barbara Novak points out, "There was a widespread belief that America's natural riches were God's blessing on a chosen people" (16). Not only was the West seen in a spiritual light, but the West was the only thing America had at the time that could compare to the cathedrals and churches built in the formative years of Europe.

America was a young and vibrant country that yearned for a heritage, something that could be held as a national treasure. The Western frontier was America's church, national treasure, and heritage. Even Europe could not boast of land as majestic as that of the American West's canyons, prairies, deserts, lush valleys, and long mountain chains. Americans finally realized that they had something to boast about.

Thus, Bierstadt not only educated a nation unfamiliar with its heritage; he imparted a spiritual vision as well. Unfortunately, towards the turn of the century when enthusiasm for spiritual grandeur was waning, Bierstadt's reputation diminished as well. However, today, as John Howat writes, Albert Bierstadt's "enthusiastic vision of nature at its grandest is one that will guarantee the lasting popularity of his work" (48).

Works Cited

Baigell, Matthew. Albert Bierstadt. New York: Watson-Guptill, 1981.

Bierstadt, Albert. Among the Sierra Nevada Mountains. National Museum of American Art. <http://nmaa.si.edu>.

---.Bridal Veil Falls. North Carolina Art Museum. <http://ncartmuseum.org>.

---.<u>Passing Storm over the Sierra Nevada</u>. CGFA.
        <http://sunsite.auc.dk/cgfa/bierstadt>.
---.<u>The Rocky Mountains</u>. Baigell, 37.
---.<u>A Storm in the Rocky Mountains</u>. Baigell, 41.
Howat, John K. <u>The Hudson River and Its Painters</u>. New
        York: Viking, 1963.
Novak, Barbara. <u>Nature and Culture: American Land-
        scape and Painting</u>. New York: Oxford UP, 1980.

PART TWO

Writing the Self

One's self I sing, a simple separate person,
Yet utter the word Democratic, the word En-Masse
                              —Walt Whitman

In a sense, it is not "I" who is writing . . . but a sometimes contradictory collection of voices: voices of beings I love and from whom I in passing borrow certain values.

                                        —Roland Barthes

If you were asked what you see when you look in the mirror, you might reply, "Myself." That simple reply has a long history, a story you depend on whenever you say, "I see my self." The concept of the self is partly a product of the Enlightenment and an age of revolution when the rights of the individual became a cause to fight for. In the American colonies, the Declaration of Independence (1776) proclaimed that "all men are created equal," and following the American Revolution, the Constitution and the Bill of Rights (1789) guaranteed the rights of the individual. In this way, the idea of the self came to life, a life the nineteenth-century poet Walt Whitman celebrated as "Democratic."

The work of the nineteenth century was to embody the self. In part, this meant giving the self an identity and a story. Writers focused on their personal feelings and experiences, both expressing and reflecting what it meant to be an individual. In novels, this interest in individual experience took the form of the *bildungsroman*, the story of the growth of a self and that self's identity. By the end of the nineteenth century, the idea that everyone had an essential, unique self to discover was firmly in place.

But this idea of the self was not without its problems. One problem is that the belief in a unique self often means alienation from others. Walt Whitman picks up this problem, explores it, and, as the epigraph by Whitman shows, tries a "both/and" solution. The opening lines of this poem, "One's-Self I Sing," assert his individuality as well as his participation in the lives of others. His poem *Song of Myself* makes this participation clear:

> I celebrate myself,
> And what I assume you shall assume,
> For every atom belonging to me as good belongs to you.

For Whitman, then, one's self merges with many other selves, but then returns to its own center. With this shape-shifting self, Whitman celebrates the individual and society, the private citizen and the bustling democracy of mid-nineteenth-century America.

Yet every solution poses a new problem. If one is many, as Whitman believed, then the identity of the self becomes a troubling issue. In the twentieth century, psychiatrist Sigmund Freud gives us a personality composed of multiple selves: an unconscious self, formed by repressed desires; a conscious self, or ego, produced by practical realities; and a superego, or conscience, shaped by both parental and social forces. Such a multilayered personality is liable to be conflicted, in part because those selves seldom speak as one.

Writing in the wake of Freud, Roland Barthes picks up on the multiple self and its contradictions: "In a sense, it is not 'I' who is writing . . . but a sometimes contradictory collection of voices: voices of beings I love and from whom I in passing borrow certain values." Here the self emerges as a contested site, a situation which seems not to trouble Barthes very much, perhaps because he believes the self to be constructed of many voices. When Barthes says "I in passing," he emphasizes writing as a process through which he constructs an "I" from other texts. In contemporary terms, he calls himself a *subject*, a term that is used sometimes interchangeably with *self*. This term implies that the self is the subject of something, or to something, or for something. When you express yourself in writing, are you to be taken as the subject *of* America, or subject *to* the idea of America, or as subject *for* the American dream?

Relatively speaking, the concept of expressing a self in writing, of writing autobiographically, is of recent origin. Earlier, we talked about the writer as role player; is writing a self one of the roles we can assume? Many writing texts encourage finding or discovering "your own voice," which suggests that writers have but one unique voice that is hiding somewhere, just waiting to be released by some mysterious turn of the key. But perhaps it is better to think of writing as the space in which we discover our *other roles*. When you think about writing the self, try to think of your self as the subject of your life.

3

Presenting the Self
Expression

In a sense, all writing is expressive. At some level, we express ourselves in every act of writing, even if it is writing carelessly because we are not interested in the assigned topic. But in another sense, writing is never completely expressive because its rules and practices are part of a social system over which we have little control. In writing, we can only say what the system of writing will let us say.

Whether or not you have thought about the problem in exactly this way, you have probably encountered it. Because modern life is so complicated, there are many barriers to full expression. We all feel a kind of censorship that prevents us from expressing things that might expose our weaknesses or show us to be different from our fellows, from leaving a durable record that may say more about ourselves than we had meant to say. We may also have trouble expressing ourselves because our language is full of ready-made expressions, clichés that can falsify and standardize whatever may be unique in our unshaped thoughts and feelings. This mixture of feelings—fear of being misunderstood and fear of being understood too well—is a major part of the anxiety about writing that most of us have.

Practice in expression is designed to ease both aspects of the writer's anxiety and to provide opportunities for thoughts to grow and deepen. Freedom of expression is particularly important because it is what makes the activity of experimenting so productive, allowing writers to explore what is in their minds as elaborately or outrageously as they wish without holding back for fear something is "wrong" or not within acceptable social limits. Eventually, of course, the limits must be considered. Writers must become more self-critical and disciplined and should work to refine the discoveries of expression within the constraints imposed by the writing situation. Such discipline, however, is not the first concern of expression.

The writing opportunities that follow are simply chances for you to write for yourself, to get started, to stretch your possibilities before you think about presenting your thoughts and feelings to anyone else. The forms of practice presented later in this chapter will begin to ask for a more public kind of expression, in which you must consider the problem of expressing *your* self *to* some other self. The purpose of expression, after all, is to broaden your powers of communication.

WHAT'S ON YOUR MIND?

"Just Do It!" says the slogan, advice that may serve you better as a writer than as a basketball player. Although your mind may seem blank, begin writing and you'll soon see that you have lots of thoughts and feelings. The mind abhors a vacuum, as you'll discover in doing the following open-ended writing practice. But first, some words of advice from an expert on how to get started with self-expression.

▨ READING

Peter Elbow, from *Writing with Power*

The open-ended writing process is ideal for the situation where 1 you sense you have something to write but you don't quite know what. Just start writing about anything at all. If you have special trouble with that first moment of writing—that confrontation with a blank page—ask yourself what you *don't* want to write about and start writing about it before you have a chance to resist. First thoughts. They are very likely to lead you to what you are needing to write.

Keep writing for at least ten or twenty or thirty minutes, de- 2 pending on how much material and energy you come up with. You have to write long enough to get tired and get past what's on the top of your mind. But not so long that you start pausing in the midst of your writing.

Then stop, sit back, be quiet, and bring all that writing to a point. 3 That is, by reading back or just thinking back over it, find the center or focus or point of those words and write it down in a sentence. This may mean different things: you can find the main idea that is there; or the new idea that is trying to be there; or the imaginative focus or center of gravity—an image or object or feeling; or perhaps some brand new thing occurs to you now as very important—it may even seem unrelated to what you wrote, but it comes to you now as a result of having done that burst of writing. Try to stand out of the way and let the center or focus itself decide to come forward. In any event don't worry about it. Choose or invent something for your focus, and then go on. The only requirement is that it be a single thing. Skip a few lines and write it down. Underline it or put a box around it so you can easily find it later. (Some people find it helpful to let themselves write down two or three focusing sentences.)

▨ PRACTICE 3.1

Open-ended Writing

Start writing, following Elbow's advice as closely as you can. That is, write as he suggests you do, read your writing, and find your point or focus. That's all you have to do. Save this material, however, for you may return to it later in the course.

FREE ASSOCIATION

Here is the opening of a book on blueness and blue things by a philosopher who is also a fiction writer (or vice versa). You may find it difficult to follow every mention of blue as you read, but you can't help but get the idea. The piece is simply a list of things that are blue or that can have the word *blue* applied to them. You may be surprised by some, feel a shock of recognition at others, and find some just too tricky to decipher. As you read, just try to follow along, noting how the word *blue* goes with everything mentioned.

▨ READING

W. H. Gass, from *On Being Blue*

Blue pencils, blue noses, blue movies, laws, blue legs and stockings, the language of birds, bees, and flowers as sung by longshoremen, that lead-like look the skin has when affected by cold, contusion, sickness, fear; the rotten rum or gin they call blue ruin and the blue devils of its delirium; Russian cats and oysters, a withheld or imprisoned breath, the blue they say that diamonds have, deep holes in the ocean and the blazers which English athletes earn that gentlemen may wear; afflictions of the spirit—dumps, mopes, Mondays—all that's dismal—low-down gloomy music, Nova Scotians, cyanosis, hair rinse, bluing, bleach; the rare blue dahlia like that blue moon shrewd things happen only once in, or the call for trumps in whist (but who remembers whist or what the death of unplayed games is like?), and correspondingly the flag, Blue Peter, which is our signal for getting under way; a swift pitch, Confederate money, the shaded slopes of clouds and mountains, and so the constantly increasing absentness of Heaven (*ins Blaue hinein*, the Germans say), consequently the color of everything that's empty: blue bottles, bank accounts, and compliments, for instance, or, when the sky's turned turtle, the blue-green bleat of ocean (both the same), and, when in Hell, its neatly landscaped rows of concrete huts and gas-blue flames; social registers, examination booklets, blue bloods, balls, and bonnets, beards, coats, collars, chips, and cheese . . . the pedantic, indecent and censorious . . . watered twilight, sour sea: through a scrambling of accidents, blue has become their color, just as it's stood for fidelity. Blue laws took their hue from the paper they were printed on. Blue noses were named for a potato.

▪ PRACTICE 3.2

On Being _____

Looking back at the passage by Gass, can you find examples of things in the world that are literally blue: things we perceive as having that color? Can you also find examples of things that are blue only in some figurative or metaphorical way? Gass is fascinated by the way language works, by the way that the name of a color is applied to all sorts of things that actually have no color at all. In the last two sentences, he explains how two things that are not literally blue came to be called blue: laws and noses. Although many of his blue things are so called for reasons lost in the history of language, Gass invents nothing here. In this passage he takes an inventory of the English language as he understands it, trying to summon up all the things that are regularly called blue. Their strange combinations, ordered by his own mind's patterns of association, make a kind of prose poem. By concentrating on the word *blue*, in all its applications, he frees his mind to roam around, to make connections that are startling, to be creative, to be expressive.

It is important to note that Gass is not being merely personal and arbitrary here. He is not calling things blue just because he wants to (like the French poet who called oranges blue). This passage is a collaboration between Gass and his language. He is thus free to associate all things that have been called blue often enough to make their blueness part of the language.

Your job is simply to work as Gass has worked, but with another color. We suggest a primary color, one that has spread throughout the language, so that you can combine in your paragraph things that are literally that color with things that we only speak of figuratively as being that color. Save this exercise; you may be returning to it later.

SPEAKING IMAGES

Art takes many forms and has many uses. One use is to provide a vehicle for the expression of feelings that many of us have but cannot express as well as an artist can. Considered in this way (which, of course, is not the only way it can be considered), art helps us organize and understand aspects of ourselves. It would be possible, in an analytic exercise, to ask you to interpret what the artist intends a work to mean. But we are definitely *not* asking you that kind of question. Instead, we ask you to imagine that each of the following three works expresses some aspect of your personality or some thoughts or feelings that you recognize as moods you have experienced or might experience.

■ **READING**

Three Images

Edvard Munch, *The Cry* **(1895).** William Francis Warden Fund, Courtesy Museum of Fine Arts, Boston

Vincent Van Gogh, *A Pair of Shoes* **(1887).** Baltimore Museum of Art, Cone Collection

Smiling Figure. Mexico, 7th–8th centuries, Metropolitan Museum of Art, Michael C. Rockefeller Collection

PRACTICE 3.3

Self-Expression through Art

Choose one of the preceding images and give it voice. Begin by writing down what the image seems to be saying. You may choose to write in first, second, or third person to do this, using the picture as a mask that you put on in order to speak. Write about what feelings the picture brings out in you. We suggest using the present tense, but if you are more comfortable with the past, use that. Just be consistent. For instance, looking at the first picture, you might begin in any of several ways: 1) He is frightened; 2) You are suffering; 3) I am in agony. Once you get started, you may look at the picture occasionally for stimulation, but do not be afraid to follow your own thoughts and feelings. If one word leads to another, write them all down.

The purpose of this exercise, like that of the others in this chapter, is to help you loosen up as a writer. There is no question of "the right answer" here, but only of writing more or less expressively. Don't quit after a few words. Keep on thinking, feeling, and writing until you have really expressed yourself about the picture. You can stop writing, think about something else for a while, and then come back to your picture. You may be surprised at how much your subconscious will dredge up while you are not thinking about the picture consciously.

TOOLS AND TOTEMS

In the passages that follow, a food expert, an artist, a journalist, and a film producer express their feelings about everyday objects. As you read each passage, follow the expression of ideas in it as well as the expression of emotions evoked by each object.

READING

Julia Child, On the Wearever No-Stick Aluminum Pan; Red Grooms, On the Umbrella; J. C. Herz, "Flying Toasters That You Can Play With"; Federico Fellini, On the Telephone

Julia Child, On the Wearever No-Stick Aluminum Pan

"Thirteen, fourteen, fifteen, sixteen, seventeen! Do you realize you   1
have 17 frying pans on this wall?" asked the lady journalist who was
interviewing me. She hadn't even seen my treasured oval cast-iron

fish sauté pan in case of Dover soles, and a few others stashed in the adjoining closet.

I love them all, even if I don't use every one. Some I just like the 2 looks of, like the darling French cast-iron pan, just big enough to sauté one jumbo egg in the best butter. The standard two- to three-egg iron omelet pan was my favorite until the no-stick came along. There's the old Griswold, heavy, squat, black, with its short handle and utterly utilitarian look. But my all-time all-purpose favorite is the Wearever no-stick aluminum pan, 10 inches top diameter and 8 inches across the bottom. Its long handle and outward slanting two-inch sides are just right for tossing eggs, mushrooms, potatoes, chicken livers and so forth. I have even made a tarte Tatin in it. It is neither so heavy you can't manipulate it easily nor so light it has no feeling. There is nothing fancy, flashy nor luxurious about it. To me it is beautiful, the perfect frying pan, the one I couldn't live without, the one that I'd take with me to that desert island.

Red Grooms, On the Umbrella

Ode to the Umbrella: a cherished and refined possession that almost always ends in loss. From Gustave Caillebotte's *Paris Street; Rainy Day* (1877) to the Morton salt girl, the umbrella is an evocative visual image. Elegant and inexpensive, a hand-operated machine, status symbol and logo-bearer, artistic or banal. Five dollars on a downtown New York street corner or $200 on Madison Avenue. Usually suffers a democratic demise pointed down in a trash can. Undoubtedly one of humanity's most common and beautiful designs, both a protector from the heavens above and a potential means of flight.

J. C. Herz, "Flying Toasters That You Can Play With"

Everyone who uses a computer has experienced that moment 1 when the screen saver turns itself on and you don't resume typing. You don't reach for the mouse. You just sit there for a minute, glassy-eyed, exhausted and brain-fried, staring at the screen, contemplating . . . flying toasters. The meditation of cubicle existence:

> *The flying toasters*
> *Migrating to better jobs*
> *This memo is late*

It's appropriate somehow that these familiar images should find 2 their way into other forms of procrastination that foster the same serene, zoned-out state of mind. To wit: After Dark Games, a candy box of games and puzzles starring characters who have traipsed across our screens for years: Hula Girl, Mowing Man, the tropical fish and yes, the flying toasters.

These are not complicated games. There are no hidden doors. 3 There are no secret combination moves. It's just solitaire, or

Sedatives: The After Dark Games package, which includes Toaster Game, top, and Mushu, Tiles, bottom, is based on classic screen savers.

jumbles of alphabet letters (tattooed on the fish), or trivia questions, or vest-pocket Pac-Man variations, or matching and memory games, or puzzles, all of which take less than 10 minutes. They're miniature experiences, simple to pick up and put down.

But these vest-pocket video games are, in their own way, as en- 4 gaging and addictive as the mega-selling 40-hour sagas with souped-up 3-D sound and state-of-the-art computer graphics.

Part of their appeal is sheer simplicity. Word puzzles are not a 5 high-octane mental experience. So it's easy to relax. It's just a hand of solitaire, and there is always another. No pressure.

You take deeper breaths. Your heart rate slows down. You blink 6 less. And pretty soon you're in a complete state of flow, immersed in a pursuit whose only purpose and consequence is to bring about this very state of mind. For nonsmokers, an easy puzzle is the closest you can get to having a cigarette. It's like doodling while you talk on the telephone. Like scribbling hatch marks on scratch paper, it's a way of slowing time. It puts a damper on the cacophony. It fosters a sense of privacy. If you're playing solitaire, the mental office door is closed.

That's why people spend so much time with the Macintosh logo 7 puzzle or Windows solitaire. It's not that the games are so exciting, it's that they're not. They function as mild mental sedatives, just as action games function as mental stimulants. Kids like action games because they're looking for all the stimulation they can get their hands on. Seeking stimulation is a child's job in life.

But in a workplace suffused with politics and deadlines and other 8 people's demands, adults are not looking for more stimulation. They're looking for stress relief. And a low-key computer game is a cheap and convenient way to cool out.

Federico Fellini, On the Telephone

Frankly, I don't see myself as the fanatical telephone user that 1 friends and colleagues have been calling me for years, with mischievous amusement. My work brings me into contact with a large number of people, which means I'm involved in an endless network of relationships, and so it's natural that a fair part of my day should be spent on the telephone. Like everyone else I consider and use the telephone as an indispensable, fast and practical means of communication. And yet this daily use of it hasn't yet managed to remove my astonishment at the fundamentally fantastic aspect of telephoning, that is, of communication at a distance. Apart from any hackneyed ideas about communication by telephone being the modern technical equivalent of ancient means of communication — telepathy, for instance — I want to make just a few odd, hurried remarks about it. I wonder, for instance, why it is easier to get out of an unexpected visit than to withstand the temptation to pick up the telephone when it keeps ringing? Just because the person speaking isn't physically present, communication on the telephone is more tenuous but more authentic, less real but more precise, more temporary but more spontaneous, more delicate but at the same time more intense. As a rule one pays more attention both to oneself and to the other person when talking on the telephone, one participates more. Feeling and impressions expand: good news becomes more exciting because right away it is more privately taken in. A disaster becomes unbearable, because the imagination is fully stretched.

Terror is terror in its purest form: nothing is more chilling than 2 a threat or a damning criticism pronounced on the telephone. Even the dullest, silliest joke on the telephone loses its dullness and pointlessness and takes on a disarming charm. For my part, I think solitude filled with voices is far preferable and far more joyful than the physical presence of others, when it has no meaning or point to it.

Questions

1. Try to describe the speaker suggested by each of the four voices. What kind of personality is suggested by each passage? What specific elements in each text are most expressive of the speaker's individuality? What text is most revealing of its speaker's personality?
2. Consider the situation of each speaker in relation to his or her chosen object. Child and Grooms were invited to express their feelings about their favorite object. Herz is expressing herself in a column for the technology section of the *New York Times*. Fellini has the most complicated feelings about the telephone. What are their reasons for liking their particular object?
3. How does each writer's ideas about his or her object compare with your ideas about that object?
4. From these four readings, can you make generalizations about the chosen objects? What is it about these objects that is so appealing?

▨ PRACTICE 3.4

Your Feelings about Something

Write a short expressive piece conveying your ideas about one of the common objects presented here or some other modern innovation, such as the cell phone, the answering machine, the remote control, the computer, the garbage disposal, or the Pokemon craze.

You might begin by writing the name of the object at the top of the page. Then either jot down a list of thoughts about that object as they occur to you, or focus on the topic through the kind of open-ended writing described in the first reading of this chapter (p. 38). Based on these notes, write a draft that will clearly convey your thoughts to a reader.

4

Representing the Self
Reflection

Reflection, like expression, foregrounds the writer. Unlike expression, however, it is not an immediate presentation of thought or feeling. It is mediated—by time, by distance, by experience and maturity. It is a *re-flection*, a looking *back* or looking again. If expression is naturally a young person's form, reflection is the opposite: a form for those who have enough perspective to look back on things and see them in a way different from the way they seemed at the time. For a child, reflection is almost an impossibility. But as soon as we are old enough to remember childhood itself as a time when we were "different"—or are able to look across the gap of any great event, like a death in the family, the loss of a friend, or a danger experienced—we can begin to reflect on our experience. Being able to think reflectively is itself a sign of maturity.

Reflection usually depends on the difference between two moments: the time of the event or situation and the time of the writing—in other words, then and now. The writer of reflection must use this difference in time to express the feelings and thoughts of *now* by recalling or imagining the emotions and ideas present *then*. Reflection is not simply the telling of a tale of the describing of a scene. These things may enter into it, but they are there only for the sake of what they are now seen to mean.

Reflection also has a crucial role to play in the writing process itself. Writing is not an instantaneous event. It takes a certain amount of time to write even a single sentence, and any serious writing project may ex-tend over a considerable period of time. During the time of writing, there are many moments of reflection in which the writer examines the words already there on the page, sometimes thinking, "But that's not what I meant to say. I really meant...." We feel the same way about deeds often enough ("I didn't mean to do *that*"), but deeds cannot be un-done; words, however, can be unwritten. We call this process *revision*, and it is an aspect of reflection that we can use in all the other forms of writing. Just as the process of revision is often helped by seeing our writing from the perspective of others, so too is the process of self-reflection. From another person's perspective, we may not look as we think we do.

IMAGES

In the following reading selections, the process of reflection is illustrated through the writers' actions: looking at photographs, recording the moment in words, and, in so doing, learning about themselves as well as others. Practice 4.1 invites you to try your hand at doing something similar.

■ READING

Three Writers Look at Pictures

Paul Auster, from *Portrait of an Invisible Man*

In [my father's] bedroom closet I had found several hundred photographs—stashed away in faded manilla envelopes, affixed to the black pages of warped albums, scattered loosely in drawers. From the way they had been stored I gathered he never looked at them, had even forgotten they were there. One very big album, bound in expensive leather with a gold-stamped title on the cover—This is Our Life: The Austers—was totally blank inside. Someone, probably my mother, had once gone to the trouble of ordering this album, but no one had ever bothered to fill it. 1

Back home, I pored over these pictures with a fascination bordering on mania. I found them irresistible, precious, the equivalent of holy relics. It seemed that they could tell me things I had never known before, reveal some previously hidden truth, and I studied each one intensely, absorbing the least detail, the most insignificant shadow, until all the images had become a part of me. I wanted nothing to be lost. 2

Death takes a man's body away from him. In life, a man and his body are synonymous; in death, there is the man and there is his body. We say, "This is the body of X," as if this body, which had once been the man himself, not something that represented him or belonged to him, but the very man called X, were suddenly of no importance. When a man walks into a room and you shake hands with him, you do not feel that you are shaking hands with his hand, or shaking hands with his body, you are shaking hands with *him*. Death changes that. This is the body of X, not this is X. The syntax 3 is entirely different. Now we are talking about two things instead of one, implying that the man continues to exist, but only as an idea, a cluster of images and memories in the minds of other people. As for the body, it is no more than flesh and bones, a heap of pure matter.

Discovering these photographs was important to me because   4
they seemed to reaffirm my father's physical presence in the world, to give me the illusion that he was still there. The fact that many of these pictures were ones I had never seen before, especially the ones of his youth, gave me the odd sensation that I was meeting him for the first time, that a part of him was only just beginning to exist. I had lost my father. But at the same time, I had also found him. As long as I kept these pictures before my eyes, as long as I continued to study them with my complete attention, it was as though he were still alive, even in death. Or if not alive, at least not dead. Or rather, somehow suspended, locked in a universe that had nothing to do with death, in which death could never make an entrance.

Most of these pictures did not tell anything new, but they helped   5
to fill in gaps, confirm impressions, offer proof where none had existed before. A series of snapshots of him as a bachelor, for example, probably taken over a number of years, gives a precise account of certain aspects of his personality that had been submerged during the years of his marriage, a side of him I did not begin to see until after his divorce: my father as prankster, as man about town, as good time Charlie. In picture after picture he is standing with women, usually two or three, all of them affecting comical poses, their arms perhaps around each other, or two of them sitting on his lap, or else a theatrical kiss for the benefit of no one but the person taking the picture. In the background: a mountain, a tennis court, perhaps a swimming pool or a log cabin. These were the pictures brought back from weekend jaunts to various Catskill resorts in the company of his bachelor friends: play tennis, have a good time with the girls. He carried on in this way until he was thirty-four.

Questions

1. What kind of truth can a photograph offer? How does the still nature of a photograph emphasize details that often go unnoticed in real life? If a photograph is mounted in an album, is it read differently?
2. For Auster, the photographs reaffirm his father's body, his physicality. Why is this so important for Auster? What is he trying to define in paragraph 4?
3. Auster speaks of his father as an "invisible man." Even while he was still alive, "I kept trying to find the father who was not

there." What kind of proof of his father's existence in the world
do the photographs offer?
4. How do the photographs help Auster see a side of his father that
he barely knew? Was this a "real" side of his father?

Sharon Olds, "I Go Back to May 1937"

I see them standing at the formal gates of their colleges,
I see my father strolling out
under the ochre sandstone arch, the
red tiles glinting like bent
plates of blood behind his head, I   5
see my mother with a few light books at her hip
standing at the pillar made of tiny bricks with the
wrought-iron gate still open behind her, its
sword-tips black in the May air,
they are about to graduate, they are about to get married,   10
they are kids, they are dumb, all they know is they are
innocent, they would never hurt anybody.
I want to go up to them and say Stop,
don't do it—she's the wrong woman,
he's the wrong man, you are going to do things   15
you cannot imagine you would ever do,
you are going to do bad things to children,
you are going to suffer in ways you never heard of,
you are going to want to die. I want to go
up to them there in the late May sunlight and say it,   20
her hungry pretty blank face turning to me,
her pitiful beautiful untouched body,
his arrogant handsome blind face turning to me,
his pitiful beautiful untouched body,
but I don't do it. I want to live. I   25
take them up like the male and female
paper dolls and bang them together
at the hips like chips of flint as if to
strike sparks from them, I say
Do what you are going to do, and I will tell about it.   30

Questions

1. What kinds of innocence is Olds evoking in this poem?
2. How would you describe the imagery she uses? Note especially
lines 5 and 9, as well as the "paper dolls" in the final lines.

3. How would you characterize Olds's reflections on these pictures? In other words, what sort of "picture" does her poem create?

Roland Barthes, "Looking for My Mother"

There I was, alone in the apartment where she had died, looking at   1
these pictures of my mother, one by one, under the lamp, gradually
moving back in time with her, looking for the truth of the face I had
loved. And I found it.

The photograph was very old. The corners were blunted from   2
having been pasted into an album, the sepia print had faded, and the
picture just managed to show two children standing together at the
end of a little wooden bridge in a glassed-in conservatory, what was
called a Winter Garden in those days. My mother was five at the
time (1898), her brother seven. He was leaning against the bridge
railing, along which he had extended one arm; she, shorter than he,
was standing a little back, facing the camera; you could tell that the
photographer had said, "Step forward a little so we can see you";
she was holding one finger in the other hand, as children often do,
in an awkward gesture. The brother and sister, united, as I knew, by
the discord of their parents, who were soon to divorce, had posed
side by side, alone, under the palms of the Winter Garden (it was
the house where my mother was born, in Chennevières-sur-
Marne).

I studied the little girl and at last rediscovered my mother. The   3
distinctness of her face, the naïve attitude of her hands, the place
she had docilely taken without either showing or hiding herself, and
finally her expression, which distinguished her, like Good from
Evil, from the hysterical little girl, from the simpering doll who
plays at being a grownup — all this constituted the future of a sover-
eign *innocence* (if you will take this word according to its etymology,
which is: "I do no harm"), all this had transformed the photographic pose into that untenable paradox which she had nonetheless
maintained all her life: the assertion of a gentleness. In this little
girl's image I saw the kindness which had formed her being immediately and forever, without her having inherited it from anyone;
how could this kindness have proceeded from the imperfect parents
who had loved her so badly — in short: from a family? Her kindness
was specifically *out-of-play*, it belonged to no system, or at least it
was located at the limits of a morality (evangelical, for instance); I
could not define it better than by this feature (among others): that
during the whole of our life together, she never made a single

"observation." This extreme and particular circumstance, so abstract in relation to an image, was nonetheless present in the face revealed in the photograph I had just discovered. "Not a just image, just an image," Godard says. But my grief wanted a just image, an image which would be both justice and accuracy—*justesse:* just an image, but a just image. Such, for me, was the Winter Garden Photograph.

Questions

1. Why is it so important for Barthes to find "the truth of the face [he] had loved"?
2. Barthes says that his mother (even in her childhood photograph) was characterized by "the assertion of a gentleness." He calls this phrase a "paradox." What does he mean by that?
3. What is a "just" image?

PRACTICE 4.1

Reflecting on a Photograph

After his father's death, Auster reflects on photographs of an "invisible" father, seeking documentary evidence of his existence in the world. His search for a father absent even in life raises the question of what sort of truth a photograph can reveal. Olds shows us how a photograph can suspend its subject in a moment of time, inducing in the writer the desire to engage in dialogue with the past. Barthes shows us one way of writing about a photograph of someone very close to the writer, someone remembered so well that the writer's reflections overwhelm the image, either filling it with the writer's feelings or noticing in it the absence of those qualities most important in the person whose image it is.

All three of these writers show how naturally photographs put us in a reflective mood. Because they freeze a moment in time, they force us to reflect in order to connect the flow of life to the frozen image reproduced by the camera. Taking these writers not as models but as inspiration, select a single photograph from your collection and reflect upon it. We suggest a group photograph of your family or a picture of yourself or a family member as a child or young adult. Try to make your writing as serious and thoughtful as what you have just read. Here are some things to remember as you prepare to write:

1. The reader will *not* have the picture, so you will not be able to depend on the visual image to work for you. You will have to put into words whatever you want the reader to know about the image you are re-

flecting upon. Before drafting, try listing the important things in the picture and those things that are left out or missing. Your draft may well turn upon the difference between what the picture reveals and what it conceals.

2. Think of the image as unchanging while everything around it changes. How does the physical presence of the image affect you as you prepare to write? Where does the image direct your thoughts? Close your eyes and think about the image. Where do your thoughts go, and what is *there?*

3. What do you remember, and what had you forgotten? What will become of this image? If you have chosen a photograph of a person, try to determine what things about the person are important to you, and make a list of them. Compare these with what the camera has caught and what it has missed. Here is space for reflection.

4. Qualities caught and missed, time frozen and moving, the simplicities of mechanism and the complexities of life — these are your starting points.

TELLING STORIES

People love to hear and to tell stories, yet stories are more than just fun. Not only do they help us make sense of the world but they also tell us how and why we came to be who and what we are. Every kind of group, including the family, has a set of stories about its past and present. By telling these stories, members of the group both relate to and shape each other, at the same time developing a sense of themselves as individuals with a shared familial and cultural heritage. In the following chapter from his book *Black Dog of Fate*, Peter Balakian tells a family story of how his grandmother came back into his life — first as poetry, then as history.

■ READING

Peter Balakian, "Words for My Grandmother"

The journey into history, into the Armenian Genocide, was for me   1
inseparable from poetry. Poetry was part of the journey and the excavation. I've never believed in poetry that expresses polemical ideas. I was a young poet devoted to immersing myself in the plasticity and lushness of words and making the best language I could. But I learned that when words collide with memory unexpected

things happen, as they did one day shortly after I began my first adult job.

I was teaching English at Dwight-Englewood School, and be-   2
cause my third-floor suite of rooms in Graham House was only a few hundred yards from my classroom, I slept as long as I could and made it to homeroom just before the students arrived. The phone was ringing early that Monday morning. It was my mother on the phone, in her cheery morning voice, informing me that on Sunday at church she and my aunts were having a *hokee hankisd* (memorial service) for the tenth anniversary of my grandmother's death.

"I can't come," I said. "I'm going to Cambridge to spend the   3
weekend with April."

"This is more important than being with some stranger."   4

"She's not a stranger."   5

"She's some girl who means nothing to any of us!"   6

I slammed down the phone and walked down the huge staircase   7
of Graham House, three flights, to the cavernous kitchen. I lit a match to start the old gas stove and boiled some water for a cup of awful instant coffee. I sat at the small Formica table staring at the long glass doors of the cabinets and the faded blue walls, sipping coffee. I was making it clear to myself that I wasn't going to let my mother force me to this *hokee hankisd*, not when April and I had a weekend planned. I kept sipping coffee and saying to myself, I'm not going. And I kept hearing the words *hokee hankisd*. A very Armenian sound. *Hokee*, soul. *Hankisd*, rest. The soul's rest: a memorial.

Armenians have a special sense of the word *hokee*. It's a word that   8
captures the Armenian feeling for the soul, for the spirit life, the invisible, the numinous. My grandmother addressing me: *hokees*, my soul, my beloved. During my night of fever in '62 when she had her flashback, she said: *Sounch* (breath). *Ott* (air). *Hokee* (soul). *Hokeet seerem*: I love your soul. *Hokeet dal*: to have soul-energy. *Hokvov yev marmenov*: body and soul. *Sourp hokee*: holy spirit. *Hokee kaloust*: coming of the spirit.

"Who the hell cares about a fucking *hokee hankisd* ten years   9
later!" I said to my mother when she called again.

Her voice turned icy. "Have you forgotten how much your   10
grandmother loved you?"

"I'll think of her all weekend," I said as I hung up.   11

On Friday afternoon after coaching J. V. football, I got into   12
my new brown Toyota Corolla and drove to Cambridge to spend the weekend with April in her dorm at the Harvard Business School, where she was finishing an MBA. I was feeling grown

up with my new paycheck and sense of independence. We took in a couple of movies and ate at a chic restaurant in Boston. We drove the streets of Cambridge after midnight in my new car, and wound up in some bars off Central Square. We slept late and lounged under the sheets reading to each other while we drank bad instant coffee.

I pulled into the long circular driveway at Graham House late on   13
Sunday night feeling good about life. As I walked up the staircase, I realized I hadn't thought once about my grandmother all weekend. Not about church, or family, or *hokee hankisd*. I opened the French doors to my apartment, chucked my knapsack on my bed, sat on my garage-sale turquoise couch, and opened my notebook. I just needed to write, and I began.

> The trees are bare
> with abandoned nests.
> Small swarms of birds
> break, dive, and rotate
> in a cloudless sky.
> I make my way through
> leaf-piles soaked by the night-rain;
> spaces between earth and sky
> cloud, field, and stone
> you too once entered
>
> It is ten years since
> you last saw your breath,
> and these shadows
> moving with day
> across the base of this oak.
>
> Ten years ago
> I walked your dark stairway,
> water hissing on the stove,
> your orientals worn
> and beaten into deep
> reds and blues by your
> half-confessed past.
>
> When you took my head
> in your arms
> and kissed my hair
> I stared as always
> at the skin of your hands

still discolored by
the arid Turkish plain.

I called it "Words for My Grandmother." This early poem—just   14
some clear images—had come out like a quiet rush of something
pent-up, and that was not how I usually wrote. Looking back, I can
see that those words came out of guilt for not having gone to the
hokee hankisd. I don't think my grandmother would have cared; her
love for me was unconditional. But I had let the family down, and
from that feeling came my personal *hokee hankisd*, a poem in which I
could arrest time and freeze memory. My grandmother had come
back to me for the first time in years.

The poem was a surprise. Out of my head came things I didn't   15
know I remembered. Images that focused and located forgotten
scenes. Those Friday afternoons at my grandmother's apartment in
East Orange when we baked *choereg.* The dark stairway, the apartment with its oriental rugs. The phrase that most startled me was
"half-confessed past." Not only didn't I know where it came from, I
wasn't even sure what it meant. The phrase was ahead of me, pointing to things I would come to know, things psychological, things
historical.

The image of my grandmother kissing my hair as she *eenched* me   16
to death was no surprise, nor her discolored hands, but the last
image, "the arid Turkish plain," also seemed to come out of
nowhere. I was twenty-three and no one had spoken to me about
the Armenian Genocide. My grandmother's flashback had been a
strange set of surrealistic images that left an imprint on me, but she
never talked about her past in rational language. This poem, then,
was a tremor from the unconscious—the historical unconscious,
the deep, shared place of ancestral pain, the place in the soul where
we commune with those who have come before us. I had written
this poem for a personal reason only. I had no historical awareness,
no political ideas, but somehow out of the collision of language
with personal memory came something larger. It was the first time
for me that poetic language became a mode of historical exploration, the first time a poem became an act of commemoration.

The next day I typed it up and sent it to my mother, with a note of   17
muted regret about having missed the *hokee hankisd.* With a bit of the
poet's ego I suggested as well that the poem was its own *hokee hankisd*,
and maybe even a better one than a church service. Mostly, I was
happy about the poem, not because I thought it was great but because
it had done what art can do: bring lost things back into your life. My
poem brought my grandmother back to me, whose love, perhaps,
meant more to me than anyone's. She was my friend and nurturer

again, now in my adult life. And with the poem's final image I had placed her at last: in the old world, the arid Turkish plain, lost Armenia. Now I would have to go and find out what that lost place was.

Questions

1. How do the Armenian words *hokee hankisd* function as an aid to memory for this young teacher of English?
2. How does Balakian explain his need to write?
3. How does the writing of the poem change Balakian's perception of his grandmother?

PRACTICE 4.2

Your Turn

Turn taking is key to the communal work of storytelling: you tell a story about the time you lost your head, and in response a friend tells you about some related incident involving a dog—an incident which in turn reminds you of the time your dog got lost and so on. Here we invite you to tell a story that connects you in some way to your family and its cultural heritage. You might want to think of your story as a response to Balakian's story—as a piece that *implicity* begins with the phrase, "That reminds me of an experience that made me feel connected with my family and our cultural heritage."

SCHOOL DAYS

In the following selection, Russell Baker recalls how a writing assignment changed him from a bored student to an engaged writer. Note that Baker re-creates the chain of associations the title of his topic sets off— associations that inspire him to write about a funny, warm family moment.

READING

Russell Baker, from *Growing Up*

The notion of becoming a writer had flickered off and on in my   1
head since the Belleville days, but it wasn't until my third year in
high school that the possibility took hold. Until then I'd been bored

by everything associated with English courses. I found English grammar dull and baffling. I hated the assignments to turn out "compositions," and went at them like heavy labor, turning out leaden, lackluster paragraphs that were agonies for teachers to read and for me to write. The classics thrust on me to read seemed as deadening as chloroform.

When our class was assigned to Mr. Fleagle for third-year English I anticipated another grim year in that dreariest of subjects. Mr. Fleagle was notorious among City students for dullness and inability to inspire. He was said to be stuffy, dull, and hopelessly out of date. To me he looked to be sixty or seventy and prim to a fault. He wore primly severe eyeglasses, his wavy hair was primly cut and primly combed. He wore prim vested suits with neckties blocked primly against the collar buttons of his primly starched white shirts. He had a primly pointed jaw, a primly straight nose, and a prim manner of speaking that was so correct, so gentlemanly, that he seemed a comic antique.

I anticipated a listless, unfruitful year with Mr. Fleagle and for a long time was not disappointed. We read *Macbeth*. Mr. Fleagle loved *Macbeth* and wanted us to love it too, but he lacked the gift of infecting others with his own passion. He tried to convey the murderous ferocity of Lady Macbeth one day by reading aloud the passage that concludes

> . . . I have given suck, and know
> How tender 'tis to love the babe that milks me.
> I would, while it was smiling in my face,
> Have plucked my nipple from his boneless gums. . . .

The idea of prim Mr. Fleagle plucking his nipple from boneless gums was too much for the class. We burst into gasps of irrepressible snickering. Mr. Fleagle stopped.

"There is nothing funny, boys, about giving suck to a babe. It is the—the very essence of motherhood, don't you see."

He constantly sprinkled his sentences with "don't you see." It wasn't a question but an exclamation of mild surprise at our ignorance. "Your pronoun needs an antecedent, don't you see," he would say, very primly. "The purpose of the Porter's scene, boys, is to provide comic relief from the horror, don't you see."

Late in the year we tackled the informal essay. "The essay, don't you see, is the...." My mind went numb. Of all forms of writing, none seemed so boring as the essay. Naturally we would have to write informal essays. Mr. Fleagle distributed a homework sheet offering us a choice of topics. None was quite so simpleminded as "What I Did on My Summer Vacation," but most seemed to be almost as dull. I took the list home and dawdled until the night before the essay was due. Sprawled on the sofa, I finally faced up to the grim task, took the list out of my notebook, and scanned it. The topic on which my eye stopped was "The Art of Eating Spaghetti."

This title produced an extraordinary sequence of mental images.   7 Surging up out of the depths of memory came a vivid recollection of a night in Belleville when all of us were seated around the supper table—Uncle Allen, my mother, Uncle Charlie, Doris, Uncle Hal— and Aunt Pat served spaghetti for supper. Spaghetti was an exotic treat in those days. Neither Doris nor I had ever eaten spaghetti, and none of the adults had enough experience to be good at it. All the good humor of Uncle Allen's house reawoke in my mind as I recalled the laughing arguments we had that night about the socially respectable method for moving spaghetti from plate to mouth.

Suddenly I wanted to write about that, about the warmth and good   8 feeling of it, but I wanted to put it down simply for my own joy, not for Mr. Fleagle. It was a moment I wanted to recapture and hold for myself. I wanted to relive the pleasure of an evening at New Street. To write it as I wanted, however, would violate all the rules of formal composition I'd learned in school, and Mr. Fleagle would surely give it a failing grade. Never mind. I would write something else for Mr. Fleagle after I had written this thing for myself.

When I finished it the night was half gone and there was no time   9 left to compose a proper, respectable essay for Mr. Fleagle. There was no choice next morning but to turn in my private reminiscence of Belleville. Two days passed before Mr. Fleagle returned the graded papers, and he returned everyone's but mine. I was bracing myself for a command to report to Mr. Fleagle immediately after school for discipline when I saw him lift my paper from his desk and rap for the class's attention.

"Now, boys," he said, "I want to read you an essay. This is titled   10 'The Art of Eating Spaghetti.'"

And he started to read. My words! He was reading *my words* out   11 loud to the entire class. What's more, the entire class was listening. Listening attentively. Then somebody laughed, then the entire class was laughing, and not in contempt and ridicule, but with open-hearted enjoyment. Even Mr. Fleagle stopped two or three times to repress a small prim smile.

I did my best to avoid showing pleasure, but what I was feeling   12 was pure ecstasy at this startling demonstration that my words had the power to make people laugh. In the eleventh grade, at the eleventh hour as it were, I had discovered a calling. It was the happiest moment of my entire school career. When Mr. Fleagle finished he put the final seal on my happiness by saying, "Now that, boys, is an essay, don't you see. It's—don't you see—it's of the very essence of the essay, don't you see. Congratulations, Mr. Baker."

For the first time, light shone on a possibility. It wasn't a very   13
heartening possibility, to be sure. Writing couldn't lead to a job after high school, and it was hardly honest work, but Mr. Fleagle had opened a door for me. After that I ranked Mr. Fleagle among the finest teachers in the school.

Questions

1. What periods of time are being reflected upon in the first two paragraphs?
2. Mr. Fleagle is described and presented to us primarily through the eyes of the sixteen-year-old Baker. Why? What do you think of Mr. Fleagle?
3. What statement is being made about reflective writing in this reflective piece?

PRACTICE 4.3

Reflection on Your School Days

Choose an event or situation from your elementary or high school years. It may be an event similar to the one in the Baker piece concerning a teacher or a subject you remember well. It may be an event of brief duration or a situation that extended over a period of time. You might list a number of events before you choose one to focus on.

Write out the event as you experienced it *then*, as if you were expressing your thoughts in a diary or in a letter to a close friend at the time the event took place. Read over what you have written, and reconsider the event from your present perspective. Then revise what you have written to emphasize this present perspective, being sure to provide a conclusion in which you reflect on what the event means to you *now*. Before you begin your draft, you might want to do some brainstorming to see what particular details you can remember—about the people involved and what they did or said, about the place where the event occurred, about your expectations, and about what you learned.

OTHER WAYS OF SEEING

When we become aware of how others see us, we may feel proud, embarrassed, confused, or even angry. These feelings, along with the experience that provoked them, can prompt self-reflection—a consideration of how our self looks to others and why it looks that way. Brent Staples, an editor at the *New York Times*, offers us just such a consideration in the following essay, which was originally published in *Ms.* magazine.

READING

Brent Staples, "Just Walk on By: A Black Man Ponders His Power to Alter Public Space"

My first victim was a woman—white, well dressed, probably in her early twenties. I came upon her late one evening on a deserted street in Hyde Park, a relatively affluent neighborhood in an otherwise mean, impoverished section of Chicago. As I swung onto the avenue behind her, there seemed to be a discreet, uninflammatory distance between us. Not so. She cast back a worried glance. To her, the youngish black man—a broad six feet two inches with a beard and billowing hair, both hands shoved into the pockets of a bulky military jacket—seemed menacingly close. After a few more quick glimpses, she picked up her pace and was soon running in earnest. Within seconds she disappeared into a cross street.

That was more than a decade ago. I was twenty-two years old, a graduate student newly arrived at the University of Chicago. It was in the echo of that terrified woman's footfalls that I first began to know the unwieldly inheritance I'd come into—the ability to alter public space in ugly ways. It was clear that she thought herself the quarry of a mugger, a rapist, or worse. Suffering a bout of insomnia, however, I was stalking sleep, not defenseless wayfarers. As a softy who is scarcely able to take a knife to a raw chicken—let alone hold it to a person's throat—I was surprised, embarrassed, and dismayed all at once. Her flight made me feel like an accomplice in tyranny. It also made it clear that I was indistinguishable from the muggers who occasionally seeped into the area from the surrounding ghetto. That first encounter, and those that followed, signified that a vast, unnerving gulf lay between nighttime pedestrians—particularly women—and me. And I soon gathered that being perceived as dangerous is a hazard in itself. I only needed to turn a corner into a dicey situation, or crowd some frightened, armed person in a foyer somewhere, or make an errant move after being pulled over by a policeman. Where fear and weapons meet—and they often do in urban America—there is always the possibility of death.

In that first year, my first away from my hometown, I was to become thoroughly familiar with the language of fear. At dark, shadowy intersections in Chicago, I could cross in front of a car stopped at a traffic light and elicit the *thunk, thunk, thunk, thunk* of the driver—black, white, male, or female—hammering down the door locks. On less traveled streets after dark, I grew accustomed to but never comfortable with people who crossed to the other side of the street rather than pass me. Then there were the standard unpleasantries with police, doormen, bouncers, cab drivers, and others whose business it is to screen out troublesome individuals *before* there is any nastiness.   3

I moved to New York nearly two years ago and I have remained an avid night walker. In central Manhattan, the near-constant crowd cover minimizes tense one-on-one street encounters. Elsewhere—visiting friends in SoHo,[1] where sidewalks are narrow and tightly spaced buildings shut out the sky—things can get very taut indeed.   4

Black men have a firm place in New York mugging literature. Norman Podhoretz[2] in his famed (or infamous) 1963 essay, "My Negro Problem—And Ours," recalls growing up in terror of black males; they "were tougher than we were, more ruthless," he writes—and as an adult on the Upper West Side of Manhattan, he continues, he cannot constrain his nervousness when he meets black men on certain streets. Similarly, a decade later, the essayist and novelist Edward Hoagland extols a New York where once "Negro bitterness bore down mainly on other Negroes." Where some see mere panhandlers, Hoagland sees "a mugger who is clearly screwing up his nerve to do more than just *ask* for money." But Hoagland has "the New Yorker's quick-hunch posture for broken-field maneuvering," and the bad guy swerves away.   5

I often witness that "hunch posture," from women after dark on the warrenlike streets of Brooklyn where I live. They seem to set   6

---

[1]A district of lower Manhattan known for its art galleries.
[2]A literary critic and editor of *Commentary* magazine.

their faces on neutral and, with their purse straps strung across their chests bandolier style, they forge ahead as though bracing themselves against being tackled. I understand, of course, that the danger they perceive is not a hallucination. Women are particularly vulnerable to street violence, and young black males are drastically overrepresented among the perpetrators of that violence. Yet these truths are no solace against the kind of alienation that comes of being ever the suspect, against being set apart, a fearsome entity with whom pedestrians avoid making eye contact.

It is not altogether clear to me how I reached the ripe old age of   7
twenty-two without being conscious of the lethality nighttime pedestrians attributed to me. Perhaps it was because in Chester, Pennsylvania, the small, angry industrial town where I came of age in the 1960s, I was scarcely noticeable against a backdrop of gang warfare, street knifings, and murders. I grew up one of the good boys, had perhaps a half-dozen fist fights. In retrospect, my shyness of combat has clear sources.

Many things go into the making of a young thug. One of   8
those things is the consummation of the male romance with the power to intimidate. An infant discovers that random flailings send the baby bottle flying out of the crib and crashing to the floor. Delighted, the joyful babe repeats those motions again and again, seeking to duplicate the feat. Just so, I recall the points at which some of my boyhood friends were finally seduced by the perception of themselves as tough guys. When a mark cowered and surrendered his money without resistance, myth and reality merged—and paid off. It is, after all, only manly to embrace the power to frighten and intimidate. We, as men, are not supposed to give an inch of our lane on the highway; we are to seize the fighter's edge in work and in play and even in love; we are to be valiant in the face of hostile forces.

Unfortunately, poor and powerless young men seem to take all   9
this nonsense literally. As a boy, I saw countless tough guys locked away; I have since buried several, too. They were babies, really—a teenage cousin, a brother of twenty-two, a childhood friend in his mid-twenties—all gone down in episodes of bravado played out in the streets. I came to doubt the virtues of intimidation early on. I chose, perhaps even unconsciously, to remain a shadow—timid, but a survivor.

The fearsomeness mistakenly attributed to me in public places   10
often has a perilous flavor. The most frightening of these confusions occurred in the late 1970s and early 1980s when I worked as

a journalist in Chicago. One day, rushing into the office of a magazine I was writing for with a deadline story in hand, I was mistaken for a burglar. The office manager called security and, with an ad hoc posse, pursued me through the labyrinthine halls, nearly to my editor's door. I had no way of proving who I was. I could only move briskly toward the company of someone who knew me.

Another time I was on assignment for a local paper and killing   11
time before an interview. I entered a jewelry store on the city's af-fluent Near North Side. The proprietor excused herself and re-turned with an enormous red Doberman pinscher straining at the end of a leash. She stood, the dog extended toward me, silent to my questions, her eyes bulging nearly out of her head. I took a cursory look around, nodded, and bade her good night. Relatively speaking, however, I never fared as badly as another black male journalist. He went to nearby Waukegan, Illinois, a couple of summers ago to work on a story about a murderer who was born there. Mistaking the reporter for the killer, police hauled him from his car at gun-point and but for his press credentials would probably have tried to book him. Such episodes are not uncommon. Black men trade tales like this all the time.

In "My Negro Problem—And Ours," Podhoretz writes that   12
the hatred he feels for blacks makes itself known to him through a variety of avenues—one being his discomfort with that "special brand of paranoid touchiness" to which he says blacks are prone. No doubt he is speaking here of black men. In time, I learned to smother the rage I felt at so often being taken for a criminal. Not to do so would surely have led to madness—via that special "paranoid touchiness" that so annoyed Podhoretz at the time he wrote the essay.

I began to take precautions to make myself less threatening. I   13
move about with care, particularly late in the evening. I give a wide berth to nervous people on subway platforms during the wee hours, particularly when I have exchanged business clothes for jeans. If I happen to be entering a building behind some people who appear skittish, I may walk by, letting them clear the lobby before I return, so as not to seem to be following them. I have been calm and ex-tremely congenial on those rare occasions when I've been pulled over by the police.

And on late-evening constitutionals along streets less traveled by,   14
I employ what has proved to be an excellent tension-reducing measure: I whistle melodies from Beethoven and Vivaldi and the more popular classical composers. Even steely New Yorkers hunching toward nighttime destinations seem to relax, and

occasionally they even join in the tune. Virtually everybody seems to sense that a mugger wouldn't be warbling bright, sunny selections from Vivaldi's *Four Seasons*. It is my equivalent of the cowbell that hikers wear when they know they are in bear country.

Questions

1. How many shifts in time do you find in this essay?
2. How does Staples use Norman Podhoretz's essay?
3. Staples tells how he has had to alter his behavior. Would you say there is a larger message in this essay? How would you state it?

■ PRACTICE 4.4

A Self-Defining Experience or Two

Recount and reflect on one or two self-defining experiences in your life. Following Brent Staples's lead, you might want to focus on an experience that made you aware of how others perceived you. But whatever kind of experience you choose to recount, be sure to reflect on the difference the experience made in your self-perception and actions.

REFLECTION AS REVISION

Joan Swift's poem "The Line-Up" began with an actual experience at the Oakland, California, Police Department, but as Swift reports, "it did not start to take form until almost a month later." The poem is itself a reflection on the strong emotions Swift felt after having to identify someone in a line-up. After writing the first draft, she "abandoned the poem for a month." She did the same after writing both the second and third drafts. Two weeks later, the final six lines were written. For Swift, revising is clearly an integral part of writing. We have included the complete first and second drafts here along with most of draft three. We end by printing the final, published version. Read the drafts carefully, noting the choices the writer made: What did she abandon? What did she retain?

█ READING

Joan Swift, "The Line-Up" and Its Drafts

   Draft #1 (4-7-70). Joan Swift notes about writing the first draft: "Its tentative beginnings were random lines in free verse. After a few of these, with the 'mother' image written and crossed out a couple of times I abandoned the poem for a month." This is a form of experimenting, of listing. It is much like free associating, yet there seems to be a dominant idea, or image, present. How many times does the mother image appear, and in what contexts?

THE LINE-UP

~~It is hard to think of them having mothers.~~

~~They stand, tall and short,~~

~~skinny and stout,~~

~~all black~~

~~all loose armed hanging at their sides,~~ *their* ... *s*

~~blinking into the glare of the lights~~

~~of the police lights~~

~~I think of their mothers.~~

~~It is hard to think of them having mothers.~~

The men ~~They~~ stand on the platform

and blink into the glare of the lights

like ~~the badly rehearsed chorus line of a~~

~~high school musical.~~

They are tall and short,

thick-necked and skinny

all black

all mothered by women

who somehow had better hopes for them.

~~Felons and doers of gross misdemeanors,~~

~~sad faced~~

~~Thieves and~~

Burglars

Draft #2 (5-8-70). In the second draft, the opening lines generate a series of attempts to work with the concept of going to sleep with the mother at the bedside and then waking anew. How many times does "wake" appear, and in what contexts? As in the first draft, Swift is trying out ways of describing the boys. Note the differences in each of these drafts between the writer's perceptions of the boys and society's.

```
THE LINE-UP
                is
Each one ^ so sad

I want to be his mother
                    glaring
tell him the ~~staring~~ lights will go down

and he will sleep ~~and dream~~ soon


~~to wake small~~

~~just beginning~~


~~to wake small~~

~~in a green field~~


~~like a wet brown calf~~


~~the platform, the police~~


No need to turn under eyes

~~to wear a number~~

~~fold and unfold black fingers~~


shuffle ~~like~~ poor soldiers

~~or~~ boys in a play

to wear numbers

~~and number all days~~

obey


~~Wake small in a new house~~

~~unguarded~~

~~tell him~~

~~wake up wake up~~

~~the sun is a~~

~~tell him~~

~~wake up wake up~~
```

~~Though their names~~

~~are Thief and Despair,~~

~~Pickpocket, Rapist,~~

Draft #3 (5-27-70). Of this draft, Swift noted, "Tackling it again three weeks later, I am astonished to see now, the lines came easily." Here in this excerpt from the third draft, which is the longest (60 lines), substantial work is accomplished, but the writer stops before ending the poem. The last six lines come two weeks later, and a few other revisions are made as Swift types up the final version of the poem. What images appear in this draft but not in the final version? What lines get reworked?

```
THE LINE-UP
                            in the glare
Each one is so sad, so _____

I want to be his mother
                white light
tell him the glaring light will go down
                sleep
and he will be home soon.


No need to turn under eyes

to shuffle, poor soldiers, boys


in a play,

obey. No need to wear numbers, obey.


only the voice of


They have hands as limp as wet leaves
                    the long
and as brown, all the fingers of their lives
         the long fingers all the dead-ends

hanging. Their eyes cannot see

past the
hanging
Their eyes cannot see past the edge


hanging. Their eyes cannot see
                    their ears
past the bright edge nor hear me
```

* * * *

~~Trees without bars, sun a wild juice.~~ *sweet*

in some utterly new place!

Trees without bars, sun a sweet juice.

* * * *

~~Now I must name him.~~

~~Now I must give him~~

~~a name.~~

* * * *

Water spilling the first ~~emeralds~~ over their_____

~~Such a field has no warden!~~

~~Can such a field have a warden?~~

A field with no warden!

But the walls come in to tell me where I am: *like police*

~~They come in like his name.~~

Captured, like him.

Caught in my accusation

Caught in the need to accuse

Caught with my accusation

~~Caught with his face like a~~ *in my throat* _____

~~forever like a chicken bone~~

The published version. Here are Joan Swift's final comments on the poem:

> The poem says: The prisoners are helpless and pitiful in their helpless-
> ness. I would like to make each one of them happy and free. But I am a

prisoner too, trapped by the same world which has trapped them, locked
in my role of accuser against my will.
  Does it say more than that?

How would you answer Joan Swift's question?

The Line-Up

Each prisoner is so sad in the glare
I want to be his mother

tell him the white light will go down
and he will sleep soon.

No need to turn under eyes   5
to shuffle   poor soldiers   boys

in a play
to wear numbers   obey.

They have hands as limp as wet leaves
the long fingers of their lives   10

hanging. They cannot see
past the sharp edge nor hear me

breathe. O I would tell each one
he will wake small again

in some utterly new place!   15
Trees without bars   sun a sweet juice

a green
field full of pardon.

The walls come in. I am
captured like him   20

locked in this world forever   unable to say   run

be free
I love you

having to accuse   25
and accuse.

Questions

1. Swift notes that she drops the prisoners' physical and racial characteristics, as well as the nature of their crimes. What effect does she gain by this?
2. Swift notes that the following revisions occurred as she typed what was to be the final version of the poem: "the field without a warden becomes a field full of pardon; 'turn' near the end becomes 'run.'" How would you describe the effects of these two changes?
3. For Swift, as we've noted, writing means allowing time for revision before a new draft. What other "rules" for revising do her drafts provide?

■ **PRACTICE 4.5**

Revising Your Own Writing

Look again at your previous expressive or reflective writing. Choose the piece that interests you the most for revision. This might be a piece whose ideas you want to further develop, that could be more effectively organized, or that you were dissatisfied with for some reason and want to rework.

Writing the Self: Two Projects

We offer here two ways of writing one's self. The first asks you to present aspects of yourself as a collage, using a form like Louise De Salvo's, in which you isolate some important moments in your life to make a story. Notice that De Salvo does not stick to a chronological order, yet her arrangement is not a random one either. Because she wants to tell the story of how she became a college professor and a scholar specializing in the work of Virginia Woolf, she chooses the important moments in her life that led her to her career choice.

For the second project, reflecting on Cyber-Chat Selves, you will have to give some thought to how selves are affected by cyberspace.

▨ READING

Louise De Salvo, from "A Portrait of the *Puttana* as a Middle-Aged Woolf Scholar"

I am thirteen years old. I have begun my adolescence with a vengeance. I am not shaping up to be the young woman I'm supposed to be. I am not docile. I am not sweet. I am certainly not quiet. And, as my father has told me dozens of times, I am not agreeable: if he says something is green, I am sure to respond that it is orange. I have mastered every conceivable method of turning my household into turmoil. I have devised a method of looking up at the ceiling when my father lectures me that instantly drives him into a frenzy.

In the middle of one of these fairly frequent outbursts, I run out of the house, feeling that I am choking, the tears hot on my cheeks. It is nighttime. I have no place to go. But I keep running. There are welcoming lights a few blocks away. It is the local library. I run up the stairs. I run up to the reading room with its engulfing brown leather chairs, pull an encyclopedia down from the shelf, and pre-

1

2

tend to read so that I won't be kicked out. It is cool and it is quiet. My rage subsides. I think that if there is a heaven, surely it must resemble a library. I think that if there is a god, surely she must be a librarian.

*

It is 1957.   3

I am fourteen years old, standing behind the window of the bak-   4
ery where I work to earn my spending money. Inside the bakery, I
have to control my appetite or I will eat everything in sight and become grotesque and obese. You can't let yourself do that because
boys only like attractive girls and attractive girls are always slim.
What I do inside the bakery is fold paper boxes before I put the pas-
tries and cakes inside. And then I tie up the boxes with the red and
white string that always tears into my flesh. What I'm doing is putting my appetitive self, which I am afraid will run out of control,
into neatly packaged, antiseptic, pure boxes—containing it and
tying it up.

Across the street, through the window, I see my friends playing   5
endless games that involve laughing, touching, rolling on the grass.
I am behind the plate-glass window, looking at life, looking at them
having fun, locked away, earning money by putting buns in bags
and cakes in boxes.

On Halloween, children come and paint the plate-glass window.   6
They paint witches and goblins in black and in primary colors. Now
I can't even see what is going on in the park across the street. But I
still put the buns in boxes. It never occurs to me to even fantasy
breaking through the window while I'm working or to wash the
paint away. Or, more simply, to open the door and cross the street
to the playground. Work is work. And work permits no play. I have
to work. That is the way it is. Opening the door to let in the sound
of laughter while working, crossing that street to the playground
after work, learning to enjoy work and learning to be able to play
will take many years. And psychoanalysis. And work on Virginia
Woolf.

*

Autumn 1963.   7

I am a senior at Douglass College. In 1963 Douglass College is   8
the kind of school a bright young working-class woman can afford.
Douglass, I think, is filled with brilliant women, and I have never
seen brilliant women before. I have studied Shakespeare with
Doris Falk, the novel with Anna Wells, philosophy with Amelie
Rorty. I now have Twentieth-Century Fiction with Carol Smith.

Carol Smith is lecturing on Virginia Woolf's *To the Lighthouse*.   9
She is talking about the relationship between Mr. and Mrs. Ramsay
in "The Window" section of the novel. I have never in my life
heard such genius. I am taking notes, watching her talk, and watching her belly. She is very pregnant. She is wearing a beige maternity
dress. I take down every word, while watching to see when the baby
she is pregnant with will kick her again.

I learn to love Virginia Woolf. I observe that it is possible to be a   10
woman, to be brilliant, to be working, to be happy, and to be pregnant. And all at the same time.

*

I am interviewed about how an Italian-American woman like me   11
became a Woolf scholar. I search my memory, think of studying
with Carol Smith, and suddenly remember my fascination with
the figure of Cam Ramsay in *To the Lighthouse*. Cam Ramsay,
the child Mrs. Ramsay virtually ignores, so busy is she with her
son James; Cam Ramsay, the child who is "wild and fierce." The
child who clenches her fist and stamps her feet. The child who is
always running away, running away. The child who will not let anyone invade the private space that she has created to protect herself
in this family with a tyrannical father who strikes out with a beak of
brass.

I remember my own adolescence. Could it be that I have   12
seen something of myself in Cam those many years ago and that
in trying to understand the relationship between Cam Ramsay
and her creator, Virginia Woolf, I am also trying to learn something
about my own past? Aren't I now in the middle of a long essay
about Virginia Woolf as an adolescent, reading her 1897 diary, a tiny
brown gilt leather volume, with a lock and key, that must be read with
a magnifying glass, so tiny and spidery is the hand, an essay that has
given me more satisfaction to write than anything I have written yet
about Virginia Woolf? And haven't I been stressing Woolf's capacity
to cope, rather than her neurosis, in that difficult year? Could it be
that in concentrating on Woolf's health, I am also trying to heal
myself?

I am married, and enduring my husband's medical internship as   13
best I can, on next to no money, with a baby who never sleeps and
who cries all the time. Although I am twenty-five, I look fifty. I
have deep circles under my eyes. I have no figure. I am still wearing
maternity clothes.

I had put my husband through medical school. (According to   14
him, I *helped* put him through medical school—his parents paid his

tuition and gave him a small allowance, and I worked as a high school English teacher and paid for everything else.) In that internship year, we came very close to a divorce. Your basic doctor-in-training-meets-gorgeous-nurse-and-wants-to-leave-his-wife-and-small-baby story.

One day, I look into the bathroom mirror and decide that I   15
will either kill myself or that I will go back to graduate school and become economically independent as quickly as I can. I look into the medicine chest, thinking that if my husband leaves me with this baby, I will probably be young, gifted, and on welfare. After wondering whether you could kill yourself by taking a year's supply of birth control pills and fantasying that, with the way my luck is running, I might grow some hair on my chest, but I probably wouldn't die, I decide that I will go back to school, get a Ph.D., and go into college teaching. I also realize that I might buy some time by squelching the young-doctor-leaves-his-young-wife-for-nurse script, at least temporarily, by announcing to my husband that if he leaves me, *he* can have the baby. Then he and his sweet young nurse can contemplate how romantic their life together will be with this baby who cries and throws up all the time.

He tells me he doesn't believe that I can part with my child.   16
I say, "Wanna bet?"   17
Shortly thereafter, he decides to hang around for a while longer.   18

*

When I first learned that Virginia Woolf had spent seven years   19
in the creation of *The Voyage Out,* her first novel, I thought that surely she must have been mad for that, if for no other reason. But as I carted off copies of *Melymbrosia,* my reconstruction of the earlier version of that novel, to the Editor's Office of The New York Public Library some seven years after *I* had begun working with her novel, I reflected that I have come to share a great deal with this woman. I have come to be a great deal like her in her attitudes toward the male establishment and art and feminism and politics; have learned from living for seven years with her to take the very best from her while managing, through the example of her life and her honesty about it, to avoid the depths of her pain.

She has been very good to me, this woman.   20

In looking back over my life, I realize that my work on Virginia   21
Woolf has helped me make some important changes.

Before I worked on Virginia Woolf, I wasn't a feminist. Before I   22
worked on Virginia Woolf, I didn't know how strong a woman I
was. Before I worked on Virginia Woolf, I whined a lot, like my
Italian foremothers, about how men got all the breaks and about
the ways they abused their women, like I felt I had been abused, but
I didn't really understand that there was a social structure that was
organized to keep men dominant and women subservient, and I really didn't understand how important it was for women to be economically independent and the potentially horrifying consequences
if they were not.

Before I worked on Virginia Woolf, I would ask the young doc-   23
tors who came to our house for dinner if I could get them another
cup of coffee, being careful to wait until there was a break in the
conversation. Now my husband, Ernie, and our children—Jason
and Justin—get up to cook me breakfast. Virginia Woolf has, in
many ways, created a monster in me, and I am proud to give
her partial credit for it. I like to think that she would have been
pleased that my reading *A Room of One's Own* has been a very important part of my emancipation from the tradition of the suffering
woman. Now I am a hell-raiser, a spitfire, and I buy and wear
"Mean Mother," "Nurture Yourself," and "I Am a Shameless Agita-
tor" buttons. And I have recently started to pump iron (much to the
amusement of fifteen-year-old Jason—the would-be writer, the
one who used to throw up all the time, who has turned out to be a
very nice kid after all—and eleven-year-old Justin, who has something to say about everything I do). But sometimes, when I'm feeling really good and have the time, I make them a bread pudding.

Questions

1. Reflection involves the manipulation of time. Look at the selection and try to determine exactly how many different moments
   in time can be distinguished. Note especially all the words that
   help keep the reader clearly oriented in time. How many of these
   paragraphs are entirely lacking in markers that indicate some
   change or shift in time?
2. The essential feature of the management of time in reflective
   writing is a distinction between the time of the events being reflected upon and the moment of reflection itself. Read through
   these paragraphs noting every phrase that indicates a difference
   between the time of the events and the time of reflection. What
   effect has De Salvo tried to attain through use of the present
   tense?

PROJECT 1: GETTING IT TOGETHER

Aspects of My Self: A Collage

We invite you to write a portrait of your life in the form of a collage. A collage is a collection of separate pieces that work together to make a story or, in the case of art, a picture. The artist Picasso created a portrait of a student by juxtaposing and superimposing fragments and cutouts of things that evoke a Parisian student: a beret, a pipe, a piece of newspaper, a rectangle to suggest a thin face, a tiny painted mustache, and so on. Similarly, De Salvo takes pieces of her life and juxtaposes them to create a story or portrait of herself.

You may have a story of discovery similar to De Salvo's, or you may still be discovering what your career will be. To get started, list memorable moments in your life as they occur to you. All lives are stories of education of one kind or another. By juxtaposing moments in your life, you will discover your own story of education and growth. As you write your drafts of particular moments, you may make further discoveries of previously hidden connections.

PROJECT 2: TAKING IT FURTHER

Look Who's Talking: Cyber-Chat Selves

What difference, if any, does the existence and proliferation of computer-mediated communication (CMC) make to our sense of self? To explore this issue, you'll need to do some research—on- and off-line. One place to begin is with a recent book on the issue of the self in cyber-space; for example, you might want to check out the first part of Sven Birkerts's *The Gutenberg Elegies* (Fawcett Columbine, 1994), Sherry Turkle's *Life on the Screen: Identity in the Age of the Internet* (Simon and Schuster, 1995), or some of the essays in Dale Spender's *Nattering on the Net* (Spinifex, 1995).

After you get some overview of the topic, you can choose a focus and put together an up-to-date bibliography of relevant books and articles. But you also need to get down to cases. More specifically, we suggest that for a week or two, you study who's talking—about what and how—in some on-line listserv, Usenet forum, or chat room. To get a list of on-going conversation groups, chats, and newsgroups, go to one of the following addresses: **<http://tile.net/lists>, <http://www.liszt.com/>,** or **<http:www.nova.edu/Inter-Links/cgi-bin/news-lists.pl>.** A list of newsgroups can also be found at **<http://sunsite.unc.edu/usenet-i/home.html>.** And don't forget that commercial services such as America

Online and CompuServe provide a variety of chat rooms for their customers' use.

To help you with your study of who's talking about what on-line, you may want to read a few of the pieces you've listed in your up-to-date bibliography on some aspect of the self in the cyberspace age. But the focus of your study should be on listening to and reflecting on the selves that are chatting in some on-line venue during a specific period of time, and your purpose is to think about what difference, if any, the existence and proliferation of CMC makes to contemporary senses of the self.

PART THREE

Writing and Knowledge

There is no doubt that all our knowledge begins with experience.
   —*Immanuel Kant,* Critique of Pure Reason *(1781)*

[W]e are well on our way to seeing conversation *as the ultimate context within which knowledge is to be understood.*
   —*Richard Rorty,* Philosophy and the Mirror of Nature *(1979)*

Every day people are asked to answer numerous questions: What time is it? Where did you buy that hat? How do I get to the subway? Usually, we answer such questions with ease and good humor. But as parents, teachers, and employers know only too well, the time always comes when something else—something other than the answer— must be said. Perhaps someone asks, "What's a platypus? Is it an animal?" To these questions, one response is bound to be, "I don't know; look it up."

The "look it up" response acknowledges the importance of book learning and, with it, the connection between writing and knowledge. Although writing may be key to knowing, for the past two hundred years the emphasis has often been on something else: amassing empirical data—information gained through the sensory experience of things. In 1781, the philosopher Immanuel Kant opened his major work on the subject of knowledge with the following sentence: "There is no doubt that all our knowledge begins with experience." But even though Kant designated experience as the beginning, he never confused the uncritical accumulation of information with the related but more significant project of *constructing* knowledge. His support and promotion of empirical science was thoughtful, not simpleminded. Experience may be first and foremost, but beginning with experience is no simple matter, in part because what makes experience possible is a set of innate cognitive categories, the two most important of which are time and space.

Time and space are the shape experience takes and therefore are basic to how we think and what we know. Perhaps that is why *narrating* and *describing* are such popular ways of representing knowledge. When we want to know what's going on, we often ask others to recount events—to tell us what happened or is happening. And, when we want a clearer sense of things, we ask for meaningful descriptive detail. In both cases, we seek knowledge that feels close to experience. As you read and write about happenings or scenes, ask yourself what kind of knowledge you are getting, how you are getting it, and why it might be valuable.

Knowledge may begin with an experience that can be narrated or described. But, as every person who has attended school can attest, it doesn't end there. In fact, schooling and knowledge are so closely associated in our culture that it is all too easy to think that only those with diplomas and degrees have knowledge, not to mention the know-how or discipline both to use what they have and to get more. This is the mistake that twelve-year-old Toni Cade Bambara is in danger of making when she brags to her "Grandma" Dorothy about knowing Einstein's theory of relativity (p. 206). But even though she must be taught a thing or two by Grandma, young Toni is right to feel that she knows some important things—things she learned from schoolbooks. For example, Toni knows unfamiliar terms such as *theory* and *relativity*. She also knows that she must define and explain unfamiliar terms to her audience. But what's really impressive is that Toni also knows how to define and explain by differentiating one kind of thing—say a theory—from another kind of thing—say a "singing tale" or a "fable" (p. 206). In short, this young girl already knows how to do what the ancient Greek philosopher Aristotle thought absolutely essential for knowledge: she knows how to classify things.

Schooling teaches the importance of classifying in a number of ways, including in its institution of different subject-matter areas such as social studies and earth sciences. In college, subject-matter areas tend to become disciplines, a transformation that usually entails further differentiations. So, for example, high school social studies becomes a number of different college-level disciplines, such as sociology, anthropology, history, and women's studies. As you probably already know, a discipline usually has its own special terminology, yet it takes more than a set of esoteric terms to make a discipline. It takes a common set of issues and one or more agreed upon ways of producing knowledge about those issues. That is why we expect to see the chemist measuring elements in a lab, the cultural anthropologist observing familial interactions in a Himalayan village, and the literary critic comparing one text with another in a library. But what we might not notice at first glance is that all of these researchers have at least one thing in common: they are all writing as they work. In so doing, they are beginning the process of producing knowledge.

Ultimately, the process that seems to begin with a researcher's experience in the lab, field, or library finds its end or purpose—and therefore its true origin—someplace else: in the context of an ongoing conversation. That, at least, is how the contemporary American philosopher Richard Rorty has invited us to understand our human interest and investment in knowledge. By making conversation first and foremost, Rorty is suggesting that what and how we know depends on our thoughtful discussions with others. To this social perspective on knowledge, we would add the idea that writing plays a significant role in getting and keeping conversations going. We invite you to test this idea out as you do the readings and practices in the next four chapters.

5

Telling What Happened or Happens
Narration

To narrate is to give an account—in speech or in writing—of a process or series of events that take place over a period of time. The period of time may be large or small, years or seconds, but time is the heart of narrative. Speech and writing themselves take time. It takes a certain amount of time to utter a sequence of sentences, or even a single sentence. It also takes time to write or to read a sentence. The art of writing narrative prose depends upon how the writer manages these two times—the time of events and the time of reading. It is possible, for instance, to describe a whole baseball season in a sentence ("The Red Sox started out well in April but faded in September—a familiar story"), but it is also possible to spend a lot of time—and a lot of words—describing a single pitch to a single batter. If you write about a single pitch, of course, you will break down that event (the pitch) into a series of sub-events (little movements of the pitcher and the batter—or even their thoughts and feelings) in order to make your account into a narrative.

A big part of the writer's task in producing narrative prose, then, is choosing a suitable **level of detail** for the events being recounted and arranging those details in a sequence that will present events clearly. The writer of narrative must also solve a few other problems. One is the problem of affect, the intensity of feeling the narrative creates. Every narrative generates some emotions. Often in academic writing, such as assignments in courses, the emotional effect sought is one of cold, dispassionate clarity. It is possible to think of this as the absence of emotion —as a pure, "natural" kind of writing. But the absence of emotion is far from natural. It is an effect achieved by writers through a considerable act of self-discipline. It is, in fact, something that every student of writing must work to achieve in order to satisfy the requirements of certain courses or instructors. The best way to gain control over the whole range of emotional possibilities in narration—from engaged to detached, from hot to cold—is to practice narrating the "same" events with different **emotional coloration.** In preparation for this kind of work, you should learn to read narrative prose with one eye on the way the writer shapes the reader's feelings about what is narrated.

Another problem facing the writer of narrative is that of **point of view.** From whose perspective will the events be recounted? As you are no doubt aware, viewpoint is closely related to the emotional quality of a narration. It is possible to tell events from the perspective of a detached observer, like a god or a scientist, but it is also possible to use the perspective of someone emotionally involved in the events. If you want to achieve an unemotional perspective about some experiments on a guinea pig, you do not recount them from the viewpoint of the guinea pig. One of the skills you should develop with respect to narrative is the ability to recount the "same" events from different points of view. Following are some examples for you to consider.

PERSPECTIVES ON STORY

Each of these samples is a short section from a longer work. They are not presented as complete texts, with beginnings, middles, and ends, but as demonstrations of how a good writer produces narrative prose. We ask you to look at them more slowly and carefully than you might if you were racing through a long book, and to think about the way in which each of them has been constructed.

READING

Five Examples

EXAMPLE 1. In the following two paragraphs from Louise Erdrich's novel *The Beet Queen,* Sita Kozka recounts a sequence of events that began one morning and ended twenty-four hours later. As you read Sita's narrative, try to notice how specific words and phrases signal the temporal sequence of events, how the focus shifts from one person to another, and how different details affect you.

Louise Erdrich, "Cousin Mary" (from *The Beet Queen*)

My cousin Mary came in on the early freight train one morning, with nothing but an old keepsake box full of worthless pins and buttons. My father picked her up in his arms and carried her down the hallway into the kitchen. I was too old to be carried. He sat her down, then my mother said, "Go clean the counters, Sita." So I don't know what lies she told them after that.

Later on that morning, my parents put her to sleep in my bed. When I objected to this, saying that she could sleep on the trundle, my mother said, "Cry sakes, you can sleep there too, you know." And this is how I ended up that night, crammed in the trundle, which is too short for me. I slept with my legs dangling out in the cold air. I didn't feel welcoming toward Mary the next morning, and who can blame me?

Questions

1. What features make this example of narration seem clear and simple? What features make this seemingly simple narrative interesting instead of just simpleminded?
2. How did Sita's narrative affect you? Did your feelings change from one moment in the narrative to another? Do you consider this a cold or a hot piece of writing? Is the narrative point of view detached or emotionally involved?

EXAMPLE 2. Richard Wright begins one of his best-known short stories, "The Man Who Lived Underground," with the following four paragraphs. As you can see, the paragraphs differ in length, with the second and fourth paragraphs being shorter than the first and third. Are there differences other than length between the longer and shorter paragraphs? As you read each paragraph, try to pay attention to what Wright does to get you involved in the feelings and actions of "the man." How does each paragraph affect you emotionally?

Richard Wright, "Going Underground" (from "The Man Who Lived Underground")

I've got to hide, he told himself. His chest heaved as he waited, crouching in a dark corner of the vestibule. He was tired of running and dodging. Either he had to find a place to hide, or he had to surrender. A police car swished by through the rain, its siren rising sharply. They're looking for me all over... He crept to the door and squinted through the fogged plate glass. He stiffened as the siren rose and died in the distance. Yes, he had to hide, but where? He gritted his teeth. Then a sudden movement in the street caught his attention. A throng of tiny columns of water snaked into the air from the perforations of a manhole cover. The columns stopped abruptly, as though the perforations had become clogged; a gray spout of sewer water jutted up from underground and lifted the circular metal cover, juggled it for a moment, then let it fall with a clang.

He hatched a tentative plan: he would wait until the siren sounded   2
far off, then he would go out. He smoked and waited, tense. At last the siren gave him his signal; it wailed, dying, going away from him. He stepped to the sidewalk, then paused and looked curiously at the open manhole, half expecting the cover to leap up again. He went to the center of the street and stooped and peered into the hole, but could see nothing. Water rustled in the black depths.

He started with terror; the siren sounded so near that he had the   3
idea that he had been dreaming and had awakened to find the car upon him. He dropped instinctively to his knees and his hands grasped the rim of the manhole. The siren seemed to hoot directly above him and with a wild gasp of exertion he snatched the cover far enough off to admit his body. He swung his legs over the opening and lowered himself into watery darkness. He hung for an eternal moment to the rim by his finger tips, then he felt rough metal prongs and at once he knew that sewer workmen used these ridges to lower themselves into manholes. Fist over fist, he let his body sink until he could feel no more prongs. He swayed in dank space; the siren seemed to howl at the very rim of the manhole. He dropped and was washed violently into an ocean of warm, leaping water. His head was battered against a wall and he wondered if this were death. Frenziedly his fingers clawed and sank into a crevice. He steadied himself and measured the strength of the current with his own muscular tension. He stood slowly in water that dashed past his knees with fearful velocity.

He heard a prolonged scream of brakes and the siren broke off.   4
Oh, God! They had found him! Looming above his head in the rain a white face hovered over the hole. "How did this damn thing get off?" he heard a policeman ask. He saw the steel cover move slowly until the hole looked like a quarter moon turned black. "Give me a hand here," someone called. The cover clanged into place, muffling the sights and sounds of the upper world. Knee-deep in the pulsing current, he breathed with aching chest, filling his lungs with the hot stench of yeasty rot.

Questions

1. What is your emotional reaction as you read this narrative of going underground? Do your feelings change from one moment to another? Does paragraph 1 affect you differently than paragraph 4?
2. Compare Sita's narration in Erdrich's "Cousin Mary" with Wright's narration of going underground. Is one more detached—or cool—than the other? Is one more detailed than the other? Does one emotionally involve you more than the other? In both cases, how much of the emotion results from the events recounted and how much from the words in which the events are recounted?

EXAMPLE 3. The following paragraphs are taken from a chapter on the nineteenth-century expansion of the American West in *The Oxford History of the American West*. Note how the writer arranges events that occur over a six-year period and beyond, as well as the amount of space he dedicates to each of two Indian tribes.

Clyde A. Milner II, "The Long Walk on the White Road"

By 1868, in the Southwest, the Navajos had fared much worse in   1
their relations with the United States. War with American forces
had come during the years that Americans were fighting each other.
The largest Civil War battle in the Far West had been fought in
New Mexico at Glorieta Pass in late March 1862. At this engagement, John M. Chivington, who would lead the slaughter at Sand
Creek in 1864, helped defeat a Confederate army. The Union's victory ended any serious threat of Confederate control in the Southwest. In August 1862, Brigadier General James H. Carleton arrived
in New Mexico in command of a column of California volunteers;
with the Confederate force already defeated, he turned to fighting
the Indians. Carleton wanted to end raids by the Mescalero
Apaches and by the Navajos. He directed his old colleague, Colonel
Kit Carson of the New Mexico volunteers, to invade first the lands
of the Apaches and then those of the Navajos. By the end of March
1863, more than four hundred Apaches had been relocated to the
new reservation at Bosque Redondo, next to the new military post
of Fort Sumner. Carson next attacked the Navajos, whose population of ten thousand may have been twenty times greater than that
of the Mescaleros. General Carleton had one message for the
Navajos: "Go to Bosque Redondo, or we will pursue and destroy
you. We will not make peace with you on any other terms."

Carson's men destroyed orchards, crops, and livestock. They   2
marched through Canyon de Chelly, the Navajos' great citadel. To
avoid starvation, six thousand Navajos surrendered by the spring of
1864. The military then organized the Navajos' Long Walk—three
hundred miles southeast to Bosque Redondo. By the end of the
year, eight thousand Indians had been relocated there. Those who
refused to surrender hid in isolated areas of their homeland or fled
west. One Navajo, Curly Tso, recounted that many of the Diné
(Navajos) saw Hweeldi (Bosque Redondo) as a place "where they
would be put to death eventually."

Carleton saw the new reservation as a place of cultural transfor-   3
mation where the Apaches and Navajos would take up farming and
where their children would learn to read and write and acquire the
"arts of peace" and the "truths of Christianity." The superintendent
of Indian affairs for New Mexico, Michael Steck, had his doubts.
He had been the agent for the Mescalero Apaches and he knew that
they considered the Navajos to be "inveterate enemies." He also
knew that the land at Bosque Redondo could not support such a
concentration of people. Carleton's grand experiment failed, destroyed by the forces of nature as much as by the forces of culture.
Drought and insects devastated the crops. The government delivered inadequate supplies. Once more the Diné faced starvation.

In 1868, the same congressionally appointed peace commission   4
that negotiated the new treaty at Fort Laramie sent two representatives to Bosque Redondo. On 1 June the representatives, who saw
the suffering of the Navajos, signed a treaty that allowed the people
to return to a reservation carved out of the Indians' old homeland.
The document still advocated programs such as schooling and
farming for the Navajos' cultural "advancement," but it recognized
the need for the Navajos to begin again on familiar ground.

What unfolded for the Diné after their return home is a remark-   5
able story. They reestablished their pastoral life-style with herds of
sheep, goats, and horses, but they did not continue to raid their
neighbors. Before removal, the Navajos had been a people divided
into extended families, bands, and clans. But the four bitter years at
Hweeldi had increased their sense of tribal unity and expanded the
Diné's familiarity with Anglo-American culture. The treaty of 1868
gave the Diné clearly defined borders for their homeland. The historian Peter Iverson has observed, "Their political boundaries
had been established: the Navajo Nation had begun." It also began
to grow. By 1870, the population reached fifteen thousand. By the
early twentieth century, the Navajo Nation was double that figure.
The reservation grew as well. From 1878 to 1886, five additions to
the original 1868 boundaries quadrupled the Navajos' territory.

Most significant, the Navajo reservation was never broken up into individual allotments. The Diné had escaped the deleterious results of the Dawes Act and its successors, and the Navajo population and Navajo lands continued to grow throughout the twentieth century.

Questions

1. Account for Milner's arrangement of time. What is his purpose in starting with conditions in 1868, then jumping back to 1862, then ending in 1886?
2. Given that the government's treatment of Native American peoples is an emotional topic, how objective is Milner's account of historical events? How much evaluative language can you find in these paragraphs?

EXAMPLE 4.   The following passage is taken from Jamaica Kincaid's book about the Caribbean island of Antigua, *A Small Place*. As you read this passage, try to think about the point of view from which the sequence of events is being narrated. Point of view is often defined in terms of the grammatical person (I, you, he/she, it, they) and the tense of the verbs (past, present, etc.). However, it can also be considered as a question of position and perspective: Whose experiences, feelings, and ideas inform and shape the narration of events?

Jamaica Kincaid, "The Tourist's Arrival" (from *A Small Place*)

You disembark from your plane. You go through customs. Since you are a tourist, a North American or European—to be frank, white—and not an Antiguan black returning to Antigua from Europe or North America with cardboard boxes of much needed cheap clothes and food for relatives, you move through customs swiftly, you move through customs with ease. Your bags are not searched. You emerge from customs into the hot, clean air: immediately you feel cleansed, immediately you feel blessed (which is to say special); you feel free. You see a man, a taxi driver; you ask him to take you to your destination; he quotes you a price. You immediately think that the price is in the local currency, for you are a tourist and you are familiar with these things (rates of exchange) and you feel even more free, for things seem so cheap, but then your driver ends by saying, "In U.S. currency." You may say, "Hmmmm, do you have a formal sheet that lists official prices and destinations?" Your driver obeys the law and shows you the sheet, and he apologises for the incredible mistake he has made in quoting you a price off the top of his head which is so vastly different (favouring him) from the one listed. You are driven to your hotel by this taxi driver in his taxi, a brand-new Japanese-made vehicle. The road on which you are travelling is a very bad road, very much in need of repair. You are feeling wonderful, so you say, "Oh, what a marvellous change these bad roads are from the splendid highways I am used to in North America." (Or, worse, Europe.) Your driver is reckless; he is a dangerous man who drives in the middle of the road when he thinks no other cars are coming in the opposite direction, passes other cars on blind curves that run uphill, drives at sixty miles an hour on narrow, curving roads when the road sign, a rusting, beat-up thing left over from colonial days, says 40 MPH. This might frighten you (you are on your holiday; you are a tourist); this might excite you (you are on your holiday; you are a tourist), though if you are from New York and take taxis you are used to this style of driving; most of the taxi drivers in New York are from places in the world like this. You are looking out the window (because you want to get your money's worth); you notice that all the cars you see are brand-new, or almost brand-new, and that they are all Japanese-made. There are no American cars in Antigua—no new ones, at any rate; none that were manufactured in the last ten years. You continue to look at the cars and you say to yourself, Why, they look brand-new, but they have an awful sound, like an old car—a very old, dilapidated car. How to account for that? Well, possibly it's because they use leaded gasoline in these brand-new cars whose engines were built to use non-leaded gasoline, but you mustn't ask the person driving the car if this is so, because he or she has never heard of unleaded gasoline. You look closely at the car; you see that it's a model of a Japanese car that you might hesitate to buy; it's a model that's very expensive; it's a model that's quite impractical for a person who has to work as hard as you do and who watches every penny you earn so that you can afford this holiday you are on. How do they afford such a car? And do they live in a luxurious house to match such a car? Well, no. You will be surprised, then, to see that most likely the person driving this brand-new car filled with the wrong gas lives in a house that, in comparison, is far beneath the status of the car; and if you were to ask why you would be told that the banks are encouraged by the government to make loans available for cars, but loans for houses not so easily available; and if you ask again why, you will be told that the two main car dealerships in Antigua are owned in part or outright by ministers in government. Oh, but you are on holiday and the sight of these brand-new cars driven by people who may or may not have really passed their driving test (there was once a scandal about driving licenses for sale) would not really stir up these thoughts in you.

Questions

1. Grammatically speaking, what is the point of view in this passage? Why do you think Kincaid uses the verb tense and person that she does?
2. In terms of position and perspective, what is the point of view of this paragraph? Is the paragraph informed and shaped by experiences, feelings, and ideas of a tourist? an Antiguan? both? neither? What is the relationship between this perspective and the grammatical person and tense of the paragraph?

EXAMPLE 5.   Our final example of narration consists of the last page (more or less) of James Joyce's famous novel *Ulysses.* This is not narration by a detached narrator, but what is called stream-of-consciousness narrative. In these lines we read the unpunctuated thoughts of Molly Bloom as she falls asleep on the night of June 16, 1904. She is thinking of her past, and in particular she recalls two different but similar events: the time she agreed to marry her husband, Leopold Bloom, while they lay together on the Hill of Howth outside of Dublin, Ireland, and an earlier moment, when she was a girl in Gibraltar and said yes to her first lover. The events narrated here are the thoughts themselves, and their order controls the order of the writing, but they are thoughts of these other two important events—each of which was a sequence leading up to the word *Yes*—so that we have a narrative within a narrative. To get the proper feeling from these lines, you should listen to them read aloud. As you study this text, try to see how the language conveys the excitement of the climactic events narrated. Pay particular attention to the use of the little words *and* and *yes*.

James Joyce, "The End of Molly's Soliloquy" (from *Ulysses*)

the sun shines for you he said the day we were lying among the rhododendrons on Howth head in the grey tweed suit and his straw hat the day I got him to propose to me yes first I gave him the bit of seedcake out of my mouth and it was leapyear like now yes 16 years ago my God after that long kiss I near lost my breath yes he said I was a flower of the mountain yes so we are flowers all a womans body yes that was one true thing he said in his life and the sun shines for you today yes that was why I liked him because I saw he understood or felt what a woman is and I knew I could always get round him and I gave him all the pleasure I could leading him on till he asked me to say yes and I wouldn't answer first only looked out over the sea and the sky I was thinking of so many things he didn't know of Mulvey and Mr Stanhope and Hester and father and old captain Groves and the sailors playing all birds fly and I say stoop and washing up dishes they called it on the pier and the sentry in front of the governors house with the thing round his white helmet poor devil half roasted and the Spanish girls laughing in their shawls and their tall combs and the auctions in the morning the Greeks and the jews and the Arabs and the devil knows who else from all the ends of Europe and Duke street and the fowl market all clucking outside Larby Sharons and the poor donkeys slipping half asleep and the vague fellows in the cloaks asleep in the shade on the steps and the big wheels of the carts of the bulls and the old castle thousands of years old yes and those handsome Moors all in white and turbans like kings asking you to sit down in their little bit of a shop and Ronda with the old windows of the posadas 2 glancing eyes a lattice hid for her lover to kiss the iron and the wineshops half open at night and the castanets and the night we missed the boat at Algeciras the watchman going about serene with his lamp and O that awful deepdown torrent O and the sea the sea crimson sometimes like fire and the glorious sunsets and the figtrees in the Alameda gardens yes and all the queer little streets and the pink and blue and yellow houses and the rosegardens and the jessamine and geraniums and cactuses and Gibraltar as a girl where I was a Flower of the mountain yes when I put the rose in my hair like the Andalusian girls used or shall I wear a red yes and how he kissed me under the Moorish wall and I thought well as well him as another and then I asked him with my eyes to ask again yes and then he asked me would I yes to say yes my mountain flower and first I put my arms around him yes and drew him down to me so he could feel my breasts all perfume yes and his heart was going like mad and yes I said yes I will Yes.

Questions

1. Try to outline the process of Molly's thoughts, beginning in this way: "First she thinks of what her husband said to her the day she got him to propose to her ('the sun shines for you') and then she remembers how they were lying among the rhododendrons...." Discuss with your fellow students any parts you have difficulty understanding.

2. Listen to some different versions of the passage read aloud. What is the right way to read it? That is, what emotional tone suits the passage best? Choose some portion of the passage and rewrite it in grammatically correct sentences that change as little of the original phrasing as possible. Does your rewrite change the emotional effect of the original? If so, how so?

Playing with Perspective and Level of Detail

We offer here some opportunities for you to use the examples of narrative we've provided as prompts for your own experiments with story-telling. We suggest you choose the one that interests you the most.

1. Rewrite the sequence of events in Erdrich's "Cousin Mary" from the mother's point of view. Imagine that you are Sita's mother writing a letter to your best friend about what happened when "poor orphaned Mary" first came to live with you.
2. a. Rewrite the sequence of events in Wright's "The Man Who Lived Underground" in a cool, direct manner. Imagine that you are "the man" and that you are now in police custody. You've confessed to having committed the crime but the police won't end the interrogation until you tell them how you eluded arrest in the first place. You are tired and want the interrogation session to end as quickly as possible, so you tell them what they want to know.
   b. How does your rewrite differ from the original? Did you change the level of detail? What about word choice? Compare paragraph 3 of the original with your rendition of the act of entering the sewer. What verbs did you use? What verbs does Wright use? What adjectives did you use? What adjectives does Wright use?
3. Write a brief, objective history of the past month or two of your life. Start with a statement of your present condition, and then choose the most important events to account for it. You will have to determine the arrangement of events as well as the amount of time each merits. Remember, you are required to be the historian of your own life and to relate its events coolly and dispassionately, no matter how busy or fraught with emotion it may have been. Take a lesson from Milner: when he wants to make a strong point, he quotes from a source.
4. Try narrating the tourist's taxi ride in Kincaid's "The Tourist's Arrival" in a way that represents it either as exciting or as frightening. Feel free to change the verb tense, person, perspective, level of detail,

and pace of Kincaid's narrative; do what you need to do to make it seem either exciting or frightening.

5. Imagine that you are Molly Bloom's psychoanalyst, and that the passage on page 95 is the transcription of her free association from your last session. For a paper you are planning to deliver at a forthcoming meeting of the Society for Psychoanalytic Study, you wish to include a description of Molly's case (with the name changed, of course). Write a version of Molly's thoughts that will be suitable for inclusion in your professional paper. If you don't know exactly what a professional paper at a psychoanalytic meeting would be like, don't worry. Use your imagination, and do your best to produce something that sounds more like a scientist and less like Molly Bloom, but that covers the material in the passage. You don't have to diagnose her case or cure her of anything; you only need to translate her free association into a scientific summary. You might begin something like this: "The patient while free-associating returned obsessively to certain scenes of her youth."

PATTERNING EVENTS

███ **READING**

Naguib Mahfouz, "Half a Day"

When a narrative emphasizes the patterning of events, it may seem peculiarly meaningful or allegorical. An *allegory* is a story with a second meaning partially hidden behind its literal account of events. The allegorical story "Half a Day" was written by Naguib Mahfouz, the prolific and popular Egyptian author who received the 1988 Nobel Prize in literature. Mahfouz is noted for writing works that can be both realistic and ambiguous. Translated into English by Denys Johnson-Davies, "Half a Day" comes from *The Time and the Place and Other Stories* (1992). As you read, pay close attention to Mahfouz's manipulation of time in the story.

> I proceeded alongside my father, clutching his right hand, running   1
> to keep up with the long strides he was taking. All my clothes were
> new: the black shoes, the green school uniform, and the red tar-
> boosh.[1] My delight in my new clothes, however, was not altogether

[1] *tarboosh:* a tasseled cloth cap, usually red, worn by Muslim men.

unmarred, for this was no feast day but the day on which I was to be cast into school for the first time.

My mother stood at the window watching our progress, and I would turn toward her from time to time, as though appealing for help. We walked along a street lined with gardens; on both sides were extensive fields planted with crops, prickly pears, henna trees, and a few date palms.   2

"Why school?" I challenged my father openly. "I shall never do anything to annoy you."   3

"I'm not punishing you," he said, laughing. "School's not a punishment. It's the factory that makes useful men out of boys. Don't you want to be like your father and brothers?"   4

I was not convinced. I did not believe there was really any good to be had in tearing me away from the intimacy of my home and throwing me into this building that stood at the end of the road like some huge, high-walled fortress, exceedingly stern and grim.   5

When we arrived at the gate we could see the courtyard, vast and crammed full of boys and girls. "Go in by yourself," said my father, "and join them. Put a smile on your face and be a good example to others."   6

I hesitated and clung to his hand, but he gently pushed me from him. "Be a man," he said. "Today you truly begin life. You will find me waiting for you when it's time to leave."   7

I took a few steps, then stopped and looked but saw nothing. Then the faces of boys and girls came into view. I did not know a single one of them, and none of them knew me. I felt I was a stranger who had lost his way. But glances of curiosity were directed toward me, and one boy approached and asked, "Who brought you?"   8

"My father," I whispered.   9

"My father's dead," he said quite simply.   10

I did not know what to say. The gate was closed, letting out a pitiable screech. Some of the children burst into tears. The bell rang. A lady came along, followed by a group of men. The men began sorting us into ranks. We were formed into an intricate pattern in the great courtyard surrounded on three sides by high buildings of several floors; from each floor we were overlooked by a long balcony roofed in wood.   11

"This is your new home," said the woman. "Here too there are mothers and fathers. Here there is everything that is enjoyable and beneficial to knowledge and religion. Dry your tears and face life joyfully."   12

We submitted to the facts, and this submission brought a sort of contentment. Living beings were drawn to other living beings, and from the first moments my heart made friends with such   13 boys as were to be my friends and fell in love with such girls as I was to be in love with, so that it seemed my misgivings had had no basis. I had never imagined school would have this rich variety. We played all sorts of different games: swings, the vaulting horse, ball games. In the music room we chanted our first songs. We also had our first introduction to language. We saw a globe of the Earth, which revolved and showed the various continents and countries. We started learning the numbers. The story of the Creator of the universe was read to us, we were told of His present world and of His Hereafter, and we heard examples of what He said. We ate delicious food, took a little nap, and woke up to go on with friendship and love, play and learning.

As our path revealed itself to us, however, we did not find it as totally sweet and unclouded as we had presumed. Dust-laden winds and unexpected accidents came about suddenly, so we had to be watchful, at the ready, and very patient. It was not all a matter of playing and fooling around. Rivalries could bring about pain and hatred or give rise to fighting. And while the lady would sometimes smile, she would often scowl and scold. Even more frequently she would resort to physical punishment.   14

In addition, the time for changing one's mind was over and gone and there was no question of ever returning to the paradise of home. Nothing lay ahead of us but exertion, struggle, and perseverance. Those who were able took advantage of the opportunities for success and happiness that presented themselves amid the worries.   15

The bell rang announcing the passing of the day and the end of work. The throngs of children rushed toward the gate, which was opened again. I bade farewell to friends and sweethearts and passed through the gate. I peered around but found no trace of my father, who had promised to be there. I stepped aside to wait. When I had waited for a long time without avail, I decided to return home on my own. After I had taken a few steps, a middle-aged man passed by, and I realized at once that I knew him. He came toward me, smiling, and shook me by the hand, saying, "It's a long time since we last met—how are you?"   16

With a nod of my head, I agreed with him and in turn asked, "And you, how are you?"   17

"As you can see, not all that good, the Almighty be praised!"   18

Again he shook me by the hand and went off. I proceeded a few steps, then came to a startled halt. Good Lord! Where was the street lined with gardens? Where had it disappeared to? When did all these vehicles invade it? And when did all these hordes   19 of humanity come to rest upon its surface? How did these hills of refuse come to cover its sides? And where were the fields that bordered it? High buildings had taken over, the street surged with children, and disturbing noises shook the air. At various points stood conjurers showing off their tricks and making snakes appear from baskets. Then there was a band announcing the opening of a circus, with clowns and weight lifters walking in front. A line of trucks carrying central security troops crawled majestically by. The siren of a fire engine shrieked, and it was not clear how the vehicle would cleave its way to reach the blazing fire. A battle raged between a taxi driver and his passenger, while the passenger's wife called out for help and no one answered. Good God! I was in a daze. My head spun. I almost went crazy. How could all this have happened in half a day, between early morning and sunset? I would find the answer at home with my father. But where was my home? I could see only tall buildings and hordes of people. I hastened on to the crossroads between the gardens and Abu Khoda. I had to cross Abu Khoda to reach my house, but the stream of cars would not let up. The fire engine's siren was shrieking at full pitch as it moved at a snail's pace, and I said to myself, "Let the fire take its pleasure in what it consumes." Extremely irritated, I wondered when I would be able to cross. I stood there a long time, until the young lad employed at the ironing shop on the corner came up to me. He stretched out his arm and said gallantly, "Grandpa, let me take you across."

Questions

1. The father describes school as a factory (par. 4), but the boy sees it as a fortress (par. 5). They both use metaphors—figures of speech in which one thing (school) is referred to as another thing (factory, fortress) that bears some resemblance to it. What other metaphors might be applied to school as it is presented in the story?
2. What is suggested by the "ranks" and the "intricate pattern" (par. 11) into which the children are separated? What resemblance does it bear to your school experience?
3. At what point in the story were you aware that this was not the story of a typical, or literal, day at school? What might the "half a day" at school be representing here?

■ PRACTICE 5.2

Finding a Pattern

Consider your own story of education both in and out of school. What metaphor or metaphors might you use in writing that story? You don't need to condense as much as Mahfouz does, but feel free to refer to his story for his selection and treatment of important moments in an education. To get started, list the most memorable events in your education, and the impression each event made on you. You may find that these impressions form a kind of pattern. Consider, for example, the father's description of school as "the factory that makes useful men out of boys." Would this be an appropriate metaphor for your educational experience? The boy uses the term *path* as a metaphor (par. 14), recalling the old metaphor "the road of life." You may find that this suits your experience or you may feel that your story of education doesn't fit a neat pattern—in which case, we say, tell it like it is.

ORGANIZING A LIFETIME

How does one go about writing a biography? Suppose we consider a person's life as a narrative, or story of a lifetime. Then, in gathering facts about the person, we look for events that appear to be related, for patterns that will form into a story. Here we've collected the facts for you so that you can compose a story of the life of writer Stephen Crane, who led a very active life as a journalist and writer of fiction and poetry. Read through the material presented here several times, making notes about what information seems most significant and where you see important connections.

■ READING

A File on Stephen Crane

Stephen Crane: A Chronology

1871   Birth of Stephen Crane on November 1 at 14 Mulberry Place, Newark, New Jersey. The fourteenth and last child of Reverend Jonathan Townley Crane, graduate of the College of New Jersey (later Princeton University) and presiding elder for the Newark district of Methodism; and

1

his wife Mary Helen, daughter of a well-known Methodist minister, George Peck.

1876   Family moves to Paterson, New Jersey, where Dr. Crane is appointed to Cross Street Church.   2

1878   Dr. Crane is appointed pastor at Port Jervis, New York. In September, Stephen begins his public school education here, the locale of his later *Whilomville Stories* and "The Monster."   3

1880   Death of Dr. Crane in Port Jervis on February 16. Mrs. Crane supports family by writing for Methodist papers and the New York *Tribune* and the Philadelphia *Press*.   4

1883   Mrs. Crane moves to Asbury Park, New Jersey, where Stephen attends school.   5

1885   Stephen writes his first story, "Uncle Jake and the Bell-Handle," never published during his lifetime. Enrolls at Pennington Seminary, Pennington, New Jersey. Withdraws from Pennington, probably December 1887, in protest of hazing charge.   6

1888   In January, Stephen enrolls at Hudson River Institute (Claverack College) in Claverack, New York, and remains there until 1890. Publishes his first sketch, "Henry M. Stanley," in school magazine *Vidette* (February 1890), and is promoted to captain in military drill. Probably hears Civil War tales from history teacher, retired General Van Petten. During the summer months (1888–92), Stephen assists his brother Townley who operates a news bureau at Asbury Park.   7

1890   Stephen enters Lafayette College in September as mining engineering student. Poor class attendance.   8

1891   Transfers to Syracuse University in January. Correspondent for the New York *Tribune* in Syracuse. Presumably sells sketches to the Detroit *Free Press*; publishes his first story, "The King's Favor," in May issue of the Syracuse *University Herald*; and begins writing *Maggie: A Girl of the Streets*. Spends little time in the classroom; ends college career in June. During the summer, he meets Hamlin Garland at Avon-by-the-Sea and reports his lecture on William Dean Howells (August 18). In love with Helen Trent. Mother dies in Paterson on December 7.   9

1892   First substantial publication of his short fiction; five of his *Sullivan County Sketches* appear in the New York *Tribune* (July 3, 10, 17, 24, 31). First of his New York City sketches published, "The Broken-Down Van" (July 10). Fired as reporter by *Tribune* for writing sardonic article on parading   10

Junior Order of United American Mechanics at Asbury Park (August 21). In love with Lily Brandon Munroe.

1893   *Maggie: A Girl of the Streets* is rejected by various publishers; Crane publishes it at his own cost under pseudonym Johnston Smith. Receives encouragement from Garland and Howells. Begins writing *The Red Badge of Courage.*   11

1894   Sells abridged version (18,000 words) of *The Red Badge* to Bacheller-Johnson Syndicate for ninety dollars; it appears first in the Philadelphia *Press* (December 3–8). Short stories and sketches on social issues appear in *The Arena* and New York *Press.*   12

1895   In January, meets and falls in love with Nelly Crouse. This same month he begins his trip to the American West and Mexico, writing special features for the Bacheller-Johnson Syndicate. Meets Willa Cather in Lincoln, Nebraska. Publishes volume of free verse in March, *The Black Riders....* The complete version (50,000 words) of *The Red Badge* is published by Appleton in October and becomes a best seller and wins a large following in England.   13

1896   *George's Mother* and revised version of *Maggie* published in May and June, respectively. In September, Crane defends Dora Clark, arrested for "soliciting"; this incident makes him continual target of New York City police. Publishes his first collection of stories, *The Little Regiment and Other Episodes of the American Civil War*, in November, his "last thing dealing with battle." Meets Cora Taylor (Howorth) in November in Jacksonville, Florida, at her establishment, Hotel de Dream.   14

1897   Shipwrecked off Florida coast on January 2 on *Commodore*, carrying contraband to Cuban insurgents; this incident is source of "The Open Boat," which appears in June. With Cora Taylor he covers short-lived Greco-Turkish War (April–May) as war correspondent for New York *Journal* and *Westminister Gazette*. Publishes *The Third Violet* in May (serialized the previous year). Resides at Ravensbrook villa (Oxted, Surrey) in England with Cora; no evidence that they were ever legally married. Friendships with Joseph Conrad, Henry James, Ford Madox Ford, Harold Frederic, and others. Travels to Ireland in September.   15

1898   To Cuba and the Spanish-American War as correspondent for Pulitzer's New York *World* and later Hearst's New York *Journal*; first dispatches in April, and last in November. Richard Harding Davis names him the best of the war correspondents in Cuba. Publishes *The Open Boat and Other Tales*   16 *of Adventure* (April). At the peak of his short story craft, with the appearance of "The Bride Comes to Yellow Sky" (February), "Death and the Child" (March), "The Monster" (August), and "The Blue Hotel" (November–December).

1899   Crane returns to England and to Cora in January; resides at   17
Brede Place (Sussex), legend-filled castle. Publishes second book of poems, *War Is Kind; The Monster and Other Stories;* and *Active Service*, a novel based on his Greek experiences. Writes at feverish pace to pay off many debts; plans a novel on the American Revolution, never finished; and starts *The O'Ruddy*, his last novel.

1900   Recurrence of earlier tubercular attacks in January and   18
periodically until his death on June 5 in a sanitarium at Badenweiler, Germany. Buried at Hillside, New Jersey. Appearance of *Whilomville Stories* and Cuban war stories, *Wounds in the Rain*.

—THOMAS A. GULLASON

1891   Crane at Syracuse University

Clarence Loomis Peaslee, a classmate of Crane's:
He has a deep regard for true learning, but not for the rubbish that   19
often passes under that name, and if he has not burned the midnight oil in search of "school" knowledge, he has worked as but few men have in the field of observation and the study of mankind. In college Crane was an omnivorous reader and sat up late at night, diligently poring over the masterpieces of literature or trying to put upon paper his own peculiar views of man and life....He wanted to produce something that would make men think, that would make men feel as he felt, and to do this he early realized that for him it must come through hard work.

Another classmate:
He gloried in talking with shambling figures who lurked in the dark   20
doorways on deserted slum streets, and his love for adventure constantly kept his feet on ill-lighted thoroughfares honeycombing the city.

1895   Reviews of Crane's Novel *The Red Badge of Courage*

From the Boston Transcript:
It is a tremendous grasping of the glory and carnage of all war; it is   21
the rendering, in phrases that reveal like lightning flashes, of the raw fighter's emotions, the blind magnificent courage and the

cowardice equally blind of a youth first possessed by the red sickness of battle.

From Outlook *magazine (December 21, 1895):*
The story is not pleasant by any means, but the author seems to lay   22
bare the very nerves of his character; practically, the book is a
minute study of one man's mind in the environment of war in all its
horrible detail.

From Book Buyer *magazine (April 1896):*
A note from Stephen Crane: "I have never been in battle, of course,   23
and I believe that I got my sense of the rage of conflict on the football field. The psychology is the same. The opposing team is an
enemy tribe."

1896 Publication of *Maggie: A Girl of the Streets*

From a note Crane wrote on the cover of Hamlin Garland's copy of
Maggie:
It is inevitable that you will be greatly shocked by this book, but   24
continue please with all possible courage to the end. For it tries to
show that environment is a tremendous thing in the world and frequently shapes lives regardless. If one proves that theory one makes
room in heaven for all sorts of souls (notably an occasional street
girl) who are not confidently expected to be there by many excellent people. It is probable that the reader of this small thing may
consider the author to be a bad man; but obviously that is a matter
of small consequence.

From an English review:
Maggie is a study of life in the slums of New York, and of the hope-   25
less struggle of a girl against the horrible conditions of her environment; and so bitter is the struggle, so black the environment, so
inevitable the end, that the reader feels a chill at his heart, and dis-
likes the book even while he admires it. Mr. Crane's realism is mer-
ciless and unsparing; in these chapters are set before us in cold
blood hideous phases of misery, brutality, drunkenness, vice; while
oaths and blasphemies form the habitual speech of the men and
women who live and move in this atmosphere of vileness. Yet every
scene is alive and has the unmistakable stamp of truth upon it. The
reader does not feel that he is reading about these horrors; he feels
as if the outer walls of some tenement houses in the slums had been
taken away and he could see—and see with comprehension—the

doings of the teeming inmates. Over the whole grimly powerful tragedy is the redeeming grace of the author's implied compassion; but he never mars the effect of the story by speaking this compassion or by pointing a moral. He has drawn a vivid picture of life at its lowest and worst; he has shown us the characters as they would be, with no false glamour of an impossible romance about them; and the moral may confidently be left to look after itself, since it stares from every page. Maggie herself is a wonderfully well-drawn character, and the book, repellent though it is, is in its way a triumph.

1897   The *Commodore* Disaster

From the New York Press, *January 5, 1897:*

CRANE'S SPLENDID GRIT

"That man Crane is the spunkiest fellow out," said Captain Murphy   26
tonight to The Press correspondent, in speaking of the wreck and incidents pertaining to it. "The sea was so rough that even old sailors got seasick when we struck the open sea after leaving the bar, but Crane behaved like a born sailor. He and I were about the only ones not affected by the big seas which tossed us about. As we went south he sat in the pilot house with me, smoking and telling yarns. When the leak was discovered he was the first man to volunteer aid.

JOKES AMID DANGER

"His shoes, new ones, were slippery on the deck, and he took them   27
off and tossed them overboard, saying, with a laugh: 'Well, captain, I guess I won't need them if we have to swim.' He stood on deck with me all the while, smoking his cigarette, and aided me greatly while the boats were getting off. When in the dinghy he suggested putting up the overcoat for a sail, and he took his turn at the oars or holding up the oar mast.

TRIES TO SAVE HIGGINS

"When we went over I called to him to see that his life preserver   28
was on all right and he replied in his usual tones, saying that he would obey orders. He was under the boat once, but got out in some way. He held up Higgins when the latter got so terribly tired and endeavored to bring him in, but the sailor was so far gone that he could hardly help himself. When we were thrown up by the waves, Crane was the first man to stagger up the beach looking for

houses. He's a thoroughbred," concluded the captain, "and a brave man, too, with plenty of grit."

1898   Crane as Correspondent in the Spanish-American War

From Langdon Smith in Cosmopolitan *magazine, September 1898:*
Crane was standing under a tree calmly rolling a cigarette; some leaves dropped from the trees, cut away by the bullets; two or three men dropped within a few feet. Crane is as thin as a lath. If he had been two or three inches wider or thicker through, he would undoubtedly have been shot. But he calmly finished rolling his cigarette and smoked it without moving away from the spot where the bullets had suddenly become so thick.   29

From Crane's report of the battle of San Juan in the New York World, *July 14, 1898:*
The road from El Paso to San Juan was now a terrible road. It should have a tragic fame like the sunken road at Waterloo. Why we did not later hang some of the gentry who contributed from the trees to the terror of this road is not known.   20

The wounded were stringing back from the front, hundreds of them. Some walked unaided, an arm or shoulder having been dressed at a field station. They stopped often enough to answer the universal hail "How is it going?" Others hobbled or clung to a friend's shoulders. Their slit trousers exposed red bandages. A few were shot horribly in the face and were led, bleeding and blind, by their mates.   31

And then there were the slow pacing stretcher-bearers with the dead or the insensible, the badly wounded, still figures with blood often drying brick color on their hot bandages.   32

Prostrate at the roadside were many others who had made their way thus far and were waiting for strength. Everywhere moved the surehanded, invaluable Red Cross men.   33

Over this scene was a sort of haze of bullets. They were of two kinds. First, the Spanish lines were firing just a trifle high. Their bullets swept over our firing lines and poured into this devoted roadway, the single exit, even as it had been the single approach. The second fire was from guerillas concealed in the trees and thickets along the trail. They had come in under the very wings of our strong advance, taken good positions on either side of the road and were peppering our line of communication   34 whenever they got a good target, no matter, apparently, what the target might be.

Red Cross men, wounded men, sick men, correspondents and 35 attaches were all one to the guerilla. The move of sending an irregular force around the flanks of the enemy as he is making his front attack is so legitimate that some of us could not believe at first that the men hidden in the forest were really blazing away at the non-combatants or the wounded. Viewed simply as a bit of tactics, the scheme was admirable. But there is no doubt now that they intentionally fired at anybody they thought they could kill.

You can't mistake an ambulance driver when he is driving 36 his ambulance. You can't mistake a wounded man when he is lying down and being bandaged. And when you see a field hospital you don't mistake it for a squadron of cavalry or a brigade of infantry.

PRACTICE 5.3

Writing Stephen Crane's Life

Here's your situation: you've just landed a job as an editorial assistant in a large publishing company. During your second day on the job, the editor you work for discovers a problem with the company's new edition of *The Collected Works of Stephen Crane*. The edition is scheduled to go to the printer tomorrow, but something is missing: the "About the Author" preface that your company always includes in editions of literary classics. Apparently, your predecessor never got around to writing the preface. In any event, it's your job now and the preface must be written by the end of the day. Fortunately, your predecessor did leave a file of material on Crane; in fact, you've just been leafing through the chronology, the comments about the man and his work by his contemporaries, and one of his articles on the Spanish-American War.

Your editor expects an account of Crane's life that college students and other readers will find both interesting and useful. He reminds you that the "About the Author" preface must give readers an idea of Crane's character, motivation, and accomplishments as well as an assessment of his life. You don't have enough information to detail all the events in the chronology, but that approach wouldn't be appropriate for this assignment anyway. Instead, you must analyze the data you have, looking for patterns of events that will enable you to narrate the story of Crane's life in two to three pages.

INTERVIEW TIME

This reading comes from *Amazing Grace* (1995), Jonathan Kozol's book about daily life in the South Bronx section of New York City. Kozol, who has been interviewing children for many years, allows the disadvantaged children in a neighborhood storefront program to tell their own stories. As compared to other written interviews, you will see that Kozol is very much present as an interviewer in this narrative. Notice how much is paraphrased and when, and how much is direct transcription of conversation. Kozol generally uses a tape recorder for his interviews, but for some interviews in *Amazing Grace* he relied on note taking when warned that tape-recording would be too off-putting for his interviewees. Also notice the narrative structure Kozol creates, how he tells the "story" of his interviews.

▓ READING

Jonathan Kozol, "An Interview with Gizelle Luke and Children of the South Bronx"

Back in New York City in late August, I find a taxi-driver at the air-   1
port who agrees to take me directly to the Bronx. Like many taxi-drivers in New York, he has a foreign accent. When I ask him where he's from, he says, "From Russia." He seems good-natured and slides open a small panel in the bulletproof partition at his back so we can chat. But when we come off the bridge into the Bronx, he opens his window, spits in the street, then rolls the window shut and locks his door. "All this is scum here. No one works. Look at this."

I ask him where he lives.   2
"I live in Queens, in a nice section."   3
The children I'm going to meet are members of a group that has   4
been organized by workers at a storefront program close to Shakespeare Avenue on Featherbed Lane, run by Covenant House, an independent Catholic organization based in midtown on the West Side of Manhattan. The program's director, Gizelle Luke, is a young black woman who has lived in Europe for some years but came back to work here in the Bronx about eight months ago.

Before the children have assembled, she takes me a couple of   5
blocks from Shakespeare Avenue to an overpass that crosses an expressway, which, she says, leads to the suburbs and the interstate,

I-95. Standing on the overpass, she gestures back toward Featherbed Lane and at a housing complex on a hill that rises just behind it. There are, she says, few economic possibilities for people who reside here. "There aren't many branches of the major banks. The 'banks' are loan sharks—or check-cashing places. If you want to open a small business, there's no banker that you've come to know that you can talk with to obtain a loan. No libraries open in the evening. Few recreational opportunities for children. Many abandoned houses and abandoned people and abandoned cars. But I want you to see something interesting."

Turning to the highway, where the cars are speeding by beneath us, she points in the direction of some buildings just beyond the road. 6

At first I can't tell what she's pointing at. Then I notice the pictures of flowers, window shades and curtains and interiors of pretty-looking rooms, that have been painted on these buildings on the sides that face the highway. It's a very strange sight, and the pictures have been done so well that when you look the first time, you imagine that you're seeing into people's homes—pleasant-looking homes, in fact, that have a distinctly middle-class appearance. I ask her if people who live here did these pictures. 7

"Nobody lives here," she replies. "Those buildings are all empty." 8

The city had these murals painted on the walls, she says, not for the people in the neighborhood—because they're facing the wrong way—but for tourists and commuters. "The idea is that they mustn't be upset by knowing too much about the population here. It isn't enough that these people are sequestered. It's also important that their presence be disguised or 'sweetened.' The city did not repair the buildings so that kids who live around here could, in fact, *have* pretty rooms like those. Instead, they *painted* pretty rooms on the facades. It's an illusion." 9

I ask if the people around here have made comments of this sort. 10

"I don't know what they say," she says. "I haven't asked. To me, it's just outrageous. The first time I saw it, I thought, 'Oh, Lord! Well, what a dirty thing to do!' Really, it is far beyond racism. It's just—'In your face! Take that!' We don't clean up your neighborhood, don't fix your buildings, fix your schools, or give you decent hospitals or banks. Instead, we paint the back sides of the buildings so that people driving to the suburbs will have something nice to look at." 11

Most people, she adds, soon realize that the pictures are just that—mere paintings—so they can't accomplish their objective. 12

"Maybe it works for tourists who are here for the first time." The city, she says, denies unkind intentions and insists it's simply decoration. "Decoration for whom? It makes me angry. Look at my hand. I'm trembling."

The children I meet a few minutes later in her office range in age   13
from seven to 12 years old. The conversation, which is desultory and a bit forced at the start, becomes more animated when I ask about the public schools that they attend, one of which is housed in a former synagogue built in 1897. Another school, to which some of the kids commute, was ranked "dead last" in reading scores of all the elementary schools in New York City two years earlier. Both schools, according to one of the children, an 11-year-old named Kimberly, have mostly Hispanic and black children—"not many white students," she says.

"How many white students—Anglo whites—do you have in   14
your class?" I ask.

"In my class?" she answers. "There is none."   15

The other children answer, "None," except for one girl who   16
says, "One."

"I used to have a white boy in my class," says Robert, nine years   17
old. "He was Irish."

"Did you like him?"   18

"He was my best friend."   19

"Since 1960," says a 12-year-old named Jeremiah, "white people   20
started moving away from black and Spanish people in New York."

The specificity of the date intrigues me. "Where do you think   21
white people went?" I ask.

"I think—to the country," says another boy.   22

"It isn't where people live. It's *how* they live," says Jeremiah.   23

"Say that again," I ask.   24

"It's *how* they live," he says again. "There are different   25
economies in different places."

When I ask him to explain this, he refers to Riverdale, a mostly   26
white and middle-class community in the northwest section of the Bronx. "Life in Riverdale is opened up," he says. "Where we live, it's locked down."

"In what way?" I ask.   27

"We can't go out and play."   28

"Why not?"   29

"You go in the park to play," he answers sharply. "You'll see   30
why."

Gizelle Luke, who is standing behind him, looks at me and lifts   31
her eyebrows when he says this.

I try to draw in the other children by asking them to tell me   32
someone they admire. Several children answer, "Marcus Garvey,"
who is hardly mentioned in most textbooks nowadays. Others speak
of Malcolm X. No one, however, mentions Martin Luther King,
even though the major street within the neighborhood is named for
him. When I comment on this, some of the children groan.

"He's mentioned too much," says Jeremiah.   33

"'Name a hero of black people,'" says Chevonne, a nine-year-   34
old, mimicking a teacher. "'Dr. Martin Luther King....I have a
dream....'"

I ask her why she doesn't like to hear of it.   35

"One," she says, "because you hear it too much. Two, because it   36
isn't true."

"If everyone looks up to him," says Jeremiah, "you have to try to   37
find somebody of your own."

"Who do *you* look up to?"   38

"I look up to God," he says, "my mother, and myself."   39

A number of sirens from police cars in the street interrupt the   40
conversation for a moment. When the sirens subside and the police
cars have moved on, I ask the children if they think of the police as
people they can trust.

"I don't," says Kimberly.   41

Virtually all the children answer, "No."   42

"You have nothing good to say about the people who protect   43
you?"

In one voice, they answer, "No."   44

Kimberly describes a night, a couple weeks before, when she and   45
her brothers thought their house was being robbed. "It was late and
we were looking at TV. We called the cops. They never came. We
called my grandmother. My grandmother came. The police never
came. They didn't come."

Feelings of distrust for the police are not unusual among young   46
people nowadays, not only in the cities; but the unanimity in the
distrust these children voice is somewhat startling.

I ask them, "Is this a good country?"   47

"No," says Chevonne.   48

"Somewhere," says Kimberly.   49

"Where?" I ask.   50

"Maybe in Connecticut," she says.   51

"Why Connecticut?"   52

"It's quiet there," she says. "They have green places."   53

"At school, do you sing 'America the Beautiful'?"   54

"We don't sing that anymore," says Kimberly.   55

"In some schools they do," says Robert.   56

"Do you think America is beautiful?"   57

"It was beautiful when they wrote that song," says Jeremiah.   58

Kimberly and Robert speak of killings that have taken place   59
within the neighborhood, and Jeremiah speaks about "the little altars in the streets" that people make by setting candles in a circle on
the sidewalk where someone has been shot down. "You hear shooting in the night," he says. "Next day, you see a lot of little card-
board boxes, each one with a candle—sometimes flowers, and you
see a picture of the person who was killed.

"Sometimes," he says, "they tie a flower to a tree and sometimes   60
they paint the person's name against the wall and put one candle
underneath."

I ask him, "Can you sleep after you hear about these things?"   61

"I pray that someone in my family will not die."   62

Like many children I have come to know in the South Bronx, Je-   63
remiah and his friends do not speak during our meeting in the jargon that some middle-class Americans identify with inner-city kids.
There's no obscenity in their speech, nor are there any of those flip
code-phrases that are almost always placed within the mouths of
poor black children in the movies—a style of speech, I sometimes
think, that may be exaggerated by the media to lend a heightened
sense of "differentness" to children in the ghetto. Children, however, are good at psyching out a stranger; it may be that these children would speak somewhat differently to someone they know
better.

As the meeting breaks up, the youngest child in the group, who   64
sat at my side but did not say a word for the entire hour, whispers to
me that she did not like what the other children said about not
trusting the police. I ask her why. She says, "My father's a policeman."

The child, who tells me her name is Monique, seems to have   65
been saving up this one idea to share with me in private. "I trust my
daddy," she says, "but I don't know my daddy." Whispering still,
she says, "I never saw him but I know that he's in the police."

I ask Monique if she lives with her mother.   66

"I never saw my mother either," she replies.   67

She's a tiny child with two pigtails and a pair of bright-red sneak-   68
ers. On the front of her jersey are these words: "The Power of
Little People."

I ask how old she is.   69

"I'm seven," she replies.   70

Standing outside on the sidewalk after the children have gone   71
home, Gizelle comments on one of the sharp-edged statements

Jeremiah made. "When you asked him about the reason that he feels 'locked down,' his answer to you was rather curt. There was an abruptness and impatience in his tone. I think it's because he didn't want to make it easy for you. He wanted to leave it for *you* to speak about racism. He didn't want to hand it to you on a platter. It's part of his maturity and dignity, I think. But you can sense the edginess in that: forcing a white person maybe to go further than you wanted, to make you name reality, not letting himself be used by you as a convenient voice. A lot of black people feel like that. They want America to name its crime and not keep squirming to avoid the risky words." She adds, "I found his description of 'the little altars in the streets' particularly moving."

Since that time, I have become more aware of just how many   72
of those little altars there are on the sidewalks all over the South Bronx. People in the neighborhoods water the flowers sometimes and replace the candles. Even when the flowers are dry, the altars often remain in place for months, sometimes for years.

▒ **PRACTICE 5.4**

Reporting from Interviews

For your interview, choose someone or some group whose work or activities interest you. If you haven't yet decided on a major, you might choose a professor in a discipline you're curious about, or you might interview several students in that discipline. Alternatively, you might interview a group of people about a particular issue or event.

Here are some suggestions for conducting an interview:

1. A tape recorder is a great help in an interview, but if you don't have access to one, try to capture the voice of the person you interview by using direct quotations in your notes.
2. You should write up some basic questions beforehand to get you started, such as: How did you become interested in this field? What do you think about increased requirements for graduation?
3. Look again at Kozol's conversational method of questioning and how he keeps the interview going by listening carefully, picking up on each child's comments, and drawing his next question from them. If you respond with interest to the person's remarks, you'll learn a lot more than if you coldly probe with a set of rigid questions.

In writing up your transcribed material, you should give your interview a narrative form. You might frame your narrative with a description of the person or group, or the locale of the interview. For example, consider what Kozol's interview gains in impact from its opening description of the dismal area, with its abandoned buildings decorated with phony window treatments. You might think about the way your subject fits or contrasts with his or her place of work. You will also need a conclusion to your narrative. Note how Kozol reflects on Gizelle Luke's last statement recalling a remark by one of the children. In this way, he shows what he has learned from his interview with them.

WHAT IS A "GOOD STORY"?

Grace Paley is an award-winning writer of short stories, many of which center on family relationships. The following story is from *Enormous Changes at the Last Minute* (1974). Note how Paley uses dialogue to structure her narrative of differing points of view about telling a story, and listen to her re-creation of the cadences of everyday (New York) conversation.

READING

Grace Paley, "A Conversation with My Father"

My father is eighty-six years old and in bed. His heart, that bloody motor, is equally old and will not do certain jobs any more. It still floods his head with brainy light. But it won't let his legs carry the weight of his body around the house. Despite my metaphors, this muscle failure is not due to his old heart, he says, but to a potassium shortage. Sitting on one pillow, leaning on three, he offers last-minute advice and makes a request.   1

"I would like you to write a simple story just once more," he says, "the kind de Maupassant wrote, or Chekhov,[1] the kind you used to write. Just recognizable people and then write down what happened to them next."   2

I say, "Yes, why not? That's possible." I want to please him, though I don't remember writing that way. I *would* like to try to tell such a story, if he means the kind that begins: "There was a woman..." fol-   3

---

[1] Guy de Maupassant (1850–93), French writer; Anton Chekhov (1860–1904), Russian writer; Ivan Turgenev (1818–83) (par. 6), Russian writer. All three writers were masters of the short-story form, and were renowned for realism of character portrayal.

lowed by plot, the absolute line between two points which I've always despised. Not for literary reasons, but because it takes all hope away. Everyone, real or invented, deserves the open destiny of life.

Finally I thought of a story that had been happening for a couple of years right across the street. I wrote it down, then read it aloud. "Pa," I said, "how about this? Do you mean something like this?"   4

Once in my time there was a woman and she had a son. They lived nicely, in a small apartment in Manhattan. This boy at about fifteen became a junkie, which is not unusual in our neighborhood. In order to maintain her close friendship with him, she became a junkie too. She said it was part of the youth culture, with which she felt very much at home. After a while, for a number of reasons, the boy gave it all up and left the city and his mother in disgust. Hopeless and alone, she grieved. We all visit her.

"O.K., Pa, that's it," I said, "an unadorned and miserable tale."   5

"But that's not what I mean," my father said. "You misunder-   6
stood me on purpose. You know there's a lot more to it. You know that. You left everything out. Turgenev wouldn't do that. Chekhov wouldn't do that. There are in fact Russian writers you never heard of, you don't have an inkling of, as good as anyone, who can write a plain ordinary story, who would not leave out what you have left out. I object not to facts but to people sitting in trees talking sense-lessly, voices from who knows where..."

"Forget that one, Pa, what have I left out now? In this one?"   7

"Her looks, for instance."   8

"Oh. Quite handsome, I think. Yes."   9

"Her hair?"   10

"Dark, with heavy braids, as though she were a girl or a for-   11
eigner."

"What were her parents like, her stock? That she became such a   12
person. It's interesting, you know."

"From out of town. Professional people. The first to be divorced   13
in their county. How's that? Enough?" I asked.

"With you, it's all a joke," he said. "What about the boy's father?   14
Why didn't you mention him? Who was he? Or was the boy born out of wedlock?"

"Yes," I said. "He was born out of wedlock."   15

"For Godsakes, doesn't anyone in your stories get married?   16
Doesn't anyone have the time to run down to City Hall before they jump into bed?"

"No," I said. "In real life, yes. But in my stories, no."   17

"Why do you answer me like that?"   18

"Oh, Pa, this is a simple story about a smart woman who came to   19
N.Y.C. full of interest love trust excitement very up to date, and
about her son, what a hard time she had in this world. Married or
not, it's of small consequence."

"It is of great consequence," he said.   20

"O.K.," I said.   21

"O.K. O.K. yourself," he said, "but listen. I believe you that she's   22
good-looking, but I don't think she was so smart."

"That's true," I said. "Actually that's the trouble with stories.   23
People start out fantastic. You think they're extraordinary, but it
turns out as the work goes along, they're just average with a good
education. Sometimes the other way around, the person's a kind of
dumb innocent, but he outwits you and you can't even think of an
ending good enough."

"What do you do then?" he asked. He had been a doctor for a   24
couple of decades and then an artist for a couple of decades and he's
still interested in details, craft, technique.

"Well, you just have to let the story lie around till some agree-   25
ment can be reached between you and the stubborn hero."

"Aren't you talking silly, now?" he asked. "Start again," he said.   26
"It so happens I'm not going out this evening. Tell the story again.
See what you can do this time."

"O.K.," I said. "But it's not a five-minute job." Second attempt: 27

Once, across the street from us, there was a fine handsome woman,
our neighbor. She had a son whom she loved because she'd known
him since birth (in helpless chubby infancy, and in the wrestling,
hugging ages, seven to ten, as well as earlier and later). This boy,
when he fell into the fist of adolescence, became a junkie. He was
not a hopeless one. He was in fact hopeful, an ideologue and successful converter. With his busy brilliance, he wrote persuasive articles for his high-school newspaper. Seeking a wider audience,
using important connections, he drummed into Lower Manhattan
newsstand distribution a periodical called *Oh! Golden Horse!*

In order to keep him from feeling guilty (because guilt is the
stony heart of nine tenths of all clinically diagnosed cancers in
America today, she said), and because she had always believed in
giving bad habits room at home where one could keep an eye on
them, she too became a junkie. Her kitchen was famous for a
while—a center for intellectual addicts who knew what they were
doing. A few felt artistic like Coleridge and others were scientific and
revolutionary like Leary[1]. Although she was often high herself, cer-

---

[1]Timothy Leary (1920–98); psychologist and promoter of psychedelic drug use.

tain good mothering reflexes remained, and she saw to it that there was lots of orange juice around and honey and milk and vitamin pills. However, she never cooked anything but chili, and that no more than once a week. She explained, when we talked to her, seriously, with neighborly concern, that it was her part in the youth culture and she would rather be with the young, it was an honor, than with her own generation.

One week, nodding through an Antonioni[2] film, this boy was severely jabbed by the elbow of a stern and proselytizing girl, sitting beside him. She offered immediate apricots and nuts for his sugar level, spoke to him sharply, and took him home.

She had heard of him and his work and she herself published, edited, and wrote a competitive journal called *Man Does Live By Bread Alone*. In the organic heat of her continuous presence he could not help but become interested once more in his muscles, his arteries, and nerve connections. In fact he began to love them, treasure them, praise them with funny little songs in *Man Does Live* . . .

> *the fingers of my flesh transcend*
> *my transcendental soul*
> *the tightness in my shoulders end*
> *my teeth have made me whole*

To the mouth of his head (that glory of will and determination) he brought hard apples, nuts, wheat germ, and soybean oil. He said to his old friends, From now on, I guess I'll keep my wits about me. I'm going on the natch. He said he was about to begin a spiritual deep-breathing journey. How about you too, Mom? he asked kindly.

His conversion was so radiant, splendid, that neighborhood kids his age began to say that he had never been a real addict at all, only a journalist along for the smell of the story. The mother tried several times to give up what had become without her son and his friends a lonely habit. This effort only brought it to supportable levels. The boy and his girl took their electronic mimeograph and moved to the bushy edge of another borough. They were very strict. They said they would not see her again until she had been off drugs for sixty days.

At home alone in the evening, weeping, the mother read and reread the seven issues of *Oh! Golden Horse!* They seemed to her as truthful as ever. We often crossed the street to visit and console. But if we mentioned any of our children who were at college or in the

---

[2]Michelangelo Antonioni (1912–), Italian film director who abandoned traditional plotting for long takes of "seemingly random events" (David Cook).

hospital or dropouts at home, she would cry out, My baby! My baby! and burst into terrible, face-scarring, time-consuming tears. The End.

First my father was silent, then he said, "Number One: You have a nice sense of humor. Number Two: I see you can't tell a plain story. So don't waste time." Then he said sadly, "Number Three: I suppose that means she was alone, she was left like that, his mother. Alone. Probably sick?"   28

I said, "Yes."   29

"Poor woman. Poor girl, to be born in a time of fools, to live among fools. The end. The end. You were right to put that down. The end."   30

I didn't want to argue, but I had to say, "Well, it is not necessarily the end, Pa."   31

"Yes," he said, "what a tragedy. The end of a person."   32

"No, Pa," I begged him. "It doesn't have to be. She's only about forty. She could be a hundred different things in this world as time goes on. A teacher or a social worker. An ex-junkie! Sometimes it's better than having a master's in education."   33

"Jokes," he said. "As a writer that's your main trouble. You don't want to recognize it. Tragedy! Plain tragedy! Historical tragedy! No hope. The end."   34

"Oh, Pa," I said. "She could change."   35

"In your own life, too, you have to look it in the face." He took a couple of nitroglycerin. "Turn to five," he said, pointing to the dial on the oxygen tank. He inserted the tubes into his nostrils and breathed deep. He closed his eyes and said, "No."   36

I had promised the family to always let him have the last word when arguing, but in this case I had a different responsibility. That woman lives across the street. She's my knowledge and my invention. I'm sorry for her. I'm not going to leave her there in that house crying. (Actually neither would Life, which unlike me has no pity.)   37

Therefore: She did change. Of course her son never came home again. But right now, she's the receptionist in a storefront community clinic in the East Village. Most of the customers are young people, some old friends. The head doctor has said to her, "If we only had three people in this clinic with your experiences…"   38

"The doctor said that?" My father took the oxygen tubes out of his nostrils and said, "Jokes. Jokes again."   39

"No, Pa, it could really happen that way, it's a funny world nowadays."   40

"No," he said. "Truth first. She will slide back. A person must   41
have character. She does not."

"No, Pa," I said. "That's it. She's got a job. Forget it. She's in   42
that storefront working."

"How long will it be?" he asked. "Tragedy! You too. When will   43
you look it in the face?"

Questions

1. What is the argument between father and daughter about?
2. What does the father mean by a "plain ordinary story"?
3. Consider the first paragraph and the last three paragraphs as a frame for the story. What effect is created by the setting described in the first paragraph?
4. How does the daughter describe her method of writing stories?

■ PRACTICE 5.5

Ways of Telling a "Good Story"

We offer four different ways of working with "A Conversation with My Father."

1. Take the daughter's first version of her story (par. 4) and rewrite it according to her father's standards for a "plain ordinary story."
2. The father and the daughter disagree about the possibility of change. The father labels the life of the woman in the story a "tragedy." He accepts the end of the story as the end of a life. The daughter sees the possibility for the story continuing, and for the possibility of change. Write a few paragraphs in which you continue the woman's story, according either to the father's prognosis or to the daughter's beliefs.
3. Retell the woman's story from her son's point of view. Remember, you will have to assess his character as it is presented in the two stories in order to assume his persona.
4. Write an analysis of the differing points of view about storytelling as they are expressed by the father and the daughter. You might also want to consider your own criteria for a "good story," as well as your own critical responses to the two stories the daughter presents.

6

Reading the Seen
Description

In a sense, narration is easy because events unfolding in time have a linear shape or structure. When someone is having difficulty in reporting an event to us, we say, "Just begin at the beginning." We can do this because both events and narratives have beginnings. Descriptions have beginnings, too. The problem is that the things being described often do not. We may describe what we hear, taste, smell, or feel, but because human beings are sight-dominated creatures, we most often describe what we see. That is, we translate our perceptions of space-bound objects with no perceivable beginning or end into a time-bound, linear form: writing.

For the writer, description of a visual object poses a number of problems: Where to begin? What to include next? Where to end? All these problems can be reduced to one: the problem of **order.** How should description be arranged? There is, however, another problem hiding behind this one: What information should be selected for inclusion in a written description? Even a blank wall presents a nearly infinite amount of information for anyone who inspects it closely enough. **Selection** and **arrangement,** the twin problems of descriptive writing, can be solved in the same way. The writer must have a *point of view* about the object being described. That is, as a writer you must see something in the object that will enable you to make a statement about it—which will in turn help you organize the impressions you are receiving from the object. Once you have a point of view, you will know what to look for, what to record, and you will have the option of moving from one item to another according to the way the objects relate to your point of view.

A scientist describing a specimen will leave out certain irrelevant details. A poet or essayist describing the same object might include much that the scientist would consider irrelevant and exclude the data of most concern to the scientist. The purpose shapes the presentation and helps to generate the point of view required for good description. Some of the following assignments are designed to develop your awareness of the way in which point of view shapes description. In others we have posed problems in translation from a visual text to a verbal one or even more complicated problems in the imitation of a verbal style and description of a visual object simultaneously.

DESCRIBING A PLACE

Here are examples of four notable writers at work describing things. The four selections serve to illustrate how a writer can organize an interior space such as a kitchen or a welfare office hearing room, an exterior urban space such as a city street, and finally an event in nature, such as a storm in a Brazilian rain forest.

In reading each selection you should consider in particular each writer's point of view. How has the writer actually organized the space to get it on paper? What has been included? What has been excluded? For instance, every room has a floor, a ceiling, and four walls. Which of these has Robinson included and excluded? Of the things that the writer has chosen to include, which are mentioned first? What pattern can you find in the movement from one object to the next? Can you tell how the writer has decided upon a particular order? If you were going to make a film based on the description of the place, could you do it with a single location? Could your camera capture everything in one steady movement, or would it have to hop around, frequently changing position, distance, and angle? You might also ask what aspects of the written description a camera could not capture.

The writer's point of view requires some consistent feeling or attitude toward the scene being described. You should try to reduce the attitude in each of the following descriptions to the shortest possible expression—a single word if you can—that expresses the dominant feeling conveyed by the description. Which of the following words best suits the Robinson selection: *pleasure, displeasure, fascination, disgust, disapproval, sympathy*? Can you find words or phrases that sum up the point of view that is used to unify each of the other three examples?

After reading and discussing all four examples, you should try to articulate the general principles of descriptive writing. What features do all four of these different writers employ in their descriptions? What is unique to each one?

■ **READING**

Marilynne Robinson, "A Kitchen" (from *Housekeeping*)

…Lucille had startled us all, flooding the room so suddenly with light, exposing heaps of pots and dishes, the two cupboard doors which had come unhinged and were propped against the boxes of china. The tables and chairs and cupboards and doors had been painted a rich white, layer on layer, year after year, but now the last layer had ripened to the yellow of turning cream. Everywhere the paint was chipped and marred. A great shadow of soot loomed up the wall and across the ceiling above the stove, and the stove pipe and the cupboard tops were thickly felted with dust. Most dispiriting, perhaps, was the curtain on Lucille's side of the table, which had been half consumed by fire once when a birthday cake had been set too close to it. Sylvie had beaten out the flames with a back issue of *Good Housekeeping*, but she had never replaced the curtain. It had been my birthday, and the cake was a surprise, as were the pink orlon cardigan with the imitation seed pearls in the yoke and the ceramic kangaroo with the air fern in its pouch. Sylvie's pleasure in this event had been intense, and perhaps the curtain reminded her of it.

Alex Kotlowitz, "The Hearing Room" (from *There Are No Children Here*)

A handwritten sign adorned the door where LaJoe was led:

HEARING ROOM ONLY
OTHERS KEEP OUT

The room itself was small, perhaps eight feet by eight feet. The combination of its fluorescent lights, four strategically placed metal chairs—one facing the other three—and a large metal desk, devoid of papers, pencils, or books, gave the room the appearance of a place meant for interrogation. There was nothing to distract the inquisitor or accused, no windows or clocks to give any sense of location or time, no pictures or posters to give the room any personality.   1

LaJoe sat in the chair clearly meant for her, the one standing apart from the others. She folded her hands and waited: Someone brought in one more chair and lined it up with the other three. "All of them on one little old me?" she whispered to herself. Ten minutes later, three women and a man filed in. They did not introduce themselves.   2

Kate Simon, "A Street" (from *Bronx Primitive*)

We lived at 2029 Lafontaine, the last house on the west side of the street from 178th to 179th, a row of five-story tenements that ended at a hat factory. To the north and solidly, interminably, along the block to 180th there stretched a bitter ugliness of high walls of big stones that held a terminal point and service barns of El trains. (It may be that my recoil from early Renaissance palaces, their pugnacious blocks of stone and fortress grimness, stems from these inimical El walls.) Across from the factory were a garage and the Italian frame houses that lined that side of the street down to 178th Street. At the corner of 178th Street, on our Jewish-German-Polish-Greek-Hungarian-Rumanian side, was Mrs. Katz's candy store. The only other store I knew at first was the grocery run by a plodding elderly couple at the corner of 179th Street and Arthur Avenue, the street to the east. In spite of their lack of English and my frail Yiddish, I eagerly ran errands there to watch their feet slide and pat in their brown felt slippers and to admire the precision with which the old man cut once, twice, into a tub of butter to dig out exactly a quarter pound. And on their side of 179th Street, about midway between Arthur and Lafontaine, there was a big tree, the only street tree in the neighborhood, which showered me, and only me, with a million white blossoms. It was my tree and I watched and touched it as carefully as the Italian grandfathers watched and touched the tomato plants in their backyards.

Edward O. Wilson, "The Storm" (from "Storm over the Amazon")

The rain forest at night is an experience in sensory deprivation, black and silent as a tomb. Life is moving out there all right, but the organisms communicate chiefly by faint chemical trails laid over the surface, puffs of odor released into the air, and body scents detected downwind. Most animals are geniuses in this chemical channel where we are idiots. On the other hand, we are masters of the audiovisual channel, matched in that category only by a few odd groups like birds and lizards. At the risk of oversimplification, I can say that this is why we wait for the dawn while they wait for the fall of darkness. 1

So I welcomed every meteorite's streak and distant mating flash from luminescent beetles. Even the passage of a jetliner five miles up was exciting, having been transformed from the familiar urban irritant to a rare sign of the continuance of my own species. 2

Then one August night in the dry season, with the moon down and starlight etching the tops of the trees, everything changed with wrenching suddenness. A great storm came up from the west and 3 moved quickly toward where I sat. It began as a flickering of light on the horizon and a faint roll of thunder. In the course of an hour the lightning grew like a menacing organism into flashes that spread across the sky and illuminated the thunderhead section by section. The sound expanded into focused claps to my left, front, and right. Now the rain came walking through the forest with a hiss made oddly soothing by its evenness of pitch. At this moment the clouds rose straight up and even seemed to tilt a little toward me, like a gigantic cliff about to topple over. The brilliance of the flashes was intimidating. Here, I knew, was the greatest havoc that inanimate nature can inflict in a short span of time: 10,000 volts dropping down an ionizing path at 500 miles an hour and a countersurge in excess of 30,000 amperes back up the path at ten times that speed, then additional back-and-forth surges faster than the eye can follow, all perceived as a single flash and crack of sound.

In the midst of the clamor something distracted my attention off   4
to the side. The lightning bolts were acting like photoflashes to illuminate the wall of the rain forest. In glimpses I studied its superb triple-tiered structure: top canopy a hundred feet off the ground, middle tree layer below that, and a scattering of lowest trees and shrubs. At least 800 kinds of trees had been found along a short transect eastward from the camp, more than occur natively in all of North America. A hundred thousand or more species of insects and other small animals were thought to live in the same area, many of which lack scientific names and are otherwise wholly unstudied. The symmetry was complete: the Amazonian rain forest is the most that life has been able to accomplish within the constraints of this stormy planet.

Large splashing drops turned into sheets of water driven by gusts   5
of wind. I retreated into the camp and waited with my *mateiros* friends under the dripping canvas roofs. In a short time leptodactylid frogs began to honk their territorial calls in the forest nearby. To me they seemed to be saying rejoice! rejoice! The powers of nature are within our compass.

PRACTICE 6.1

Making and Changing an Impression

A. Describe a place that you know. Choose a place you can look at as you write or a place so strong in your memory that you don't need to look at it. Begin by jotting down details of the scene or words that capture your feeling about it. Don't hurry yourself, but take some time accumulating bits of language that serve to capture some aspect of the place for you.

When you have enough material, read it over and begin drafting your written description. As you write, ask yourself if you are making the right choices for selection and arrangement of details. Are you leaving out something important? Are you mentioning things that are not necessary to convey the impression you want to convey? What impression *do* you want to convey?

B. Revise the description you wrote in (A) to create the opposite impression. If, for example, you described a city street to give an impression of its unpleasantness, try to see the same street from a more pleasant point of view. Suppose the street's crowded sidewalks and noisy people led you to describe it in unpleasant terms; now revise from the point of view of one for whom crowds and noise are a positive sign of lively city life.

CHANGING PLACES

In the following selection from *Gemini*, her autobiography, Nikki Giovanni gives us an example of how knowledge of the history of a place can make that place interesting. In this case, personal and family history are interwoven with urban history. She also provides an example of how physical details are integrated with historical information. As you read her essay, think about some place of historical interest that you might describe, paying particular attention to the ways she has found to include the past — what is *not* there now — with the present.

READING

Nikki Giovanni, from "400 Mulvaney Street"

When we were growing up Knoxville didn't have television, let   1
alone an airport. It finally got TV but the airport is in Alcoa. And is now called Tyson Field. Right? Small towns are funny. Knoxville even has a zip code and seven-digit phone numbers. All of which seems strange to me since I mostly remember Mrs. Flora Ford's white cake with white icing and Miss Delaney's blue furs and Armetine Picket's being the sharpest woman in town — she attended our church — and Miss Brooks wearing tight sweaters and Carter-Roberts Drug Store sending out Modern Jazz Quartet sounds of "Fontessa" and my introduction to Nina Simone by David Cherry, dropping a nickel in the jukebox and "Porgy"

coming out. I mostly remember Vine Street, which I was not allowed to walk to get to school, though Grandmother didn't want
me to take Paine Street either because Jay Manning lived on it and
he was home from the army and very beautiful with his Black face
and two dimples. Not that I was going to do anything, because I
didn't do anything enough even to think in terms of not doing anything, but according to small-town logic "It looks bad."

The Gem Theatre was on the corner of Vine and a street that   2
runs parallel to the creek, and for 10 cents you could sit all day and
see a double feature, five cartoons and two serials plus previews for
the next two weeks. And I remember Frankie Lennon would come
in with her gang and sit behind me and I wanted to say, "Hi. Can I
sit with you?" but thought they were too snooty, and they, I found
out later, thought I was too Northern and stuck-up. All of that is
gone now. Something called progress killed my grandmother.

Mulvaney Street looked like a camel's back with both humps   3
bulging—up and down—and we lived in the down part. At the top
of the left hill a lady made ice balls and would mix the flavors for
you for just a nickel. Across the street from her was the Negro center, where the guys played indoor basketball and the little kids went
for stories and nap time. Down in the valley part were the tennis
courts, the creek, the bulk of the park and the beginning of the
right hill. To enter or leave the street you went either up or down. I
used to think of it as a fort, especially when it snowed, and the
enemy would always try to sneak through the underbrush nurtured
by the creek and through the park trees, but we always spotted
strangers and dealt. As you came down the left hill the houses were
up on its side; then people got regular flat front yards; then the
right hill started and ran all the way into Vine and Mulvaney was
gone and the big apartment building didn't have a yard at all.

Grandmother and Grandpapa had lived at 400 since they'd left   4
Georgia. And Mommy had been a baby there and Anto and Aunt
Agnes were born there. And dated there and sat on the swing on the
front porch and fussed there, and our good and our bad were
recorded there. That little frame house duplicated twice more
which overlooked the soft-voiced people passing by with "Evening,
'Fessor Watson, Miz Watson," and the grass wouldn't grow between our house and Edith and Clarence White's house. It was said
that he had something to do with numbers. When the man tried to
get between the two houses and the cinder crunched a warning to
us, both houses lit up and the man was caught between Mr. White's
shotgun and Grandfather's revolver, trying to explain he was lost.
Grandpapa would never pull a gun unless he intended to shoot and
would only shoot to kill. I think when he reached Knoxville he was

just tired of running. I brought his gun to New York with me after he died but the forces that be don't want anyone to keep her history, even if it's just a clogged twenty-two that no one in her right mind would even load.

Mr. and Mrs. Ector's rounded the trio of houses off. He always wore a stocking cap till he got tied back and would emerge very dapper. He was in love with the various automobiles he owned and had been seen by Grandmother and me on more than one occasion sweeping the snow from in front of his garage before he would back the car into the street. All summer he parked his car at the bottom of the hill and polished it twice a day and delighted in it. Grandmother would call across the porches to him, "Ector, you a fool 'bout the car, ain't cha?" And he would smile back. "Yes, ma'am." We were always polite with the Ectors because they had neither children nor grandchildren so there were no grounds for familiarity. I never knew Nellie Ector very well at all. It was rumored that she was a divorcée who had latched on to him, and to me she became all the tragic heroines I had read about, like *Forever Amber* or the *All This and Heaven Too* chick, and I was awed but kept my distance. He was laughs, though. I don't know when it happened to the Ectors but Mr. White was the first to die. I considered myself a hot-shot canasta player and I would play three-hand with Grandmother and Mrs. White and beat them. But I would drag the game on and on because it seemed so lonely next door when I could look through my bedroom window and see Mrs. White dressing for bed and not having to pull the shade anymore.

You always think the ones you love will always be there to love you. I went on to my grandfather's alma mater and got kicked out and would have disgraced the family but I had enough style for it not to be considered disgraceful. I could not/did not adjust to the Fisk social life and it could not/did not adjust to my intellect, so Thanksgiving I rushed home to Grandmother's without the bitchy dean of women's permission and that dean put me on social probation. Which would have worked but I was very much in love and not about to consider her punishment as anything real I should deal with. And the funny thing about that Thanksgiving was that I knew everything would go down just as it did. But I still wouldn't have changed it because Grandmother and Grandpapa would have had dinner alone and I would have had dinner alone and the next Thanksgiving we wouldn't even have him and Grandmother and I would both be alone by ourselves, and the only change would have been that Fisk considered me an ideal student, which means little on a life scale. My grandparents were surprised to see me in my brown slacks and beige sweater nervously chain-smoking and being

5

6

so glad to touch base again. And she, who knew everything, never once asked me about school. And he was old so I lied to him. And I went to Mount Zion Baptist with them that Sunday and saw he was going to die. He just had to. And I didn't want that. Because I didn't know what to do about Louvenia, who had never been alone in her life.

I left Sunday night and saw the dean Monday morning. She   7
asked where I had been. I said home. She asked if I had permission. I said I didn't need her permission to go home. She said, "Miss Giovanni," in a way I've been hearing all my life, in a way I've heard so long I know I'm on the right track when I hear it, and shook her head. I was "released from the school" February 1 because my "attitudes did not fit those of a Fisk woman." Grandpapa died in April and I was glad it was warm because he hated the cold so badly. Mommy and I drove to Knoxville to the funeral with Chris— Gary's, my sister's, son—and I was brave and didn't cry and made decisions. And finally the time came and Anto left and Aunt Agnes left. And Mommy and Chris and I stayed on till finally mommy had to go back to work. And Grandmother never once asked me about Fisk. We got up early Saturday morning and Grandmother made fried chicken for us. Nobody said we were leaving but we were. And we all walked down the hill to the car. And kissed. And I looked at her standing there so bravely trying not to think what I was trying not to feel. And I got in on the driver's side and looked at her standing there with her plaid apron and her hair in a bun, her feet hanging loosely out of her mules, sixty-three years old, waving good-bye to us, and for the first time having to go into 400 Mulvaney without John Brown Watson. I felt like an impotent dog. If I couldn't protect this magnificent woman, my grandmother, from loneliness, what could I ever do? I have always hated death. It is unacceptable to kill the young and distasteful to watch the old expire. And those in between our link commit the little murders all the time. There must be a better way. So Knoxville decided to become a model city and a new mall was built to replace the old marketplace and they were talking about convention centers and expressways. And Mulvaney Street was a part of it all. This progress....

Gay Street is to Knoxville what Fifth Avenue is to New York.   8
Something special, yes? And it looked the same. But Vine Street, where I would sneak to the drugstore to buy *Screen Stories* and watch the men drink wine and play pool—all gone. A wide, clean military-looking highway has taken its place. Austin Homes is cordoned off. It looked like a big prison. The Gem Theatre is now some sort of nightclub and Mulvaney Street is gone. Completely wiped out. Assassinated along with the old people who made it live.

I looked over and saw that the lady who used to cry "HOT FISH! GOOD HOT FISH!" no longer had a Cal Johnson Park to come to and set up her stove in. Grandmother would not say, "Edith White! I think I'll send Gary for a sandwich. You want one?" Mrs. Abrum and her reverend husband from rural Tennessee wouldn't bring us any more goose eggs from across the street. And Leroy wouldn't chase his mother's boyfriend on Saturday night down the back alley anymore. All gone, not even to a major highway but to a cutoff of a cutoff. All the old people who died from lack of adjustment died for a cutoff of a cutoff.

And I remember our finding Grandmother the house on Linden 9 Avenue and constantly reminding her it was every bit as good as if not better than the little ole house. A bigger back yard and no steps to climb. But I knew what Grandmother knew, what we all knew. There was no familiar smell in that house. No coal ashes from the fireplaces. Nowhere that you could touch and say, "Yolande threw her doll against this wall," or "Agnes fell down these steps." No smell or taste of biscuits Grandpapa had eaten with the Alaga syrup he loved so much. No Sunday chicken. No sound of "Lord, you children don't care a thing 'bout me after all I done for you," because Grandmother always had the need to feel mistreated. No spot in the back hall weighted down with lodge books and no corner where the old record player sat playing Billy Eckstine crooning, "What's My Name?" till Grandmother said, "Lord! Any fool know his name!" No breeze on dreamy nights when Mommy would listen over and over again to "I Don't See Me in Your Eyes Anymore." No pain in my knuckles where Grandmother had rapped them because she was determined I would play the piano, and when that absolutely failed, no effort on Linden for us to learn the flowers. No echo of me being the only person in the history of the family to curse Grandmother out and no Grandpapa saying, "Oh, my," which was serious from him, "we can't have this." Linden Avenue was pretty but it had no life.

And I took Grandmother one summer to Lookout Mountain in 10 Chattanooga and she would say I was the only grandchild who would take her riding. And that was the summer I noticed her left leg was shriveling. And she said I didn't have to hold her hand and I said I liked to. And I made ice cream the way Grandpapa used to do almost every Sunday. And I churned butter in the hand churner. And I knew and she knew that there was nothing I could do. "I just want to see you graduate," she said, and I didn't know she meant it. I graduated February 4. She died March 8.

And I went to Knoxville looking for Frankie and the Gem and 11 Carter-Roberts or something and they were all gone. And 400

Mulvaney Street, like a majestic king dethroned, put naked in the streets to beg, stood there just a mere skeleton of itself. The cellar that had been so mysterious was now exposed. The fireplaces stood. And I saw the kitchen light hanging and the peach butter put up on the back porch and I wondered why they were still there. She was dead. And I heard the daily soap operas from the radio we had given her one birthday and saw the string beans cooking in the deep well and thought how odd, since there was no stove, and I wanted to ask how Babbi was doing since I hadn't heard or seen "Brighter Day" in so long but no one would show himself. The roses in the front yard were blooming and it seemed a disgrace. Probably the tomatoes came up that year. She always had fantastic luck with tomatoes. But I was just too tired to walk up the front steps to see. Edith White had died. Mr. Ector had died, I heard. Grandmother had died. The park was not yet gone but the trees looked naked and scared. The wind sang to them but they wouldn't smile. The playground where I had swung. The courts where I played my first game of tennis. The creek where our balls were lost. "HOT FISH! GOOD HOT FISH!" The hill where the car speeding down almost hit me. Walking barefoot up the hill to the center to hear stories and my feet burning. All gone. Because progress is so necessary. General Electric says, "Our most important product." And I thought Ronald Reagan was cute.

▪ PRACTICE 6.2

A Place with a History

Provide a description, long or short as your instructor assigns, of a place that is interesting partly because of its history. Ideally, there should be some visible remains of that history in addition to the things that would be quite unperceivable without your historical knowledge.

Your job is to integrate what *is* there with what *was* there, to describe both the present and the absent, the present and the past. Before you write, take another look at the way Nikki Giovanni solved the problem of integrating past and present in her essay. For instance, you might examine paragraphs 8 and 9, where she uses negative constructions to include in her text what no longer exists in the place she is describing. Note how much emphasis is placed on what people did and what they no longer do as well as on places and things that are gone or changed.

INTERPRETING A SCENE

William Hogarth was England's leading caricaturist and visual satirist in the eighteenth century. He is famous for *The Rake's Progress* and *The Harlot's Progress*—his series of engravings depicting male and female degeneration and disaster. The engraving we are reprinting here is from a much milder series called *The Four Times of Day.* This one is "Noon," first printed in 1738. Along with the engraving, we are providing a sample description of it to give you some ideas on how to write your own description.

▨ READING

A Reading of Hogarth's "Noon"

This is a picture of a street scene in a bustling city, full of people in eighteenth-century clothing. The street itself is made of cobblestones, and has an open sewer or gutter running down the middle of it. A dead cat lies in the gutter near some broken stones.

The right side of the picture is dominated by a large brick building with windows of leaded glass. A crowd is emerging from a small door in the building, half of them coming closer to our viewpoint, the other half walking away with their backs turned. Some of this crowd have severe expressions on their faces and carry black books. They may be coming from a rather puritanical church after services.

In the right foreground, among this crowd, are a man, woman, and child dressed in what must have been the height of fashion. The man is wearing shoes with buckles, stockings, knee breeches, an immense bow tie, and a long coat with frills and over twenty buttons. He is making elegant gestures with his hands, pointing his feet like a dancer, with a cane dangling by a ribbon from his ruffled wrist and a sword hanging from his other side.

This elegant fop is speaking to a richly dressed lady, while in front of them is a creature like a midget but probably a small boy, dressed like a miniature of the man, complete with a cane, a wig, and a toy sword. He has a hand inside his long vest as he gazes downward, smiling, possibly at the dead cat. These three seem to be a family group.

On the other side of the gutter there is a group of people who have obviously not been to church. They stand in front of a sign that says "Good Eating" between two very large teeth topped with a picture of a man's head on a platter. From a window

above, a woman is throwing an old piece of meat from a platter toward the gutter, while a man grabs for it from behind her and misses. Near the window hangs a sign with a picture of a woman standing so that the top of the sign is at the level of her neck, leaving her headless.

Down below in the street a boy is scratching his bushy head and bellowing over a huge pie he has apparently just dropped, while a poorly dressed girl scrambles at his feet for the broken pieces, stuffing them into her mouth. Just behind these two stand another couple, a woman holding a hot pie with her apron and a black man reaching around her from behind to fondle her breasts and kiss her cheek. She seems to be encouraging this but her pie is tilting, dripping its liquid center toward the cobblestones. The whole pie may soon be headed that way.

The gutter seems to divide the well-to-do from the less affluent, the pious from the boisterous. This division gives a sense of the diversity of city life. But it is a very unflattering picture. There are no attractive people in the picture except the young woman who is losing her pie and perhaps more than that. Even a building in the background has a huge crack, parallel to the gutter, running down its side.

PRACTICE 6.3

Your Reading of a Hogarth Street Scene

On page 136 is a London street scene done by Hogarth a few years after the one just presented and discussed. Your assignment is to write a description of this scene that is about as complete and accurate as our description of the other scene by Hogarth.

You should not try to follow the other description. That one was organized partly by the gutter that Hogarth used to divide his picture. (Such gutters were called "kennels" in Hogarth's day.) You must find an organizing principle in this engraving that will guide you in writing your description of it.

This one seems to tell a bit more of a story than the first. Certainly it offers a thematic way of organizing and interpreting the material. Note that in the last paragraph of the description of Hogarth's "Noon," a move to interpretation is made, as if to answer the questions, What was Hogarth trying to show in this picture? What do all the elements of the picture add up to? There is no single correct way of doing this, but rather several possible ways. Your job is to find one and use it here.

READING THE IMAGE OF CELEBRITY

Here are two excerpts from Graham McCann's book *Marilyn Monroe*. In these two paragraphs, McCann conjectures about Monroe's photographic image, and describes her face and what her look seems to promise to the spectator. McCann refers to Monroe's "celebrity body" and then describes what he means by that. As you read, try to analyze how McCann achieves his effect. What physical features does he describe? Notice how he links description with his analysis of Monroe's body image.

READING

Graham McCann, from *Marilyn Monroe*

Select a typical photograph of Marilyn Monroe. Study it, scruti-   1
nize its features, sense its execution. Was this one pose unique,
snapped between its forming and dissolving, or was it an achingly
familiar pose, shot successively, here as merely one amongst many?
Monroe, as a still image, excites the most intense reaction from the

George Barris, from *Marilyn*

spectator: what happened before, after, who was in the room with her, who was behind the camera, what was she thinking, saying, feeling? The single image sparks off a series of questions (every caption trails off into three dots...). A typical pose displays her with glistening blonde hair, brightly dressed, her face set with half-closed eyes and half-opened mouth (not quite seeing, not quite speaking)—a picture of sheer promise. Parts of her body—the dark red lips, the long black eyelashes, the shaped and elongated eyebrows—are heavily outlined, whilst other parts—her neck and torso—are traced with trinkets and clothing that accentuate the roundness and fullness of her figure. The bent-forward attitude of her head and upper body, the slanting seductiveness of the eyes and lips, fashion an alluring self-image quite distinct from the cryptic off-camera self Monroe spent her life striving to define. As seen in portraits, Monroe intrigues us, invites us to ponder on our peculiar relationship to her....

In her early stills, Monroe is seen as interesting because of her body; in later portraits, it is a "celebrity body" that is the interesting sight. In the silent movies stylization of both gesture and looks was necessary for narrative, and prompted not only new ways of walking, sitting and using the hands, but also the development of styles to suit personalities. Fashions became part of a mammoth tie-up between the cinema and big business; the two influenced each other in the interests of the "image industry." Glamour contains a charm enhanced by means of illusion. A glamour image of a woman is particularly impressive in that it plays on the desire of the viewer in a peculiarly pristine way: beauty or sexuality is desirable exactly to the extent that it is idealized and unattainable. Monroe suffered because of this image: "People expected so much of me, I sometimes hated them. It was too much of a strain...Marilyn Monroe has to look a certain way—be *beautiful*—and act in a certain way, be talented. I wondered if I could live up to their expectations." [W. J. Weatherby, *Conversations with Marilyn*. London: Robson Books, 1976, 146.]

2

PRACTICE 6.4

Reading a Celebrity's Image

Using what you have learned from studying McCann's techniques, try a reading of your own. Select a well-known figure who appears regularly in the media—a recording artist, an actress, a comedian, an athlete, an anchorperson, a politician, a talk-show host—and try to capture the special qualities of his or her performance, particularly those that can be treated in terms of facial expressions and posture (rather than voice or language). The idea is to include the necessary minimum of physical details, but to go beyond such details to the impression, idea, or issue they convey. Make your reading about as long as McCann's.

PRACTICE 6.5

Reading the Image of Someone You Know Well

In the chapter on reflection, we asked you to reflect on a photographic image. Now we ask you to take that photograph—or another if you choose—and describe the person in it. McCann describes a person who is posing as a celebrity, and who is very assuredly and professionally "working" the camera. Your subject may be self-consciously posing, too—especially if the photograph is a professional product. A snapshot may tell you more.

Connecting Ideas and Things
Classification

Classifying is a way of connecting ideas and things through the use of categories. When we don't like the process, we call it pigeonholing, implying that things are being stuffed into categories whether they fit or not. But this kind of organization is basic to language itself. Nouns like *sheep* and *goats* or adjectives like *red* and *green* are themselves categories that enable us to know our world. Classifying is simply a more systematic use of the power that language gives us to organize the flood of information or data we encounter every day.

Classifying depends on our ability to compare and contrast, to find common features that link all the members of one group of things, along with other features that distinguish all the members of *this* group from *that* group. This way of thinking is as old as Aristotle, but was developed extensively during the period when biology was becoming a science. Classification enabled the modern theories of evolution and the origin of the species to be generated. In other areas of study, especially the social sciences, a good classification system such as the one that identifies an upper class, a corporate class, a middle class, a working class, and a lower class enables an investigator to perceive relationships that are not readily apparent and to give data meaning. As a way of knowing, classifying is often key to the research and experimenting phase of a writing project.

One of the most important research skills is the ability to play with the data being collected. This is true of the most serious professional projects as well as amateur practices. But perhaps we should clarify what we mean by "play." We are not suggesting fakery or carelessness, but rather that one should play as a child plays with blocks or construction sets, trying out different arrangements to see what can be made of them. In academic research, *play* means trying out various classifications in order to find the categories that enable you to bring together a group of things that would otherwise have been separate.

For any classifier, the first question is how many levels of classification are needed, and the second is how many categories at each level are required to cover all the material.

In biology, for example, the basic category is life itself, which brings all living things together and excludes stones, machines, and all those things that we call inorganic. The basic class is then refined and refined again, yielding smaller groups at every level until the smallest biological group (the species) is reached. Thus, human beings are classified this way:

Kingdom: Animalia
  Phylum: Chordata
    Subphylum: Vertebrata
      Class: Mammalia
        Subclass: Eutheria
          Order: Primates
            Family: Hominidae
              Genus: Homo
                Species: Sapiens

Let us look a little more closely at the way this biological classification system works. At the fourth level, class, mammals are distinguished from all the other creatures in the category above it—that is, all the other living things that have vertebrae or backbones (fish, birds, reptiles, and amphibians). Mammals, the class mammalia, are defined in biology books as "warm-blooded animals whose skin is covered with hair; the females have mammary glands that secrete milk for the nourishment of the young." Within the class of mammals there are three subclasses that are distinguished by the way they give birth: eggs, like the platypus; pouches, like the possum; or a womb or uterus, like the rat, bat, whale, human, and many others. This third subclass, Eutheria, is then broken down into twelve orders, so that even-toed mammals with hooves (cows and hippopotamuses, for instance) can be distinguished from odd-toed mammals with hooves (horses and rhinoceroses, for instance). One of these twelve orders is distinguished as the first, the highest, and is therefore called Primates. This order includes humans, those members of the great ape family (Pongidae) who devised the whole system. There is a lesson here: those who write, rank. The "highest" order, Primates, is distinguished by having hands and large brains, both of which may be used to "grasp" things. The human brain grasps powerfully by naming and classifying things. The "highest" primate is the classifying primate, the one who knows: genus, *Homo*; species, *sapiens*.

It is possible to divide *Homo sapiens* into smaller groups, but once we get below the level of species, we are moving into areas of less interest to biologists and more interest to anthropologists and other social scientists: races, nations, classes, tribes, occupational groups, kinship groups, and so on. This is the level of classifying that sometimes provokes the charge of stereotyping and, with it, resistance to being typed or to knowing through typing. But is there any other way to know—or be known? Is the problem classification or something else—say, for example, ranking? Can there be classification without ranking, or do the two automatically go together? These are some questions to think about as you work through the following readings and practices.

CATEGORIES

The following short excerpt illustrates the difference between everyday or casual classification and the more systematic classification of a professional social scientist. Besides providing a clear and consistent basis for his categories, Packard tries to make his classification system more complete and more significant than the groupings offered by the businessman and the transferee's wife.

READING

Vance Packard, from *A Nation of Strangers*

A Darien businessman who has lived there all his life said: "The   1
town is divided between commuters and locals and they seldom cross paths except in the stores; and there is a certain amount of resentment." The wife of a transferee who had lived in Darien two years told me: "You feel you are not really accepted here because they expect you to move and so they don't care about getting acquainted."

A somewhat more precise picture of the divisions would show   2
three major groups, with little interaction between them:

1. The locals—people who were raised in Darien and make their   3
   living there, as merchants, contractors, etc. Some are of old Irish-Yankee stock, many are of Italian ancestry.
2. The Darien people—families from somewhere else who have   4
   made it by living in Darien more than five years. They dominate the town socially.
3. The transients—who will be moving on after one to four years   5
   of residence.

Questions

1. What are the main differences between the classification suggested by the businessman and Packard's "more precise picture"?
2. Assume that Packard started with the genus of "all residents of Darien." On what basis has he distinguished the three species he finds within that genus?
3. Packard says of his first group that they "make their living" in Darien. How does this distinguish them from the others?
4. Packard's second group is said to "dominate the town socially." What does this mean? How does this relate to what the businessman and the transferee's wife told Packard? Are the businessman and the wife distinguishable in terms of Packard's categories?
5. One of the uses of classification is to prepare the way for interesting questions. For instance, if Packard's grouping is accurate and his information is correct, we are now in a position to ask *why* Group 2 dominates. We may not be able to answer on the basis of the information we have, but we can now formulate our need for more information or we can speculate and suggest answers on the basis of what we already know.

    Two questions: Why do you suppose Group 2 dominates? What additional information might help you answer this question?

■ **PRACTICE 7.1**

Social Categories in an Institution

This practice is meant to be a thought experiment rather than an occasion for polished prose.

1. Using Packard's sample as a model, construct a relatively brief and general classification of all the people in your college or university.
2. Consider the following questions: What principle did you use to construct your categories? What other classifying principles are possible? Is your classification system complete? Is there a category for all the people a visitor to your campus might see? Do any of the categories overlap?
3. Try one or two alternative classifications or compare your set of classes with those devised by a few of your classmates. Try to come up with the most complete and logically clear set of categories that you can.
4. Take one of the general categories you've constructed and subdivide it to account for distinct groups within that category. What principles

did you use to subdivide members of the category? What other principles of subdivision are possible?
5. Which level of classification do you think would be most useful to an
incoming student? Why?

TYPES

All classifying entails some kind of articulation between the general and the
specific. In constructing a system of classification, we sometimes begin
with large, general categories, as in Practice 7.1; then we subdivide, working our way down toward more and more specific groupings. At other
times, we work in the opposite direction, beginning with the specifics we
observe and then grouping those specifics into distinct types that can, in
turn, be considered in terms of more general categories, and so on.

In the following excerpt, psychologist Monica M. Moore recounts
types of nonverbal behavior that young women use to signal their lack of
interest in being courted by this or that man. Do women you know use
signals other than the ones Moore documents?

■ READING

Monica M. Moore, "Rejection Signaling" (from "Nonverbal Courtship Patterns in Women")

Recent ethological[1] studies of nonlinguistic communication in   1
human courtship have begun to establish the existence of a nonverbal signaling system for negotiating sexual relationships. Previous
research has shed some light on the nonverbal behaviors women
employ to signal interest in potential male partners. This study
shows that women also use nonverbal displays to *end* courtship interaction.

The participants in this study were 200 randomly selected   2
women judged to be between the ages of eighteen and thirty-five
years. The women were covertly observed late in the evening at
bars known for high levels of singles' activity in a Midwestern college town.

Gaze avoidance occurred when the woman did not make eye con-   3
tact with the man, despite the fact that he was looking directly at
her. Instead, she looked at other people, made eye contact with
someone else at the table, or directed her gaze to another point in

---

[1]*Ethology:* The study of animal behavior in natural environments. *Eds.*

the room. Other signals included the *upward gaze*, in which the woman looked directly at the ceiling, lifting her head approximately one-quarter inch, and the *hair gaze*, in which the woman drew her hair across her face and looked at the ends. All of these behaviors consisted of prolonged (more than ten seconds) inattention on the part of the woman.

Sometimes, a woman would turn her head and *look away* from a man while he was speaking or engaging in some other behavior to draw her attention. In contrast, other women would *stare* at a man for a long period of time, often until he looked away. This behavior was frequently combined with another facial pattern: the *frown* or the *sneer*. In the *frown*, the corners of the woman's mouth were turned downward with compressed lips and her brow was furrowed. In the *sneer*, the woman's mouth was twisted and her nose was wrinkled.   4

Two other facial patterns that met the criteria for rejection sig-naling were the *negative head shake* and the *yawn*. When women flirt with men they often engage in a great deal of affirmative head nod-ding. Here, women shook their heads negatively, moving their faces from side to side by rotating their heads on their necks. They also yawned. In this signal, the mouth was opened wide and the nose was wrinkled while the eyes were squinted or, in some cases, closed. Sometimes a woman covered her mouth with her hand.   5

Women also engaged in self-grooming behaviors. However, un-like behaviors displayed by flirtatious women, these gestures were exhibited not to draw attention to the body (such as *primping* or *hair flipping*) but to engage in self-care behaviors more commonly done in private. In this regard, women sometimes *cleaned* their *nails* or *picked* their *teeth*.   6

These nonverbal behaviors are a powerful tool, since they allow women to exert selectivity in partner choice. Women can judge a man's attractiveness and value as a mate through observations of his status, ambition, lack of other commitments, intelligence, and in-come. Mixing rejection signals with nonverbal courtship behaviors buys women time to make these evaluations.   7

▓ **PRACTICE 7.2**

Social Types in a Particular Place

In this practice, you are to work from observation of specifics to classifi-cation into types. Choose one of the places and focuses listed on the next page and go there prepared to take notes about what you see. Your note taking may go better if you plan ahead: What types do you expect to see? What behaviors are significant to note? Be sure to leave space for notes on behaviors and types you didn't anticipate. Based on your notes and observations, try classifying and commenting on what you have seen. Choose one of the following:

1. the eating habits of people in a college cafeteria or a mall food court
2. the spectatorial habits of people who attend a sports event
3. the study habits of students in a college library
4. the interpersonal habits of people at a party, dance, or similar social gathering
5. the in-class habits of students in a college course
6. the shopping habits of people in a specific kind of store
7. the play habits of children in a day-care center or a neighborhood park

FROM ABSTRACT TO CONCRETE

To help ourselves and others understand something, we often try to define it. Defining involves classifying, as a look at any dictionary entry will illustrate. Usually, a dictionary entry identifies the kind of thing at issue, notes its distinctive features, and provides an illustration or example. This use of classifying is especially important when the item to be understood is an abstraction, such as *freedom, knowledge, love,* or *power.* Classifying is a way to make the abstract more concrete.

As an example, we offer you an excerpt from Bertrand Russell's book *Power.* As you read the selection, pay particular attention to the way it is organized. Russell is exceptionally careful to name the processes of thought he is using:

> *First Paragraph:* "Power may be defined…"
> *Second:* "There are various ways of classifying…"
> *Third:* "Power…may be classified…"
> *Fifth:* "These forms of power are…displayed…"
> *Sixth:* "All these forms…are exemplified…"
> *Seventh–tenth:* "illustrates," "typifies," "show," "are illustrative"
> *Eleventh:* "Let us apply these…analogies…"
> *Twelfth:* "…organizations are…distinguishable…"

■ READING

Bertrand Russell, from *Power*

Power may be defined as the production of intended effects. It is   1
thus a quantitative concept: given two men with similar desires, if
one achieves all the desires that the other achieves, and also others,

he has more power than the other. But there is no exact means of comparing the power of two men of whom one can achieve one group of desires, and another another; e.g., given two artists of whom each wishes to paint good pictures and become rich, and of whom one succeeds in painting good pictures and the other in becoming rich, there is no way of estimating which has the more power. Nevertheless, it is easy to say, roughly, that A has more power than B, if A achieves many intended effects and B only a few.

There are various ways of classifying the forms of power, each of which has its utility. In the first place, there is power over human beings and power over dead matter or nonhuman forms of life. I shall be concerned mainly with power over human beings, but it will be necessary to remember that the chief cause of change in the modern world is the increased power over matter that we owe to science. 2

Power over human beings may be classified by the manner of influencing individuals, or by the type of organization involved. 3

An individual may be influenced: A. By direct physical power over his body, e.g., when he is imprisoned or killed; B. By rewards and punishments as inducements, e.g., in giving or withholding employment; C. by influence on opinion, i.e., propaganda in its broadest sense. Under this last head I should include the opportunity for creating desired habits in others, e.g., by military drill, the only difference being that in such cases action follows without any such mental intermediary as could be called opinion. 4

These forms of power are most nakedly and simply displayed in our dealings with animals, where disguises and pretenses are not thought necessary. When a pig with a rope round its middle is hoisted squealing into a ship, it is subject to direct physical power over its body. On the other hand, when the proverbial donkey follows the proverbial carrot, we induce him to act as we wish by persuading him that it is to his interest to do so. Intermediate between these two cases is that of performing animals, in whom habits have been formed by rewards and punishments; also, in a different way, that of sheep induced to embark on a ship, when the leader has to be dragged across the gangway by force, and the rest then follow willingly. 5

All these forms of power are exemplified among human beings. 6

The case of the pig illustrates military and police power. 7

The donkey with the carrot typifies the power of propaganda. 8

Performing animals show the power of "education." 9

The sheep following their unwilling leader are illustrative of party politics, whenever, as is usual, a revered leader is in bondage to a clique or to party bosses. 10

Let us apply these Aesopian analogies to the rise of Hitler. The carrot was the Nazi program (involving, e.g., the abolition of 11 interest); the donkey was the lower middle class. The sheep and their leader were the Social Democrats and Hindenburg. The pigs (only so far as their misfortunes are concerned) were the victims in concentration camps, and the performing animals are the millions who make the Nazi salute.

The most important organizations are approximately distinguishable by the kind of power that they exert. The army and the police exercise coercive power over the body; economic organizations, in the main, use rewards and punishments as incentives and deterrents; schools, churches, and political parties aim at influencing opinion. But these distinctions are not very clear-cut, since every organization uses other forms of power in addition to the one which is most characteristic.

12

Questions

1. Try diagramming Russell's classification scheme for power. Do you think Russell used a top-down or a bottom-up method to generate his set of classifications?

2. In paragraph 4, Russell identifies three ways "an individual may be influenced." After defining the third way as "by influence on opinion," Russell notes that in cases such as "military drill," habits are formed without the "mental intermediary . . . called opinion." Why doesn't Russell posit a fourth type of power to account for such cases? Do you think he should have? Why or why not?

3. Although Russell says that he is concerned with forms of "power over human beings," he uses animal analogies to explain his classifications. In this context, do you think animal analogies are appropriate? To what extent do people who are treated like pigs, donkeys, performing animals, or sheep become pigs, donkeys, performing animals, or sheep? Do people have powers that are not available to these animals? Do these animals have powers that remain unaccounted for in Russell's taxonomy of power? In short, is Russell's taxonomy of power complete or does it leave out important forms of power?

▉ PRACTICE 7.3

Power in an Institution You Know

Classify and discuss the forms of power that are characteristic of an institution you know well, such as a school, a family, a youth group, a military organization, or a business. In developing your classification, you might want to use Russell's categories as a point of departure. However, if you do so, be sure to test their applicability to your topic and modify them as necessary to fit your purpose. In planning and organizing your essay, you should remember that Russell's work not only classifies but also defines and exemplifies. What definitions and examples do you need to make your classifications informative and interesting?

PRACTICE 7.4

Forms of _____

Using Russell's very clear structure as a model (definition, classification, exemplification), write a short essay in which you take some other large abstraction—love, faith, service, education—and produce your own discussion of it. To get started, brainstorm by writing down your definitions of the abstraction you have chosen. Compare your definitions with those of a dictionary. Then, work out the definition that will best suit your project. It is quite likely that you will want to revise your definition once you start the process of classifying the forms of the abstraction you have selected. You will, in fact, be testing the usefulness of your definition in the process of classification. Remember to follow the pattern of Russell's essay, in which the definition of *power* is followed by classification, and classification is supported by illustration and exemplification.

Title your essay "Forms of _____."

THE TYPE AND THE INDIVIDUAL

Like all strategies, classifying can be used for good or for ill. It can help us get to know and therefore understand both people and things. But when classifying becomes stereotyping, it may block understanding and obstruct interaction. Where do stereotypes come from? How and why do people use stereotypes in relating to one another? What might one do about the predicaments stereotypes produce? In the following essay from her book *The Latin Deli* (1993), Judith Ortiz Cofer suggests some answers to these questions as she tells the story of her body in terms of four categories: skin, color, size, and looks.

▨ READING

Judith Ortiz Cofer, "The Story of My Body"

Migration is the story of my body.
     —*Víctor Hernández Cruz*

Skin

I was born a white girl in Puerto Rico but became a brown   1
girl when I came to live in the United States. My Puerto Rican
relatives called me tall; at the American school, some of my
rougher classmates called me Skinny Bones, and the Shrimp because I was the smallest member of my classes all through grammar
school until high school, when the midget Gladys was given the
honorary post of front row center for class pictures and score-
keeper, bench warmer, in P.E. I reached my full stature of five feet
in sixth grade.

I started out life as a pretty baby and learned to be a pretty girl   2
from a pretty mother. Then at ten years of age I suffered one of the
worst cases of chicken pox I have ever heard of. My entire body, including the inside of my ears and in between my toes, was covered
with pustules which in a fit of panic at my appearance I scratched
off my face, leaving permanent scars. A cruel school nurse told me I
would always have them—tiny cuts that looked as if a mad cat had
plunged its claws deep into my skin. I grew my hair long and hid
behind it for the first years of my adolescence. This was when I
learned to be invisible.

Color

In the animal world it indicates danger: the most colorful creatures   3
are often the most poisonous. Color is also a way to attract and se-
duce a mate. In the human world color triggers many more complex and often deadly reactions. As a Puerto Rican girl born of
"white" parents, I spent the first years of my life hearing people
refer to me as *blanca*, white. My mother insisted that I protect myself from the intense island sun because I was more prone to sun-
burn than some of my darker, *trigueño*[1] playmates. People were
always commenting within my hearing about how my black hair
contrasted so nicely with my "pale" skin. I did not think of the color
of my skin consciously except when I heard the adults talking about
complexion. It seems to me that the subject is much more common

---

[1]*trigueño:* swarthy, dark.

in the conversation of mixed-race peoples than in mainstream United States society, where it is a touchy and sometimes even embarrassing topic to discuss, except in a political context. In Puerto Rico I heard many conversations about skin color. A pregnant woman could say, "I hope my baby doesn't turn out *prieto*" (slang for "dark" or "black") "like my husband's grandmother, although she was a good-looking *negra* in her time." I am a combination of both, being olive-skinned—lighter than my mother yet darker than my fair-skinned father. In America, I am a person of color, obviously a Latina. On the Island I have been called everything from a *paloma blanca*, after the song (by a black suitor), to *la gringa.*[2]

My first experience of color prejudice occurred in a supermarket   4
in Paterson, New Jersey. It was Christmastime, and I was eight or nine years old. There was a display of toys in the store where I went two or three times a day to buy things for my mother, who never made lists but sent for milk, cigarettes, a can of this or that, as she remembered from hour to hour. I enjoyed being trusted with money and walking half a city block to the new, modern grocery store. It was owned by three good-looking Italian brothers. I liked the younger one with the crew-cut blond hair. The two older ones watched me and the other Puerto Rican kids as if they thought we were going to steal something. The oldest one would sometimes even try to hurry me with my purchases, although part of my pleasure in these expeditions came from looking at everything in the well-stocked aisles. I was also teaching myself to read English by sounding out the labels in packages: L&M cigarettes, Borden's homogenized milk, Red Devil potted ham, Nestle's chocolate mix, Quaker oats, Bustelo coffee, Wonder bread, Colgate toothpaste, Ivory soap, and Goya (makers of products used in Puerto Rican dishes) everything—these are some of the brand names that taught me nouns. Several times this man had come up to me, wearing his blood-stained butcher's apron, and towering over me had asked in a harsh voice whether there was something he could help me find. On the way out I would glance at the younger brother who ran one of the registers and he would often smile and wink at me.

It was the mean brother who first referred to me as "colored." It   5
was a few days before Christmas, and my parents had already told my brother and me that since we were in Los Estados[3] now, we would get our presents on December 25 instead of Los Reyes,

[2]*paloma blanca:* white dove; *la gringa:* North American, foreigner.

[3]*Los Estados:* the United States.

Three Kings Day, when gifts are exchanged in Puerto Rico. We were to give them a wish list that they would take to Santa Claus, who apparently lived in the Macy's store downtown—at least that's where we had caught a glimpse of him when we went shopping. Since my parents were timid about entering the fancy store, we did not approach the huge man in the red suit. I was not interested in sitting on a stranger's lap anyway. But I did covet Susie, the talking schoolteacher doll that was displayed in the center aisle of the Italian brothers' supermarket. She talked when you pulled a string on her back. Susie had a limited repertoire of three sentences: I think she could say: "Hello, I'm Susie Schoolteacher," "Two plus two is four," and one other thing I cannot remember. The day the older brother chased me away, I was reaching to touch Susie's blonde curls. I had been told many times, as most children have, not to touch anything in a store that I was not buying. But I had been looking at Susie for weeks. In my mind, she was my doll. After all, I had put her on my Christmas wish list. The moment is frozen in my mind as if there were a photograph of it on file. It was not a turning point, a disaster, or an earth-shaking revelation. It was simply the first time I considered—if naively—the meaning of skin color in human relations.

I reached to touch Susie's hair. It seems to me that I had to get on tiptoe, since the toys were stacked on a table and she sat like a princess on top of the fancy box she came in. Then I heard the booming "Hey, kid, what do you think you're doing!" spoken very loudly from the meat counter. I felt caught, although I knew I was not doing anything criminal. I remember not looking at the man, but standing there, feeling humiliated because I knew everyone in the store must have heard him yell at me. I felt him approach, and when I knew he was behind me, I turned around to face the bloody butcher's apron. His large chest was at my eye level. He blocked my way. I started to run out of the place, but even as I reached the door I heard him shout after me: "Don't come in here unless you gonna buy something. You PR kids put your dirty hands on stuff. You always look dirty. But maybe dirty brown is your natural color." I heard him laugh and someone else too in the back. Outside in the sunlight I looked at my hands. My nails needed a little cleaning as they always did, since I liked to paint with watercolors, but I took a bath every night. I thought the man was dirtier than I was in his stained apron. He was also always sweaty—it showed in big yellow circles under his shirt-sleeves. I sat on the front steps of the apartment building where we lived and looked closely at my hands, which showed the only skin I could see, since it was bitter cold and I was wearing my quilted play coat, dungarees, and a knitted navy

6

cap of my father's. I was not pink like my friend Charlene and her sister Kathy, who had blue eyes and light brown hair. My skin is the color of the coffee my grandmother made, which was half milk, *leche con café* rather than *café con leche*. My mother is the opposite mix. She has a lot of café in her color. I could not understand how my skin looked like dirt to the supermarket man.

I went in and washed my hands thoroughly with soap and hot water, and borrowing my mother's nail file, I cleaned the crusted watercolors from underneath my nails. I was pleased with the results. My skin was the same color as before, but I knew I was clean. Clean enough to run my fingers through Susie's fine gold hair when she came home to me.   7

Size

My mother is barely four feet eleven inches in height, which is average for women in her family. When I grew to five feet by age twelve, she was amazed and began to use the word tall to describe me, as in "Since you are tall, this dress will look good on you." As with the color of my skin, I didn't consciously think about my height or size until other people made an issue of it. It is around the preadolescent years that in America the games children play for fun become fierce competitions where everyone is out to "prove" they are better than others. It was in the playground and sports fields that my size-related problems began. No matter how familiar the story is, every child who is the last chosen for a team knows the torment of waiting to be called up. At the Paterson, New Jersey, public schools that I attended, the volleyball or softball game was the metaphor for the battlefield of life to the inner city kids—the black kids versus the Puerto Rican kids, the whites versus the blacks versus the Puerto Rican kids; and I was 4F, skinny, short, bespectacled, and apparently impervious to the blood thirst that drove many of my classmates to play ball as if their lives depended on it. Perhaps they did. I would rather be reading a book than sweating, grunting, and running the risk of pain and injury. I simply did not see the point in competitive sports. My main form of exercise then was walking to the library, many city blocks away from my barrio.   8

Still, I wanted to be wanted. I wanted to be chosen for the teams. Physical education was compulsory, a class where you were actually given a grade. On my mainly all A report card, the C for compassion I always received from the P.E. teachers shamed me the same as a bad grade in a real class. Invariably, my father would say: "How can you make a low grade for *playing games?*" He did not understand. Even if I had managed to make a hit (it never happened) or get the ball over that ridiculously high net, I already had a reputation as a "shrimp," a   9 hopeless nonathlete. It was an area where the girls who didn't like me for one reason or another—mainly because I did better than they on academic subjects—could lord it over me; the playing field was the place where even the smallest girl could make me feel powerless and inferior. I instinctively understood the politics even then; how the *not* choosing me until the teacher forced one of the team captains to call my name was a coup of sorts—there, you little show-off, tomorrow you can beat us in spelling and geography, but this afternoon you are the loser. Or perhaps those were only my own bitter thoughts as I sat or stood in the sidelines while the big girls were grabbed like fish and I, the little brown tadpole, was ignored until Teacher looked over in my general direction and shouted, "Call Ortiz," or, worse, "Somebody's *got* to take her."

No wonder I read Wonder Woman comics and had Legion of   10
Super Heroes daydreams. Although I wanted to think of myself as "intellectual," my body was demanding that I notice it. I saw the little swelling around my once-flat nipples, the fine hairs growing in secret places; but my knees were still bigger than my thighs, and I always wore long- or half-sleeve blouses to hide my bony upper arms. I wanted flesh on my bones—a thick layer of it. I saw a new product advertised on TV. Wate-On. They showed skinny men and women before and after taking the stuff, and it was a transformation like the ninety-seven-pound-weakling-turned-into-Charles-Atlas ads that I saw on the back covers of my comic books. The Wate-On was very expensive. I tried to explain my need for it in Spanish to my mother, but it didn't translate very well, even to my ears—and she said with a tone of finality, eat more of my good food and you'll get fat—anybody can get fat. Right. Except me. I was going to have to join a circus someday as Skinny Bones, the woman without flesh.

Wonder Woman was stacked. She had a cleavage framed by the   11
spread wings of a golden eagle and a muscular body that has become fashionable with women only recently. But since I wanted a body that would serve me in P.E., hers was my ideal. The breasts were an indulgence I allowed myself. Perhaps the daydreams of bigger girls were more glamorous, since our ambitions are filtered through our needs, but I wanted first a powerful body. I daydreamed of leaping up above the gray landscape of the city to where the sky was clear and blue, and in anger and self-pity, I fantasized about scooping my enemies up by their hair from the playing fields and dumping them on a barren asteroid. I would put the P.E. teachers each on their own rock in space too, where they would be the loneliest people in the universe, since I knew they had no "inner resources," no imagination, and in outer space, there would be no air

for them to fill their deflated volleyballs with. In my mind all P.E. teachers have blended into one large spiky-haired woman with a whistle on a string around her neck and a volleyball under one arm. My Wonder Woman fantasies of revenge were a source of comfort to me in my early career as a shrimp.

I was saved from more years of P.E. torment by the fact that in   12 my sophomore year of high school I transferred to a school where the midget, Gladys, was the focal point of interest for the people who must rank according to size. Because her height was considered a handicap, there was an unspoken rule about mentioning size around Gladys, but of course, there was no need to say anything. Gladys knew her place: front row center in class photographs. I gladly moved to the left or to the right of her, as far as I could without leaving the picture completely.

Looks

Many photographs were taken of me as a baby by my mother to   13 send to my father, who was stationed overseas during the first two years of my life. With the army in Panama when I was born, he later traveled often on tours of duty with the navy. I was a healthy, pretty baby. Recently, I read that people are drawn to big-eyed round-faced creatures, like puppies, kittens, and certain other mammals and marsupials, koalas, for example, and, of course, infants. I was all eyes, since my head and body, even as I grew older, remained thin and small-boned. As a young child I got a lot of attention from my relatives and many other people we met in our barrio.[4] My mother's beauty may have had something to do with how much attention we got from strangers in stores and on the street. I can imagine it. In the pictures I have seen of us together, she is a stunning young woman by Latino standards: long, curly black hair, and round curves in a compact frame. From her I learned how to move, smile, and talk like an attractive woman. I remember going into a bodega for our groceries and being given candy by the proprietor as a reward for being *bonita*, pretty.

I can see in the photographs, and I also remember, that I was   14 dressed in the pretty clothes, the stiff, frilly dresses, with layers of crinolines underneath, the glossy patent leather shoes, and, on special occasions, the skull-hugging little hats and the white gloves that were popular in the late fifties and early sixties. My mother was proud of my looks, although I was a bit too thin. She could dress me up like a doll and take me by the hand to visit relatives, or go to the Spanish mass at the Catholic church, and show me off. How

---

[4]*barrio:* district, quarter.

was I to know that she and the others who called me "pretty" were representatives of an aesthetic that would not apply when I went out into the mainstream world of school?

In my Paterson, New Jersey, public schools there were still quite   15
a few white children, although the demographics of the city were changing rapidly. The original waves of Italian and Irish immigrants, silk-mill workers, and laborers in the cloth industries had been "assimilated." Their children were now the middle-class parents of my peers. Many of them moved their children to the Catholic schools that proliferated enough to have leagues of basketball teams. The names I recall hearing still ring in my ears: Don Bosco High versus St. Mary's High, St. Joseph's versus St. John's. Later I too would be transferred to the safer environment of a Catholic school. But I started school at Public School Number 11. I came there from Puerto Rico, thinking myself a pretty girl, and found that the hierarchy for popularity was as follows: pretty white girl, pretty Jewish girl, pretty Puerto Rican girl, pretty black girl. Drop the last two categories; teachers were too busy to have more than one favorite per class, and it was simply understood that if there was a big part in the school play, or any competition where the main qualification was "presentability" (such as escorting a school visitor to or from the principal's office), the classroom's public address speaker would be requesting the pretty and/or nice-looking white boy or girl. By the time I was in the sixth grade, I was sometimes called by the principal to represent my class because I dressed neatly (I knew this from a progress report sent to my mother, which I translated for her) and because all the "presentable" white girls had moved to the Catholic schools (I later surmised this part). But I was still not one of the popular girls with the boys. I remember one incident where I stepped out into the playground in my baggy gym shorts and one Puerto Rican boy said to the other: "What do you think?" The other one answered: "Her face is OK, but look at the toothpick legs." The next best thing to a compliment I got was when my favorite male teacher, while handing out the class pictures, commented that with my long neck and delicate features I resembled the movie star Audrey Hepburn. But the Puerto Rican boys had learned to respond to a fuller figure: long necks and a perfect little nose were not what they looked for in a girl. That is when I decided I was a "brain." I did not settle into the role easily. I was nearly devastated by what the chicken pox episode had done to my self-image. But I looked into the mirror less often after I was told that I would always have scars on my face, and I hid behind my long black hair and my books.

After the problems at the public school got to the point where   16
even nonconfrontational little me got beaten up several times, my

parents enrolled me at St. Joseph's High School. I was then a minority of one among the Italian and Irish kids. But I found several
good friends there—other girls who took their studies seriously.
We did our homework together and talked about the Jackies. The
Jackies were two popular girls, one blonde and the other red-
haired, who had women's bodies. Their curves showed even in the
blue jumper uniforms with straps that we all wore. The blonde
Jackie would often let one of the straps fall off her shoulder, and although she, like all of us, wore a white blouse underneath, all the
boys stared at her arm. My friends and I talked about this and practiced letting our straps fall off our shoulders. But it wasn't the same
without breasts or hips.

My final two and a half years of high school were spent in Au-   17
gusta, Georgia, where my parents moved our family in search of a
more peaceful environment. There we became part of a little community of our army-connected relatives and friends. School was yet
another matter. I was enrolled in a huge school of nearly two thousand students that had just that year been forced to integrate. There
were two black girls and there was me. I did extremely well academically. As to my social life, it was, for the most part, uneventful—
yet it is in my memory blighted by one incident. In my junior year,
I became wildly infatuated with a pretty white boy. I'll call him
Ted. Oh, he was pretty: yellow hair that fell over his forehead, a
smile to die for—and he was a great dancer. I watched him at Teen
Town, the youth center at the base where all the military brats
gathered on Saturday nights. My father had retired from the navy,
and we had all our base privileges—one other reason we had
moved to Augusta. Ted looked like an angel to me. I worked on
him for a year before he asked me out. This meant maneuvering to
be within the periphery of his vision at every possible occasion. I
took the long way to my classes in school just to pass by his locker, I
went to football games, which I detested, and I danced (I too was a
good dancer) in front of him at Teen Town—this took some fancy
footwork, since it involved subtly moving my partner toward the
right spot on the dance floor. When Ted finally approached me, "A
Million to One" was playing on the jukebox, and when he took me
into his arms, the odds suddenly turned in my favor. He asked me
to go to a school dance the following Saturday. I said yes, breath-
lessly. I said yes, but there were obstacles to surmount at home. My
father did not allow me to date casually. I was allowed to go to
major events like a prom or a concert with a boy who had been
properly screened. There was such a boy in my life, a neighbor who
wanted to be a Baptist missionary and was practicing his anthropo-
logical skills on my family. If I was desperate to go somewhere and
needed a date, I'd resort to Gary. This is the type of religious nut

that Gary was: when the school bus did not show up one day, he put his hands over his face and prayed to Christ to get us a way to get to school. Within ten minutes a mother in a station wagon, on her way to town, stopped to ask why we weren't in school. Gary informed her that the Lord had sent her just in time to find us a way to get there in time for roll call. He assumed that I was impressed. Gary was even good-looking in a bland sort of way, but he kissed me with his lips tightly pressed together. I think Gary probably ended up marrying a native woman from wherever he may have gone to preach the Gospel according to Paul. She probably believes that all white men pray to God for transportation and kiss with their mouths closed. But it was Ted's mouth, his whole beautiful self, that concerned me in those days. I knew my father would say no to our date, but I planned to run away from home if necessary. I told my mother how important this date was. I cajoled and pleaded with her from Sunday to Wednesday. She listened to my arguments and must have heard the note of desperation in my voice. She said very gently to me: "You better be ready for disappointment." I did not ask what she meant. I did not want her fears for me to taint my happiness. I asked her to tell my father about my date. Thursday at breakfast my father looked at me across the table with his eyebrows together. My mother looked at him with her mouth set in a straight line. I looked down at my bowl of cereal. Nobody said anything. Friday I tried on every dress in my closet. Ted would be picking me up at six on Saturday: dinner and then the sock hop at school. Friday night I was in my room doing my nails or something else in preparation for Saturday (I know I groomed myself nonstop all week) when the telephone rang. I ran to get it. It was Ted. His voice sounded funny when he said my name, so funny that I felt compelled to ask: "Is something wrong?" Ted blurted it all out without a preamble. His father had asked who he was going out with. Ted had told him my name. "Ortiz? That's Spanish, isn't it?" the father had asked. Ted had told him yes, then shown him my picture in the yearbook. Ted's father had shaken his head. No. Ted would not be taking me out. Ted's father had known Puerto Ricans in the army. He had lived in New York City while studying architecture and had seen how the spics lived. Like rats. Ted repeated his father's words to me as if I should understand *his* predicament when I heard why he was breaking our date. I don't remember what I said before hanging up. I do recall the darkness of my room that sleepless night and the heaviness of my blanket in which I wrapped myself like a shroud. And I remember my parents' respect for my pain and their gentleness toward me that weekend. My mother did not say "I warned you," and I was grateful for her understanding silence.

In college, I suddenly became an "exotic" woman to the men   18
who had survived the popularity wars in high school, who were now
practicing to be worldly: they had to act liberal in their politics, in
their lifestyles, and in the women they went out with. I dated heavily for a while, then married young. I had discovered that I needed
stability more than social life. I had brains for sure and some talent
in writing. These facts were a constant in my life. My skin color, my
size, and my appearance were variables—things that were judged
according to my current self-image, the aesthetic values of the
times, the places I was in, and the people I met. My studies, later
my writing, the respect of people who saw me as an individual person they cared about, these were the criteria for my sense of self-
worth that I would concentrate on in my adult life.

Questions

1. To tell her body story, Cofer uses four categories: skin, color,
   size, and looks. How did Cofer come to think of these categories
   as key? To what extent do you think we are supposed to see them
   as key to Cofer's self? to her body? to her story?
2. At the end of her essay, Cofer claims that her skin color, size, and
   appearance were "variables" (par. 18). What does the term *variable* mean and why does Cofer use it here? To what extent is
   Cofer's claim supported by the rest of her essay? Does anything
   about Cofer's body remain invariable?
3. As she was growing up, how did Cofer deal with stereotyping?
   To what extent did she use stereotypes? resist stereotypes? As a
   grown-up, how does Cofer deal with stereotypes? Does she use
   them? resist them?
4. Another essay in this book that deals explicitly with stereotyping
   is Brent Staples's "Just Walk On By." Do you think that Cofer's
   and Staples's ideas about stereotyping are more alike or more
   different? Were the ways they dealt with stereotypes in their
   own lives similar?

▨ PRACTICE 7.5

Resisting Stereotypes

Write an essay that resists some stereotype. As Cofer's essay demonstrates, there are many ways to resist a stereotype, including *demonstrat-
ing* how stereotypes are not natural but learned, *showing* how the key
features of a particular stereotype change their meaning and value from
one context to another, and *revealing* how a specific individual is actually

quite different from some stereotypical idea or image. The way you choose to resist will depend on the stereotype you choose as your focus as well as on your particular experiences, feelings, and ideas in regard to that stereotype. You need not choose an ethnic, racial, sexual, religious, or political stereotype. Instead, you might choose a familial stereotype like "the kid sister," a vocational stereotype like "the used car salesman," an avocational stereotype like "the computer hacker," or a pop-cultural stereotype like "the Gen-Xer." In fact, you may use stereotypes of animals, things, or events rather than persons, even though the reason to resist stereotyping is more readily apparent when people are at issue. No matter what stereotype you choose as a topic, you will want to think about its key features, as Cofer clearly did when she used skin, color, size, and looks to structure her resistance to the stereotyping of her body.

8

Taking Things Apart
Analysis

Analysis is a systematic way of knowing that characterizes schooling, especially at the college level. It entails studying how the key parts of some whole function relate to each other. We can analyze most things in a systematic way, including living creatures, machines, events, social groups, ecosystems, and texts. But being systematic is not really the point of analyzing. In academia, we analyze in order to understand how or why something is as it is and to explain what we've discovered to others.

So, analytical writing is not just what you do to report what you know to others—it is also what you do when you are trying to understand something. For example, you might begin analyzing something by writing an outline of its key parts and the order in which you will study them. As you fill in your outline with details, you may find complex ideas that need to be broken down into simpler elements, specifics that require the addition of new parts to your outline, and patterns or relationships that you hadn't noted before. All these findings should be recorded for possible use later, when you are presenting to others what you have learned through analysis.

Usually, analysis proceeds in two ways: comparatively and dialectically. In a comparative analysis, you take two or more specific things—say apples and oranges—that belong to the same general class—in this case, fruit—and examine their key parts. But how do you know which of the parts are key—the shape, color, skin, seeds, flesh, taste, geographical distribution, resistance to blight, etc.? Since you are working comparatively, the key parts will be those that enable you to see and say something subtle and significant about how specific items are both alike and different, and why their likeness and difference might matter to those interested in some more general issue, such as the nutritional value of various fruits.

In a dialectical analysis, you examine the parts of something specific, such as an advertisement, a recent tuition increase, or a chemical reaction, in order to figure out the extent to which it can be understood in terms of something bigger, such as some scholarly generalization about media portrayals of women, some well-known socioeconomic theory about the rising cost of higher education, or the prevailing principles and assumptions of the academic discipline known as chemistry. Generalizations, theories, and disciplinary frameworks usually tell you what parts of something should be considered key, but when you analyze dialectically, you are putting big ideas to the test. So, you should note not only what a generalization, theory, or disciplinary framework helps you to see but also what it hides from view or overlooks.

The practices in this chapter offer opportunities for both comparative and dialectical analysis. The first practice asks you to analyze a short comparison, while the next two invite you to try your hand at writing a comparative analysis. The last two practices challenge you to undertake a dialectical analysis of advertising, first by examining one such text in terms of Robert Scholes's generalizations about video ads, and then by developing your own generalization based on an analysis of a number of print ads. As you do some or all of these practices, consider analysis as a systematic way of knowing. In other words, analyze analysis. William Wordsworth once wrote, "we murder to dissect." As a way of knowing, do you think analysis and dissection are more alike or more different? To what extent does the systematic study of something entail murder?

LIKENESS AND DIFFERENCE

The following brief essay appeared in the New York *Tribune* in February 1892. It was the work of Stephen Crane, a young man of twenty, who had recently left college to pursue a career as a writer. This was the first of a series of sketches of Sullivan County in New York's Catskill Mountains, which began Crane's career.

▒ READING

Stephen Crane, "The Last of the Mohicans"

Few of the old, gnarled and weather-beated inhabitants of the pines   1
and boulders of Sullivan County are great readers of books or students of literature. On the contrary, the man who subscribes for the

county's weekly newspaper is the man who has attained sufficient position to enable him to leave his farm labors for literary pursuits. The historical traditions of the region have been handed down from generation to generation, at the firesides in the old homesteads. The aged grandsire recites legends to his grandson; and when the grandson's head is silvered he takes his corncob pipe from his mouth and transfixes his children and his children's children with stirring tales of hunter's exploit and Indian battle. Historians are wary of this form of procedure. Insignificant facts, told from mouth to mouth down the years, have been known to become of positively appalling importance by the time they have passed from behind the last corncob in the last chimney corner. Nevertheless, most of these fireside stories are verified by books written by learned men, who have dived into piles of moldy documents and dusty chronicles to establish their facts.

This gives the great Sullivan County thunderbolt immense weight. And they hurl it at no less a head than that which once evolved from its inner recesses the famous Leatherstocking Tales. The old storytellers of this district are continually shaking metaphorical fists at *The Last of the Mohicans* of J. Fenimore Cooper. Tell them that they are aiming their shafts at one of the standard novels of American literature and they scornfully sneer; endeavor to oppose them with the intricacies of Indian history and they shriek defiance. No consideration for the author, the literature or the readers can stay their hands, and they claim without reservation that the last of the Mohicans, the real and only authentic last of the Mohicans, was a demoralized, dilapidated inhabitant of Sullivan County.

The work in question is of course a visionary tale and the historical value of the plot is not a question of importance. But when the two heroes of Sullivan County and J. Fenimore Cooper, respectively, are compared, the pathos lies in the contrast, and the lover of the noble and fictional Uncas is overcome with great sadness. Even as Cooper claims that his Uncas was the last of the children of the Turtle, so do the sages of Sullivan County roar from out their rock-bound fastnesses that their nondescript Indian was the last of the children of the Turtle. The pathos lies in the contrast between the noble savage of fiction and the sworn-to-claimant of Sullivan County.

All know well the character of Cooper's hero, Uncas, that bronze god in a North American wilderness, that warrior with the eye of the eagle, the ear of the fox, the tread of the catlike panther, and the tongue of the wise serpent of fable. Over his dead body a warrior cries:

"Why has thou left us, pride of the Wapanachki? Thy time   5
has been like that of the sun when in the trees; thy glory brighter
than his light at noonday. Thou art gone, youthful warrior, but
a hundred Wyandots are clearing the briers from thy path to
the world of spirits. Who that saw thee in battle would believe that
thou couldst die? Who before thee has ever shown Uttawa the way
into the fight? Thy feet were like the wings of eagles; thine arm heavier than falling branches from the pine; and thy voice like the Manitto
when he speaks in the clouds. The tongue of Uttawa is weak and his
heart exceedingly heavy. Pride of the Wapanachki, why hast thou
left us?"

The last of the Mohicans supported by Sullivan County is a   6
totally different character. They have forgotten his name. From
their description of him he was no warrior who yearned after
the blood of his enemies as the hart panteth for the water-brooks;
on the contrary he developed a craving for the rum of the
white men which rose superior to all other anxieties. He had the
emblematic Turtle tattooed somewhere under his shirtfront.
Arrayed in tattered, torn and ragged garments which some white
man had thrown off, he wandered listlessly from village to village
and from house to house, his only ambition being to beg, borrow or
steal a drink. The settlers helped him because they knew his story.
They knew of the long line of mighty sachems sleeping under the
pines of the mountains. He was a veritable "poor Indian." He
dragged through his wretched life in helpless misery. No one could
be more alone in the world than he and when he died there was no
one to call him pride of anything nor to inquire why he had left
them.

PRACTICE 8.1

Analyzing a Comparison

Crane's sketch, as you have no doubt noticed, works by comparison
and contrast. Your assignment is to analyze how Crane's sketch is put
together. You might begin by examining paragraphs 3 through 6, the
most explicitly comparative part of the sketch. To see how this part
works, consider writing down, in two columns, phrases from Crane's text
that balance one another. For instance, the contrasting phrases that conclude the final two paragraphs could come at the bottom of your
columns:

Noble Savage	*Poor Indian*
....	....
....	....
why hast thou left us?	no one . . . to inquire why he had left them.

Next, you will want to consider how the phrases in these columns relate to Crane's statement that "the pathos lies in the contrast." To what extent do the formal features and language of paragraphs 3 through 6 support Crane's statement?

Finally, consider the relationship between the first two paragraphs and the rest of the sketch. What do these paragraphs do? To what extent do they prepare the way for the comparative analysis in paragraphs 3 through 6? To what extent do they complicate or change the point of the comparative analysis in paragraphs 3 through 6?

MAKING COMPARISONS

Our minds work in terms of relationships. It is very hard—perhaps impossible—for us to consider a thing by itself. Inevitably, we make analogies or invent metaphors whenever we are forced to discuss a single thing in isolation.

The method of comparison and contrast simply formalizes what we all do when thinking. In using this method, we look separately for points of resemblance (comparison) between two objects and for points of difference (contrast). If there are no points of resemblance, then there is no reason to discuss the two things together. On the other hand, if two things are too similar, there is not much to say about them. The method of comparison and contrast is of most use when we wish to distinguish the specific differences between two things that are members of the same category: humans and monkeys (same genus, different species), men and women (same species, different sex), this shortstop and that shortstop (same function, different performance).

The following reading assignment consists of two modern poems, both inspired by Pieter Brueghel's *The Fall of Icarus.* This painting is based on the Greek legend of Icarus and his father, Daedalus, who tried to escape from imprisonment on the island of Crete. A master craftsman, Daedalus made wings for himself and his son out of birds' feathers held together with wax. He warned the boy not to fly too low or the water would wet the wings and weigh him down, nor too high or the heat of the sun would melt the wax. But Icarus was a high-spirited lad and ignored his father's advice. He flew too high, his wings came apart, and he fell into the sea and drowned.

▨ READING

Pieter Brueghel, *The Fall of Icarus*

W. H. Auden, "Musée des Beaux Arts"[1]

About suffering they were never wrong,
The Old Masters: how well they understood
Its human position; how it takes place
While someone else is eating or opening a window or just walking
    dully along;
How, when the aged are reverently, passionately waiting   5
For the miraculous birth, there always must be
Children who did not specially want it to happen, skating
On a pond at the edge of the wood:
They never forgot
That even the dreadful martyrdom must run its course   10
Anyhow in a corner, some untidy spot
Where dogs go on with their doggy life and the torturer's horse
Scratches its innocent behind on a tree.

In Brueghel's *Icarus*, for instance: how everything turns away
Quite leisurely from the disaster; the ploughman may   15
Have heard the splash, the forsaken cry,
But for him it was not an important failure; the sun shone
As it had to on the white legs disappearing into the green
Water; and the expensive delicate ship that must have seen
Something amazing, a boy falling out of the sky,   20
Had somewhere to get to and sailed calmly on.

William Carlos Williams, "Landscape with the Fall of Icarus"

According to Brueghel
when Icarus fell
it was spring

[1]Museum of Fine Arts.

Pieter Brueghel, *The Fall of Icarus*

a farmer was ploughing
his field   5
the whole pageantry

of the year was
awake tingling
near

the edge of the sea   10
concerned
with itself

sweating in the sun
that melted
the wings' wax   15

unsignificantly
off the coast
there was

a splash quite unnoticed
this was   20
Icarus drowning

▓ PRACTICE 8.2

Two Poets and a Painting

Write a comparative analysis of Auden's "Musée des Beaux Arts" and Williams's "Landscape with the Fall of Icarus." Your specific task is to discuss the similarities and differences between the two poems in terms of their ideas and the language in which the ideas are conveyed. You are not being asked to judge which is the better poem. The thesis of your paper should simply be a statement as to whether the *similarities* or *differences* seem to you most significant. For example, you might argue, "The most striking thing about these two poems is that they treat the same painting in such different ways," or "The interesting thing about these two poems is that, despite superficial differences in style, they treat the painting in essentially the same way."

Read the poems several times, take notes, and sort out your thoughts before you begin. For inspiration, we present on page 169 Jeff Mac-Nelly's cartoon version of young Skyler Fishawk at work on a similar project. Please do *not* follow his method of composition; he understands

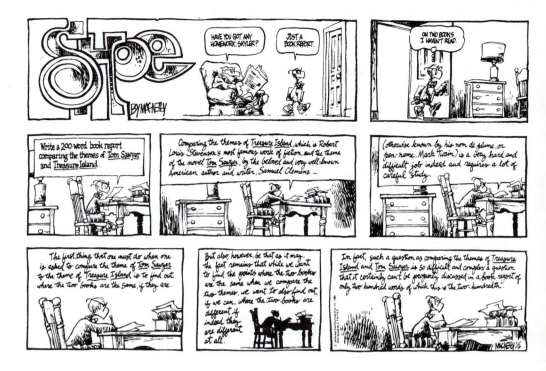

the theory of comparison and contrast very well, but he manages to avoid the practice completely.

COMPARATIVE THINKING

As MacNelly's cartoon suggests, comparative analysis is a common academic writing assignment that is very much in danger of turning into a mechanical exercise. Unfortunately, the repetition of mechanical exercises seems to have been precisely what high school was all about for Mark Edmundson—at least until Doug Meyers came along and provoked a handful of seniors to think seriously about conformity, rebellion, school, and intellectual vision. In "My First Intellectual," Mark Edmundson, a high school jock who eventually became a college English professor, writes a profile of Doug Meyers, "the teacher who changed his life." Comparative thinking permeates Edmundson's profile, ultimately coming to a head—or, more accurately, to a face-off between Meyers and O'Mara. How are Meyers and O'Mara alike and different? What's at issue for Edmundson and for us in their confrontation?

▨ **READING**

Mark Edmundson, "My First Intellectual: An Ex-Jock Remembers the Teacher Who Changed His Life"

Doug Meyers came to Medford High School with big plans for his 1
philosophy course. Together with a group of self-selected seniors,
he was going to ponder the eternal questions: beauty, truth, free
will, fate, that sort of thing. The class would start out reading *The
Story of Philosophy*, by Will Durant, then go on to Plato's dialogues,
some Aristotle, Leibniz (a particular favorite of Meyers's), maybe
just a little bit of Kant, then into a discussion of Bertrand Russell's
effort to clear the whole thing up with an injection of clean scientific logic. Meyers had just graduated from Harvard. All of his intellectual aspirations were intact.

On the first day of class, we saw a short, slight man, with olive 2
skin — we thought he might be Mexican — wearing a skinny tie and
a moth-eaten legacy suit with a paper clip fastened to the left lapel.
On his feet were Ivy League gunboat shoes, lace-ups designed in
homage to the *Monitor* and the *Merrimack*.[1] He had hunched shoulders, a droopy black mustache, and Valentino-type eyes, deep
brown, sensuous, and penitential. Even when he strove for some
dynamism, as he did that first day, explaining his plans for the
course, he still had a melancholy Castilian presence, the air of an instinctively comprehending reader of *Don Quixote*.

Having outlined the course, he turned away from us and began 3
writing on the blackboard, in a script neater than any we would see
from him again. It was a quotation from Nietzsche. He told us to
get out our papers and pens and spend a couple of pages interpreting the quote "as a limbering-up exercise." I had never heard of
Nietzsche. I had never read all the way through a book that was
written for adults and that was not concerned exclusively with football.

The day before, I'd sat in the office of Mrs. Olmstead, the senior 4
guidance counselor, whose perfume conjured up the sound of
Mantovani's string section, sentimental, lush, and all-conquering,
and been informed that I ranked 270th in a class of nearly 700. My
prospects were not bright. We talked about Massachusetts Bay
Community College, Salem State Teachers College; we discussed
my working for the city of Medford — perhaps I'd start by collecting barrels, then graduate in time to a desk job (my father had some

[1]*Monitor and Merrimack:* Civil War opponents in the first battle between ironclad
ships.

modest connections); I mentioned joining the Marines (I might have made it in time for the Cambodia invasion[2]). Nothing was resolved.

As I was mumbling my way out the door, Mrs. Olmstead began talking about a new teacher who was coming to the school, "someone we're especially proud to have." He was scheduled to teach philosophy. I didn't know what philosophy was, but I associated it with airy speculation, empty nothing; it seemed an agreeable enough way of wasting time.

So there I was in a well-lit top-floor room, wearing, no doubt, some sharp back-to-school ensemble, pegged pants and sporty dice-in-the-back-alley shoes, mildly aching from two or three football-inflicted wounds, and pondering the Nietzsche quotation, which I could barely understand. I felt dumb as rock, a sentiment with which I, at seventeen, had no little prior experience. But by putting the quotation on the board, Meyers showed me that in at least one department his powers of comprehension were a few notches lower than mine. He had misunderstood Medford High School entirely. The appearance had taken him in. No doubt he'd strolled through the building on the day before students arrived; he'd seen desks, chalkboards, large windows that slid up and open with a cheering metallic gurgle, supply closets stocked full of paper and books, all the paraphernalia of education. He had seen these things and he'd believed that he was in a school, a place where people quested, by their lights and by fits and starts, for the truth, its elaborations and its antitheses.

But I had acquired a few facts that Meyers would not have been primed to receive at Harvard, or at prep school, or at any of the other places where he had filled his hours. Medford High School, whatever its appearances, was not a school. It was a place where you learned to do—or were punished for failing in—a variety of exercises. The content of these exercises mattered not at all. What mattered was form, repetition and form. You filled in the blanks, conjugated, declined, diagrammed, defined, outlined, summarized, recapitulated, positioned, graphed. It did not matter what: English, geometry, biology, history, all were the same. The process treated your mind as though it were a body part capable of learning a number of protocols, simple choreographies, then repeating, repeating.

Our bodies themselves were well monitored. When the bell rang, we rose and filed into the corridor, stayed in line, spoke quietly if at all, entered the next class, were ordered to sit down, sit quietly, feet beneath the desk, all day long presided over by teachers, a significant fraction of whom were going, at greater or less ve-

[2]March 1970; a major event of the Vietnam War.

locities, ending sometimes with a bang, sometimes with subdued, heart-emptying sobs, out of their minds. At least two that I can remember had been mastered by a peculiar form of speech: You couldn't say that they were talking to themselves, but they were clearly not addressing anyone on the outside, either. Poetry, Mill famously said, is not heard but overheard. This was overheard, but no way close to poetry. This was the way souls in purgatory mutter and carry on. When these teachers were overwhelmed—it wasn't hard to do: We stole Miss McDougle's rank book; we locked her once, briefly, in the supply closet—they called for a sub-master, Sal Todaro, or, more feared, Dan O'Mara, Dandy Dan, to restore order. The place was a shabby Gothic cathedral consecrated to Order, and maybe it was not without its mercies. If you'd done what you should have at Medford High, the transition into a factory, into an office, into the Marines would be something you'd barely notice; it would be painless, sheer grease.

Before Meyers arrived, I never rebelled against the place, at least   9
not openly. I didn't in part because I believed that Medford High was the only game there was. The factories where my father and uncles worked were extensions of the high school; the TV shows we watched were manufactured to fit the tastes for escape that such places form; the books we were assigned to read in class, *Ivanhoe*, *Silas Marner*, *The Good Earth*, of which I ingested about fifty pages each, could, as I saw it then (I've never had the wherewithal to check back into them), have been written by the English teachers, with their bland, babbling goodness and suppressed hysterias. Small bursts of light came through in the Beethoven symphonies my father occasionally played at volume on our ancient stereo (the music sounded like it was coming in over a walkie-talkie) and the Motown tunes I heard on Boston's black radio station, WILD, but these sounds were not connected to any place or human possibility I knew about. So I checked out. I went low to the ground, despondent, suspicious, asleep in the outer self, barely conscious within.

This condition Doug Meyers changed. That now, however im-   10
perfectly, I can say what's on my mind, and that I know what kind of life I hope for, I owe not to him alone, of course, but to many. Doug Meyers pushed open the door to those others, though, other worlds, other minds. And pretty much on his own, Meyers taught me how to teach. I'm not sure if I've ever heard his sort of approach described before, but I think it's as good now as it was when I first encountered him almost thirty years ago.

For three months, Meyers did his best with Will Durant and *The*   11
Story of Philosophy. We barely gave him an inch. Gubby Shea (Kevin

Shea on his report cards and disciplinary citations) made enormous daisy chains out of the elastics he used to bind the advertising circulars he delivered in Jamaica Plain and Mattapan on Saturday mornings or sat, his body tight with concentrated energy, inking in all of the *o*'s in the textbook, a brilliant, futile parody of life at Medford High. Jeff Stanwick pried tufts of grass off the soles of his soccer cleats; Michael de Leo and John Aquino, wide receiver and quarterback for the Medford Mustangs (I blocked for them, sporadically), contemplated pass plays and the oncoming game with Newton, or Somerville, or Everett. Carla Masse was high-school beautiful. Susan Rosenberg, the school's only hippie—she wore wire-rim glasses and work boots and was of no social consequence at all— conversed with Meyers on subjects no one else cared about. She and Joseph Jones were about the only ones with anything to say.

Joseph was a hater. He hated communism, hated drugs, hated   12
women's lib (as it was then called), hated Susan, hated Meyers. He was stumpy and strong as a boss troll, with acne on his face so livid it looked like someone had sprayed it on that morning. He wore Sears, Roebuck short-sleeve, stain-holding shirts that reeked of the night shift. Joseph called himself conservative, but he was only that because he hadn't yet encountered a recruiter from a Brownshirt[3] operation.

Meyers wrote him off from the start. He didn't try to convert   13
Joseph, or to understand his painful home life, or to contact his suppressed inner self. By indulging Joseph a little, putting his blather into cogent form for him and us, Meyers might have "gotten a good discussion going"—every teacher's dream. Instead, Meyers talked with serene intelligence to Susan and anyone else who cared to volunteer and treated Joseph with subtle, and occasionally not so subtle, derision.

For Meyers thought well of himself. He wouldn't pander. And   14
we all wondered, if unspokenly, where this guy might have gotten his considerable lode of self-esteem. Teachers, as we could have told him, were losers out-and-out. And this one in particular wasn't strong or tough or worldly. He wore ridiculous clothes, old formal suits and that weird paper clip in his lapel; he talked like a dictionary; his accent was over-cultivated, queer, absurd. He was a compendium of odd mannerisms, starting with the way he swung his right hand from the wrist laterally as he spoke. Yet he thought highly of himself. And not much at all, it wasn't difficult to see, of us. Except for Susan, whom he addressed in affectionate tones, Meyers spoke to the class with perpetual irony. He mocked us, and

[3]*Brownshirts:* German Nazi storm troopers.

not always so genially, for never doing the reading, never knowing the answer, never having a thought in our heads. We were minor fools, his tone implied, for ignoring this chance to learn a little something before being fed live and whole to what was waiting. For our part, we sat back, let him wrangle with Joseph, and waited to see what would turn up.

One day in mid-December or so, Meyers walked in and told us 15 to pass back our copies of *The Story of Philosophy*. Then he told us that he had some other books for us to read but that we'd have to pay for them ourselves. (Gubby Shea piped up immediately to say that this was fine with him, since he'd finished with the Durant, finished inking in the *o*'s.) Meyers, it turned out, had asked no one's permission to do this; it just struck him as a good idea to try to get people who never picked up a book to do some reading by giving them work that might speak to their experience. At Medford High, this qualified as major educational innovation, real breakthrough thinking. And of course there were plenty of rules against using books that hadn't been approved by the school board, weren't purchased through public funding, and so on.

The books that Meyers picked were on a theme, though I had no 16 idea of that at the time. *The Stranger, One Flew Over the Cuckoo's Nest, Group Psychology and the Analysis of the Ego, Siddhartha*: The first three were about the oppressions of conformity (among other things), the last about the Buddha's serene, fierce rebellion against it. We were all weighed down by conformity, Meyers knew. And he also knew that we, his self-selected seniors, were oppressors in our own rights, passing on the ways of the system to the weaker, homelier, duller kids. These were revelations that emerged slowly for us as we talked not just about the high school and its day-to-day machinations but also about sports, sororities, circles of friends and family and what they closed out. We learned to use some unfamiliar language to talk about ourselves, and so became, for a few moments at a time, strangers in our own lives, the subjects of new kinds of understanding and judgment.

I don't want to idealize this process. For the first few weeks, 17 since virtually no one but Susan would read a book at home, we simply sat in a circle and read the pages aloud in turn. Periodically, Meyers would ask a question, and usually, in the beginning, it was he that would answer it or decide finally to let it drop. One day, when we were reading *The Stranger*, Meyers asked us about solitude. What does it mean to be alone? Is it possible? What would it mean to be genuinely by oneself? Susan Rosenberg raised her hand, no doubt ready to treat us to a description of Zen meditation and its capacity to melt the ego beyond solitude into pure nothingness. But Meyers must have seen something ripple across Carla Masse's beautiful face. He gestured in her direction, though she hadn't volunteered.

Carla was a high-school princess, a sorority girl, whose autobiography, I'd have guessed, would have translated into a graph peaking from prom to prom, with soft valleys of preparation in between. She spoke in a teasing nasal voice acquired from Karen Laidlaw (vitally alive in my memory for having given a thirty-minute talk on the subject of the pencil in the English class of Miss McDougle — she of the stolen rank book and the supply-closet imprisonment; she whose glasses Mark Castle snatched from off her desk and wore through most of a fifty-minute class period). What Carla did was to run through a litany of defenses against being alone. She mentioned listening to the radio and talking on the phone, then playing the songs and conversations over in her mind, and a myriad of other strategies, ending, perceptively enough, with expectation, our habit of blocking out the present by waiting for things to happen in the future. But Carla did not express herself with detachment. She said "I." "This is how I keep from being alone." "And why," asked Meyers, "is it hard to be alone?" "Because," Carla answered, "I might start to think about things."

Carla had been, up until that point, one of the Elect, predestined for all happiness; suddenly she had gone over to the terminally Lost. One of the great sources of grief for those who suffer inwardly is their belief that others exist who are perpetually and truly happy. From the ranks of the local happy few, Carla had just checked out, leaving some effective hints about those she'd left behind.

The book that mattered to me wasn't *The Stranger*, which had gotten Carla going, or Freud's book on the herd instinct (when I was writing my dissertation, a literary critical reading of Freud, my working text of *Group Psychology* was, somehow, the one that had belonged to Gubby Shea, with the *o*'s colored in to about page 20), but Kesey's *One Flew Over the Cuckoo's Nest*. It's a hard book for me to read now, with its pumped-up, cartoon hero, Randall Patrick McMurphy. But at the time it was all in all. I read it in a lather, running through it in about ten hours straight, then starting in again almost immediately.

But that didn't happen right off. It was probably on the fifth day of reading the book out loud in class that a chance remark Meyers made caught my attention, or what there was of it then to catch. He said that prisons, hospitals, and schools were on a continuum, controlling institutions with many of the same protocols and objectives, and that Kesey, with his bitter portrait of the mental hospital, might be seen as commenting on all these places.

This idea, elementary as it was, smacked me with the force   22
of revelation. Here was a writer who was not on the side of the teachers, who in fact detested them and their whole virtuous apparatus. That the book was in part crude and ugly I knew even at the time: Blacks in it are twisted sadists, the women castrators or sweet whores. But it was the anti-authoritarian part that swept me in; here was someone who found words, gorgeous, graffiti-sized, and apocalyptic, for what in me had been mere inchoate impulses, dumb groans of the spirit laboring away in its own darkness.

"You can't like that book anymore," said a well-meaning,   23
department-broken professor of English I ran into after giving a lecture in California. "You used to be able to like it, but not anymore" he said, not smugly, not knowingly, but a little wistfully. I understood what he meant, but I couldn't share the genteel sentiment. That book pulled me out of where I was. So it wasn't angelic: If you'll only consent to being saved by an angel, you may have some time to wait.

During the period when we were reading Kesey aloud and   24
discussing him, Doug Meyers started bringing things into class. Every Friday we got some music: I remember hearing Billie Holiday, Mozart, the Incredible String Band, the Velvet Underground. The selection standard was simple — things he liked that we probably would not have heard. He also showed us art books, read a poem from time to time, and brought in friends of his to explain themselves. Meyers loved the things he offered us, but he loved them in a quirky way: He seemed to look affectionately askance at everything he cared about. What love you could find in Medford culture, where you could find it, wasn't always so easy to distinguish from the mechanisms of hunger and satiety.

A panel of Students for a Democratic Society members appeared   25
one day to debate the Vietnam War with us. (Most of us were in favor.) One February day, a group of black students burst into the room during class and announced that this was the anniversary of Malcolm X's death. Meyers looked up mildly from his place in the circle and asked the foremost of them, "And when was he born, Malcolm Little?" The young man knew, or said he did, and gave a date. Meyers nodded and invited them to sit down and talk about politics. It was the first time I'd had an extended conversation about

these things with blacks, and more than a few followed. These discussions didn't stop the ongoing racial guerrilla war at Medford High, but they were something.

As time went on, word spread around the school that odd things were happening in Meyers's classroom. It was known that once, on a torpid winter day, he brought us all outside for a snowball fight. Joseph—no surprise—got it going by heaving a jagged ice chunk, caveman-style, at Meyers. Meyers, who looked that day like a Mexican padre, with his long black coat and broadbrimmed black hat, responded by trying to pitch Joseph into a snowbank. Meyers was ill-coordinated but determined. From where I stood, it looked like Joseph was being attacked by a giant crow. When Joseph shook the snow off his parka and stepped up for retaliation, a bunch of us pelted him with snowballs.

As the weather warmed up, the class occasionally went outside to sit on the grass and hold discussions there. This sometimes resulted in one or two of us nodding off, but Meyers didn't much care; he had most of us most of the time now. He sat cross-legged, wise-medicine-man-style, and swung his wrist and laughed, and we answered the questions he asked, because what he thought mattered perhaps did. It was a first, this outdoors business; no one at Medford High would have imagined doing it.

One Thursday afternoon, just as we were wrapping up a discussion of Thoreau, Meyers gave us a solemn, mischievous look, the sort of expression shrewd old rabbis are supposed to be expert in delivering, and said, "There's been some doubt expressed about our going outside." Then he told a story. In the faculty cafeteria, with plenty of the other teachers milling around, Meyers had been approached by Dandy Dan O'Mara, the sub-master, the disciplinarian. O'Mara had the sly bullying style of a hard Irish cop. He had a barroom face, red nose, watery eyes, the hands of someone who worked for a living. He was stepping up to put Meyers in his place.

O'Mara got rapidly to the point. What would happen, he'd asked Meyers, if everyone held class outside? Now this was familiar stuff to us all. O'Mara's question came out of that grand conceptual bag that also contained lines like "Did you bring gum for everyone?" and "Would you like to share that note with the whole class?" O'Mara was trying to treat Meyers like a student, like one of us, and in front of his colleagues. At Medford High, there were two tribes, us and them. Meyers had defied the authorities; clearly he had become one of them, a student, of no use or interest whatever. But in fact, Meyers was of no particular clan but his own, the tribe of root-

26

27

28

29

less, free-speculating readers and talkers and writers who owe allegiance first to a pile of books that they've loved, and then, only secondly, to other things.

O'Mara did not know this. Nor did he know that Meyers, 30 however diminutive, mild, and Mandarinly self-effacing, thought himself something of a big deal. So O'Mara would not have been prepared when Meyers drew an easy breath and did what every high-school kid would like to do when confronted with this sort of bullying. He didn't fight it, didn't stand on his dignity. He simply ran with it. What if everyone held class outside on sunny days? Suppose that happened? And from there, Meyers went on to draw a picture of life at Medford High School—a picture that had people outside on the vast lawn talking away about books and ideas and one thing and another, hanging out, being lazy and being absorbed, thinking hard from time to time, and reveling in the spring. It was Woodstock and Socrates' agora fused,[4] and Meyers spun it out for us, just as he had for O'Mara. What if that happened, he asked us (and the sub-master)? How tragic would it be?

This vision of the renovated school took a long time to un- 31 fold, and it had something like a musical form, ebbing and rising, threading back through major themes and secondary motifs. And in my mind's eye, I could see O'Mara wilting, growing too small for his wrinkled, sad clothes. He would soon know, as we did, that Meyers could produce plenty more of this (he was the most eloquent man I'd met) and that it was time to cut and run. What struck me about the performance (and I believed Meyers's rendition of it, word for word—he was unfailingly, often unflatteringly honest) was that it was done with words alone, nothing equivalent to the body blows Kesey's R. P. McMurphy specializes in.

We went outside whenever we chose to after that. It was very 32 odd: I had been at Medford High for three years, and I had never seen O'Mara's side lose a round. I'd seen a kid from the city's preeminent street gang, the South Medford Bears, spit in a teacher's face; but soon enough the police wagon was there and the big boy was trussed and bawling and on the way to jail. After class was over on the day that Meyers told us the O'Mara story, John Aquino, the quarterback of the football team and very little in line with the stereotype, said to me, "You know, Meyers can really be an asshole when he wants to be." In Medford, there were fifty intonations you

---

[4]*Woodstock:* free outdoor music festival of August 1969; Socrates taught his philosophy in the marketplace (agora).

could apply to the word "asshole." Spun right, the word constituted high praise.

O'Mara was a broad target. America was in crisis then; people were assuming intense allegorical identities: pig, peacenik, hawk, dove. O'Mara had turned into an ugly monolith, at least in our eyes. In Asia, the Vietcong were making fools of his spiritual brethren, Johnson, Westmoreland, McNamara, and the rest. His sort was on the run. In the next few years, it would get even worse for them. But Meyers, for his part, hadn't treated O'Mara as among the lost, even though he probably had it coming. Instead he'd invited him to a party, an outdoor extravaganza. At the time, O'Mara surely couldn't discern the invitation in Meyers's extended aria, but who knows what he might have seen later on as he turned it all over in his mind.

That year of teaching was the last for Doug Meyers. He got married, went to law school, and, I heard, eventually moved to Maine, where he could pursue a life a little akin to the one Thoreau, his longtime idol, managed to lead during his stay at Walden. I haven't seen Meyers in about twenty-five years. But I do carry around with me the strong sense that the party he invited us to, me and Carla and Gubby and Michael de Leo and Dandy Dan O'Mara (but not Joseph, no, not everyone quite), is still a live possibility. Sometimes I even stumble on an installment of it, or help make one.

I had great teachers after Doug Meyers, some of the world's most famous in fact, but I never met his equal. What I liked most about him, I suppose, was that for all the minor miracle of what he accomplished with us, he was no missionary: He served us but also himself. He got what he wanted out of Medford High, which was a chance to affront his spiritual enemies, though with some generosity, and to make younger people care about the sorts of things he cared about, to pull them out of their parents' orbit and into his. All good teaching entails some kidnapping; there's a touch of malice involved.

As well as some sorrow: Good teachers have many motivations, but I suspect that loneliness is often one of them. You need a small group, a coterie, to talk to; unable to find it in the larger world, you try to create it in the smaller sphere of a classroom. Meyers, who seemed at times a little lost in his life, a brilliant orphan, did something like that with us. (When he saw the material he had to work with on that first day, he must have been on the verge of stepping out the window.) Whatever his motives, part of what I admired about him was his streak of arrogance. His goodness had some edge to it.

It would be a mistake to believe that what Meyers taught about teaching was that always and until the end of time you should draw the chairs into a circle, read pop-cult marvels like *Cuckoo's Nest*, and apply them directly to the situation at hand. No, Meyers taught something else entirely. When I call him to mind in that long black padre coat, he reminds me of Groucho Marx in *Horse Feathers*, duckwalking at top throttle back and forth in front of a whole congress of professors, singing out his Marxian ditty with the gorgeous refrain "Whatever it is, I'm against it!"

What Meyers taught—or at least what I gleaned from him—is   38 that anything that's been successfully institutionalized, however rebellious it may seem or however virtuous, is stifling. What's called subversion only lasts for an instant in a school or a hospital or a home; it's quickly swept up to become part of the protocol, an element in "the way we do things around here." At the time, Kesey and Camus collided well enough with the dead protocols of Medford High, but now, for all I know, they fit in fine—alienation has become standard issue. What to do then? When Bacchus is ascendant, when all the world is a pop-cult blast, as it can seem now, then maybe you become a high priest of Apollo, with his hard graces. Teachers, freelance spirit healers that they are or ought to be, make a diagnosis, pour out a cure or two, then see what happens. Or so Meyers did with us.

Such teaching incites friction. Many students, the successes in   39 particular, resent it and respond with civil venom. And teachers, under-compensated as they usually are, often yearn for some adulation to balance the books. It's tough to be both broke and unloved.

"Whenever others agree with me," the sublime Oscar Wilde   40 said, "I know that I must be wrong." When students love you from Day One, when you succeed too fast, chances are that Wilde's dictum applies. And when the world does eventually come around to your way of thinking, maybe then it's time to deliver your premises a salutary whack: "Whatever it is," chants Groucho from the wings, "I'm against it."

This approach isn't without its costs. One pays for the kind of   41 mental exhilaration that Meyers initiated. One pays in self-doubt and isolation, in the suspicion that what seems to be true resistance is merely a perverse substitute for genuine talent, a cheap way of having something to say. Meyers's path, so appealing in its first steps, separated me from my family, cut me loose from religion and popular faith, sent me adrift beyond the world bordered by TV and piety and common sense. One step down that road followed another, and now, at forty-six, I probably could not turn around if I wished to.

Still, the image I most often hit on when I think about Meyers   42 glows brightly enough. It's late spring, a gloomy dead day.

He's brought in a record by the Incredible String Band. He's at the back of the room standing beside the beat-up phonograph. I dislike the record and open my book, *The Autobiography of Malcolm X*, which has not been assigned in any class, and disappear into it. Meyers cranks the music just a little louder. I keep reading. But then, curious, I raise my head. The racket of the string Band floods in. And there in the back of the room, Meyers is dancing away. He's a terrible dancer, stiff and arrhythmic. Not until I saw Bob Dylan in concert did I ever see anyone dance so self-consciously. It struck me that this was probably the first time anyone had ever danced in this building, or at least in this classroom. The air was too heavy with invisible gray weight: Most bodies, given instructions, probably couldn't have responded.

But here was Meyers, bringing it off. It was like a few good new words coming into the language, some strokes of light rendered by a painter for the first time, though with an unsteady enough hand. Sometime in the future, maybe, they'd have everyone at Medford High School up and dancing to the Incredible String Band in geometric unison or in spontaneous disarray. They'd teach minicourses in the band's kind of music, whatever that might be. But not then, and not for a little while to come, either. Meyers had scored a benevolent victory over the place. (You could say he'd beaten them at their game, but really he'd shown them a new one.) He had a right to a little celebration. 43

Questions

1. As you see it, what is Edmundson implicitly comparing and contrasting when he recounts the confrontation between Meyers and O'Mara? What was at stake back then? What is at stake now—or, what do you think Edmundson's point and aim are in writing about Meyers today?
2. Besides the central confrontation and comparison between Meyers and O'Mara, there are a number of other comparisons that Edmundson makes in passing, including comparing Meyers's dress with his own "back-to-school ensemble." Make a list of these other comparisons and consider their relationship to the central contrast: Do they reinforce, complicate, or undercut the point of the Meyers/O'Mara contrast?
3. What does Edmundson mean when he says that all good teaching involves some kind of "kidnapping" and that it "incites friction"? Do you agree with him?

PRACTICE 8.3

Schooling — Take Two

This practice invites you to think comparatively about your schooling. Taking your cue from Edmundson, you might try your hand at writing a profile of a teacher — a profile that speaks to some broader issue such as what constitutes good teaching. Edmundson obviously spent lots of time analyzing teaching, and as his profile of Meyers shows, he discovered that good teaching has many important aspects or parts, including content, style, motive, practice, location, timing, and effect. In your experience, is one or more of these parts more key to good teaching than the others? How was your experience of school similar to and different from Edmundson's? How does the teacher you're profiling compare with Meyers? with other teachers you have had? These questions should get you thinking comparatively, which is part of what this practice is all about.

Of course, people aren't the only topics for profiles. Courses, programs, and even whole schools can be profiled, but if you would prefer one of these other topics, we suggest that you talk about it first with your instructor. As Edmundson's essay shows, detailed descriptions are as important to profiles as the comparative analysis of various parts or aspects of a whole. Often, it's easier to be detailed, comparative, and analytic about a teacher than about a course, program, or school.

TESTING A GENERALIZATION

"On Video Texts" is an example of critical analysis as well as an argument for the necessity for such analytical skills in everyday life. Read this text first for its sense, and then, during your second reading, make notes on the process of critical analysis used by the writer.

READING

Robert Scholes, "On Video Texts" (from *Protocols of Reading*)

The moments of surrender proposed to us by video texts come in   1
many forms, but all involve a complex dynamic of power and pleasure. We are, for instance, offered a kind of power through the enhancement of our vision. Close-ups position us where we could never stand. Slow motion allows us an extraordinary penetration into the mechanics of movement, and, combined with music, lends

a balletic grace to ordinary forms of locomotion. Filters and other devices cause us to see the world through jaundiced or rose-colored optics, coloring events with emotion more effectively than verbal pathetic fallacy and less obtrusively. These derangements of normal visual processing can be seen as either constraints or extensions of visual power—that is, as power over the viewer or as extensions of the viewer's own optical power, or both. Either way they offer us what is perhaps the greatest single virtue of art: change from the normal, a defense against the ever-present threat of boredom. Video texts, like all except the most utilitarian forms of textuality, are constructed upon a base of boredom, from which they promise us relief.

Visual fascination—and I have mentioned only a few of its obvious forms—is just one of the matrices of power and pleasure that are organized by video texts. Others include narrativity and what I should like to call, at least tentatively, cultural reinforcement. By narrativity, of course, I mean the pleasures and powers associated with the reception of stories presented in video texts. By cultural reinforcement, I mean the process through which video texts confirm viewers in their ideological positions and reassure them as to their membership in a collective cultural body. This function, which operates in the ethical-political realm, is an extremely important element of video textuality and, indeed, an extremely important dimension of all the mass media. This is a function performed throughout much of human history by literature and the other arts, but now, as the arts have become more estranged from their own culture and even opposed to it, the mass media have come to perform this role. What the epic poem did for ancient cultures, the romance for feudalism and the novel for bourgeois society, the media—and especially television—now do for the commodified, bureaucratized world that is our present environment. 2

It is time, now, to look at these processes as they operate in some specific texts. Let us begin with a well-known Budweiser commercial, which tells—most frequently in a format of twenty-eight seconds, though a longer version also exists—the life story of a black man pursuing a career as a baseball umpire. In this brief period of time, we are given enough information to construct an entire life story—provided we have the cultural knowledge upon which this construction depends. The story we construct is that of a young man from the provinces, who gets his "big break," his chance to make it in the big city, to rise to the top of his profession. We see him working hard in the small-time, small-town atmosphere of the minor leagues, where the pace of events is slower and more relaxed than it is "at the top." He gets his chance for success—the voice- 3 over narrator says. "In the minors you got to make all the calls, and then one day you *get* the call"—after which we see him face his first real test. He must call an important and "close" play correctly and then withstand the pressure of dispute, neither giving ground by changing his mind (which would be fatal) nor reacting too vigorously to the challenge of his call by an offended manager. His passing of this test and being accepted is presented through a later scene in a bar, in which the manager who had staged the protest "toasts" the umpire with a bottle of Budweiser beer, with a chorus in the background singing, "You keep America working. This Bud's for you." From this scene we conclude that the ump has now "made it" and will live happily ever after. From a few scenes, then, aided by the voice-over narration and a music track, we construct an entire life. How do we do this? We draw upon a storehouse of cultural information that extends from fairy tales and other basic narrative structures to knowledge about the game and business of baseball.

In processing a narrative text we actually construct the story, bringing a vast repertory of cultural knowledge to bear upon the text that we are contemplating. Our pleasure in the narrative is to some extent a constructive pleasure, based upon the sense of accomplishment we achieve by successfully completing this task. By "getting" the story, we prove our competence and demonstrate our membership in a cultural community. And what is the story that we "get"? It is the myth of America itself, of the racial melting pot, of upward mobility, of justice done without fear or favor. The corporate structure of baseball, with minor leagues offering a path for the talented to the celebrity and financial rewards of the majors, embodies values that we all possess, we Americans, as one of the deepest parts of our cultural heritage or ideology. It is, of course, on the playing field that talent triumphs most easily over racial or social barriers. Every year in baseball new faces arrive. Young men, having proved themselves in the minors, get their chance to perform at the highest level. Yale graduates and high-school dropouts who speak little or no English are judged equally by how well they hit, run, throw, and react to game situations. If baseball is still the national pastime, it is because in it our cherished myths materialize— or appear to materialize.   4

The commercial we are considering is especially interesting because it shows us a black man competing not with his body but with his mind, his judgment and his emotions, in a cruelly testing public arena. Americans who attend to sports are aware that black athletes are just beginning to find acceptance at certain "leadership" positions, such as quarterback in professional football, and that there is still an active scandal over the slender representation of blacks at   5 baseball's managerial and corporate levels. The case of the black umpire reminds viewers of these problems, even as it suggests that here, too, talent will finally prevail. The system works, America works. We can take pride in this. The narrative reduces its story to the absolutely bare essentials, making a career turn, or seem to turn, on a single decision. The ump must make a close call, which will be fiercely contested by a manager who is deliberately testing him. This is a story of initiation, in that respect, an ordeal that the ump must meet successfully. The text ensures that we know this is a test, by showing us the manager plotting in his dugout, and it gives us a manager with one of those baseball faces (Irish? German?) that have the history of the game written on them. This is not just partisan versus impartial judge, it is old man against youth, and white against black. We root for the umpire because we want the system to work—not just baseball but the whole thing: America. For the story to work, of course, the ump must make the right call, and we must know it to be right. Here, the close-up and slow motion come into play—just as they would in a real instant replay—to let us see both how close the call is and that the umpire has indeed made the right call. The runner is out. The manager's charge from the dugout is classic baseball protest, and the ump's self-control and slow walk away from the angry manager are gestures in a ritual we all know. That's right, we think, that's the way it's done. We know these moves the way the contemporaries of Aeschylus and Sophocles knew the myths upon which the Greek tragedies were based. Baseball is already a ritual, and a ritual we partake of mostly through the medium of television. The commercial has only to organize these images in a certain way to create a powerful narrative.

At the bar after the game, we are off stage, outside that ritual of baseball, but we are still in the world of myth. The manager salutes the ump with his tilted bottle of beer; the old man acknowledges that youth has passed its test. The sword on the shoulder of knighthood, the laying on of hands, the tilted Bud—all these are ritual gestures in the same narrative structure of initiation. To the extent that we have wanted this to happen we are gratified by this closing scene of the narrative text, and many things, as I have suggested, conspire to make us want this ending. We are dealing with an archetypal narrative that has been adjusted for maximum effect within a particular political and social context, and all this has been deployed with a technical skill in casting, directing, acting, photographing, and editing that is of a high order. It is very hard to resist the pleasure of this text, and we cannot accept the pleasure without, for the bewildering minute at least, also accepting the ideology that is so richly and closely entangled with the story that we construct from the video text. To accept the pleasure of this text is to believe that America works; and this is a comforting belief, itself a pleasure of an even higher order—for as long as we can maintain it. Does the text also sell Budweiser? This is something only market research (if you believe it) can tell. But it surely sells the American way first and then seeks to sell its brand of beer by establishing a metonymic[1] connection between the product and the nation: a national beer for the national pastime.

An audience that can understand this commercial, successfully   7
constructing the ump's story from the scenes represented in the text and the comments of the narrative voice, is an audience that understands narrative structure and has a significant amount of cultural knowledge as well, including both data (how baseball leagues are organized, for instance, and how the game is played) and myth (what constitutes success, for example, and what initiation is). At a time when critics such as William Bennett and E. D. Hirsch are bewailing our ignorance of culture, it is important to realize that many Americans are not without culture; they simply have a different culture from that of Bennett and Hirsch. What they really lack, for the most part, is any way of analyzing and criticizing the power of a text like the Budweiser commercial—not its power to sell beer, which is easily resisted, especially once you have tasted better beer—but its power to sell America. For the sort of analysis that I am suggesting, it is necessary to recover (as Eliot says) from the surrender to this text, and it is also necessary to have the tools of ideological criticism. Recovery, in fact, may depend upon critical analysis, which is why the analysis of video texts needs to be taught in all our schools.

Before moving on to the consideration of a more complex textual   8
economy, we would do well to pause and consider the necessity of ideological criticism. One dimension of the conservative agenda for this country has been conspicuously anticritical. The proposals of William Bennett and E. D. Hirsch, for instance, different as they are in certain respects, are both recipes for the indoctrination of young people in certain cultural myths. The great books of past ages, in the eyes of Bennett, Hirsch, and Allan Bloom, are to be mythologized, turned into frozen monuments of Greatness in which our "cultural heritage" is embodied. This is precisely what Bloom does to Plato, for instance, turning the dialectical search for truth into a fixed recipe for "greatness of soul." The irony of this is that Plato can only die in this process. Plato's work can better be

---

[1]*Metonymy:* a figure of speech that works by association. Here, beer becomes associated with baseball, which is already associated with the myth of America.

kept alive in our time by such irreverent critiques as that of Jacques Derrida, who takes Plato seriously as an opponent, which is to say, takes him dialectically. In this age of massive manipulation and disinformation, criticism is the only way we have of taking something seriously. The greatest patriots in our time will be those who explore our ideology critically, with particular attention to the gaps between mythology and practice. Above all, we must start with our most beloved icons, not the ones we profess allegiance to, but those that really have the power to move and shake us.

Questions

1. Robert Scholes states that all video texts "involve a complex dynamic of power and pleasure (par. 1)." What examples of power and pleasure does he present? Trace his use of one of these terms in his discussion of the Budweiser commercial.
2. What stories do other beer commercials tell? What stories do soda commercials tell?
3. What are some of "our most beloved icons" (par. 8)? Why is it patriotic to critically examine them?
4. What is "the dialectical search for truth" (par. 8)?

PRACTICE 8.4

Analyzing a Video Text

Write an analysis of a video text. Examine your response to a commercial that has caught your attention (we suggest videotaping it so that you can replay and study it). As you watch the commercial, make notes of what happens, what the story is. Your next move is to interpret the story: What does it mean? What cultural knowledge enables you to "get" the story? What is the chain of associations connected to the product? How will you benefit if you buy this product?

DEVELOPING A GENERALIZATION

The following selection is from a book called *Media Culture* (1995), in which the writer argues that media is the dominant form of culture that socializes us and shapes our identity. In this excerpt, the writer analyzes the intended effects of print advertising.

▓ **READING**

Douglas Kellner, "Advertising Images"
(from *Media Culture*)

Like television narratives, advertising too can be seen as providing   1
some functional equivalents of myth. Like myths, ads frequently resolve social contradictions, provide models of identity, and
celebrate the existing social order. Barthes (1972 [1957]) saw that
advertising provided a repertoire of contemporary mythologies,
and in the following discussion I depict how cigarette ads
contribute to identity formation in contemporary society. The
following analysis is intended to show that even the static images
of advertising contain subject positions[1] and models for identification that are heavily coded ideologically.[2] As in the previous discussion, I argue here—against a certain type of postmodern[3]
formal analysis—that the images of media culture are important
both in the mode of their formal image construction and address, as
well as in terms of the meanings and values which they communicate. Accordingly, I discuss some print ads which are familiar,
are readily available for scrutiny, and lend themselves to critical
analysis.

Print ads are an important sector of the advertising world with   2
about 50 percent of advertising revenues going to various print
media while 22 percent is expended on television advertising. Let us
look first, then, at some cigarette ads, including Marlboro ads
aimed primarily at male smokers and Virginia Slims ads which try
to convince women that it is cool to smoke and that the product
being advertised is perfect for the "modern" woman (see the illustration following).[4] Corporations such as those in the tobacco industry undertake campaigns to associate their product with positive

[1] *subject positions:* the identities, roles, looks, or images established by media models
that audiences are invited or induced to identify with.
[2] *heavily coded ideologically:* the advertisement represents through words and images
the beliefs or myths of a particular group or society.
[3] *postmodern:* the condition of post-1960's culture, featuring fragmentary images
and disconnected styles. Here, Kellner is rejecting a type of analysis of images
that describes only "the surface...rather than seeking meanings or significance"
(236).
[4] Publishers now have difficulty obtaining permission to reproduce tobacco ads;
thus we have not included the ads Douglas Kellner is referring to. We assume you
are sufficiently familiar with them; if not, they may be found on p. 249 of his book,
Media Culture (Routledge, 1995).

and desirable images and gender models. Thus, in the 1950s, Marlboro undertook a campaign to associate its cigarette with masculinity, associating smoking its product with being a "real man." Marlboro had been previously packaged as a milder women's cigarette, and the "Marlboro man" campaign was an attempt to capture the male cigarette market with images of archetypically masculine characters. Since the cowboy, Western image provided a familiar icon of masculinity, independence, and ruggedness, it was the preferred symbol for the campaign. Subsequently, the "Marlboro man" became a part of American folklore and a readily identifiable cultural symbol.

Such symbolic images in advertising attempt to create an association between the products offered and socially desirable and meaningful traits in order to produce the impression that if one wants to be a certain type of person—for instance, to be a "real man"—then one should buy Marlboro cigarettes. Consequently, for decades, Marlboro used the cowboy figure as the symbol of masculinity and the center of their ads. In a postmodern image culture, individuals get their very identity from these figures, thus advertising becomes an important and overlooked mechanism of socialization, as well as manager of consumer demand.

Ads form textual systems with basic components which are interrelated in ways that positively position the product. The main components of the classical Marlboro ads are the conjunction of nature, the cowboy, horses, and the cigarette (see Figure 1). This system associates the Marlboro cigarette with masculinity, power, and nature. Note, however, in the Marlboro ad in Figure 2, how the cowboys decline in size, dwarfed by the images of desert and sky. Whereas in earlier Marlboro ads, the Marlboro man loomed largely in the center of the frame, now images of nature are highlighted. Why this shift?

All ads are social texts which respond to key developments during the period in which they appear. During the 1980s, media reports concerning the health hazard of cigarettes became widespread—a message highlighted in the mandatory box at the bottom of the ad that "The Surgeon General Has Determined That Cigarette Smoking is Dangerous to Your Health." As a response to this attack, the Marlboro ads now feature images of clean, pure, wholesome nature, as if it were "natural" to smoke cigarettes, as if cigarettes were a healthy "natural" product, an emanation of benign and healthy nature. The ad, in fact, hawks *Marlboro Lights* and one of the captions describes it as a "low tar cigarette." Many 1980s Marlboro ads deployed imagery that was itself "light," white, green, snowy, and airy. Through the process of metonymy, or contiguous association, the ads tried to associate the cigarettes with "light," "natural," healthy deserts, clean snow, horses, cowboys, trees, and sky, as if they were all related "natural" artifacts, sharing the traits of "nature," thus covering over the fact that cigarettes are an artificial, synthetic product, full of dangerous pesticides, preservatives, and other chemicals.

Thus, the images of healthy nature are a Barthesian mythology (1972) which attempt to cover over the image of the dangers to health from cigarette smoking. The Marlboro ad also draws on images of tradition (the cowboy), hard work, caring for animals, and other desirable traits, as if smoking were a noble activity, metonymically equivalent to these other positive social activities. The images, texts, and product shown in the ad thus provide a symbolic construct which tries to cover over and camouflage contradictions between the "heavy" work and the "light" cigarette, between the "natural" scene and the "artificial" product, between the cool and healthy outdoors scene and between the hot and unhealthy activity of smoking, and the rugged masculinity of the Marlboro man and the Light cigarette, originally targeted at women. In fact, this latter contradiction can be explained by the marketing ploy of suggesting to men that they can both be highly masculine, like the Marlboro man, and smoke a (supposedly) "healthier" cigarette, while also appealing to macho women who might enjoy smoking a "man's" cigarette which is also "lighter" and "healthier," as women's cigarettes are supposed to be.

The 1983 Virginia Slims ad pictured in Figure 3 attempts in a similar fashion to associate its product with socially desired traits and offers subject positions with which women can identify. The Virginia Slims textual system classically includes a vignette at the top of the ad with a picture underneath of the Virginia Slims woman next to the prominently displayed package of cigarettes. In the example pictured, the top of the ad features a framed box that contains the narrative images and message, which is linked to the changes in the situation of women portrayed through a contrast with the "modern" women below. The caption under the boxed image of segregated male and female exercise classes in 1903 contains the familiar Virginia slims slogan "You've come a long way, baby." The caption, linked to the Virginia slims woman, next to the package of cigarettes, connotes a message of progress, metonymically linking Virginia Slims to the "progressive woman" and "modern" living. In this ad, it is the linkages and connections between the parts that establish the message which associates

Virginia Slims with progress. The ad tells women that it is progressive and socially acceptable to smoke, and it associates Virginia Slims with modernity, social progress, and the desired social trait of slimness.

In fact, Lucky Strike carried out a successful advertising campaign in the 1930s which associated smoking with weight reduction ("Reach for a Lucky instead of a sweet!"), and Virginia Slims plays on this tradition, encapsulated in the very brand name of the product. Note too that the cigarette is a "Lights" variety and that, like the Marlboro ad, it tries to associate its product with health and well-being. The pronounced smile on the woman's face also tries to associate the product with happiness and self-contentment, struggling against the association of smoking with guilt and dangers to one's health. The image of the slender woman, in turn, associated with slimness and lightness, not only associates the product with socially desirable traits, but in turn promotes the ideal of slimness as the ideal type of femininity.

Later in the 1980s, Capri cigarettes advertised its product as "the slimmest slim!", building on the continued and intensified association of slimness with femininity. The promotion of smoking and slimness is far from innocent, however, and has contributed to eating disorders, faddish diets and exercise programs, and a dramatic increase in anorexia among young women, as well as rising cancer rates. As Judith Williamson points out (1978), advertising "addresses" individuals and invites them to identify with certain products, images, and behavior. Advertising provides a utopian image of a new, more attractive, more successful, more prestigious "you" through purchase of certain goods. Advertising magically offers self-transformation and a new identity, associating changes in consumer behavior, fashion, and appearance with metamorphosis into a new person. Consequently, individuals are taught to identify with values, role models, and social behavior through advertising which is thus an important instrument of socialization as well as a manager of consumer demand.

Advertising sells its products and view of the world through images, rhetoric, slogans, and their juxtaposition in ads to which tremendous artistic resources, psychological research, and marketing strategies are devoted. These ads express and reinforce dominant images of gender and position men and women to assume highly specific subject positions. A 1988 Virginia Slims ad (shown in Figure 4), in fact, reveals a considerable transformation in its image of women during the 1980s and a new strategy to persuade women that it is all right and even "progressive" and ultramodern

to smoke. This move points to shifts in the relative power between
men and women and discloses new subject positions for women validated by the culture industries.

Once again the sepia-colored framed box at the top of the   11
ad contains an image of a woman serving her man in 1902; the
comic pose and irritated look of the woman suggests that such
servitude is highly undesirable and its contrast with the Virginia
Slims woman (who herself now wears the leather boots and leather
gloves and jacket as well) suggests that women have come a
long way while the ever-present cigarette associates woman's right
to smoke in public with social progress. This time the familiar
"You've come a long way, baby" is absent, perhaps because the
woman pictured would hardly tolerate being described as "baby"
and because women's groups had been protesting the sexist and
demeaning label in the slogan. Note, too, the transformation of
the image of the woman in the Virginia Slims ad. No longer the
smiling, cute, and wholesome potential wife of the earlier ad, she is
now more threatening, more sexual, less wifely, and more masculine. The sunglasses connote the distance from the male gaze which
she wants to preserve and the leather jacket with the military insignia connotes that she is equal to men, able to carry on a masculine role, and is stronger and more autonomous than women of the
past.

The 1988 ad is highly antipatriarchal and even expresses hostility   12
toward men with the overweight man with glasses and handle-
bar mustache looking slightly ridiculous while it is clear that
the woman is being held back by ridiculous fashion and intolerable social roles. The "new" Virginia Slims woman, however,
who completely dominates the scene, is the epitome of style
and power. This strong woman can easily take in hand and enjoy the phallus (i.e., the cigarette as the sign of male power accompanied by the male dress and military insignia) and serve as
an icon of female glamour as well. This ad links power, glamour,
and sexuality and offers a model of female power, associated
with the cigarette and smoking. Ads work in part by generating dissatisfaction and by offering images of transformation, of a new
personal identity. This particular ad promotes dissatisfaction
with traditional images and presents a new image of a more powerful woman, a new lifestyle and identity for the Virginia Slims
smoker. In these ways, the images associate the products advertised
with certain socially desirable traits and convey messages concerning the symbolic benefits accrued to those who consume the
product.

Although Lights and Ultra Lights continue to be the dominant   13
Virginia Slims types, the phrase does not appear as a highlighted
caption in the 1988 ad as it used to and the package does not
appear either. No doubt this "heavy" woman contradicts the
"light" image and the ad connotes instead power and (a dubious)
progress for women rather than slimness or lightness. Yet
the woman's teased and flowing blonde hair, her perfect teeth
which form an obliging smile, and especially, her crotch positioned
in the ad in a highly suggestive and inviting fashion code her as
a symbol of beauty and sexuality, albeit more autonomous and
powerful.

The point I am trying to make is that it is precisely the images   14
which are the vehicles of the subject positions and that therefore
critical literacy in a postmodern image culture requires learning
how to read images critically and to unpack the relations between
images, texts, social trends, and products in commercial culture
(Kellner 1989d). My reading of these ads suggests that advertising
is as concerned with selling lifestyles and socially desirable identities, which are associated with their products, as with selling the
product themselves—or rather, that advertisers use the symbolic
constructs with which the consumer is invited to identify to try to
induce her to use their product. Thus, the Marlboro man (i.e., the
consumer who smokes the cigarette) is smoking masculinity or natural vigor as much as a cigarette, while the Virginia Slims woman is
exhibiting modernity, thinness, or female power when she lights up
her "slim."

This sort of reading of advertising not only helps individuals to   15
resist manipulation, but it also depicts how something as seemingly
innocuous as advertising can depict significant shifts in modes and
models of identity. For example, the two Virginia Slims ads suggest
that at least a certain class of women (white, upper-middle and
upper class) were gaining more power in society and that women
were being attracted by stronger, more autonomous, and more
masculine images. Advertising campaigns attempt to incorporate
such images to associate their products with the socially desired
traits which are then further promoted with the ads' attempts to
promote their products.

Questions

1. In the first paragraph, Kellner talks about his approach to reading advertisements. In your own words, describe the generalization he is going to develop in this excerpt.

2. Outline Kellner's main ideas and the evidence he uses to develop each idea.
3. Write a one-paragraph summary of this excerpt. Begin it with, "In 'Advertising Images,' Douglas Kellner argues that…"
4. According to Kellner, what's the purpose of analyzing advertising? To what extent do advertisers assume a naive or unthinking audience for their ads?
5. Compare some very recent Virginia Slims and Marlboro ads with those Kellner analyzes. What desirable identities are these cigarette companies trying to sell to women and men? Have there been any significant changes in the persuasive appeals of these cigarette advertisements over the past ten years or so?

■ **PRACTICE 8.5**

Analyzing Images of Women in Advertising

The following pages present a selection of ads featuring women. As you look at these ads, ask yourself what desirable transformations of self are being offered to the woman who reads these advertisements. How is femininity being defined? What socially desirable traits are being offered with each product? In what ways are these ads about social relations rather than objects?

Try reading these ads as a sort of historical narrative of advertising. Do you notice any significant differences in the image of woman created by advertising over the years? While it's obvious that clothing and hairstyles have changed during the twentieth century, has there been any significant change in the way advertisements work and what they work for? How valid are Kellner's generalizations about advertising? Remember, to make an effective generalization, you need to gather and present sufficient evidence. The more carefully you consider these specific advertisements, the richer your analysis will be.

If your instructor wishes to include some library research in this assignment so that you can consider the topic in greater depth, you might concentrate on the image of women in a particular decade, such as the 1950s, by looking at the advertising in a number of popular magazines of that period. Or, if you wish to enlarge your historical survey, concentrate on advertising over a period of several decades in a magazine with a fairly long publishing history, such as *Ladies' Home Journal, Redbook, Cosmopolitan,* or *Seventeen.*

1913

1922

Make that dream come true

WHAT woman lives who has not at some time enjoyed the vision of herself a bride. For many the dream has been fulfilled. Don't allow a bad complexion to place you among the others!

Your beauty of feature, becoming dress, graceful bearing, keen wit, can be completely overshadowed by a blotchy or otherwise unattractive skin. But there is no excuse for submission to such a condition, when to correct it is so easy.

Usually all that nature requires to make a clear pleasing complexion is right living—and—proper, regular cleansing of the skin. It is this knowledge that has made Resinol Soap a favorite in thousands of homes where it is now in daily use.

If you are neglected and humiliated because of a red, oily, or otherwise repellent skin, begin today the following treatment:

Gently work the profuse foamy lather of Resinol Soap well into the pores with the finger tips. It rinses easily and completely with a little clear warm water. A dash of cold water to close the pores completes the treatment. Now see how velvety your skin looks and feels—how invigorated it is—and what a delicate glow it has. These are only the first happy effects of this delightful toilet soap.

At all drug and toilet goods counters. May we send you a free trial? Write now. Dept. 5-A, Resinol, Baltimore, Md.

Resinol Soap

1934

Never Beyond This Shore

HERE at the sea's edge is as near to Jim as I can go.

Other women have gone farther than this. There were women on Corregidor; women have gone to Ireland and Australia and Iceland; women have been lost in the Battle of the Atlantic.

But I know I would be foolish to dream of serving as they have. For a woman to go farther than this shore demands a special skill, complete independence—and I have neither.

No, my task is here, here in the little storm-tight house that sits back from the cove, here with my son.

And if I become discontent with the seeming smallness of my task, Jim's words come back to steady me. "I'm leaving you a very important job, Mary. Until this war is won, there won't be any more evenings when we can sit by the fireside and plan our tomorrows together. It will be up to you to make the plans for the three of us.

"Mary," he said, "keep our dreams alive."

* * *

MAKE no little plans, you who build the dream castles here at home. When you try to imagine the future, after he returns, be sure your imaginings are full of bright and cheerful hues, for that world of tomorrow will be resplendent in things you don't know—never even imagined. Allow for wonderful new developments in such fields as television, fluorescent lighting, plastics. And leave a flexible horizon for the marvels that are sure to come from the new science of electronics. When you're dreaming of your better tomorrow, count on us. General Electric Company, Schenectady, N. Y.

* * *

THE VOLUME *of General Electric war production is so high and the degree of secrecy required is so great that we can tell you little about it now. When it can be told completely we believe that the story of industry's developments during the war years will make one of the most fascinating chapters in the history of industrial progress.*

GENERAL ELECTRIC

1942

IF YOU WANT TO WIN THE BOYS . . .

Stay Sweet As You Are!

There are good times, good friends, and gaiety ahead if you do. And laughter and love . . . and marriage almost before you know it. But if you don't . . . you're headed for boredom and loneliness.

And it's so easy to stay sweet . . . stay adorable . . . if you let Listerine Antiseptic look after your breath. Every morning. Every night. And especially before every date when you want to be at your best. Listerine instantly stops bad breath, and keeps it stopped for hours, usually . . . *four times better than any tooth paste.*

No Tooth Paste Kills Odor Germs
Like This . . . Instantly

Listerine Antiseptic does for you what no tooth paste does. Listerine instantly kills bacteria . . . by millions—stops bad breath instantly, and usually for hours on end.

You see, far and away the most common cause of offensive breath is the bacterial fermentation of proteins which are always present in the mouth. *And research shows that your breath stays sweeter longer, depending upon the degree to which you reduce germs in the mouth.*

Listerine Clinically Proved
Four Times Better Than Tooth Paste

No tooth paste, of course, is antiseptic. Chlorophyll does not kill germs—but Listerine kills bacteria by millions, gives you lasting antiseptic protection against bad breath.

Is it any wonder Listerine Antiseptic in recent clinical tests averaged at least four times more effective in stopping bad breath odors than the chlorophyll products or tooth pastes it was tested against? With proof like this, it's easy to see why Listerine belongs in your home. Every morning . . . every night . . . before every date, make it a habit to always gargle Listerine, the most widely used antiseptic in the world.

A Product of
The Lambert Company

LISTERINE ANTISEPTIC STOPS BAD BREATH
4 times better than any tooth paste

Every week 2 different shows, Radio & Television—"THE ADVENTURES OF OZZIE & HARRIET" See your paper for times and stations

1954

Beautiful but dumb...that's how pretty girls used to be referred to in the thirties and forties, and actually a lot of them were kind of dumb. If a girl looked like anything, she just sat there like a cup-cake and never opened her mouth. I guess some people still expect a pretty girl to be marshmallow-brained and doe-eyed but they're often in for a shock! Some of the best-looking girls I know are also the brightest...they work at it. My favorite magazine says, "If you have a brain, use it...it's the best gift nature ever gave a girl ...yes, even better than beauty!" I love that magazine. I guess you could say I'm That COSMOPOLITAN Girl.

Photographed by Jim Houghton

If you want to reach me you'll find me reading
COSMOPOLITAN

1966

"I have 23 people working for me...and 4 against me"

It takes a woman's touch.

Sometimes...to really know what's going on...it takes a woman's touch. It's as true in business as it is in the home.

The fact that almost half the women in the country work is no longer news. But the "why" still might be. Women work because they want to. Because they have to. For much the same reasons men do. It depends on the *individual*. Which is what women have been saying all along.

Over the past 20 years, Redbook has evolved, kept pace with the young women it serves. It has grown into one of the major women's magazines—from 308 advertising pages in 1956 to 1,415 last year. And 1977 started with the biggest first four months in Redbook's history.

Which shows that advertisers know what we know. Sometimes to get things done, it takes a woman's touch. Especially women 18–34.

It takes a woman's touch...especially 18-34

1977

1987

1993

1999

Writing and Knowledge: Two Projects

Two groups of specialists study knowing: epistemologists and cognitive psychologists. As philosophers, epistemologists explore the origins, nature, methods, and limits of human knowledge. Cognitive psychologists tend to investigate learning or how people come to know what they know through imitating, memorizing, thinking, and communicating.

Of course, you don't have to be a philosopher or a psychologist to be interested in ways of knowing. As the following essay by Toni Cade Bambara shows, knowledge is so important to who we are and what we see, do, and say that it makes sense for us to think about the goals of education in relation to the ways we learn, including listening to lectures, engaging in conversation, and telling stories. As you read Bambara's essay, note how she presents her ideas. Do you think Miss Dorothy would have approved of this mode of presentation? The project following this reading asks you to write about the act of acquiring knowledge.

The second project, "Reading On- and Offline," focuses on how "hypertext" sources may or may not alter our ways of knowing.

READING

Toni Cade Bambara, "The Education of a Storyteller" (from *Deep Sightings and Rescue Missions*)

Back in the days when I wore braids and just knew I knew or would soon come to know *everything* onna counna I had this grandmother who was in fact no kin to me, but we liked each other.

And she had this saying designed expressly for me, it seemed, for moments when I my brain ground to a halt and I couldn't seem to

1

2

205

think my way out of a paper bag—in other words, when I would dahh you know play like I wasn't intelligent.

She'd say, "What are you pretending not to know today, Sweet-   3
heart? Colored gal on planet earth? Hmph know everything there is to know, anything she/we don't know is by definition the unknown."

A remark she would deliver in a wise-woman voice not unlike   4
that of Toni Morrison's as I relisten to it. And it would encourage me to rise to quit being trifling.

As I say, we weren't blood kin but I called her Grandma Dorothy   5
or Miss Dorothy or M'Dear (I was strictly not allowed by progres-sive parents to call anybody Ma'am or Sir or to refer to anybody as a Lady or a Gentleman or—the very worst-of-all-worst feudalistic self-ambushing-back for one's political health—refer to a fascist pig dog rent-gouging greedy profiteering cap as a "landlord").

Miz D called me Sweetheart, Peaches, You Little Honey, Love,   6
Chile, Sugar Plum, Miz Girl, or Madame depending on what she was calling me for or what she was calling me out about.

One day, I came bounding into her kitchen on the sunny side of   7
Morningside Park in Harlem, all puff-proud straight from the li-brary—and I stood over her with my twelve-year-old fast self watching her shuck corn over the *Amsterdam News* and I then an-nounced, standing hipshot, a little bony fist planted on my little bony hip and the other splayed out sophisticated like I said.

"Grandma Dorothy, I know Einstein's theory of relativity."   8

And she say, "Do tell," shoving the ears of corn aside and giving   9
me her full attention. "Well do it, Honey, and give me a signal when it's my turn to join in the chorus."

Well, straightaway I had to *explain* that this was not a call-and-   10
response deal but a theory, "an informed hunch as how the universe is put together in terms of space and time."

"Uh-hunh," she says, "well get on with it and make it lively,   11
'cause I haven't tapped my foot or switched my hips all day."

So I had to *explain* that this was not a song or a singing tale...but   12
a theory.

And she say, "Uh-hunh, well, Sugar, be sure to repeat the 'free-   13
dom part' two times like in the blues so I'll get it."

"The freedom part," I mumble, kinda deflated at this point, and   14
sort of slumping against her ladder-back chair.

"Sure," she says, "the lesson that I'm to take away to tell my   15
friends 'cause you know uneducated and old-timey women tho' we may be, we still soldiers in the cause of freedom, Miz Girl."

So I just go ahead and slump on down in the chair she's pulled   16
out for me, and I say, voice real feeble like, "Grandma Dorothy, relativity is not one of them fables, ya know, with a useful moral at

the end. It's not one of them uplift-the-race speeches like they give on Speakers' Corner. It's a ahhhh…"

"Hmm, Chile," she says, giving me a worried look like she's real concerned about my welfare. "What kind of theory is this? Is Br'er Rabbit in it, or one of them other rascals I dearly love?"   17

"Miss Dorothy, Mr. Einstein, one of those white guys from Europe, I don't think he know from Br'er Rabbit."   18

"Uh-hunh. Well, Sugar Plum, am *I* in it?"   19

"Ahhhh." I'm about to give up on my whole program for self-development at this point. But she, Miz Dorothy, is not concerned with my distress. She has tugged her dress down between her knees, dug her heels into the ruts in the linoleum, is leaning over, her wrists loose against her kneecaps, and she is just rattling on, encouraging me about the many ways I can tell this theory—in terms of air, earth, fire, and water, for example—or in terms of the saints, or the animals of the zodiac, or the orishas of the voudou pantheon, or as a parable assuming my scientific/progressive mother would allow her children (us) to read the Bible and assuming I could remember a parable that might have enough similarities to the theory blah blah blah.   20

Finally she says, "Well, let me hush, Precious, and you just go on and tell it however Cynthia would tell it or one of your other scatter-tooth girlfriends."   21

And I come alive at that point—jump up switching hands on hips.   22

"Well, my girlfriends don't know it. Cynthia don't know it and Rosie don't know it and Carmen don't know it—just I know it."   23

And she say, "Madame, if your friends don't know it, then you don't know it, and if you don't know that, then you don't know nothing. Now, what else are you pretending not to know today, Colored Gal?"   24

It was Grandma Dorothy who taught me critical theory, who steeped me in the tradition of Afrocentric aesthetic regulations, who trained me to understand that a story should be informed by the emancipatory impulse that characterizes our storytelling trade in these territories as exemplified by those freedom narratives which we've been trained to call slave narratives for reasons too obscene to mention, as if the "slave" were an identity and not a status interrupted by the very act of fleeing, speaking, writing, and countering the happy-darky propaganda. She taught that a story should contain mimetic devices so that the tale is memorable, shareable, that a story should be grounded in cultural specificity and shaped by the modes of Black art practice—call-and-response but one modality that bespeaks a communal ethos.   25

I would later read Fanon on the subject—"To speak is to assume a culture and to bear responsibility for a civilization."   26

Later still, I read Paolo Freire, speaking on activist pedagogy, engaged cultural work. "The purpose of educational forms is to reflect and encourage the practice of freedom."   27

While Grandma Dorothy was teaching me theory, and the bebop musicians I eavesdropped on while hanging around fire escapes and in hallways were teaching me about pitch, structure, and beat, and the performers and audiences at the Apollo and the Harlem Opera House were teaching me about the community's high standards regarding expressive gifts, I was privy to a large repertoire of stories.   28

As told by women getting their heads done in beauty parlors, or stretching curtains on those prickly racks on the roofs, by women and men on Speakers' Corner—the outdoor university on Seventh Avenue and 125th Street in front of Micheaux's Liberation Memorial Bookstore—men from trade unions, from the Socialist party, the Communist party, the African Blood Brotherhood, the National Negro Congress, women from Mary McLeod Bethune clubs, the women's department of Sanctified Church, women of the Ida B. Wells Club, from trade unions, Popular Front organizations formed in the mid to late thirties.   29

Representatives from the Abyssinia Movement whose membership grew as a result of political mobilization in 1935 in support of Ethiopia's struggle to oust invasionary forces from Italy and Mussolini.   30

Representatives from the temple men—what we called Muslims in those days.   31

Stories that shaped my identity as a girl, as a member of the community, and as a cultural worker.   32

Two types of stories struck me most at the time. One, about women's morality. Now, outside the community and in too many places within the community, "women's morality" had a very narrow context and meant sexual morality. One was taught not to be slack, sluttish, low-down, but rather upright, knees locked, and dress down.   33

But in the storytelling arenas, from kitchen tales to outdoor university anecdotes, "women's morality" was much more expansive, interesting, it took on the heroic—Harriet T. and Ida B. and the women who worked with W. E. B. Du Bois, the second wife of Booker T. and the Mother Divine of the Peace and Co-op Movement, and Claudia Jones, organizer from Trinidad who was deported during the Crackdown, when the national line shifted from "blacks as inferior" to "blacks as subversive" and wound up in a stone quarry prison and wrote "In every bit as hard as they hit me."   34

These women were characterized as "morally exemplary," mean-   35
ing courageous, disciplined, skilled and brilliant, responsive to responsibility for and accountable to the community.

The other type of memorable tale bound up in these women   36
heroics was tales of resistance—old and contemporary—insurrec-
tions, flight, abolition, warfare in alliance with Seminoles and Nar-
ragansetts during the period of European enslavement; the critical
roles men and women played in the revolutionary overthrow of
slavery; and in the Reconstruction self-help enterprises founded,
the self-governing townships founded, the political convention con-
vened and progressive legislation pressed through; and in days
since—the mobilization, organization, agitation, legislation, economic boycotts, protest demonstrations, rent strikes, parades,
consumer-cooperative organizations.

One tale heard in girlhood that I do believe informs me, trans-   37
forms me, is still told today in the islands off the coast of Georgia
and the Carolinas. A tale about that moment of landing on those
shores not as in very old times when we came as invited guests of
the leaders of Turtle Island territories, those days when we came in
ships with spices, gold books, and other gifts of friendship and solidarity, visiting the Cheyenne, the Aztecs, the Zapotec, the Aleuts.

Not then, but later.   38

In that terrible time when we were kidnapped, herded in ships,   39
and brought here in chains as enslaved labor.

The tale goes: 40

And when the boat brought the Africans from the big ships to   41
the shore, those Africans stepped out onto the land, took a look
around, and with deep-sight vision saw what the European further
had in store for them, whereupon they turned right around and
walked all the way home, all the way home to the motherland.

That's the story version. The historical events on which the story   42
is based, on which a cycle of stories is derived, is used by numerous
writers and independent Black film- and video-makers. Paule
Marshall in *Praisesong for the Widow*, and Toni Morrison in *Song of
Solomon* and *Tar Baby*, Richard Perry in *Montgomery's Children*, Julie
Dash in her film masterpiece *Daughters of the Dust*. And are docu-
mented in ship's logs and journals, and bodies of correspondence
written by numerous European slavers.

"The ship foundered off the coast and much of the barreled   43
cargo was lost. The Africans stampeded and went overboard with
the horses. Many drowned, some reached the shoreline and were
never seen again, but most of the Africans who reached the shallows
returned themselves to the depths weighted down within their
irons. And the sight of hundreds of men, women, and children,

holding themselves under as the waves washed over them, drove
onlookers quite mad indeed.

"And when we saw what was further in store for us, we turned   44
right around and walked all the way home to Africa."

OR   45

"And there on deck, we looked to shore and saw what was fur-   46
ther in store, and we flew away to Guinea."

OR   47

"They took one look and were struck blind by the abomination,   48
and when they hit the depths, they hung on to the horses till they
reached land—and till this day, you can hear those Blind African
Riders thundering in the hills, thundering in the hills."

OR   49

"And when the horrible news grazed the ear of the goddess,   50
she turned, and in turning, the hems of her skirt swept the sands in
patterns meter neter nu, and swiftly running across the savannahs
on newly bruised feet, streaking red across the outdoor altars
burning, tearing bark from the trees with her teeth, rising, ripping
roofs from the homes with her nails, whooping, tumbling birds bald
and beakless from the clouds shrieking, she was chasing the ships,
chasing the ships from the tropic of Capricorn to the Horse
Latitudes.

"And there on deck a girlchild in one yard of cloth bent back   51
over the rail of the ship; across her throat an arm as stout as the
mast of a man who would brand her or break her, pressing out her
breath, wood splintering into her spine, hate poring into her pores,
her eyes lifting to the red eye of the twister; then up she rose, from
the fingers that clutched and claimed, up from the rust of the anchor chain, up from the nick of seashells in the salt museums, up
past the sails that snapped like teeth, she bore her bronchia to the
gusts, and was swept up in the skirts of Oye Mawu, blowing all the
way home, blowing all the way home, all the way home, blown
home."

Grandma Dorothy, in an effort to encourage our minds to leap,   52
would tell us, "Of course we know how to walk on the water, of
course we know how to fly; fear of sinking, though, sometimes
keeps us from the first crucial move, then too, the terrible educa-
tions you liable to get is designed to make you destruct the journey
entire. So send your minds on home to the motherland and just tell
the tale, you little honeys." And my mama—not one to traffic in
metaphors usually, being a very scientific woman—would add,
"Yeah, speak your speak, 'cause every silence you maintain is liable
to become *first* a lump in your throat, then a lump in your lym-
phatic system."

Questions

1. What does Miss Dorothy mean when she tells twelve-year-old Toni, "Madame, if your friends don't know it, then you don't know it" (par. 24)?

2. Bambara makes use of various writing strategies including reflection, narration, description, classification, and analysis. Review the essay and note when and how these strategies are used. Does Bambara's essay emphasize one of these strategies?

3. What kinds of education are presented here? Does Bambara value one of these kinds more than the others? How do stories figure in Bambara's education?

▓ PROJECT 1: GETTING IT TOGETHER

Ways of Learning

The preceding four chapters have offered you numerous opportunities to read, think, and write about knowing and learning, two of the issues that concern Bambara in "The Education of a Storyteller." Bambara's essay reminds us that we learn in different ways and in different places, such as at home, at school, through books, through media, or through conversation. And the way we learn about the functioning of the human brain in a psychology class differs from the way we learn about it in an anatomy class or in a literature class.

We ask you to review the practices you did in the preceding four chapters and to think about what you learned and how and where you learned it in the process of writing the practices. Perhaps, in the process of gathering information and writing, you had an experience like Bambara's, in which your college learning collided with another kind of knowledge, and you learned something new from another—perhaps unexpected—source.

Write about how you came to know different things in different ways, analyzing the differences and similarities.

▓ PROJECT 2: TAKING IT FURTHER

Reading On- and Offline: Text and Hypertext

What difference, if any, will the invention of hypertext make in traditional conceptions of knowledge? To explore this issue, you'll need to do some research, both off- and online about what's traditional and what's new. Traditionally, knowledge has been conceived in terms of print technology and its institutions, including the library, the book, and the article. But as you know, computer technology is producing new kinds of texts and institutions of writing, including the Internet, Web sites, and hypertexts.

One way to begin this project is to find and read a few recent pieces about the shift from bookish ways of writing and knowing to hypertextual ways of writing and knowing. For example, you might read one or more of the following:

- Chapter 1 in George Landow's *Hypertext 2.0* (Johns Hopkins University Press, 1997)
- Jerome McGann's "The Rationale of HyperText" (**http://jefferson.village.virginia.edu/public/jjm2f/rationale.html**)
- Kimberly Amaral's "Hypertext: An Overview" (**http:www.umassd .edu/Public/People/KAmaral/Thesis/hypertext.html**)
- Chapters 8 and 11 in Sven Birkerts's *The Gutenberg Elegies* (Fawcett Columbine, 1994)
- Chapter 4 of Richard Lanham's *The Electronic Word* (Univ. of Chicago Press, 1993)

As you read, note how print text and hypertext are described, defined, and analyzed. What story do these scholarly works tell or imply about the relationship and progress of writing and knowledge?

After you get a general sense of the issues, it is time to analyze each of the two kinds of textual practice more closely. Here are two suggestions for such a close analysis:

1. Focusing on hypertext, compare a book introduction to the topic with an online introduction to the topic. For the book introduction, use Chapter 1 of George Landow's *Hypertext 2.0* (Johns Hopkins University Press, 1997). For the online introduction, go to the "Hypertext" section of Landow's Web site *Cyberspace, Hypertext, and Critical Theory* at **<http://www.stg.brown.edu/projects/hypertext/landow/ cpace/cspaceov.html>**; at the "Hypertext" site, choose "Definitions," and once there, read the following hypertexts by Landow: "History of the Concept of Hypertext" and "Reading and Writing in a Hypertext Environment." Now that you've read different kinds of texts on the same topic by the same writer, compare the two. In what ways are these two kinds of texts—a print text and a hypertext—different? In what ways are they similar? Does what you know about hypertext change as you go from book to Web? What difference, if any, does the medium of communication make to what you learn and know?

2. Taking ways of reading as your focus, go to *Dogstory* by Herbert Lindenberger at **<http://www.stanford.edu/~hslinden/dogstory/ index.html>.** You will see that Lindenberger offers you three ways of reading this hypertext: a linear or chronological way; a postmodern or associative way; and an alpha or bit-by-bit way. Read the hypertext in each way, beginning with whichever way of reading appeals to you most. Keep in mind that linear reading is usually identified with traditional print texts while associative reading is linked with hypertexts; the bit-by-bit reading looks both ways—back to print and forward to the electronic millennium. Be sure to take notes on each of your reading experiences, including what you do to get from one screen to another and how this way of reading feels.

Write a paper that compares the three ways of reading *Dogstory*. How does each way of reading relate to what you get from the text—both what you understand and what you think it means to know "Mickey," beagles, and dogstories? What you discover during your close analysis will be central to the paper. However, as you present your findings, you will also want to use and acknowledge relevant ideas from the writers you consulted on the difference hypertext may make in traditional conceptions of knowledge.

Writing and Power

First question: who is speaking? Who, among the totality of speaking individuals, is accorded the right to use this sort of language?
　　　　　—Michel Foucault, The Archaeology of Knowledge

Knowledge, power, and the self are the triple foundation of thought.
　　　　　—Gilles Deleuze, Foucault

"I now pronounce you man and wife." Who has the right to say these words? The priest, the rabbi, or the judge, to name several members of a privileged group, some of whom preface their pronouncement with the words, "By the powers vested in me"—words that assert the speaker's privileged status as one who has been granted the legal right to perform the marriage ceremony.

In this section of *The Practice of Writing*, you will focus on writing that has the power to influence readers to do or think something: to follow directions, to buy a product, to give you a job, or to accept your point of view. As we make clear in the introductions to chapters 9 and 10, the ability to write persuasively and to organize and present a well-reasoned argument confer both power and knowledge upon the writer: the power to move readers and the knowledge of how persuasion works. Michel Foucault, the writer we've quoted above, spent much of his life studying how knowledge and power function in various social institutions, such as medicine, psychiatry, and the penal system. His study of institutional practices showed how particular sets of beliefs come to be formed and accepted, and how they shape people within a given system, such as inmates in a penitentiary or a hospital for the insane. Power is gained by those who know the way the system works. One has to be considered qualified, like a doctor acquiring a medical degree, to be granted the right to speak—or to have one's writing read. Those who have power in an academic system are those who have learned its discourse: those who know how to use the language and the forms of writing appropriate to the academic community.

In his autobiography, *Narrative of the Life of Frederick Douglass: An American Slave*, Douglass related how, when he was a boy, his owner tried to prevent him from learning to read and write. When the boy heard his master say that his learning to read would be dangerous and "would forever unfit him to be a slave," Douglass understood for the first time "the white man's power to enslave the black man." At the same time, he saw that "the pathway from slavery to freedom" lay in acquiring those forbidden skills. Through subterfuge, Douglass did learn to read and write, and at the age of twelve, he managed to get hold of a schoolbook that contained a dialogue between a master and a slave who had three times tried to run away. The slave's arguments on behalf of freedom so impress his master that he emancipates him. In the same book, Douglass found a speech to the British Parliament by Richard Brinsley Sheridan (1751–1816), an Irish-born playwright and member of parliament whose eloquent arguments for Catholic emancipation strengthened Douglass's desire to be free. Finally, in 1838, when he was twenty, Douglass managed to escape to New England. He then went on to become a powerful speaker and writer, working on behalf of emancipation for blacks and, after the Civil War, working for civil rights for blacks.

However, Douglass was such an eloquent speaker that some people doubted he was ever a slave, so well had he learned the language of the educated white middle class. In 1845, he wrote his *Narrative* to give proof of his life as a slave, and proof of his ability to employ the discourse of middle-class power in order to denounce slavery. On the title page, "Written by Himself" appears as an assertion of Douglass's command of the discourse of his former oppressors and of his present, supposedly enlightened, northern audience. Douglass's case is one of knowledge and power combined with truth and morality—a combination all writers should honor.

Guiding and Moving Readers
Direction and Persuasion

We use the strategies of directing and persuading when we wish to guide or move the reader to do something. With direction, the goal is to *show* the reader how to do something, or how to get from point A to point B. With persuasion, the goal is to *convince* an audience through clever manipulation of rhetoric to do or to buy something they might not have thought of doing or buying on their own.

Direction

In writing directions, we assume that the reader wants to follow them. We do not have to engage in persuasion. All we have to do is make our verbal presentation so clear that the reader can get all the necessary information from our words. This is not as easy as it sounds. If you have ever tried to follow the directions that come with various unassembled products, you know something about how difficult it is. Inadequate directions are extremely frustrating and can almost always be traced to one problem: the writer's failure to imagine the reader clearly and to understand what the reader already knows and what new information must be provided.

Here are a few rules (or directions) for you to follow when writing directions.

1. Always imagine the reader trying to perform your words, depending on them for success.
2. Give the reader as much information and explanation as is necessary, but don't confuse the reader with too much information or repetition.
3. Go step by step, taking the reader through the procedure so that he or she can follow your words with deeds.
4. Consider the morale of the reader, and offer encouragement as well as information when needed.

WRITING DIRECTIONS

The writer of directions has to imagine the reader out there somewhere, holding the directions in one hand and coming back to them every step of the way. How much explanation does the reader need? How much can be taken for granted? Cookbooks, for instance, often take a lot for granted.

READING

Craig Claiborne, "Basic Pie Pastry" (from *The New York Times Cookbook*)

BASIC PIE PASTRY   Pastry for 9-inch pie or 6 tarts

2 cups sifted all-purpose flour   ⅓ cup cold water,
1 teaspoon salt   approximately
⅔ cup shortening

1. Sift together the flour and salt.
2. Using a pastry blender or two knives, chop in the shortening until the mixture resembles coarse cornmeal.
3. Sprinkle water slowly over the top of the flour, while tossing the mixture up from the bottom of the bowl with a fork. After about three-quarters of the water has been added, press the dampened part of the dough into a ball and set aside. Add only enough water to dampen the remaining flour mixture. Press all the dough together and divide into two portions, one slightly larger than the other. If the kitchen is hot, chill the dough for one-half hour before rolling.
4. Place the larger ball of dough on a lightly floured pastry cloth or board, pat in all directions with a floured rolling pin and then roll from the center out in all directions, loosening the pastry and reflouring the cloth and rolling pin as necessary. Roll into a round one-eighth inch thick and two inches larger in diameter than the top of the pie pan.
5. Fold gently into quarters, place in the pan and unfold. Fit the dough into the pan loosely and press against the pan without stretching it. Trim the edge slightly larger than the outside rim of the pan. Add desired filling.
6. Stack the pastry trimmings on the remaining dough and roll until about one inch larger than the top of the pan. Fold gently into quarters and cut several small gashes to allow steam to escape.

7. Moisten the rim of the lower crust, place top crust on the filled pan and unfold. Do not stretch the pastry. Tuck the rim of the top beneath the edge of the undercrust and flute with the fingers, making a tight seal.
8. Bake as directed for the filling used.

For the uninitiated, Craig Claiborne's "Basic Pie Pastry" will present some mysteries. How does one "chop in" shortening? What does coarse cornmeal look like? Why is the dough dampened in two steps, then pressed together, and then divided? What temperature must the kitchen be to be "hot"? Are the "pastry trimmings" the same thing as the dough cut off the edge of the pan? If so, when does "dough" become "pastry"? Moisten the rim with what? How do you "flute with the fingers"?

Now look at Marion Cunningham's "Basic Master Recipe." Which of Claiborne's "mysteries" do her instructions address?

Marion Cunningham, from "Basic Master Recipe: American Apple Pie" (from *The Fannie Farmer Baking Book*)

Mixing with a Pastry Blender

A fast and fairly dependable method, especially for beginners.

Begin by making small circular downward motions around the sides and bottom of the bowl with the wires of the blender, thus "cutting" the shortening into the flour. Scrape the flour down from the sides of the bowl occasionally, and as the flour and shortening collect on the wires of the cutter, wipe them off into the bowl. If you find you can do better with the bowl at an angle, tip one side up as you work. Just be sure to move the pastry blender through the flour and all  around the bowl, scraping down the sides so that all the particles of shortening get worked in. When you've mixed enough, all the flour will have been "touched" by the shortening, and the mixture will have irregular granules of fat—about the size of soft bread crumbs—or for those of you of the appropriate age, old-fashioned soap flakes.

Mixing with Two Knives

This method is just as effective as the above, but a bit slower and perhaps a little more awkward.

Hold a table knife almost upright in each hand. Cut into the flour and shortening with the knives, rapidly drawing them through the mixture, toward one another, so they scrape as they pass. Rapidly repeat about 15 or 20 times, scraping the shortening off the blades as it collects. The initial cuts break the shortening into more manageable pieces. Continue drawing the knives through in the same way, giving the bowl a quarter turn with every 15 or 20 cuts, and scraping down the sides of the bowl so that  all the particles of fat and flour are combined. Repeat the motion until the mixture looks like fresh bread crumbs.

Questions

1. Compare Cunningham's directions with Claiborne's. How does each set of directions conform to the four rules for writing directions that we listed in the introduction to this chapter?
2. Based on the two examples we've given you, how would you describe the audience for each of these cookbooks?

▪ PRACTICE 9.1

How to Make or Do Something

This exercise has three stages: writing, testing, and revising.

A. *Writing.* Think of something that you know more about than the average person. It can't simply be "knowledge of" in this case; it must be "knowing how to" make something or do something. It must also be something that another person might conceivably want to learn how to do. It can be anything from how a football guard should pull out of the line and block the opposing linebacker or safety on a sweep, to how to change a diaper, tune a guitar, braid hair, paper-train a dog, or figure out a statistical mean.

   The first part of your task is to describe clearly the sort of person you are writing this for. How familiar or unfamiliar is he or she with the background? In choosing your audience, try not to make your task too hard or too easy. Choose some type of person who knows something about the subject but doesn't know how this particular thing is done. Remember to write a description of this person first. Then name your project: How to _____. Make a list of all the steps required to complete the task. Next, consider this list in terms of the audience you have described: Will any further explanation be necessary? Can any explanations be simplified? Are there places where you will need to consider your reader's morale? Finally, produce the best set of directions you can for the task you have chosen.

B. *Testing.* Exchange your set of directions with another person in your class. Then, each of you should mark every point at which you feel in doubt about the writer's intentions or feel that you could not follow the directions. Do this, imagining that each of you is exactly the type of person chosen as the audience. Ideally, you should give your paper to the person in the class who fits your audience profile the most closely, though this may not always be possible; do the best you can in any case. Your reader should provide you with a set of written directions for the revision of your directions.

C. *Revising.* Follow your reader's directions and revise your original directions as best you can. Resubmit them to your reader for approval. If you ran into problems following your reader's directions for revision, just tell him or her about them. Don't write directions for revising the directions—enough is enough.

WRITING DIRECTIONS FOR UNNATURALLY DIFFICULT EVERYDAY ACTS

Simple objects sometimes require elaborate directions in order to free them from their complicated wrappers.

READING

Tibor Kalman and Lulu Kalman, "Problem: How to Open a CD Box"

1. Remove the plastic wrap. How? With a knife? Better yet, buy a special 99-cent EZ-CD opener tool designed precisely for this purpose. Ain't America grand? (Now, where did you put that thing?)
2. Peel off the special sticker that seals the CD case. Don't bother with the little pull tab—it'll tear off and become useless if you dare touch it. Just start peeling the plastic off with your nails instead. The pieces are superglued, so they will stick to your fingers. Roll them into a ball and flick it against the wall. Then ask a neighbor to remove the little ball of sticky plastic and throw it away.
3. Open the plastic box. It's snapped tight on itself. Insert your index finger at the opening opposite the hinge and pry carefully. Try very hard not to break the box. The box, called a jewel box probably because of the jewels that the packaging executives were able to purchase with their profits, is five-sixteenths of an inch thick. You can fit about 50 into a foot of drawer space. A CD that is slipped into a cardboard sleeve the way LP's were packaged is about one-sixteenth of an inch thick. You can fit nearly 200 in a foot of drawer space.
4. Ah. Now you can see the CD! Try to remove it. Go ahead. It's plugged onto that little plastic thing with the little plastic fingers—plugged on really tight to secure it for shipping. In the

next two weeks, those little, tiny plastic fingers will break off, one at a time, and fall on the floor. Your dog will eat them. ("It might be food. If not, I'll just throw up.")

5. The CD itself has a colorful label with a stunning color photo of a boot. No artist's name, no title, no song list, just this beautiful, shiny boot. The back cover of the CD box has the other boot. To find the song list, you must try to remove the CD booklet. This will take considerable ingenuity because it is wedged into position by several cleverly designed plastic tabs and a special device that is a last-ditch attempt to block you when you try to remove it. This will cost you a cuticle.

6. Open the CD booklet. Turn to the last page. There, among the copyright notices, publishing credits and assistant tape-engineer credits, you'll find the song list. Isn't it fun reading with a magnifying glass?

7. Enjoy the CD.

8. Return the CD to its shelf. Since the boxes are slippery, carry them one at a time and never stack them, to avoid the consequences of No. 9. Make appointments with your optometrist and chiropractor if you amass a shelved collection.

9. In two weeks, you'll drop the plastic box while trying to open it. Its hinges will break, challenging you to find another solution to the problem of storing your now naked CD.

10. In a couple of years, you'll put them in the basement, next to your LP's, replacing them with mini-CCDVDCVDX's, the new state-of-the-art format. The guys with the jewels have the packaging already figured out. Just 14 steps.

Questions

1. How do the Kalmans' directions conform to our rules for writing directions (p. 217)?
2. How would you describe their attitude toward their audience? What is their purpose in writing?
3. How would you describe the CD packagers' attitude toward buyers of CDs?

PRACTICE 9.2

Helping Others Cope

The Kalmans have provided useful directions for a small but nasty chore. We ask you to draw on your expertise in dealing with a similar problem—for example, how to extract a small gift from a large carton filled with styrofoam packing peanuts without covering yourself and your home with them; how to convince a small, overexcited child to gracefully exit a large toy store; or how to bathe a large, recalcitrant dog. Choose one of these or come up with your own easy-to-follow directions for another common problem, being sure to describe the difficulties your reader will encounter, as the Kalmans do.

GUIDING CONDUCT

Since the Middle Ages, conduct literature has been an important forum for directive writing. Such literature tells how to act in various social situations. In so doing, it also promotes certain cultural ideals or virtues. Until the end of the seventeenth century, most conduct literature was addressed to male members of the aristocracy. In the eighteenth and nineteenth centuries, the amount and popularity of such literature increased as women became the preferred audience for conduct-book writers. During the twentieth century, etiquette manuals, self-help books, and advice columns in newspapers and magazines proliferated. As a result, conduct literature is now very specialized in both the readers it addresses and the topics it takes up. Nevertheless, it continues to imply a reader who is — or should be — concerned with self-presentation and self-improvement.

READING

Direction through the Ages

Andreas Capellanus, from *The Art of Courtly Love* (1174–86)

The man who wants to keep his love affair for a long time untroubled should above all things be careful not to let it be known to any outsider, but should keep it hidden from everybody; because when a number of people begin to get wind of such an affair, it ceases to develop naturally and even loses what progress it has already made. Furthermore a lover ought to appear to his beloved wise in every respect and restrained in his conduct, and he should do nothing disagreeable that might annoy her. Moreover every man is bound, in time of need, to come to the aid of his beloved, both by sympathizing with her in all her troubles and by acceding to all her reasonable desires. Even if he knows sometimes that what she wants is not so reasonable, he should be prepared to agree to it after he has asked her to reconsider. And if inadvertently he should do something improper that offends her, let him straightway confess with downcast face that he has done wrong, and let him give the excuse that he lost his temper or make some other suitable explanation that will fit the case. And every man ought to be sparing of praise of his beloved when he is among other men; he should not talk about her often or at great length, and he should not spend a great deal of time in places where she is. When he is with other men, if he meets her in a group of women, he should not try to communicate with her by signs, but should treat her almost like a stranger, lest some person spying on their love might have opportunity to spread malicious gossip. Lovers should not even nod to each other unless they are sure that nobody is watching them. Every man should also wear things that his beloved likes and pay a reasonable amount of attention to his appearance—not too much because excessive care for one's looks is distasteful to everybody and leads people to despise the good looks that one has. If the lover is lavish in giving, that helps him retain a love he has acquired, for all lovers ought to despise all worldly riches and should give alms to those who have need of them. Nothing is considered more praiseworthy in a lover than to be known to be generous, and no matter how worthy a man may be otherwise, avarice degrades him, while many faults are excused if one has the virtue of liberality. Also, if the lover is one who is fitted to be a warrior, he should see to it that his courage is apparent to everybody, for it detracts very much from the good character of a man if he is timid in a fight. A lover should always offer his services and obedience freely to every lady, and he ought to root out all his pride and be very humble. He ought to give a good deal of attention to acting toward all in such fashion that no one may be sorry to call to mind his good deeds or have reason to censure anything he has done. Then, too, he must keep in mind the general rule that lovers must not neglect anything that good manners demand or good breeding suggests, but they should be very careful to do everything of this sort.

Dr. John Gregory, from *A Father's Legacy to His Daughters* (1774)

Consider every species of indelicacy in conversation as shameful in itself, and as highly disgusting to us. All double *entendre* is of this sort. The dissoluteness of men's education allows them to be diverted with a kind of wit, which yet they have delicacy enough to be shocked at when it comes from your mouths, or even when you hear it without pain and contempt. Virgin purity is of that delicate nature, that it cannot hear certain things without contamination. It is always in your power to avoid these. No man, but a brute or a fool, will insult a woman with conversation which he sees gives her pain; nor will he dare to do it if she resent the injury with a becoming spirit. There is a dignity in conscious virtue which is able to awe the most shameless and abandoned of men.

You will be reproached, perhaps, with prudery: by prudery is 2 usually meant, an affectation of delicacy. Now I do not wish you to affect delicacy; I wish you to possess it. At any rate, it is better to run the risk of being thought ridiculous than disgusting.

The men will complain of your reserve; they will assure you that 3 a franker behaviour would make you more amiable; but, trust me, they are not sincere when they tell you so. I acknowledge, that on some occasions it might render you more agreeable as companions, but it would make you less amiable as women—an important distinction which many of your sex are not aware of. After all, I wish you to have great ease and openness in your conversation. I only point out some considerations which ought to regulate your behaviour in that respect.

Constance Cary Harrison, from *The Well-Bred Girl in Society* (1898)

A fashion safe to stamp a young girl in general society as but ill- 1 equipped with knowledge of good form is that of "vanishing" in company with her attendant after a dance and remaining in unfrequented corners until remark is thereby created. Such is the young woman whose chaperon is in continual speculation as to her whereabouts, or else in active exercise to find her. She is no doubt often innocent of intention to offend, but at large and mixed entertainments the better part of wisdom in a woman is to keep in view of her fellows. A witty Frenchwoman, Mme. De Girardin, once wrote, "Amuse yourselves, O young beauties, but flutter your wings in the broad light of day. Avoid shadows in which suspicion hides." The "vanishing woman" act, made famous by a clever Hungarian magician in fashionable séances in drawing-rooms last season, should be limited in performance to a platform in full view of the audience. The prompt return of a young woman to the side or vicinity of her chaperon after dancing is not only a graceful and well-bred action, but affords an opportunity to the man, who too often is embarrassed in this respect, to withdraw and fulfil some other engagement.

Conspicuous mannerisms in dancing are offensive to good form. 2 I refer to certain tricks of holding the left arm and hand, of carrying the train of the dress (which should be what is called "dancing length," and then forgotten utterly), of dipping the knees when waltzing, etc. These habits, contracted through heedlessness, perhaps, have been seen to mar the otherwise charming grace of maidens whose youth and beauty called attention to their movements on the floor. A dancing-master in New York, whose pupils are known throughout Europe for their admirable form, would never tolerate an approach to either affectation or hoydenism among the young ladies of his classes. Most of these girls had afterward occasion to discover that what he thus taught them was of the first importance in shaping the verdict of the jury of chaperons, who, sitting on the benches around the ball-room walls, make or mar a maiden's claim to a place in the front ranks of good society.

Letitia Baldridge, from *Amy Vanderbilt's Everyday Etiquette* (1978)

Our fourteen-year-old son wants to begin dating. He is shy and awkward, an only child, and we ourselves are confused about the mores of today's dating. How can we help him launch forth into the dating world?   1

The first thing to master is how to make the date in the first place. Sometimes asking a girl for a date on the telephone is easier for a young man than in a face-to-face meeting.   2

Before he makes that call, he should jot down on a piece of paper all the information he must communicate, so that no important details will be omitted: the occasion, where is it, when is it, what will everyone be wearing, is a meal included, what time will she be picked up, by whom, how, and when will she be taken home?   3

When the big night arrives, he should give special attention to his grooming. If he's paying for the whole date, he should have his money safely in hand; if they are splitting the costs, all of that should have been arranged ahead of time, so that no embarrassing moments occur.   4

He should be on time to pick up his date. He should not sit in the car with whoever is driving and simply honk to announce his arrival; he should go up to her house or apartment and ring the bell. Her parents will probably ask him inside, and he should sit down with them to make conversation until she arrives on the scene. If sports, for example, is the only subject about which he talks with ease, he should ask her parents what they think of such and such a team. That conversation might last well beyond the time she appears, ready to go.   5

During their date, he should not leave her alone or go off with
other friends. He should make sure she has enough to eat and drink
(unless she's the independent type who takes care of that herself). If
it's a dance, he should see to it she's not standing alone on the sidelines.

He should get her home on time, exactly. If anything happens,
such as transportation problems, he should assure that her parents
are called immediately with an explanation of the delay.

At the end of the evening he should say, "Thank you for coming
with me tonight." If the young woman doesn't thank him in return
and say that *she* had a great time, then she is the one who needs to
look to her manners!

Ellen Fein and Sherrie Schneider, "Rule #20: Be Honest but Mysterious," from *The Rules: Time-Tested Secrets for Capturing the Heart of Mr. Right* (1995)

Men love mystery! Fifty years ago it was easier to be mysterious
with men. Women lived at home and their mothers answered the
phone and never told the men who else called their daughters.
Dates didn't see women's bedrooms so soon. Today, men pick up
women at their apartments, see their lingerie in the bathroom, their
romance novels in the living room, and hear their phone messages.
While such openness is good for marriage, it's important to project
a certain amount of mystery during the dating period.

We are all looking for someone to share our lives, thoughts, and
feelings with, but as we suggested in *Rule #19* wait until he says he
loves you to share your innermost secrets. When he is in your
apartment, don't listen to your answering machine. Let him wonder
who called you besides him! You might know that the messages are
probably from girlfriends feeling suicidal about their dating situations, but he doesn't!

If your date is at your place and one of your friends calls and asks
how everything is going, don't say, "*Scott's* over. I can't talk." That
means you've been talking about Scott to your friends and he's
somehow important. Even if that is the case, Scott should not know
that he is the subject of your thoughts and conversations or he
might think he doesn't have to work so hard to get you. Simply say,
"I can't talk right now. I'll call you later." After you hang up, don't
tell him who called or why.

Before he comes to your apartment, tuck this book away in your
top drawer and make sure any self-help books are out of sight. Have
interesting or popular novels or nonfiction books in full view. Hide

in the closet any grungy bathrobes or something you don't want him to see, such as a bottle of Prozac.

In general, don't give away any information that is not absolutely   5
necessary. If you are busy on the night he asks you for a date, don't tell him what you are planning to do. Just say you are busy. If he asks you out for the weekend, don't say, "I'm visiting my brother this weekend. His wife just had a baby." Simply say, "I'm sorry, but I already have plans." Less is more. Let him wonder what you are doing. You don't have to be an open book. This is good for him and it's good for you. It keeps the intrigue going. You don't want to make dating you so easy and predictable that he loses interest in you. Always remember that in time you will be able to tell him just about anything!

On the other hand, *Rules* girls don't lie either. Don't tell a Mel   6
Gibson–type guy that you love hiking and shop at L.L. Bean all the time when you can't stand trees, insects, and backpacks. And certainly don't tell your boyfriend that you love and want children because he does when you really don't. Take our advice. Don't lie. It's a law of the universe.

Questions

1. Most conduct books are divided into subsections, each bearing a subtitle that indicates what's at issue. Fein and Schneider's piece follows that custom. Assume for a moment that each of the previous excerpts constitutes a complete subsection; give each excerpt a "How to _____" or "The art of _____" subtitle. What problems did you have in coming up with subtitles? How did you deal with these problems? Compare your subtitles with those composed by your classmates; which subtitles do you like best? Why?
2. Which of these excerpts is most like basic-directive writing as we have described it on pages 217–18? Which excerpt is least like basic-directive writing? Do any of the excerpts strike you as nondirective in form or purpose?
3. Which excerpt seems most attentive to the reader? How is this attention expressed? Are some parts of each excerpt aimed more at the reader's morale than at information or instruction? Which parts? How important are these parts?
4. The readings here present a brief survey of eight centuries of conduct books. What historical changes, if any, do you find in rules of conduct for men (Capellanus and Baldridge)? for women (Gregory, Harrison, and Fein and Schneider)?
5. Directive writing aims at influencing its reader's actions. Presumably, it succeeds in being informative when the reader acts

out the directions. We doubt, however, that you will act out all the directions in these excerpts. Must we then conclude that for you, these directive pieces of writing are not informative? What, if anything, do you know now that you didn't know before reading these samples of directive writing?

▧ PRACTICE 9.3

How to Conduct Yourself

The dean of students has asked you to help put together a "Social Survival Skills Manual" for newcomers to the college. You will be working on the manual with some twenty other students, each of whom has been assigned the same general task: to choose some particular social situation that is likely to pose a problem for the incoming student and to compose a directive piece of writing that will enable the newcomer to act appropriately. Since the project interests you—and pays well—you agree to draft a contribution for consideration by both the student group and the dean. But what to write about? Meeting people? Getting a date? Dressing for campus success? Making the grade with professors or with a particular group of peers? Dealing with campus police? librarians? roommates? Cafeteria etiquette? Although there are many possibilities, you decide to do the one that you think is really important. So do it.

Persuasion

As you have seen, when writing directions, you keep in mind an audience that wants to know how to do something. With persuasion, on the other hand, you must imagine an audience that you want to sway through the power of your words. In a democratic and capitalistic society, we depend upon persuasion to do what coercion does in a totalitarian society. Thus persuasion is used to move us to vote in certain ways and to spend in certain ways. We are, in fact, bombarded with persuasive texts, visual as well as verbal, by all the media of mass communication: newspapers, magazines, radio, and television. Written persuasion is also used in more personal ways: to seek employment, to redress grievances, to make changes in an organization or group. In public life, persuasion pervades our law courts as well as our halls of government.

Although many political speeches and some advertisements do, in fact, mix rational argument with the emotional appeal of persuasive language, we can make a clear distinction between argument and persuasion. Argument seeks to make an informed case for or against something; it tries to prove by logical connection that one view of a topic is right and another is wrong—it does not necessarily seek to motivate the reader to action. Persuasion, on the other hand, is always concerned with action and motivation: "trust me," "fear them," "buy this product," "vote for this candidate." At its most insidious, persuasion can even spur readers to action that is contrary to reason.

Every citizen needs to be able to deal with persuasion in two ways: (1) to produce it when necessary and (2) to defend oneself against it constantly. For purposes of defense, it is best to know how persuasion is put together from the inside. One who has written it knows firsthand how it works. These persuasive exercises, then, are designed with a double purpose: to improve your writing skills and to make you a more alert and critical reader of persuasive texts.

There are certain aspects of persuasion that are neither nice nor fair. Persuasion tries to subdue thought by appealing to emotion, and persuasive writing, in its most extreme forms, tries to ignore the alternatives to whatever cause it is pleading. Advertisers of cigarettes are not happy to include that little message from the surgeon general in their ads. They would much prefer to ignore the dangerous side of their product. As it is, they will do everything they can to counter those ominous words about ill health by projecting images of healthy outdoor life associated with the product.

PERSUADING THROUGH ADVERTISING

The persuasive manner of the following ad may seem ludicrously obvious now, but its techniques are still used. Notice how the visual and verbal aspects of the ad reinforce one another. Few contemporary ads would rely so heavily on verbal copy. (Because the verbal print is so small in our reduced copy, we have reproduced the language of the fine print from the ad.) After you have examined the pictures and text, consider the questions that follow.

READING

Fly-Tox Advertisement, 1926

In many finely appointed homes spraying every room with Fly-Tox   1
is a daily summertime accomplishment. This is not just an exceptional refinement. Indeed, it is considered a requisite to good housekeeping.

Spraying the entire room with Fly-Tox reaches and kills offen-   2
sive household insects even in their places of hiding. That insures unmolested summer comfort. Musty, fly-tainted odors are dis-

What is your baby worth?

Priceless! A great gift that can never be replaced! Innocent and defenseless. Its comfort and health, even life itself, depend on little duties that constitute vigilant care and loving thoughtfulness.

In the summertime no greater service can be rendered than to shield the child and its food from the perilous contact with flies and mosquitoes.

The fly is the filthiest insect known. Literally hundreds—some scientists say, thousands—of deadly bacteria swarm in the putrescent ooze of a fly's spongy foot. It contaminates everything it touches. Sows the germs of disease on the very delicacies a child likes to eat.

The mosquito is no less an assassin. Whole epidemics have been traced by its ravages. Penetrating a child's tender skin, the bite is bitterly painful. And with the germ of fever firing their blood, little bodies writhe in the burning torture of flaming torment. The end—sometimes is tragic.

Flies and mosquitoes transmit typhoid fever, dysentery infantile paralysis. Safety is only possible when these insects are killed. That is why devoted parents in millions of homes use Fly-Tox. It destroys flies and mosquitoes. It safeguards the health and comfort of our most precious possession—little children.

Wherever there are flies, use Fly-Tox

In many finely appointed homes spraying every room with Fly-Tox is a daily summertime accomplishment. This is not just an exceptional refinement. Indeed, it is considered a requisite to good housekeeping.

Spraying the entire room with Fly-Tox reaches and kills offensive household insects even in their places of hiding. That insures unmolested summer comfort. Musty, fly-tainted odors are displaced by an atmosphere of cleanliness. The draperies are unsoiled, spotless, beautiful. The upholstery fresh and bright, radiant with cleanliness. In the absence of unclean household insects, every room in the house glows with a refreshing, cleanly charm—a charm in which every housewife enjoys a rightful pride.

The Modern Safeguard to Health and Comfort

Fly-Tox is an established, efficient household insecticide. It was developed at Mellon Institute of Industrial Research. Stainless. Harmless to humans. Yet when its cleanly fragrant spray touches them these insect enemies to man's health and comfort crumple up and die. Fly-Tox has brought to millions of homes a new summer comfort—a house without flies or mosquitoes. Most people prefer the hand sprayer. It gives better satisfaction. However, a trial sprayer is given free with every small bottle.

| HALF PINT - 50C | PINT - 75C | QUART - $1.25 | GALLON - $4.00 |

Gallons in glass jugs are especially suitable for hotels, restaurants, summer camps, institutions

FLY-TOX
KILLS FLIES
MOSQUITOES
MOTHS, ROACHES, ANTS, FLEAS

placed by an atmosphere of cleanliness. The draperies are unsoiled, spotless, beautiful. The upholstery fresh and bright, radiant with cleanliness. In the absence of unclean household insects, every room in the house glows with a refreshing, cleanly charm—a charm in which every housewife enjoys a rightful pride.

Fly-Tox is an established, efficient household insecticide. It was developed at Mellon Institute of Industrial Research. Stainless. Harmless to humans. Yet when its cleanly fragrant spray touches them these insect enemies to man's health and comfort crumple up and die. Fly-Tox has brought to millions of homes a new summer comfort—a house without flies or mosquitoes. 3

Most people prefer the hand sprayer. It gives better satisfaction. However, a trial sprayer is given free with every small bottle. 4

In the summertime no greater service can be rendered than to shield the child and its food from the perilous contact with flies and mosquitoes. The fly is the filthiest insect known. Literally hundreds—some scientists say, thousands—of deadly bacteria swarm in the putrescent ooze of a fly's spongy foot. It contaminates everything it touches. Sows the germs of disease on the very delicacies a child likes to eat. 5

The mosquito is no less an assassin. Whole epidemics have been traced by its ravages. Penetrating a child's tender skin, the bite is bitterly painful. And with the germ of fever firing their blood, little bodies writhe in the burning torture of flaming torment. The end—sometimes is tragic. 6

Flies and mosquitoes transmit typhoid fever, dysentery, infantile paralysis. Safety is only possible when these insects are killed. That is why devoted parents in millions of homes use Fly-Tox. It destroys flies and mosquitoes. It safeguards the health and comfort of our most precious possession—little children. 7

Questions

1. Advertising is usually aimed at a specific audience. How would you describe the target group for this ad? What details in the ad indicate the audience the copywriter had in mind?
2. Persuasion often appeals to "absolutes," or accepted standards of value or behavior. How many different appeals of this sort can you detect in the Fly-Tox ad? What emotions are most directly evoked by the text?
3. Consider the use of connotative language in the text of the ad. What connotations are most frequently and powerfully evoked? How are contrasting connotations used to motivate the prospective buyer? How much information about the composition

of the product is actually given? Where do you suspect the ad to be furthest from the truth? Where is it most accurate?

4. How do the visual images work to persuade? What is the function of each of the five separate pictures presented? Can you link certain images with specific words in the text?

PRACTICE 9.4

The Ghastly Resort Hotel

You have just landed a job writing advertising copy for a resort hotel on a small island off the coast of the United States. The hotel management has brought you to the island for a few days of exploration, during which you have noted the following features:

1. The hotel seems made of plastic. It features shiny, new, bright, loud colors and wildly patterned wallpaper.
2. The rooms are very small, the walls are thin, and music from the hotel bar can be heard all night long.
3. Hot water for bathing is seldom available.
4. The hotel band, a group of local kids playing on garbage can lids and harmonicas, seems to know only three songs.
5. The island is run by a dictator whose soldiers are everywhere. You saw three of them savagely beat a ragged child who tried to steal a loaf of bread.
6. The one town on the island is really a small village full of battered shacks with outdoor plumbing facilities.
7. The beach consists of a small amount of imported white sand spread over the local mud.
8. A swimmer at the beach was recently attacked and badly wounded by a barracuda.
9. At two minutes after sunset, hordes of large, vicious mosquitoes come out.
10. It is blazing hot while the sun is out but damp and cold at night.
11. The hotel owns one large motor launch. Every few days, when the launch is in good repair, it takes a crowded group of tourists to a small sand bar where they look for shells but mostly find cans and bottles left by other tourists.
12. The food in the hotel is highly flavored with some mysterious local herb that lingers on your taste buds for days. The most frequently featured dish is a local specialty: squid.

All in all, this is not a place you would choose for yourself or recommend to a friend. But the job is important to you, and you have already run up a large bill that you cannot pay until you receive your fee for writing the copy. You decide that you will not leave out any of the material from the above list (to satisfy your conscience), but you will try to put everything in the most favorable light possible (to appease your employer). You sit down in your room to write the most attractive copy you can. You can hear the band playing one of their three tunes. You begin to write....

But before you begin, let us give you some technical advice. You have several problems to contend with here. One is organizational. The twelve items you have to cover must be grouped in paragraphs according to some system. You must look for natural groupings and then organize your writing accordingly, with an appropriate introduction and conclusion. Another problem is connotation. Nothing in your copy must have an unpleasant connotation. The word *barracuda*, for instance, would be as out of place as the word *cancer* in a cigarette ad. This problem, in turn, leads to a denotative problem. To satisfy what is left of your conscience, you must use some word or phrase that points to the barracuda you happen to know about, although this reference must be disguised or prettied-up in some way. And so it is for every detail.

CHANGING THE PERSUASIVE PATTERN

The advertisement described below appeared in 1954, in a campaign designed to change the image of Marlboro cigarettes. Marlboro cigarettes were identified as a "feminine high-style cigarette" when the company decided to go masculine. This is the way that marketing researcher Pierre Martineau described that campaign in *Motivation in Advertising* (1957): "1. No women were shown in the advertising. 2. All models were very virile men.... 3. The models were also chosen as successful, forceful personalities to inspire emulation, identification with an admirable figure.... 4. To reinforce the notion of virility and also to hint of a romantic past, each man had a plainly visible tattoo on his hand.... This symbol gave richness to the product image, bringing it all into focus."

▒ READING

The Marlboro Man, 1954

Because of the current legal climate, publishers now find it difficult to obtain permission to reproduce tobacco advertisements; thus for this edition of *The Practice of Writing*, we have not reproduced this advertisement. The ad may be found in 1954 issues of *Life* magazine, or see **http://www.chickenhead.com/truth/1950s.html** for similar Marlboro ads. Here is a description of the ad: A rugged-looking young man with a buzz cut is leaning on his elbow, his tattooed fist against his right cheek. The tattoo appears to be of an anchor with two stars below its crossbar. You can see the straps of his dark undershirt, the hair on his chest, and the whistle around his neck, which suggests that he might very well be a marine drill sergeant. He is meant to exude masculinity as he stares straight at the reader through narrowed eyes, a slim column of smoke curling upward from the cigarette set in the left-hand corner of his mouth. In the upper right-hand corner of the ad is his title, "The Marlboro Man," and under his picture are the words: "A lot of man...a lot of cigarette." In the lower right-hand corner, there's a small picture of the "New 'Self-Starter'" flip-top box, and to the left of it, we read "'He gets a lot to like—filter, flavor, flip-top box.' The works."

■ PRACTICE 9.5

Reaching a Different Audience

Pierre Martineau's analysis makes clear the motivation behind the Marlboro Man ad. Your job in this assignment is to produce an ad for a different but similar advertising campaign.

First find a product that is clearly associated with one particular type of person (a certain sex, age, class, race, profession). Then construct an ad designed to make that same product appeal to a very different type of person. Make an entire full-page ad, with visual and verbal material laid out in the most effective way. (This is a cut-and-paste job, or you can design it on your computer.)

Along with the ad, submit a paragraph in which you explain what you have done. Describe the association pattern you are trying to change, and the sort of consumer you are trying to persuade to buy your product.

GETTING A JOB

When you apply for a job, most business and professional organizations require you to submit a letter of application and a résumé of your educational and work experience. On the basis of these two documents, they decide whether or not to grant you an interview, so it's important that your letter of application be direct, sincere, persuasive, and well-written (neat and free of errors), and that your résumé be factual and neat in appearance.

READING

The Job Letter and Résumé

The Résumé

On page 238 is a sample résumé presenting the facts about Jennifer Hazard, who is seeking a management trainee position at a bank. Her résumé follows one of the standard formats. In drawing up your own résumé, remember that clarity and simplicity go further than color photographs and fancy fonts. Here are some general rules:

Try to keep to one or two pages in length.

Use white or cream bond paper.

Use a standard font, such as courier or Times Roman.

The Letter

Your letter of application should elaborate on the information in your résumé that is most pertinent to the job for which you are applying. Letters of application also follow a fairly standard format:

Paragraph 1: State the job for which you are applying. Explain where you saw the advertisement or who told you about the job.

Paragraph 2. Describe your college training, stressing those courses and activities most relevant to the job for which you are applying.

Paragraph 3. Describe your previous work experience and how it relates to the position you want.

Paragraph 4. Tell why you'd like to work for the particular company or organization.

Paragraph 5. State that your résumé is enclosed (and any other material requested, such as letters of recommendation), and that you are available for an interview.

PRACTICE 9.6

The Job Letter and Résumé

To prepare to write a job letter and to construct a résumé, you must first decide what kind of position you are applying for. The next step is very important: do some research on that position. You might interview someone

Résumé

JENNIFER HAZARD

65 Bridge Road
Warlock, Rhode Island 02885
Phone: 401-249-8694

Education

1992–1996	Warlock High School, Warlock, Rhode Island
1996–1998	Ocean State Community College, Cranberry, Rhode Island
	Major: Accounting
1998–2000	Pawtuxet College, Providence, Rhode Island
	B.A. expected May 2000
	Major: Economics; Minor: Sociology GPA: 3.75

Extracurricular Activities

1996–	Volunteer, Providence Children's Hospital
1998–2000	Pawtuxet College Women's Varsity Swim Team
1998–2000	Business Manager, *Pawtuxet College Clarion*

Experience

1999–	Teller, Warlock Savings Bank, Warlock, Rhode Island
1998–1999	Bookkeeper, Mercury Hardware Store, Warlock, Rhode Island
Summer 1997	Counselor, Swimming Instructor, Stone Hill Camp, Rumstick, Rhode Island
1995–1996	Cashier, Buddy's Family Restaurant, Nayatt, Rhode Island

References

Professor John McNulty, Department of Economics, Pawtuxet College, Providence, Rhode Island 02903

Professor Marilyn Vargas, Department of Sociology, Pawtuxet College, Providence, Rhode Island 02903

Mr. Joseph DiSano, Manager, Warlock Savings Bank, Warlock, Rhode Island 02885

65 Bridge Road
Warlock, Rhode Island
May 1, 2000

Mr. Harold O'Brien
Personnel Department
Friendly National Bank
Providence, Rhode Island 02905

Dr. Mr. O'Brien:
  I wish to apply for the position of Branch Manager
Trainee, which was advertised in the <u>Providence Daily
Bugle</u> on April 30.
  This month I shall be graduating from Pawtuxet College,
where I've been majoring in economics. Because I've been
interested in a career in banking, I decided to research
the functions of the two banks in my hometown of Warlock
for my economics honors thesis. I wanted to know what
services were most used by the customers of these banks
and how the banks were working with small businesses to
help them expand or to improve their facilities. Warlock,
like so many older towns, has had to revitalize its downtown business area in order to compete with the new malls
outside town. Such renewal has been possible because of
the cooperation of the banks, the town planning committee,
and the businesspeople. Writing this thesis showed me how
important a part of a community a bank can be when it
takes an active interest in the growth of that community.
  I've had practical experience in financial affairs as
Business Manager of the college newspaper and in my summer
and part-time work as a bookkeeper and as a teller. In fact,
doing the books for a small hardware store that wanted to
expand gave me a good picture of small business problems. It
was this experience that started my thesis research.
  I'd especially enjoy working for Friendly National Bank
because of the innovations in banking you've introduced
and because I am looking for a challenging position in a
bank that gives the same attention to the small busi-
nessperson as to a large corporation.
  I have enclosed my résumé, and if my credentials interest
you, I am available for an interview at your convenience.

Sincerely yours,

Jennifer Hazard

JENNIFER HAZARD

in a similar position to find out what the job entails, or visit your college's job placement office to see what information they have on file and what services they provide for job seekers. If you are interested in a particular organization or company, check to see if it has a Web site. On the other hand, if you simply want to practice writing the letter and résumé, we have included some sample newspaper ads for you to practice with.

Next, draw up a résumé following the model in this book or another standard format. You can list your own qualifications or, if you're practicing, imagine you are just right for the job and invent suitable qualifications.

Now write a letter applying for the job. Remember to be direct and sincere, and be sure to read the job advertisement or notice very carefully. Look again at Jennifer Hazard's letter. It's clear she's done research on Friendly National Bank and its business policies in Rhode Island. She also shows a particular interest in the needs of small businesses, and her résumé shows that she has relevant work experience as a cashier and bookkeeper for small businesses. In her letter, she briefly stresses the importance of this practical experience. You may not have such closely related experience, but you should stress the qualities you do have, and how they can be useful in the position you desire. Remember, your hobbies, your volunteer work, your extracurricular activities, and your special interests can be as valuable and relevant as your academic work.

Now choose your job and start writing.

WEB PRODUCER

Fastpace Internet (www.fastpace. net), a leading national network of local portal Web sites, is seeking part-time producer with strong writing and information organization skills for editorial, classified, and e-commerce content development. Responsibilities: transform concepts into detailed site maps; work with designers and coders to create Web pages; implement projects across the network. 1–2 yrs. Web experience required. Excellent growth potential for a motivated, entrepreneurial individual. E-mail letter and résumé to Lance_Lucky@FastpaceInternet .com.

Accessories Assistant

The Federic Fickel Co. is seeking an Assistant to work with the Vice President for Accessories of our growing luxury-goods company. To qualify, you must have a strong sense of style and an interest in fashion, and be detail-oriented and highly organized; strong computer skills (Word/Excel) necessary. Some experience in a fast-paced office environment like ours is highly desirable. Recent college graduate preferred. Excellent benefits and opportunity for growth in the world of fashion. Send letter and résumé to Evelyn Woods, Human Resources Dept., The Federic Fickel Co., 599 Fifth Avenue, New York, NY 10777.

10

Reasoning with Readers
Argumentation

Where persuasion seeks to put the mind to sleep, so that its appeal to emotion will be effective, argumentation aims to awaken thought by appealing to reason. Persuasion is most at home in the rough and tumble worlds of advertising and politics. Argumentation is mainly an intellectual or academic use of language, requiring patience and moderation. In principle, an argument can always be reversed. New evidence or new reasoning can convince even the arguer that the **issue** under discussion should be seen in a different way. But you cannot convince an advertiser not to want your money or a politician to reject your vote.

For various reasons, persuasion and argumentation are often mixed in actual speech and writing, both in academic discourse and in the world of affairs. But for the purposes of study and practice, it is useful to treat them separately. The purest forms of argumentation appear in philosophy. Here, for instance, is Bertrand Russell reflecting (in *My Philosophical Development*, 1975) on one of his earlier books:

> In *The Analysis of Mind* I argued the thesis that the "stuff" of mental occurrences consists entirely of sensations and images. I do not know whether this thesis was sound....(p. 111)

As Russell indicates, a **thesis** is essential to argumentation. Although he is not arguing in this passage but reflecting upon his earlier argument, he summarizes the thesis he had argued in the past, adding the interesting comment that he is no longer certain that his thesis was sound. This kind of second thought is, as you know, typical of reflection, but it is also built into the process of argumentation. A person writing advertising copy has a set goal: sell that product! The copywriter can revise to make the copy more persuasive but cannot rethink the point of the writing. A person writing an argument, on the other hand, begins with a thesis that may be qualified during the writing or even, as Russell indicates, rethought after its publication in a book.

A thesis, then, is the point or organizing principle of an argument: "I argued the thesis," Russell says. But there is always something tentative about a thesis. The writers of arguments often consider counterarguments against the theses they are supporting. Sometimes this is only a gesture, a persuasive trick, but in serious argumentation it is also a way of testing. If you do this scrupulously while writing, it should lead you to qualify your thesis. For example, Russell might then write: "The 'stuff' of mental occurrences consists *mostly* of sensations and images." Or, if Russell were to modify his thesis in an important way, it might then read: "The 'stuff' of mental occurrences consists of sensations, images, and concepts."

Here is an example of another philosopher introducing a long and serious argument:

> Let me start with a confession.
>
> I wrote this paper in a fit of anger and self-righteousness caused by what I thought were certain disastrous developments in the sciences. The paper will therefore sound a little harsh, and it will perhaps also be a little unjust. Now while I think that self-righteousness has no positive function whatever and while I am convinced that it can only add to the fear and to the tensions that already exist, I also think that a little anger can on occasions be a good thing and can make us see our surroundings more clearly.
>
> I think very highly of science, but I think very little of experts, although experts form about 95 percent or more of science today. It is my belief that science was advanced, and is still being advanced, by *dilettantes* and that experts are liable to bring it to a standstill. I may be entirely wrong in this belief of mine, but the only way to find out is to tell you. Therefore, with my apologies, here is my paper. (Paul Feyerabend, "Experts in a Free Society," *The Critic* [November–December 1970])

This is unusually personal and informal for philosophical argument, but there are reasons for that. The author doesn't want to sound like an expert, so he makes a personal confession. He refers to his thesis as a "belief," but his attitude toward his belief is the attitude toward argumentation we have been describing. Even in his anger, his passionate concern, he does not want to carry the day by emotion. In fact, by confessing his own emotion he is putting the reader on guard against it. He has written in anger, but he will not appeal to anger in his readers. Above all, he does not want to bully readers into thinking that there are no alternatives to his own attitude. "I may be entirely wrong," he says, "but the only way to find out is to tell you." This is the true spirit of argumentation: make a case for your thesis as strongly as you can, but be prepared to rethink it on the basis of new evidence or an argument that you haven't foreseen.

Learning to argue well is a complex process, and there are no real shortcuts. The study of formal logic sometimes helps, but this is a demanding discipline that does not guarantee effective writing. It is our belief that argumentation, like other kinds of writing, is not so much a theory to be acquired as it is a practice to be worked at. The relation of argumentative practice and theory has been well described by the philosopher Gilbert Ryle in his book *The Concept of Mind* (1949). Describing a man arguing a case before a court, Ryle says the following:

> He probably observes the rules of logic without thinking about them. He does not cite Aristotle's formulae[1] to himself or to the court. He applies in his practice what Aristotle abstracted in his theory of such practices. He reasons with a correct method but without considering the prescriptions of a methodology. The rules that he observes have become his way of thinking, when he is taking care. (48)

Elsewhere, Ryle points out that "knowing how" is different from "knowing that." And he adds, a "surgeon must indeed have learned from instruction, or by his own indications and observations, a great number of truths; but he must also have learned by practice a great number of aptitudes" (49).

Like surgery, reasoning well in writing is best learned through guided practice. This chapter offers you guided practice in reading and writing arguments, beginning with three assignments that focus respectively on debating issues, presenting reasons, and supplying evidence. Exploring these three aspects of argumentation should prepare you well for the next three practices, each of which asks you to take and support a reasonable position on an arguable issue. But before you examine the practice of others and undertake some arguments of your own, we would like to offer you the following brief list of features common to good arguments:

1. A clear thesis that states the writer's position on a debatable issue
2. An organized set of reasons that develops the thesis
3. An orderly presentation of evidence that supports the reasons
4. The fair consideration of reasons and evidence that run counter to the thesis
5. A conclusion that emphasizes the thesis

It is our thesis that these five features characterize all reasonable arguments. Of course, you should check for yourself to see if we are right.

---

[1]Aristotle, one of the best-known classical Greek philosopher-teachers, completed a treatise entitled *Rhetoric* in 330 B.C. In that treatise, Aristotle formulates various means of arguing, including three kinds of logical appeals as well as pathetic and ethical appeals. *Eds.*

WHAT'S THE ARGUMENT?

In everyday speech, the term *argument* is often used to refer to a face-off between two people that involves shouting, name calling, personal attacks, emotional outbursts, slamming doors, and closed minds. In the domain of writing, however, argument refers to something else—to the strategy reasonable people use in situations where there are important disagreements about debatable issues. Not all disagreements are about debatable issues. You and a classmate may disagree about exactly when the next English paper is due but arguing with one another about it won't do any good. The due date is a simple matter of fact, which you can find out by asking your instructor. Like matters of fact, personal feelings and opinions are also not debatable. Your personal dislike of some television show can't be disputed, if only because you are the one who actually knows how you feel. What we can debate, however, are the show's thematic purpose, its aesthetic quality, and its effects on children. In more general terms, we can and do disagree about three kinds of debatable issues: what's true, what's good, and what's possible.

The reading selection below includes pieces by five different writers and represents a field of disagreement or controversy. The controversy about women's nature and women's rights has been going on for quite some time—certainly more than 150 years. The field is crowded with disputants and that makes it harder for all of us to get our bearings. But one way to figure out where you stand in this or any field of debate is to listen carefully to a few participants—especially those who disagree with each other, as some of the following writers do. The reporter Patricia Cohen opens the selection by explaining how these four letters came to be written and published in the July 18, 1998, edition of the *New York Times*. As you read the letters, try to figure out what position each writer takes. To what extent are these women arguing about the same issue? What is at stake in their disagreements? Finally, keep in mind that all but one of these five pieces are letters, a kind of writing that doesn't lend itself to full-blown argumentation.

■ READING

Patricia Cohen, "A Woman's Worth: 1857 Letter Echoes Still"

It wasn't until three years after the first women's rights convention at Seneca Falls in 1848 that Susan B. Anthony and Elizabeth Cady Stanton met. Yet the partnership they formed blossomed into an independent women's rights movement that won women the right

1

to vote and set the foundation for 20th-century feminism's critique of American society.

Throughout their decades-long friendship, the two women maintained an intense and fascinating correspondence. There is an uncanny sense of recognition in reading these letters today. Science advances, laws are rewritten, the economy is transformed, but the debates about differences between the sexes and the role of women in marriage and the workplace remain. 2

With that immediacy in mind, *The New York Times* asked three writers to respond to excerpts from a letter Anthony wrote more than 140 years ago. Katha Pollitt is a columnist for *The Nation* and author of "Reasonable Creatures: Essays on Women and Feminism" (Alfred A. Knopf, 1994). Dorothy Patterson is married to Paige Patterson, president of the Southern Baptists, and was on the seven-member committee that amended the denomination's essential statement of beliefs at the Southern Baptists' convention last month to include a declaration that a woman should "submit herself graciously" to her husband. Lynn Margulis, a scientist at the University of Massachusetts at Amherst, is an author of "Slanted Truths: Essays on Gaia, Symbiosis and Evolution" (Springer-Verlag, 1997) and "What Is Sex?" (Simon & Schuster, 1997). 3

Reprinted on page 248, Anthony's letter to Stanton describes a debate Anthony had with the spiritualist and reformer Andrew Jackson Davis over the differences between men and women. Stanton had spoken on this issue in her address to the Seneca Falls convention, her first on women's rights, delivered 150 years ago tomorrow. In that speech, she scorned the notion that men were intellectually, morally or physically superior to women, and attacked the idea that the sexes were different but equal, saying that men "soon run this difference into the old groove of superiority." 4

Anthony argues that differences between men and women are not inborn, but a result of society's influence. And she adds that reproduction is the "highest and holiest function." 5

This 1857 letter is included in a collection of correspondance and speeches by Stanton and Anthony and edited by Ellen Carl DuBois. Their writings trace the trajectory of their remarkable relationship. 6

At first glance, the two might seem something of an odd couple. Stanton, a member of one of New York's blue-blood families, married a prominent abolitionist and bore seven children. Plump and square, with a head of curls lined up like bedrolls and a penchant for naps, Stanton was known for her brilliance, education and cutting wit. Pictures of Anthony, on the other hand, invariably show her in a 7 dark, somber dress, her hair tightly drawn into a severe bun and wire-rimmed spectacles perched on her nose. Unmarried her entire life, Anthony became a teacher after her father was wiped out in the economic panic of 1837. Though she fiercely believed that women should be able to support themselves independently, her first reformist efforts were not on behalf of her gender but of temperance.

Anthony, egged on by Stanton, eventually became fed up with the male leaders of the temperance movement, however, who bestowed second-class status on their female colleagues. Although it was Stanton who originally stoked Anthony's interest in feminism, it was Anthony who then drew her mentor more deeply into political reform: "In turning the intense earnestness and religious enthusiasm of this great-souled woman into this channel, I soon felt the power of my convert goading me forward to more untiring work." Stanton was the philosopher, Anthony the organizer.   8

Stanton often complained to Anthony of the difficulties of balancing her commitment to work with her family duties. Saying she would have to sit up all night to finish her speech on women's rights for the New York State Legislature in 1854, Stanton wrote to Anthony of the distractions at home: "Yesterday one of the boys shot an arrow into my baby's eye. The eye is safe, but oh! my fright when I saw the blood come and the organ swell and witnessed her suffering! What an escape! ... Then, today, my nurse has gone home with a felon [abscess] on her finger. So you see how I am bound here." At another moment, she wrote, "It is in vain to look for the elevation of woman, so long as she is degraded in marriage."   9

Anthony served as Stanton's on-the-scene reporter, detailing the ins and outs of the reformers' struggles. Anthony's insecurity often comes through in her letters as she would appeal to Stanton for guidance. She fretted over a speech she had to give to the New York State Teachers Convention in 1856, writing: "If I get all the time the world has, I can't get up a decent document. So for the love of me and for the saving of the reputation of womanhood, I beg you, with one baby on your knee and another at your feet and four boys whistling, buzzing, hallooing Ma, Ma, set yourself about the work. It is but of small moment who writes the address, but of vast moment that it be well done.... Now will you load my gun, leaving me only to pull the trigger and let fly the powder and ball?"   10

The power of their intellect and vigor of their arguments make it seem natural to speak to them across the years. Pity that we can't hear their latest response.   11

Susan B. Anthony, from an 1857 letter to Mrs. Stanton

Collins, Sept. 29/57

Dear Mrs. Stanton,

How I do long to be with you this very minute, to have one look   1
into your very soul, and one sound of your soul-stirring voice.

For a week, I was in such a home whirl. On Friday the 25th I left   2
for the Collins Progressive Friends Meeting. Arrived Saturday A.M.

Mr. Davis set forth his idea of the nature of the sexes and their   3
relation to each [other]....He said woman's inherent nature *is Love
and Man's Wisdom.* That Love reaches out to Wisdom—Man—
and Wisdom reaches out to Love—Woman—and the two meet
and make a beautiful blending of the two principles.

My soul was on fire. This is but a *revamp* of the world's idea from   4
the beginning, the very same doctrine that consigned woman from
the beginning to the sphere of the affections, that subjugated her to
man's wisdom.

I said *women.* If you accept the theory given you by Davis, you   5
may give up all talk of a change for woman: she is now where God
and nature intended she should be....such a doctrine makes my
heart *sink* within me, said I. And did I accept it, I would return to
my own father's house, and never again raise my voice for woman's
right to the control of her own person, the ownership of her own
earnings, the guardianship of her own children. For if this be true,
she ought not to possess those rights. She ought to make final appeal to the wisdom of her husband, father and brother.

All day yesterday, the likeness and unlikeness of the sexes has   6
been the topic of discussion. Phillip D. Moore of Newark took sides
with me. Well on the love and wisdom side, we had [Aaron M.]
Powell, George Taylor, Dr. Mary Taylor of Buffalo and a Mr.
Lloyd of Pa. The discussion has been loud and long, and how I
wished that *you* could be there. I tell you, Mrs. Stanton, after all, it
is very precious to the soul of man, that he shall *reign supreme in intellect,* and it will take centuries if not ages to dispossess him of the
fancy that he is born to do so.

The female doctor urged as a physiological fact that girl babies   7
have from their births less physical vigor than the boy body. Then
she claimed that there is ever passing from the woman out to man a
"female arrow," an influence, she meant, that thrills his soul, all
unlike that of man to man, etc. Well then here is a fact, a girl
dressed in boy's clothes stands side by side with a young man and
this "female arrow" is never perceived, at least not sufficiently to
cause the recipient to suspect the sex at his side [is] other than his
own.

Take that same being, array her in woman's dress, and tomorrow   8
morning place her at the same [spot]. While the tones of her voice,
the move of her hand, the glance of her are all the same as yesterday, her presence causes the sensuous thrill to rush to his very fingers and toes end. Now tell me the cause. Is the "arrow" in the
being, does it go out to that young man from the brain, the soul,
the femininity of that young woman, or is it in the flowing robes
and waving tresses, in the *knowledge* of the *difference of sex. The latter
I say.* At least to a very great extent. But say our opponents, such an
admission is so gross, so animal. Well I can't help that. *If it is fact,*
there it is. To me it is not coarse or gross, it is simply the answering
of the highest and holiest function of the physical organism, that is
that of reproduction. To be a *mother*, to be a *father* is the last and
highest wish of any human being, to *reproduce himself or herself.*

> With best love,
> SUSAN B. ANTHONY

Lynn Margulis, "Dear Susan B."

Dear Susan B.,
You have battled so nobly for the rights of your gender mates (to   1
vote, to control the destiny of their own bodies, to act as guardians
of their offspring and to manage their own financial resources)
against the fancy that Man, in his Wisdom, is born to reign
supreme in intellect.

Still, you provoke my response. Yes, there is the sensuous "thrill   2
to rush to the man's very fingers and toes end" due to the "knowledge of the difference of sex," as you put it. But I disagree that your
young man is fooled. He knows full well the "girl standing at his
side and dressed in boy's clothes" has a triangular pubis. Her gait,
her hip waddle, her peripheral glances betray her gender more profoundly than her long hair. Certainly if she were to don flowing
robes open to the air and wafted by her waving tresses these might
enhance his pleasure but they would not create his excitement in
the first place. The urgency to mate persists in all people as in all
other mammals because of the evolutionary drive to continue the
species; the inborn imperative for genes to reproduce and hormonal
differences that evolved over millions of years.

Both genders to a great degree are superficial. Some organisms I   3
work with have four genders; some even more. (To biologists, genders are complementary mating types. In other words, an organism
can mate and produce fertile offspring with a mature member of the
same species who is of a different gender, but never with one of its

same gender.) Hormonal differences lead to differences in men's and women's reproductive and other organs, metabolism, circulatory system, brain size and structure, and many aspects of behavior. Differences between men and women are never permanent and unchanging, but rather reflect frequencies in populations. For example, you'll find more tall people among a population of 20-year-old male basketball players than, say, 20-year-old female skaters. Similarly you'll find more weepers in the group of scorned lovers among women than men of the same age. But since the great gender differences are of relative number, rather than fixed type, generalizations are dangerous and the overgeneralizations (women=love; men= wisdom) are wicked.

A wonderful scientist friend of mine confided in me after he was   4
diagnosed with prostate cancer how his life had changed. He had long since lost his sexual appetite and capacity to perform. With treatment, his raging hormones had subsided. Now for the first time in a long life he could, as he put it, relate to women as people. This reality of this ability to take each person as an individual was not only new, it was delightful. Before the cancer, he confessed, we females, all of us, and not just his beloved wife, were to him titillating objects of potential pleasure. He now did not miss his once-active sex life. Sexually debilitated but strangely happy and encouraged, he remarked that his loss inspired him to listen to women undistractedly. Suffering a genital tumor ironically led him to enhance to twice the number of his many friends.

Although the detail of our sexual energies and their objects and ob-   5
jectives vastly vary, the existence of our sexuality itself is an undeniable truth. For two billion years, at least, all our ancestors have been sexual beings or they simply never would have survived. To me, a lover of knowledge, this truth so "gross," so "animal" deserves celebration not denial. All of us from fertile egg to embryo to corpse, are exactly that: warm, wet, furry animals compelled by the sexuality of our forefathers and foremothers to be, either directly or indirectly, our own exciting and excitable, provocative and provocable selves.

With fond admiration for the truth and beauty of your own rig-   6
orous efforts on our behalf.

LYNN

Dorothy Patterson, "Dear Ms. Anthony"

Dear Ms. Anthony,
You are to be commended for your untiring efforts in behalf of   1
women, your intervention in cases of injustice, your successful ef-

forts in securing for women the right to vote and your opposition to infanticide and abortion as "disgusting and degrading crimes."

Your letter to Elizabeth Stanton has crossed my desk with a request that I reply to some of the thoughts presented. You are precisely correct when you argue that the differences between men and women cannot be explained with "love" (as representative of women) and "wisdom" (as representative of men). This conclusion cannot be supported from the Bible, in which husbands are directed to "love their wives as Christ loved the church" (Ephesians 5:25) and wives are admonished to follow the example of the Proverbs' "woman of strength" who "opened her mouth with wisdom" (Proverbs 31:26). Women do indeed have a tremendous natural capacity to love. Wisdom is presented in Scripture as a spiritual gift (1 Corinthians 12:8) and is thus available to women or men, according to divine distribution. Physiological differences obviously are present in the design of the human body. Modern diapers even accommodate gender differences! Required skill tests in the military have been adjusted to reflect different standards for women in order to accommodate those physiological differences from men.

Preoccupation with a personal agenda or political cause can blur the remarkable genders and can prohibit an appreciation of the role assignments God has given as well as open the door to personal bitterness not only toward the opposite sex but also toward God Himself.

We must indeed insist that women have protection from injustices in every venue, freedom to express themselves, and the opportunity to pursue the highest levels of achievement. However, in pursuing these goals, we dare not "throw out the baby with the bath;" i.e., we must not abrogate the directives God has given for relationships between husbands and wives and for responsibilities of parents to their children. To do so opens the door for a society in which the marriages fail, children become violent and society itself abandons all absolutes.

Biblical directives to men and women are based upon their equality. Both are created in the image of God; both are ultimately responsible to God. However, from the moment of creation, differences are evident in how men and women are to function in the world. God created the woman as a "helper comparable to him" (the man). This compound expression describes perfectly the complementarity God designed—the woman is "comparable" or like the man—also in God's image; but the woman is a "helper": she has a different function or role assignment than the man. Thus, when they become "one flesh" in marriage, their union brings commonality of personhood and uniqueness of role assignments, enabling them to function better together than either could do alone.

One other danger is to suggest that the union of one man and one woman in marriage is primarily for reproduction. There is a unique joy and reward in linking hands with the Creator Himself to produce offspring, the next generation. However, wedded bliss is not limited to procreation but includes spiritual fellowship, loving companionship and sexual satisfaction.

So, my dear Mrs. Anthony, we agree on the value of women to their families, to society, and especially to God, whose children they are! We agree that they are to be protected from injustices, respected, honored, and encouraged to reach their highest potential. We would probably disagree on defining that highest potential. From my perspective, for a woman who chooses to marry, happiness and productivity will come from willingly submitting herself to the servant leadership of her husband, thereby coming under his provision and protection, and willingly making herself available to conceive and nurture offspring if God so blesses.

For me as a wife, these responsibilities surpass all others and demand my freshest energies, greatest creativity and complete commitment. My determination to accept these priorities and the responsibilities associated therewith are ultimately in obedience to God, and thus my obedience is ultimately to Him.

MRS. DOROTHY PATTERSON
Magnolia Hill

Katha Pollitt, "Dear Susan B. Anthony"

Dear Susan B. Anthony,
How I wish you could see the way the women's movement you helped to start has transformed our society—for the better. The life patterns of men and women have altered unrecognizably since your day.

We go to school together, work together, share a vastly enlarged terrain of common interests, even borrow from each other's wardrobes. Women are professors, Supreme Court justices, union organizers, bus drivers and bartenders. Most of the flagrant legal injustices you fought—the unequal marriage laws, for instance, that gave men automatic custody of children, despite much sentimental swooning over motherhood—have been swept away. Your generation of feminists, who in an age without reliable contraception put their faith in "voluntary motherhood," i.e., marital celibacy, and who tended to emphasize the dangers of sex over its pleasures, might blanch a bit at the vast enthusiasm of both sexes for nonmarital and nonreproductive sex, abortion and birth control, small families, divorce, dirty dancing and sexy underwear—even homosexuality.

In your day prostitution was a major industry, but even the most   3
dissolute roué felt entitled to marry a virgin. Today a man who made such a demand would sound like a religious maniac or a pervert—or someone who feared he couldn't measure up to comparison. Feminism is not the only cause of these momentous changes, but it has helped women to shape them according to their own needs and experiences.

Some things haven't changed, though. Women are still the sec-   4
ond sex—on the receiving end of a great deal of sexual violence, discrimination and cultural misogyny. Feminism is still blamed for every social problem under the sun, from juvenile crime (everything to do with children is still women's fault) to poverty. Tom Edsall, a respected political commentator with The Washington Post, even linked feminism with the Oklahoma City bombing, implying that once women discovered their clitorises (ask Mrs. Stanton), they no longer needed men, who had to compensate by joining violent militia groups that stressed "hyper-masculinity." There are plenty of people (including some women) who would like to see women put back in their place: subject to their husbands and dependent on marriage for a decent life, punished for having children out of wedlock or seeking a divorce, marginalized in the work place. "Stigma" is a popular word in policy circles these days.

Another thing that hasn't changed is the importance attached by   5
many to the question of differences between the sexes. It seems that the more our actual lives converge, the more tightly we cling to the notion that inalterable bedrock natural principles prove that the process has reached its outer limit. Few men could get away with claiming, like your self-satisfied Mr. Davis, that women's "inherent nature" was love and man's wisdom. But men are from Mars and women from Venus? The double standard permanently imprinted on our genes by evolution? Biological differences in the brain that explain why women can't excel at math or chess, enjoy pornography, find their car in the parking lot—even though lots of women do all those things? No one would deny that biological differences exist between the sexes, although it's not so easy to pin them down or explain why they matter. And here the historical record ought to give us pause. After all, in your day expert opinion was positive that college education made women infertile and drove them insane.

People are always saying feminism is dead—in fact, Time maga-   6
zine put a very unflattering dead-looking photo of you on its cover

just the other week. But of course, that's nonsense. Millions of women today proudly claim to be feminists, and millions more (the great majority) support the movement's goals even if they reject the label. I think the sociologist Arlie Hochschild had it right when she said we are in the middle of a stalled revolution, in which women's demands for equality at work and home, for social respect have come up against some rather resistant features of American life, from the lack of reliable high-quality child care to men who don't do their fair share at home. The good news: the Treasury put your face on the dollar coin. The bad news: the coin looks like a quarter and annoys everybody. I'd say we need another 150 years.

In sisterhood,
KATHA POLLITT

Questions

1. Review each of the four letters, looking for the sentence or two that most clearly states the writer's position. Write down what you find. If you can't find such a thesis statement, compose one that fits what the writer says in the letter.
2. What's at stake in these four letters on the issue of sexual difference? Identify the key areas of agreement and disagreement, paying close attention to concerns about what is true or good or possible.
3. With which of the four letter writers do you agree (or disagree) most? Give one reason for your agreement (or disagreement).
4. Why doesn't Patricia Cohen discuss the three letters by Margulis, Patterson, and Pollitt, or explicitly take a position on the issues of sexual difference and women's rights? Where do you think she stands?

PRACTICE 10.1

Identifying Issues and Positions

Reasonable arguments require an understanding of where people stand on the issues at stake in a particular debate. One way to develop your understanding is to report the issues and positions to others. Another way is to get involved in the ongoing debate. This practice offers you the opportunity to choose one of these ways (as outlined below) to develop your understanding of the debates about sexual difference, women's roles, and women's rights.

1. Cohen's introductory report summarizes the argument of Anthony's letter but says next to nothing about the content of the letters by Margulis, Patterson, and Pollitt. Taking up where Cohen leaves off, summarize the arguments of Margulis, Patterson, and Pollitt, and identify what's at issue in their letters. Keep in mind that your report is to be a continuation of Cohen's article and therefore should be suitable for publication in the *New York Times*.
2. Become a participant in the discussion by responding to one of the letter writers: Anthony, Margulis, Patterson, or Pollitt. We suggest that you choose the writer with whom you agree or disagree most. Be sure to state your position clearly and present a few reasons why you stand where you do. Remember that you are writing a letter, not a formal argument. Look at the various ways these four letter writers explain their positions and try one or two similar tactics.

POWERFUL APPEALS

In constructing and analyzing arguments, we still rely on the methods of appeal distinguished by Aristotle: ethical, emotional, and logical. All three may be used in one argument, although a writer may rely on one kind more than another. In an **ethical** appeal, the writer must convince his audience of his good character, of his knowledge of the issues at hand and the strength of his claims and evidence, and that he has the good of his audience in mind. In evaluating an **emotional** appeal, we look to see whether the writer offers nothing but simple responses to a complex problem; relies on stereotyping, or sets one group against another; or relies on emotion in place of facts or reason. In evaluating a **logical** appeal, we look for a well-structured argument with a thesis, as well as reasons that develop that thesis, including supporting evidence. An argument is greatly weakened by the use of **fallacies,** such as:

hasty generalization: to generalize from too little evidence.
  Example: Deaths from bicycle accidents have doubled in Middletown in the past year. Therefore, more Americans than ever are dying in bicycle accidents.

false cause: assuming that one thing caused another simply by association.
  Example: wearing your Yankees cap to every Yankees game because the first time you wore it, they won.

either/or: assuming that only two alternatives exist, one of which is clearly less desirable than the other, when in fact other possibilities exist.

Example: Either learn double-entry bookkeeping or never get a decent job after college.

non sequitur ("it does not follow"): the conclusion does not follow from the premises of the argument; i.e., the progression of thought is not logical.

Example: All men are mortal.
Socrates is a man.
My dog is named Socrates.

In evaluating an argument, then, you must analyze not only the structure of the argument—*how* it works—but also *what* its claims are, and whether they are well supported with evidence.

The following speech was given by President Woodrow Wilson to the United States Senate July 10, 1919. World War I, probably the bloodiest war in history, had ended in November 1918, leaving much of Europe devastated and an estimated 10 million dead. At the Paris Peace Conference in 1919 President Wilson insisted that a League of Nations be an integral part of the peace treaty. The function of the league, a forerunner of today's United Nations, was "to promote international cooperation and to achieve international peace and security." Wilson was a fervent supporter of the league, but in the Senate, he faced strong opposition to such an international treaty from proponents of a policy that would keep America isolated from European affairs. Wilson's aim in this speech was to convince the United States Senate to ratify the peace treaty and thus support a League of Nations. As you read his speech, note the kinds of appeals Wilson is making. Identify his reasons and consider how well he supports them with evidence.

READING

Woodrow Wilson, "An Address to the Senate," July 10, 1919

Gentlemen of the Senate: The treaty of peace with Germany was signed at Versailles on the twenty-eighth of June. I avail myself of the earliest opportunity to lay the treaty before you for ratification and to inform you with regard to the work of the Conference by which that treaty was formulated. 1

The treaty constitutes nothing less than a world settlement. 2

* * * *

The hopes of the nations allied against the central powers were at a very low ebb when our soldiers began to pour across the sea. 3

There was everywhere amongst them, except in their stoutest spirits, a sombre foreboding of disaster. The war ended in November, eight months ago, but you have only to recall what was feared in midsummer last, four short months before the armistice, to realize what it was that our timely aid accomplished alike for their morale and their physical safety. That first, never-to-be-forgotten action at Château-Thierry had already taken place. Our redoubtable soldiers and marines had already closed the gap the enemy had succeeded in opening for their advance upon Paris,—had already turned the tide of battle back towards the frontiers of France and begun the rout that was to save Europe and the world. Thereafter the Germans were to be always forced back, back, were never to thrust successfully forward again. And yet there was no confident hope. Anxious men and women, leading spirits of France, attended the celebration of the fourth of July last year in Paris out of generous courtesy,—with no heart for festivity, little zest for hope. But they came away with something new at their hearts: they have themselves told us so. The mere sight of our men,—of their vigour, of the confidence that showed itself in every movement of their stalwart figures and every turn of their swinging march, in their steady comprehending eyes and easy discipline, in the indomitable air that added spirit to everything they did,—made everyone who saw them that memorable day realize that something had happened that was much more than a mere incident in the fighting, something very different from the mere arrival of fresh troops. A great moral force had flung itself into the struggle. The fine physical force of those spirited men spoke of something more than bodily vigour. They carried the great ideals of a free people at their hearts and with that vision were unconquerable. Their very presence brought reassurance; their fighting made victory certain.

They were recognized as crusaders, and as their thousands 4 swelled to millions their strength was seen to mean salvation. And they were fit men to carry such a hope and make good the assurance it forecast. Finer men never went into battle; and their officers were worthy of them. This is not the occasion upon which to utter a eulogy of the armies America sent to France, but perhaps, since I am speaking of their mission, I may speak also of the pride I shared with every American who saw or dealt with them there. They were the sort of men America would wish to be represented by, the sort of men every American would wish to claim as fellow countrymen and comrades in a great cause. They were terrible[1] in battle, and gentle and helpful out of it, remembering the mothers and the

---

[1] *terrible:* in the sense of causing terror or fear.

sisters, the wives and the little children at home. They were free men under arms, not forgetting their ideals of duty in the midst of tasks of violence. I am proud to have had the privilege of being associated with them and of calling myself their leader.

But I speak now of what they meant to the men by whose sides they fought and to the people with whom they mingled with such utter simplicity, as friends who asked only to be of service. They were for all the visible embodiment of America. What they did made America and all that she stood for a living reality in the thoughts not only of the people of France but also of tens of millions of men and women throughout all the toiling nations of a world standing everywhere in peril of its freedom and of the loss of everything it held dear, in deadly fear that its bonds were never to be loosed, its hopes forever to be mocked and disappointed. 5

And the compulsion of what they stood for was upon us who represented America at the peace table. It was our duty to see to it that every decision we took part in contributed, so far as we were able to influence it, to quiet the fears and realize the hopes of the peoples who had been living in that shadow, the nations that had come by our assistance to their freedom. It was our duty to do everything that it was within our power to do to make the triumph of freedom and of right a lasting triumph in the assurance of which men might everywhere live without fear. 6

* * * *

The Turkish Empire...had fallen apart, as the Austro-Hungarian had. It had never had any real unity. It had been held together only by pitiless, inhuman force. Its people cried aloud for release, for succour from unspeakable distress, for all that the new day of hope seemed at last to bring within its dawn. Peoples hitherto in utter darkness were to be led out into the same light and given at last a helping hand. Undeveloped peoples and peoples ready for recognition but not yet ready to assume the full responsibilities of statehood were to be given adequate guarantees of friendly protection, guidance, and assistance. 7

And out of the execution of these great enterprises of liberty sprang opportunities to attempt what statesmen had never found the way before to do; an opportunity to throw safeguards about the rights of racial, national, and religious minorities by solemn international covenant; an opportunity to limit and regulate military establishments where they were most likely to be mischievous; an opportunity to effect a complete and systematic internationalization of waterways and railways which were necessary to the free eco- 8 nomic life of more than one nation and to clear many of the normal channels of commerce of unfair obstructions of law or of privilege; and the very welcome opportunity to secure for labour the concerted protection of definite international pledges of principle and practice.

These were not tasks which the Conference looked about it to find   9
and went out of its way to perform. They were thrust upon it by circumstances which could not be overlooked. The war had created them. In all quarters of the world old established relationships had been disturbed or broken and affairs were at loose ends, needing to be mended or united again, but could not be made what they were before. They had to be set right by applying some uniform principle of justice or enlightened expediency. And they could not be adjusted by merely prescribing in a treaty what should be done. New states were to be set up which could not hope to live through their first period of weakness without assured support by the great nations that had consented to their creation and won for them their independence. Ill governed colonies could not be put in the hands of governments which were to act as trustees for their people and not as their masters if there was to be no common authority among the nations to which they were to be responsible in the execution of their trust. Future international conventions with regard to the control of waterways, with regard to illicit traffic of many kinds, in arms or in deadly drugs, or with regard to the adjustment of many varying international administrative arrangements could not be assured if the treaty were to provide no permanent common international agency, if its execution in such matters was to be left to the slow and uncertain processes of cooperation by ordinary methods of negotiation.

* * * *

A league of free nations had become a practical necessity. Exam-   10
ine the treaty of peace and you will find that everywhere throughout its manifold provisions its framers have felt obliged to turn to the League of Nations as an indispensable instrumentality for the maintenance of the new order it has been their purpose to set up in the world, — the world of civilized men.

That there should be a league of nations to steady the counsels   11
and maintain the peaceful understandings of the world, to make, not treaties alone, but the accepted principles of international law as well, the actual rule of conduct among the governments of the world, had been one of the agreements accepted from the first as the basis of peace with the central powers. The statesmen of all the belligerent countries were agreed that such a league must be cre-

ated to sustain the settlements that were to be effected. But at first I think there was a feeling among some of them that, while it must be attempted, the formulation of such a league was perhaps a counsel of perfection which practical men, long experienced in the world of affairs, must agree to very cautiously and with many misgivings. It was only as the difficult work of arranging an all but universal adjustment of the world's affairs advanced from day to day from one stage of conference to another that it became evident to them that what they were seeking would be little more than something written upon paper, to be interpreted and applied by such methods as the chances of politics might make available if they did not provide a means of common counsel which all were obliged to accept, a common authority whose decisions would be recognized as decisions which all must respect.

And so the most practical, the most skeptical among them turned   12
more and more to the League as the authority through which international action was to be secured, the authority without which, as they had come to see it, it would be difficult to give assured effect either to this treaty or to any other international understanding upon which they were to depend for the maintenance of peace. The fact that the Covenant of the League was the first substantive part of the treaty to be worked out and agreed upon, while all else was in solution, helped to make the formulation of the rest easier. The Conference was, after all, not to be ephemeral. The concert of nations was to continue, under a definite Covenant which had been agreed upon and which all were convinced was workable. They could go forward with confidence to make arrangements intended to be permanent. The most practical of the conferees were at last the most ready to refer to the League of Nations the superintendence of all interests which did not admit of immediate determination, of all administrative problems which were to require a continuing oversight. What had seemed a counsel of perfection had come to seem a plain counsel of necessity. The League of Nations was the practical statesman's hope of success in many of the most difficult things he was attempting.

And it had validated itself in the thought of every member of the   13
Conference as something much bigger, much greater every way, than a mere instrument for carrying out the provisions of a particular treaty. It was universally recognized that all the peoples of the world demanded of the Conference that it should create such a continuing concert of free nations as would make wars of aggression and spoliation such as this that has just ended forever impossible. A cry had gone out from every home in every stricken land from which sons and brothers and fathers had gone forth to the great sacrifice that such a sacrifice should never again be exacted. It was

manifest why it had been exacted. It had been exacted because one nation desired dominion and other nations had known no means of defence except armaments and alliances. War had lain at the heart of every arrangement of the Europe,—of every arrangement of the world,—that preceded the war. Restive peoples had been told that fleets and armies, which they toiled to sustain, meant peace; and they now knew that they had been lied to: that fleets and armies had been maintained to promote national ambitions and meant war. They knew that no old policy meant anything else but force, force,—always force. And they knew that it was intolerable. Every true heart in the world, and every enlightened judgment demanded that, at whatever cost of independent action, every government that took thought for its people or for justice or for ordered freedom should lend itself to a new purpose and utterly destroy the old order of international politics. Statesmen might see difficulties, but the people could see none and could brook no denial. A war in which they had been bled white to beat the terror that lay concealed in every Balance of Power must not end in a mere victory of arms and a new balance. The monster that had resorted to arms must be put in chains that could not be broken. The united power of free nations must put a stop to aggression, and the world must be given peace. If there was not the will or the intelligence to accomplish that now, there must be another and a final war and the world must be swept clean of every power that could renew the terror. The League of Nations was not merely an instrument to adjust and remedy old wrongs under a new treaty of peace; it was the only hope for mankind. Again and again had the demon of war been cast out of the house of the peoples and the house swept clean by a treaty of peace; only to prepare a time when he would enter in again with spirits worse than himself. The house must now be given a tenant who could hold it against all such. Convenient, indeed indispensable, as statesmen found the newly planned League of Nations to be for the execution of present plans of peace and reparation, they saw it in a new aspect before their work was finished. They saw it as the main object of the peace, as the only thing that could complete it or make it worth while. They saw it as the hope of the world, and that hope they did not dare to disappoint. Shall we or any other free people hesitate to accept this great duty? Dare we reject it and break the heart of the world?

＊ ＊ ＊ ＊

America may be said to have just reached her majority as a world power. It was almost exactly twenty-one years ago that the results of the war with Spain put us unexpectedly in possession of rich islands   14 on the other side of the world and brought us into association with other governments in the control of the West Indies. It was regarded as a sinister and ominous thing by the statesmen of more than one European chancellery that we should have extended our power beyond the confines of our continental dominions. They were accustomed to think of new neighbours as a new menace, of rivals as watchful enemies. There were persons amongst us at home who looked with deep disapproval and avowed anxiety on such extensions of our national authority over distant islands and over peoples whom they feared we might exploit, not serve and assist. But we have not exploited them. And our dominion has been a menace to no other nation. We redeemed our honour to the utmost in our dealings with Cuba. She is weak but absolutely free; and it is her trust in us that makes her free. Weak peoples everywhere stand ready to give us any authority among them that will assure them a like friendly oversight and direction. They know that there is no ground for fear in receiving us as their mentors and guides. Our isolation was ended twenty years ago; and now fear of us is ended also, our counsel and association sought after and desired. There can be no question of our ceasing to be a world power. The only question is whether we can refuse the moral leadership that is offered us, whether we shall accept or reject the confidence of the world.

The war and the Conference of Peace now sitting in Paris seem   15
to me to have answered that question. Our participation in the war established our position among the nations and nothing but our own mistaken action can alter it. It was not an accident or a matter of sudden choice that we are no longer isolated and devoted to a policy which has only our own interest and advantage for its object. It was our duty to go in, if we were indeed the champions of liberty and of right. We answered to the call of duty in a way so spirited, so utterly without thought of what we spent of blood or treasure, so effective, so worthy of the admiration of true men everywhere, so wrought out of the stuff of all that was heroic, that the whole world saw at last, in the flesh, in noble action, a great ideal asserted and vindicated, by a nation they had deemed material and now found to be compact of the spiritual forces that must free men of every nation from every unworthy bondage. It is thus that a new role and a new responsibility have come to this great nation that we honour and which we would all wish to lift to yet higher levels of service and achievement.

The stage is set, the destiny disclosed. It has come about by no   16
plan of our conceiving, but by the hand of God who led us into this way. We cannot turn back. We can only go forward, with lifted eyes and freshened spirit, to follow the vision. It was of this that we

dreamed at our birth. America shall in truth show the way. The light streams upon the path ahead, and nowhere else.

PRACTICE 10.2

But Is It Reasonable?

To assess the strength of Wilson's argument, consider yourself a member of the United States Senate in July 1919. Make an outline of Wilson's speech to see how it is structured. Now look at the argument in terms of the three appeals we discussed in the introduction:

Ethical: How does Wilson present himself? How does he perceive his audience; i.e., what is his manner in addressing them? On what authority are his claims based?

Emotional: To what extent does Wilson appeal to emotions aroused by fear, hope, patriotism, religious faith, righteousness, moral duty, children, and so on?

Logical: What is Wilson's thesis? What reasons or claims does he give to support it, and what evidence does he present to develop those reasons or claims? Can you find any fallacies in his argument?

Does he rely on one kind of appeal more than another? As a member of the audience for this speech, how would you react to paragraphs 3, 4, and 5, for example? In what ways are the American soldiers described? Now look at paragraph 6: What is Wilson's purpose in praising the American soldiers who fought in World War I?

Write an analysis of Wilson's argument that considers the strength and validity of his appeals and concludes with your reasons why you would or would not be convinced to vote to support the League of Nations.

CLAIMS AND EVIDENCE

Logical arguments use reasons to develop a thesis. A reason consists of two parts: a claim, and evidence supporting that claim. Suppose, for example, that the thesis you want to argue is "Contemporary women are still the second sex" and that someone asks, "What makes you think so?" If you answer that you think as you do because of what feminist authorities like Katha Pollitt have said and because of persistent, gender-based income inequities, you are developing your thesis by presenting two claims. To make those claims reasonable, supporting evidence is needed. To support your first claim, you'll need to quote or paraphrase some specific statements by Katha Pollitt. As for the second claim, you'll need to supply evidence that gender-based income inequities do in fact exist. Without evidence, claims aren't actually reasonable.

There are many kinds of evidence, including examples, personal experiences, expert testimony, experimental findings, statistics, and facts. Many people consider statistics and facts more objective and therefore more trustworthy than either a personal experience or a single example. But in truth, no type of evidence is beyond question. When you are writing or reading arguments, always evaluate the evidence that supports each claim: How *relevant, accurate, typical,* and *sufficient* is it? And keep in mind that there are different ways of presenting the same evidence. For example, the number of homeless Americans might be given as three million or as 1%. Do these two numbers affect you in the same way? Which form of the homeless number does Mantsios use in the following piece? Does his choice fit in with the rest of his argument? As you read that argument, notice how Mantsios uses evidence, especially statistics, to support his claims about class realities in the United States.

READING

Gregory Mantsios, from "Class in America: Myths and Realities"

People in the United States don't like to talk about class. Or so it would seem. We don't speak about class privileges, or class oppression, or the class nature of society. These terms are not part of our everyday vocabulary, and in most circles they are associated with the language of the rhetorical fringe. Unlike people in most other parts of the world, we shrink from using words that classify along economic lines or that point to class distinctions: phrases like *working class, upper class,* and *ruling class* are rarely uttered by Americans.

For the most part, avoidance of class-laden vocabulary crosses class boundaries. There are few among the poor who speak of themselves as lower class; they identify, rather, with their race, ethnic group, or geographic location. Workers are more likely to identify with their employer, industry, or occupational group than with other workers, or with the working class.[1]

Neither are those at the other end of the economic spectrum likely to identify with the word *class.* In her study of 38 wealthy and socially prominent women, Susan Ostrander asked participants if they considered themselves members of the upper class. One participant responded,

I hate to use the word 'class.' We are responsible, fortunate people, old families, the people who have something.

Another said,

I hate [the term] upper class. It is so non–upper class to use it. I just call it 'all of us,' those who are wellborn.[2]

It is not that Americans, rich or poor, aren't keenly aware of class differences—those quoted above obviously are—it is that class is not in the domain of public discourse. Class is not discussed or debated in public because class identity has been stripped from popular culture. The institutions that shape mass culture and define the parameters of public debate have avoided class issues. In politics, in primary and secondary education, and in the mass media, formulating issues in terms of class is unacceptable, perhaps even un-American.   4

There are, however, two notable exceptions to this phenomenon. First, it is acceptable in the United States to talk about "the middle class." Interestingly enough, such references appear to be acceptable precisely because they mute class differences. References to the middle class by politicians, for example, are designed to encompass and attract the broadest possible constituency. Not only do references to the middle class gloss over differences, but also these references avoid any suggestion of conflict or exploitation.   5

This leads us to the second exception to the class avoidance phenomenon. We are, on occasion, presented with glimpses of the upper class and the lower class (the language used is "the wealthy" and "the poor"). In the media, these presentations are designed to satisfy some real or imagined voyeuristic need of "the ordinary person." As curiosities, the ground-level view of street life and the inside look at the rich and the famous serve as unique models, one to avoid and one to aspire to. In either case, the two models are presented without causal relation to each other: One is not rich because the other is poor. Similarly, when social commentators or liberal politicians draw attention to the plight of the poor, they do so in a manner that obscures the class structure and denies class exploitation. Wealth and poverty are viewed as one of several natural and inevitable states of being: Differences are only differences. One may even say differences are the American way, a reflection of American social diversity.   6

We are left with one of two possibilities: Either talking about class and recognizing class distinctions are not relevant to U.S. society, or we mistakenly hold a set of beliefs that obscure the reality of class differences and their impact on people's lives.   7

Let us look at four common, albeit contradictory, beliefs about the United States.   8

Myth Number 1: The United States is fundamentally a classless   9
society. Class distinctions are largely irrelevant today, and whatever
differences do exist in economic standing are, for the most part, insignificant. Rich or poor, we are all equal in the eyes of the law, and
such basic needs as health care and education are provided to all regardless of economic standing.

Myth Number 2: We are, essentially, a middle-class nation. De-   10
spite some variations in economic status, most Americans have
achieved relative affluence in what is widely recognized as a consumer society.

Myth Number 3: We are all getting richer. The American public as   11
a whole is steadily moving up the economic ladder, and each generation propels itself to greater economic well-being. Despite some fluc-
tuations, the United States position in the global economy has
brought previously unknown prosperity to most, if not all, North
Americans.

Myth Number 4: Everyone has an equal chance to succeed. Suc-   12
cess in the United States requires no more than hard work, sacrifice, and perseverance: "In America, anyone can be president." And
with a little luck (a clever invention or a winning lottery ticket),
there are opportunities for the easygoing as well. "In America, anyone can become a millionaire; it's just a matter of being in the right
place at the right time."

In trying to assess the legitimacy of these beliefs, we want to ask   13
several important questions. Are there significant class differences
among Americans? If these differences do exist, are they getting
bigger or smaller, and do these differences have a significant impact
on the way we live? Finally, does everyone in the United States really have an equal opportunity to succeed?

The Economic Spectrum

We will begin by looking at differences. An examination of official   14
census material reveals that variations in economic well-being are in
fact immense. Consider the following:

- The wealthiest 15 percent of the American population holds
  nearly 75 percent of the total household wealth in the country.
  That is, they own three-quarters of all the consumer durables
  (such as houses, cars, and stereos) and financial assets (such as
  stocks, bonds, property, and savings accounts).[3]
- Approximately 17,000 Americans declared more than $1 million
  of *annual* income on their 1985 tax returns; that is more money
  than most Americans expect to earn in an entire lifetime.[4]

Affluence and prosperity are clearly alive and well in certain seg- 15
ments of the United States population. However, this abundance is
in contrast to the poverty and despair that is also prevalent in the
United States. At the other end of the spectrum:

- A total of 15 percent of the American population—that is, one
  of every seven—live below the government's official poverty line
  (calculated in 1984 at $5,278 for an individual and $10,600 for a
  family of four).[5] These poor include a significant number of
  homeless people—approximately three million Americans.[6]
- Nearly a quarter of all the children in the United States under
  the age of six live in poverty.[7]

The contrast between rich and poor is sharp, and with nearly 16
one-third of the American population living at one extreme or the
other, it is difficult to argue that we live in a classless society. The
income gap between rich and poor in the United States (measured
as the percentage of total income held by the wealthiest 20 percent
of the population versus the poorest 20 percent) is approximately 11
to 1, one of the highest ratios in the industrialized world.[8] (For example, the ratio in Great Britain is 7 to 1; in Japan, it is 4 to 1.)

Reality 1: There are enormous differences in the economic status 17
of American citizens. A sizable proportion of the United States
population occupies opposite ends of the economic spectrum.

Nor can it be said that the majority of the American population 18
fares very well. In the middle range of the economic spectrum:

- 50 percent of the American population holds less than 3.5 percent of the nation's wealth.[9]
- The median household income (that is, half the American population made more and the other half made less) was $22,420 in
  1984. This is a margin of approximately $225 per week above the
  poverty level.[10]

The level of inequality is sometimes difficult to comprehend fully 19
with dollar figures and percentages. To help his students visualize the
distribution of income, the well-known economist Paul Samuelson
asked them to picture an income pyramid made of children's blocks,
with each layer of blocks representing $1000. If we were to construct
Samuelson's pyramid today, the peak of the pyramid would be much
higher than the Eiffel Tower, yet almost all of us would be within six
feet of the ground.[11] In other words, the distribution of income is
heavily skewed; a small minority of families take the lion's share of national income, and the remaining income is distributed among the

vast majority of middle-income and low-income families. Keep in mind that Samuelson's pyramid represents the distribution of income, not wealth. The distribution of wealth is skewed even further.

Reality 2: The middle class in the United States holds a very   20
small share of the nation's wealth.

Lottery millionaires and Horatio Alger stories notwithstanding,   21
evidence suggests that the level of inequality in the United States is getting higher. Statistically, it is getting harder to make it big and more difficult to even stay in the middle-income level. Census data show the gap between the rich and the poor to be the widest since the government began collecting information in 1947. Furthermore, the percentage of households earning at a middle-income level (that is, between 75% and 125% of the median income) has been falling steadily since 1967.[12] Most of those who disappeared from the middle-income level moved downward, not upward. And economic polarization is expected to increase over the next several decades.[13]

Reality 3: The middle class is shrinking in size, and most of those   22
leaving the ranks of the middle class are falling to a lower economic standing....

Class affects more than life-style and material well-being. It has a   23
significant impact on our physical and mental well-being as well.

Researchers have found an inverse relation between social class   24
and health. Lower-class standing is correlated to higher rates of infant mortality,[14] eye and ear disease, arthritis, physical disability, diabetes, nutritional deficiency,[15] respiratory disease,[16] mental illness,[17] and heart disease.[18] In all areas of health, poor people do not share the same life chances as those in the social class above them. Furthermore, lower-class standing is correlated to a lower quality of treatment for illness and disease. The results of poor health and poor treatment are born out in the life expectancy rates within each class. Aaron Antonovsky found that the higher your class standing, the higher your life expectancy.[19] Conversely, Lillian Guralnick studied the relationship between class and the death rate per 1000 in each of six age categories. Within each age group, she found that the lower one's class standing, the higher the death rate; in some age groups, the figures were as much as two and three times as high.[20]

Reality 4: From cradle to grave, class standing has a significant   25
impact on our chances for survival.

The lower one's class standing, the more difficult it is to secure   26
appropriate housing, the more time is spent on the routine tasks of everyday life, the greater is the percentage of income that goes to pay for food and other basic necessities,[21] and the greater is the likelihood of crime victimization.[22] Class can predict chances for both survival and success.

Notes

1. See Oscar Glantz, "Class Consciousness and Political Solidarity," *American Sociological Review*, vol. 23, August 1958, pp. 375–382; Robert Nisbet, "The Decline and Fall of Social Class," *Pacific Sociological Review*, vol. 2, Spring 1959, pp. 11–17; Charles W. Tucker, "A Comparative Analysis of Subjective Social Class: 1945–1963," *Social Forces*, no. 46, June 1968, pp. 508–514; and Ira Katznelson, *City Trenches: Urban Politics and Patterning of Class in the United States*, New York, Pantheon Books, 1981.

2. Susan Ostander, "Upper-Class Women: Class Consciousness as Conduct and Meaning," in *Power Structure Research*, by G. William Domhoff, Beverly Hills, California, Sage Productions, 1980, pp. 78–79.

3. Steven Rose, *The American Profile Poster*, New York, Pantheon Books, 1986, p. 31.

4. Barbara Kallen, "Getting By on $1 Million a Year," *Forbes*, October 27, 1986, p. 48.

5. "Characteristics of the Population Below the Poverty Level: 1984," from *Current Population Reports, Consumer Income Series P-60, no. 152*, Washington, D.C., U.S. Department of Commerce, Bureau of the Census, June 1986.

6. Constance Holden, "Homelessness: Experts Differ on Root Causes," *Science*, May 2, 1986, pp. 569–570.

7. "New Class of Children Is Poorer and the Prospects of Advancement Are Dim," *New York Times*, October 20, 1985, p. 56.

8. "United Nations National Accounts Statistics," *Statistical Papers, Series M no. 79*, New York, United Nations, 1985, pp. 1–11. See also Ira C. Magaziner and Robert B. Reich, *Minding America's Business: The Decline and Rise of the American Political Economy*," New York, Vintage, 1983, p. 23.

9. Steven Rose, *The American Profile Poster*, p. 31.

10. "Money Income of Households, Families, and Persons in the United States: 1984," *Current Population Reports P-60, no. 151*, Washington D.C., Department of Commerce, Bureau of Census, 1986, p. 1.

11. Paul Samuelson, *Economics*, 10th ed., New York, McGraw-Hill, 1976, p. 84.

12. Chris Tilly, "U-Turn on Equality," *Dollars and Sense*, May 1986, p. 11.

13. Paul Blumberg, *Inequality in an Age of Decline*, Oxford University Press, 1980.

14. Kyriakos S. Markides and Connie McFarland, "A Note on Recent Trends in the Infant Mortality–Socioeconomic Status Relationship," *Social Forces*, 61:1, September 1982, pp. 268–276.

15. Stanley D. Eitzen, *In Conflict and Order: Understanding Society*, Boston, Allyn and Bacon, 1985, p. 265. Lucile Duberman, *Social Inequality: Class and Caste in America*, New York, J. B. Lippincott, 1976, p. 200.

16. *Statistical Abstracts of the U.S.*, 1986, p. 116.

17. August Hollingshead and Frederick Redlick, *Social Class and Mental Illness: A Community Study*. New York, John Wiley, 1958. Also Leo Srole, *Mental Health in the Metropolis: The Midtown Manhattan Study*, New York, McGraw-Hill, 1962.

18. U.S. Bureau of the Census, *Social Indicators III*, Washington D.C., U.S. Government Printing Office, 1980, p. 101.

19. Aaron Antonovsky, "Social Class, Life Expectancy and Overall Mortality," *The Impact of Social Class*, New York, Thomas Crowell, 1972, pp. 467–491.

20. Lillian Guralnick, "Socioeconomic Differences in Mortality by Cause of Death," in *International Population Conference, Ottawa, 1963*, Liège, International Union for the Scientific Study of Population, 1964, p. 298, quoted in Antonovsky, op. cit. See also Steven Caldwell and Theodore Diamond, "Income Differentials in Mortality" in Linda Del Bene and Fritz Scheuren, eds. *Statistical Uses of Administrative Records*, Washington, D.C., United States Social Security Administration, 1979, p. 58. Harriet Duleep, "Measuring the Effect of Income on Adult Mortality Using Longitudinal Administrative Record Data," *Journal of Human Resources*, vol. 21, no. 2, Spring 1986.

21. Paul Jacobs, "Keeping the Poor, Poor?" in Jerome H. Skolnick and Elliot Currie, *Crisis in American Institutions*, Boston, Little, Brown and Company, 1982, pp. 104–114.

22. Dennis W. Roncek, "Dangerous Places: Crime and Residential Environment," *Social Forces*, 60:1, September 1981, pp. 74–96.

Questions

1. Why don't Americans like to use the term *class*?
2. What is Mantsios's main argument against the myth of a classless society?
3. What are the realities? Do numbers always qualify as bearers of reality? What other statistics might Mantsios have used in his argument?

■ **PRACTICE 10.3**

What's True Now?

In stating his four claims or "realities," Mantsios uses the present tense. But if you look at the endnotes, you'll see that the statistical evidence comes from sources published in 1986 or earlier. Clearly, that evidence was relevant when Mantsios first published his essay in 1988, but that evidence is no longer current enough for us to accept Mantsios's realities as reasonable renditions of what's true *now*, in the present time. These days, is it really true that "a sizable proportion" of Americans are either rich or poor? that only a "very small share" of the nation's wealth belongs to the middle class? that the middle class is decreasing in numbers and economic power? that class standing affects one's "chances for survival and success"?

To answer these questions, you need to consult some up-to-date statistics. More specifically, we invite you to choose *one* of Mantsios's claims and see to what extent it is true nowadays. List the evidence Mantsios uses to support his claim and then consult current versions of the same *kinds* of statistical sources.

Mantsios uses two main kinds of sources for his statistics: government census reports and published books and articles. Nowadays, you can get government census data on-line as well as in print. The reference section of your college's library probably has the current edition of *Statistical Abstracts of the United States* in print or on CD-Rom. Online, you may find what you're looking for at one of the following government sites: **<http://www.census.gov>** or **<http://www.census.gov/stat_abstract>** or for labor statistics, **<http://stats.bls.gov>**. If you want links to additional online sources for statistics, go to **<http://odwin.ucsd.edu/ idata/>**. As for published books and articles, we recommend checking out the most current volume of *The State of Working America*, a biennial report written under the auspices of the Economic Policy Institute (**<http://www .epinet.org/>**) and published as a book in 1999 by Cornell University Press. Of course, there are many other books and articles that include relevant statistics, some of which are listed in the "Find Out More" section of a Web site devoted to the issue of inequality: **<http://www.inequality.org>**.

As you consult one or more of these sources, keep your goal in mind. You are updating Mantsios's evidence and, if need be, modifying his claim so that it fits the current statistics. In a paragraph or two, write out your update; begin with the claim and then present the supporting statistical evidence you found to support that claim. Don't forget to document your sources.

ARGUING ABOUT THE VALUE OF INEQUALITY

Arguments about what's true have a way of turning into arguments about what's good. At first, we may disagree about the true state of things — the realities. Arguing may then occasion a meeting of the minds about what's true, but when it does, it doesn't mean there will be nothing left to debate. What you make of the truth may not be the same as what I make of it, perhaps because our values differ. To some extent, values are always implicated in our arguments, but sometimes they become what is explicitly at stake: How should this or that situation be evaluated? To what extent is it good or bad?

People don't always agree on the answers to value questions, as the following two pieces attest. Both George Will, an editorial commentator for *Newsweek* magazine, and Isabel V. Sawhill, a research fellow at the Brookings Institute, agree that income inequality exists and is increasing in the United States. But is this state of affairs bad? Will doesn't think so, as the title of his editorial suggests. Does Sawhill agree with Will's argument about what's good about inequality? To what extent do she and Will share the same values?

READING

George Will, "Healthy Inequality," from *Newsweek*, October 28, 1996

Economists today perform the stern duty formerly done by dour   1
Calvinist divines, that of telling many complainers that nothing can be done about their complaints and, besides, the suffering is good for them. Now pastors Jeremy Greenwood and Mehmet Yorukoglu argue convincingly that something currently decried as a social dysfunction and injustice—the combination of slowing productivity growth and widening income inequality—is actually a recurring and benign phenomenon.

Greenwood and Yorukoglu, economists at the universities of   2
Rochester and Chicago respectively, date the onset of current discontents about both productivity and inequality from 1974, when two lines on a graph began moving in ways which, taken together, looked peculiar. One line charted labor productivity. It had been ascending steeply since the mid-1950s. In 1974 the line began a modest decline. The other line charted investment in information technology. What had been an irregular and modest ascent since the mid-1950s began a dramatically steep ascent that continues to this day. It did so because of what a third graph line records—a steep decline in the price of information technology.

These three developments seemed counterintuitive. Should not   3
rapid investment in new technology both explain, and be explained

by, the increased productivity of labor equipped with the technology? Quite the contrary, say Greenwood and Yorukoglu. They say that often one consequence of new technology is an initial decline in productivity associated with the cost of learning to use the new machines. And the learning process puts a premium on quick learners, meaning skilled labor. This widens the gap between the incomes of the skilled and the unskilled.

So 1974 in America resembled 1770 in Britain, and 1840 in   4
America. At those times, new technologies began appearing, machines that would eventually enhance the productivity of labor, but not before a period of costly learning. Information technologies are causing economic turbulence—discomforting but creative turbulence—much as steam and, later, electricity did.

When around 1770 Watt's engine brought steam power to   5
British manufacturing, the mechanization of manufacturing spread rapidly, as did complementary inventions, such as new machines for spinning cotton. And the price of spun cotton fell two thirds by 1841. New methods of producing wrought iron caused production to increase 500 percent between 1788 and 1815 and prices to fall 36 percent between 1801 and 1815, although the general price level rose 50 percent between 1770 and 1815.

Then industrialism came to America. Between 1774 and 1815 the   6
per capita stock of equipment grew just 0.7 percent per year. But between 1815 and 1860 annual growth quadrupled to 2.8 percent, and it soared to 4.5 percent between 1860 and 1900. In 1830 there were just 30 miles of railroad tracks. By 1840 there were 2,808. In 1860 there were 30,000. The aggregate capacity of steam engines quadrupled between 1840 and 1860. All of which put a premium on the skills of engineers, machinists, boilermakers, carpenters and joiners, whose wages grew relative to those of common laborers.

Was this inequality a bad thing? No, it was an incentive for   7
people to invest in self-improvement. And it advanced the nation's economic sophistication. (The increased industrial sophistication was concentrated primarily in the North. Was that inequality a bad thing? Not after Fort Sumter.)[1]

At the dawn of this century, industrial applications of electricity   8
were slowed by the existence of large stocks of equipment and structures for water and steam power. So at first electricity was used primarily in rapidly expanding industries that were designing new plants adapted to electricity. So the rapid-growers grew still more rapidly. More inequalities. And more social benefits.

[1]On April 12, 1861, the Confederates fired the first shot of the Civil War against the Union-held Fort Sumter in Charleston, South Carolina.

By one estimate, since the Second World War 60 percent of U.S.   9
economic growth has derived from the introduction of increasingly
efficient equipment, the most important of which have been information machines. Around 1950 computers entered the economy, essentially as calculating devices, and the cost of crunching numbers
plummeted. Between 1950 and 1980 the cost of a MIP (million instructions per second) fell between 27 and 50 percent *annually*. In the
1960s computers became labor-saving devices for storing, sorting
and retrieving data, the cost of which probably fell at an annual rate of
25 to 30 percent between 1960 and 1985. But the labor-saving applications were job-creating: by 1980 there were 1.13 times as many information workers as production workers, up from 0.22 in 1900.

Now computers have become communication devices, produc-   10
ing myriad streamlinings in business organizations, and other economic efficiencies. Information technologies also are producing
additional inequality, as those people who are talented at using information technologies reap rewards that are, in turn, incentives for
other people to invest time and money in increasing their inventories of talents. Thus does society progress to higher levels of sophistication. Such progress is, as usual, accompanied by a chorus from
laments of sentimentalists who consider it a cosmic injustice that
progress has a price. And the laments are loudest from those who
make a fetish of equality.

Equality—other than equality before the law—is a problematic,   11
and often pernicious, social value. The celebration of equality of
condition often is merely envy tarted up in the clothing of compassion. Furthermore, when equality of outcomes, rather than equal
opportunity, is regarded as a matter of moral urgency, this often
disposes society to a surly resentment of virtues and talents that, for
good reasons, receive high rewards.

A society that chafes against stratifications derived from dispari-   12
ties of talents will be a society that discourages individual excellence. Such a society also will resent the excellence it cannot
discourage, and hence such a society will have a curdled spirit. As a
character in Mary McCarthy's novel "Birds of America" says, "I've
decided that may be why the Parisians are so sullen and why they
drink. They thought of equality first."

Questions

1. Write a one-paragraph summary of Will's argument that answers the following questions: What thesis is Will arguing?
   What are the main reasons Will presents to develop and support
   his thesis?

2. Will opens with an analogy between contemporary economists and Calvinist pastors (par. 1). He follows this analogy with another one between 1974 in the United States and 1770 in Britain (pars. 4 and 5). Which of these analogies strikes you as more convincing? How and why is it more convincing?
3. What does Will value most? Why does he value it more than other things?

READING

Isabel V. Sawhill, "Still the Land of Opportunity?" (from *The Public Interest,* Spring 1999)

America is known as "the land of opportunity." But whether it deserves this reputation has received too little attention. Instead, we seem mesmerized by data on the distribution of incomes which show that incomes are less evenly distributed than they were 20 or 30 years ago. In 1973, the richest 5 percent of all families had 11 times as much income as the poorest one-fifth. By 1996, they had almost 20 times as much. But it is not only the distribution of income that should concern us. It is also the system that produces that distribution.

Indeed, I would argue that one cannot judge the fairness of any particular distribution without knowing something about the rules of the game that gave rise to it. Imagine a society in which incomes were as unequal as they are in the United States but where everyone had an equal chance of receiving any particular income—that is, in which the game was a completely unbiased lottery. Although some, especially those who are risk adverse, might blanch at the prospect of losing, and might wish for a more equal set of outcomes a priori (as most famously argued by John Rawls),[1] others might welcome the chance to do exceedingly well. But—and this is the important point—no one could complain that they hadn't had an equal shot at achieving a good outcome. So the perceived fairness of the process is critical, and the rules governing who wins and who loses matter as much as the outcomes they produce.

In talking about this issue, we often invoke the phrase "equal opportunity," but we seldom reflect on what we really mean by "opportunity," how much of it we really have, and what we should do if

---

[1]John Rawls: a contemporary moral philosopher; author of *A Theory of Justice* (1971).

it's in short supply. Instead, we have an increasingly sterile debate over income equality. One side argues for a redistribution of existing incomes, through higher taxes on the wealthy and more income support for the poor. The other side argues that inequality reflects differences in individual talent and effort, and as such is a spur to higher economic growth, as well as just compensation for unequal effort and skill. If there is any common ground between these two views, it probably revolves around the idea of opportunity and the measures needed to insure that it exists.

Opportunity first

The American public has always cared more about equal opportunity than about equal results. The commitment to provide everyone with a fair chance to develop their own talents to the fullest is a central tenet of the American creed. This belief has deep roots in American culture and American history and is part of what distinguishes our public philosophy from that of Europe. Socialism has never taken root in American soil.

Public opinion is only one reason to refocus the debate. Another is that the current emphasis on income inequality begs the question of how much inequality is too much. Virtually no one favors a completely equal distribution of income. Inequality in rewards encourages individual effort and contributes to economic growth. Many would argue that current inequalities far exceed those needed to encourage work, saving, and risk taking, and further that we need not worry about the optimal degree of inequality in a society that has clearly gone beyond that point. But the argument is hard to prove and will not satisfy those who believe that inequality is the price we pay for a dynamic economy and the right of each individual to retain the benefits from his or her own labor. In light of these debates, if any public consensus is to be found, it is more likely to revolve around the issue of opportunity than around the issue of equality.

A final reason why opportunity merits our attention is that it gets at the underlying processes that produce inequality. It addresses not just the symptoms but the causes of inequality. And a deeper understanding of these causes can inform not only one's sense of what needs to be done but also one's sense of whether the existing distribution of income is or is not a fair one.

Three societies

Consider three hypothetical societies, all of which have identical distributions of income as conventionally measured. The first society is a meritocracy. It provides the most income to those who work

4

5

6

7

the hardest and have the greatest talent, regardless of class, gender, race, or other characteristics. The second one, I will call a "fortune-cookie society." In this society, where one ends up is less a matter of talent or energy than pure luck. The third society is class-stratified. Family background in this society is all important, and thus you need to pick your parents well. The children in this society largely end up where they started, so social mobility is small to nonexistent.

The United States and most other advanced countries are a mixture of these three ideal types. Given a choice between the three, most people would probably choose to live in a meritocracy. Not only do the rules determining success in a meritocracy produce greater social efficiency but, in addition, most people consider them inherently more just. Success is dependent on individual action. In principle, by making the right choices, anyone can succeed, whereas in a class-stratified or fortune-cookie society, people are buffeted by forces outside their control. So, even if the distribution of income in each case were identical, most of us would judge them quite differently. We might even prefer to live in a meritocracy with a less equal distribution of income than in a class-stratified or fortune-cookie society with a more equal distribution. Indeed, social historians have found this to be the case. The American public accepts rather large disparities in income and wealth because they believe that such disparities are produced by a meritocratic process. Even those at the bottom of the distribution believe that their children will do better than they have. It is this prospect, and the sense of fairness that accompanies it, that has convinced the American body politic to reject a social-welfare state.

For the last 25 years, the top one-fifth of the population has been improving their prospects while the other 80 percent has lagged behind. Yet no one has rebelled. The many have not imposed higher taxes on the few. (Small steps in this direction were taken in 1993, but the Democratic president who proposed them later apologized to a group of wealthy donors for doing so.) Even welfare recipients tell survey researchers that they consider the new rules requiring them to work at whatever job they can get fair. They plan on "bettering themselves." Such optimism flies in the face of studies suggesting that women on welfare (and those similar to them) will earn poverty-level wages for most of their lives. But it is an optimism that is characteristically, if in this case poignantly, American.

Several points need to be made about our purported meritocracy. The first is that even a pure meritocracy leaves less room for individual agency than is commonly believed. Some of us are blessed with good genes and good parents while others are not. The second is that the United States, while sharing these inherent flaws with other meritocracies, remains a remarkably dynamic and fluid society. Although it is not a pure meritocracy, it has moved closer to that ideal than at any time in its past. The third point is that, in the past, a rapid rate of economic growth provided each new generation with enhanced opportunities. It was this fact, in large part, that contributed to our image as the land of opportunity. But a mature economy cannot count on this source of upward mobility to leaven existing disparities; it needs instead to repair its other two opportunity-enhancing institutions: families and schools. The remainder of this essay elaborates on each of these points.

The inherent limits of a meritocracy

In a meritocracy, one would expect to find considerable social and economic fluidity. In such a system, the abler and more ambitious members of society would continually compete to occupy the top rungs. Family or class background, per se, should matter little in the competition while education should matter a lot.   11

The social-science literature contains a surprising amount of information on this topic. Based on my own reading of this literature, I would argue that social origins or family background matter a good deal. Not everyone begins the race at the same starting line. The kind of family into which a child is born has as much or more influence on that child's adult success than anything else we can measure. Yes, education is important too, but when we ask who gets a good education, it turns out to be disproportionately those from more advantaged backgrounds. Well-placed parents are much more likely to send their children to good schools and to encourage them to succeed academically. In short, although not as evident as in a class-stratified society, even in a meritocracy one had better pick one's parents well.   12

Why do families matter so much? There are at least three possibilities. The first is that well-placed parents can pass on advantages to their children without even trying: They have good genes. The second is that they have higher incomes, enabling them to provide better environments for their children. The third is that they are simply better parents, providing their children an appropriate mix of warmth and discipline, emotional security and intellectual stimulation, and preparation for the wider world.   13

It has proved difficult to discover which of these factors is most important. However, as Susan Mayer demonstrates in her recent book, *What Money Can't Buy*, the role of material resources has probably been exaggerated. Most studies have failed to adjust for the fact that parents who are successful in the labor market have competencies that make them good parents as well. It is these com-   14 petencies, rather than the parents' income, that help their children succeed. I don't want to leave the impression that income doesn't matter at all. It enables families to move to better neighborhoods; it relieves the stresses of daily living that often produce inadequate parenting; and, most obviously, it enables parents to purchase necessities. Still, additional income assistance, although possibly desirable on other grounds, is not likely to produce major changes in children's life prospects.

Genes clearly matter. We know this from studies of twins or siblings who have been raised apart. However, IQ or other measures of ability are at least somewhat malleable, and differences in intelligence only partially explain who ends up where on the ladder of success. Good parenting and an appropriate home environment are much harder to measure, but studies suggest that they may explain a substantial portion of the relationship between family background and later success in school or in the labor market. In addition, children with two parents fare much better than those with only one, in part because they have higher incomes but also because the presence of a second parent appears, according to all of the evidence, to be beneficial in and of itself.

So, for whatever reason, families matter. Unless we are willing to take children away from their families, the deck is stacked from the beginning. And even if one could remove children from their homes, there would still be the pesky little matter of differences in genetic endowments. Since a meritocracy has no good way of dealing with these two fundamental sources of inequality, it is a pipe dream to think that it can provide everyone with an equal chance. If we want a society in which there is less poverty and more equality, we will have to work harder and more creatively to compensate for at least some of these initial advantages and disadvantages.

* * * *

Class stratification

Not only has economic growth slowed but its benefits now accrue almost entirely to those with the most education. Simply being a loyal, hard-working employee no longer guarantees that one will achieve the American dream. Whatever progress has been made in extending educational opportunities, it has not kept pace with the demand. Men with a high-school education or less have been particularly hard hit. The combination of slower growth and a distribution of wage gains that have favored women over men and the college educated over the high-school educated since the early 1970s has hurt poorly educated men. Their real incomes are less than one-half what they otherwise would have been in 1995. Education is, to put it simply, the new stratifying variable in American life. This, of course, is what one would hope for in a meritocracy, but only if everyone has a shot at a good education.

It is said that Americans would rather talk about sex than money.   18
But they would rather talk about money than class, and some would rather not talk about the underclass at all. Many people consider the label pejorative, but research completed in the past decade suggests that such a group may indeed exist. Its hallmark is its lack of mobility. This group is not just poor but persistently poor, often over several generations. It is concentrated in urban neighborhoods characterized by high rates of welfare dependency, joblessness, single parenthood, and dropping out of school. It is disproportionately made up of racial and ethnic minorities. Although still relatively small (a little under three million people in 1990, according to an Urban Institute analysis of Census data), it appears to be growing. Anyone who doubts the existence of such a group need only read the detailed first-hand portrayals of ghetto life in Alex Kotlowitz's *There Are No Children Here*, Leon Dash's *Rosa Lee*, or Ron Suskind's *A Hope in the Unseen*. These accounts suggest that dysfunctional families, poor schools, and isolation from mainstream institutions are depriving a significant segment of our youth of any prospect of one day joining the middle class.

All of this is by way of a caution: Whatever the broader trends in   19
economic and social mobility, there may be enclaves that get left behind. Moreover, one can argue that it is this subgroup—and their lack of mobility—that should be our main concern. The very existence of such a group threatens our sense of social cohesion and imposes large costs on society. Its nexus with race is particularly disturbing.

Questions

1. Sawhill is interested in judging the "fairness" of income and wealth distribution, but believes that to do so, one needs to refer to "the rules of the game" that gave rise to the distribution (par. 2). According to Sawhill, what are the rules that gave rise to the current state of income and wealth distribution?
2. Why does Sawhill believe that "equal opportunity" (par. 5) is a better focus for debate than income inequality?
3. Although Sawhill is less explicit than Will about what she values, what's good—or fair—is the key issue of her piece. As you see it, what does Sawhill value most? Why does she value that above other possibilities?

■ **PRACTICE 10.4**

Taking a Position

When values are at stake, it is often hard to take a position, in part because our values are multiple and complex, rather than singular and simpleminded. To help college students recognize and work through ethical dilemmas, the Markkula Center for Applied Ethics has developed a Web site that you might want to check out: it is called the *Ethics Connection* and can be found at the following address: **<http://scuish.scu.edu/Ethics/>**.

Other sites on the Web offer you a chance to participate in socio-political arguments that are value laden. For example, the Politics and Society section of the *Atlantic Unbound* site (**<http://www.theatlantic.com/unbound/>**) allows visitors to take part in an ongoing forum by posting and riposting messages, some of which are provoked by current or previous roundtable discussions. The roundtables are online debates by a handful of invited participants, each of whom states a position on the topic at issue and later responds to another participant's position.

For this practice, consider yourself a participant in a roundtable debate on the following issue: Would the United States be a better place to live or would Americans be better off as a people if income were more equally distributed? You may participate in this roundtable either by writing a paper that states and explains your position on the issue or by responding in writing to one of the other two participants' statements: Will's "Healthy Inequality" or Sawhill's "Still the Land of Opportunity?" Argumentative responses usually take one of two forms: a defense or a critique of the other writer's reasoning. Since this is a debate, be sure to frame your position statement or response as an argument.

ARGUING ABOUT SCHOOL CHOICE

The need for educational reform is one of today's most important topics. Policy debates center on exactly what should be done, with school choice emerging as a key issue. The following selections contribute to both sides of the debate surrounding school choice. This issue produces multilevel arguments because the writers not only present reasons and evidence for their positions but also address assumptions and counterarguments. The first reading, Chubb and Moe's pro-choice argument, appeared in the *Brookings Review* in 1990 and has been cited frequently by both sides in the school choice argument. In the second reading, Nancy Kanode argues that the use of vouchers for private schools will undermine the public education system and that the use of public funds to support religious education is a violation of the Constitution. You should consider the following as material to be used when you consider what policy you might advocate.

READING

John E. Chubb and Terry M. Moe, "Choice *Is* a Panacea" (1990)

For America's public schools, the last decade has been the worst of times and the best of times. Never before have the public schools been subjected to such savage criticism for failing to meet the nation's educational needs—yet never before have governments been so aggressively dedicated to studying the schools' problems and finding the resources for solving them.

The signs of poor performance were there for all to see during the 1970s. Test scores headed downward year after year. Large numbers of teenagers continued to drop out of school. Drugs and violence poisoned the learning environment. In math and science, two areas crucial to the nation's success in the world economy, American students fell far behind their counterparts in virtually every other industrialized country. Something was clearly wrong.

During the 1980s a growing sense of crisis fueled a powerful movement for educational change, and the nation's political institutions responded with aggressive reforms. State after state increased spending on schools, imposed tougher requirements, introduced more rigorous testing, and strengthened teacher certification and training. And, as the decade came to an end, creative experiments of various forms—from school-based management to magnet schools—were being launched around the nation.

We think these reforms are destined to fail. They simply do not get to the root of the problem. The fundamental causes of poor academic performance are not to be found in the schools, but rather in the institutions by which the schools have traditionally been governed. Reformers fail by automatically relying on these institutions to solve the problem—when the institutions are the problem.

The key to better schools, therefore, is institutional reform. What we propose is a new system of public education that eliminates most political and bureaucratic control over the schools and relies instead on indirect control through markets and parental choice. These new institutions naturally function to promote and nurture the kinds of effective schools that reformers have wanted all along.

Schools and Institutions

Three basic questions lie at the heart of our analysis. What is the relationship between school organization and student achievement? What are the conditions that promote or inhibit desirable forms of organization? And how are these conditions affected by their institutional settings? 6

Our perspective on school organization and student achievement is in agreement with the most basic claims and findings of the "effective schools" literature, which served as the analytical base of the education reform movement throughout the 1980s. We believe, as most others do, that how much students learn is not determined simply by their aptitude or family background—although, as we show, these are certainly influential—but also by how effectively schools are organized. By our estimates, the typical high school student tends to learn considerably more, comparable to at least an extra year's worth of study, when he or she attends a high school that is effectively organized rather than one that is not. 7

Generally speaking, effective schools—be they public or private—have the kinds of organizational characteristics that the mainstream literature would lead one to expect: strong leadership, clear and ambitious goals, strong academic programs, teacher professionalism, shared influence, and staff harmony, among other things. These are best understood as integral parts of a coherent syndrome of organization. When this syndrome is viewed as a functioning whole, moreover, it seems to capture the essential features of what people normally mean by a team—principals and teachers working together, cooperatively and informally, in pursuit of a common mission. 8

How do these kinds of schools develop and take root? Here again, our own perspective dovetails with a central theme of educational analysis and criticism: the dysfunctions of bureaucracy, the value of autonomy, and the inherent tension between the two in American public education. Bureaucracy vitiates the most basic requirements of effective organization. It imposes goals, structures, and requirements that tell principals and teachers what to do and how to do it—denying them not only the discretion they need to exercise their expertise and professional judgment but also the flexibility they need to develop and operate as teams. The key to effective education rests with unleashing the productive potential already present in the schools and their personnel. It rests with granting them the autonomy to do what they do best. As our study of American high schools documents, the freer schools are from external control the more likely they are to have effective organizations. 9

Only at this late stage of the game do we begin to part company with the mainstream. While most observers can agree that the public 10 schools have become too bureaucratic and would benefit from sub-stantial grants of autonomy, it is also the standard view that this transformation can be achieved within the prevailing framework of democratic control. The implicit assumption is that, although polit-ical institutions have acted in the past to bureaucratize, they can now be counted upon to reverse course, grant the schools auton-omy, and support and nurture this new population of autonomous schools. Such an assumption, however, is not based on a systematic understanding of how these institutions operate and what their con-sequences are for schools.

Political Institutions

Democratic governance of the schools is built around the imposi-tion of higher-order values through public authority. As long as that authority exists and is available for use, public officials will come under intense pressure from social groups of all political stripes to use it. And when they do use it, they cannot blithely as-sume that their favored policies will be faithfully implemented by the heterogeneous population of principals and teachers below — whose own values and professional views may be quite different from those being imposed. Public officials have little choice but to rely on formal rules and regulations that tell these people what to do and hold them accountable for doing it.   11

These pressures for bureaucracy are so substantial in themselves that real school autonomy has little chance to take root throughout the system. But they are not the only pressures for bureaucracy. They are compounded by the political uncertainty inherent in all democratic politics: those who exercise public authority know that other actors with different interests may gain authority in the future and subvert the policies they worked so hard to put in place. This knowledge gives them additional incentive to embed their policies in protective bureaucratic arrangements — arrangements that re-duce the discretion of schools and formally insulate them from the dangers of politics.   12

These pressures, arising from the basic properties of democratic control, are compounded yet again by another special feature of the public sector. Its institutions provide a regulated, politically sensi-tive setting conducive to the power of unions, and unions protect the interests of their members through formal constraints on the governance and operation of schools — constraints that strike di-rectly at the schools' capacity to build well-functioning teams based on informal cooperation.   13

The major participants in democratic governance — including the unions — complain that the schools are too bureaucratic.   14

And they mean what they say. But they are the ones who bureaucratized the schools in the past, and they will continue to do so, even as they tout the great advantages of autonomy and professionalism. The incentives to bureaucratize the schools are built into the system.

Market Institutions

This kind of behavior is not something that Americans simply have to accept, like death and taxes. People who make decisions about education would behave differently if their institutions were different. The most relevant and telling comparison is to markets, since it is through democratic control and markets that American society makes most of its choices on matters of public importance, including education. Public schools are subject to direct control through politics. But not all schools are controlled in this way. Private schools—representing about a fourth of all schools—are subject to indirect control through markets.

15

What difference does it make? Our analysis suggests that the difference is considerable and that it arises from the most fundamental properties that distinguish the two systems. A market system is not built to enable the imposition of higher-order values on the schools, nor is it driven by a democratic struggle to exercise public authority. Instead, the authority to make educational choices is radically decentralized to those most immediately involved. Schools compete for the support of parents and students, and parents and students are free to choose among schools. The system is built on decentralization, competition, and choice.

16

Although schools operating under a market system are free to organize any way they want, bureaucratization tends to be an unattractive way to go. Part of the reason is that virtually everything about good education—from the knowledge and talents necessary to produce it, to what it looks like when it is produced—defies formal measurement through the standardized categories of bureaucracy.

17

The more basic point, however, is that bureaucratic control and its clumsy efforts to measure the unmeasurable are simply *unnecessary* for schools whose primary concern is to please their clients. To do this, they need to perform as effectively as possible, which leads them, given the bottom-heavy technology of education, to favor decentralized forms of organization that take full advantage of strong leadership, teacher professionalism, discretionary judgment, informal cooperation, and teams. They also need to ensure that they provide the kinds of services parents and students want and that they have the capacity to cater and adjust to their clients' special-

18

ized needs and interests, which this same syndrome of effective organization allows them to do exceedingly well.

Schools that operate in an environment of competition and   19
choice thus have strong incentives to move toward the kinds of
"effective-school" organizations that academics and reformers
would like to impose on the public schools. Of course, not all
schools in the market will respond equally well to these incentives.
But those that falter will find it more difficult to attract support,
and they will tend to be weeded out in favor of schools that are better organized. This process of natural selection complements the
incentives of the marketplace in propelling and supporting a population of autonomous, effectively organized schools.

Institutional Consequences

No institutional system can be expected to work perfectly under   20
real-world conditions. Just as democratic institutions cannot offer
perfect representation or perfect implementation of public policy,
so markets cannot offer perfect competition or perfect choice. But
these imperfections, which are invariably the favorite targets of
each system's critics, tend to divert attention from what is most crucial to an understanding of schools: as institutional systems, democratic control and market control are strikingly different in their
fundamental properties. As a result, each system structures individual and social choices about education very differently, and each has
very different consequences for the organization and performance
of schools. Each system puts its own indelible stamp on the schools
that emerge and operate within it.

What the analysis in our book suggests, in the most practical   21
terms, is that American society offers two basic paths to the emergence of effective schools. The first is through markets, which
scarcely operate in the public sector, but which act on private schools
to discourage bureaucracy and promote desirable forms of organization through the natural dynamics of competition and choice.

The second path is through "special circumstances,"—homoge-   22
neous environments free of problems—which, in minimizing the
three types of political pressures just discussed, prompt democratic
governing institutions to impose less bureaucracy than they otherwise would. Private schools therefore tend to be effectively organized because of the way their system naturally works. When public
schools happen to be effectively organized, it is in spite of their system—they are the lucky ones with peculiarly nice environments.…

The way to get schools with effective organizations is not to in-   23
sist that democratic institutions should do what they are incapable
of doing. Nor is it to assume that the better public schools, the
lucky ones with nice environments, can serve as organizational

models for the rest. Their luck is not transferable. The way to get effective schools is to recognize that the problem of ineffective performance is really a deep-seated institutional problem that arises from the most fundamental properties of democratic control.

The most sensible approach to genuine education reform is therefore to move toward a true institutional solution—a different set of institutional arrangements that actively promotes and nurtures the kinds of schools people want. The market alternative then becomes particularly attractive, for it provides a setting in which these organizations take root and flourish. That is where "choice" comes in.   24

Educational Choice

It is fashionable these days to say that choice is "not a panacea." Taken literally, that is obviously true. There are no panaceas in social policy. But the message this aphorism really means to get across is that choice is just one of many reforms with something to contribute. School-based management is another. So are teacher empowerment and professionalism, better training programs, stricter accountability, and bigger budgets. These and other types of reforms all bolster school effectiveness in their own distinctive ways—so the reasoning goes—and the best, most aggressive, most comprehensive approach to transforming the public school system is therefore one that wisely combines them into a multifaceted reformist package.   25

Without being too literal about it, we think reformers would do well to entertain the notion that choice *is* a panacea. Of all the sundry education reforms that attract attention, only choice has the capacity to address the basic institutional problem plaguing America's schools. The other reforms are all system-preserving. The schools remain subordinates in the structure of public authority—and they remain bureaucratic.   26

In principle, choice offers a clear, sharp break from the institutional past. In practice, however, it has been forced into the same mold with all the other reforms. It has been embraced half-heartedly and in bits and pieces—for example, through magnet schools and limited open enrollment plans. It has served as a means of granting parents and students a few additional options or of giving schools modest incentives to compete. These are popular moves that can be accomplished without changing the existing system in any fundamental way. But by treating choice like other system-preserving reforms that presumably make democratic control work better, reformers completely miss what choice is all about.   27

Choice is not like the other reforms and should not be combined with them. Choice is a self-contained reform with its own rationale   28 and justification. It has the capacity *all by itself* to bring about the kind of transformation that reformers have been seeking to engineer for years in myriad other ways. Indeed, if choice is to work to greatest advantage, it must be adopted *without* these other reforms, since they are predicated on democratic control and are implemented by bureaucratic means. The whole point of a thoroughgoing system of choice is to free the schools from these disabling constraints by sweeping away the old institutions and replacing them with new ones. Taken seriously, choice is not a system-preserving reform. It is a revolutionary reform that introduces a new system of public education.

A Proposal for Real Reform

... Our guiding principle in the design of a choice system is this: 29
public authority must be put to use in creating a system that is almost entirely beyond the reach of public authority. Because states have primary responsibility for American public education, we think the best way to achieve significant, enduring reform is for states to take the initiative in withdrawing authority from existing institutions and vesting it directly in the schools, parents, and students. This restructuring cannot be construed as an exercise in delegation. As long as authority remains "available" at higher levels within state government, it will eventually be used to control the schools. As far as possible, all higher-level authority must be eliminated.

What we propose, more specifically, is that state leaders create a   30
new system of public education with the following properties.

The Supply of Schools

The state will be responsible for setting criteria that define what   31
constitutes a "public school" under the new system. These criteria should be minimal, roughly corresponding to the criteria many states now use in accrediting private schools—graduation requirements, health and safety requirements, and teacher certification requirements. Any educational group or organization that applies to the state and meets these minimal criteria must then be chartered as a public school and granted the right to accept students and receive public money.

Existing private schools will be among those eligible to partici-   32
pate. Their participation should be encouraged, because they constitute a supply of already effective schools. Our own preference would be to include religious schools too, as long as their sectarian functions can be kept clearly separate from their educational functions. Private schools that do participate will thereby become public

schools, as such schools are defined under the new choice system.

School districts can continue running their present schools, as-   33
suming those schools meet state criteria. But districts will have authority over only their own schools and not over any of the others
that may be chartered by the state.

Funding

The state will set up a Choice Office in each district, which, among   34
other things, will maintain a record of all school-age children and
the level of funding—the "scholarship" amounts—associated with
each child. This office will directly compensate schools based on
the specific children they enroll. Public money will flow from funding sources (federal, state, and district governments) to the Choice
Office and then to schools. At no point will it go to parents or students.

The state must pay to support its own Choice Office in each dis-   35
trict. Districts may retain as much of their current governing apparatus as they wish—superintendents, school boards, central offices,
and all their staff. But they have to pay for them entirely out of the
revenue they derive from the scholarships of those children who
voluntarily choose to attend district-run schools. Aside from the
governance of these schools, which no one need attend, districts
will be little more than taxing jurisdictions that allow citizens to
make a collective determination about how large their children's
scholarships will be.

As it does now, the state will have the right to specify how much,   36
or by what formula, each district must contribute for each child.
Our preference is for an equalization approach that requires
wealthier districts to contribute more per child than poor districts
do and that guarantees an adequate financial foundation to students
in all districts. The state's contribution can then be calibrated to
bring total spending per child up to whatever dollar amount seems
desirable; under an equalization scheme, that would mean a larger
state contribution in poor districts than in wealthy ones.

While parents and students should be given as much flexibility as   37
possible, we think it is unwise to allow them to supplement their
scholarship amounts with personal funds. Such "add-ons" threaten
to produce too many disparities and inequalities within the public
system, and many citizens would regard them as unfair and burden-
some.

Complete equalization, on the other hand, strikes us as too sti-   38
fling and restrictive. A reasonable trade-off is to allow collective
add-ons, much as the current system does. The citizens of each
district can be given the freedom to decide whether they want to

spend more per child than the state requires them to spend. They can then determine how important education is to them and how much they are willing to tax themselves for it. As a result, children from different districts may have different-sized scholarships.

Scholarships may also vary within any given district, and we strongly think that they should. Some students have very special educational needs—arising from economic deprivation, physical handicaps, language difficulties, emotional problems, and other disadvantages—that can be met effectively only through costly specialized programs. State and federal programs already appropriate public money to address these problems. Our suggestion is that these funds should take the form of add-ons to student scholarships. At-risk students would then be empowered with bigger scholarships than the others, making them attractive clients to all schools—and stimulating the emergence of new specialty schools.   39

Choice among Schools

Each student will be free to attend any public school in the state, regardless of district, with the student's scholarship—consisting of federal, state, and local contributions—flowing to the school of choice. In practice most students will probably choose schools in reasonable proximity to their homes. But districts will have no claim on their own residents.   40

To the extent that tax revenues allow, every effort will be made to provide transportation for students who need it. This provision is important to help open up as many alternatives as possible to all students, especially the poor and those in rural areas.   41

To assist parents and students in choosing among schools, the state will provide a Parent Information Center within its local Choice Office. This center will collect comprehensive information on each school in the district, and its parent liaisons will meet personally with parents in helping them judge which schools best meet their children's needs. The emphasis here will be on personal contact and involvement. Parents will be required to visit the center at least once, and encouraged to do so often. Meetings will be arranged at all schools so that parents can see firsthand what their choices are.   42

The Parent Information Center will handle the applications process in a simple fashion. Once parents and students decide which schools they prefer, they will fill out applications to each, with parent liaisons available to give advice and assistance and to fill out the applications themselves (if necessary). All applications will   43 be submitted to the Center, which in turn will send them out to the schools.

Schools will make their own admissions decisions, subject only to   44
nondiscrimination requirements. This step is absolutely crucial. Schools must be able to define their own missions and build their own programs in their own ways, and they cannot do that if their student population is thrust on them by outsiders.

Schools must be free to admit as many or as few students as they   45
want, based on whatever criteria they think relevant—intelligence, interest, motivation, special needs—and they must be free to exercise their own, informal judgments about individual applicants.

Schools will set their own "tuitions." They may choose to do so   46
explicitly, say, by publicly announcing the minimum scholarship they are willing to accept. They may also do it implicitly by allowing anyone to apply for admission and simply making selections, knowing in advance what each applicant's scholarship amount is. In either case, schools are free to admit students with different-sized scholarships, and they are free to keep the entire scholarship that accompanies each student they have admitted. That gives all schools incentives to attract students with special needs, since these children will have the largest scholarships. It also gives schools incentives to attract students from districts with high base-level scholarships. But no school need restrict itself to students with special needs, nor to students from a single district.

The application process must take place within a framework   47
that guarantees each student a school, as well as a fair shot at getting into the school he or she most wants. That framework, however, should impose only the most minimal restrictions on the schools.

We suggest something like the following. The Parental Informa-   48
tion Center will be responsible for seeing that parents and students are informed, that they have visited the schools that interest them, and that all applications are submitted by a given date. Schools will then be required to make their admissions decisions within a set time, and students who are accepted into more than one school will be required to select one as their final choice. Students who are not accepted anywhere, as well as schools that have yet to attract as many students as they want, will participate in a second round of applications, which will work the same way.

After this second round, some students may remain without   49
schools. At this point, parent liaisons will take informal action to try to match up these students with appropriate schools. If any students still remain unassigned, a special safety-net procedure—a lottery,

for example—will be invoked to ensure that each is assigned to a specific school.

As long as they are not "arbitrary and capricious," schools must   50
also be free to expel students or deny them readmission when, based on their own experience and standards, they believe the situation warrants it. This authority is essential if schools are to define and control their own organizations, and it gives students a strong incentive to live up to their side of the educational "contract."

Choice as a Public System

. . . We are proposing that the state put its democratic authority to   51
use in creating a new institutional framework. The design and legitimation of this framework would be a democratic act of the most basic sort. It would be a social decision, made through the usual processes of democratic governance, by which the people and their representatives specify the structure of a new system of public education.

This framework, as we set it out, is quite flexible and admits of   52
substantial variation on important issues, all of them matters of public policy to be decided by representative government. Public officials and their constituents would be free to take their own approaches to taxation, equalization, treatment of religious schools, additional funding for disadvantaged students, parent add-ons, and other controversial issues of public concern, thus designing choice systems to reflect the unique conditions, preferences, and political forces of their own states.

Once this structural framework is democratically determined,   53
moreover, governments would continue to play important roles within it. State officials and agencies would remain pivotal to the success of public education and to its ongoing operation. They would provide funding, approve applications for new schools, orchestrate and oversee the choice process, elicit full information about schools, provide transportation to students, monitor schools for adherence to the law, and (if they want) design and administer tests of student performance. School districts, meantime, would continue as local taxing jurisdictions, and they would have the option of continuing to operate their own system of schools.

The crucial difference is that direct democratic control of the   54
schools—the very *capacity* for control, not simply its exercise—would essentially be eliminated. Most of those who previously held authority over the schools would have their authority permanently withdrawn, and that authority would be vested in schools, parents, and students. Schools would be legally autonomous: free to govern themselves as they want, specify their own goals and programs and

methods, design their own organizations, select their own student bodies, and make their own personnel decisions. Parents and students would be legally empowered to choose among alternative schools, aided by institutions designed to promote active involvement, well-informed decisions, and fair treatment.

Democracy and Educational Progress

We do not expect everyone to accept the argument we have made here. In fact, we expect most of those who speak with authority on educational matters, leaders and academics within the educational community, to reject it. But we will regard our effort as a success if it directs attention to America's institutions of democratic control and provokes serious debate about their consequences for the nation's public schools. Whether or not our own conclusions are right, the fact is that these issues are truly basic to an understanding of schools, and they have so far played no part in the national debate. If educational reform is to have any chance at all of succeeding, that has to change.

In the meantime, we can only believe that the current "revolution" in public education will prove a disappointment. It might have succeeded had it actually been a revolution, but it was not and was never intended to be, despite the lofty rhetoric. Revolutions replace old institutions with new ones. The 1980s reform movement never seriously thought about the old institutions and certainly never considered them part of the problem. They were, as they had always been, part of the solution—and, for that matter, part of the definition of what democracy and public education are all about.

This identification has never been valid. Nothing in the concept of democracy requires that schools be subject to direct control by school boards, superintendents, central offices, departments of education, and other arms of government. Nor does anything in the concept of public education require that schools be governed in this way. There are many paths to democracy and public education. The path America has been trodding for the past half-century is exacting a heavy price—one the nation and its children can ill afford to bear, and need not. It is time, we think, to get to the root of the problem.

55

56

57

Questions

1. In paragraph 5, Chubb and Moe present the thesis of their argument for "institutional reform" as the "key to better schools." The system they propose relies on "indirect control through markets

and parental choice." What do they mean by "indirect control"? What do they see as the consequences of a market-based system?

2. What are the key aspects of Chubb and Moe's pro-choice argument? (Look particularly at pars. 29–50.) Given your own experience with an educational system, which of their proposals do you agree with? Which seem problematic to you? Why?

3. What do Chubb and Moe mean when they say "public authority must be put to use in creating a system that is almost entirely beyond the reach of public authority" (par. 29)?

4. Chubb and Moe describe their proposal as "revolutionary" (par. 28). What challenges does such a revolution face? Do you think these challenges can be overcome?

Nancy Kanode, "Private School Vouchers: Bad for America"

Educational vouchers or school choice, as many of its promoters like to call it, is an effort to create educational choices for parents of elementary through high school children. Whether at the city, state, or federal level, legislation is being introduced with the hope of making the private-school choice idea into reality. This discussion will focus on the more controversial matter of private school vouchers when exploring the school choice issue, rather than discussing choice among public schools or that of charter schools. The backbone of the school choice movement involves vouchers given to parents by the government allowing them to use the voucher (an amount normally used to fund a student at public school) at private schools, including sectarian schools. On the surface it sounds too good to be true, enabling parents, rich or poor, black or white, to select the highest quality education for their children, and best of all, to have it paid for by taxes. However, upon further examination, this particular movement may, unwittingly, ruin our public educational system, create bigger chasms in race, religion, and caste, and most importantly, violate our Constitution. The argument for school choice comes primarily from two different camps. The first is the group of Americans concerned that public schools are "insufficiently rigorous in their methods, do not stress math and science" and "emphasize individuality at the expense of discipline" (Goldberg 26). Public education in this country has come under a barrage of criticism, much of it from many Americans who feel our schools don't provide kids with a good education. Some will say there is much to criticize: falling SAT scores over the last 20 years, many unsafe inner-city schools, and poor test scores when compared to students in other countries (Smith, Meier 15). Additionally, many from this group want private school choice

1

because of the problems of some unsafe, inner-city schools. Besides low academic performance there, the lack of a safe environment has made many parents want to send their children to safer schools outside their districts. For many of these people the cause for educational vouchers would be eliminated if they had the freedom to send their children to any public school (public school choice), even if it was outside their district. The very general term "school choice," including private school vouchers, addresses these problems, they feel, and should be more prominent on the agenda for educational reform.

By contrast, there is a mistrust of the agenda from those representing the second camp. This group is largely composed of conservatives, especially Christian conservatives. Many opponents of school choice believe the attacks against public education by many from this group are propaganda to lay the foundation for their ultimate goal: getting back to less culturally diverse schools (segregation and injecting religious instruction, Judeo-Christian style, into the curriculum at the expense of taxpayers).   2

Many public school defenders claim critics have unfairly used statistics to paint a negative situation in public schools and have quite possibly created a crisis where there really isn't one. As a result of the negative propaganda, many Americans' perception of public schools has changed and they now see school vouchers as the only way to solve our educational problems. Some of the so-called evidence against the public school system, in the form of statistics, may not fully represent the facts.   3

For example, the fact that SAT scores have fallen over the last 20 years has been used to demonstrate that our public educational system is in a crisis. However, upon a closer look at SAT test takers one can't help but notice that there is an increasing number of minorities taking the SAT than there used to be (Smith, Meier 16). The percentage of minorities taking the SAT in 1975 was 14%, and 86% for whites (17). But by 1990 the percentage of minorities taking the SAT had risen to 27% and had dropped for whites to 73% (17). Minorities don't always score well because of background and language difficulties (18). But, nevertheless, in the last 15 years all minority subgroups have improved their scores (18). Furthermore, the SAT scores of white students, rather than falling as we've all been led to believe, have really remained stable (16). Quite possibly, it could be a case of changing demographics rather than a declining educational system. And in fact, when Sandia National Laboratories weighted the 1990 SAT scores to show the demographic makeup of those who took the SAT in 1975, they showed that scores actually went up by 30 points in only 15 years (16). By slanting statistics,   4 some proponents of school choice have created an artificial need that requires their remedy.

There are problems in public schools, as well as in private   5
schools, that reflect the complex problems of our changing society. Some of the problems in these schools revolve around racial conflicts. However, shipping kids out of these schools may only polarize the different races by creating segregation. Public school officials admit things have changed in public schools, especially in some inner-city schools, but they blame parents and not the system. They believe it is a solvable problem. Parental involvement is what is really needed, according to public school officials, but they feel no one can force parents—certainly not vouchers. Teachers claim they see more children than ever from abusive and neglectful homes (Houston). Rather than punish public schools for these problems (by diverting funds to private schools), school officials feel more should be done to change conditions for children at home, along with more education to improve racial relations.

Many advocates of school choice point to the large number of   6
private schools, especially in southern states, as evidence that people are unhappy with public education and have, therefore, chosen private education. However, private schools may have cropped up for another reason. The number of private Christian schools, as well as enrollment, increased dramatically in the 1960's in areas of segregation when the desegregation policy began (Smith, Meier 69). Many attribute this to racial reasons, rather than legitimate complaints against the educational system. As Dr. Menendez put it in his study of a large number of textbooks from conservative private schools, "They idealize an American past that itself was intolerant or unjust or, in some cases, simply imaginary." He goes on to say, "the views and attitudes expressed are sharply at variance with the major tenets of American democracy: respect for diversity, intellectual freedom, maximum choice in lifestyle, religious tolerance, racial and cultural pluralism, appreciation for modernity, experimentation, and pragmatism" (Menendez 4).

To the average American the word "choice" connotes freedom   7
and when coupled with the word "school" evokes images of a wide array of educational opportunities. The idea of choice in the education reform movement may sound good, but it is not realistic. It is only a realistic perspective for some Americans who want to inculcate a particular type of religious instruction to their children. For parents who feel vouchers will ensure parental choice in education the facts are disappointing.

Most Americans, when thinking of the private school sector, en-   8
vision many different types of private schools. They believe the pri-

vate school sector is made up of Montessori-type schools, college-prep schools, along with religious schools. But the truth is, a whopping 85% of private schools are religious in nature (A.U.S.C.S.). So the choice for most parents, should vouchers become reality, will ultimately be among religious schools. For these schools, religion permeates their entire curriculum. The fact that proponents of this movement have renamed it "school choice" is an effort to make it more enticing to Americans.

Only private school administrators will have the real choice, because unlike public education, they decide who gets into their schools and who doesn't. They may reject, as they do now, any student who they feel won't fit in for whatever reason. None of the proposed new legislation changes this policy. It will be far more discriminatory than any public school could ever be. One of the reasons test scores from private schools are sometimes higher than their public school counterparts is because of their right to exclude students. This undoubtedly gives private schools an edge when it comes down to test score competition. Because they are legally entitled to exercise discrimination in who they accept, private schools don't have the burden of having to average in low scores from slow students or students with disabilities. Therefore, when evaluating the quality of a private school using test scores, it may not necessarily be the better teaching staff or facility a private school offers, but rather it may be better students the private school has selected.

Private religious schools routinely select students with like-minded views, which means schools will not be diverse, but will reflect whatever the majority of its student body believes. This narrowness will only be amplified if we go to the educational voucher system. Furthermore, these schools are just as discriminating in who they hire to teach. Parents who assume their children will get a broad education could be in for a shock when they discover that many schools will probably be limited and myopic in the education they offer, only offering their own particular worldview based on the particular brand of religion sponsoring that school. Vouchers will not change any of this, but insure that discrimination happens on a larger scale at public expense. As if this Isolationist-type thinking is not bad enough, other areas besides religious, political, and racial domains of the American melting pot will also be differentiated.

Voucher legislation permits private schools to continue to discriminate, not only on the basis of religion, gender, and disability, but could also encourage a caste system in our country. Many Americans don't fully appreciate the low emphasis on caste in our country as compared with many other nations. It is difficult in most countries, and impossible in others, for a person from a poor or un-educated class to get a formal education and rise to a different position in class structure. In the United States, while there is some class distinction, anyone who truly desires to rise to another class has a good chance at doing so. This is in large part due to our philosophy regarding public education for everyone all the way up through college.

One facet of the strong caste system in other countries is seen in   12
their educational institutions. These institutions which cater mostly to a specific class perpetuate the class distinction by insuring that each of their students meet a certain profile criteria. In many of those schools, wealth and class level solely determine whether a student can attend. Even in this country, there are some private schools that tend to accept students from a certain class. And in those situations, parents have that freedom as long as they pay for it, monetarily as well as socially. But it is wrong for taxpayers to have to finance someone else's right to exclusivism.

However, with the voucher system possibility, class distinction   13
will be supported in that parents will be subsidized with tax dollars to send their children to exclusive schools with other students of similar status. One must use the term "subsidy" because there is no way the average American could afford the high tuition of many private schools. Many proponents of school choice are under the mistaken impression their children can attend any private school, notwithstanding cost. This is not how the voucher proposal reads. What will likely happen is that these same Americans will not be able to afford the difference between the voucher amount and the school tuition cost when considering exclusive private schools and will end up putting their children in some of the mediocre private schools which charge less tuition, whereas those middle-to-uppers who now have their children in public schools will be able to afford exclusive schools because of the voucher subsidy. It follows then that school vouchers could make the problem of class distinction in our society even worse by separating even more "the Haves" from the "Have Nots." Yet, there is the even bigger issue of constitutionality.

Many uninformed Americans see nothing constitutionally wrong   14
with assisting parochial and other private schools by way of vouchers. Our Constitution insures that religious institutions can teach their beliefs. However, it also insures that government tax dollars will not fund religious institutions, including their schools. This is because our forefathers wanted to keep the business of religion apart from the business of government, including using tax dollars to aid schools in proselytizing. When they drafted the First Amend-

ment to our Constitution they created a document that prohibits financial support of religious institutions. Interestingly, many states later followed suit in their state constitutions. In the past, most private schools seemed content with this arrangement because it also insured little interference or intrusion from the government in the operations of their schools.

In other words, the Constitution provides protection for private   15
schools to teach their own curriculum (provided it meets minimum educational requirements), but it very clearly, in its First Amendment, sets up a wall between church and state where no tax dollars are to support religious organizations or those teaching or proselytizing their beliefs in the elementary and secondary years of education. The educational voucher plan draws upon public funds to support religious education, a direct violation of our Constitution and most state constitutions.

Over the years there have been many attempts to turn religious   16
schools into pseudo-public schools, in order to get state funding, but they have always been struck down, sometimes by other religious organizations themselves, hoping to maintain America's religious liberty. This has changed over the years, for now many religious organizations can't wait to get their hands on voucher money. Note the sentiment for keeping private schools free of tax or state support in 1947: after a Cincinnati school board turned a Catholic school into a pseudo-public school (Johnson, Yest 110), the Council of Churches for Greater Cincinnati issued the following statement:

> The principle of the separation of church and state was established on the basis that any support, however slight, for any church or religious establishment would lead first to bitter wrangling between the adherents of different religions for tax favors and ultimately to the worst of all tyrannies, religious persecution. As President Madison pointed out in his famous "Memorial Against Religious Assessments," the first step towards church support, direct or indirect, from tax funds is the first step towards a return of the Spanish inquisition.... The principle of separation of church and state is not a worn out slogan to be evaded by legal fiction. It is the keynote of our religious freedom. As such, it is worth protecting. For that reason we shall support wholeheartedly the move to stop tax support for any church school, North College Hill or any other place. (Johnson, Yest 111)

Many proponents of school choice don't see the concern over the   17
diversion of money away from public education because they believe

public schools will be forced to improve or close up (Kirkpatrick 47–61). Some people erroneously believe vouchers will make public schools better by promoting competition in education. But there is no evidence to support this notion. Numerous studies have concluded that the positive things our public school system has accomplished could only have been done by having one large, centralized system (Houston). Competition may be great for soft drinks, but it could be terrible for schools. Many Americans feel it is our public educational system that makes our country so great. The difference between our democracy and those of many other nations is our education-of-the-masses philosophy, instituted by such men as Thomas Jefferson, Horace Mann, and John Dewey. As a result the United States can boast that 26% of our population graduates from college —the highest percentage in the world, including Japan (Houston).

While critics of our educational system point to higher test scores   18
by other nations, they forget that unlike other nations, we offer high school and college education to everyone—even mediocre students. By contrast, other countries screen and weed out mediocre students to vocational tracks early on, so that they are left with the most academically inclined students at the high school level. It follows, therefore, that their students' scores, when compared to our "teach-everyone policy" scores, are higher. But notwithstanding this mitigating circumstance, American students still shine. For example, at the 1994 International Mathematical Olympiad in Hong Kong, the U.S. high school team, with only a month of preparation (compared to a year-long preparation by other teams), accomplished a feat never done before. Each member of our team got a perfect score on the two-day exam. And each member was public school educated (Smith, Meier 138). This confirms what a *Money* magazine report concluded after an exhaustive study of public schools and private schools. "Students who attend the best public schools outperform most private schools. The average public school teacher has stronger academic qualifications than most private schools. Public school class sizes are no larger than most private schools and are smaller than in most Catholic schools. Shocked? So were we" (Topolnicki 98). The article went on to say that, based on their study, the average private school was no better than the average public school. Those mediocre and poor public schools will improve only if our government leaders and the public decide to make a serious commitment to educational quality for every school and commit to making all inner-city schools safe. Diverting money away from public schools will not accomplish this objective.

One argument that comes up frequently in favor of the voucher   19
school choice plan is the myth that vouchers will correct the injus-

tice of "double taxation" for parents who now send their children to private school and who must still support a public school system they don't use. What these parents don't realize is that private school tuition is not a tax. It is an added expense they have chosen to pay. In fact, there is no such thing as a double tax. We are all expected to support certain basic services whether we use them or not. For example, we pay for police services, our fire departments, our libraries and, of course, our public schools. And yet many of us rarely use these services. Single people and couples without children must still pay school taxes even though they don't have children to utilize public schools. Most of us believe it is in our best interest, as a nation and individually, to make sure our people are educated. But the truth is under a voucher plan there will be double taxation. This is because Americans will still have to pay to maintain quality in public schools and then pay increased taxes to make up for the money being given to parochial and other private schools (Lieberman 7–14; Americans United for Separation of Church and State).

Additionally, Americans already voluntarily support, through churches, charities, and other religious organizations, a wide variety of religious institutions and schools. It is wrong to make them pay taxes for the purpose of supporting schools teaching religious views they disagree with.

20

Clearly, educational vouchers for private schools are wrong for America. Not only does this idea violate our Constitution by funding religious schools, but it allows discrimination on the basis of religion, disability, and gender, not to mention other characteristics. Covertly, it promotes discrimination in race and in caste. It dictates that those who do not "fit" will likely be labeled misfits or losers and will all be left to cluster in what remains of our public education system should we adopt this program. Voucher legislation doesn't require private schools to admit any student with a voucher. Therefore, there is no real choice for students, only for private schools.

21

Many of the issues facing the public education reform movement are complex and vary from area to area. And while we have a responsibility to improve our public educational system, we must be careful, like the early promoters of public education, to get agreement that can lead to common action and not a separatist way of thinking. We need to have a greater loyalty to not only our Constitution, but to a commitment to diversity in our institutions and to dissolving conflicts there.

22

Our greatest commitment should be to provide children with worldviews different from those of their parents. Private schools,

23

for the most part, don't accomplish this. Many of them are only an extension of the same viewpoints as home and provide little opportunity for kids to experience diversity. Instead, they insure that adults who grow up this way are comfortable only within their own political, racial and socioeconomic strata. And it follows that children educated in this restrictive world will be less tolerant of different attitudes and viewpoints as adults. What we need is unity in the midst of our diversity, rather than isolation. We can't allow television to be the only thing that unifies us. Our public schools should be what they have been for the last century: the best institution for shaping and conveying a common culture.

Works Cited

Goldberg, Bruce, "A Liberal Argument for School Choice." *American Enterprise*, Sept./Oct. 1996.

Houston, Paul, "What's Right with Schools?" *American School Board Journal*, April 1992, 24–27.

Johnson, Alvin, and Frank Yest. *Separation of Church and State*. Minneapolis: University of Minnesota, 1948.

Kirkpatrick, David. *Choice in Schooling*. Chicago, Ill.: Loyola University Press, 1990.

Lieberman, Myron. *Public Education: An Autopsy*. Cambridge: Harvard University Press, 1993.

Menendez, Albert J. *Visions of Reality: What Fundamentalist Schools Teach*. Buffalo, N.Y.: Prometheus Books, 1993.

"Private School Vouchers: Myth vs. Fact." Americans United for Separation of Church and State (A.U.S.C.S.), Washington, D.C., Oct. 1996.

Smith, Kevin B., and Kenneth J. Meier. *The Case against School Choice*. Armonk, N.Y.: M.E. Sharpe, 1995.

Topolnicki, Denise M. "Why Private Schools Are Rarely Worth the Money." *Money*, Oct. 1994, 98+.

Questions

1. List Kanode's main arguments against the use of vouchers for private schools. What evidence does she present for each point?
2. How does Kanode address Chubb and Moe's major argument in favor of competition as a way to improve public education?
3. How would you define the kind of public education that Kanode is arguing for?

▨ PRACTICE 10.5

A Policy Memo

You are a member of the campaign staff for someone who's running for the state legislature from your home district. Your district is composed of a city with overcrowded, deteriorating schools surrounded by suburbs with good, relatively uncrowded school systems. Because the city has less taxable property than the suburbs, the city spends far less per pupil than the suburbs do. A majority of voters agree that something must be done to improve their children's education, but there is little agreement on what should be done. Your candidate will be expected to present a policy for educational reform. Here are the major issues being discussed in your district:

A number of city voters are calling for an end to the inequity in spending per pupil. Some want school funding centralized by the state; others want vouchers given to low-income city families to help equalize spending.

Many suburban voters oppose the use of vouchers for school choice, fearing that their schools will be overrun with disadvantaged city children.

City and suburban parents with children in private and parochial schools favor vouchers as a way of defraying their expenses.

Most teachers in your district have supported your candidate in the past. They consider the voucher system a threat to public education, and are calling for more federal and state funds to improve the public school system.

Some voters favor schools run by private corporations in competition with public schools. A number of these corporations have been lobbying the state legislature.

Your job is to write a policy memo to inform your candidate about the issues and to present a position to be taken. You can argue for or against school choice, or you can argue for or against a particular system of choice or education. Use the arguments put forth and the information provided in the previous selections as source material for your position. You will need evidence to back up your position, so some research will be necessary. You'll find plenty of references to school choice in general sources such as the *New York Times Index* and the *National Newspaper Index*, or in more specialized sources such as the *Social Sciences Index*.

In addition, there is plenty of information online, as at **<www.policy .com>,** which provides information, links to related sites, and links to ongoing discussions on numerous issues, including school choice. However, when consulting a Web site, be wary. Try to judge whether you're getting objective information or just propaganda from one point of view. Your knowledge of the positions taken in the previous readings should help you decipher the politics of your Web source.

Writing and Power: Two Projects

We offer two projects dealing with power and the media as opportunities for you to bring together the strategies you've practiced thus far. Both projects draw on the following selection, which is taken from Jane Shattuc's book on television talk shows, *The Talking Cure: TV Talk Shows and Women* (1997). Shattuc poses the question of whether daytime talk shows are "simply sensational commercialism" or whether they might be "a new form of political debate." As you follow her development of ideas, note how Shattuc must reexamine the terms *political* and *debate*, as they apply to the structure of talk-show argumentation.

■ READING

Jane Shattuc, from "The 'Oprahfication' of America? Identity Politics and Public Sphere Debate"

> *Today I am sitting between two people who have never been this close face to face since one very unforgettable night two years ago. Debbie says that the man sitting across from her locked her in a closed room, held a gun to her, and violently raped her. Jawad says Debbie is lying.*
> —*Oprah Winfrey*, Oprah, *May 3, 1994*

Are daytime TV talk shows simply sensational commercialism or could they be a new form of political debate? The visceral description by Winfrey of an *Oprah* program on May 3, 1994, seemingly relegates the social issues involved in rape to the realm of cheap thrills. But on another level, the program's dramatic and individualized account allows ordinary citizens — in the studio and at home — to enter into a debate about sexual power in their everyday lives, a rare moment on network television.

Traditionally, democratic thought assumes that there must be an   2
independent public arena where political opinion can be formed
freely. The arena should be entirely free of the taint of government
control as well as that of corporate capitalism. For many Americans,
the town meeting is the ideal of participatory democracy: the citizen
takes part in the politics of the local community by standing up and
speaking up. But such direct communication is becoming less tenable
in the age of information technology and global communication.

If TV has become the central communicator of information, no   3
other public forum replicates the town-meeting democratic sensibil-
ity better than the first generation of daytime TV talk shows, born in
the 1970s through the 1980s: the *Oprah Winfrey Show*, *Sally Jesse
Raphaël*, the *Phil Donahue Show*, and even *Geraldo*. Here, "average"
Americans debate important, albeit sensationalized, issues that are
central to their political lives: racism, sexuality, welfare rights, and religious freedom. Would Jürgen Habermas, one of the leading theo-
reticians of the public sphere, have included such shows as part of the
public sphere, which he defined as "the realm of our social life in
which something approaching public opinion can be formed.... A
portion of the public sphere comes into being in every conversation
in which private individuals assemble to form a public body"?[1] The
answer depends on whose definition of politics one invokes.

The concept of the public sphere — the place where public opin-   4
ion can be formed — looms over all analyses of talk shows. From
"The Talk Show Report" in *Ladies Home Journal*[2] to think pieces
about tabloid culture in the *New York Times*,[3] to a Marxist collective
analysis of the genre in *Sociotext*,[4] to an article on talk and female
empowerment in *Genders*,[5] our culture is hyperconscious that daytime TV talk shows are involved in the political arena. They are a
rare breed: highly popular programs that depend on social topics
and the participation of average citizens. However, there is the fear
that the shows may be trivializing "real" politics by promoting irra-
tional, victimized, and anomalous individuals as representative of
the citizenry. The print press has pejoratively alluded to the
"oprahfication" of America. Yet the popularity of the shows continually begs two questions: Can the content of the shows be defined
as "political"? And, more important, can the shows — the children
of corporate media interests — be considered public arenas where
"the people" form opinion freely?

Even though the women's movement has shown that politics in   5
the late twentieth century includes the personal, American culture
still is uncomfortable in describing the content of daytime talk shows
as political. The term *political* is derived from the Latin *politicus*, which
means relating to a citizen.[6] A citizen is defined by his or her alle-

giance to a state and protection by it. Obviously, the shows, with their dependence on spectacle, individualism, and sensation, deviate radically from the traditional political discussions about social policy that define citizenship, such as Oxford debates, congressional deliberations, union-hall meetings, and even network news, with its emphasis on established political institutions. Although debate has shifted from the Aristotelian model of speaker and listener to the coordinated discussion of the twentieth century, the shows are more personal and emotional in their content and vertiginous in structure than traditional forms of political discussion. Still, Rivera asserts continually on air: "Our studio is a representation of the country at large." And Ron Rosenbaum argues that the shows "have become the American equivalent of the Athenian agora, where citizens, sophists and philosophers bat around questions of behavior. They can be barometers of public feeling on questions of good and evil."[7]

No other TV genre—not news, prime time drama, or soap opera—generates more ongoing social controversy than daytime talk shows. Beyond the headline-grabbing *Jenny Jones* murder[8] or Winfrey's cocaine confession,[9] the shows evoke endless debates about everyday experience. Not only does viewer give-and-take take place as part of the show but discussions continue on the news, in the workplace, and at home: the popularization of current political, social, and theoretical topics. The shows raise questions of fact versus fiction as the audience tests the credibility of the stories presented. (In the common vernacular: "Are those people for real?") They test the demarcation between entertainment and news as they mix political issues and personal drama. Further, they use ordinary people to stage social issues that are infrequently discussed elsewhere on television: homosexuality, familial conflict, sexual relations, and racial divisions.   6

As the 1990s bring into the political arena an angry African-American underclass, gay activists, and employed women, might *Oprah*'s audience and those of other daytime talk shows be the newest incarnation of the public sphere? This chapter looks at the concept of the active audience in media studies and the political change brought on by identity politics.   7

The Social Sphere: Democracy, Debate, and Public Participation

Historically, open debate has been a fundamental ideal of capitalist democracies. The public sphere, as articulated by Habermas, exists in opposition to the sphere of the nuclear family and domestic activity, which is governed not by public discussion but by privacy. The concept of the public sphere emanates from the agora of democratic ancient Greece, part marketplace and public forum. Its   8 modern manifestation arose in Britain in the seventeenth and eighteenth centuries out of the development of competitive capitalism and the corresponding rise of liberal democratic thought. A new political class, the bourgeoisie, emerged to formulate these economic and political theories and initiate their implementation. These people became the intellectuals and technicians who articulated the ideas of civil society separate from its dominant institutions.

A series of institutions also developed, such as debating societies,   9
coffeehouses, salons, the press, libraries, and universities, where public opinion was fashioned. The bourgeois public sphere came to be demarcated by its separation from the interests of the church and the state; its activities were carried out by citizens who had independent sources of income. All members of the civil society were equal. Rational discourse defined the debate; arguments were won not on power but evidence. The public sphere's authority was derived from the fact that the ideas therein generated had to do not with private interests but with the public good.

Ultimately, for Habermas, the advent of monopoly capitalism in   10
the twentieth century has destroyed the independence of the public sphere as a universalist institution. The new economy has led to an uneven distribution of wealth and rising entry costs to the social sphere and, accordingly, unequal access to it and control over it. Instead of public opinion, private-interest advertising and public relations have taken over. What was the free press has become the mass media. Instead of fostering a free flow of rational debate, these public-sphere institutions manipulate the populace. Government emerged as the welfare state: a giant with its own bureaucratic self-interests, one of which is sustaining capitalism. The independent public sphere as the generator of "critical" information has been slowly squeezed by late capitalism and the state.

For Habermas, as well as recent media critics,[10] the change has   11
become more obvious. The mammoth, corporate mass media serve as a "tranquilizing substitute for action" for the "uncritical masses."[11] The former divisions between the public sphere, capitalism, and the state have collapsed as the mass media increasingly substitute for independent public thought. As fewer and fewer citizens vote, the media "produce" the concept of the "public." U.S. journalism—now "a mouthpiece for officialdom"—engineers consensus by manipulating public opinion; in the case of the Gulf War, for example, the news could not be distinguished from the official state's line.[12]

Even though Habermas concedes that the public sphere has been   12
more an ideal than fact down through history, the concept still

serves as a powerful element in the assumptions of capitalist democracy. Hopes of a public sphere are evoked whenever a writer be-
moans the passing of considered discussion of public issues is where
the commercial pressures for "entertainment" have destroyed objectivity and truth.[13] The *New York Times* often stands as the principal defender of "real" news. Janet Maslin commented in its pages,
"In the world of daytime talk shows, only one topic is truly off limits: America's fascination with escapist trivia as a means of avoiding
real discourse."[14] John J. O'Connor, the paper's TV critic, warns:
"There's a battle being waged in television these days and broadly
speaking, it's taking place along lines of 'us versus them' cultural
lines. Depending on your vantage point, the results so far could be
interpreted as either democracy taking the offensive or the barbar-
ians." He maintains that the tabloid-style TV shows "are in the
business of inventing emotional 'wallops' and are openly contemptuous of what they like to refer to as 'pointy-headed' journalists,
meaning for the most part the college-educated kind that works in
non-tabloid print."[15] Here, a newspaperman writing a column for a
traditional news medium suppresses questions about the objectivity
in all news reporting in favor of charges that tabloids or talk shows
are manipulative or that they are promoting what another *New York
Times* writer calls "the new kind of dumbness."[16] This nostalgia for
the loss of the bourgeois public sphere is deeply intertwined with a
kind of politics where clear categories of power are maintained: a
class, culture, and gender hierarchy based on the centrality of the
educated white bourgeois male.[17] Not surprisingly, Donahue is
often nominated by the press as the most "responsible" or "trusted"
daytime host.[18]

At issue is whether a popular audience can enjoy but be critical of   13
TV. Or whether TV is a commercial Moloch swallowing up the
minds of viewers and creating passive consumers. The public
sphere tradition calls for a liberal or educated elite to lead the uneducated masses for their own good by steering media content and the
social agenda toward democratic values. This patrician style of leadership or public service assumes ordinary people do not have the
ability to comprehend the mass media's power and control....

The daytime talk shows, whose audience is predominantly   14
women at home, are easy to denigrate as well, as a non-culture. The
shows are feminine in that they are experienced as sites of emotion
and consumerist values by domestic labor within the home. Such
distinctions allow Walter Goodman of the *New York Times* to brand
the shows as "the nation's picture window onto domestic dysfunction." He decries [their practices]: "No week passes that Oprah or
Phil or Sally Jesse or Geraldo or Montel or one of the lesser practi-

tioners does not conduct a public examination of private abominations like wife beating, husband slashing and, most relevant to the Menendez case, child abuse."[19] The division between what is public and what is private is much more complex and historically controversial than Goodman's dichotomy connotes.

Feminist questions about culture and the social relevance of the personal and psychological realms emanate from a larger shift brought on by identity politics in the second half of the twentieth century. Identity politics asserts the centrality of identity in carrying out radical change. Although related to nineteenth century movements of suffrage, abolitionism, and unionism, with their interest in governmental and institutional reform, identity politics places equal if not greater emphasis on an understanding of the psychology of repression, or social subjectivity, in political activism. That is, political change must begin with labor on how we learn racism, sexism, and classism by challenging previously nonpolitical issues, such as lifestyle, sexual relations, and everyday culture.... 15

Many feminists have come to champion daytime talk shows as a new public sphere or counter public sphere. The shows not only promote conversation and debate but do away with the distance between audience and stage. They do not depend on the power of expertise or bourgeois education. They elicit common sense and everyday experience as the mark of truth. They confound the distinction between the public and the private. The shows are about average women as citizens talking about and debating issues and experience. As a lesbian transsexual who has been on *Geraldo*, *Donahue*, and *Jane Whitney*, Kate Bornstein states that she sees the appearances as a battle to establish how her cultural identity is to be represented. She likens the shows to the nineteenth-century freak-show circuses but declares: "What's different now is that we, as freaks, are doing the speaking. It isn't the barker telling our story for us."...[20] 16

Of course, the daytime talk shows are not simply progressive or regressive. They do not represent the death of the public sphere. Although they do not often discuss specific governmental or social institutions, they are clear debates about the public sphere's growing intercession into the family, the home, and regulation of the individual's body. Further, the genre most explicitly enters the public sphere debate through its gesture toward participatory democracy: its town-meeting structure. Further, it maintains the organization of the social debate by always placing the private issue within a social matrix. As a result, the talk show participates in a debate arena comparable to Habermas's public sphere. However, the evidence of social injustice has shifted from rational and distant forms to an in- 17 tersection that collapses personal experience, physical evidence, and emotion.

Reinventing Debate as Talk on the Oprah Winfrey Show

Oprah exemplifies this new form of evidence. Here, there is a continual tension between rational educated forms of evidence and the direct "authentic" experience of the audience. *Oprah does* challenge the supposed objectivity of traditional patriarchal power. The host—a black woman—undercuts the authority of the debate format with her self-confessional style; she routinely admits her early sexual and drug abuse and her erstwhile struggle to lose weight. *Oprah* also represents potentially a radical public sphere that privileges process over a single truth or closure. It often presents what Masciarotte calls an "irritated middle."[21]

Nevertheless, the structure of an *Oprah* program is typical of most daytime talk shows: problem solution. Most often, the problem is introduced as a personal problem (for example, obesity, HIV+, a bisexual spouse) but then generalized to a larger social issue. For instance, an April 15, 1994, program on mothers who want to give up their violent children becomes generalized by Winfrey to "What really makes a child act this way?" Either by taking the opposite side or teasing out other views, Winfrey questions the guests to flesh out the problem. The identifications of guests underline their social representativeness; for example, one is a "mother who wants to give away a violent child," another is a "convicted woman who plotted her husband's death." The labeling offers a popularized version of the logic of identity politics, wherein identity is constructed as a series of sectional needs (black, woman, lesbian, worker). Mary Louise Adams and Linda Briskin detail how identity politics began as an attempt to break down the hegemonic notion of homogeneity, that we all are one."[22] On talk shows these social identities become broader. The labeling tends toward more generic or psychosociological characterizations ("man who raped woman at gun point") than the social topology produced by identity politics (race, gender, nation, class). It is not understanding social identity but creating identification with the participants that is paramount for the narratives of commercial television.

Nevertheless, Winfrey slowly invokes the audience as a larger social collectivity. She directs the debate toward social issues through her selection of questioners and specifically through the rhetorical use of the pronouns "you," "I," and "we." To illustrate: she says, "I am sure what mothers out there are thinking," or "When I first heard about this, like everybody, I wondered what the big deal is," or (my favorite because it's Winfrey at her most self-

18

19

20

aggrandizing), "The question we all have, I am speaking for the audience here and the audience around the world listening to you..."
Or consider Donahue's well-known address to the audience:
"Ladies and gentlemen of the jury." As the above quotations reveal,
the audience represents not only society at large, but a society that
thinks and adjudicates.

Another aspect indicated by the quotations is when the host   21
moves from authority—controller of the program—to positioning
herself or himself with the audience as one of the observers or
judges who has a social or personal stake. But control is not thereby
relinquished. What many people applaud as Winfrey's debunking
of her authority—she will even sit in the audience—can also be
seen as a move that subtly allows her to orchestrate a collective response from the audience.

When Wendy Kaminer says of her experience on *Oprah*, "If all   22
issues are personalized, we lose our capacity to entertain ideas, to
generalize from our own or someone else's experiences, to think abstractly,"[23] she has missed the point. Such shows continually move
from personal identification to larger group identification in order
to be popular on a broad commercial medium. The host generalizes
the particular experience into a larger social frame to capture the
interest of a larger audience. For all their individualized narratives,
the shows speak in social generalities, but not about changing specific social and political institutions.

As much as daytime talk show audiences are purveyed as a repre- 23
sentative random sample of American women, they are not democratic entities. First, during segment breaks, producers monitor,
guide, and select questioners: Oprah often segues with "As you
were saying during the break,..." Second, some shows selectively
hand out tickets to particular programs in order to get a certain
type of audience makeup. *Donahue*'s NBC pages seek out middle-
class, well-dressed, women tourists on nearby streets in a quest for
articulate guests. Often the audience coordinators call and invite
people who have a personal stake in an issue. Audience guests move
from being identified guests (relatives, representatives of social organizations, or similar victims) to part of the microcosm, the studio
audience, a stand-in for the larger society.

Yet the show creates a flow between stage guests, audience   24
guests, and audience members that empowers audience authority.
For example, on a *Oprah* program on violence in schools on April 7,
1994, the audience was dominated by angry schoolteachers. Or on a
Oprah show about HIV on February 17, 1994, 60 percent of the audience were HIV positive. A debate about the morality of homosexuality or certain sexual practices did not take place on the latter

because HIV-positive people were normalized as the majority of this microcosm. Hence, guests and studio audience were united in their acceptance of homosexuality.

To a large degree, the constitution of the audience draws from   25
the identity politics movement. Identity politics has institutionalized around organizations that represent particular political issues. Producers book a guest based on the perception that he or she is involved in a topical social problem, calling upon such organizations as ACT-UP, the National Organization for Women, various battered women's shelters, and the National Association for the Advancement of Colored People to line up experts, guests, or audience members. For example, for a program on nonsafe sex, *Geraldo* producers worked closely with the New York gay rights organizations not only to arrange for participants but to produce a program free of stereotype. It is advantageous for these organizations to stack the audience and the debate, and thereby create the rare opportunity for their members to have a "majority" experience. Even so, the program will encourage nonmembers or off-the-street audience recruits to speak up if they disagree. As one *Donahue* producer commented during the warm-up of the studio audience: "We like emotion and controversy."

Oprah usually stacks the debate in a clear direction, allowing for a   26
subtle form of closure based on a selected majority rule. Winfrey's monitoring of questions confers on her the gatekeeping function. On a March 8, 1994, program on why girls fall behind in high school, audience questioners were overwhelmingly women teachers and female students who had experienced sexism; only two of twelve speakers resisted the premise that sexism was a problem for teenage girls.

Most *Oprah* programs end with solutions offered by the experts   27
and underlined by a pithy remark by Winfrey and/or an audience member. Sometimes the programs, such as the problem-child program, do not end in a resolution/solution; this one closed as the debate between mothers continued. This is the "irritated middle," or the "cacophony of 'I's," with no sense of a sociological answer that Masciarotte asserts makes daytime talk shows radical. But in general *Oprah* offers a subtle form of "we," achieved through her slow process of consensus building. . . .

The shows do not follow the tradition of the bourgeois public   28
sphere, where J. B. Thompson says, "the authority of the state could be criticized by an informed and reasoning public or 'publicness.'"[24] Rather, the shows rely on testimonials, emotions, and the body as well as laughter, facial expression, and tears. These are forms of argument and evidence available to nonexperts or the

lower classes, and they are gaining acceptance as the shows test the centrality of the educated bourgeoisie in defining politics and debate. In this postmodern age of simulations, daytime talk shows demand a belief in the authenticity of lived experience as a social truth. Perhaps such raw physical directness is what makes the educated middle class so uncomfortable with the so-called "oprahfication" of America. As one *Oprah* audience member stated on April 14, 1994: "Don't tell me how to feel. I am my experience.". . .

It is naive to assume that daytime talk shows are a public sphere   29 untainted by capitalism, the state, or even the bourgeois intellectual. Because they are based in commercialism, popular culture, and the identity politics of the 1970s, they stage a contradictory set of tensions where groups that normally do not have a voice are allowed a powerful platform. The genre challenges accepted notions of political discussion. Not only do the shows question what constitutes politics, they challenge who is allowed to speak. As we move from the age of mechanically reproduced debates to one of electronically reproduced discussions, the shows represent an uncomfortable public sphere. They reveal a profound political change: the authority of everyday lived experience, whether in reactionary or progressive form. As they manifest this change with programs on militias, domestic violence, and black pride, among other topics, the empowerment of the knowledge of people who are not formally educated can be seen as the failure or the triumph of liberal democratic thought.

* * * *

Notes

1. Jürgen Habermas, "The Public Sphere: An Encyclopedia Article," *New German Critique*, Autumn 1984, 49.

2. Barbara Lippert, "The Talk Show Report," *Ladies Home Journal*, April 1994, 154–156, 210.

3. John Corry, "A New Age of Television Tastelessness?" *New York Times*, 29 May 1988, 1; and John J. O'Connor, "Defining What's Civilized and What's Not," *New York Times*, 25 April 1989, C18.

4. P. Carpignano, R. Andersen, S. Aronowitz, and W. Difazio, "Chatter in the Age of Electronic Reproduction: Talk Television and the 'Public Mind,'" *Sociotext* 25/26 (1990): 33–55.

5. Gloria-Jean Masciarotte, "C'mon Girl: Oprah Winfrey and the Discourse of Feminine Talk," *Genders* 11 (Fall 1991): 81–110.

6. *Webster's New World Unabridged Dictionary*, 2d ed. (New York: Simon & Schuster, 1983), 1392.

7. Ron Rosenbaum, "Staring into the Heart of Darkness," *New York Times Magazine*, 4 June 1995, 41.

8. On 6 March 1995, a Michigan man, Scott Amedure, surprised a male friend, Jon Schmitz, by admitting that he had a crush on Schmitz during a taping of a *Jenny Jones* program on secret admirers. The next day Schmitz murdered Amedure, declaring that he had been "humiliated" by the exposure on national TV. *Jenny Jones* and talk shows in general were blamed in the press for being irresponsible in misleading guests. See the cover story: Michelle Green, "Fatal Attraction," *People*, 27 March 1995, 40–44.

9. Winfrey, host of *Oprah*, "confessed" her use of cocaine in front of a live audience during the taping of a program in late January 1995. The statement was reported on the evening news as well as in the printed press. For the tabloid coverage, see cover stories: Jim Nelson, "Oprah and Cocaine: The Shocking Story She Didn't Tell You on TV," *National Enquirer*, 31 January 1995, 5; and Ken Harrell, "Oprah: 'How a Man Made Me Slave to Cocaine,'" *Globe*, 31 January 1995, 37.

10. For examples, see Nicholas Garnham, *Capitalism and Communication: Global Culture and the Economics of Information* (London: Sage, 1990), 1–19; and David Sholle, "Resistance and Pinning Down a Wandering Concept in Cultural Studies," *Journal of Urban and Cultural Studies* 1.1 (1990): 87–105.

11. Jürgen Habermas, *The Structural Transformation of the Public Sphere*, trans. Thomas Burger (Cambridge: MIT Press, 1989), 164.

12. Carpignano et al., "Chatter in the Age of Electronic Reproduction," 40.

13. For a discussion of how the established press maintains these distinctions between high and low news, see John Hartley, *Tele-ology: Studies in Television* (London: Routledge, 1992).

14. Janet Maslin, "In Dirty Laundryland," *New York Times*, 10 October 1993, sec. 9, 7.

15. John J. O'Connor, "Defining What's Civilized and What's Not," *New York Times*, 25 April 1989, C18.

16. John Corry, "A New Age of Television Tastelessness?" *New York Times*, 29 May 1988, sec. 2.1.

17. Consider how a series of binary oppositions surface in these discussions of the liberal news tradition and the exploitive talk show genre: democratic versus bias; independent versus profit-oriented; serious versus trivial; educated versus uneducated; and masculine versus feminine.

18. For an example, see Eric Sherman, "Who's the Best? Donahue? Oprah? Someone Else?" *TV Guide*, 26 March 1986, 26.

Newsweek, 29 October 1979, describes him as "America's most trusted tour guide across today's constantly shifting social and cultural terrain."

19. Walter Goodman, "As TV Sows Outrage, Guess What It Reaps," *New York Times*, 28 March 1995, C14.

20. Elizabeth Jensen, "Tales Are Oft Told as TV Talk Shows Fill Up Air Time," *Wall Street Journal*, 25 May 1993, 1.

21. Masciarotte, "C'mon Girl," 90.

22. Mary Louise Adams, "There's No Place Like Home: On the Place of Identity in Feminist Politics," *Feminist Review* 31 (spring 1989): 22–33; and Linda Briskin, "Identity Politics and the Hierarchy of Oppression: A Comment," *Feminist Review* 35 (1990): 102–108.

23. Wendy Kaminer, *I'm Dysfunctional, You're Functional: The Recovery Movement and Other Self-Help Fashions* (New York: Vintage, 1993), 38.

24. J. B. Thompson, *Ideology and Modern Culture: Critical Social Theory* (Cambridge: Polity Press, 1990), 112.

Questions

1. *Public sphere* is an important term in this essay. In paragraph 3, Shattuc presents Jürgen Habermas's definition, and then poses the question of whether talk shows can "be considered public arenas where 'the people' form opinion freely" (par. 4). Make an outline showing how she sets about answering this question.

2. What do you understand from Shattuc's use of the term *identity politics*? This term is commonly defined as "the tendency to base one's politics on a sense of personal identity—as gay, as Jewish, as black, as female" (Diana Fuss, *Essentially Speaking*, p. 96). See paragraph 15 for Shattuc's definition, and paragraph 19 for Oprah's version. What is Shattuc's objection to Oprah's version of identity politics?

3. What are Shattuc's identity politics? Is she speaking for a particular political class? Do you find that she has tried to present impartially evidence for both the positive and negative aspects of daytime talk shows in general, and *Oprah* in particular?

PROJECT 1: GETTING IT TOGETHER

Ways of Appealing

1. Take a look at the work you've done previously, especially in the persuasion and argument sections, in light of Shattuc's concern with rational argument. What kinds of appeals were used the most by the

writers in each section? Consider the differences between presenting an argument in written form and presenting one orally, as on television. What kind of appeal are you most likely to encounter on television?

For this project, we ask you to compare the way an issue is treated on a daytime talk show with the way the same or a similar issue is treated either on another daytime talk show or on a regular evening news program on PBS or one of the major commercial networks. Write a comparative evaluation of the kinds of appeals made on the talk shows or on the talk show and the news program. In your conclusion, you might consider whether it is or is not possible to hold a rational discussion on television.

2. Look again at Peter Balakian's "Words for My Grandmother" (p. 57), Louise De Salvo's "Portrait of the *Puttana* as a Middle-Aged Woolf Scholar" (p. 76), or Toni Cade Bambara's "The Education of a Storyteller" (p. 205). Re-read one of these in light of Shattuc's comments on identity politics and the reliance on experience as a basis for argument. Write a response to Shattuc from the point of view of either Balakian, De Salvo, or Bambara. In your response, compare your writer's politics with those of Oprah Winfrey.

PROJECT 2: TAKING IT FURTHER

Online Politics and Public Opinion

Like many other TV shows, *The Oprah Winfrey Show* has an official Web site: **<http://www.oprah.com/>**. Besides transcripts from recent shows, the Web site includes a message board where viewers can post their responses to a show's issues and to each other. This message board is one small part of that new electronic public sphere known as the Internet.

Like a talk show, the Internet is composed of discourses (talk) and images (show), much of which is intent on influencing public opinion and shaping political discussion. Take newsgroups, for example. Newsgroups such as soc.politics and alt.current-events.usa are two among tens of thousands of discussion forums on Usenet, one of the oldest and most diverse parts of the Internet. Accessible to anyone who can log on, Usenet discussion groups strike some as quintessentially democratic and therefore politically progressive; they are the participatory town meetings of an emerging electronic democracy. Others, however, think existing online political discussions further the degradation of the public sphere and in so doing, undermine the possibility of a civil society based on rational argument rather than mindless manipulation.

What do you think? Using what you've learned from reading Shattuc's paper on the politics of talk shows, investigate some online discussion forum as a place where public opinion is being formed. If you want to explore what happens when a talk show goes online, visit *Oprah Online* at **<http://www.oprah.com/>**; once there, click on "message boards," "talk about the show," and a topic. If you want to study a newsgroup, go to **<http://tile.net>** for a list of such groups. You can also find newsgroup postings by topic if you use a search engine like AltaVista (**<http://altavista.com>**) or Dogpile (**<http://dogpile.com>**) and indicate that you want your topic searched on Usenet. Another option is to study an online chat for members provided by a company like AOL; if you choose this option, be sure to search for a chat related to some sociopolitical issue or event like school choice; the shootings in Columbine, Colorado; or gun control.

As you study the postings in the discussion forum, consider the following questions: To what extent is the discussion rational? What seems to be at issue? What claims are being made and what kind of evidence is presented? What role do appeals to feelings, personal experience, and experts play? To what extent do participants interact with each other? What seems to be the purpose and the structure of the discussion? Having worked through these questions, write a paper that states, develops, and supports your position on the kinds and quality of online public discussion.

PART FIVE

Writing with Personality, Knowledge, and Power

11

Putting It Together
Synthesis

The production of a synthetic text calls upon all of an individual's writing skills. A synthesis is not just an argument, for it seeks to make sense of a complex body of material rather than to argue for one point of view over another; in fact, a synthesis may even conclude that two opposing views are both partly right. Still less is synthesis an explicit act of persuasion, since it makes its appeal more to reason than to emotion. Nevertheless, a strong synthetic text has some of the cohesive qualities of an argument and some of the liveliness of persuasion. It also displays the kind of personal engagement associated with reflective writing, even though it focuses on ideas rather than experiential events.

In constructing a synthesis, the writer must examine a body of material and apply the processes of analysis and classification in such a way that he or she can develop a hypothesis about this material. In a synthetic text, the thesis is always a hypothesis—a provisional idea to be explored, explained, supported, and qualified by reference to the material at issue. Although a synthetic text may be organized like an argument, it is usually just as concerned with raising questions as it is with providing answers. A major fault in this kind of writing can be claiming to have proved the hypothesis once and for all.

In order to generate a hypothesis, you need to understand a body of material, but in order to understand a body of material, you need some hypothesis or organizing principle. This seems to present a problem so circular that it cannot be solved, but in practice, you begin to work through your materials with one or more possible ideas already in mind. You try classification and analysis to see if they can help you shape the material in a way that will lead you to formulate a clearer, working hypothesis. Sometimes you'll find that more material must be gathered before you can develop and support a certain hypothesis. In doing this, you may discover new questions and new directions to explore. The hypothesis you eventually settle on will be limited by the data you're working with, and you must acknowledge this limitation in two ways: by not claiming more than your data will support and by not ignoring significant material you've gathered.

Writing a synthesis paper involves a process of moving back and forth from your material to your writing. It may well involve starting to write, stopping, returning to the material, discarding some of what you have done, beginning again. For some people, written outlines are helpful. For others, sketchy notes, diagrams, and mental outlines will be more important. Each individual must find the appropriate way. Practice helps, but as every writer of synthetic essays discovers, you can't simply gather material aimlessly and then sit down and write. You must think about the text you will write as you work through the material you've gathered.

PROJECT 1

How Should Photographs Be "Read"?

The special nature of the photographic image has led to a wide difference of opinion about how photographs should be interpreted, or read. With this synthesis project, we aim to involve you in that controversy. Before presenting you with any pictures, however, we want to offer a brief sketch of the nature of the controversy about photography. As time goes on, you may find this sketch too neat and simple, but it should serve you—and us—as a place to start.

A photograph can be seen as a document—a record of a moment snatched from history—or as a work of art—a text free of simple connections to its origin and open to multiple interpretations. Knowing this, you might consider it a simple matter to divide all photographs into one category or the other, with documents here and art works there. But in practice, such division would lead to many problems; some photographs would refuse to rest nicely in one category or the other. Some could be seen either as documents or as works of art and, in fact, would seem most properly described as belonging to both categories at the same time.

Another way to regard this problem is to see it not as a matter of categorizing individual photographs but as a matter of interpretation. How should a given photograph be interpreted? Must it be connected to its time and place of origin? Do we need to know where and when it was taken? Do we need to know what was "really" going on in front of the camera, or can we use the image for our own purposes? Can we simply go where the photograph stimulates us to go, using it as a key to our own thoughts, feelings, and dreams?

The material in this section should make the issues involved in reading photographs both more concrete and more complicated for you. We ask you to consider and discuss these materials as the basis for an essay on the interpretation of photographic images. Later we will offer some advice about how to proceed in writing. For the moment, however, you need only read and consider. Take your time. Stop and think about the words and images that follow.

READING 1

Jean Mohr, "A Photo and Some Reactions" (from *Another Way of Telling*)

On one occasion, the photographer and teacher Jean Mohr showed a group of people a particular photograph and asked them to interpret it. He gives us their reactions and then tells us what was actually happening. Before you read any of the responses, jot down what comes into your mind when you look at the picture on page 324.

Market-gardener: (*Laughs*) This one makes me think of a little 1
girl who already has a maternal capacity, and who's treating her doll like it was her own baby. All right, the doll is not pretty and is undressed, but it's hers!

Clergyman: An odd photo. Should one protect children from see- 2
ing the cruelty of the world? Should one hide certain aspects of reality from them? Her hands over the doll's eyes shouldn't be there. One ought to be able to show everything, to see all.

Schoolgirl: She's crying because her doll hasn't any clothes. 3

Banker: Well-fed, well-dressed, such a child is probably spoilt. 4
Given the luxury of no material worries, people can give in to any whim or fancy.

Actress: "My baby is crying but doesn't want to show it." What 5
surprises me is how she hides the doll's face. There's a strong sense of identification between the doll and the child. The girl is playing

out what is happening to the doll and what the doll feels. The vine in the background is strange....

Dance-teacher: She has everything, yet she doesn't realize it, she is 6 crying with her eyes shut. And the tree behind. The doll is as big as she is.

Psychiatrist: It puzzles me. She's crying as if she has a pain, and 7 yet she's well. She's crying on behalf of her doll, and she covers the eyes as if there was a sight which shouldn't be seen.

Hairdresser: It's a child and somebody has tried to take her doll, 8 which is precious to her. She's going to hold on to it. Perhaps she's German, she's blonde. It makes me think of myself when I was that age.

Factory worker: It's sweet. It reminds me of my niece when her 9 sister tries to take her doll away from her. She's crying, screaming, because someone wants to take her doll away.

What was happening: Great Britain, in the country. A small girl 10 was playing with her doll. Sometimes sweetly, sometimes brutally. At one moment she even pretended to eat her doll.

Questions

1. Compare your written response to the picture with those of Mohr's respondents and with your classmates' responses. Which responses do you find most interesting? Why?
2. What makes a "good" response good? Is it a matter of "correctness" or "imagination" or something else?

Allan Sekula, from "On the Invention of Photographic Meaning"

I would like to conclude with a rather schematic summary. All photographic communication seems to take place within the conditions of a kind of binary folklore. That is, there is a "symbolist" folk-myth and a "realist" folk-myth. The misleading but popular form of this opposition is "art photography" vs. "documentary photography." Every photograph tends, at any given moment of reading in any given context, toward one of these two poles of meaning. The oppositions between these two poles are as follows: photographer as seer vs. photographer as witness, photography as expression vs. photography as reportage, theories of imagination (and inner truth) vs. theories of empirical truth, affective value vs. informative value....

Questions

1. Summarize in your own words the differences between the two notions of photography that Sekula describes.
2. Is Sekula talking about two kinds of photography or two ways of seeing photographs?
3. Can photographs be described in any other way than those Sekula defines? Can these two opposing descriptions be combined or surpassed? What is a photograph?

John Berger Reads a Photograph (from *Another Way of Telling*)

A mother with her child is staring intently at a soldier. Perhaps they   1
are speaking. We cannot hear their words. Perhaps they are saying
nothing and everything is being said by the way they are looking at
each other. Certainly a drama is being enacted between them.

The caption reads: "A Red Hussar leaving, June 1919, Bu-   2
dapest." The photograph is by André Kertész.

So, the woman has just walked out of their home and will shortly   3
go back alone with the child. The drama of the moment is expressed
in the difference between the clothes they are wearing. His for travelling, for sleeping out, for fighting; hers for staying at home.

The caption can also entail other thoughts. The Hapsburg   4
monarchy had fallen the previous autumn. The winter had been

one of extreme shortages (especially of fuel in Budapest) and economic disintegration. Two months before, in March, the socialist Republic of Councils had been declared. The Western allies in Paris, fearful lest the Russian and now the Hungarian example of revolution should spread throughout Eastern Europe and the Balkans, were planning to dismantle the new republic. A blockade was already imposed. General Foch himself was planning the military invasion being carried out by Rumanian and Czech troops. On June 8th Clemenceau telegraphed an ultimatum to Béla Kun demanding a Hungarian military withdrawal which would have left the Rumanians occupying the eastern third of their country. For another six weeks the Hungarian Red Army fought on, but it was finally overwhelmed. By August, Budapest was occupied and very soon after, the first European fascist regime under Horthy was established.

If we are looking at an image from the past and we want to relate   5
it to ourselves, we need to know something of the history of that past. And so the foregoing paragraph—and much more than that might be said—is relevant to the reading of Kertész's photograph. Which is presumably why he gave it the caption he did and not just the title "Parting." Yet the photograph—or rather, the way this photograph demands to be read—cannot be limited to the historical.

Everything in it is historical: the uniforms, the rifles, the corner   6
by the Budapest railway station, the identity and biographies of all the people who are (or were) recognizable—even the size of the trees on the other side of the fence. And yet it also concerns a resistance to history: an opposition.

This opposition is not the consequence of the photographer hav-   7
ing said Stop! It is not that the resultant static image is like a fixed post in a flowing river. We know that in a moment the soldier will turn his back and leave; we presume that he is the father of the child in the woman's arms. The significance of the instant photographed is already claiming minutes, weeks, years.

The opposition exists in the parting look between the man and   8
the woman. This look is not directed towards the viewer. We witness it as the older soldier with the moustache and the woman with the shawl (perhaps a sister) do. The exclusivity of this look is further emphasized by the boy in the mother's arms; he is watching his father, and yet he is excluded from their look.

This look, which crosses before our eyes, is holding in place what   9
is, not specifically what is there around them outside the station, but what *is* their life, what *are* their lives. The woman and the soldier are looking at each other so that the image of what *is* now shall remain for

them. In this look their being *is* opposed to their history, even if we assume that this history is one they accept or have chosen.

Questions

1. Using Sekula's terminology, describe Berger's way of reading the photograph. Now, describe it in your own words.
2. What do you like and dislike in Berger's way of reading? How important do you think it is to know the historical context of a photograph?

John Berger on the Use of Photography (from *About Looking*)

We need to return to the distinction I made between the private and public uses of photography. In the private use of photography, the context of the instant recorded is preserved so that the photograph lives in an ongoing continuity. (If you have a photograph of Peter on your wall, you are not likely to forget what Peter means to you.) The public photograph, by contrast, is torn from its context, and becomes a dead object which, exactly because it is dead, lends itself to any arbitrary use.

In the most famous photographic exhibition ever organized, *The Family of Man* (put together by Edward Steichen in 1955), photographs from all over the world were presented as though they formed a universal family album. Steichen's intuition was absolutely correct: the private use of photographs can be exemplary for their public use. Unfortunately the shortcut he took in treating the existing class-divided world as if it were a family, inevitably made the whole exhibition, not necessarily each picture, sentimental and complacent. The truth is that most photographs taken of people are about suffering, and most of that suffering is man-made.

"One's first encounter," writes Susan Sontag, "with the photographic inventory of ultimate horror is a kind of revelation, the prototypically modern revelation: a negative epiphany. For me, it was photographs of Bergen-Belsen and Dachau which I came across by chance in a bookstore in Santa Monica in July 1945. Nothing I have seen—in photographs or in real life—ever cut me as sharply, deeply, instantaneously. Indeed, it seems plausible to me to divide my life into two parts, before I saw those photographs (I was twelve) and after, though it was several years before I understood fully what they were about."

Photographs are relics of the past, traces of what has happened. If the living take that past upon themselves, if the past becomes an integral part of the process of people making their own history, then all photographs would reacquire a living context, they would continue to exist in time, instead of being arrested moments. It is just possible that photography is the prophecy of a human memory yet to be socially and politically achieved. Such a memory would encompass any image of the past, however tragic, however guilty, within its own continuity. The distinction between the private and public uses of photography would be transcended. The Family of Man would exist.

Questions

1. What do you think Berger means about *The Family of Man* exhibition being "sentimental and complacent"? Have you seen that exhibit or the book made from it? If so, what is your own view of the matter?
2. Berger makes a distinction between the private and public uses of photography. Do you understand what he means by these two kinds of use? Can you put his definitions in your own words? Does it make sense to you? Is this the same as the distinction described by Sekula between the photograph as document and as symbol?

READING 2

Three Photographs in Context

Gisèle Freund on Doisneau's Photograph (from *Photography and Society*)

The photographer Robert Doisneau saw one of his photographs   1
used in a different context from his intention. For him, Parisians had always been the most fascinating of subjects. He loved to wander the streets and stop at cafés. One day, in a small café on the rue de Seine where he was accustomed to meeting his friends, he noticed a delightful young woman at the bar drinking a glass of wine. She was seated next to a middle-aged gentleman who was looking at her with a smile that was both amused and greedy. Doisneau asked and received permission to photograph them. The photograph appeared in the magazine *Le Point*, in an issue devoted to cafés illustrated with Doisneau's photographs. He handed this photograph, among others, to his agency.

All sorts of publications call on agencies when they need pictures   2
to illustrate an article. Sometime later, Doisneau's photograph appeared in a small magazine published by the temperance league to illustrate an article on the evils of alcohol. The gentleman in the

photograph, who was a drawing instructor, was not pleased. "I shall be taken for a boozer," he complained to the apologetic photographer who had no control over how his photographs were used. Things went from bad to worse when the same photograph appeared in a scandal sheet which had reproduced it from *Le Point* without the permission of either the agency or the photographer. The caption accompanying the photograph read: "*Prostitution in the Champs-Elysées.*" This time the drawing teacher was furious and sued the magazine, the agency, and the photographer. The court fined the scandal magazine a large sum of money for fraud, and the agency, which had not released the photograph, was also found guilty. But the court acquitted the photographer, ruling that he was an "innocent artist." [Doisneau's photograph is reproduced on page 331.]

From an Interview with Robert Doisneau (in *Dialogue with Photography*)

Don't you think that there is a certain historical value in your picture?   1

    Well, if this is correct, it is despite me, it wasn't a conscious aim of   2
mine. But if my work is of historical interest, so much the better. My
idea was much more egotistic, it was to hold the world that I loved! . . .

    You just said that your photographic purpose was egotistic. Was that a   3
conscious intent?

    "Intent" is often unconscious. It is the game of seizing and delay-   4
ing! There is something in Prévert that is wonderful—the "small
second of eternity." Nothing is more beautiful than this expression
for me. It appears in a poem called "Jardin" in *Parc Montsouris:*

> The bench of the Montsouris park
> Where you kissed me and I kissed you
> In the Montsouris park in Paris
> On the earth that is astral and that is all
> And this small second of eternity.

    And this is it! This "small second of eternity" that we are lucky   5
enough to be able to find! The understanding of this is not yet
visible for all people. But when a tiny bit of this "small second" is
captured by photography, when it is put in a rectangle that has a
form accepted by culture or scholastic training, then people look
and say, "Oh, yes!" Maybe it would be ideal to think that, afterward,
these same people would want to go out and see for themselves.
That would really be success! But I don't think it will happen. I be-

Robert Doisneau, *A Parisian Café*

lieve that the more time goes by, the more people will use substitute experts. People will delegate their eyes to the eye specialists! It is easier and more comfortable to let specialists be accountable for filtering our responses to life than to face them ourselves. Already, people seem willing to delegate *all* their senses to specialists.

You were suggesting a while ago that you would like people to take photographs and photographers more seriously.   6

I hate collectors, the ones who take something just for them-   7
selves. Me, I like to give. I like to discover something and show it. I'm the village idiot who goes off to the forest and comes back with a bird in his hat and walks around everywhere saying, "Look and see what I've unearthed!" And this bird of an unknown species immediately bothers notable people simply because they don't know how to categorize it. They never saw that kind of bird before, so they say: "Yes, it's amusing. Now go play elsewhere and let us be, because we're talking about serious things." This is a bit like the photographer's role now.

I do pictures as gifts for my friends. They are people who are my   8
accomplices, and I am very happy to tell them: "Here, just look at what I've unearthed!" I am happy that it might make them chuckle a little bit, like the way I chuckled inside when I took the picture. Or maybe it's an emotion more delicate than chuckling. I want to give, *always* to give.

There are certain things that you seek, situations that you wait for?   9

I am not interested in refined culture, but rather in instinctive   10
things. I wait for surprise, to be surprised, I do not ever want to have a preconceived idea, or to bring back mere pictorial souvenirs.

Often, you find a scene, a scene that already is evoking some-   11
thing—either stupidity, or pretentiousness, or, perhaps, charm. So you have a little theater. Well, all you have to do is wait there in front of this little theater for the actors to present themselves. I often operate in this way. Here I have my setting and I wait. What I am waiting for, I don't know exactly. I can stay half a day in the same place. And it's very rare that I come home with a completely empty bag.

Photography is very subjective. Photography is not a document   12
on which a report can be made. It is a *subjective* document. Photography is a false witness, a lie. People want to prove the universe is there. It is a physical image that contains a certain amount of documentation, which is fine, but it isn't evidence, a testimony upon which a general philosophy can be based. People can say, "Here is a fellow who has seen such and such facets of life, but not the whole."

If it is not about reality, what does photography mean to you?   13

It might involve the principle of the committed photographer   14
who thinks of himself as socially responsible. There may be something there that is important. You may choose to report on a socially deprived area. Most people would not take their cameras to
these places. But the committed photographer may reveal a certain
aspect of the condition of people's lives there. Photographers have
done this, and I find that this is one of the great merits of photography. Beforehand, apart from the few paintings, there were no documents of the actual social environment. The people of Viva who
took pictures of low-income-housing projects did work that was
very interesting. Whether it is reality or not, it is, nevertheless, the
penetration of an environment that had never been seen in a picture
before. The fact that the photographer may have this social responsibility is very important because he will be showing something that
most people hold in contempt, that they may want to hide.

You take a certain type of picture — how do you relate this to your polit-   15
ical ideology?

I am not militant. The photography profession doesn't permit me   16
to be militant. When you're militant you really have to spend a lot of
time at it. You really have to found your life on it. Whereas my mili-
tancy is photographic and *all* my life, if I can, if I have enough will, if
I am not overwhelmed by paperwork and red tape, I spend taking pictures. Thus, I do have convictions that are, if you like, political. My
photos are not pictures that say, "Here is good and evil, right and
wrong." If my work speaks, it does so by being a little less serious, a
little less solemn, and by its lightness it helps people to live. I think
that this is a social role that isn't negligible. I don't say that it is important, but just that it isn't negligible. I would rather *help* people
through photography than produce "symbolic images" for propaganda purposes. I work more in everyday chronicles and with "smallness." I would not be at ease doing violent or "heavy" things.

From an Interview with Gordon Parks (in *The Photographs of Gordon Parks*)

Bush: Your work at the [Chicago] South Side Community Art Cen-   1
ter won you a Julius Rosenwald Fellowship in 1941. It was $200 a
month, and you chose to go to Washington in January 1942 to
work with Roy Stryker at the Farm Security Administration.

Parks: Yes, those were the photographers whose work I had seen   2
while I was working on the railroad. I went to work for Roy Stryker

at the Farm Security Administration. That's where I met Ben Shahn, Russell Lee, Dorothea Lange and a number of others. Walker Evans had gone by then. That was a great time in my life. And Stryker taught me the importance of the camera in terms of being a documentary tool.

Bush: You also learned that Washington was a southern city, didn't you?   3

Parks: I found out what prejudice was really like. I expected Washington, D.C., as the seat of our government, to be the one place where I could find democracy. And that was the one place I didn't find democracy. I found that discrimination and bigotry were worse there than any place I had yet seen.   4

Bush: This was the time when you took the picture of the woman in front of the American flag.   5

Parks: Yes, Stryker had taken my camera away from me when I got to D.C. and told me to go out and get to know Washington. I went to the motion pictures and was refused; I went to a place called Julius Garfinkel, a big department store, and the clerk wouldn't sell me a coat. They wouldn't feed me at several restaurants. I was furious. I wanted to photograph discrimination. Roy said, "You just don't go out and photograph discrimination. How do you do it? This is what you have to learn. I want you to sit down and write me a long set of plans about how you would attempt to do it." Of course, it was very difficult for me. I didn't know how to do it. Finally, he sent me to talk with a black charwoman who worked in the building. "You will find out a lot from the lady," he said. And I did. I found out that she had been a charwoman there for many years. Yet, she had been to high school, and she deserved a much better job. I took her into a room where there was an American flag draped on a wall. I posed her against it—Grant Wood style—with a mop in one hand and a broom in the other. When Roy saw that photograph, he said, "You're going to get us all fired." I thought the photograph had been destroyed, but I found it in the Library of Congress. I realize now that it is possibly the most popular photograph of that whole series. I thought that it had long since been destroyed.   6

Bush: You have often said since then: "I had learned how to fight the evil of poverty—along with the evil of racism—with a camera." How did you learn to do this? How have your feelings changed over the years, if indeed they have, since you first became a photographer?   7

Parks: The photograph of the black cleaning woman standing in front of the American flag with a broom and a mop expresses that more than any other photograph I have taken. It was the first one I took in Washington, D.C. I thought then, and Roy Stryker eventually proved it to me, that you could not photograph a person who   8

Gordon Parks, *American Gothic* (Washington, D.C., 1942)

turns you away from the motion picture ticket window, or someone who refuses to feed you, or someone who refuses to wait on you in a store. You could not photograph him and say, "This is a bigot," because bigots have a way of looking just like everybody else. What the camera had to do was expose the evils of racism, the evils of poverty, the discrimination and the bigotry, by showing the people who suffered most under it. That was the way it had to be done....

Bush: What were your basic assignments [when you joined the   9
Farm Security Administration]?

Parks: I was a documentary man. Roy wanted me to show the   10
"face of America." He wasn't just interested in showing the poverty-stricken. He wanted to capture on film the character of the New England farmer, the upstate New York businessman — whatever. There were other things to photograph besides poverty-stricken people ....

Bush: When you met Alexander Lieberman and people in the   11
fashion business, you must admit, in retrospect, that you really were not yet an experienced fashion photographer. But, when you freelanced for Vogue and Glamour, you were really in the "big time." Was it just nerve, confidence, or had you just learned that fast? You learn things very fast.

Parks: I learned very fast, Martin. I had to learn fast. After my   12
mother died, it was a matter of survival. I had to learn fast. I didn't have a formal education. I had to do it on plain dreams, guts and hope. That's what it was. The determination that, by God, I'm going to do it. I wanted to be somebody. For some reason or other, I don't know why, even today—I sometimes attribute it to my mother—I never thought of my blackness when I did anything. Even today, I don't think of my blackness. I work as an artist who happens to be black. And I tell the kids that this is the only way....

Bush: When did you begin writing as well as photographing Life   13
magazine articles?

Parks: I did my own research sometimes. I did my research in   14
Chicago while I was doing a story called, "The Modern Shouting Baptist." The white lad who was with me offended people there by not taking off his hat. The kid was very nice. He didn't mean any offense. But the members of the church were very uptight about it. So he told me that he had better not go back. I had better do it all; and I did. That's how I happened to start writing....

Bush: You took an extraordinary photograph of an old woman   15
five minutes before she died. Was that an invasion of her privacy?

Parks: Oh, yes, but she had been conscious enough to know it. She   16
knew I was there. There were situations that I feel were more private, incidents while I was with Roberto Rosellini and Ingrid Bergman on Stromboli and while I was with Muhammad Ali. Ali had a busted jaw.

He had invited me to his room, but I would not take the picture. George Plimpton (in his book) wondered why I never took that picture because he was sitting there with me. But, at the moment, I thought more of my friendship with Ali than I did about being a reporter, and my responsibilities as a reporter. This was a guy who had befriended me over the years. I would not photograph him that way.

Martin Bush on Gordon Parks (from *The Photographs of Gordon Parks*)

People are Gordon Parks' passion, all kinds of people: hungry   1
people, fashionable people, famous people.…They speak to us about ourselves and about the world around us, and the viewer is constantly reminded that poverty, hunger and intolerance are still three of the most awful things that mankind has to endure.

Parks is no stranger to frustration and despair. He witnessed   2
firsthand how easily crime, drugs, prostitution and apathy claimed their victims as he fought his way through the violent streets of urban ghettos to emerge in places where few blacks dared to go— or even aspired to go. But Parks freed himself from the past and turned his own bitterness and violence into something positive. "When I felt I couldn't say what was in me, I turned to photography," he said. "I learned that it would enable me to show what was right and wrong about America, the world and life. I wanted my children and my children's children to be able to look at my pictures and know what my world was like. My purpose has been to communicate, to somehow evoke the same response from a seamstress in Paris or a housewife in Harlem."…

Parks' big breakthrough came…later when Life magazine of-   3
fered him a full-time staff position as a photographer. "When I first went to Life in 1949, I was the worst photographer they had," said Parks. "I asked for and accepted help whenever I needed it, knowing that I walked a tightrope; feeling the pressure of succeeding for blacks, because I was black, and proving myself to certain whites who resented my presence."

Later on, Parks could look back with pride on what he had   4
achieved, secure in the knowledge that he had become one of the magazine's most versatile and talented photographers, a man who was at home in the raw and often dangerous arena of photojournalism, or in the lush world of high fashion.

But Life was only a step toward more significant things. What   5
things? Parks had no idea at the time. Still, that did not seem to matter. "I felt," he said, "that I was working on a larger canvas.…" That larger canvas would soon include a three-volume autobiography,

three books of poetry that were illustrated with his own photographs, a novel, a ballet, several sonatas and symphonies, and musical scores for two films. Parks eventually left Life to pursue an entirely new form of expression — the motion pictures — and successfully directed five major films. In recent years he has continued to seek an even wider artistic expression by combining painting with his photography.

Eve Arnold on Her Work (from *The Unretouched Woman*)

Twenty-five years ago, when I became a photojournalist, I was looked on as someone apart — a "career lady," a "woman photographer." My colleagues were not spoken of in inverted commas; they were not "career men" or "men photographers." I was not happy about it, but realized as have women before me that it was a fundamental part of female survival to play the assigned rôle. I could not fight against those attitudes. I needed to know more about other women to try to understand what made me acquiesce in this situation.

It was then that I started my project, photographing and talking to women. I became both observer and participant. I photographed girl children and women; the rich and the poor; the migratory potato picker on Long Island and the Queen of England; the nomad bride in the Hindu Kush waiting for a husband she had never seen, and the Hollywood Queen Bee whose life was devoted to a regimen of beauty care. There was the Zulu woman whose child was dying of hunger and women mourning their dead in Hoboken, New Jersey. I filmed in harems in Abu Dhabi, in bars in Cuba, and in the Vatican in Rome. There was birth in London and betrothal in the Caucasus, divorce in Moscow and protest marches of black women in Virginia. There were the known and the unknown — and always those marvelous faces.

I am not a radical feminist, because I don't believe that siege mentality works. But I know something of the problems and the inequities of being a woman, and over the years the women I photographed talked to me about themselves and their lives. Each had her own story to tell — uniquely female but also uniquely human.

Themes recur again and again in my work. I have been poor and I wanted to document poverty; I had lost a child and I was obsessed with birth; I was interested in politics and I wanted to know how it affected our lives; I am a woman and I wanted to know about women.

I realize now that through my work these past twenty-five years I have been searching for myself, my time, and the world I live in....

I was anxious not to take just pretty pictures. I wanted my work to have a purpose, to make a social comment, no matter how slight; to say something about the world I lived in....

When Bob Capa saw my photographs for the first time he said   7
that for him—metaphorically, of course—my work fell between
Marlene Dietrich's legs and the bitter lives of migrant potato pickers. I wonder if he knew how close to the mark he was about me.

I want to deal with the "migrants" part first. As a second-   8
generation American, daughter of Russian immigrants, growing up
during the Depression, the reality I knew well was poverty and deprivation. So I could identify easily with laborers who followed the
potato crop north along the Eastern seaboard, settling in each new
area as the harvest was ready for them.

Now, about Marlene's legs—metaphorically, of course. I also grew   9
up with Hollywood movies. Although I was a reluctant host to their
imagery, I could not deny their impact on me and on other women.
They affected the way we saw ourselves and the way men saw us. The
traditional still photograph was an idealized portrait. The subject was
posed in the most flattering position, and the features were lit—eyes,
lips, teeth, cheekbones, breasts, and in Dietrich's case, legs—like so
many commodities. Wrinkles and blemishes were removed by the re-
toucher. Everything that life had deposited was penciled out.

When I photographed Marlene recording the songs she had   10
sung to the soldiers during World War II—"Lilli Marlene," "Miss
Otis Regrets," etc.—I wanted the working woman, the unretouched woman.

From an Interview with Eve Arnold (in *Master Photographers*)

Eve Arnold's photographs demonstrate her passionate interest in   1
people, in the human and particularly the female predicament. She
brings to her observations the sharply inquisitive, but at the same time
uncensoring, eye of the journalist. She seeks to reveal inner meanings
and truths by drawing attention to the unguarded moment when the
subject has all but forgotten the presence of the camera, and she produces her vignettes unretouched, unposed, un-selfconscious....

Would you call yourself a feminist?   2

I suppose I *am* a sort of half-baked feminist, and I do believe in   3
the feminist movement, but I have to say that it's been an enormous
help to me to be a woman. You see, men like to be photographed
by women, and women don't feel that they have to carry on a flirta-
tion, which they often do with a male photographer.

Do you like commercial assignments?   4

I love the discipline that they demand. It teaches you great control,   5
and you have to draw on all your technical knowledge. Working with

art directors isn't always easy, and sometimes you seem to be just clicking a shutter, but the organization that must precede the shoot is very comprehensive. I tend to be a very organized photographer, even when doing editorial work. I like to organize everything first, so that during the actual shoot I can loosen up and "play."

For example, when I first went to China in 1979 I had to rely on the Chinese to show me things, but I'd done my homework and I knew exactly what I wanted to see. So I asked them about religion and their art schools and their millionaires, because I knew that some capitalistic principles had been reestablished. They hadn't been asked those sorts of questions before, and having been asked, they were quite happy to oblige. If I hadn't known what to ask for I would have seen all the usual sights that they had come to believe foreign journalists were interested in being shown. Preparation is the most important aspect of photojournalism—if you know what you want, most people will help you.

China is about as far removed from your photographs of the glamour and superficiality of Hollywood as anyone could imagine. Marlene Dietrich is perhaps the epitome of the glamorous woman and yet in these pictures you appear deliberately to have deglamorized her—why did you want to do that?

In this series of pictures I wanted to show her as she really was—a working woman, quite different from the idealized version. Robert Capa got it right when he said, metaphorically, that my work fell between Marlene Dietrich's legs and the lives of migratory potato pickers!

Are you a technically minded person?

Not at all. I'm much more intuitive. For instance I never remember what exposure I have given a picture—I just don't care. I bracket a lot, taking different exposures of the same subject, and I take pictures in situations and light conditions in which people say it can't be done. Often it works.

I remember one time when I took a photograph of a black girl in a dark hallway lit only by a 60 watt bulb. It shouldn't have come out, but it did, and I was happy with the result which was used as a double-page spread. If I had gone by the book and strobed it I wouldn't have got the picture I wanted.

I play these games because it's fun to play. After all, it's only film, and when it works it can be wonderful. I like to work on the edges of the film. With very little light and very slow film you can get some great images. It's dicey, and it doesn't always work, but when it does the rewards are enormous. I would far rather do anything than play it safe. I'm a gambler by nature and I think it has paid off.

Eve Arnold, *Marlene Dietrich* (United States, 1942)

Of course I lose a lot of images, and I use up a lot more film, but it's vital to get something that is entirely my own.

How do you feel that magic working for you, when you are taking pictures?   13

Even now when I work I may think that I've got something really   14
great, only to find that I haven't. It's not something I can explain. Perhaps it's best to let the images speak for themselves—at the end of the day they are the only things that matter.

I love photography. Maybe mystery is too big a word, but it has   15
that unknown quantity about it. One thing I find interesting, and have only recently started to think about, is that in that split second when I actually press the shutter absolutely anything can happen. Other images are forming that perhaps I hadn't noticed. In that moment in time a new figure might appear—one that I hadn't anticipated. So I always get what I see, but often something else as well. Sometimes colour foxes me, too. There can be marvellous surprises, and disappointments, but it's the element of the unknown that keeps up my interest in photography.

Photography is now a recognized form of art, and prints sell for large   16
sums. What do you feel about that?

It's sad that a few elitist art pundits have made photography "es-   17
tablishment," and I think that its commercialization in terms of collecting limited editions and signed photographs is pretentious. I would prefer photographs to be cheap and available to everyone—students should be able to buy them to stick on their walls. I once asked a dear friend of mine—a gifted photographer—what the difference was between the photography of the fifties and that of today. He replied "That's easy. Photography in the fifties was about people. Now it's about photography."

Questions

1. Consider the titles to the photographs by Doisneau, Parks, and Arnold. In what ways are the titles similar? In what ways are they different? Does each title fit its photograph well? If it were up to you, how would you title each photograph?
2. Do these three pictures represent different approaches to photography? Can you relate them to the distinctions made earlier in this section by Sekula and Berger?
3. How does knowing something about the methods and purposes of each photographer affect the way you see and understand the pictures?

4. Do you prefer one of the pictures to the others? Why or why not?
5. What are your thoughts about photography after working through the materials presented here?

PRACTICE 11.1

Writing about Photographs

We would like you to write a synthesis paper about the reading or inter-preting of photographs. In this paper, you should consider the various ways in which photographs can be read, and you should present your own theory about the best way to approach the interpretation of photographs. Your discussion should be based upon specific pictures. You may restrict yourself to those presented in this book, or you may introduce others, provided you supply copies of them with your finished paper. To help you get started, the following pages present a few additional photographs and some basic information about them.

In writing your paper, you need not discuss every picture that we present. Above all, you should not feel obliged to plod through discussions of each one in the order in which you find them here. Let your thoughts organize your essay, and let your discussions of individual photographs come where they are most appropriate to support your theory of inter-pretation. You should feel free to discuss more than one picture at a time, for the sake of comparison and contrast, or to discuss a number of works together to illustrate a point. If you wish, you may take up the question of an individual photographer's style, since you will have more than one picture by several well-known photographers to consider.

You need not confine yourself to the pictures immediately following, but may refer to others already presented in this book. For purposes of comparison and contrast, you may also refer to other kinds of visual im-ages presented in this book, including images drawn from the worlds of art and advertising, but remember to emphasize photography. For many reasons, we have concentrated on black-and-white photography here, leaving the issue of color aside. We strongly suggest that you, too, ac-cept this limitation. Remember that your task is to propose and demon-strate a theory about how photographs should be regarded, interpreted, or read, paying some attention to both their social and personal dimen-sions. You may, of course, cite statements about photography from ma-terial presented in this book or from other sources, provided you document such material according to whatever form your instructor rec-ommends. The basic questions you should answer are, What are photo-graphs for? How should we look at them? and Why should we look at them in that way?

Three More Photographs by Doisneau, Parks, and Arnold

Robert Doisneau, *Sidelong Glance* **(Paris, 1948)**

Gordon Parks, *Muslim School Children* (1963)

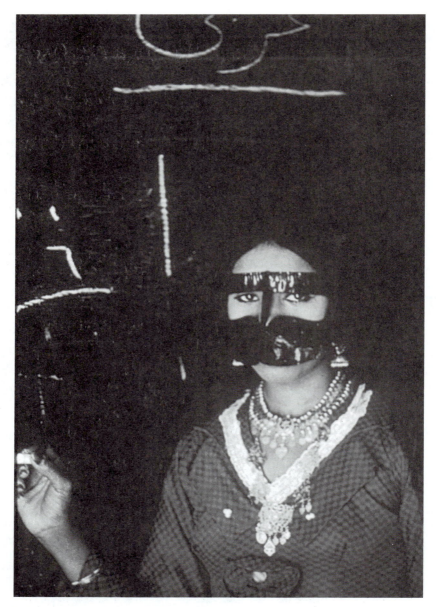

Eve Arnold, *A Literacy Teacher in Abu Dhabi* (1976)

Three Pictures from the Vietnam War Period

Associated Press, *A Paratrooper Works to Save the Life of a Buddy*

John Paul Filo, *Student Killed by National Guardsmen, Kent State University, May 4, 1970*

Huynh Cong (Nick) Ut, *Children Fleeing a Napalm Strike* (June 8, 1972)

A Picture Album

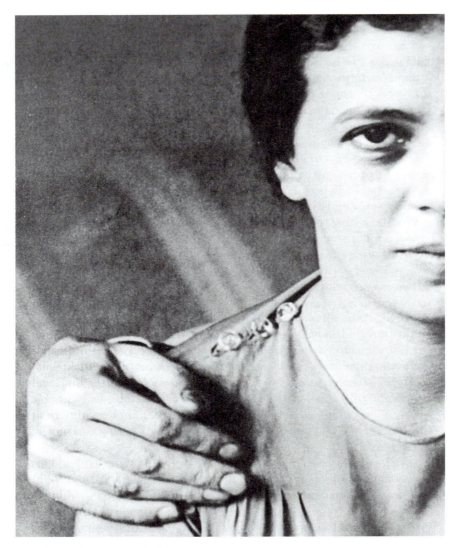

André Kertész, *Elizabeth and I* (Paris, 1931)

Dorothea Lange, *Drought Refugees Hoping for Cotton Work* **(Blythe, California, 1936)**

Unknown (March 27, 1945)
As U.S. Seventh Army troops advance, a German woman surveys the wreckage of her home in Bensheim, Germany.

Abbey Rowe (Washington DC, March 31, 1956)
Birthday party for David Eisenhower, grandson of President Dwight Eisenhower. In
attendance were movie and television stars Roy Rogers and Dale Evans.

Garry Winogrand, *World's Fair, New York City* (1964)

Automatic Reconnaissance Camera, *Mirage Jet* (July 1967)

W. Eugene Smith, *Tomoko in the Bath* **(1972)**

This is one of a series Smith made for his book Minimata, in which he recorded the victims of industrial pollution in a Japanese community. In this picture, a mother bathes her deformed child.

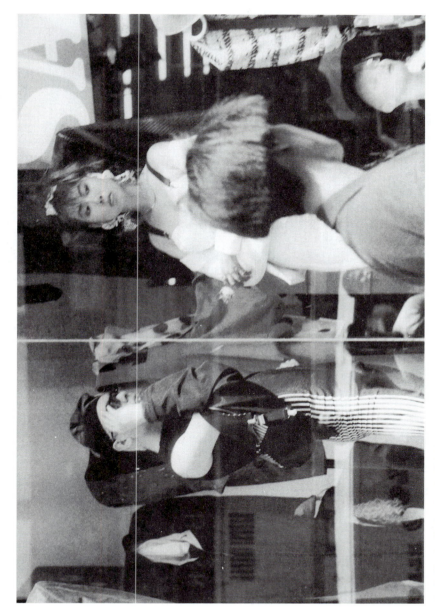

Charles Martin, *Window Dressing* (1989)

357

Dayna Smith, *Woman Comforted by Relatives and Friends at Husband's Funeral.* Izbica, Kosovo (1998).

▧ PROJECT 2

The American Frontier and American Culture

We have gathered six readings on the American frontier for you to use as source material for a synthesis paper on the impact of the American western frontier on American culture, and as a basis for further exploration of a specific area that interests you.

In the first two readings, we pair Frederick Jackson Turner, an American historian writing in 1893 on the "significance of the frontier," with Richard Slotkin, a professor of American studies writing in 1992 about "the myth of the frontier." These selections are followed by two fictional works—an excerpt from Edward L. Wheeler's highly popular dime novel featuring Deadwood Dick (1877), and Stephen Crane's "The Blue Hotel" (1898). Finally, historian Patricia Nelson Limerick examines the Disneyfied frontier.

▧ READING 1

Frederick Jackson Turner's "The Significance of the Frontier in American History" is frequently cited as "the most influential single piece of historical writing ever done in the United States" (William Prescott Webb). Writing in 1893, when the American frontier no longer existed, Turner asserted—in fellow historian Webb's words—"the overwhelming importance of the frontier as the dominant force in creating a democracy" and in shaping a national character. As you read, note which forces Turner considered most formative.

Frederick Jackson Turner, from "The Significance of the Frontier in American History"

In a recent bulletin of the Superintendent of the Census for 1890   1
appear these significant words: "Up to and including 1880 the country had a frontier of settlement, but at present the unsettled area has been so broken into by isolated bodies of settlement that there can hardly be said to be a frontier line. In the discussion of its extent, its westward movement, etc., it can not, therefore, any longer have a place in the census reports." This brief official statement marks the closing of a great historic movement. Up to our

own day American history has been in a large degree the history of the colonization of the Great West. The existence of an area of free land, its continuous recession, and the advance of American settlement westward, explain American development.

Behind institutions, behind constitutional forms and modifications, lie the vital forces that call these organs into life and shape them to meet changing conditions. The peculiarity of American institutions is the fact that they have been compelled to adapt themselves to the changes of an expanding people — to the changes involved in crossing a continent, in winning a wilderness, and in developing at each area of this progress out of the primitive economic and political conditions of the frontier into the complexity of city life. Said Calhoun in 1817, "We are great, and rapidly — I was about to say fearfully — growing!" So saying, he touched the distinguishing feature of American life. All peoples show development; the germ theory of politics has been sufficiently emphasized. In the case of most nations, however, the development has occurred in a limited area; and if the nation has expanded, it has met other growing peoples whom it has conquered. But in the case of the United States we have a different phenomenon. Limiting our attention to the Atlantic coast, we have the familiar phenomenon of the evolution of institutions in a limited area, such as the rise of representative government; the differentiation of simple colonial governments into complex organs; the progress from primitive industrial society, without division of labor, up to manufacturing civilization. But we have in addition to this a recurrence of the process of evolution in each western area reached in the process of expansion. Thus American development has exhibited not merely advance along a single line, but a return to primitive conditions on a continually advancing frontier line, and a new development for that area. American social development has been continually beginning over again on the frontier. This perennial rebirth, this fluidity of American life, this expansion westward with its new opportunities, its continuous touch with the simplicity of primitive society, furnish the forces dominating American character. The true point of view in the history of this nation is not the Atlantic coast, it is the Great West. Even the slavery struggle, which is made so exclusive an object of attention by writers like Professor von Holst, occupies its important place in American history because of its relation to westward expansion.

In this advance, the frontier is the outer edge of the wave — the meeting point between savagery and civilization. Much has been written about the frontier from the point of view of border warfare and the chase, but as a field for the serious study of the economist and the historian it has been neglected.

The American frontier is sharply distinguished from the European frontier—a fortified boundary line running through dense populations. The most significant thing about the American frontier is, that it lies at the hither edge of free land. In the census reports it is treated as the margin of that settlement which has a density of two or more to the square mile. The term is an elastic one, and for our purposes does not need sharp definition. We shall consider the whole frontier belt, including the Indian country and the outer margin of the "settled area" of the census reports. This paper will make no attempt to treat the subject exhaustively; its aim is simply to call attention to the frontier as a fertile field for investigation, and to suggest some of the problems which arise in connection with it.

In the settlement of America we have to observe how European life entered the continent, and how America modified and developed that life and reacted on Europe. Our early history is the study of European germs developing in an American environment. Too exclusive attention has been paid by institutional students to the Germanic origins, too little to the American factors. The frontier is the line of most rapid and effective Americanization. The wilderness masters the colonist. It finds him a European in dress, industries, tools, modes of travel, and thought. It takes him from the railroad car and puts him in the birch canoe. It strips off the garments of civilization and arrays him in the hunting shirt and the moccasin. It puts him in the log cabin of the Cherokee and Iroquois and runs an Indian palisade around him. Before long he has gone to planting Indian corn and plowing with a sharp stick; he shouts the war cry and takes the scalp in orthodox Indian fashion. In short, at the frontier the environment is at first too strong for the man. He must accept the conditions which it furnishes, or perish, and so he fits himself into the Indian clearings and follows the Indian trails. Little by little he transforms the wilderness, but the outcome is not the old Europe, not simply the development of Germanic germs, any more than the first phenomenon was a case of reversion to the Germanic mark. The fact is, that here is a new product that is American. At first, the frontier was the Atlantic coast. It was the frontier of Europe in a very real sense. Moving westward, the frontier became more and more American. As successive terminal moraines result from successive glaciations, so each frontier leaves its traces behind it, and when it becomes a settled area the region still partakes of the frontier characteristics. Thus the advance of the

4

5

frontier has meant a steady movement away from the influence of Europe, a steady growth of independence on American lines. And to study this advance, the men who grew up under these conditions, and the political, economic, and social results of it, is to study the really American part of our history.

* * * *

The Atlantic frontier was compounded of fisherman, fur-trader, miner, cattle-raiser, and farmer. Excepting the fisherman, each type of industry was on the march toward the West, impelled by an irresistible attraction. Each passed in successive waves across the continent. Stand at Cumberland Gap and watch the procession of civilization, marching single file — the buffalo following the trail to the salt springs, the Indian, the fur-trader and hunter, the cattle-raiser, the pioneer farmer — and the frontier has passed by. Stand at South Pass in the Rockies a century later and see the same procession with wider intervals between. The unequal rate of advance compels us to distinguish the frontier into the trader's frontier, the rancher's frontier, or the miner's frontier, and the farmer's frontier. When the mines and the cow pens were still near the fall line the traders' pack trains were tinkling across the Alleghanies, and the French on the Great Lakes were fortifying their posts, alarmed by the British trader's birch canoe. When the trappers scaled the Rockies, the farmer was still near the mouth of the Missouri.

Why was it that the Indian trader passed so rapidly across the continent? What effects followed from the trader's frontier? The trade was coeval with American discovery. The Norsemen, Vespuccius, Verrazani, Hudson, John Smith, all trafficked for furs. The Plymouth pilgrims settled in Indian cornfields, and their first return cargo was of beaver and lumber. The records of the various New England colonies show how steadily exploration was carried into the wilderness by this trade. What is true for New England is, as would be expected, even plainer for the rest of the colonies. All along the coast from Maine to Georgia the Indian trade opened up the river courses. Steadily the trader passed westward, utilizing the older lines of French trade. The Ohio, the Great Lakes, the Mississippi, the Missouri, and the Platte, the lines of western advance, were ascended by traders. They found the passes in the Rocky Mountains and guided Lewis and Clark, Frémont, and Bidwell. The explanation of the rapidity of this advance is connected with the effects of the trader on the Indian. The trading post left the un-armed tribes at the mercy of those that had purchased fire-arms — a truth which the Iroquois Indians wrote in blood, and so the remote

6

7

and unvisited tribes gave eager welcome to the trader. "The savages," wrote La Salle, "take better care of us French than of their own children; from us only can they get guns and goods." This accounts for the trader's power and the rapidity of his advance. Thus the disintegrating forces of civilization entered the wilderness. Every river valley and Indian trail became a fissure in Indian society, and so that society became honeycombed. Long before the pioneer farmer appeared on the scene, primitive Indian life had passed away. The farmers met Indians armed with guns. The trading frontier, while steadily undermining Indian power by making the tribes ultimately dependent on the whites, yet, through its sale of guns, gave to the Indian increased power of resistance to the farming frontier. French colonization was dominated by its trading frontier; English colonization by its farming frontier. There was an antagonism between the two frontiers as between the two nations. Said Duquesne to the Iroquois, "Are you ignorant of the difference between the king of England and the king of France? Go see the forts that our king has established and you will see that you can still hunt under their very walls. They have been placed for your advantage in places which you frequent. The English, on the contrary, are no sooner in possession of a place than the game is driven away. The forest falls before them as they advance, and the soil is laid bare so that you can scarce find the wherewithal to erect a shelter for the night."

And yet, in spite of this opposition of the interests of the trader and the farmer, the Indian trade pioneered the way for civilization. The buffalo trail became the Indian trail, and this became the trader's "trace;" the trails widened into roads, and the roads into turnpikes, and these in turn were transformed into railroads. The same origin can be shown for the railroads of the South, the Far West, and the Dominion of Canada. The trading posts reached by these trails were on the sites of Indian villages which had been placed in positions suggested by nature; and these trading posts, situated so as to command the water systems of the country, have grown into such cities as Albany, Pittsburgh, Detroit, Chicago, St. Louis, Council Bluffs and Kansas City. Thus civilization in America has followed the arteries made by geology, pouring an ever richer tide through them, until at last the slender paths of aboriginal intercourse have been broadened and interwoven into the complex mazes of modern commercial lines; the wilderness has been interpenetrated by lines of civilization growing ever more numerous. It is like the steady growth of a complex nervous system for the originally simple, inert continent. If one would understand why we are to-day one nation, rather than a collection of isolated states, he must study

8

this economic and social consolidation of the country. In this progress from savage conditions lie topics for the evolutionist.

Questions

1. In paragraph 2, Turner sets out the "different phenomenon" of national development as crucial to the formation of the "American character." Paraphrase his thesis in this paragraph.
2. Turner clearly indicates the thrust of his history of the American frontier when he sets aside the "point of view of border warfare and the chase" for that of "the economist and the historian" (par. 3). Make an outline of his argument.
3. What does Turner mean when he says that "the frontier is the line of most rapid and effective Americanization" (par. 5)? What is Turner's concept of the American character?
4. Write a short summary of Turner's argument, in order to be able to compare his story of the American West with the essays and fictional stories you will be reading.

READING 2

Richard Slotkin points out in *Gunfighter Nation: The Myth of the Frontier in Twentieth-Century America* (1992) that by the time Turner presented his speech in Chicago in 1893, the frontier's "significance as a *mythic space* began to outweigh its importance as a real place.... the West became a landscape known through, and completely identified with, the fictions created about it." Also in Chicago at exactly the same time as Turner was one of the great propagators of the myth, William F. Cody (1846–1917)—better known as Buffalo Bill—the star of his own "Wild West" show. The following excerpt, which describes Cody's background and rise to fame, is taken from *Gunfighter Nation*.

Richard Slotkin, "Buffalo Bill's Wild West" (from *Gunfighter Nation: The Myth of the Frontier in Twentieth-Century America*)

In 1893 the Frontier was no longer (as [Frederick Jackson] Turner   1
saw it) a geographical place and a set of facts requiring a historical explanation. Through the agency of writers like Turner and [Theodore] Roosevelt, it was becoming a set of symbols that

constituted an explanation of history. Its significance as a *mythic space* began to outweigh its importance as a real place, with its own peculiar geography, politics, and cultures.

The Frontier had always been seen through a distorting-lens of mythic illusion; but until 1893 it had also been identified with particular geographical regions, actual places capable of generating new and surprising information as a corrective to mythic presupposition. As a region with a distinct geography, ecology, and social landscape, "the West" has continued to exist. But after 1893 regional realities no longer affected the development of the mythology identified with "the West." For most Americans—to the perpetual dismay of westerners—the West became a landscape known through, and completely identified with, the fictions created about it. Indeed, once that mythic space was well established in the various genres of mass culture, the fictive or mythic West became the scene in which new acts of mythogenesis would occur—in effect displacing both the real contemporary region and the historical Frontier as factors in shaping the on-going discourse of cultural history.

It was in that mythic space, defined by the genres of commercial popular culture, that the rival ideological claims of the "school of Turner" and the "school of Roosevelt"—of the populist and the progressive versions of liberal ideology—would be played out.

* * * *

"Buffalo Bill's Wild West" was for more than thirty years (1883–1916) one of the largest, most popular, and most successful businesses in the field of commercial entertainment. The Wild West was not only a major influence on American ideas about the frontier past at the turn of the century; it was a highly influential overseas advertisement for the United States during the period of massive European emigration. It toured North America and Europe, and its creator William F. Cody became an international celebrity on terms of friendship with European royalty and heads of state as well as with the leaders of the American military establishment. With its hundreds of animals, human performers, musicians, and workmen, its boxcars filled with equipment and supplies, it was nearly as large and difficult to deploy as a brigade of cavalry; and since it went everywhere by railroad (or steamship) it was far more mobile. The staff of the Imperial German army was said to have studied Buffalo Bill's methods for loading and unloading trains in planning their own railroad operations.

William F. Cody, "Buffalo Bill," was the creator, leading manager, and until the turn of the century the chief attraction of the

Buffalo Bill's Wild West and Congress of Rough Riders of the World: Historical Sketches and Programme, Chicago, 1893.

Wild West. Over the years he worked with a series of partners whose ideas and decisions influenced the development of the enterprise and who often assumed a greater share of control over the design of the production. But it was Cody and his ideas that provided the most coherent and continuous line of development. Certainly Cody himself was primarily responsible for establishing the Wild West's commitment to historical authenticity and to its mission of historical education.

The management of Cody's enterprise declared it improper to   6
speak of it as a "Wild West show." From its inception in 1882 it was called "The Wild West" (or "Buffalo Bill's Wild West"), a name that identified it as a "place" rather than a mere display or entertainment. A "Salutatory" notice that was added to the Program of the 1886 Wild West and that appeared in every Program thereafter, declared:

> It is the aim of the management of Buffalo Bill's Wild West to do more than present an exacting and realistic entertainment for public amusement. Their object is to PICTURE TO THE EYE, by the aid of historical characters and living animals, a series of animated scenes and episodes, which had their existence in fact, of the wonderful pioneer and frontier life of the Wild West of America.

The Wild West was organized around a series of spectacles   7
which purported to re-enact scenes exemplifying different "Epochs" of American history: "Beginning with the Primeval Forest, peopled by the Indian and Wild Beasts only, the story of the gradual civilization of a vast continent is depicted." The first "Epoch" displayed Plains Indian dancers but represented them as typical of the woodland Indians who greeted the colonists on the Atlantic shore (a tableau depicting either the Pilgrims at Plymouth Rock or John Smith and Pocahontas). The historical program then cut abruptly to the settlement of the Great Plains, displaying life on a Cattle Ranch, a grand "Buffalo Hunt," and Indian attacks on a settler's cabin and the "Deadwood Stage." Between these episodes were displays of "Cowboy Fun," or trick riding and roping, and spectacular feats of marksmanship by featured performers like Annie Oakley ("Little Sure Shot") and Buffalo Bill himself.

...Over the years Buffalo Bill managed to engage such figures as   8
Sitting Bull and Geronimo as performers, and a great number of Indians who had fought against the cavalry less than a year before, as well as the services of regular units of the U.S. Cavalry to perform opposite them. But the center of the Wild West, as both

premier performer and veteran of historical reality, was Buffalo Bill himself:

> The central figure in these pictures is that of THE HON. W. F. CODY (Buffalo Bill), to whose sagacity, skill, energy, and courage...the settlers of the West owe so much for the reclamation of the prairie from the savage Indian and wild animals, who so long opposed the march of civilization.

It is the most extraordinary tribute to the skill of the Wild   9
West's management that its performances were not only accepted as entertainment but were received with some seriousness as exercises in public education. The leading figures of American military history, from the Civil War through the Plains Indian wars, testified in print to the Wild West's accuracy and to its value as an inculcator of patriotism. Brick Pomeroy, a journalist quoted in the 1893 Program, used the newly minted jargon of the educational profession to praise Buffalo Bill with the wish that "there were more progressive educators like William Cody in this world." He thought the show ought to be called "Wild West Reality," because it had "more of real life, of genuine interest, of positive education... [than] all of this imaginary Romeo and Juliet business."

But despite its battery of authentications, the Wild West wrote   10
"history" by conflating it with mythology. The re-enactments were not re-creations but reductions of complex events into "typical scenes" based on the formulas of popular literary mythology: the "Forest Primeval" Epoch reads colonial history in Fenimore Cooper's terms, the Plains episodes in terms drawn from the dime novel. If the Wild West was a "place" rather than a "show," then its landscape was a mythic space in which past and present, fiction and reality, could coexist; a space in which history, translated into myth, was re-enacted as ritual. Moreover, these rituals did more than manipulate historical materials and illustrate an interpretation of American history; in several rather complex ways, the Wild West and its principals managed not only to comment on historical events but to become actors themselves.

Staging Reality: The Creation of Buffalo Bill, 1869–1883

Until 1869 William F. Cody had been a minor actor on the stage of   11
western history, a frontier jack of all trades who had been a farmer, teamster, drover, trapper, Civil War soldier in a Jayhawk regiment, Pony Express rider, stagecoach driver, posse-man, meat hunter for the Kansas Pacific Railroad, and army scout. The upsurge of interest in the Plains that accompanied construction of the transconti-

nental railroads brought numerous tourists to the region, along with journalists, gentlemen-hunters in search of big game, and dime novelists looking for material. There was money to be made guiding such folk on hunting trips, and fame (and more hunting clients) to be garnered when the trips were written up back east. Wild Bill Hickok and Cody both achieved early fame in this way— Hickok as the subject of an article written for *Harper's Weekly* by G. W. Nichols, Cody in a Ned Buntline dime novel published in 1869 and a stage melodrama that premiered in 1871. Cody had already acquired a word-of-mouth reputation as an excellent scout and hunting guide, but after 1869 his newly acquired dime-novel celebrity made his name familiar to a national audience while linking it with spectacular and utterly fictitious adventures.

In 1871 James Gordon Bennett, Jr., editor and publisher of the New York *Herald*, hired Cody as a guide on one of the more elaborate celebrity hunting trips of the era (covered of course by a *Herald* reporter). The next year General Philip Sheridan named Cody to guide the hunting party of the Russian Grand Duke Alexis, who was in the country on a state visit. General Custer was among the American notables who accompanied the expedition, and Cody again figured prominently in the elaborate press coverage of the event. When Bennett, hoping to capitalize on this journalistic coup, urged Cody to visit him in New York, Cody, encouraged by his army superiors and friends, seized the opportunity to cash in on his celebrity. The visit was a turning point in Cody's career. In New York he took control of the commodity of his fame by forming a partnership with Ned Buntline for the production of Buffalo Bill dime novels and stage melodramas.

Between 1872 and 1876 Cody alternated between his career as scout for the U.S. Cavalry and his business as star of a series of melodramas in the East. His theatrical enterprises prospered, so that by 1873 he was able to form his own "Buffalo Bill Combination" with Wild Bill Hickok and "Texas Jack" Omohundro. The plays themselves were trivial and the acting amateurish, but the success of the "Combination" was evidence of the public's deep and uncritical enthusiasm for "the West," which could best be addressed through a combination of dime-novel plots and characters with "authentic" costumes and personages identified with "the real thing." A poster for the 1877 edition of the "Combination" advertises the main feature of the entertainment as a performance of *May Cody or, Lost and Won*, a melodramatic variation on the captivity narrative featuring both Indians and Mormons as villains. An actor impersonates Brigham Young, but two genuine Sioux chiefs appear in the play and in the dance performances "inciden-

12

13

tal" to the drama which "introduc[e] ... THE RED MEN OF THE FAR WEST."

Cody's continuing engagement with the Plains wars strength-   14 ened his claims of authenticity and in 1876 provided him with a windfall of public celebrity. The outbreak of war with the Sioux and Northern Cheyenne had been expected since the failure in 1875 of government attempts to compel the sale of the Black Hills, and preparations for three major expeditions into "hostile" territory began in the winter of 1875–76. Cody was then performing in the East, but his services as Chief of Scouts had been solicited for the column led by General Crook out of Fort Fetterman. His theatrical engagements prevented his joining Crook, whose command moved out in May, but General Carr had also been trying to recruit him for the 5th Cavalry. On the 11th of June Cody announced from the stage in Wilmington, Delaware, that he was abandoning "play act- ing" for "the real thing" and within the week had joined the 5th (now commanded by Merritt) in southern Wyoming. While the three main columns under Terry (with Custer), Gibbon, and Crook attempted to encircle and engage the main body of "hostiles," Merritt's command moved toward the Black Hills to prevent addi- tional warriors from leaving the reservation to join Sitting Bull and Crazy Horse. On July 7 the command learned of Custer's disas- trous defeat at the Little Big Horn (June 25). Ten days later a bat- talion of the 5th under Captain Charles King—a professional soldier with literary ambitions—caught up with a band of off- reservation Cheyenne which it had been tracking. In a rapid sequence of ambush and counter-ambush, Cody and his scouts en- gaged a small party of Cheyenne outriders. Merritt and his officers, watching from a low hill, saw Cody and one of the Cheyenne meet —seemingly in mutual surprise—and spontaneously fire. They saw Cody's horse stumble and fall (the horse had stepped in a prairie- dog hole). But Cody extricated himself from the saddle, took a kneeling position and deliberate aim, and shot the charging Indian from his horse. Then, as King's advancing troopers swept by him, he walked over to the corpse, scalped it, and waved his trophy in the air.

This scene became the core of the Buffalo Bill legend and the   15 basis of his national celebrity. Before the year was over he would be hailed as the man who took "The First Scalp for Custer." It would be claimed that the Indian he slew was a leading chief, one of the leaders at the Little Big Horn, and even that Cody had announced his intention to avenge Custer from the stage in Wilmington—an absurdity, since the Last Stand did not occur until three weeks later. Although the fight itself had elements of exciting drama, it was in fact a small skirmish in a dusty, empty place. The Signal Corps observer who had the best sight of the action said only that he saw "just a plain Indian riding a calico or a paint pony." But the dusty details were immediately transformed into melodrama by Captain King, whose literary ambitions reveal themselves in the sensational prose with which he described Cody's fight in his official report (and later in a book). King's report was given to a correspondent of Bennett's New York *Herald*, who added his own touches.

But the chief mythologizer of the event was Cody himself. That   16 winter he would star in *The Red Right Hand; or, The First Scalp for Custer*, a melodrama in which the "duel" with Yellow Hand becomes the climax of a captivity-rescue scenario. (The story also appeared as a dime novel.) Moreover, it seems that Cody approached the event itself with just such a performance in mind. On the morning of July 17, knowing that the proximity of the Indians made battle probable, Cody abandoned his usual buckskin clothing for one of his stage costumes, "a brilliant Mexican *vaquero*[1] outfit of black velvet slashed with scarlet and trimmed with silver buttons and lace"—the sort of costume that dime-novel illustrations had led the public to suppose was the proper dress of the wild Westerner. He was preparing for that moment when he would stand before his audience, wearing the figurative laurels of the day's battle and the *vaquero* suit, able to declare with truth that he stood before them in a plainsman's authentic garb, indeed the very clothes he had worn when he took "The First Scalp for Custer." In that one gesture he would make "history" and fictive convention serve as mutually authenticating devices: the truth of his deeds "historicizes" the costume, while the costume's conventionality allows the audience—which knows the West only through such images—to recognize it as genuine.

Cody also displayed the relics of Yellow Hand—a warbonnet,   17 shield, gun, and scabbard, and the dried human scalp itself—outside theaters in which the "Combination" performed, as indisputable evidence of his claims as a historical actor. Their impact was augmented when the display was condemned as obscene and barbaric by the self-appointed keepers of public morality. Even the anti-Indian and sensation-loving *Herald* criticized Cody; and in Boston, where Friends of the Indian were numerous and influential, the "Combination" was banned. The effect of this action was roughly the same as the banning of *Huckleberry Finn* by the Boston Library Committee— or better, the advertisement in that novel of "The Royal Nonesuch" as a show to which women and children would not be admitted. It brought sensation-seekers to the show in droves.

---

[1]*vaquero*: cowboy.

Here the Buffalo Bill signature appears clearly, in its characteris-   18
tic confusion of the theatrical and the historical or political. The
deed itself is unquestionably real—blood was shed, a battle won—
but the event is framed by fiction from start to finish, and its ultimate meaning is determined by its re-enactment in the theater. It
soon ceased to matter that the skirmish itself was unimportant, that
Yellow Hand was not a war chief, that his was not "the first scalp
for Custer," and that the "revenge" symbolized by Cody's deed had
no counterpart in reality (since the Indians he fought had not been
at the Little Big Horn)....The "duel" itself became even more sensational in Cody's 1879 autobiography, where it culminated in a
hand-to-hand knife fight. The image of Cody waving the scalp in
the air was reduced to a crude woodcut, which became a permanent
feature of Buffalo Bill iconography. It appeared in most of the Wild
West Programs, as a dime-novel cover, a poster, and—elaborated
in oils—as the centerpiece of several heroic paintings.

After 1876, the Buffalo Bill mythology developed in two forms,   19
the dime novel and (after 1882) the Wild West. Buffalo Bill was the
protagonist of more dime novels than any other character, real or
fictional, with the possible exception of Jesse James. But after 1883,
the Wild West was the basis of his fame and of his increasingly leg-
endary status. The early Buffalo Bill dime novels (written by Cody
himself, as well as by Buntline and Prentiss Ingraham) were based
(loosely) on his frontier exploits; they placed Buffalo Bill in the traditional pantheon of frontier heroes derived from Boone, Hawkeye,
Carson, and Crockett. But the Wild West framed Cody in a mythic
spectacle that enlarged and transformed this legend; eventually
even his dime novels celebrated him as the proprietor of the Wild
West rather than as an old-time plainsman.

The Wild West and the Ritualization of American History
The Wild West itself was Buffalo Bill's most important myth-   20
making enterprise, the basis of his later celebrity and continuing
dime-novel fame. It began in 1882 as part of a July 4th celebration
in Cody's hometown of North Platte, Nebraska. Its primary features were rodeo-like displays of cowboy skills—feats of marksmanship, riding and roping, horse races—framed by an elaborate
parade. To this base were added elements that would appeal to the
larger audience that had been drawn to the Buffalo Bill Combination, scenes "typical" of Western life, developed around a standard
melodramatic narrative scheme like the captivity/rescue. Many of
these scenes were drawn from Buffalo Bill dime novels: the attack
on the Deadwood Stage, the Pony Express display, the raid on the
settler's cabin, the "Grand Buffalo Hunt on the Plains." As in the

Combination, authentic historical celebrities were recruited to lend credibility and to exploit public curiosity: Major North and his Pawnee battalion were early favorites, Sitting Bull appeared in 1884–85, *métis*[2] veterans of the Riel Rebellion in Canada (1886). In later years the Wild West would feature appearances by Rain-in-the-Face ("the Indian who killed Custer"), chief Joseph of the Nez Perce, Jack Red Cloud (son of a famous Sioux chief), and (over the years) assorted sheriffs and outlaws whose exploits had attracted the attention of the newspapers.

21   Cody was of course well aware that his representation of historical events was inaccurate, to say the least. But he seems to have been sincere in his belief that the Wild West offered something like a poetic truth in its representation of the frontier. His "truth" had two aspects, the pictorial and the moral. Within the boundaries of good showmanship he strove for the greatest accuracy of detail, because he wished to memorialize a period of his own life (and a regional life style) which he loved and from which time increasingly estranged him. This concern pervades both his public and private writing and shows as well in the care and consideration with which he treated his Indian performers and the wild animals used in the Wild West.

22   But the "moral truth" of the frontier experience, which the Wild West emphasized, was its exemplification of the principle that violence and savage war were the necessary instruments of American progress. Even the displays of marksmanship by Buffalo Bill and Annie Oakley are framed by the Program's essay on "The Rifle as an Aid to Civilization":

> [While it is] a trite saying that "the pen is mightier than the sword," it is equally true that the bullet is the pioneer of civilization, for it has gone hand in hand with the axe that cleared the forest, and with the family Bible and school book. Deadly as has been its mission in one sense, it has been merciful in another; for without the rifle ball we of America would not be to-day in the possession of a free and united country, and mighty in our strength.

23   Cody exploited his connection with Wounded Knee in advertising posters which alternately showed him overseeing the making of the Peace Treaty and charging into a village to rescue White captives. He also reconstructed on the Wild West's grounds the cabin in which Sitting Bull lived at the time of his assassination. There Cody staged a ceremony of reconciliation between cavalry and Indian veterans of

---

[2]*métis:* people of French and Indian ancestry.

the two battles of the Little Big Horn and Wounded Knee. The Crow scout "Curly," famed as the last man to see Custer alive, shook hands with Rain-in-the-Face, the Sioux who had been unjustly accused (and immortalized by Longfellow) as the man who killed Custer and then cut out his heart and ate it. These ceremonies of reconciliation transfer to the Indian wars a species of public ritual previously associated with the reunion on Civil War battlefields of veterans of the Blue and the Gray. Of course, the Indian-war ceremony occurs not on the "real" battleground of the West, but on the fictive "battleground" of Buffalo Bill's Wild West. Nonetheless, the ideological import of the gesture was seriously intended. Cody framed the ceremony with a set of overt appeals for reconciliation between Whites and Indians. The Program now represented the "savages" as "The Former Foe— Present Friend— the *American.*"

This shift in the role assigned to the Indians signaled a change in   24
the historical scenario enacted by the Wild West. In its original appearance, "Custer's Last Fight" had concluded the Wild West's first half and was followed by scenes displaying the peaceful life and labor of the ranch and mining camp. In the new program, the "Last Fight" was the last act in the Wild West and served as an elegy for the *entire* period of American pioneering.

Questions

1. Like Frederick Jackson Turner, Buffalo Bill Cody had a view of history. What similarities and differences do you find between Turner's and Cody's views?
2. Trace Buffalo Bill's construction of himself as hero. Would he feel at home with today's celebrities? Who might you compare him with?
3. Summarize the version of the frontier that Buffalo Bill promoted.
4. In "The Significance of the Frontier in American History," Frederick Jackson Turner describes the process of the making of the "new product that is American" (par. 5). How does Buffalo Bill's life and character fit that description?

READING 3

The following selection is taken from a popular dime novel of 1877 featuring Deadwood Dick, a fictional hero second only in popularity to Buffalo Bill. Author Edward L. Wheeler, who lived in Philadelphia and never went West, produced thirty-three Deadwood Dick novels. As Bill Brown has pointed out, "Wheeler's Deadwood Dick was a new type of Western hero: the bandit, the vengeful outlaw who refuses to comply with what he [sees as] a corrupt legal system." This masked man, dressed all in black, would provide the model for other masked Western heroes who existed on the margins of society, such as the Lone Ranger. Dime novels, with their emphasis on action-packed adventure, were criticized in their day for corrupting the young, much as violence on TV is today. If you are interested in this topic, we suggest you read a group of dime novels to analyze their presentation of violence. A representative group may be found in Bill Brown, ed, *Reading the West: An Anthology of Dime Westerns*, Boston: Bedford Books, 1997, along with a bibliography listing sources for further reading.

As you read the two chapters of *Deadwood Dick*, you will find that the action in one chapter seems unrelated to the next. Concentrate instead on the types of characters, actions, and settings, all of which would continue to appear in fiction and film featuring the West, and would be taken as truth by such impressionable readers as the Swede in Stephen Crane's "The Blue Hotel."

Edward L. Wheeler, from *Deadwood Dick, the Prince of the Road; or, The Black Rider of the Black Hills*

Chapter II. Deadwood Dick, The Road-Agent

"$500 Reward: For the apprehension and arrest of a notorious young desperado who hails to the name of Deadwood Dick. His present whereabouts are somewhat contiguous to the Black Hills. For further information, and so forth, apply immediately to 1

Hugh Vansevere,
At Metropolitan Saloon, Deadwood City."

Thus read a notice posted up against a big pine tree, three miles above 2
Custer City, on the banks of French creek. It was a large placard tacked up in plain view of all passers-by who took the route north through Custer gulch in order to reach the infant city of the Northwest—Deadwood.

Deadwood! the scene of the most astonishing bustle and activity, this 3
year (1877). The place where men are literally made rich and poor in one day and night. Prior to 1877 the Black Hills have been for a greater part undeveloped, but now, what a change! In Deadwood districts, every foot of

Front page of the opening number of *Beadle's Half Dime Library*. Courtesy of The Library of Congress.

available ground has been "claimed" and staked out; the population has increased from fifteen to more than twenty-five hundred souls.

The streets are swarming with constantly arriving new-comers;   4
the stores and saloons are literally crammed at all hours; dance-houses and can-can dens exist; hundreds of eager, expectant, and hopeful miners are working in the mines, and the harvest reaped by them is not at all discouraging. All along the gulch are strung a profusion of cabins, tents and shanties, making Deadwood in reality a town of a dozen miles in length, though some enterprising individual has paired off a couple more infant cities above Deadwood proper, named respectively Elizabeth City and Ten Strike. The quartz formation in these neighborhoods is something extraordinary, and from late reports, under vigorous and earnest development are yielding beyond the most sanguine expectation.

The placer mines west of Camp Crook are being opened to very   5
satisfactory results, and, in fact, from Custer City in the south, to Deadwood in the north, all is the scene of abundant enthusiasm and excitement.

A horseman riding north through Custer gulch, noticed the plac-   6
ard so prominently posted for public inspection, and with a low whistle, expressive of astonishment, wheeled his horse out of the stage road, and rode over to the foot of the tree in question, and ran his eyes over the few irregularly-written lines traced upon the notice.

He was a youth of an age somewhere between sixteen and   7
twenty, trim and compactly built, with a preponderance of muscular development and animal spirits; broad and deep of chest, with square, iron-cast shoulders; limbs small yet like bars of steel, and with a grace of position in the saddle rarely equaled; he made a fine picture for an artist's brush or a poet's pen.

Only one thing marred the captivating beauty of the picture.   8

His form was clothed in a tight-fitting habit of buck-skin, which   9
was colored a jetty black, and presented a striking contrast to anything one sees as a garment in the wild far West. And this was not all, either. A broad black hat was slouched down over his eyes; he wore a thick black vail over the upper portion of his face, through the eye-holes of which there gleamed a pair of orbs of piercing intensity, and his hands, large and knotted, were hidden in a pair of kid gloves of a light color.

The "Black Rider" he might have been justly termed, for his thor-   10
oughbred steed was as black as coal, but we have not seen fit to call him such — his name is Deadwood Dick, and let that suffice for the present.

It was just at the edge of evening that he stopped before, and   11
proceeded to read the placard posted upon the tree in one of the loneliest portions of Custer's gulch.

Above and on either side rose to a stupendous hight the tree-fringed mountains in all their majestic grandeur.   12

In front and behind, running nearly north and south, lay the deep, dark chasm—a rift between mighty walls—Custer's gulch.   13

And over all began to hover the cloak of night, for the sun had already imparted its dying kiss on the mountain craters, and below, the gloom was thickening with rapid strides.   14

Slowly, over and over, Deadwood Dick, outlaw, road-agent and outcast, read the notice, and then a wild sardonic laugh burst from beneath his mask—a terrible, blood-curdling laugh, that made even the powerful animal he bestrode start and prick up its ears.   15

"Five hundred dollars reward for the apprehension and arrest of a notorious young desperado who hails to the name of Deadwood Dick! Ha! ha! ha! isn't that rich, now? Ha! ha! ha! *arrest* Deadwood Dick! Why, 'pon my word it is a sight for sore eyes. I was not aware that I had attained such a desperate notoriety as that document implies. They will make me out a murderer before they get through, I expect. Can't let me alone—everlastingly they must be punching after me, as if I was some obnoxious pestilence on the face of the earth. Never mind, though—let 'em keep on! Let them just continue their hounding game, and see which comes up on top when the bag's shook. If more than one of 'em don't get their fingers burned when they snatch Deadwood Dick bald-headed, why I'm a Spring creek sucker, that's all. Maybe I don't know who foots the bill in this reward business; oh, no; maybe I can't ride down to Deadwood and frighten three kind o' ideas out of this Mr. Hugh Vansevere, whoever he may be. Ha! ha! the fool that h'isted that notice didn't *know* Deadwood Dick, or he would never have placed his life in jeopardy by performing an act so uninteresting to the party in question. Hugh Vansevere; let me see—I don't think I've got that registered in my collection of appellatives. Perhaps he is a new tool in the employ of the old mechanic."   16

Darker and thicker grew the night shadows. The after-harvest moon rose up to a sufficient hight to send a silvery bolt of powerful light down into the silent gulch; like an image carved out of the night that horse and rider stood before the placard, motionless, silent.   17

The head of Deadwood Dick was bent, and he was buried in a deep reverie. A reverie that engrossed his whole attention for a long, long while; then the impatient pawing of his horse aroused him, and he sat once more erect in his saddle.   18

A last time his eyes wandered over the notice on the tree—a last time his terrible laugh made the mountains ring, and he guided his horse back into the rough, uneven stage-road, and galloped off up the gulch.   19

"I will go and see what this Hugh Vansevere looks like!" he said, applying the spurs to his horse. "I'll be dashed if I want him to be so numerous with my name, especially with five hundred dollars affixed thereto, as a reward." 20

*   *   *   *

Midnight. 21

Camp Crook, nestling down in one of the wildest gulch pockets of the Black Hills region—basking and sleeping in the flood of moonlight that emanates from the glowing ball up afar in heaven's blue vault, is suddenly and rudely aroused from her dreams. 22

There is a wild clatter of hoofs, a chorus of strange and varied voices swelling out in a wild mountain song, and up through the very heart of the diminutive city, where the gold-fever has dropped a few sanguine souls, dash a cavalcade of masked horsemen, attired in the picturesque garb of the mountaineer, and mounted on animals of superior speed and endurance. 23

At their head, looking weird and wonderful in his suit of black, rides he whom all have heard of—he whom some have seen, and he whom no one dare raise a hand against, in single combat—Deadwood Dick, Road-Agent Prince, and the one person whose name is in everybody's mouth. 24

Straight on through the single northerly street of the infant village ride the dauntless band, making weirdly beautiful music with their rollicking song, some of the voices being cultivated, and clear as the clarion note. 25

A few miners, wakened from their repose, jump out of bed, come to the door, and stare at the receding cavalcade in a dazed sort of way. Others, thinking that the noise is all resulting from an Indian attack, seize rifles or revolvers, as the case may be, and blaze away out of windows and loopholes at what ever may be in the way to receive their bullets. 26

But the road-agents only pause a moment in their song to send back a wild, sarcastic laugh; then they resume it, and merrily dash along up the gulch, the ringing of iron-shod hoofs beating a strange tattoo on the sound of the music. 27

Sleepily the miners crawl back to their respective couches; the moon smiles down on mother earth, and nature once more fans itself to sleep with the breath of the fragrant breeze. 28

*   *   *   *

Deadwood—magic city of the West! 29

Not dead, nor even sleeping, is this headquarters of the Black   30
Hills population at midnight, twenty-four hours subsequent to the
rush of the daring road-agents through Camp Crook.

Deadwood is just as lively and hilarious a place during the inter-   31
val between sunset and sunrise as during the day. Saloons, dance-
houses, and gambling dens keep open all night, and stores do not
close until a late hour. At one, two and three o'clock in the morning
the streets present as lively an appearance as at any period earlier in
the evening. Fighting, shooting, stabbing and hideous swearing are
features of the night; singing, drinking, dancing and gambling another.

Nightly the majority of the miners come in from such claims as   32
are within a radius of from six to ten miles, and seldom is it that
they go away without their "load." To be sure, there are some men
in Deadwood who do not drink, but they are so few and scattering
as to seem almost entirely a nonentity.

It was midnight, and Deadwood lay basking in a flood of mellow   33
moonlight that cast long shadows from the pine forest on the peaks,
and glinted upon the rapid, muddy waters of Whitewood creek,
which rumbles noisily by the infant metropolis on its wild journey
toward the south.

All the saloons and dance-houses are in full blast; shouts and   34
maudlin yells rend the air. In front of one insignificant board, "ten-
by-twenty," an old wretch is singing out lustily:

"Right this way, ye cum, pilgrims, ter ther great Black Hills   35
Thee'ter; only costs ye four bits ter go in an' see ther tender sex, already a-kickin' in their striped stockin's; only four bits, recollect, ter
see ther greatest show on earth, so heer's yer straight chance!"

But, why the use of yelling? Already the shanty is packed, and   36
judging from the thundering screeches and clapping of hands, the
entertainment is such as suits the depraved tastes of the ruffianly
"bums" who have paid their "four bits," and gone in.

But look!   37

Madly out of Deadwood gulch, the abode of thousands of lurk-   38
ing shadows, dashes a horseman.

Straight through the main street of the noisy metropolis, he   39
spurs, with hat off, and hair blowing backward in a jetty cloud.

On, on, followed by the eyes of scores curious to know the   40
meaning of his haste—on, and at last he halts in front of a large
board shanty, over whose doorway is the illuminated canvas sign:
"Metropolitan Saloon, by Tom Young."

Evidently his approach is heard, for instantly out of the "Metro-   41
politan" there swarms a crowd of miners, gamblers and bummers to
see "what the row is."

"Is there a man among you, gentlemen, who bears the name of   42
Hugh Vansevere?" asks the rider, who from his midnight dress we
may judge is no other than Deadwood Dick.

"That is my handle, pilgrim!" and a tall, rough-looking customer   43
of the Minnesotian order steps forward. "What mought yer lay be
ag'in me?"

"A *sure* lay!" hisses the masked road-agent, sternly. "You are advertis-   44
ing for one Deadwood Dick, and he has come to pay you his respects!"

The next instant there is a flash, a pistol report, a fall and a   45
groan, the clattering of iron-shod hoofs, and then, ere anyone
scarcely dreams of it, *Deadwood Dick is gone!*

Chapter III. The "Cattymount" — a Quarrel and Its Results

The "Metropolitan" saloon in Deadwood, one week subsequent to   46
the events last narrated, was the scene of a larger "jamboree" than
for many weeks before.

It was Saturday night, and up from the mines of Gold Run, Bob-   47
tail, Poor Man's Pocket, and Spearfish, and down from the Deadwood in miniature, Crook City, poured a swarm of rugged, grisly
gold-diggers, the blear-eyed, used-up-looking "pilgrim," and the
inevitable wary sharp, ever on the alert for a new buck to fleece.

The "Metropolitan" was then, as now, the headquarters of the   48
Black Hills metropolis for arriving trains and stages, and as a natural consequence received a goodly share of the public patronage.

A well-stocked bar of liquors in Deadwood was *non est*,[1] yet the sa-   49
loon in question boasted the best to be had. Every bar has its clerk at a
pair of tiny scales, and he is ever kept more than busy weighing out the
shining dust that the toiling miner has obtained by the sweat of his
brow. And if the deft-fingered clerk cannot put six ounces of dust in his
own pouch of a night, it clearly shows that he is not long in the business.

Saturday night!   50

The saloon is full to overflowing — full of brawny, rough, and   51
grisly men; full of ribald songs and maudlin curses; full of foul at-
mospheres, impregnated with the fumes of vile whisky, and worse
tobacco, and full of sights and scenes, exciting and repulsive.

As we enter and work our way toward the center of the apart-   52
ment, our attention is attracted by a coarse, brutal, "tough," evidently just fresh in from the diggings; who, mounted on the summit
of an empty whiskey cask, is exhorting in rough language, and in
the tones of a bellowing bull, to an audience of admiring miners assembled at his feet, which, by the way, are not of the most diminutive pattern imaginable. We will listen:

---

[1]*non est:* not to be found.

"Feller coots and liquidarians, behold before ye a lineal descen-   53
dant uv Cain and Abel. Ye'll reckolect, ef ye've ever bin ter camp-
meetin', that Abel got knocked out o' time by his cuzzin Cain, all
becawse Abel war misproperly named, and warn't *able* when the
crysis arriv ter defen' himsel' in an able manner.

"Hed he bin 'heeled' wi' a shipment uv Black Hills sixes, thet   54
would hev enabled him to distinguish hisself fer superyer ability.
Now, as I sed before, I'm a lineal descendant uv ther notorious Ain
and Cable, and I've lit down hyar among yer ter explain a few p'ints
'bout true blessedness and true cussedness.

"Oh! brethren, I tell ye I'm a snorter, I am, when I git a-goin'—a   55
wild screechin' cattymount, right down frum their sublime spheres up
Starkey—ar' a regular epizootic uv religyun, sent down frum cloud-
dum and scattered permiscously ter ther forty winds uv ther earth."

We pass the "cattymount," and presently come to a table at   56
which a young and handsome "pilgrim," and a ferret-eyed sharp are
engaged at cards. The first mentioned is a tall, robust fellow, somewhere in the neighborhood of twenty-three years of age, with clear-
cut features, dark lustrous eyes, and teeth of pearly whiteness. His
hair is long and curling, and a soft brown mustache, waxed at the
ends, is almost perfection itself.

Evidently he is of quick temperament, for he handles the cards   57
with a swift, nervous dexterity that surprises even the professional
sharp himself, who is a black, swarthy-looking customer, with "vil-
lain" plainly written in every lineament of his countenance; his eyes,
hair, and a tremendous mustache that he occasionally strokes, are of
a jetty black; did you ever notice it?—dark hair and complexion
predominate among the gambling fraternity.

Perhaps this is owing to the condition of the souls of some of   58
these characters.

The professional sharp in our case was no exception to the rule.   59
He was attired in the hight of fashion, and the diamond cluster, inevitably to be found there, was on his shirt front; a jewel of wonderful size and brilliancy.

"Ah! curse the luck!" exclaimed the sharp, slapping down the   60
cards; "you have won again, pilgrim, and I am five hundred out. By
the gods, your luck is something astonishing!"

"*Luck!*" laughed the other, coolly; "well, no. I do not call it luck,   61
for I never have luck. We'll call it chance!"

"Just as you say," growled the gambler, bringing forth a new   62
pack. "Chance and luck are then twin companions. Will you continue longer, Mr.—"

"Redburn," finished the pilgrim.   63

"Ah! yes—Mr. Redburn, will you continue?"   64

"I will play as long as there is anything to play for," again fin-   65
ished Mr. R., twisting the waxed ends of his mustache calmly.
"Maybe you have got your fill, eh?"

"No; I'll play all night to win back what I have lost."   66

A youth, attired in buck-skin, and apparently a couple of years   67
younger than Redburn, came sauntering along at this juncture, and
seeing an unoccupied chair at one end of the table (for Redburn and
the gambler sat at the sides, facing each other), he took possession
of it forthwith.

"Hello!" and the sharp swore roundly. "Who told *you* to mix in   68
your lip, pilgrim?"

"Nobody, as I know of. Thought I'd squat right here, and watch   69
your *sleeves!*" was the significant retort, and the youth laid a cocked
six-shooter on the table in front of him.

"Go on, gentlemen; don't let me be the means of spoiling your fun."   70

The gambler uttered a curse, and dealt out the pasteboards.   71

The youth was watching him intently, with his sharp black eyes.   72

He was of medium hight, straight as an arrow, and clad in a   73
loose-fitting costume. A broad sombrero was set jauntily upon the
left side of his head, the hair of which had been cut close down to
the scalp. His face—a pleasant, handsome, youthful face—was devoid of hirsute covering, he having evidently been recently handled
by the barber.

The game between Mr. Redburn and the gambler progressed;   74
the eyes of he whom we have just described were on the card sharp
constantly.

The cards went down on the table in vigorous slaps, and at last   75
Mr. Pilgrim Redburn raked in the stakes.

"Thunder 'n' Moses!" ejaculated the sharp, pulling out his   76
watch—an elegant affair, of pure gold, and studded with diamonds—and laying it forcibly down upon the table.

"There! what will you plank on that!"   77

Redburn took up the time-piece, turned it over and over in his   78
hands, opened and shut it, gave a glance at the works, and then
handed it over to the youth, whom he instinctively felt was his
friend. Redburn had come from the East to dig gold, and therefore
was a stranger in Deadwood.

"What is its money value?" he asked, familiarizing his tone.   79
"Good, I suppose."

"Yes, perfectly good, and cheap at two hundred," was the unhesi-   80
tating reply. "Do you lack funds, stranger?"

"Oh! no. I am three hundred ahead of this cuss yet, and—"   81

"You'd better quit where you are!" said the other, decisively.   82
"You'll lose the next round, mark my word."

"Ha! ha!" laughed Redburn, who had begun to show symptoms   83
of recklessness. "I'll take my chances. Here, you gamin, I'll cover
the watch with two hundred dollars."

Without more ado, the stakes were planked, the cards dealt, and   84
the game began.

The youth, whom we will call Ned Harris, was not idle.   85

He took the revolvers from the table, changed his position so   86
that his face was just in the opposite direction of what it had been,
and commenced to pare his finger nails. The fingers were as white
and soft as any girl's. In his hand he also held a strangely-angled
little box, the sides of which were mirror-glass. Looking at his fin-
ger-nails he also looked into the mirror, which gave a complete
view of the card-sharp, as he sat at the table.

Swiftly progressed the game, and no one could fail to see how it   87
was going by watching the cunning light in the gambler's eye. At
last the game-card went down, and next instant, after the sharp had
raked in his stakes, a cocked revolver in either hand of Ned Harris
covered the hearts of the two players.

"Hello!" gasped Redburn, quailing under the gaze of a cold steel   88
tube — "what's the row, now?"

"Draw your revolver!" commanded Harris, sternly, having an   89
eye on the card-sharp at the same time. "Come! don't be all night
about it!"

Redburn obeyed; he had no other choice.   90

"Cock it and cover your man!"   91

"Who do you mean?"   92

"The cuss under my left-hand aim."   93

Again the "pilgrim" felt that he could not afford to do otherwise   94
than obey.

So he took "squint" at the gambler's left breast after which   95
Harris withdrew the siege of his left weapon, although he still covered the young Easterner the same. Quietly he moved around to
where the card-sharp sat, white and trembling.

"Gentlemen!" he yelled, in a clear, ringing voice, "will some of   96
you step this way a moment?"

A crowd gathered around in a moment: then the youth resumed: 97

"Feller-citizens, all of you know how to play cards, no doubt.   98
What is the penalty of cheating, out here in the Hills?"

For a few seconds the room was wrapt in silence; then a chorus   99
of voices gave answer, using a single word:

"Death!"   100

"Exactly," said Harris, calmly. "When a sharp hides cards in Chi-   101
naman fashion up his sleeve, I reckon that's what you call cheatin',
don't you?"

"That's the size of it," assented each bystander, grimly.   102

Ned Harris pressed his pistol-muzzle against the gambler's fore- 103
head, inserted his fingers in each of the capacious sleeves, and a moment later laid several high cards upon the table.

A murmur of incredulity went through the crowd of spectators. 104
Even "pilgrim" Redburn was astonished.

After removing the cards, Ned Harris turned and leveled his re- 105
volver at the head of the young man from the East.

"Your name?" he said, briefly, "is—" 106

"Harry Redburn." 107

"Very well. Harry Redburn, that gambler under cover of your pis- 108
tol is guilty of a crime, punishable in the Black Hills by death. As you
are his victim—or, rather, were to be—it only remains for you to
aim straight and rid your country of an A No. 1 dead-beat and
swindler!"

"Oh! no!" gasped Redburn, horrified at the thought of taking the 109
life of a fellow-creature—"I cannot, I cannot!"

"You *can!*" said Harris, sternly; "go on—*you must salt that card-* 110
sharp, or I'll certainly salt you!"

A deathlike silence followed. 111

"*One!*" said Harris, after a moment. 112

Redburn grew very pale, but not paler was he than the card- 113
sharp just opposite. Redburn was no coward; neither was he accustomed to the desperate character of the population of the Hills.
Should he shoot the tricky wretch before him, he knew he should
be always calling himself a murderer. On the contrary, in the natural laws of Deadwood, such a murder would be classed justice.

"*Two!*" said Ned Harris, drawing his pistol-hammer back to full 114
cock. "Come, pilgrim, are you going to shoot?"

Another silence; only the low breathing of the spectators could 115
be heard.

"*Three!*" 116

Redburn raised his pistol and fired—blindly and carelessly, not 117
knowing or caring whither went the compulsory death-dealing bullet.

There was a heavy fall, a groan of pain, as the gambler dropped 118
over on the floor; then for the space of a few seconds all was the
wildest confusion throughout the mammoth saloon.

Revolvers were in every hand, knives flashed in the glare of the 119
lamplight, curses and threats were in scores of mouths, while some
of the vast surging crowd cheered lustily.

At the table Harry Redburn still sat, as motionless as a statue, the 120
revolver still held in his hand, his face white, his eyes staring.

There he remained, the center of general attraction, with a hun- 121
dred pair of blazing eyes leveled at him from every side.

"Come!" said Ned Harris, in a low tone, tapping him on the 122
shoulder—"come, pardner; let's git out of this, for times will be

brisk soon. You've wounded one of the biggest card-devils in the Hills, and he'll be rearin' pretty quick. Look! d'ye see thet feller comin' yonder, who was preachin' from on top of the barrel, a bit ago? Well, that is Catamount Cass, an' he's a pard of Chet Diamond, the feller you salted, an' them fellers behind him are his gang. Come! follow me, Henry, and I'll nose our way out of here."

Redburn signified his readiness, and with a cocked six-shooter in   123
either hand Ned Harris led the way.

Questions

1. List the particular qualities of the characters and places in these two chapters. How do the characters compare as types with characters in present-day popular fiction, film, or TV?
2. Describe the lesson that Harry Redburn, the "pilgrim" from the East, is given in the codes of the Wild West.
3. Buffalo Bill's Wild West presented the "violent and savage war" of the frontier as necessary to progress. What message regarding violence is present in *Deadwood Dick?*

READING 4

In his short story "The Blue Hotel" (1898), Stephen Crane examined the effects of the Western dime novel on a highly impressionable person. You should note which features of the dime novel Crane makes use of in developing his story. Also, you may want to compare Crane's journalistic writing about the West with this fictional representation.

Stephen Crane, "The Blue Hotel"

The Palace Hotel at Fort Romper was painted a light blue, a shade   1
that is on the legs of a kind of heron, causing the bird to declare its position against any background. The Palace Hotel, then, was always screaming and howling in a way that made the dazzling winter landscape of Nebraska seem only a grey swampish hush. It stood alone on the prairie, and when the snow was falling the town two hundred yards away was not visible. But when the traveller alighted at the railway station he was obliged to pass the Palace Hotel before he could come upon the company of low clapboard houses which composed Fort Romper, and it was not to be thought that any traveller could

pass the Palace Hotel without looking at it. Pat Scully, the proprietor, had proved himself a master of strategy when he chose his paints. It is true that on clear days, when the great transcontinental expresses, long lines of swaying Pullmans, swept through Fort Romper, passengers were overcome at the sight, and the cult that knows the brown-reds and the subdivisions of the dark greens of the East expressed shame, pity, horror, in a laugh. But to the citizens of this prairie town and to the people who would naturally stop there, Pat Scully had performed a feat. With this opulence and splendor, these creeds, classes, egotisms, that streamed through Romper on the rails day after day, they had no color in common.

As if the displayed delights of such a blue hotel were not sufficiently enticing, it was Scully's habit to go every morning and evening to meet the leisurely trains that stopped at Romper and work his seductions upon any man that he might see wavering, gripsack in hand. 2

One morning, when a snow-crusted engine dragged its long string of freight cars and its one passenger coach to the station, Scully performed the marvel of catching three men. One was a shaky and quick-eyed Swede, with a great shining cheap valise; one was a tall bronzed cowboy, who was on his way to a ranch near the Dakota line; one was a little silent man from the East, who didn't look it, and didn't announce it. Scully practically made them prisoners. He was so nimble and merry and kindly that each probably felt it would be the height of brutality to try to escape. They trudged off over the creaking board sidewalks in the wake of the eager little Irishman. He wore a heavy fur cap squeezed tightly down on his head. It caused his two red ears to stick out stiffly, as if they were made of tin. 3

At last, Scully, elaborately, with boisterous hospitality, conducted them through the portals of the blue hotel. The room which they entered was small. It seemed to be merely a proper temple for an enormous stove, which, in the center, was humming with god-like violence. At various points on its surface the iron had become luminous and glowed yellow from the heat. Beside the stove Scully's son Johnnie was playing High-Five with an old farmer who had whiskers both grey and sandy. They were quarrelling. Frequently the old farmer turned his face toward a box of sawdust — colored brown from tobacco juice — that was behind the stove, and spat with an air of great impatience and irritation. With a loud flourish of words Scully destroyed the game of cards, and bustled his son upstairs with part of the baggage of the new guests. He himself conducted them to three basins of the coldest water in the world. The cowboy and the Easterner burnished themselves fiery red with this water, until it seemed to be some kind of metal-polish. 4

The Swede, however, merely dipped his fingers gingerly and with trepidation. It was notable that throughout this series of small cere-monies the three travellers were made to feel that Scully was very benevolent. He was conferring great favors upon them. He handed the towel from one to another with an air of philanthropic impulse.

Afterward they went to the first room, and, sitting about the   5
stove, listened to Scully's officious clamor at his daughters, who were preparing the midday meal. They reflected in the silence of experienced men who tread carefully amid new people. Neverthe-less, the old farmer, stationary, invincible in his chair near the warmest part of the stove, turned his face from the sawdust-box fre-quently and addressed a glowing commonplace to the strangers. Usually he was answered in short but adequate sentences by either the cowboy or the Easterner. The Swede said nothing. He seemed to be occupied in making furtive estimates of each man in the room. One might have thought that he had the sense of silly suspicion which comes to guilt. He resembled a badly frightened man.

Later, at dinner, he spoke a little, addressing his conversation en-   6
tirely to Scully. He volunteered that he had come from New York, where for ten years he had worked as a tailor. These facts seemed to strike Scully as fascinating, and afterward he volunteered that he had lived at Romper for fourteen years. The Swede asked about the crops and the price of labor. He seemed barely to listen to Scully's extended replies. His eyes continued to rove from man to man.

Finally, with a laugh and a wink, he said that some of these   7
Western communities were very dangerous; and after his statement he straightened his legs under the table, tilted his head, and laughed again, loudly. It was plain that the demonstration had no meaning to the others. They looked at him wondering and in silence.

II

As the men trooped heavily back into the front room, the two little   8
windows presented views of a turmoiling sea of snow. The huge arms of the wind were making attempts — mighty, circular, futile — to em-brace the flakes as they sped. A gate-post like a still man with a blanched face stood aghast amid this profligate fury. In a hearty voice Scully announced the presence of a blizzard. The guests of the blue hotel, lighting their pipes, assented with grunts of lazy masculine contentment. No island of the sea could be exempt in the degree of this little room with its humming stove. Johnnie, son of Scully, in a tone which defined his opinion of his ability as a card-player, chal-lenged the old farmer of both grey and sandy whiskers to a game of High-Five. The farmer agreed with a contemptuous and bitter scoff.

They sat close to the stove, and squared their knees under a wide board. The cowboy and the Easterner watched the game with interest. The Swede remained near the window, aloof, but with a countenance that showed signs of an inexplicable excitement.

The play of Johnnie and the grey-beard was suddenly ended by another quarrel. The old man arose while casting a look of heated scorn at his adversary. He slowly buttoned his coat, and then stalked with fabulous dignity from the room. In the discreet silence of all the other men the Swede laughed. His laughter rang somehow childish. Men by this time had begun to look at him askance, as if they wished to inquire what ailed him.

A new game was formed jocosely. The cowboy volunteered to become the partner of Johnnie, and they all then turned to ask the Swede to throw in his lot with the little Easterner. He asked some questions about the game, and, learning that it wore many names, and that he had played it when it was under an alias, he accepted the invitation. He strode toward the men nervously, as if he expected to be assaulted. Finally, seated, he gazed from face to face and laughed shrilly. This laugh was so strange that the Easterner looked up quickly, the cowboy sat intent and with his mouth open, and Johnnie paused, holding the cards with still fingers.

Afterward there was a short silence. Then Johnnie said, "Well, let's get at it. Come on now!" They pulled their chairs forward until their knees were punched under the board. They began to play, and their interest in the game caused the others to forget the manner of the Swede.

The cowboy was a board-whacker. Each time that he held superior cards he whanged them, one by one, with exceeding force, down upon the improvised table, and took the tricks with a glowing air of prowess and pride that sent thrills of indignation into the hearts of his opponents. A game with a board-whacker in it is sure to become intense. The countenances of the Easterner and the Swede were miserable whenever the cowboy thundered down his aces and kings, while Johnnie, his eyes gleaming with joy, chuckled and chuckled.

Because of the absorbing play none considered the strange ways of the Swede. They paid strict heed to the game. Finally, during a lull caused by a new deal, the Swede suddenly addressed Johnnie: "I suppose there have been a good many men killed in this room." The jaws of the others dropped and they looked at him.

"What in hell are you talking about?" said Johnnie.

The Swede laughed again his blatant laugh, full of a kind of false courage and defiance. "Oh, you know what I mean all right," he answered.

"I'm a liar if I do!" Johnnie protested. The card was halted, and   16
the men stared at the Swede. Johnnie evidently felt that as the son
of the proprietor he should make a direct inquiry. "Now, what
might you be drivin' at, mister?" he asked. The Swede winked at
him. It was a wink full of cunning. His fingers shook on the edge of
the board. "Oh, maybe you think I have been to nowheres. Maybe
you think I'm a tenderfoot?"

"I don't know nothin' about you," answered Johnnie, "and I don't   17
give a damn where you've been. All I got to say is that I don't know what
you're driving at. There hain't never been nobody killed in this room."

The cowboy, who had been steadily gazing at the Swede, then   18
spoke: "What's wrong with you, mister?"

Apparently it seemed to the Swede that he was formidably men-   19
aced. He shivered and turned white near the corners of his mouth.
He sent an appealing glance in the direction of the little Easterner.
During these moments he did not forget to wear his air of advanced
pot-valor. "They say they don't know what I mean," he remarked
mockingly to the Easterner.

The latter answered after prolonged and cautious reflection. "I   20
don't understand you," he said, impassively.

The Swede made a movement then which announced that he   21
thought he had encountered treachery from the only quarter where
he had expected sympathy, if not help. "Oh, I see you are all against
me. I see—"

The cowboy was in a state of deep stupefaction. "Say," he cried,   22
as he tumbled the deck violently down upon the board, "say, what
are you gittin' at, hey?"

The Swede sprang up with the celerity of a man escaping from a   23
snake on the floor. "I don't want to fight!" he shouted, "I don't
want to fight!"

The cowboy stretched his long legs indolently and deliberately.   24
His hands were in his pockets. He spat into the sawdust-box. "Well,
who the hell thought you did?" he inquired.

The Swede backed rapidly toward a corner of the room. His   25
hands were out protectingly in front of his chest, but he was making
an obvious struggle to control his fright. "Gentlemen," he qua-
vered, "I suppose I am going to be killed before I can leave this
house! I suppose I am going to be killed before I can leave this
house!" In his eyes was the dying-swan look. Through the windows
could be seen the snow turning blue in the shadow of dusk. The
wind tore at the house, and some loose thing beat regularly against
the clapboards like a spirit tapping.

A door opened, and Scully himself entered. He paused in sur-   26
prise as he noted the tragic attitude of the Swede. Then he said,
"What's the matter here?"

The Swede answered him swiftly and eagerly: "These men are going to kill me." 27

"Kill you!" ejaculated Scully. "Kill you! What are you talkin'?" 28

The Swede made the gesture of a martyr. 29

Scully wheeled sternly upon his son. "What is this, Johnnie?" 30

The lad had grown sullen. "Damned if I know," he answered. "I can't make no sense to it." He began to shuffle the cards, fluttering them together with an angry snap. "He says a good many men have been killed in this room, or something like that. And he says he's goin' to be killed here too. I don't know what ails him. He's crazy, I shouldn't wonder." 31

Scully then looked for explanation to the cowboy, but the cowboy simply shrugged his shoulders. 32

"Kill you?" said Scully again to the Swede. "Kill you? Man, you're off your nut." 33

"Oh, I know," burst out the Swede. "I know what will happen. Yes, I'm crazy—yes. Yes, of course, I'm crazy—yes. But I know one thing—" There was a sort of sweat of misery and terror upon his face. "I know I won't get out of here alive." 34

The cowboy drew a deep breath, as if his mind was passing into the last stages of dissolution. "Well, I'm doggoned," he whispered to himself. 35

Scully wheeled suddenly and faced his son. "You've been troublin' this man!" 36

Johnnie's voice was loud with its burden of grievance. "Why, good Gawd, I ain't done nothin' to 'im." 37

The Swede broke in. "Gentlemen, do not disturb yourselves. I will leave this house. I will go away, because"—he accused them dramatically with his glance—"because I do not want to be killed." 38

Scully was furious with his son. "Will you tell me what is the matter, you young divil? What's the matter, anyhow? Speak out!" 39

"Blame it!" cried Johnnie in despair, "don't I tell you I don't know? He—he says we want to kill him, and that's all I know. I can't tell what ails him." 40

The Swede continued to repeat: "Never mind, Mr. Scully; never mind. I will leave this house. I will go away, because I do not wish to be killed. Yes, of course, I am crazy—yes. But I know one thing! I will go away. I will leave this house. Never mind, Mr. Scully; never mind. I will go away." 41

"You will not go 'way," said Scully. "You will not go 'way until I hear the reason of this business. If anybody has troubled you I will take care of him. This is my house. You are under my roof, and I will not allow any peaceable man to be troubled here." He cast a terrible eye on Johnnie, the cowboy, and the Easterner. 42

"Never mind, Mr. Scully; never mind. I will go away. I do not wish to be killed." The Swede moved toward the door which 43 opened upon the stairs. It was evidently his intention to go at once for his baggage.

"No, no," shouted Scully peremptorily; but the white-faced man slid by him and disappeared. "Now," said Scully severely, "what does this mane?"   44

Johnnie and the cowboy cried together: "Why, we didn't do nothin' to 'im!"   45

Scully's eyes were cold. "No," he said, "you didn't?"   46

Johnnie swore a deep oath. "Why, this is the wildest loon I ever see. We didn't do nothin' at all. We were jest sittin' here playin' cards, and he—"   47

The father suddenly spoke to the Easterner. "Mr. Blanc," he asked, "what has these boys been doin'?"   48

The Easterner reflected again. "I didn't see anything wrong at all," he said at last, slowly.   49

Scully began to howl. "But what does it mane?" He stared ferociously at his son. "I have a mind to lather you for this, me boy."   50

Johnnie was frantic. "Well, what have I done?" he bawled at his father.   51

III

"I think you are tongue-tied," said Scully finally to his son, the cowboy, and the Easterner; and at the end of this scornful sentence he left the room.   52

Upstairs the Swede was swiftly fastening the straps of his great valise. Once his back happened to be half turned toward the door, and, hearing a noise there, he wheeled and sprang up, uttering a loud cry. Scully's wrinkled visage showed grimly in the light of the small lamp he carried. This yellow effulgence, streaming upward, colored only his prominent features, and left his eyes, for instance, in mysterious shadow. He resembled a murderer.   53

"Man! man!" he exclaimed, "have you gone daffy?"   54

"Oh, no! Oh, no!" rejoined the other. "There are people in this world who know pretty nearly as much as you do—understand?"   55

For a moment they stood gazing at each other. Upon the Swede's deathly pale cheeks were two spots brightly crimson and sharply edged, as if they had been carefully painted. Scully placed the light on the table and sat himself on the edge of the bed. He spoke ruminatively. "By cracky, I never heard of such a thing in all   56 my life. It's a complete muddle. I can't, for the soul of me, think how you ever got this idea into your head." Presently he lifted his eyes and asked: "And did you sure think they were going to kill you?"

The Swede scanned the old man as if he wished to see into   57 his mind. "I did," he said at last. He obviously suspected that this answer might precipitate an outbreak. As he pulled on a strap his whole arm shook, the elbow wavering like a bit of paper.

Scully banged his hand impressively on the footboard of the bed.   58 "Why, man, we're goin' to have a line of ilictric streetcars in this town next spring."

"'A line of electric streetcars,'" repeated the Swede, stupidly.   59

"And," said Scully, "there's a new railroad goin' to be built down   60 from Broken Arm to here. Not to mintion the four churches and the smashin' big brick schoolhouse. Then there's the big factory, too. Why, in two years Romper'll be a met-tro-*pol*-is."

Having finished the preparation of his baggage, the Swede   61 straightened himself. "Mr. Scully," he said, with sudden hardihood, "how much do I owe you?"

"You don't owe me anythin'," said the old man, angrily.   62

"Yes, I do," retorted the Swede. He took seventy-five cents from   63 his pocket and tendered it to Scully; but the latter snapped his fingers in disdainful refusal. However, it happened that they both stood gazing in a strange fashion at three silver pieces on the Swede's open palm.

"I'll not take your money," said Scully at last. "Not after what's   64 been goin' on here." Then a plan seemed to strike him. "Here," he cried, picking up his lamp and moving toward the door. "Here! Come with me a minute."

"No," said the Swede, in overwhelming alarm.   65

"Yes," urged the old man. "Come on! I want you to come and   66 see a picter—just across the hall—in my room."

The Swede must have concluded that his hour was come. His jaw   67 dropped and his teeth showed like a dead man's. He ultimately followed Scully across the corridor, but he had the step of one hung in chains.

Scully flashed the light high on the wall of his own chamber.   68 There was revealed a ridiculous photograph of a little girl. She was leaning against a balustrade of gorgeous decoration, and the formidable bang to her hair was prominent. The figure was as graceful as an upright sled-stake, and, withal, it was of the hue of lead. "There," said Scully, tenderly, "that's the picter of my little girl that died. Her name was Carrie. She had the purtiest hair you ever saw! I was that fond of her, she—"

Turning then, he saw that the Swede was not contemplating the picture at all, but, instead, was keeping keen watch on the gloom in the rear.   69

"Look, man!" cried Scully, heartily. "That's the picter of my little gal that died. Her name was Carrie. And then here's the picter of my oldest boy, Michael. He's a lawyer in Lincoln, an' doin' well. I gave that boy a grand eddication, and I'm glad for it now. He's a fine boy. Look at 'im now. Ain't he bold as blazes, him there in Lincoln, an honored an'respicted gintleman! An honored and respicted gintleman," concluded Scully with a flourish. And, so saying, he smote the Swede jovially on the back.   70

The Swede faintly smiled.   71

"Now," said the old man, "there's only one more thing." He dropped suddenly to the floor and thrust his head beneath the bed. The Swede could hear his muffled voice. "I'd keep it under me piller if it wasn't for that boy Johnnie. Then there's the old woman—Where is it now? I never put it twice in the same place. Ah, now come out with you!"   72

Presently he backed clumsily from under the bed, dragging with him an old coat rolled into a bundle. "I've fetched him," he muttered. Kneeling on the floor, he unrolled the coat and extracted from its heart a large yellow-brown whisky bottle.   73

His first maneuver was to hold the bottle up to the light. Reassured, apparently, that nobody had been tampering with it, he thrust it with a generous movement toward the Swede.   74

The weak-kneed Swede was about to eagerly clutch this element of strength, but he suddenly jerked his hand away and cast a look of horror upon Scully.   75

"Drink," said the old man affectionately. He had risen to his feet, and now stood facing the Swede.   76

There was a silence. Then again Scully said: "Drink!"   77

The Swede laughed wildly. He grabbed the bottle, put it to his mouth; and as his lips curled absurdly around the opening and his throat worked, he kept his glance, burning with hatred, upon the old man's face.   78

IV

After the departure of Scully the three men, with the card-board still upon their knees, preserved for a long time an astounded silence. Then Johnnie said: "That's the doddangedest Swede I ever see."   79

"He ain't no Swede," said the cowboy, scornfully. 80

"Well, what is he then?" cried Johnnie. "What is he then?" 81

"It's my opinion," replied the cowboy deliberately, "he's some 82
kind of a Dutchman." It was a venerable custom of the country to
entitle as Swedes all light-haired men who spoke with a heavy
tongue. In consequence the idea of the cowboy was not without its
daring. "Yes, sir," he repeated. "It's my opinion this feller is some
kind of a Dutchman."

"Well, he says he's a Swede, anyhow," muttered Johnnie, sulkily. 83
He turned to the Easterner: "What do you think, Mr. Blanc?"

"Oh, I don't know," replied the Easterner. 84

"Well, what do you think makes him act that way?" asked the 85
cowboy.

"Why, he's frightened." The Easterner knocked his pipe against 86
a rim of the stove. "He's clear frightened out of his boots."

"What at?" cried Johnnie and the cowboy together. 87

The Easterner reflected over his answer. 88

"What at?" cried the others again. 89

"Oh, I don't know, but it seems to me this man has been reading 90
dime novels, and he thinks he's right out in the middle of it—the
shootin' and stabbin' and all."

"But," said the cowboy, deeply scandalized, "this ain't Wyoming, 91
ner none of them places. This is Nebrasker."

"Yes," added Johnnie, "an' why don't he wait till he gits *out* 92
West?"

The travelled Easterner laughed. "It isn't different there 93
even—not in these days. But he thinks he's right in the middle of
hell."

Johnnie and the cowboy mused long. 94

"It's awful funny," remarked Johnnie at last. 95

"Yes," said the cowboy. "This is a queer game. I hope we don't 96
git snowed in, because then we'd have to stand this here man bein'
around with us all the time. That wouldn't be no good."

"I wish pop would throw him out," said Johnnie. 97

Presently they heard a loud stamping on the stairs, accompanied 98
by ringing jokes in the voice of old Scully, and laughter, evidently
from the Swede. The men around the stove stared vacantly at each
other. "Gosh!" said the cowboy. The door flew open, and old
Scully, flushed and anecdotal, came into the room. He was jabber-
ing at the Swede, who followed him, laughing bravely. It was the
entry of two roisterers from a banquet hall.

"Come now," said Scully sharply to the three seated men, "move 99
up and give us a chance at the stove." The cowboy and the
Easterner obediently sidled their chairs to make room for the

newcomers. Johnnie, however, simply arranged himself in a more indolent attitude, and then remained motionless.

"Come! Git over there," said Scully.   100

"Plenty of room on the other side of the stove," said Johnnie.   101

"Do you think we want to sit in the draft?" roared the father.   102

But the Swede here interposed with a grandeur of confidence.   103
"No, no. Let the boy sit where he likes," he cried in a bullying voice
to the father.

"All right! All right!" said Scully, deferentially. The cowboy and   104
the Easterner exchanged glances of wonder.

The five chairs were formed in a crescent about one side of the   105
stove. The Swede began to talk; he talked arrogantly, profanely, angrily. Johnnie, the cowboy, and the Easterner maintained a morose
silence, while old Scully appeared to be receptive and eager, breaking in constantly with sympathetic ejaculations.

Finally the Swede announced that he was thirsty. He moved in   106
his chair, and said that he would go for a drink of water.

"I'll git it for you," cried Scully at once.   107

"No," said the Swede, contemptuously. "I'll get it for myself."   108
He arose and stalked with the air of an owner off into the executive
parts of the hotel.

As soon as the Swede was out of hearing Scully sprang to his feet   109
and whispered intensely to the others: "Upstairs he thought I was
tryin' to poison 'im."

"Say," said Johnnie, "this makes me sick. Why don't you throw   110
'im out in the snow?"

"Why, he's all right now," declared Scully. "It was only that he   111
was from the East, and he thought this was a tough place. That's all.
He's all right now."

The cowboy looked with admiration upon the Easterner. "You   112
were straight," he said. "You were on to that there Dutchman."

"Well," said Johnnie to his father, "he may be all right now, but I   113
don't see it. Other time he was scared, but now he's too fresh."

Scully's speech was always a combination of Irish brogue and   114
idiom, Western twang and idiom, and scraps of curiously formal
diction taken from the storybooks and newspapers. He now hurled
a strange mass of language at the head of his son. "What do I keep?
What do I keep? What do I keep?" he demanded, in a voice of
thunder. He slapped his knee impressively, to indicate that he himself was going to make reply, and that all should heed. "I keep a
hotel," he shouted. "A hotel, do you mind? A guest under my roof
has sacred privileges. He is to be intimidated by none. Not one
word shall he hear that would prijudice him in favor of goin' away.
I'll not have it. There's no place in this here town where they can

say they iver took in a guest of mine because he was afraid to stay here." He wheeled suddenly upon the cowboy and the Easterner. "Am I right?"

"Yes, Mr. Scully," said the cowboy, "I think you're right." 115

"Yes, Mr. Scully," said the Easterner, "I think you're right." 116

V

At six-o'clock supper, the Swede fizzed like a fire-wheel. He some- 117
times seemed on the point of bursting into riotous song, and in all his madness he was encouraged by old Scully. The Easterner was encased in reserve; the cowboy sat in wide-mouthed amazement, forgetting to eat, while Johnnie wrathily demolished great plates of food. The daughters of the house, when they were obliged to replenish the biscuits, approached as warily as Indians, and, having succeeded in their purpose, fled with ill-concealed trepidation. The Swede domineered the whole feast, and he gave it the appearance of a cruel bacchanal. He seemed to have grown suddenly taller; he gazed, brutally disdainful, into every face. His voice rang through the room. Once when he jabbed out harpoon-fashion with his fork to pinion a biscuit, the weapon nearly impaled the hand of the Easterner, which had been stretched quietly out for the same biscuit.

After supper, as the men filed toward the other room, the Swede 118
smote Scully ruthlessly on the shoulder. "Well, old boy, that was a good, square meal." Johnnie looked hopefully at his father; he knew that shoulder was tender from an old fall; and, indeed, it appeared for a moment as if Scully was going to flame out over the matter, but in the end he smiled a sickly smile and remained silent. The others understood from his manner that he was admitting his responsibility for the Swede's new viewpoint.

Johnnie, however, addressed his parent in an aside. "Why don't 119
you license somebody to kick you downstairs?" Scully scowled darkly by way of reply.

When they were gathered about the stove, the Swede insisted on 120
another game of High-Five. Scully gently deprecated the plan at first, but the Swede turned a wolfish glare upon him. The old man subsided, and the Swede canvassed the others. In his tone there was always a great threat. The cowboy and the Easterner both remarked indifferently that they would play. Scully said that he would presently have to go to meet the 6:58 train, and so the Swede turned menacingly upon Johnnie. For a moment their glances crossed like blades, and then Johnnie smiled and said, "Yes, I'll play."

They formed a square, with the little board on their knees. The 121
Easterner and the Swede were again partners. As the play went on,

it was noticeable that the cowboy was not board-whacking as usual. Meanwhile, Scully, near the lamp, had put on his spectacles and, with an appearance curiously like an old priest, was reading a newspaper. In time he went out to meet the 6:58 train, and, despite his precautions, a gust of polar wind whirled into the room as he opened the door. Besides scattering the cards, it chilled the players to the marrow. The Swede cursed frightfully. When Scully returned, his entrance disturbed a cosy and friendly scene. The Swede again cursed. But presently they were once more intent, their heads bent forward and their hands moving swiftly. The Swede had adopted the fashion of board-whacking.

Scully took up his paper and for a long time remained immersed   122
in matters which were extraordinarily remote from him. The lamp burned badly, and once he stopped to adjust the wick. The newspaper, as he turned from page to page, rustled with a slow and comfortable sound. Then suddenly he heard three terrible words: "You are cheatin'!"

Such scenes often prove that there can be little of dramatic im-   123
port in environment. Any room can present a tragic front; any room can be comic. This little den was now hideous as a torture-chamber. The new faces of the men themselves had changed it upon the instant. The Swede held a huge fist in front of Johnnie's face, while the latter looked steadily over it into the blazing orbs of his accuser. The Easterner had grown pallid; the cowboy's jaw had dropped in that expression of bovine amazement which was one of his important mannerisms. After the three words, the first sound in the room was made by Scully's paper as it floated forgotten to his feet. His spectacles had also fallen from his nose, but by a clutch he had saved them in air. His hand, grasping the spectacles, now remained poised awkwardly and near his shoulder. He stared at the card-players.

Probably the silence was while a second elapsed. Then, if the   124
floor had been suddenly twitched out from under the men they could not have moved quicker. The five had projected themselves headlong toward a common point. It happened that Johnnie, in rising to hurl himself upon the Swede, had stumbled slightly because of his curiously instinctive care for the cards and the board. The loss of the moment allowed time for the arrival of Scully, and also allowed the cowboy time to give the Swede a great push which sent him staggering back. The men found tongue together, and hoarse shouts of rage, appeal, or fear burst from every throat. The cowboy pushed and jostled feverishly at the Swede, and the Easterner and Scully clung wildly to Johnnie; but through the smoky air, above the swaying bodies of the peace-compellers, the eyes of the two

warriors ever sought each other in glances of challenge that were at once hot and steely.

Of course the board had been overturned, and now the whole company of cards was scattered over the floor, where the boots of the men trampled the fat and painted kings and queens as they gazed with their silly eyes at the war that was waging above them. 125

Scully's voice was dominating the yells. "Stop now! Stop, I say! Stop, now——" 126

Johnnie, as he struggled to burst through the rank formed by Scully and the Easterner, was crying, "Well, he says I cheated! He says I cheated! I won't allow no man to say I cheated! If he says I cheated he's a——!" 127

The cowboy was telling the Swede, "Quit, now! Quit, d'ye hear——" 128

The screams of the Swede never ceased: "He did cheat! I saw him! I saw him——" 129

As for the Easterner, he was importuning in a voice that was not heeded: "Wait a moment, can't you? Oh, wait a moment. What's the good of a fight over a game of cards? Wait a moment——" 130

In this tumult no complete sentences were clear. "Cheat"— "Quit"—"He says"—these fragments pierced the uproar and rang out sharply. It was remarkable that, whereas Scully undoubtedly made the most noise, he was the least heard of any of the riotous band. 131

Then suddenly there was a great cessation. It was as if each man had paused for breath; and although the room was still lighted with the anger of men, it could be seen that there was no danger of immediate conflict, and at once Johnnie, shouldering his way forward, almost succeeded in confronting the Swede. "What did you say I cheated for? What did you say I cheated for? I don't cheat, and I won't let no man say I do!" 132

The Swede said, "I saw you! I saw you!" 133

"Well," cried Johnnie, "I'll fight any man what says I cheat!" 134

"No, you won't," said the cowboy. "Not here." 135

"Ah, be still, can't you?" said Scully, coming between them. 136

The quiet was sufficient to allow the Easterner's voice to be heard. He was repeating, "Oh, wait a moment, can't you? What's the good of a fight over a game of cards? Wait a moment!" 137

Johnnie, his red face appearing above his father's shoulder, hailed the Swede again. "Did you say I cheated?" 138

The Swede showed his teeth. "Yes." 139

"Then," said Johnnie, "we must fight." 140

"Yes, fight," roared the Swede. He was like a demoniac. "Yes, fight! I'll show you what kind of man I am! I'll show you who you want to fight! Maybe you think I can't fight! Maybe you think I 141 can't! I'll show you, you skin, you card-sharp! Yes, you cheated! You cheated! You cheated!"

"Well, let's go at it, then, mister," said Johnnie, coolly.   142

The cowboy's brow was beaded with sweat from his efforts in in-   143
tercepting all sorts of raids. He turned in despair to Scully. "What
are you goin' to do now?"

A change had come over the Celtic visage of the old man. He   144
now seemed all eagerness; his eyes glowed.

"We'll let them fight," he answered, stalwartly. "I can't put up   145
with it any longer. I've stood this damned Swede till I'm sick. We'll
let them fight.

VI

The men prepared to go out of doors. The Easterner was so   146
nervous that he had great difficulty in getting his arms into the
sleeves of his new leather coat. As the cowboy drew his fur cap
down over his ears his hands trembled. In fact, Johnnie and old
Scully were the only ones who displayed no agitation. These preliminaries were conducted without words.

Scully threw open the door. "Well, come on," he said. Instantly a   147
terrific wind caused the flame of the lamp to struggle at its wick, while
a puff of black smoke sprang from the chimney-top. The stove was in
mid-current of the blast, and its voice swelled to equal the roar of the
storm. Some of the scarred and bedabbled cards were caught up from
the floor and dashed helplessly against the farther wall. The men lowered their hands and plunged into the tempest as into a sea.

No snow was falling, but great whirls and clouds of flakes, swept   148
up from the ground by the frantic winds, were streaming southward
with the speed of bullets. The covered land was blue with the sheen
of an unearthly satin, and there was no other hue save where, at the
low, black railway station—which seemed incredibly distant—one
light gleamed like a tiny jewel. As the men floundered into a thigh-
deep drift, it was known that the Swede was bawling out something.
Scully went to him, put a hand on his shoulder, and projected an
ear. "What's that you say?" he shouted.

"I say," bawled the Swede again, "I won't stand much show   149
against this gang. I know you'll all pitch on me."

Scully smote him reproachfully on the arm. "Tut, man!" he   150
yelled. The wind tore the words from Scully's lips and scattered
them far alee.

"You are all a gang of—" boomed the Swede, but the storm also   151
seized the remainder of this sentence.

Immediately turning their backs upon the wind, the men had   152
swung around a corner to the sheltered side of the hotel. It was the

function of the little house to preserve here, amid this great devastation of snow; an irregular V-shape of heavily encrusted grass, which crackled beneath the feet. One could imagine the great drifts piled against the windward side. When the party reached the comparative peace of this spot it was found that the Swede was still bellowing.

"Oh, I know what kind of a thing this is! I know you'll all pitch   153
on me. I can't lick you all!"

Scully turned upon him panther-fashion. "You'll not have to   154
whip all of us. You'll have to whip my son Johnnie. An' the man what troubles you durin' that time will have me to dale with."

The arrangements were swiftly made. The two men faced each   155
other, obedient to the harsh commands of Scully, whose face, in the subtly luminous gloom, could be seen set in the austere impersonal lines that are pictured on the countenances of the Roman veterans. The Easterner's teeth were chattering, and he was hopping up and down like a mechanical toy. The cowboy stood rock-like.

The contestants had not stripped off any clothing. Each was in   156
his ordinary attire. Their fists were up, and they eyed each other in a calm that had the elements of leonine cruelty in it.

During this pause, the Easterner's mind, like a film, took lasting   157
impressions of three men — the iron-nerved master of the ceremony; the Swede, pale, motionless, terrible; and Johnnie, serene yet ferocious, brutish yet heroic. The entire prelude had in it a tragedy greater than the tragedy of action, and this aspect was accentuated by the long, mellow cry of the blizzard, as it sped the tumbling and wailing flakes into the black abyss of the south.

"Now!" said Scully.   158

The two combatants leaped forward and crashed together like   159
bullocks. There was heard the cushioned sound of blows, and of a curse squeezing out from between the tight teeth of one.

As for the spectators, the Easterner's pent-up breath exploded   160
from him with a pop of relief, absolute relief from the tension of the preliminaries. The cowboy bounded into the air with a yowl. Scully was immovable as from supreme amazement and fear at the fury of the fight which he himself had permitted and arranged.

For a time the encounter in the darkness was such a perplexity of   161
flying arms that it presented no more detail than would a swiftly revolving wheel. Occasionally a face, as if illumined by a flash of light, would shine out, ghastly and marked with pink spots. A moment later, the men might have been known as shadows, if it were not for the involuntary utterance of oaths that came from them in whispers.

Suddenly a holocaust of warlike desire caught the cowboy, and   162
he bolted forward with the speed of a bronco. "Go it, Johnnie! Go it! Kill him! Kill him!

Scully confronted him. "Kape back," he said; and by his glance   163
the cowboy could tell that this man was Johnnie's father.

To the Easterner there was a monotony of unchangeable fight-   164
ing that was an abomination. This confused mingling was eternal to
his sense, which was concentrated in a longing for the end, the
priceless end. Once the fighters lurched near him, and as he
scrambled hastily backward he heard them breathe like men on the
rack.

"Kill him, Johnnie! Kill him! Kill him! Kill him!" The cowboy's   165
face was contorted like one of those agony masks in museums.

"Keep still," said Scully, icily.   166

Then there was a sudden loud grunt, incomplete, cut short, and   167
Johnnie's body swung away from the Swede and fell with sickening
heaviness to the grass. The cowboy was barely in time to prevent the
mad Swede from flinging himself upon his prone adversary. "No, you
don't," said the cowboy, interposing an arm. "Wait a second."

Scully was at his son's side. "Johnnie! Johnnie, me boy!" His   168
voice had a quality of melancholy tenderness. "Johnnie! Can you go
on with it?" He looked anxiously down into the bloody, pulpy face
of his son.

There was a moment of silence, and then Johnnie answered in   169
his ordinary voice, "Yes, I—it—yes."

Assisted by his father he struggled to his feet. "Wait a bit now till   170
you git your wind," said the old man.

A few paces away the cowboy was lecturing the Swede. "No, you   171
don't! Wait a second!"

The Easterner was plucking at Scully's sleeve. "Oh, this is   172
enough," he pleaded. "This is enough! Let it go as it stands. This is
enough!"

"Bill," said Scully, "git out of the road." The cowboy stepped   173
aside. "Now." The combatants were actuated by a new caution as
they advanced toward collision. They glared at each other, and then
the Swede aimed a lightning blow that carried with it his entire
weight. Johnnie was evidently half stupid from weakness, but he
miraculously dodged, and his fist sent the overbalanced Swede
sprawling.

The cowboy, Scully, and the Easterner burst into a cheer that   174
was like a chorus of triumphant soldiery, but before its conclusion
the Swede had scuffled agilely to his feet and come in berserk abandon at his foe. There was another perplexity of flying arms, and
Johnnie's body again swung away and fell, even as a bundle might
fall from a roof. The Swede instantly staggered to a little wind-
waved tree and leaned upon it, breathing like an engine, while his
savage and flame-lit eyes roamed from face to face as the men bent

over Johnnie. There was a splendor of isolation in his situation at this time which the Easterner felt once when, lifting his eyes from the man on the ground, he beheld that mysterious and lonely figure, waiting.

"Are you any good yet, Johnnie?" asked Scully in a broken voice. 175

The son gasped and opened his eyes languidly. After a moment 176 he answered, "No—I ain't—any good—any—more." Then, from shame and bodily ill, he began to weep, the tears furrowing down through the blood stains on his face. "He was too—too—too heavy for me."

Scully straightened and addressed the waiting figure. "Stranger," 177 he said, evenly, "it's all up with our side." Then his voice changed into that vibrant huskiness which is commonly the tone of the most simple and deadly announcements. "Johnnie is whipped."

Without replying, the victor moved off on the route to the front 178 door of the hotel.

The cowboy was formulating new and unspellable blasphemies. 179 The Easterner was startled to find that they were out in a wind that seemed to come direct from the shadowed arctic floes. He heard again the wail of the snow as it was flung to its grave in the south. He knew now that all this time the cold had been sinking into him deeper and deeper, and he wondered that he had not perished. He felt indifferent to the condition of the vanquished man.

"Johnnie, can you walk?" asked Scully. 180

"Did I hurt—hurt him any?" asked the son. 181

"Can you walk, boy? Can you walk?" 182

Johnnie's voice was suddenly strong. There was a robust impa- 183 tience in it. "I asked you whether I hurt him any!"

"Yes, yes, Johnnie," answered the cowboy, consolingly; "he's 184 hurt a good deal."

They raised him from the ground, and as soon as he was on his 185 feet he went tottering off, rebuffing all attempts at assistance. When the party rounded the corner they were fairly blinded by the pelting of the snow. It burned their faces like fire. The cowboy carried Johnnie through the drift to the door. As they entered, some cards again rose from the floor and beat against the wall.

The Easterner rushed to the stove. He was so profoundly chilled 186 that he almost dared to embrace the glowing iron. The Swede was not in the room. Johnnie sank into a chair and, folding his arms on his knees, buried his face in them. Scully, warming one foot and then the other at a rim of the stove, muttered to himself with Celtic mournfulness. The cowboy had removed his fur cap, and with a dazed and rueful air he was running one hand through his tousled locks. From overhead they could hear the creaking of boards, as the Swede tramped here and there in his room.

The sad quiet was broken by the sudden flinging open of a door   187
that led toward the kitchen. It was instantly followed by an inrush of women. They precipitated themselves upon Johnnie amid a chorus of lamentation. Before they carried their prey off to the kitchen, there to be bathed and harangued with that mixture of sympathy and abuse which is a feat of their sex, the mother straightened herself and fixed old Scully with an eye of stern reproach. "Shame be upon you, Patrick Scully!" She cried. "Your own son, too. Shame be upon you!"

"There, now! Be quiet now!" said the old man, weakly.   188

"Shame be upon you, Patrick Scully!" The girls, rallying to this   189
slogan, sniffled disdainfully in the direction of those trembling accomplices, the cowboy and the Easterner. Presently they bore Johnnie away, and left the three men to dismal reflection.

VII

"I'd like to fight this here Dutchman myself," said the cowboy,   190
breaking a long silence.

Scully wagged his head sadly. "No, that wouldn't do. It wouldn't   191
be right. It wouldn't be right."

"Well, why wouldn't it?" argued the cowboy. "I don't see no   192
harm in it."

"No," answered Scully, with mournful heroism. "It wouldn't be   193
right. It was Johnnie's fight, and now we mustn't whip the man just because he whipped Johnnie."

"Yes, that's true enough," said the cowboy; "but—he better not   194
get fresh with me, because I couldn't stand no more of it."

"You'll not say a word to him," commanded Scully, and even   195
then they heard the tread of the Swede on the stairs. His entrance was made theatric. He swept the door back with a bang and swaggered to the middle of the room. No one looked at him. "Well," he cried, insolently, at Scully, "I s'pose you'll tell me now how much I owe you?"

The old man remained stolid. "You don't owe me nothin'."   196

"Huh!" said the Swede, "huh! Don't owe 'im nothin'."   197

The cowboy addressed the Swede. "Stranger, I don't see how   198
you come to be so gay around here."

Old Scully was instantly alert. "Stop!" he shouted, holding his   199
hand forth, fingers upward. "Bill, you shut up!"

The cowboy spat carelessly into the sawdust-box. "I didn't say a   200
word, did I?" he asked.

"Mr. Scully," called the Swede, "how much do I owe you?" It   201
was seen that he was attired for departure, and that he had his valise
in his hand.

"You don't owe me nothin'," repeated Scully in the same imper-   202
turbable way.

"Huh!" said the Swede. "I guess you're right. I guess if it was any   203
way at all, you'd owe me somethin'. That's what I guess." He
turned to the cowboy. "'Kill him! Kill him! Kill him!'" he mim-
icked, and then guffawed victoriously. "'Kill him!'" He was con-
vulsed with ironical humor.

But he might have been jeering the dead. The three men were   204
immovable and silent, staring with glassy eyes at the stove.

The Swede opened the door and passed into the storm, giving   205
one derisive glance backward at the still group.

As soon as the door was closed, Scully and the cowboy leaped to   206
their feet and began to curse. They trampled to and fro, waving
their arms and smashing into the air with their fists. "Oh, but that
was a hard minute!" wailed Scully. "That was a hard minute! Him
there leerin' and scoffin'! One bang at his nose was worth forty dollars to me that minute! How did you stand it, Bill?"

"How did I stand it?" cried the cowboy in a quivering voice.   207
"How did I stand it? Oh!"

The old man burst into sudden brogue. "I'd loike to take that   208
Swade," he wailed, "and hold 'im down on a shtone floor and bate
'im to a jelly wid a shtick!"

The cowboy groaned in sympathy. "I'd like to git him by the   209
neck and ha-ammer him"—he brought his hand down on a chair
with a noise like a pistol-shot—hammer that there Dutchman until
he couldn't tell himself from a dead coyote!"

"I'd bate 'im until he—"   210

"I'd show *him* some things—"   211

And then together they raised a yearning, fanatic cry—"Oh-o-   212
oh! if we only could—"

"Yes!"   213

"Yes!"   214

"And then I'd—"   215

"O-o-oh!"   216

VIII

The Swede, tightly gripping his valise, tacked across the face of   217
the storm as if he carried sails. He was following a line of little
naked, grasping trees which, he knew, must mark the way of the
road. His face, fresh from the pounding of Johnnie's fists, felt more

pleasure than pain in the wind and the driving snow. A number of square shapes loomed upon him finally, and he knew them as the houses of the main body of the town. He found a street and made travel along it, leaning heavily upon the wind whenever, at a corner, a terrific blast caught him.

He might have been in a deserted village. We picture the world   218
as thick with conquering and elate humanity, but here, with the bugles of the tempest pealing, it was hard to imagine a peopled earth. One viewed the existence of man then as a marvel, and conceded a glamor of wonder to these lice which were caused to cling to a whirling, fire-smitten, ice-locked, disease-stricken, space-lost bulb. The conceit of man was explained by this storm to be the very engine of life. One was a coxcomb not to die in it. However, the Swede found a saloon.

In front of it an indomitable red light was burning, and the   219
snowflakes were made blood-color as they flew through the circumscribed territory of the lamp's shining. The Swede pushed open the door of the saloon and entered. A sanded expanse was before him, and at the end of it four men sat about a table drinking. Down one side of the room extended a radiant bar, and its guardian was leaning upon his elbows listening to the talk of the men at the table. The Swede dropped his valise upon the floor and, smiling fraternally upon the barkeeper, said, "Gimme some whisky, will you?" The man placed a bottle, a whisky-glass, and a glass of ice-thick water upon the bar. The Swede poured himself an abnormal portion of whisky and drank it in three gulps. "Pretty bad night" remarked the bartender, indifferently. He was making the pretension of blindness which is usually a distinction of his class; but it could have been seen that he was furtively studying the half-erased blood stains on the face of the Swede. "Bad night," he said again.

"Oh, it's good enough for me," replied the Swede, hardily, as he   220
poured himself some more whisky. The bartender took his coin and maneuvered it through its reception by the highly nickelled cash-machine. A bell rang; a card labelled "20 cts." had appeared.

"No," continued the Swede, "this isn't too bad weather. It's good   221
enough for me."

"So?" murmured the barkeeper, languidly.   222

The copious drams made the Swede's eyes swim, and he   223
breathed a trifle heavier. "Yes, I like this weather. I like it. It suits me." It was apparently his design to impart a deep significance to these words.

"So?" murmured the bartender again. He turned his gaze dream-   224
ily at the scroll-like birds and bird-like scrolls which had been drawn with soap upon the mirrors in back of the bar.

"Well, I guess I'll take another drink," said the Swede, presently.   225
"Have something?"

"No, thanks; I'm not drinkin'," answered the bartender. After-   226
ward he asked, "How did you hurt your face?"

The Swede immediately began to boast loudly. "Why, in a fight.   227
I thumped the soul out of a man down here at Scully's hotel."

The interest of the four men at the table was at last aroused.   228

"Who was it?" said one.   229

"Johnnie Scully," blustered the Swede. "Son of the man what   230
runs it. He will be pretty near dead for some weeks, I can tell you. I
made a nice thing of him, I did. He couldn't get up. They carried
him in the house. Have a drink?"

Instantly the men in some subtle way encased themselves in re-   231
serve. "No, thanks," said one. The group was of curious formation.
Two were prominent local businessmen; one was the district attorney; and one was a professional gambler of the kind known as
"square." But a scrutiny of the group would not have enabled an
observer to pick the gambler from the men of more reputable pursuits. He was, in fact, a man so delicate in manner, when among
people of fair class, and so judicious in his choice of victims, that in
the strictly masculine part of the town's life he had come to be explicitly trusted and admired. People called him a thoroughbred.
The fear and contempt with which his craft was regarded were undoubtedly the reason why his quiet dignity shone conspicuous
above the quiet dignity of men who might be merely hatters,
billiard-markers, or grocery clerks. Beyond an occasional unwary
traveller who came by rail, this gambler was supposed to prey solely
upon reckless and senile farmers, who, when flush with good crops,
drove into town in all the pride and confidence of an absolutely in-
vulnerable stupidity. Hearing at times in circuitous fashion of the
despoilment of such a farmer, the important men of Romper invariably laughed in contempt of the victim, and if they thought of the
wolf at all, it was with a kind of pride at the knowledge that he
would never dare think of attacking their wisdom and courage. Besides, it was popular that this gambler had a real wife and two real
children in a neat cottage in a suburb, where he led an exemplary
home life; and when anyone even suggested a discrepancy in his
character, the crowd immediately vociferated descriptions of this
virtuous family circle. Then men who led exemplary home lives,
and men who did not lead exemplary home lives, all subsided in a
bunch, remarking that there was nothing more to be said.

However, when a restriction was placed upon him—as, for in-   232
stance, when a strong clique of members of the new Pollywog Club
refused to permit him, even as a spectator, to appear in the rooms

of the organization—the candor and gentleness with which he accepted the judgment disarmed many of his foes and made his friends more desperately partisan. He invariably distinguished between himself and a respectable Romper man so quickly and frankly that his manner actually appeared to be a continual broadcast compliment.

And one must not forget to declare the fundamental fact of his entire position in Romper. It is irrefutable that in all affairs outside his business, in all matters that occur eternally and commonly between man and man, this thieving card-player was so generous, so just, so moral, that, in a contest, he could have put to flight the consciences of nine tenths of the citizens of Romper.   233

And so it happened that he was seated in this saloon with the two prominent local merchants and the district attorney.   234

The Swede continued to drink raw whisky, meanwhile babbling at the barkeeper and trying to induce him to indulge in potations. "Come on. Have a drink. Come on. What—no? Well, have a little one, then. By gawd, I've whipped a man tonight, and I want to celebrate. I whipped him good, too. Gentlemen," the Swede cried to the men at the table, "have a drink?"   235

"Ssh!" said the barkeeper.   236

The group at the table, although furtively attentive, had been pretending to be deep in talk, but now a man lifted his eyes toward the Swede and said, shortly, "Thanks. We don't want any more."   237

At this reply the Swede ruffled out his chest like a rooster. "Well," he exploded, "it seems I can't get anybody to drink with me in this town. Seems so, don't it? Well!"   238

"Ssh!" said the barkeeper.   239

"Say," snarled the Swede, "don't you try to shut me up. I won't have it. I'm a gentleman, and I want people to drink with me. And I want 'em to drink with me now. *Now*—do you understand?" He rapped the bar with his knuckles.   240

Years of experience had calloused the bartender. He merely grew sulky. "I hear you," he answered.   241

"Well," cried the Swede, "listen hard then. See those men over there? Well, they're going to drink with me, and don't you forget it. Now you watch."   242

"Hi!" yelled the barkeeper, "this won't do!"   243

"Why won't it?" demanded the Swede. He stalked over to the table, and by chance laid his hand upon the shoulder of the gambler. "How about this?" he asked wrathfully. "I asked you to drink with me."   244

The gambler simply twisted his head and spoke over his shoulder. "My friend, I don't know you."   245

"Oh, hell!" answered the Swede, "come and have a drink."   246

"Now, my boy," advised the gambler, kindly, "take your hand off   247
my shoulder and go 'way and mind your own business." He was a
little, slim man, and it seemed strange to hear him use this tone of
heroic patronage to the burly Swede. The other men at the table
said nothing.

"What! You won't drink with me, you little dude? I'll make you,   248
then! I'll make you!" The Swede had grasped the gambler frenziedly at the throat, and was dragging him from his chair. The
other men sprang up. The barkeeper dashed around the corner of
his bar. There was a great tumult, and then was seen a long blade in
the hand of the gambler. It shot forward, and a human body, this
citadel of virtue, wisdom, power, was pierced as easily as if it had
been a melon. The Swede fell with a cry of supreme astonishment.

The prominent merchants and the district attorney must have at   249
once tumbled out of the place backward. The bartender found himself hanging limply to the arm of a chair and gazing into the eyes of
a murderer.

"Henry," said the latter, as he wiped his knife on one of the tow-   250
els that hung beneath the bar rail, "you tell 'em where to find me.
I'll be home, waiting for 'em." Then he vanished. A moment afterward the barkeeper was in the street dinning through the storm for
help and, moreover, companionship.

The corpse of the Swede, alone in the saloon, had its eyes fixed   251
upon a dreadful legend that dwelt atop of the cash-machine: "This
registers the amount of your purchase."

IX

Months later, the cowboy was frying pork over the stove of a   252
little ranch near the Dakota line, when there was a quick thud of
hoofs outside, and presently the Easterner entered with the letters
and the papers.

"Well," said the Easterner at once, "the chap that killed the   253
Swede has got three years. Wasn't much was it?"

"He has? Three years?" The cowboy poised his pan of pork,   254
while he ruminated upon the news. "Three years. That ain't much."

"No. It was a light sentence," replied the Easterner as he un-   255
buckled his spurs. "Seems there was a good deal of sympathy for
him in Romper."

"If the bartender had been any good," observed the cowboy,   256
thoughtfully, "he would have gone in and cracked that there
Dutchman on the head with a bottle in the beginnin' of it and
stopped all this here murderin'."

"Yes, a thousand things might have happended," said the East-   257
erner, tartly.

The cowboy returned his pan of pork to the fire, but his philoso-   258
phy continued. "It's funny, ain't it? If he hadn't said Johnnie was
cheatin' he'd be alive this minute. He was an awful fool. Game
played for fun, too. Not for money. I believe he was crazy."

"I feel sorry for the gambler," said the Easterner.   259

"Oh, so do I," said the cowboy. "He don't deserve none of it for   260
killin' who he did."

"The Swede might not have been killed if everything had been   261
square."

"Might not have been killed?" exclaimed the cowboy. "Every-   262
thin' square? Why, when he said that Johnnie was cheatin' and
acted like such a jackass? And then in the saloon he fairly walked up
to git hurt?" With these arguments the cowboy browbeat the Easterner and reduced him to a rage.

"You're a fool!" cried the Easterner, viciously. "You're a bigger   263
jackass than the Swede by a million majority. Now let me tell you
one thing. Let me tell you something. Listen! Johnnie *was* cheating!"

"'Johnnie,'" said the cowboy, blankly. There was a minute of si-   264
lence, and then he said, robustly, "Why, no. The game was only for
fun."

"Fun or not," said the Easterner, "Johnnie was cheating. I saw him.   265
I know it. I saw him. And I refused to stand up and be a man. I let the
Swede fight it out alone. And you—you were simply puffing around
the place and wanting to fight. And then old Scully himself! We are
all in it! This poor gambler isn't even a noun. He is kind of an adverb.
Every sin is the result of a collaboration. We, five of us, have collabo-
rated in the murder of this Swede. Usually there are from a dozen to
forty women really involved in every murder, but in this case it seems
to be only five men—you, I, Johnnie, old Scully; and that fool of an
unfortunate gambler came merely as a culmination, the apex of a
human movement, and gets all the punishment."

The cowboy, injured and rebellious, cried out blindly into this   266
fog of mysterious theory: "Well, I didn't do anythin', did I?"

Questions

1. The Swede arrives in Fort Romper looking like "a badly frightened man" (par. 5). Discuss the story as a study in fear.
2. Compare the description of the professional gambler in "Deadwood Dick" (chap. 3) with that of Crane's gambler (pars.

231–250). Also consider their places in their respective communities.

3. The card game abruptly ceases with "three terrible words: 'You are cheatin'!'" (par. 122). How and why does the fight come about? What is its effect on the Swede?

4. Discuss Crane's story as a commentary on conceptions of the West as promoted by popular culture, such as dime novels and Wild West shows. How would you describe Crane's representation of the West in this story?

READING 5

In this excerpt from her essay "The Adventures of the Frontier in the Twentieth Century," historian Patricia Nelson Limerick examines the Disney version of the frontier. Frontierland exemplifies popular culture's use of the term *frontier*, which "carries a persistently happy affect, a tone of adventure, heroism, and even fun very much in contrast" with historical fact.

Patricia Nelson Limerick, "Travels in Frontierland"

Limerick's complete essay may be found in Richard White and Patricia Nelson Limerick, *The Frontier in American Culture*. Berkeley: University of California Press, 1994. Limerick goes on to consider political use of the term (John F. Kennedy's "New Frontier"); the media's use; and Third World and African American applications.

The year 1988 signified the fortieth anniversary of humanity's escape from zippers and buttons. In May of that year a journal of science and technology called *Discover* published an article commemorating this occasion. "Velcro," the headline read: "The Final Frontier."

To the specialist in Western American history, this is a title to ponder. In what sense might Velcro constitute a frontier? In his 1893 essay "The Significance of the Frontier in American History," Frederick Jackson Turner left his central term curiously befogged: The word "frontier," he said, "is an elastic one, and for our purposes does not need sharp definition."[1] But Turner did join the director of the United States census in offering one clear and concrete definition: the frontier was a place occupied by fewer than two people per square mile. Thus, if the headline writer were a strict follower of Turner's quantitative definition, then the Velcro Frontier would be a place where fewer than two people per square mile used Velcro. The writer, on the other hand, might have been following one of the more poetic and less precise Turnerian definitions, finding in a society's choice of fasteners a symbolic line of division between wilderness and human culture, backwardness and progress, savagery and civilization. The habit-bound users of zippers would now represent the primitive and backward people of North America, with the hardy, adventurous users of Velcro living on the cutting edge of progress.

Historians of the American West might puzzle over the shifting definitions of the word "frontier," but few readers experience any confusion when they see this headline. To them, the frontier analogy says simply that makers, marketers, and users of Velcro stand on the edge of exciting possibilities. Velcro is a frontier because Velcro has thousands of still-to-be-imagined uses. No normal reader, if one defines "normal reader" as a person who is not a Western American historian, would even notice the peculiar implications of the analogy. For most Americans in the twentieth century, the term "frontier" is perfectly clear, reliable, and simple in its meanings. 3

"Frontier," the historian David Wrobel writes, "has become a metaphor for promise, progress, and ingenuity."[2] And yet, despite the accuracy of this summation, the relation between the frontier and the American mind is not a simple one. Clear and predictable on most occasions, the idea of the frontier is still capable of sudden twists and shifts of meaning, meanings considerably more interesting than the conventional and familiar definition of the frontier as a zone of open opportunity. 4

Conventional thinking is at its most powerful, however, in twentieth-century reconstructions of the nineteenth-century experience of westward expansion, reconstructions quite explicitly designed for sale. To see this commercialized vision of the Old Frontier in concrete, three-dimensional form, the best place to go is Disneyland in Anaheim, California. When they enter Frontierland, visitors might ask Disneyland employees for directions, but they do not have to ask for a definition of the frontier. The frontier, every tourist knows, was the edge of Anglo-American settlement, the place where white Americans struggled to master the continent. This frontier, as everything in Frontierland confirms, was populated by a colorful and romantic cast of characters—mountain men, cowboys, prospectors, pioneer wives, saloon girls, sheriffs, and outlaws. Tepees, log cabins, and false-front stores were the preferred 5 architecture of the frontier; coonskin caps, cowboy hats, bandannas, buckskin shirts and leggings, moccasins, boots, and an occasional sunbonnet or calico dress constituted frontier fashion; canoes, keel-boats, steamboats, saddle horses, covered wagons, and stagecoaches gave Americans the means to conquer the rivers, mountains, deserts, plains, and other wide-open spaces of the frontier; firearms, whether long rifles or six-shooters, were everywhere and in frequent use. These images are very well understood. Tourists do not need any assistance in defining Frontierland.

And yet, even in the tightly controlled world of Disneyland, the idea of the frontier has encountered complications. At the Golden Horseshoe, Frontierland's saloon, every show once had a "spontaneous" gunfight in which Black Bart and Sheriff Lucky blazed away at each other. In 1958, as a reporter for the *Saturday Evening Post* watched, the gunfight underwent some slippage at the joint that connects fantasy to reality: "As the sheriff advanced toward the wounded bandit," the writer said, "a tow-headed five-year-old, wearing a cowboy suit and holding a cap pistol, came running from the crowd," asking earnestly, "'Can I finish him off, sheriff, can I?'" The sheriff consented, and everyone fired.

> Black Bart shuddered, then lay deathly still.
> The lad took one look, dropped his gun and fled, screaming, "Mommy, mommy! I didn't mean to! I didn't mean to!"

Scholars with a penchant for interpreting signs, symbols, and signifiers could go to town with this incident, pondering the way in which the appeal to "mommy" follows hard and fast on the attempted initiation into the manly sport of gunplay. But my own attention fixes on the line, "I didn't mean to!" Since the child wanted to kill Black Bart, and, with an impressive deference to authority, asked the sheriff for permission to kill him, why would he then make the claim, "I didn't mean to"? His worries of intention and outcome were, in any case, soon ended: "His tears stopped a moment later, however, when he turned and saw Black Bart and Sheriff Lucky walking into the Golden Horseshoe to get ready for their next performance."[3] Rather than feeling soothed, another sort of child might at that moment have conceived a long-range ambition to kill *both* Black Bart and Sheriff Lucky for their complicity in tricking him.

In the twentieth century, as this boy learned, the image of the frontier balances precariously between too much reality and too little. Properly screened and edited, the doings of the Old Frontier are quite a bit of fun. But when encounters with death, or injury, or

6

7

conflict, or loss become unexpectedly convincing and compelling, then fun can make an abrupt departure, while emotions considerably more troubling take its place.

The outlaw-killing lad was not the only child encountering the limits of Frontierland's fun, not the only one to stumble in the uncertain turf along the border between the imagined and the actual. As the *Saturday Evening Post* writer described it, one "seven-year-old boy was certain he could tell the real from the unreal."

8

> As they jogged along on the burro ride, the leathery mule-skinner warned, "Look out for them thar cactus plants. Them needles is mighty sharp."
>
> The skeptical boy leaned over and took a swipe at the cactus. On the way to the first-aid station, he decided all was not fantasy at Disneyland. The management has since moved the cactus out of reach.[4]

Moving the cactus — finding the place where its thorns could *look* sharp and scary but not *be* sharp and scary — can serve as a fine representation of the whole process of getting authenticity into the proper adjustment at Frontierland. When too many surprised innocents made visits to the first-aid stand, the frontier was clearly out of alignment, and a repositioning was in order.

And yet, in other parts of Frontierland's turf, wounds and injuries were a taken-for-granted dimension of frontier life. At Tom Sawyer's Island, as the *Saturday Evening Post* writer put it, kids "can fire air-operated, bulletless rifles at the plastic Indians."[5] A writer for the *Reader's Digest* described the same opportunity in 1960: "From the top of a log fort you can sight in with guns on a forest in which Indians lurk. The guns don't fire bullets — they're hydraulically operated — but the recoil is so realistic that you'd never guess they aren't the genuine article."[6]

9

The Indians of this frontier were not, however, the sort to hold a grudge. Visitors could fire away at the Indians and then move on to a voyage in "Indian canoes paddled by real Indians."[7] "Realness" was not, in this case, an easy matter to arrange. "Wanting authentic Native Americans to paddle canoes full of guests around the rivers of the theme area, Disneyland recruited employees from southwestern tribes," the historian John Findlay writes in his book *Magic Lands*. "These Indians, of course, came from the desert rather than a riverine or lakes environment, so they had to be taught how to paddle canoes by white employees of the park who had learned the skill at summer camp."[8]

10

11

Over the decades, life at Frontierland has become, if anything, more confusing for those rare individuals who stop and think about what they are seeing. There is, for instance, the question of the frontier's geographical location. On one side of a path, a roller coaster rushes through a southwestern mesa, carved into a mine. On the other side of the path, the great river, with its stately steamboat, rolls by. Where is the frontier? Evidently where New Mexico borders on the Mississippi River, where western gold and silver miners load their ore directly onto steamboats heading to New Orleans.

In recent times, even the ritualized violence between whites and Indians has become a matter of some awkwardness. On the various rides along the Rivers of America, one passes a settler's cabin, wildly in flames. In my childhood, the guides announced that the cabin was on fire because Indians had attacked it. In current times, the cabin is just on fire, usually without commentary or blame. At the further reaches of cultural change lies the recent experience of an acquaintance: the guide told his group that the cabin was on fire because the settler had been ecologically and environmentally careless.[9]

Consider, as well, the curious politics of the shooting gallery encountered at the entrance to Frontierland. Visitors can take firearm in hand and shoot at a variety of targets—including a railroad train, winding its way through a sculpted landscape. But if you are shooting at a railroad train, then *who*—in this frontier role-play—*are you?* Which side are you on? If you are firing on the train, then you seem to be either a hostile Indian or a murderous and larcenous outlaw. What is going on here? Is the visitor receiving an invitation to play with point of view, to reconsider the whole question of the identity and interests of good guys and bad guys, champions of progress and opponents of progress? Or is this casting of the railroad as target simply the product of Disneyland's designers working under the mandate to create a scene chock-full of the shapes and forms that will say "frontier," with the assumption that any visitor so stimulated visually will fall into step with the mythic patterns of frontier life, pick up a gun, and blast away at whatever is in sight?

If professional Western American historians find themselves conceptually without anchor when they visit Frontierland, the reason is clear: with the possible exception of the suggestion that environmental carelessness produced the settler's cabin fire, the work of academic historians has had virtually no impact either on Disneyland's vision of the frontier or on the thinking of Disneyland's visitors. That cheerful and complete indifference to the work of frontier historians may, in truth, be the secret of the place's success....

12

13

14

Notes

I would like to thank Kim Gruenwald, Stephen Sturgeon, and Jon Coleman for their help in following the trail of the frontier. I would also like to thank my colleague Mark Pittenger, whose book *American Socialists and Evolutionary Thought, 1870–1920* (Madison: University of Wisconsin Press, 1993) showed me how to think about the habits, ways, and customs of analogy-users.

1. In Frederick Jackson Turner, *The Frontier in American History* (1920; rpt. Tucson: University of Arizona Press, 1986), 2.

2. David M. Wrobel, *The End of American Exceptionalism: Frontier Anxiety from the Old West to the New Deal* (Lawrence: University Press of Kansas, 1993), 145.

3. Robert Cahn, "The Intrepid Kids of Disneyland," *Saturday Evening Post*, June 18, 1958, 22–23.

4. Ibid., 120.

5. Ibid., 119.

6. Ira Wolfert, "Walt Disney's Magic Kingdom," *Reader's Digest*, April 1960, 147.

7. Ibid., 147.

8. John M. Findlay, *Magic Lands: Western Cityscapes and American Culture after 1940* (Berkeley: University of California Press, 1992), 93–94.

9. Change seems to have been equally dramatic in Disney thinking about Indians. In 1993, the Walt Disney Company announced plans for a new American history theme park in Virginia. The section called "Native America," one company representative said, would now display "the sophisticated, intelligent societies that existed here before European settlers came, and in fact wiped out their societies" (Michael Wines, "Disney Will 'Recreate' U.S. History Next to a Place Where It Was Made," *New York Times*, November 12, 1993).

Questions

1. In light of Limerick's reading of Velcro as a frontier, consider other present-day uses of the term and their implications.

2. Limerick notes that some changes have been made at Frontierland over the years. How would you describe the experience that a visitor is supposed to have? Is Frontierland supposed to be "educational" in the same way that Buffalo Bill's Wild West was?

3. If possible, go to visit Frontierland at Disneyland to see whether it has changed in any way since Limerick wrote her description of it. Write a report on your reaction to Frontierland and give your interpretation of the historical point of view Disney is promoting.

Otherwise, visit Disneyland on the various Web sites devoted to it, to see how Frontierland is promoted. You can find brief descriptions of Disneyland attractions at **<http://disney.go.com/ Disneyland/explore/frontierland/attractions/index.html>**. Just feed "Disneyland" to your search engine, and a number of other sites will be listed. One site, "Disneyland Inside and Out" **<http://ccnet.simplenet.com/disneyland/itp_attractions.html>**, tells you which attractions are most crowded, and which least crowded. Investigate these. Do the most popular attractions offer different varieties of wild frontiers? How do they compare with Frontierland's attractions?

PRACTICE 11.2

The Frontier as American Mythology

We have gathered the texts here as a small database for you to use in thinking about the American frontier and its impact on American history and mythology. We offer two suggestions for projects below, and though there is enough material here for substantial essays, your instructor can decide whether further research is desirable.

1. As Richard Slotkin has pointed out, once the frontier was officially declared closed, "'Frontier' became primarily a term of ideological rather than geographical reference" (*Gunfighter Nation*, 4). Slotkin defines *ideology* as "the basic system of concepts, beliefs, and values that defines a society's way of interpreting its place in the cosmos and the meaning of its history." This meaning is expressed "in the symbolic narratives of *mythology*" (5). He finds the Myth of the Frontier "our oldest and most characteristic myth" (10). Though written before the official closing of the American Frontier, *Deadwood Dick* may be considered an early narrative of mythology, especially because its author had never been west. What aspects of the myth do Buffalo Bill and his Wild West show enact? How does Crane's "The Blue Hotel" both enact and critique the frontier myth? How does Disney interpret the myth?

   In your conclusion, consider whether the myth of the frontier is alive and well, or whether it is being supplanted by some other American mythology.

2. According to Frederick Jackson Turner, "American social development has been continually beginning over again on the frontier. This perennial rebirth, this fluidity of American life, this expansion westward with its new opportunities, its continuous touch with the simplicity of primitive society, furnish the forces dominating the

American character" (par. 2). Apply Turner's theory of American character to exemplary characters in *Deadwood Dick*, "The Blue Hotel," to Buffalo Bill and his Wild West show, and of course, conclude by examining the Disney version of an ideal American. (For quite a while, it was Davy Crockett; who's the latest?)

PROJECT 3

Virtual Relationships

The Internet and the technologies associated with it are transforming how we live, including how we relate to others and therefore to ourselves. Nowadays, people often "meet" each other for the first time in cyberspace—the on-line world composed, in part, of Web sites, discussion lists, newsgroups, chatrooms, MOOs, and e-mail. But when we meet someone in cyberspace, how real is the relationship? Are we actually relating to others when we send or receive typed text, or should we consider all cyber-relationships as virtual, not actual, and therefore as essentially unreal? Does the forum and kind of typed text affect the quality of communications and relations? Taking the time to compose an e-mail text means being out of sync with another, and yet that difference may be key to real communication—if not true romance. To what extent do you agree with those who think that e-mail relationships often have more depth and therefore more reality than the abbreviated interactions of synchronous chats or the back and forth repartee of instant messages?

These are some of the issues raised by the readings in this synthesis project. As you will see, all these readings have something to do with e-mail relationships: how they get started and change, what they offer people, and why they appeal to so many. Working through these readings will increase your understanding of virtual relationships and prepare you to share that understanding in writing. To help you formulate a focused hypothesis, the practice poses a question for you to consider: What are the benefits and limitations of e-mail relationships? Keep this question in mind as you move through the following readings.

READING 1

A Collection of Quotations on Online Communication and Relations

The way you meet people in cyberspace puts a different spin on affiliation: In traditional kinds of communities, we are accustomed to meeting people, then getting to know them; in virtual communities,   1 you can get to know people and *then* choose to meet them. Affiliation also can be far more ephemeral in cyberspace because you can get to know people you might never meet on the physical plane.

How does anybody find friends? In the traditional community, we search through our pool of neighbors and professional colleagues, of acquaintances and acquaintances of acquaintances, in order to find people who share our values and interests. We then exchange information about one another, disclose and discuss our mutual interests, and sometimes we become friends. In a virtual community we can go directly to the place where our favorite subjects are being discussed, then get acquainted with people who share our passions or who use words in a way we find attractive. In this sense, the topic is the address: You can't simply pick up a phone and ask to be connected with someone who wants to talk about Islamic art or California wine, or someone with a 3-year-old daughter or a 40-year-old Hudson; you can, however, join a computer conference on any of those topics, then open a public or private correspondence with the previously unknown people you find there. Your chances of making friends are increased by several orders of magnitude over the old methods of finding a peer group.

—HOWARD RHEINGOLD, from *The Virtual Community* (1993)

There is, finally, a tremendous difference between communication in the instrumental sense and communion in the affective, soul-oriented sense. Somewhere we have gotten hold of the idea that the more all-embracing we can make our communications networks, the closer we will be to that connection that we long for deep down. For change us as they will, our technologies have not yet eradicated that flame of a desire—not merely to be in touch, but to be, at least figuratively, embraced, known and valued not abstractly but in presence. We seem to believe that our instruments can get us there, but they can't. Their great power is all in the service of division and acceleration. They work in—and create—an unreal time that has nothing to do with the deep time in which we thrive: the time of history, tradition, ritual, art, and true communion.

—SVEN BIRKERTS, from *The Gutenberg Elegies* (1994)

E-mail deepened my friendship with Ralph. Though his office was next to mine, we rarely had extended conversations because he is shy. Face to face he mumbled so, I could barely tell he was speaking. But when we both got on e-mail, I started receiving long, self-revealing messages; we poured our hearts out to each other. A friend discovered that e-mail opened up that kind of communication with her father. He would never talk much on the phone (as her mother would), but they have become close since they both got on line.

Why, I wondered, would some men find it easier to open up on e-mail? It's a combination of the technology (which they enjoy) and the obliqueness of the written word, just as many men will reveal feelings in dribs and drabs while riding in the car or doing something, which they'd never talk about sitting face to face. It's too intense, too bearing-down on them, and once you start you have to keep going. With a computer in between, it's safer.

—DEBORAH TANNEN, from "The Gender Gap in Cyberspace," *Newsweek*, May 16, 1994

Who is actually reading our e-mail? As we type in cyberspace, whom do we imagine, or invoke, as our audience? And how does this imagined audience shape and constrain our writing? E-mail is, simultaneously, the most intimate and the most public form of correspondence. Online correspondences can over time create a sense of intimacy that rivals the intimacy of paper mail correspondence, and yet, with e-mail, there is no envelope. The opaque paper envelope (and, not so long ago the wax seal) and the laws that prohibit tampering with paper mail go some distance toward ensuring that the letter's first reader is the intended reader.... E-mail seems a tremendously intimate form of correspondence, one where the writer and reader seem to be directly connected in a world that excludes everyone else. This is an illusion that is important to us, not unconnected, perhaps, with Richard Nixon's belief that somehow all those tapes he was making were really private self-communion, or Robert Packwood's belief that his diaries (read and transcribed by his secretaries, I understand!) were private documents. The privacy, even the intimacy of e-mail seems to be an important illusion. When the illusion is broken, we are disturbed.

—CHARLES MORAN, "Notes Towards a Rhetoric of E-Mail," *Computers and Composition*, 12 (1995)

If you have been in love, if your lover could write, you know what I mean: it appears every day. It's transactive—not plain exposition, not pure narrative. It's a letter, but then, not the sort of letter you get from the bank or university. It's more like conversation. It's not conversation: it's one-way, and it's written. And it's written in the knowledge that days may pass between the writing and the reading—that in fact (though heaven forbid) it may be lost before it reaches you. As you read it, it speaks in the familiar voice of news, disappointments, and desires. It's affectionate—full of affect. Sometimes it's telegraphic, sometimes oblique, sometimes it includes a sort of lover's code: silly abbreviations <imho> <rotfl>, smiley faces:), Xs and Os.

> loved your smiley run over by a truck:..-_<lffunkhouser>   8

I want to argue that what email writers are doing on the net does   9
not in essence or in genre differ from what writers do off line. In some cases, it looks like a business letter. Sometimes it's a bulletin, sometimes a broadside, sometimes a joke, a memo, a grafitto, a book. In many one-to-one postings, email shows all the features of the lovers' correspondence you used to read (or did you write it?) every day.

—MICHAEL SPOONER AND KATHLEEN YANCY,
"Postings on a Genre of Email,"
College Composition and Communication, 47 (1996)

Is Anybody There? The first time I made contact with someone   10
on a Web site was with a guy who said his interests were music and sand. And I said, "Sand?" I have a kind of special interest in sand. When I was on my first and only LSD trip, I went to the beach and I spent 12 hours lying there looking at grains of sand. I had decided to make a collection of the sand, and the idea was to choose six of the most perfect and representative grains—a project that took all day and well into the night. I still have this collection in a small box lined with velvet. And I took some pictures of it with an electron microscope and sent them to this guy at his Web site.

And it took a few days to discover that the person I was talking to   11
was actually a 4-year-old kid and that his interest in sand was going out into his backyard and playing in his sandbox. And it was great— I would never have come up to this guy at a party and said, "Hey, let's talk music and sand."

—LAURIE ANDERSON, from "Dazed and Bemused,"
New York Times Magazine, Sept. 28, 1997

The truly interesting thing here is that using a word processor   12
changes how we write—not just because we're relying on new tools to get the job done, but also because the computer fundamentally transforms the way we conjure up our sentences, the thought process that runs alongside the writing process. You can see this transformation at work on a number of levels. The most basic is one of sheer volume: the speed of digital composition—not to mention the undo commands and the spell checker—makes it a great deal easier to churn out ten pages where we might once have scratched out five using pen and paper (or a Smith-Corona). The perishability of certain digital formats—e-mail being the most

obvious example—has also created a more casual, almost conversational writing style, a fusion of written letter and telephone-speak.
                                    —STEVEN JOHNSON, from *Interface Culture* (1997)

Questions

1. Which of these quotations do you like or agree with most? Why?
2. What does Rheingold mean when he says that "the topic is the
   address" (par. 2)? To what extent does Anderson see topics (pars.
   10–11) in the same way as Rheingold?
3. How do you think Tannen (pars. 4–5) would respond to Birkerts's claim that computers can't give us what we really want
   from communication (par. 3)?
4. Both Moran (par. 6) and Birkerts (par. 3) have something interesting to say about our longing for "connection," yet they don't
   see or say the same thing. Who do you think is more right about
   our longing for connection?
5. In what ways is e-mail style conversational? What do Spooner
   and Yancy (pars. 7–9) as well as Johnson (par. 12) have to say
   about this issue?

READING 2

In the following excerpt, sociologist Sherry Turkle relates changes in our
notions of the self and identity to the emergence of cyberspace—a new
kind of virtual reality. As you read this piece, circle unfamiliar terms.
Also note when and how Turkle uses both quotations from people she
interviewed as well as references to other texts on her topic.

Sherry Turkle, from *Life on the Screen: Identity in the Age of the Internet* (1995)

We come to see ourselves differently as we catch sight of our im-   1
ages in the mirror of the machine. A decade ago, when I first called
the computer a second self, these identity-transforming relationships were almost always one-on-one, a person alone with a machine. This is no longer the case. A rapidly expanding system of
networks, collectively known as the Internet, links millions of
people in new spaces that are changing the way we think, the nature
of our sexuality, the form of our communities, our very identities.

   At one level, the computer is a tool. It helps us write, keep track   2
of our accounts, and communicate with others. Beyond this, the

computer offers us both new models of mind and a new medium on which to project our ideas and fantasies. Most recently, the computer has become even more than tool and mirror: We are able to step through the looking glass. We are learning to live in virtual worlds. We may find ourselves alone as we navigate virtual oceans, unravel virtual mysteries, and engineer virtual skyscrapers. But increasingly, when we step through the looking glass, other people are there as well.

The use of the term "cyberspace" to describe virtual worlds   3
grew out of [Gibson's] science fiction, but for many of us, cyberspace is now part of the routines of everyday life. When we read our electronic mail or send postings to an electronic bulletin board or make an airline reservation over a computer network, we are in cyberspace. In cyberspace, we can talk, exchange ideas, and assume personae of our own creation. We have the opportunity to build new kinds of communities, virtual communities, in which we participate with people from all over the world, people with whom we converse daily, people with whom we may have fairly intimate relationships but whom we may never physically meet....

In the story of constructing identity in the culture of simulation,   4
experiences on the Internet figure prominently, but these experiences can only be understood as part of a larger cultural context. That context is the story of the eroding boundaries between the real and the virtual, the animate and the inanimate, the unitary and the multiple self, which is occurring both in advanced scientific fields of research and in the patterns of everyday life. From scientists trying to create artificial life to children "morphing" through a series of virtual personae, we shall see evidence of fundamental shifts in the way we create and experience human identity. But it is on the Internet that our confrontations with technology as it collides with our sense of human identity are fresh, even raw. In the real-time communities of cyberspace, we are dwellers on the threshold between the real and virtual, unsure of our footing, inventing ourselves as we go along.

On [the Internet] people are able to build a self by cycling   5
through many selves. An interior designer nervously admits in my interview with her that she is not at her best because she is about to have a face-to-face meeting with a man with whom she has shared months of virtual intimacy in chat sessions on America Online. She says she is "pretty sure" that her electronic lover is actually a man (rather than a woman pretending to be a man) because she does not think "he" would have suggested meeting if it were otherwise, but she worries that neither of

them will turn out to be close enough to their very desirable cyber-selves:

> I didn't exactly lie to him about anything specific, but I feel very different online. I am a lot more outgoing, less inhibited. I would say I feel more like myself. But that's a contradiction. I feel more like who I wish I was. I'm just hoping that face-to-face I can find a way to spend some time being the online me.

A thirty-year-old teacher describes her relationship to Internet   6
Relay Chat (or IRC), a live forum for online conversations, as being "addicted to flux." On IRC one makes up a name, or handle, and joins any one of thousands of channels discussing different issues. Anyone can start a new channel at any time. In the course of the past week, this woman has created channels on East Coast business schools (she is considering applying), on the new editorial policy of *The New Yorker,* and on a television situation comedy about a divorced woman having an affair with her ex-husband. She has concerns about her involvement with IRC that do not stem from how much time she spends ("about five hours a day, but I don't watch television any more") but from how many roles she plays.

> It is a complete escape....On IRC, I'm very popular. I have three handles I use a lot....So one [handle] is serious about the war in Yugoslavia, [another is] a bit of a nut about *Melrose Place,* and [a third is] very active on sexual channels, always looking for a good time....Maybe I can only relax if I see life as one more IRC channel.

In the past, such rapid cycling through different identities was   7
not an easy experience to come by. Earlier in this century we spoke of identity as "forged." The metaphor of iron-like solidity captured the central value of a core identity, or what the sociologist David Riesman once called inner direction. Of course, people assumed different social roles and masks, but for most people, their lifelong involvement with families and communities kept such cycling through under fairly stringent control. For some, this control chafed, and there were roles on the margins where cycling through could be a way of life. In tribal societies, the shaman's cycling through might involve possession by gods and spirits. In modern times, there was the con artist, the bigamist, the cross-gender impersonator, the "split personality," the Dr. Jekyll and Mr. Hyde.

Now, in postmodern times, multiple identities are no longer so   8
much at the margins of things. Many more people experience iden-

tity as a set of roles that can be mixed and matched, whose diverse demands need to be negotiated. A wide range of social and psychological theorists have tried to capture the new experience of identity. Robert Jay Lifton has called it protean. Kenneth Gergen describes its multiplication of masks as a saturated self. Emily Martin talks of the flexible self as a contemporary virtue of organisms, persons, and organizations.

The Internet has become a significant social laboratory for experimenting with the constructions and reconstructions of self that characterize postmodern life. In its virtual reality, we self-fashion and self-create. What kinds of personae do we make? What relation do these have to what we have traditionally thought of as the "whole" person? Are they experienced as an expanded self or as separate from the self? Do our real-life selves learn lessons from our virtual personae? Are these virtual personae fragments of a coherent real-life personality? How do they communicate with one another? Why are we doing this? Is this a shallow game, a giant waste of time? Is it an expression of an identity crisis of the sort we traditionally associate with adolescence? Or are we watching the slow emergence of a new, more multiple style of thinking about the mind?

9

Works Cited

Gergen, Kenneth. *The Saturated Self: Dilemmas of Identity in Contemporary Life.* New York: Basic Books, 1991.

Gibson, William. *Neuromancer.* New York: Ace, 1984.

Lifton, Robert Jay. *The Protean Self: Human Resilience in an Age of Fragmentation.* New York: Basic Books, 1993.

Martin, Emily. *Flexible Bodies: Tracking Immunity in American Culture from the Days of Polio to the Age of AIDS.* Boston: Beacon Pr, 1994.

Riesman, David, Nathan Glazer, and Reuel Denney. *The Lonely Crowd.* New York: Doubleday Anchor, 1950.

Questions

1. In paragraph 2, Turkle names three ways of thinking about computers. What are the three ways and which of the three ways best describes how you most often use or think about computers?
2. Make a list of the main roles you play every day. Instead of role playing, Turkle talks about "cycling through many selves" (par. 5). What's the difference between role playing and cycling through selves? To what extent are the different roles you play actually different selves?

3. In paragraph 4, Turkle refers to our culture as a "culture of simulation." What features does she consider characteristic of our culture? What is the relationship between a "culture of simulation" and the "postmodern times" referred to in paragraph 7?
4. This excerpt from Turkle's well-known book ends with a paragraph of questions. Take one of these questions and respond to it in a ten-minute focused freewrite. If you need some reminders about how to freewrite, see p. 18 as well as p. 38.

READING 3

The following excerpt is from an online work-in-progress called *The Psychology of Cyberspace*. John Suler, a professor of psychology at Rider University, has designed and written this work, which includes links to related resources that can be found on the Web.

John Suler, from "E-Mail Communication and Relationships," in *The Psychology of Cyberspace*

E-mail may be the most important, unique method for communicating and developing relationships since the telephone. First of all, it is easy to use. People also find it familiar and safe because it is similar in many respects to writing letters—minus the annoyances of addressing envelopes, licking stamps, and trips to the mail box. Of all the methods for developing relationships on the internet, it is the most common—and perhaps the most powerful. Although friendships and romances may indeed begin in text-driven chat rooms, MOOs, MUDs, or the newer multimedia chat environments, these relationships almost always progress to e-mail as a way to deepen the communication. It is a more private, more reliable, less chaotic way to talk. Even when other methods improve greatly by becoming more effectively visual and auditory—as in video teleconferencing—e-mail will not disappear. Many people will prefer it BECAUSE it is a non-visual and non-auditory form of communication. After all, we don't see people rushing out to buy video equipment to accessorize their telephone —even though that technology has been available for some time.

E-mail is not just electronic mail sent via the internet. E-mail communication creates a psychological space in which pairs of people—or groups of people—interact. It creates a context and boundary in which human relationships can unfold.

The basic features of e-mail communication include the follow-   3
ing:

Typed Text (TextTalk)—People type words to communicate   4
via e-mail. More technologically sophisticated methods enable you
to incorporate pictures and sounds into the message, but that's a
more complicated process that destroys the simplicity and ease of
use that attracts many people to e-mailing. On the other hand,
some people may not be attracted to e-mail BECAUSE it involves
typing. While everyone knows how to talk, not everyone knows
how to type. Some people also may not feel comfortable or skilled
in expressing themselves through writing. The typing/writing barrier filters some people out of the e-mail world. For those who love
to write, e-mail is heaven. It's even possible that there is a difference in cognitive style between people who love to communicate
with written words and those who don't. "Text talk," as I like to call
it, is a language unto itself.

No Face-to-Face Cues—In the typed text of e-mail, you can't see   5
other people's faces or hear them speak. All those subtle voice and
body language cues are lost, which can make the nuances of communicating more difficult. But humans are creative beings. Avid
e-mailers have developed all sorts of innovative strategies for expressing themselves through typed text. A skilled writer may be able to
communicate considerable depth and subtlety in the deceptively simple written word. Despite the lack of face-to-face cues, conversing via
e-mail has evolved into a sophisticated, expressive art form.

Anonymity—People may not know who you are or where you   6
are when you send them an e-mail. If you want, you can use a pseudonym in the message. And the return address contains only general information about where you are. The average user doesn't
know how to track down the origin and identity of a mysterious
message. Those who are determined to remain hidden can send
their mail through an anonymous mailer service that will strip away
all identifying information from the e-mail. This potential for
anonymity in e-mailing disinhibits some people. They say things
they wouldn't ordinarily say. The lack of face-to-face cues amplifies
this disinhibiting effect. In some cases the result may be people who
speak in an aggressive, antisocial manner. Sometimes it encourages
people to be more open, honest, and affectionate. Anonymity isn't
intrinsically a "good" or "bad" thing. It cuts both ways.

Asynchronous Interaction—E-mail conversations do not occur   7
in "real time." You and your partner do not have to be sitting at the
computer at the same moment in order to talk. Unlike face-to-face
encounters, which are synchronous, e-mail discussions do not require you to respond on-the-spot to what the other has said. You

have time to think, evaluate, and compose your reply. Some people take advantage of this convenient "zone for reflection." Some do not. When I receive a message that emotionally stirs me up, I apply my "Hold On!" rule of thumb. I compose a reply without sending it (or write nothing), wait 24 hours, then go back to reread the other person's message and my unsent reply. Very often, I interpret the other person's message differently—usually less emotionally—the second time around. Very often, the reply I do send off is very different (much more rational and mature) than the one I WOULD have sent the day before. The "Hold On!" rule of thumb has saved me from unnecessary misunderstandings and arguments.

Adjustable Conversing Speed—Because e-mail communication   8
is asynchronous, the rate at which you converse is maneuverable. A conversation may occur over the course of minutes, days, weeks, or months. Interactive time can be shortened or stretched, as needed. Changes in the pacing of the e-mail exchange between two people reflects the dynamics of their relationships.

Adjustable Group Size—Most e-mail programs allow you to cc   9
people or create a mailing list. These features make it very easy to expand a dyad conversation into a group discussion. Large groups of dozens or more people can be managed through such programs as "listserv." The membership boundary of the e-mail interactive space is as flexible as its members want it to be. Sometimes the boundaries are hidden: people can be dropped from a discussion without their even knowing it. Many of the ideas discussed in this article apply to e-mail dyads as well as groups. But the topic of mailing lists is a whole universe unto itself, involving all the subtleties and complexities of group dynamics. For example, through what stages does an e-mail group progress? What is it like being a member of an online working group, such as a wizard mailing list? How can decisions be made in a mailing list? What are the pros and cons of online support groups?

Spam—Inevitably, e-mail users are subjected to the "spam" of   10
unrequested messages designed to sell an idea or a product. Junk mail. To internet oldtimers, spam is anathema. It's the apocalyptic sign of the commercialization of cyberspace. People subjectively experience e-mail as a personal space in which they interact with friends and colleagues. Spam is the commercial that pops up in your face, intruding on that private zone. In the list of incoming mail, it stands out like a wart. One of the very few good things about spam is that it reminds you of how e-mail is NOT a totally private space. Unwelcomed others can inject their irrelevance. And although it rarely happens, technically clever sociopathic and other nosy people can secretly listen in on your conversations.

* * * *

A person's ability to communicate effectively via e-mail depends   11
highly on his or her writing skills. People who hate to write probably will not become consistent e-mail users. Regular and avid users
usually enjoy writing. Some even report that they PREFER writing
as a way to express themselves. They take delight in words, sentence structure, and the opportunity to craft exactly how they wish
to express their thoughts and moods. They enjoy that "zone of reflection" where they can ponder and self-reflect before expressing
themselves. As such, e-mail usually is a less spontaneous form of
communicating than speech. Unlike verbal conversation—where
words issue forth and immediately evaporate—writing places one's
thoughts in a more visible, permanent, concrete, and objective format. An e-mail message is a tiny packet of self-representation that is
launched off into cyberspace. Some even experience it as a creative
work, a gift sent to one's internet pal. It's a piece of oneself that experienced e-mail users enjoy constructing.

The quality of the relationship between e-mail correspondents   12
rests on their writing skills. The better people can express themselves
through writing, the more the relationship can develop and deepen.
Poor writing can result in misunderstandings and possibly conflicts.
In the absence of an accurate perception of what the other is trying to
say, people tend to project their own expectations, anxieties, and fantasies onto the other. A disparity in writing ability between e-mail
partners also can be problematic. The equivalent in in-person encounters would be one person who is very eloquent and forthcoming,
talking to another who speaks awkwardly and minimally. The loqua-
cious one eventually may resent putting so much effort into the relationship and taking all the risks of self-disclosure. The quiet one may
feel controlled, ignored, and misunderstood.

We tend to think of writing abilities as a fixed skill—a tool for   13
expressing oneself that is either sophisticated or not. It's also possible that the quality of one's writing is affected by the quality of the
relationship with the other. As an e-mail relationship deepens—
and trust develops—a person may open up to more expressive
forms of writing. They are more willing to experiment, take risks—
not just in what specific thoughts or emotions they express, but also
in the words and composition used. Spelling and grammar conjure
up all sorts of memories and emotions from the school years of
one's childhood. Your self-concept may ride on those memories. In
the course of an e-mail relationship, those issues from the past may
be stirred up. Writing isn't just a tool for developing the e-mail relationship. Writing affects the relationship, and the relationship

influences the quality of the writing. Writing effectiveness changes as a result of what is happening in the ongoing e-mail encounter. Composition advances when people feel safe and are ready to explore; it regresses when they feel threatened, hurt, or angry. Those changes reflect the developmental changes in the relationship.

In addition to writing skill, writing STYLE also affects the e-mail relationship and is in turn affected by it. Concrete, emotional and abstract expression, complexity of vocabulary and sentence structure, the organization and flow of thought—all reflect one's cognitive/personality style and influence how the other reacts to you. Compulsive people may construct highly organized, intellectualized messages with little emotional revelation. Histrionic people may show less concern about organization and much more for the emotions they express. Narcissists may write extremely long, rambling blocks of paragraphs. Schizoids may produce very short but penetrating messages. Different writing/personality styles may be compatible, incompatible, or complementary to other styles.   14

An e-mail message can be dissected into six components: (1) the sender's name as indicated in your incoming mailbox, (2) the subject line, as indicated in your incoming mailbox, (3) the greeting that introduces the body of the message, (4) the body of the message, including quoted text, (5) the sign-off line and name, and, (6) the signature block. The body of the message is what most people consider the actual "message" itself. Surely, it is the most lengthy, complex, and changing aspect of the exchange between e-mail partners. However, the other components of the message also can be tiny gems of communication. Much meaning can be packed into those little nuggets. How those deceptively simple components of the message change over time may signal important changes in the relationship.   15

* * * *

Often there are several stages in the development of an e-mail relationship. First, the people must come in contact with each other. That may seem like a serendipitous or uneventful occurrence—they just "happened" to run into each other on the Internet, or that first round of e-mail involved some "simple" request for information. But often there is more going on below the surface. Although, theoretically, people can connect with everyone else on the Internet, they don't. They establish ongoing relationships with only a handful of people. Consciously—and often unconsciously—we filter through the hundreds and thousands of names that scroll down our monitor and select out those people that have similar interests to ours, those that address our psychological and emotional needs.... those that fit our transference dynamics. When reflecting   16 on one of your ongoing e-mail relationships, it's interesting to open your archive and look up those first few messages that were exchanged. Exactly when and where did you meet? Exactly what was said? Those first few messages can reveal the needs and emotional dynamics that sparked the relationship.

As in all relationships, the momentum begins with those sparked   17
dynamics and evolves from there. The people gradually reveal more about themselves to each other, which adds more layers of complexity onto the core dynamics that drew them together. The lack of face-to-face cues encourages them to discuss thoughts and feelings that they otherwise might not reveal — which helps solidify the bond between them. But filling in for that lack of face-to-face cues also deepens the relationship. Describing how one looks, for example, is a powerful way of saying, "I want you to see the real me." The same principle holds true for disclosing facts about your in-person life. Because cyberspace easily can be a world isolated from one's "real" life — a world where you can remain anonymous or take on an imaginative identity — revealing your ACTUAL identity is taken as a sign of intimacy and commitment. The more people start to share that kind of real-world information in their e-mail, the more the relationship is deepening.

The developmental path in e-mail relationships is one that leads   18
towards becoming more and more real to the other person. For the relationship to move beyond a certain point, the couple will want and need to have more real-time and face-to-face contact. They might try meeting in online chat, which can make the other person's "presence" seem more powerful and thereby enhance the feeling of actually "being together" in real time. It also tests each other's commitment to the relationship, because you both have to be there at a specific time. If they have the technical skills, they might try communicating with video or audio streaming. They might attach pictures of themselves to their e-mail. An even bigger move forward is to step outside the sometimes invisible psychological boundary that "we are ONLINE friends." You break the cyberspace barrier by sending letters, photos, and gifts via postal mail.... or telephone the other person....or you take the final, inevitable step of actually meeting your friend in-person.

Each of these moves towards becoming more real to the e-mail   19
partner is a significant turning point in the relationship. The thoughts and feelings that are discussed during and after each of these more intimate contacts builds new dimensions to the relationship. This is especially true of taking that big step forward by meeting your e-mail companion in-person. Both of you are taking that decisive step OUT of cyberspace and into the face-to-face encounter. It can be a bit anxiety-provoking. Will he be what I've

imagined him to be? What will she think of me? Why did we decide to meet each other NOW in the relationship? What are we both expecting from the rendezvous? All of these are important questions.

Questions

1. In paragraph 1, Suler notes that nowadays, people seem to prefer "non-visual and non-auditory form[s] of communication." Do you think he is right? If so, why do you suppose people would prefer the textual over the visual or auditory?
2. Suler lists and comments on seven key features of e-mail communication (par. 3–9). Which of these seven features do you think is most important for the formation of intimate online relationships? Why?
3. Discuss two specific and significant ways that writing skill and writing style can affect e-mail relationships (pars. 10–13).
4. According to Suler, how do e-mail relationships become more and more real? What is gained and what is lost as the virtual becomes more real?

▊ READING 4

In the following essay, the writer Meghan Daum recounts and reflects on her cyber-romance with another writer she calls "Pete." As you read this essay, be on the lookout for turning points in the relationship between the two writers and ask yourself why the relationship turns out as it does.

Meghan Daum, "Virtual Love," *The New Yorker,* Aug. 25/Sept. 1, 1997

It was last November; fall was drifting away into an intolerable chill. I was at the end of my twenty-sixth year, and was living in New York City, trying to support myself as a writer, and taking part in the kind of urban life that might be construed as glamorous were it to appear in a memoir in the distant future. At the time, however, my days felt more like a grind than like an adventure: hours of work strung between the motions of waking up, getting the mail, watching TV with my roommates, and going to bed. One morning, I logged on to my America Online account to find a message under the heading "is this the real meghan daum?" It came from someone with the screen name PFSlider. The body of the message consisted of five sentences, written entirely in lower-case letters, of perfectly

1

turned flattery: something about PFSlider's admiration of some newspaper and magazine articles I had published over the last year and a half, something about his resulting infatuation with me, and something about his being a sportswriter in California.

I was engaged for the thirty seconds that it took me to read the   2
message and fashion a reply. Though it felt strange to be in the position of confirming that I was indeed "the real meghan daum," I managed to say, "Yes, it's me. Thank you for writing." I clicked the "Send Now" icon, shot my words into the void, and forgot about PFSlider until the next day, when I received another message, this one headed "eureka."

"wow, it is you," he wrote, still in lower case. He chronicled the   3
various conditions under which he'd read my few-and-far-between articles—a boardwalk in Laguna Beach, the spring-training pressroom for a baseball team that he covered for a Los Angeles newspaper. He confessed to having a crush on me. He referred to me as "princess daum." He said he wanted to have lunch with me during one of his two annual trips to New York.

The letter was outrageous and endearingly pathetic, possibly the   4
practical joke of a friend trying to rouse me out of a temporary writer's block. But the kindness pouring forth from my computer screen was bizarrely exhilarating, and I logged off and thought about it for a few hours before writing back to express how flattered and "touched"—this was probably the first time I had ever used that word in earnest—I was by his message.

I am not what most people would call a computer person. I have   5
no interest in chat rooms, newsgroups, or most Web sites. I derive a palpable thrill from sticking a letter in the United States mail. But I have a constant low-grade fear of the telephone, and I often call people with the intention of getting their answering machines. There is something about the live voice that I have come to find unnervingly organic, as volatile as live television. E-mail provides a useful antidote for my particular communication anxieties. Though I generally send and receive only a few messages a week, I take comfort in their silence and their boundaries.

PFSlider and I tossed a few innocuous, smart-assed notes back   6
and forth over the week following his first message. Let's say his name was Pete. He was twenty-nine, and single. I revealed very little about myself, relying instead on the ironic commentary and forced witticisms that are the conceit of so many E-mail messages. But I quickly developed an oblique affection for PFSlider. I was excited when there was a message from him, mildly depressed when there wasn't. After a few weeks, he gave me his phone number. I did not give him mine, but he looked it up and called me one Friday

night. I was home. I picked up the phone. His voice was jarring, yet not unpleasant. He held up more than his end of the conversation for an hour, and when he asked permission to call me again I granted it, as though we were of an earlier era.

Pete—I could never wrap my mind around his name, privately   7
thinking of him as PFSlider, "E-mail guy," or even "baseball boy"—began phoning me two or three times a week. He asked if he could meet me, and I said that that would be O.K. Christmas was a few weeks away, and he told me that he would be coming back East to see his family. From there, he would take a short flight to New York and have lunch with me.

"It is my off-season mission to meet you," he said.   8

"There will probably be a snowstorm," I said.   9

"I'll take a team of sled dogs," he answered.   10

We talked about our work and our families, about baseball and Bill   11
Clinton and Howard Stern and sex, about his hatred for Los Angeles and how much he wanted a new job. Sometimes we'd find each other logged on simultaneously and type back and forth for hours.

I had previously considered cyber-communication an oxymoron,   12
a fast road to the breakdown of humanity. But, curiously, the Internet—at least in the limited form in which I was using it—felt anything but dehumanizing. My interaction with PFSlider seemed more authentic than much of what I experienced in the daylight realm of living beings. I was certainly putting more energy into the relationship than I had put into many others. I also was giving Pete attention that was by definition undivided, and relishing the safety of the distance between us by opting to be truthful instead of doling out the white lies that have become the staple of real life. The outside world—the place where I walked around avoiding people I didn't want to deal with, peppering my casual conversations with half-truths, and applying my motto "Let the machine take it" to almost any scenario—was sliding into the periphery of my mind.

For me, the time on-line with Pete was far superior to the phone.   13
There were no background noises, no interruptions from "call waiting," no long-distance charges. Through typos and misspellings, he flirted maniacally. "I have an absurd crush on you," he said. "If I like you in person, you must promise to marry me." I was coy and conceited, telling him to get a life, baiting him into complimenting me further, teasing him in a way I would never have dared to do in person, or even on the phone. I would stay up until 3 A.M. typing with him, smiling at the screen, getting so giddy that when I quit I couldn't fall asleep. I was having difficulty recalling what I used to do at night. It was as if he and I lived together in our own quiet space—a space made all the more intimate because of our con-

scious decision to block everyone else out. My phone was tied up for hours at a time. No one in the real world could reach me, and I didn't really care.

Since my last serious relationship, I'd had the requisite number   14
of false starts and five-night stands, dates that I wasn't sure were dates, and emphatically casual affairs that buckled under their own inertia. With PFSlider, on the other hand, I may not have known my suitor, but, for the first time in my life, I knew the deal: I was a desired person, the object of a blind man's gaze. He called not only when he said he would call but unexpectedly, just to say hello. He was protected by the shield of the Internet; his guard was not merely down but nonexistent. He let his phone bill grow to towering proportions. He told me that the thought about me all the time, though we both knew that the "me" in his mind consisted largely of himself. He talked about me to his friends, and admitted it. He arranged his holiday schedule around our impending date. He managed to charm me with sports analogies. He didn't hesitate. He was unblinking and unapologetic, all nerviness and balls to the wall.

And so PFSlider became my everyday life. All the tangible stuff   15
fell away. My body did not exist. I had no skin, no hair, no bones. All desire had converted itself into a cerebral current that reached nothing but my frontal lobe. There was no outdoors, no social life, no weather. There was only the computer screen and the phone, my chair, and maybe a glass of water. Most mornings, I would wake up to find a message from PFSlider, composed in Pacific time while I slept in the wee hours. "I had a date last night," he wrote. "And I am not ashamed to say it was doomed from the start because I couldn't stop thinking about you."

I fired back a message slapping his hand. "We must be careful   16
where we tread," I said. This was true but not sincere. I wanted it, all of it. I wanted unfettered affection, soul-mating, true romance. In the weeks that had elapsed since I picked up "is this the real meghan daum?" the real me had undergone some kind of meltdown—a systemic rejection of all the savvy and independence I had worn for years, like a grownup Girl Scout badge.

Pete knew nothing of my scattered, juvenile self, and I did my   17
best to keep it that way. Even though I was heading into my late twenties, I was still a child, ignorant of dance steps and health insurance, a prisoner of credit-card debt and student loans and the nagging feeling that I didn't want anyone to find me until I had pulled myself into some semblance of an adult. The fact that Pete had literally seemed to discover me, as if by turning over a rock, lent us an aura of fate which I actually took half-seriously. Though skepticism seemed like the obvious choice in this strange situation,

I discarded it precisely because it was the obvious choice, because I wanted a more interesting narrative than cynicism would ever allow. I was a true believer in the urban dream: the dream of years of struggle, of getting a break, of making it. Like most of my friends, I wanted someone to love me, but I wasn't supposed to need it. To admit to loneliness was to smack the face of progress, to betray the times in which we lived. But PFSlider derailed me. He gave me all of what I'd never even realized I wanted.

My addiction to PFSlider's messages indicated a monstrous narcissism, but it also revealed a subtler desire, which I didn't fully understand at the time. My need to experience an old-fashioned kind of courtship was stronger than I had ever imagined. And the fact that technology was providing an avenue for such archaic discourse was a paradox that both fascinated and repelled me. Our relationship had an epistolary quality that put our communication closer to the eighteenth century than to the impending millennium. Thanks to the computer, I was involved in a well-defined courtship, a neat little space in which he and I were both safe to express the panic and the fascination of our mutual affection. Our interaction was refreshingly orderly, noble in its vigor, dignified despite its shamelessness. It was far removed from the randomness of real-life relationships. We had an intimacy that seemed custom-made for our strange, lonely times. It seemed custom-made for me.   18

The day of our date, a week before Christmas, was frigid and sunny. Pete was sitting at the bar of the restaurant when I arrived. We shook hands. For a split second, he leaned toward me with his chin, as if to kiss me. He was shorter than I had pictured, though he was not short. He struck me as clean-cut. He had very nice hands. He wore a very nice shirt. We were seated at a very nice table. I scanned the restaurant for people I knew, saw none, and couldn't decide how I felt about that.   19

He talked, and I heard nothing he said. I stared at his profile and tried to figure out whether I liked him. He seemed to be saying nothing in particular, but he went on forever. Later, we went to the Museum of Natural History and watched a science film about storm chasers. We walked around looking for the dinosaurs, and he talked so much that I wanted to cry. Outside, walking along Central Park West at dusk, through the leaves, past the yellow cabs and the splendid lights of Manhattan at Christmas, he grabbed my hand to kiss me and I didn't let him. I felt as if my brain had been stuffed with cotton. Then, for some reason, I invited him back to my apartment. I gave him a few beers and finally let him kiss me on the lumpy futon in my bedroom. The radiator clanked. The phone rang and the machine picked up. A car alarm blared outside. A key   20 turned in the door as one of my roommates came home. I had no sensation at all—only a clear conviction that I wanted Pete out of my apartment. I wanted to hand him his coat, close the door behind him, and fight the ensuing emptiness by turning on the computer and taking comfort in PFSlider.

When Pete finally did leave, I berated myself from every angle: 21
for not kissing him on Central Park West, for letting him kiss me at all, for not liking him, for wanting to like him more than I had wanted anything in such a long time. I was horrified by the realization that I had invested so heavily in a made-up character—a character in whose creation I'd had a greater hand than even Pete himself. How could I, a person so self-congratulatingly reasonable, have been sucked into a scenario that was more akin to a television talk show than to the relatively full and sophisticated life I was so convinced I led? How could I have received a fan letter and allowed it to go this far?

The next day, a huge bouquet of FTD flowers arrived from him.   22
No one had ever sent me flowers before. I forgave him. As human beings with actual flesh and hand gestures and Gap clothing, Pete and I were utterly incompatible, but I decided to pretend otherwise. He returned home and we fell back into the computer and the phone, and I continued to keep the real world safely away from the desk that held them. Instead of blaming him for my disappointment, I blamed the earth itself, the invasion of roommates and ringing phones into the immaculate communication that PFSlider and I had created.

When I pictured him in the weeks that followed, I saw the image   23
of a plane lifting off over an overcast city. PFSlider was otherworldly, more a concept than a person. His romance lay in the notion of flight, the physics of gravity defiance. So when he offered to send me a plane ticket to spend the weekend with him in Los Angeles I took it as an extension of our blissful remoteness, a three-dimensional E-mail message lasting an entire weekend.

The temperature on the runway at J.F.K. was seven degrees   24
Fahrenheit. Our DC-10 sat for three hours waiting for deicing. Finally, it took off over the frozen city, and the ground below shrank into a drawing of itself. Phone calls were made, laptop computers were plopped onto tray tables. The recirculating air dried out my contact lenses. I watched movies without the sound and told myself that they were probably better that way. Something about the plastic interior of the fuselage and the plastic forks and the din of the air and the engines was soothing and strangely sexy.

Then we descended into LAX. We hit the tarmac, and the seat-   25
belt signs blinked off. I hadn't moved my body in eight hours, and now I was walking through the tunnel to the gate, my clothes

wrinkled, my hair matted, my hands shaking. When I saw Pete in the terminal, his face seemed to me just as blank and easy to miss as it had the first time I'd met him. He kissed me chastely. On the way out to the parking lot, he told me that he was being seriously considered for a job in New York. He was flying back there next week. If he got the job, he'd be moving within the month. I looked at him in astonishment. Something silent and invisible seemed to fall on us. Outside, the wind was warm, and the Avis and Hertz buses ambled alongside the curb of Terminal 5. The palm trees shook, and the air seemed as heavy and palpable as Pete's hand, which held mine for a few seconds before dropping it to get his car keys out of his pocket. He stood before me, all flesh and preoccupation, and for this I could not forgive him.

Gone were the computer, the erotic darkness of the telephone, 26 the clean, single dimension of Pete's voice at 1 A.M. It was nighttime, yet the combination of sight and sound was blinding. It scared me. It turned me off. We went to a restaurant and ate outside on the sidewalk. We strained for conversation, and I tried not to care that we had to. We drove to his apartment and stood under the ceiling light not really looking at each other. Something was happening that we needed to snap out of. Any moment now, I thought. Any moment and we'll be all right. These moments were crowded with elements, with carpet fibres and automobiles and the smells of everything that had a smell. It was all wrong. The physical world had invaded our space.

For three days, we crawled along the ground and tried to pull 27 ourselves up. We talked about things that I can no longer remember. We read the Los Angeles *Times* over breakfast. We drove north past Santa Barbara to tour the wine country. I felt like an object that could not be lifted, something that secretly weighed more than the world itself. Everything and everyone around us seemed imbued with a California lightness. I stomped around the countryside, an idiot New Yorker in my clunky shoes and black leather jacket. Not until I studied myself in the bathroom mirror of a highway rest stop did I fully realize the preposterousness of my uniform. I was dressed for war. I was dressed for my regular life.

That night, in a tiny town called Solvang, we ate an expensive 28 dinner. We checked into a Marriott and watched television. Pete talked at me and through me and past me. I tried to listen. I tried to talk. But I bored myself and irritated him. Our conversation was a needle that could not be threaded. Still, we played nice. We tried to care, and pretended to keep trying long after we had given up. In the car on the way home, he told me that I was cynical, and I didn't have the presence of mind to ask him just how many cynics he had met who would travel three thousand miles to see someone they barely knew.

Pete drove me to the airport at 7 A.M. so I could make my eight-o'clock flight home. He kissed me goodbye—another chaste peck that I recognized from countless dinner parties and dud dates. He said that he'd call me in a few days when he got to New York for his job interview, which we had discussed only in passing and with no reference to the fact that New York was where I happened to live. I returned home to frozen January. A few days later, he came to New York, and we didn't see each other. He called me from the plane taking him back to Los Angeles to tell me, through the static, that he had got the job. He was moving to my city.

PFSlider was dead. There would be no meeting him in distant hotel lobbies during the baseball season. There would be no more phone calls or E-mail messages. In a single moment, Pete had completed his journey out of our mating dance and officially stepped into the regular world—the world that gnawed at me daily, the world that fostered those five-night stands, the world where romance could not be sustained, because so many of us simply did not know how to do it. Instead, we were all chitchat and leather jackets, bold proclaimers of all that we did not need. But what struck me most about this affair was the unpredictable nature of our demise. Unlike most cyber-romances, which seem to come fully equipped with the inevitable set of misrepresentations and false expectations, PFSlider and I had played it fairly straight. Neither of us had lied. We'd done the best we could. Our affair had died from natural causes rather than virtual ones.

Within a two-week period after I returned from Los Angeles, at least seven people confessed to me the vagaries of their own E-mail affairs. This topic arose, unprompted, in the course of normal conversation. I heard most of these stories in the close confines of smoky bars and crowded restaurants, and we all shook our heads in bewilderment as we told our tales, our eyes focussed on some point in the distance. Four of these people had met their correspondents, by travelling from New Haven to Baltimore, from New York to Montana, from Texas to Virginia, and from New York to Johannesburg. These were normal people, writers and lawyers and scientists. They were all smart, attractive, and more than a little sheepish about admitting just how deeply they had been sucked in. Mostly, it was the courtship ritual that had seduced us. E-mail had become an electronic epistle, a yearned-for rule book. It allowed us to do what was necessary to experience love. The Internet was not responsible for our remote, fragmented lives. The problem was life itself.

29

30

31

The story of PFSlider still makes me sad, not so much because   32
we no longer have anything to do with each other but because it
forces me to see the limits and the perils of daily life with more
clarity than I used to. After I realized that our relationship would
never transcend the screen and the phone — that, in fact, our face-
to-face knowledge of each other had permanently contaminated the
screen and the phone — I hit the pavement again, went through the
motions of everyday life, said hello and goodbye to people in
the regular way. If Pete and I had met at a party, we probably
wouldn't have spoken to each other for more than ten minutes, and
that would have made life easier but also less interesting. At the
same time, it terrifies me to admit to a firsthand understanding of
the way the heart and the ego are snarled and entwined like dis-
eased trees that have folded in on each other. Our need to worship
somehow fuses with our need to be worshipped. It upsets me still
further to see how inaccessibility can make this entanglement so
much more intoxicating. But I'm also thankful that I was forced to
unpack the raw truth of my need and stare at it for a while. It was a
dare I wouldn't have taken in three dimensions.

The last time I saw Pete, he was in New York, three thousand   33
miles away from what had been his home, and a million miles away
from PFSlider. In a final gesture of decency, in what I later realized
was the most ordinary kind of closure, he took me out to dinner. As
the few remaining traces of affection turned into embarrassed regret, we talked about nothing. He paid the bill. He drove me home
in a rental car that felt as arbitrary and impersonal as what we now
were to each other.

Pete had known how to get me where I lived until he came to   34
where I lived: then he became as unmysterious as anyone next door.
The world had proved to be too cluttered and too fast for us, too pol-
luted to allow the thing we'd attempted through technology ever to
grow in the earth. PFSlider and I had joined the angry and exhausted
living. Even if we met on the street, we wouldn't recognize each other,
our particular version of intimacy now obscured by the branches and
bodies and falling debris that make up the physical world.

Questions

1. List the turning points in the story of the relationship between
   Daum and Pete. To what extent does this e-mail romance develop along the path Suler identifies as typical (par. 17, p. 431)?

2. In paragraph 4, Daum says that never before had she used the
   term *touched* seriously. What does this detail tell you about Daum's

personality and style? How do you feel about her at this point in the essay? Do your feelings about her change as the essay goes on? Do her personality and style seem to change? From what to what?

3. Daum seems genuinely surprised to find that e-mail is not "dehumanizing" (par. 12). How and why does she find it so different from what she expected?

4. Why do you think that Daum doesn't reprint any of her correspondence with PFSlider? Do you think she should have done so?

READING 5

The following set of e-mail messages come from a recent novel by Sylvia Brownrigg called *The Metaphysical Touch* (FSG, 1998). The novel is about the virtual love affair of two characters: J. D., a former computer instructor living in New York City, and Pi, a woman temporarily living in Mendocino, California, with a friend named Abbie and Abbie's daughter Martha. Online, J. D. uses "Hamlet" as his signature while Pi uses "Sylvia"—for Sylvia Plath. The following correspondence occurs relatively early on in the e-mail relationship between Hamlet and Sylvia. As you read this excerpt, pay attention not only to the body of the message but to other e-mail components as well. What do these components tell you about these two characters and the relationship they are creating?

Sylvia Brownrigg, from *The Metaphysical Touch* (1998)

```
Re: Something deep
   If I might add to this depth, Hamlet. Just to note       1
something I have discovered recently, largely
through reading aloud to Martha, or by sneaking in
and reading her books behind her back: Many of the
world's best truths are hidden in children's books.
Were you aware of this? It's something of a shock to
me, because you aren't necessarily able to appreci-
ate it at that age (youth is wasted on the young:
THAT'S what they meant when they said that) but it
turns out that that's where everyone's stashed much
of the good stuff, the stuff you need to make sense
of the world.
   This happens to be of special interest to me in my    2
life because of my odd and tormented relation to the
adult book world, which I'll explain another time.
```

Suffice it to say that the best of the kids' books also say something deep about our need for evil in an amoral et cetera.

Thought you should know.   3

S.

Re: Youth is wasted

Re: This. I quite agree. Why can't we all have it   4
back, now that we'd know what to do with it better?
Mine without the divorce trauma and that terrible
third-grade teacher, though, please.

Re: the wit and wisdom of kids' books: I've always   5
suspected that kids get the best deal in many aspects of life, so it doesn't surprise me that their
literature is quietly superior to ours in peddling
the answers to life's problems.

There are times in the ritzier areas of the great   6
park in my city, when I see these kids and think: Now
there's the life. These are rich kids I'm talking
about, obviously, and I'm sure half of them actually
have miserable mothers who are quietly addicted to
Valium or coke and probably fathers--or again mothers, for that matter--off vacationing with their secretaries in the Bahamas. My point simply being:

These kids do look great in their clothes.   7

You take your standard adult outfit--tennis shoes,   8
leather jacket, jeans--and you make it tiny and perfect, and suddenly it's adorable. What is that
about? Everything looks better on kids--baseball
caps, tennis shoes, goofy T-shirts. I have fashion
envy I guess. I want to be able to put on ordinary
schleppy clothing and look adorable, like they do.

This is not impressive, is it? Kids' clothing   9
envy.

Sorry to be so damn shallow.   10

Hamlet

Re: Hidden depths

No, no, I know what you mean. Martha has a pair of   11
pyjamas with little constellations all over them
that I completely covet. I'm aware that I would not
be able to wear them with the panache she has, but
still I'd like a pair.

Equally shallowly,   12

Sylvia

Re: Shallow waters

Hey, you can't be that shallow. I mean, think of your 13
poetry! Specifically, you did write some pretty nifty

suicide poems. Plus, no offense, but you're dead,
aren't you? Right there that guarantees you some depth.
Hamlet

Re: Dead Poets Society
   It's true that dead is possibly the only way to be   14
if you're a poet--it makes people much more likely
to read you. Do you think everyone would know
"Ariel" as well as they do if it weren't for my
stunt with the gas oven?
   But enough about me. Let's talk about you. How is   15
life in Denmark, anyway? Still rotten?
Sylvia

Re: Rottenness
   What can I tell you about Denmark? Denmark is a   16
state of mind--like every other place, I guess. Right
at this minute it is seeming more floral and breezy
than rotten, but that could change at any time.
Hamlet

Re: The state of the state
   (Do they have magnolia trees in Denmark?) Here's a   17
question.--If Denmark is a state of mind, what does
that make California?
S.

Re: California
   A state of denial? That's my best effort.   18
   So may I assume that you, like the g. of P., re-   19
side in California? I happen to know a thing or two
about that state myself. I mean, of Calif., though
also of denial.
Hamlet

Re: state of Calif.
   Yes, California, but an unfamiliar northern edge   20
of it where the living is easy and the people long-
haired. I'm newish to town and it hasn't yet altogether grown on me. Though it is a place, if I may
quote from a storefront I passed not too long ago
here, with "a little magic--and a lot of style."
   It's important to know that "a lot of style" is in   21
italics.
Sylvia

Re: a little magic
   That's so touching, as a description. I wish some-   22
one would say the same thing about me.

So I know that poets guard their privacy, which I   23
can certainly respect, and Lord knows you Sylvia
Plath have already had about 10 salacious biographies published about you which is a lot for someone
who's only been dead 30 years or whatever it is.

But I'm curious. Why the unfamiliar edge? Or is   24
that getting too personal? I don't want to pry.

Hamlet

Re: and a lot of style

No, no, pry away. I was a confessional poet, don't   25
forget. I laid it all on the line for people. I
haven't been in this particular (small h) hamlet
long -- just long enough to begin to figure out my way
around. I came up here to deal with the major Life
Change. Yours clearly fishing for more curiosity on
your part but not wanting to assume you want to hear
the whole damn thing, Sylvia

Re: Fishing

OK, I'm biting, I'm biting.   26

Re: The whole damn thing. Do it, tell it. I'm   27
guessing, as a careful reader, it may have to do
with the dark reference you made earlier? I think
"odd and tormented" was the phrase you used, as in
an "o. and t. relation to the adult book world."

Hamlet

Re: Tormented relations

Well spotted.   28

I won't belabor the tale. Doubtless I should hold   29
off altogether and write more nifty poetry out of it.
(If only I could.) Basically, I used to live and work
with many dead philosophers -- more than you could
shake a stick at, as my fifth-grade teacher used to
say -- and they all died in a fire. A second death, a
permanent, existential one, if you see what I mean.
Stacks and stacks of them. A career's worth. I had
been planning to become one myself, and had been
trundling along for years in grad student ignominy to
that end.

And along with Kant, Hume, and the other guys, the   30
fire took everything else too: furniture, photographs, sanity, cat -- Zeno, my black and white cat
who went the same way as the philosophers. I was
left with a whole lot of nothing. (Was that a pop
song?) So I have been Coping with Catastrophe, as my
mother's ohsohelpful self-help book would have it.

These days I live with no dead philosophers but instead with young Martha and her nice alive mother,
who is part employer, part charity officer. Also, of
course, the g.s. of Pinsk and of Zeno.

And that's the story, in a nutshell.   31
Sylvia

Re: Whole lotta nothin
Dear Sylvia

Yes it was a pop song. Written as above, in the   32
original.

But listen: 33

Re: The fire. The philosophers. Zeno. I'm so   34
sorry.

I don't even know you, and I'm sorry.   35

Which isn't that unusual, in a sense, because I was   36
raised on a healthy diet of guilt (Wasp and Jewish
both, as was once pointed out to me) and am liable to
feel sorry about almost anything, if given half a
chance, whether or not I bear any responsibility for
it. But I really am sorry. What does that make you, a
recovering ex-philosopher? A philosopher from scratch?

I was a philosopher once too, of course. Though I   37
had my disillusionments with it. I'm sure you're familiar with the old saw, "There are more things on
heaven and earth, Horatio, than are dreamt of in
your philosophy."

But back to the main point. What a very dramatic   38
and sad nutshell that was, Sylvia.

In sympathy, Hamlet   39

Re: The nutshell

I know. It's an attention grabber, that fire. But   40
thanks for the sympathy. We try to keep very tough
and resilient about it all, me and the ghosts, but a
little sympathy every now and then helps the tragedy
go down, as Mary Poppins might have said but didn't.
Mary Poppins, help. I'm regressing. Must have been
my inner child interrupting the flow. Don't you hate
it when that happens?
Sylvia

Questions

1. Pick two messages by Sylvia. Using the six e-mail components
   that Suler identifies (par. 15, p. 430), analyze the messages to see

what they tell you about Sylvia's character. What kind of person is she? What does she care about? Why is she writing to Hamlet?

2. According to Suler, style is not only an important aspect of e-mail relationships but also a clue to the personality of the writer (par. 14, p. 430). Examine Hamlet's style to see what it can tell you about this character's personality.

3. There's a lot about children and fiction in these messages. Why do you think this is so? What's the relationship between these two topics and the romance of e-mail?

4. In this excerpt, how and why does the relationship between Hamlet and Sylvia change? What do you think will happen next? Do you think their relationship is likely to last for a long time? Why or why not?

PRACTICE 11.3

The Value of Virtual Relationships

What are the benefits and the limitations of e-mail relationships? To answer this question, you should work through the readings collected here, noting what the writers say or imply about the value of e-mail relationships as well as where they disagree with each other. But even though you should take note of disagreements, you are not being asked to argue for or against e-mail relationships. Your purpose is to understand and help us to understand both the positive and the negative aspects of virtual relations. Strategically speaking, you should emphasize analysis, interpretation, and reflection rather than argument.

In thinking about the value of virtual relationships, consider their social and cultural as well as their personal dimensions. And, if you are permitted or required to do additional research, think about interviewing some people who are devoted e-mail users as well as analyzing e-mail relationships in which you are—or have been—a participant. The more specific details you have on hand, the more likely it is that your hypothesis—your answer to the question—will be well developed.

Acknowledgments

Eve Arnold. "On Her Work." From *The Unretouched Woman*. Copyright © 1976 by Eve Arnold. Reprinted with the permission of Alfred A. Knopf, a division of Random House, Inc.

W. H. Auden. "Musee Des Beaux Arts." From *W. H. Auden: Collected Poems*, edited by Edward Mendelson. Copyright © 1940 and renewed 1968 by W. H. Auden. Reprinted with the permission of Random House, Inc. and Faber & Faber Ltd.

Paul Auster. "Portrait of an Invisible Man." From *The Invention of Solitude*. Copyright © 1998 by Paul Auster. Reprinted with the permission of the Carol Mann Agency.

Russell Baker. Excerpt from *Growing Up*. Copyright © 1982 by Russell Baker. Reprinted with the permission of Contemporary Books, Inc.

Peter Bakakian. "Words for My Grandmother." From *Black Dog of Fate*. Copyright © 1998 by Peter Bakakian. Reprinted with the permission of Basic Books, a member of Perseus Books, LLC.

Letitia Baldridge. Excerpt from *Amy Vanderbilt's Everyday Etiquette*. Copyright © 1978 by Letitia Baldridge. Reprinted with the permission of Bantam Books, a division of Random House, Inc.

Toni Cade Bambara. "The Education of a Storyteller." From *Deep Sightings and Rescue Missions*. Copyright © 1996 by Toni Cade Bambara. Reprinted with the permission of Pantheon Books, a Division of Random House, Inc.

Roland Barthes. "Looking for My Mother." From *A Lover's Discourse*, translated by Richard Howard. Translation copyright © 1979 by Farrar, Straus & Giroux. Excerpt from Chapter 28 in *Camera Lucida* translated by Richard Howard. Translation © 1981 by Hill & Wang, a division of Farrar, Straus & Giroux. Reprinted with the permission of Farrar, Straus & Giroux, LLC.

John Berger. "John Berger Reads a Photograph." From *Another Way of Telling*. Copyright © 1982

John Berger and Jean Mohr. "On the Use of Photography. " From *About Looking* by John Berger. Copyright © 1980 by John Berger. Reprinted by permission of Pantheon Books, a division of Random House, Inc. Excerpt from *The Ways of Seeing*. Copyright © 1972 by Penguin Books Ltd. Reprinted with the permission of Penguin Putnam, Inc.

Pat Booth. Excerpt from an interview with Eve Arnold from *Master Photographers: Great Photographers on Their Art and Technique* edited by Pat Booth. Copyright © 1983 by Pat Booth. Reprinted with the permission of Crown Publishers, Inc. and Macmillan London.

Sylvia Brownrigg. Excerpt from *the Metaphysical Touch*. Copyright © 1998 by Sylvia Brownrigg. Reprinted with the permission of Farrar, Straus & Giroux, LLC.

Martin Bush. Excerpts from an interview with Gordon Parks published in *The Photographs of Gordon Parks*. Copyright © 1983 by Wichita State University. Reprinted with the permission of The Edwin A.Ulrich Museum of Art, Wichita State University, Wichita, Kansas.

Andreas Capellanus. Excerpt from *The Art of Courtly Love* translated by John Jay Parry. Copyright © 1990 by Columbus University Press, New York. Reprinted with permission of the publisher.

John E. Chubb and Terry M. Moe. "Choices *Is* a Panacea." From *The Brookings Review*, summer 1990. Copyright © 1990 by The Brookings Institution. Reprinted with the permission of the Publishers.

Craig Claiborne. "Basic Pie Pastry." From *The New York Times Cookbook*. Copyright © 1961 by Craig Claiborne. Reprinted by permission of HarperCollins Publishers, Inc.

Judith Ortiz Cofer. "The Story of My Body." From *The Latin Deli*. Copyright © 1993 by Judith Ortiz Cofer. Reprinted with the permission of The University of Georgia Press.

Patricia Cohen. "A Woman's Worth: 1857 Letter Echoes Still." From *The New York Times*, July 18, 1998, pp. B7, B9. Copyright © 1998 by The New York Times Company. Reprinted by permission.

Peter W. Cookson. "The Market Metaphor." From *School Choice: The Struggle for the Soul of American Education*. Copyright © 1994 by Peter W. Cookson. Reprinted with the permission of Yale University Press.

Marion Cunningham. "Basic Master Recipe: American Apple Pie." From *The Fannie Farmer Baking Book*. Copyright © 1984 by Marion Cunningham. Reprinted with the permission of Alfred A. Knopf, a division of Random House, Inc.

Meghan Daum. Excerpt from "Virtual Love." Published in *The New Yorker*, August 25/September 1, 1997, pp. 80-83. Copyright © 1997 by Meghan Daum. Reprinted with the permission of International Creative Management Incorporated.

Louise DeSalve. Excerpt from "A Portrait of the *Puttana* as a middle-aged Woolf Scholar," excerpt From "It Is 1957," and "autumn 1963." From *Between Women: Biographers, Novelists, Teachers, and Artists Write About Their Work on Women*, edited by Carol Ascher, Louise DeSalvo and Sara Rudnick. Copyright © 1983 by Louise De-Salvo. Reprinted with the permission of the author.

Mark Edmundson. "My First Intellectual: An Ex-Jock Remembers the Teacher Who Changed His Life." From *Linga Franca*, March 1999, pp. 55-60. Copyright © 1999 by Mark Edmundson. Reprinted with the permission of the author.

Peter Elbow. Excerpt from *Writing with Power: Techniques for Mastering the Writing Process* Copyright © 1981 by Oxford University Press, Inc. Reprinted with the permission of the publishers.

Louise Erdrich. "Cousin Mary." From *The Beet Queen*. Copyright © 1986 by Louise Erdrich. Reprinted by permission of Henry Holt and Company, LLC.

Ellen Fein and Sherrie Schneider. "Rule #20: Be Honest but Mysterious." From *The Rules: Time-Tested Secrets for Capturing the Heart of Mr. Right*. Copyright © 1995 by Ellen Fein and Sherrie Schneider. Reprinted with the permission of Warner Books, Inc.

Federico Fellini. "On the Telephone." Excerpt from *Fellini on Fellini* by Frederico Fellini, edited by Christian Strich. Italian translation copyright © 1976 by Isabel Quigley. Reprinted with the Permission of Delacorte Press, a division of Random House, Inc.

Gisele Freund. "On Doisneau's Photograph." From *Photography and Society*. Copyright © 1980 by Gisele Freund. Reprinted with the permission of David R. Godine, Publishers, Inc.

W. H. Gass. Excerpt from *On Being Blue*. Copyright © 1976 by William H. Gass. Reprinted with the permission of David R. Godine, Publisher, Inc.

Nikki Giovanni. "400 Mulvaney Street." From *Gemini*. Copyright © 1971 by Nikki Giovanni. Reprinted with the permission of Scribner, a division of Simon & Schuster, Inc.

Thomas A. Gullason. "Stephen Crane—A Chronology." From *Stephen Crane's Career: Perspectives and Evaluations* edited by Thomas A. Gullason. Copyright © 1972 Thomas A. Gullason. Reprinted with the permission of the author.

J. C. Herz. "Flying Toasters That You Can Play With." From *The New York Times*, Thursday, April 29, 1999, p. G4. Copyright © 1999 by J.C. Herz. Reprinted with permission.

Paul Hill and Thomas Cooper. Excerpt from "Robert Doisneau." From *Dialogue with Photography*. Copyright © 1979 by Paul Hill and Thomas Cooper. Reprinted with the permission of Farrar, Straus & Giroux LLC.

James Joyce. "The End of Molly's Soliloquy." From *Ulysses* by James Joyce. Copyright © 1934 And renewed 1962 by Lucia & George Joyce. Published by Random House and The Bodley Head. Reprinted with the permission of Random House, Inc.

Tibor Kalman and Lulu Kalman. "How to Open a CD Box." From *The New York Times Magazine*, December 13, 1998. Copyright © 1998 by Tibor Kalman and Lulu Kalman. Reprinted with Permission.

Nancy Kanode. "Private School Vouchers: Bad for America." Reprinted with the permission of the author.

Douglas Kellner. "Advertising Images." From *Media Culture: Cultural Studies, Identity and Politics between the Modern and the Postmodern*. Copyright © 1995 by Douglas Kellner. Reprinted with the permission of Routledge and the author.

Jamaica Kincaid. "The Tourist's Arrival." From *Annie John*. Copyright © 1985 by Jamaica Kincaid. Reprinted with the permission of Farrar, Straus & Giroux, LLC.

Alex Kotlowitz. "The Hearing Room." Excerpts from *There Are No Children Here*. Copyright © 1992 by Alex Kotlowitz. Reprinted with the permission of Doubleday, division of Random House, Inc.

Jonathan Kozel. "An Interview with Gizelle Luke and Children of the South Bronx." From *Amazing Grace*. Copyright © 1995 by Jonathan Kozel. Reprinted by permission of Crown Publishers, a Division of Random House, Inc.

Patricia Nelson Limerick. "Travels in Frontierland." Reprinted in *The Adventures of the Frontier in the Twentieth Century*, from *The Frontier in American Culture* by Richard White and Patricia Nelson Limerick. Copyright © 1994 by the Regents of the University of California. Reprinted by permission of the University of California Press. This selection contains excerpts from Robert Cahn, "The Intrepid Kids of Disneyland" from *The Saturday Evening Post*, June 18, 1958. Copyright © 1958. Reprinted with the permission of The Saturday Evening Post Society.

Naguib Mahfouz. "Half a Day." From *The Time and the Place and Other Stories*, translated by Naguib Mahfouz and Denis Johnson-Davies. Copyright © 1991 by the American University in Cairo Press. Reprinted with the permission of Doubleday, a division Random House, Inc.

Gregory Mantsios. Excerpt from "Class in America: Myths and Realities." From *Race, Class, and Gender in the United States*, Fifth Edition by Paula S. Rothenberg. Copyright © 1998 St. Martin's Press. Reprinted with the permission of the author.

Graham McCann. Excerpt from *Marilyn Monroe*. Copyright © 1987 by Graham McCann. Reprinted with the permission of Rutgers University Press.

Clyde A. Milner II. "The Long Walk on the White Road." From *The Oxford History of the American West* edited by Clyde A. Milner, Carol O'Connor, and Martha A. Sandweiss. Copyright © 1994 by Oxford University Press, Inc. Reprinted by permission of Oxford University Press.

Jean Mohr. "A Photo and Some Reactions." From *Another Way of Telling*. Copyright © 1982 by John Berger and Jean Mohr. Reprinted by permission of Pantheon Books, a division of Random House, Inc.

Monica M. Moore. "Rejection Signaling." From *Nonverbal Patterns in Women: Rejection Signaling*. Published in *Semiotica*, February 1998. Copyright © 1998 by Monica M. Moore. Reprinted with the permission of Monica M. Moore, Department of Psychology, Webster University, St. Louis, MO 63119.

William Carlos Williams. "Landscape with the Fall of Icarus." From *The Collected Poems of William Carlos Williams, 1939-1962, vol II*. Copyright © 1958 by William Carlos Williams. Reprinted by permission of New Directions Publishing.

Garry Wills. "American Adam." From *John Wayne's America*. Copyright © 1997 by Literary Research, Inc. Reprinted with the permission of Simon & Schuster, Inc.

Edward O. Wilson. "The Storm." From "Storm over the Amazon" in *On Nature: Nature, Landscape and Natural History* edited by David Halpern. Copyright © 1987 by Edward O. Wilson. Reprinted with the permission of Farrar, Straus & Giroux, LLC.

Wisconsin Education Association Council. "A Private School Choice as a Solution." From *Private Schools and Private School Vouchers: What the Research Shows*. Reprinted with the permission of the Wisconsin Education Association Council.

Richard Wright. "Going Underground." From "The Man Who Lived Underground" in *Eight Men*. Copyright © 1940, 1961 by Richard Wright. Renewed 1989 by Ellen Wright. Reprinted with the permission of HarperCollins Publishers, Inc.

Art:

p. 42. "The Cry." Edvard Munch, artist. William Francis Warden Fund. Courtesy of Museum of Fine Arts, Boston.

p. 43. "A Pair of Boots." Vincent Van Gogh, artist. The Baltmore Museum of Art: The Cone Collection formed by Dr. Claribel Cone and Miss Etta Cone of Baltimore, Maryland.

p. 44. "Smiling Figure", ceramics dating to VII-IX century. From Veracruz, Mexico. The Metropolitan Museum of Art. The Michael C. Rockefeller Memorial Collection. Bequest of Nelson A. Rockefeller, 1979.

p. 47. "After Dark" Games package. Courtesy of After Dark Games.

p. 134. "Noon." William Hogarth, artist. The Granger Collection, New York.

p. 136. "London" (editor's title). William Hogarth, artist. "The Musician," The Granger Collection, New York.

p. 137. Photo of "Marilyn Monroe." World copyright © George Barris.

p. 167. "The Fall of Icarus." Pieter Brueghel, artist. Brussels, Collection of Van Bueren. Scala/Art Resource, N.Y.

p. 169. "Shoe" cartoon by Jeff McNelly. Reprinted with the permission of Jefferson Communications, Inc., Reston, VA.

p. 200. *Cosmopolitan* advertisement, 1966. Reprinted with the permission of *Cosmopolitan* Magazine.

p. 201. *Redbook* advertisement, 1977. Reprinted with the permission of *Redbook* magazine. Copyright © 1993 by The Hearst Corporation. All rights reserved.

p. 202. "Charlie" advertisement. © 1987 Revlon, Inc. Courtesy of Revlon, Inc.

p. 203. "Bisou Bisou" advertisement, 1993. Mark Hanaeur. © Bisou Bisou/No Comment! Reproduced with permission.

p. 204. Calvin Klein Jeans billboard ad, February 23, 1999. Corbis SYGMA.

p. 220. "Pastry blender" and "Knives" line art illustrated by Lauren Jarrett. From *The Fannie Farmer Baking Book*. © 1996 by Marion Cunningham. Reprinted with the permission of Random House, Inc.

p. 232. "Fly-tox" advertisement. From *Ladies Home Journal*, June 1926. Courtesy of General Research Division, The New York Public Library and the Astor, Lenox, and Tilden Foundation.

p. 324. "Little girl crying" photo. Jean Mohr, photographer. From *Another Way of Telling* by John Berger and Jean Mohr, p. 54. Copyright © 1982 by John Berger and

Jean Mohr. Reprinted with the permission of Pantheon Books, a division of Random House, Inc.

p. 326. "A Red Hussar Leaving, June 1919, Budapest." Andre Kertesz, photographer. © Ministere de la Culture—France. Courtesy of Mission du Patrimoine Photographique, Paris.

p. 331. "Parisian Café." Courtesy Robert Doisneau/Black Star/Rapho.

p. 335. " American Gothic, 1942." Washington, D.C. Gordon Parks, photographer. Photograph courtesy of the Edwin A. Ulrich Museum of Art, The Wichita State University, Kansas. Reproduced with the permission of Gordon Parks.

p. 341. "Marlene Dietrich." Eve Arnold, photographer. Courtesy of Eve Arnold/Magnum Photos.

p. 344. "Sidelong Glance." Courtesy of Robert Doisneau/Black Star/Rapho.

p. 345. "Muslim School Children, 1963." Photograph courtesy of the Edwin A. Ulrich Museum of Art, The Wichita State University, Kansas. Reproduced with the permission of Gordon Parks.

p. 346. "A Literacy Teacher in Abu Dhabi." Eve Arnold, photographer. Courtesy of Eve Arnold/Magnum Photos.

p. 347. "A Paratrooper Works to Save the Life of a Buddy." Courtesy AP/Wide World Photos.

p. 348. "Student Killed by National Guardsmen, Kent State University, May 4, 1970." © 1970 John Paul Filo.

p. 349. "Children Fleeing a Napalm Strike, June 8, 1972." Nick Ut, photographer. AP/Wide World Photos.

p. 350. "Elizabeth and I, Paris 1931." Andre Kertesz, photographer. © Ministere de la Culture—France. Courtesy of Mission du Patrimoine Photographique, Paris.

p. 351. "Draught Refugees Hoping for Cotton Work, Blythe, California, 1936." Courtesy of The Library of Congress.

p. 352. "U.S. Seventh Army troops advance as woman surveys wreckage of her home, March 1945, Bensheim, Germany." Courtesy Records of the Office of the Chief Signal Officer, National Archives and Records Administration.

p. 353. "Birthday Party for David Eisenhower, March 31, 1956, Washington, D.C." Abbey Rowe, photographer. Courtesy Dwight D. Eisenhower Library, National Archives and Records Administration.

p. 354. "World's Fair, New York City, 1964." Gelatin-silver print. Garry Winogrand, photographer. © The Estate of Garry Winogrand, courtesy Fraenkel Gallery, San Francisco.

p. 356. "Tomoko in the Bath, 1972." Eugene W. Smith, photographer. Courtesy Black Star.

p. 357. "Window Dressing, 1989." © Charles Martin. Reproduced with the permission of Charles Martin.

p. 358. "Woman Comforted by Relatives and Friends at Husband's Funeral, Izbica, Kosovo, 1998." Dayna Smith, photographer. © 1998 The Washington Post. Reprinted with permission.

p. 366. "Buffalo Bill's Wild West and Congress of Rough Riders of the World." Courtesy Buffalo Bill Memorial Museum, Denver Colorado.

p. 376. *Beadle's Half Dime Library* front page. © Bettmann/CORBIS. Courtesy of the Library of Congress.

Index

Instructor's Notes

The Practice of

Writing

Fifth Edition

Robert Scholes • Nancy R. Comley • Janice Peritz

Prepared by Stuart Cochran

The Practice of Writing

INSTRUCTOR'S NOTES
FIFTH EDITION

The Practice of Writing

Stuart Cochran

BEDFORD/ST. MARTIN'S   Boston   ◆   New York

For information, write: Bedford/St. Martin's, 75 Arlington Street, Boston, MA 02116   (617-399-4000)

ISBN: 0-312-25958-1

Contents

A Few Words about
The Practice of Writing

This manual is addressed primarily to the person who needs it most—the instructor with relatively little experience in the composition classroom. We hope that some of the material here will be of use as well to experienced teachers, but we must cheerfully run the risk of boring them in order to give the newcomer the sort of assistance that he or she will need in teaching writing.

It is a truism of marine architecture that no boat can be built for comfort and speed. It is similar with composition texts and, indeed, with composition courses. No teacher can teach everything about writing in one quarter or one semester, and no textbook can cover every aspect of writing successfully. It is with books as it is with boats: much better for all concerned if the makers are honest about what their creation is intended to accomplish.

The Practice of Writing undertakes to solve one major problem that besets all writing classrooms—the morale problem. All language teaching includes some degree of repetition. To this, writing adds an element of psychological stress for the student and the burden of reading and responding for the teacher. And yet, the creation of written works, like all constructive processes, has a dimension of pleasure and satisfaction that is the true reward for the effort required. As we saw it, our task was to find a way of locating and using the compositional joy that is locked into every well-made piece of writing.

By emphasizing the pleasure of composition, we do not mean to slight the results that a writing course should achieve. Rather, we wish to assert that promoting a healthy and appreciative *attitude* toward writing is a major goal of teaching English. The student's growth as a writer does not end with the completion of a course. We hope that students—ours and yours—will show visible improvement after working with us, and that they will want to become better writers still. Above all, we hope that they can see how their own practice is the key to improvement.

In composing this fifth edition of our text, we have organized our materials into five parts: Practicing Writing, Writing the Self, Writing and Knowledge, Writing and Power, and Three Writing Projects. Under each of these categories, separate chapters explore particular writing strategies, focusing on how writing is situated and the writing process, as well as how we as writers express ourselves, reflect, narrate, describe, etc. This organization will, we hope, clarify the approach we take and have taken in *The Practice of Writing*, which is to see writing as situated in discourse and not merely as discreet modes of rhetoric. We have continued to emphasize visual material, and for this edition have added material on video texts as well, because we think the ability to read these texts critically is crucially important. We have also added considerable material involving the Internet and, whenever possible, introduced those materials in the context of the questions they raise about how we experience our selves, our writing, and discourse in and through that medium. All of these readings, including many other new ones, are the points of departure for practice in writing. We have included a number of texts from the fields of advertising, art, literature, and photography, as well as the more expository and argumentative kinds of writing. The readings are designed both to provide interesting texts for class discussion and to function as bases for written assignments. There is enough reading here so that no "reader" is needed to accompany this text, and we usually provide questions to help you get class discussion going. The questions aim to treat the readings as a writing instructor must—that is, to emphasize *how* the text can be used by a writer rather than *what* it means to a literary critic. When appropriate, we suggest possibilities of additional research if you decide to enlarge the scope of any particular writing assignment or project.

The Practice of Writing is not a handbook of grammar, and you may well wish to order one for that aspect of your composition course. This is also not a text that concentrates on a single form of discourse or seeks to develop the student's skill at a single method of composition. We have emphasized range and variety, but we have tried to arrange things so as to lead up to and emphasize the kind of argumentative and synthetic writing most required of the college student.

We would like to thank all the graduate assistants and adjunct instructors with whom we've taught over the years for their suggestions for improving *The Practice of Writing* and for using the text effectively in the classroom. We'd especially like to thank the following past and present colleagues at Queens College: Stuart Cochran, Jane Collins, Ann Davison, Deborah Nelson, Susan O'Brian, Jay Prosser, Danny Sexton, Christine Timm, James Werner, and Carl Whithaus; also, from her days as a graduate assistant at Brown University, Lori Lefkovitz, whose classroom experiences you will find interspersed with our own throughout this manual.

PREPARING YOURSELF TO TEACH WRITING

It would be unthinkable for a teacher to enter a literature class without some training in the history and theory of the subject. Yet teachers enter composition classes every year with nothing but their native wit and their own history as writers to guide them. The occasional genius aside—this is not enough. To manage a writing classroom with the confidence that brings ease and allows the students to relax and grow, some preparation is needed. Formal course work in language and discourse is the ideal solution, but the ideal is not always attainable. Therefore we list a few texts here that we recommend most strongly to every new writing teacher for orientation in the field and the classroom, and to experienced writing teachers for inspiration and encouragement.

- Richard Graves, ed., *Rhetoric and Composition: A Sourcebook for Teachers and Writers* (Upper Montclair, N.J.: Boynton/Cook, 1984).

- Theresa Enos, ed., *A Sourcebook for Basic Writing Teachers* (New York: Random House, 1987).

- Gary Tate, ed., *Teaching Composition: Twelve Bibliographic Essays* (Fort Worth: Texas Christian University Press, 1987).

- Chris Anson, ed., *Writing and Response: Theory, Practice, and Research* (Urbana, Ill.: NCTE, 1988).

- *Focus on Collaborative Learning* (Urbana, Ill.: NCTE, 1988).

- Gary Tate and Edward P. J. Corbett, eds., *The Writing Teacher's Sourcebook* (New York: Oxford University Press, 1988).

- Amy Tucker, *Decoding ESL* (New York: McGraw-Hill, 1991). (Note: This is a well-researched critical discussion of teaching writing to students of diverse linguistic backgrounds. Especially helpful for understanding how cultural difference manifests itself rhetorically.)

- Patricia Bizzell, "Composing Processes: An Overview," in *Academic Discourse and Critical Consciousness* (Pittsburgh: University of Pittsburgh Press, 1992).

- Lester Faigley, *Fragments of Rationality: Postmodernity and the Subject of Composition* (Pittsburgh: University of Pittsburgh Press, 1992). (Note: This is a survey of contemporary theories and their pedagogical implications. Includes stimulating discussions of the student's writing "self," computer networking, teacher authority.)

- John C. Bean, *Engaging Ideas: The Professor's Guide to Integrating Writing, Critical Thinking, and Active Learning in the Classroom* (San Francisco: Jossey-Bass, 1996).

- Patricia Bizzell and Bruce Herzberg, *The Bedford Bibliography for Teachers of Writing*, 4th ed. (Boston: Bedford/St. Martin's, 1996).

- Victor Villanueva Jr., ed., *Cross-Talk in Comp Theory: A Reader* (Urbana, Ill.: NCTE, 1997).

- Lisa Ede, ed., *On Writing Research: The Braddock Essays 1975–1998* (Boston: Bedford/St. Martin's, 1999).

- *Journals*. Writing teachers should regularly see two journals available to members of the National Council of Teachers of English: *College English*, which frequently publishes important essays on writing, and *College Composition and Communication*, which is devoted primarily to this field. *The Journal of Advanced Composition* is also highly recommended.

SUGGESTED SYLLABUS

We present on page xii a syllabus for a 15-week course, as an example of how to use *The Practice of Writing*. Use this syllabus or develop your own according to the needs of your students. Keep in mind that the book is not meant to be covered in any comprehensive sense but is rather meant as a collection of resources from which you may pick and choose to design your own course. In planning your syllabus for a semester's work, start with a general outline of what you want to cover. After you are better acquainted with your students' writing abilities, you will be able to refine the syllabus. During the first few weeks of the course, have your students write frequently, both in class and out, so that you can make an early assessment. If your students work easily with the practices in part 2, "Writing the Self," you may wish to spend more time with part 3, "Writing and Knowledge," and part 4, "Writing and Power." On the other hand, if your students come to you after having been drilled in what might be called teacher-oriented writing ("never use *I* or *you*"; passive constructions; more generalities than specifics), they will benefit from the time spent on writer-oriented (chapters 3 and 4) or reader-oriented (chapter 9) writing. Such writing will help them develop more confidence in their own voices and ideas.

In the syllabus, we have tried to leave adequate time for discussion of the readings and of strategies for approaching the writing assignments, as well as for discussion of student papers. We have also included suggestions for writing practice in the classroom. Students need experience in writing under time limitations (especially for essay exams in other courses), and shorter practices can usefully provide this experience. Starting a writing practice in class is also valuable. The instructor is available for help during the composing process, and thus serves a more creative and helpful role than when he or she functions simply as judge of final products. Remember that you can't accomplish everything you wish to in one semester. In writing up this suggested syllabus, we're fully aware of our own practice of adjusting a syllabus during the semester as we discover more about our students' strengths and weaknesses—and interests. Also, there will be days when you will find it necessary to deviate from your syllabus to discuss some issues of grammar or to let your students engage in a discussion of some issue that will go on longer than expected because you see them teaching each other what argumentation is all about. Such days are not wasted, so allow for them when designing your own syllabus.

PORTFOLIOS

We suggest you consider a modified portfolio approach in organizing your assignments and syllabus. Your students should keep everything they write—all prewriting, drafts, revisions, peer work, etc.—and collect it in a portfolio that will be available for your review either periodically during the course of the term or at the end of the term, when you make a final assessment. Most students are uncomfortable without some sense of their grade until the course is over, so in the modified portfolio approach, you assign a grade to a paper only after it has been developed through a process of drafting, peer work, revision, editing, and proofreading. Some instructors comment on drafts; others choose not to do so. If you do, focus on issues of substance and how well the student is expressing ideas and addressing the writing situation, rather than hunting for errors. Also remember to encourage the writer by pointing out strengths as well as weaknesses. Once you grade papers and return them to the class, let them know what you intend them to do with those papers. May they revise them once again for a re-grade? *Must* they revise them to earn the grade you tentatively assign? May they rework the papers and at the end of the course select a prescribed number on which you will base the final, overall portfolio grade? If you can delay grading even final versions of papers for a while, it will go a long way to establishing the kind of supportive writing environment students need to practice and grow. Some instructors believe it makes more sense to assess the complete body of a student's work at the end of the term, in order to give credit for where the student winds up—not where she begins. If you choose this approach, plan on reviewing the portfolio with the student a few times during the term so that she has some idea of where she stands before the final grade is due.

A 15-WEEK SYLLABUS

This course is based on readings and practices, three complete papers, plus a final culminating synthesis project in part 5. In order to relate the practices throughout the term to the synthesis project, we have assigned project 1, "How Should Photographs Be Read" as the fourth paper. If you want to leave open the option of the final project, point students to that work early on and have them make a choice by midterm, so that they can begin additional research, if necessary, or focus in that area whenever practices allow.

I Getting Started/Writing the Self

WEEK 1

- First day writing sample: Practice 1.2 ("Imagining Your Reader"). Give overview of the course and course policies. Homework (HW): Read chap. 1 ("Writing as a Human Act"). Bring newspaper article for Practice 1.1.

- Discuss writing portfolio. Test a few directions from Practice 1.2. In-class Practice 1.1 and/or 1.3. HW: Read chap. 2 through Practice 2.1 ("Experimenting in Writing"); introduction to part 2; introduction to chap. 3, "What's on Your Mind."

WEEK 2

- Introduce freewriting (focused and unfocused): in-class Practice 2.1 or 3.1. "Speaking Images": in-class Practice 3.3 ("Self-Expression through Art"). Read aloud and comment. HW: Read introduction to chap. 4 ("Representing the Self"), "Images"/Reading: "Three Writers Look at Pictures"; respond to questions. Bring in a photograph for Practice 4.1.

- Discuss "Three Writers Look at Pictures." Begin in-class Practice 4.1. HW: Finish Practice 4.1; read "Other Ways of Seeing/Reading"; respond to questions.

WEEK 3

- Discuss/read aloud Practice 4.1. Discuss "Other Ways of Seeing"; begin in-class Practice 4.4 ("A Self-Defining Experience or Two"). HW: Finish Practice 4.4; read De Salvo; read "Planning and Drafting" in chap. 2.

- Discuss De Salvo. Assign paper 1: "Aspects of My Self: A Collage." Begin prewriting. Discuss "Planning and Drafting." HW: Compose draft paper 1.

WEEK 4

- Peer review paper 1. Discuss "Revising and Editing" in chap. 2. HW: Continue revising/editing paper 1. Read introduction to part 3 ("Writing and Knowledge") and chap. 5 ("Telling What Happened or Happens—Narration").

- Discuss process of revising/editing paper 1—address concerns. Introduce "Writing and Knowledge." HW: Complete revision/editing of paper 1. Read "Perspectives on Story"; respond to questions.

II Writing and Knowledge

WEEK 5

- Paper 1 plus portfolio due. Discuss "Perspectives on Story." In-class Practice 5.1 (1 or 2). Read aloud and discuss. HW: Read introduction to chap. 6 ("Reading the Seen: Description") and "Describing a Place." Begin Practice 6.1A. Bring in celebrity photo.

WEEK 6

- Discuss description and assigned readings. In-class practice 6.1B. In-class "Reading the Image of Celebrity." In-class Practice 6.4. Read aloud and comment. HW: Revise Practice 6.4. Read introduction to chap. 7 ("Connecting Ideas and Things: Classification"); read "The Type and the Individual"; respond to questions.

- Discuss revised Practice 6.4. Introduce classification, discuss Cofer and questions. HW: Read introduction to chap. 8 ("Taking Things Apart: Analysis"); read "Testing a Generalization." Read "Developing a Generalization." Begin Practice 8.5. ("Analyzing Images of Women in Advertising").

WEEK 7

- Discuss assigned readings and questions. Assign paper 2 on analysis: Practice 8.5. HW: Draft paper 2.

- Peer review for revising and editing paper 2. HW: Revise/edit paper 2. Read introduction to part 4 and "Writing Directions for Unnaturally Difficult Acts"/Reading; respond to questions.

III   Writing and Power

WEEK 8

- Paper 2 plus portfolio due. Discuss direction, persuasion. Begin in-class Practice 9.2. Read aloud and comment. HW: Revise Practice 9.2. Read introduction to persuasion. Reading: "The Marlboro Man, 1954." Begin Practice 9.5 (identify possible product and obtain, if feasible.)

- Discuss persuasion. Compare Reading: "Fly-Tox Advertisement, 1926" and "The Marlboro Man, 1954." In-class Practice 9.5. Discuss. HW: Read introduction to chap. 10 ("Reasoning with Readers: Argumentation"). Read "What's the Argument"; respond to questions.

WEEK 9

- Introduce argumentation. Discuss "What's the Argument." In-class Practice 10.1A or B. HW: Read "Powerful Appeals," "Claims and Evidence" (introductions only). Read "Arguing about the Value of Inequality."

- Introduce final synthesis project part 5, chap. 11—Project 1: "How Should Photographs Be 'Read'" for paper 4. Discuss questions following "Arguing about the Value of Inequality." HW: Read introduction to part 5 and chap. 11. Read Jane Shattuc. Respond to questions.

WEEK 10

- Discuss Shattuc and questions. Assign paper 3: Project 1: "Getting It Together: Ways of Appealing" 1 (kinds of appeals in TV programs. HW: Decide on a program topic for paper 3. Begin prewriting.

- Discuss and approve paper 3 program topic. Begin in-class drafting. HW: Continue drafting paper 3.

WEEK 11

- Library orientation and exercise. HW: Complete draft of paper 3. Do Reading 1 for paper 4: Project 1: "How Should Photographs Be 'Read'."

- Peer review paper 3 for revising/editing. HW: Finish paper 3.

IV Writing with Personality, Knowledge, and Power: Synthesis

WEEK 12

- Paper 3 plus portfolio due. Introduce synthesis. Discuss Reading 1 for "How Should Photographs Be 'Read'." HW: Respond to questions. Reading 2: "Three Photographs in Context."

- Discuss "Three Photographs in Context." In-class respond to questions. HW: Begin Practice 11.1.

WEEK 13

- Class discussion on Practice 11.1. Small group work on planning and drafting synthesis papers. HW: Begin draft of synthesis paper 4: "Writing about Photographs."

- Continue work on project 1 synthesis paper.

WEEK 14

- Peer review of synthesis paper 4: "Writing about Photographs." HW: Begin revision and editing of paper 4.

- In-class revision and editing of paper 4. HW: Review and complete portfolio and paper 4.

WEEK 15

- Paper 4 and portfolio due.

The Practice of Writing

PART ONE

Practicing Writing

We do not believe that reading about writing does much to help students become better writers. That is why this book emphasizes practice. In this first chapter, then, we are not telling students how to write but explaining—very briefly—how writing works and why this book has the shape it has. Above all, this chapter is designed to help the student understand why certain kinds of assignments will be given later on, and how the forms of writing and the process of writing are related. Our experience in the classroom has shown that students work much better when they understand fully the purpose of the work they are doing. In a writing course, the student's effort to improve is the crucial ingredient. Without that, everything else will fail. It is important for you to understand this chapter as well. Knowing what is here, you can decide what to emphasize for your students. We have provided three practices early in this chapter to help students begin to think about how all writing is situated in the role of communication and in language and culture, and how it has identifiable conventions. Following the practices, we give brief explanations of how we have organized *The Practice of Writing* and the strategies we include under those rubrics.

1

Writing as a Human Act
Situations and Strategies

This chapter is intended to provide a sense of writing as communication. It's important to vary the activities you plan for each class, so you might want to assign readings for two parts for discussion in class, separated by a practice. One of our aims throughout this book is to give you the maximum amount of flexibility, so both the level and interests of your students and your purposes may be considered. Students should not have a difficult time relating to writing in terms of self, knowledge, and power. If you choose to discuss the early origins of the alphabet or the printed text, you might point to those historical developments as being similar to the change now underway from print to electronic media. In any event, you may want to emphasize what writing does (and can do) both in the world and to (create) the world, since many students come to college with an interest in power and a focus on their future work.

■ **PRACTICE 1.1 PURPOSEFUL PIECES (P. 5)**

Students should have no trouble finding suitable newspaper articles for this practice, both in tabloids and in newspapers of record. For examples on representing a self, they may want to look at Letters to the Editor, op-ed pieces, or advertising; for documenting knowledge, articles on developments in science or even the narrative of a crime may make good examples; and for influencing beliefs, editorials, op-ed pieces, and political speeches will work. The most interesting part of this practice may be discussing how writing can accomplish more than one task. An obituary, for example, documents biographical knowledge on one level, but can also be read as a commentary on self-representation.

■ PRACTICE 1.2   IMAGINING YOUR READER (P. 7)

This brief, writing-to-learn practice is a simple way to demonstrate three things about language and communication: an understanding of audience/reader, what the audience/reader needs to know, and how to convey that knowledge as clearly as possible. To write effective directions, students will have to imagine for whom they are writing; what she or he already knows and needs to learn; how to convey what the reader needs to know without unnecessary, confusing details; and how to be as clear as possible in doing so. It's our experience that students really enjoy the practical challenge of this task.

■ PRACTICE 1.3   RECOGNIZING CONVENTIONS (P. 8)

Here's a practice you could have students do on their own or in small groups. Get them started early in this kind of work to show them how much they already know.

Newspaper Articles

1. "Beyond the Bounce in Bond Yields"
2. "Community Members Honored"
3. "Mayor Pushes Voucher Plan"
4. "Sprewell Goes from a Misfit to a Nice Fit"
5. "Video Legacies Are Preserved"
6. "Orphans Who Weren't Recall Care That Wasn't"
7. "Trustees Pick Site for New Library"
8. "Objection to Nude Statue Prompts Bus Stop Change"
9. "Salvadoran Ruling Party Gains Early Edge"
10. "Deeper Look into the Tale of a Daughter and an Ax"

Scholarly Journals

1. "Federalism and Urban Revolt in France, 1793"
2. "Taking Economic Power Seriously in a Time of Sectoral Change"
3. "Epistemological Crises, Dramatic Narrative, and the Philosophy of Science"
4. "The Antecedents of Beethoven's *Liederkreis*"
5. Medusa's Head: Male Hysteria under Political Pressure"
6. "Shadow-Hunting: Romantic Irony, *Sartor Resartus*, and Victorian Romanticism"
7. "Changes in Prison Culture: Prison Gangs and the Case of the 'Pepsi Generation'"
8. "The Scientific Status of Causality"
9. "Coping with Post-Colonialism"
10. "Lechtin Release by Soybean Seeds"

With a few exceptions, careful attention to the length, topicality, diction, syntax, and typography (font size and style) will enable students to classify these titles appropriately. Titles 7–10 under *Scholarly Journals* and title 10 under *Newspaper Articles* may provide more of a challenge and could probably appear under either category. It might be helpful, even before you ask your students to write a set of rules, to make some observations as a class on the differences between these two kinds of titles. For instance, someone may note how the scholarly articles tend to use colons in their titles (3 of the 10 do so), while it's rare to see a newspaper headline with one. This is a good opportunity to point out the differences between the sciences and humanities, as well as how to distinguish academic from popular discourse. You might also want to explain the meaning of *syntax* (word order). But the best way to get started may simply be to ask the students which of the titles are most readily understandable, and why.

2

Writing as a Process
Experimenting, Planning and Drafting, Revising, Editing

While we don't believe one can learn how to write by only reading about writing, we do believe that a good understanding of how successful writers proceed is crucial, particularly to inexperienced writers. Much of the anxiety connected with writer's block or the frustration some students feel when they are not able to transcribe their thoughts directly onto paper results from misconceptions about the writing process.

This chapter has been designed to work well in conjunction with other chapters. Rather than working through chapter 2 from beginning to end, try referring back to it over the first few weeks as students approach their first paper. They will take up the brief explanations and practices with more interest when they can apply them directly to a writing assignment.

■ PRACTICE 2.1   EXPERIMENTING IN WRITING (P. 20)

This practice also works well when taken up with the practices on getting started in chapter 3, "Presenting the Self: Expression." Whether students practice on their own, in small groups, or as a class, with you acting as the recorder, emphasize the prolific generation of ideas and the excitement that can attend the earliest stages of writing. There's probably no better antidote to the anxiety of the blank white page than the fun of a fast-paced, uncensored brainstorming session. If your course is online and you can spend a session in a computer lab or a wired classroom, you can use the possibilities of CMC (computer mediated communication) to great effect at this stage of writing. For example, have your students go to a chat room (most Web-based online course software now include this facility) and then brainstorm ideas. Or you could direct your students on the Internet to certain OWLs (online writing labs) that provide interactive prewriting activities such as focused freewriting, listing, and clustering—for example, the CUNY WriteSite <http://writesite.cuny.edu/projects/stages/start.html>. By whatever means you enable experimenting in writing, your students will feed off of your and each other's positive energy at this stage, and that in itself can propel them into the challenge of composing their first draft.

■ PRACTICE 2.2 PLANNING AND DRAFTING (P. 26)

This is a practice you may want to go back to when your students are facing a draft of their first paper. Imagining the audience, defining the purpose, and constructing a working thesis or controlling idea are critical parts of the planning stage, and you should go over these practices in detail. Remind your students of what they learned in Practice 1.2 ("Imagining Your Reader") about the need to consider the audience for whom they write. Most students assume that they are writing solely for the instructor. We find it helpful to broaden that conception to each other and even the academic community at large, for two reasons. First, it will impress upon them the need for appropriate context and help them to avoid telegraphing their ideas if they don't think the reader is intimately familiar with the topic and even the sources of a subject as it has been developed in class. Second, it will reinforce the idea that there *is* an academic community and that the conversation of that community is in a discourse with its own conventions and expectations. So their purpose is not only to understand their writing in terms of self, knowledge, and power or a particular mode of rhetoric appropriate to one of those rubrics (self: expression, reflection; knowledge: narration, description, etc.), but also to understand how to present their intellectual work as a form of academic discourse.

You might have students put their attempts at drafting thesis statements on the board (or post them to an online discussion forum), then discuss them as a group to distinguish statements of fact, purpose, or questions from true thesis statements. Although at the early stages many of the thesis statements may be a little vague, you can point out the need to refine the statement for greater specificity as the student clarifies her own thinking during the drafting process itself. How many times have we seen an unrevised first attempt at a thesis statement wind up contradicting the student's conclusion in the draft? We don't want to get ahead of ourselves here, but it's useful right at the start to emphasize the tentative nature of an early thesis statement and the need to revisit it throughout the composing process.

You'll find that some students, like some writers, prefer writing from an outline, while others would rather proceed more intuitively. You'll have to judge what parts of the planning stage to require or emphasize. It may be a good idea to give everyone at least the experience of working on an outline, even if they don't all go ahead and write from one. Certain writing tasks, such as timed exam essays—almost demand outlines as a test-taking strategy, so you'll do your students a service if you help them improve this important skill.

■ PRACTICE 2.3   REVISING (P. 28)

Again, use this practice on its own or take this part of the writing process up when your students have completed the first draft of their paper. Depending on how extensive a draft your students have and your purpose in this chapter, you may want to use all or part of what follows to prompt your students in the revision process or to engage each other in that activity. If you choose the latter—the peer review process—a few words on candid but supportive feedback are probably in order. Early in the semester, students are shy about commenting on one another's writing. You can help the revision process along by reading an effective draft to the class and asking them what's good about it and what areas need clarification. If your students remain silent, ask your own questions to give them an idea of how to respond to one another. In your own written response to a draft, we suggest you point your comments toward further revision rather than dwelling on finding and correcting errors (more on editing below). The trick in teaching revision is to get them to realize that revision involves further discoveries with respect to any topic. (Make sure that students present all versions of their writing with each revision, so that you can see whether they've really revised and not simply edited.) Finally, as far as peer work is concerned, you should also emphasize to your students that, as writers, they must be the final *author*ity on their own work and thus evaluate and decide whether or not to follow the suggestions of a peer reviewer.

Here is a menu of some prompts you might want to include on a peer review sheet. Pick and choose from these or add your own to design a handout for in-class peer work. It is preceded by some useful instructions.

Read through the entire draft once quietly to yourself. Then reread the draft, looking at the particular issues below. Note your annotations in the margins of the draft, and make your comments on a separate sheet of paper clearly numbered as to your responses.

- What are the main ideas this paper tries to develop? What questions does it seek to answer? How satisfactory are those answers? In other words, give the writer some feedback about *your overall response* to the draft. What part of the paper do you find the most interesting? The least interesting? What surprises you? What would you like to know more about?

- A good introduction should capture your interest right from the start. After reading this introduction, are you interested in reading any further? If not, why not? Does the writer give you any idea of the ground she intends to cover, or map out how she plans on doing so? Do you have any suggestions on how to improve the introduction, perhaps with a more effective "hook"?

- Can you identify the thesis by underlining or circling it and writing "thesis" in the margin? Is the sentence you underlined merely an opinion ("I like this painting") or a simple statement of fact or of purpose? If so, how could it be transformed into something that admits debate and needs to be argued or supported by the writer? Is the thesis in the first paragraph or does it appear less effectively somewhere else in the body of the essay? If the thesis is too broad or vague, how could the writer narrow it or be more specific about it?

- The body of the paper should focus on developing the thesis and coherently presenting support for it. How well does the writer do this? Can you discern a pattern of organization or is the organization confusing?

  - Identify the writer's major points in the margins (pt. 1, pt. 2, etc.), and then list those points as an outline, using a phrase or one sentence at most to identify each one. How does the writer appear to have organized her draft? Is there a discernible line of argument or just a random collection of different points? Does each paragraph present you with a complete thought? Is the organization, or the way the discussion progresses from paragraph to paragraph, clear or confusing? Could it be improved?

  - Identify the support the writer uses to illustrate the thesis in the margins (sup. pt.1, sup. pt. 2, etc.). Is the support relevant? If not, why not? Which examples or illustrations need to be expanded and which should be taken out?

A. Identify the writer's conclusion in the margin. Does it reinforce the thesis? Does it provide a satisfying sense of closure as well as present the reader with a summary of what has been shown? If not, why not? Is the problem with the conclusion itself or with the body of the paper? Help the writer think about a revision of this essay. What points could or should be developed further? Are there new areas the writer could fruitfully explore within the overall approach he or she has taken?

B. Is the writing style of this draft appropriate to its purpose? Who is the implied audience? Does the writer assume the reader knows too much or too little? Is the writing too informal for a college essay? (In other words, does the tone of voice sound too casually conversational, or "spoken," rather than "written"?) Is the choice of words appropriate? Circle words you think the writer should reconsider and write "*wc*" (word choice) in the margin.

EDITING

All new teachers (and many not so new) struggle with how to deal with sentence level (sometimes referred to as surface level) difficulties in their students' writing. However you ultimately approach this feature of writing, we think it is important that you keep some principles in mind. Don't take the responsibility for correcting or line editing their writing away from your students. Quite the opposite, everything you do should help them take that responsibility on as their own. Most of us have felt somewhat overwhelmed when faced with a poorly written paper, and to seek out and correct every error is nonproductive. To return a paper to a student that has been completely redlined (at considerable time and effort to the instructor) is overwhelming and discouraging to the student, and it is a rare student indeed who will even read all those corrections carefully. It is far more effective to try to isolate in a hierarchy of significance the most important impediments to communication in your students' sentences early in the term. Then be sure your students understand that it's their responsibility to focus on those two or three problem areas and to make progress in resolving them during the rest of the term. If you use an assigned handbook, you may want to note an applicable code in the margins next to a problem sentence or to name or point to the particular issue of concern. Let your student correct her own grammar, whenever possible. If you decide to try to address some editing issues in peer review sessions, we suggest you avoid technical vocabulary whenever possible. Emphasize, once again, that students are not expected to edit each other's work but to point to areas that need attention. Here are some of the editing prompts you might want to include, preceded by some instructions:

> If necessary, help the writer edit the draft by pointing out (with the marginal annotations in italics below) some of these syntactical and grammatical issues:
>
> A. Are sentence boundaries observed, i.e., are sentences too long (*run-on*) or incomplete (*fragment*)? Are any words or punctuation missing?
>
> B. Does each subject and *verb agree*? Does the writer shift *verb tense*s without reason?
>
> C. Are *pronouns* consistent in person and number with their unambiguous antecedents (the words for which they stand)? Are the parts of each sentence clearly and closely connected or are some pronouns and modifiers *disconnected* from the words to which they refer?
>
> D. Are words used (*word choice*) or *spell*ed incorrectly?

PART TWO

Writing the Self

We believe a basic understanding of the idea of "self" in the West is important. Students are naturally interested in the self, and we try here to give it a conceptual and cultural context. Ask your students when they first became conscious of their selves. You might want to mention the last writing project in Chapter 11, which will afford them an opportunity to consider how we experience our selves in cyberspace. In any event, the material in this chapter is meant to enable a student to locate the written representation of a self (or persona) in relation to his or her self as author and an imagined reader/audience. Understanding the distances between the author, the written persona, and the audience helps students bridge or navigate those distances more effectively in the act of communication.

3

Presenting the Self
Expression

The materials in this chapter are designed to emphasize two aspects of writing: the satisfaction of self-expression and the ways that writers begin to write. There is a mechanical dimension to self-expression as well as a playful dimension. Writing in the expressive mode helps students learn how to get their minds in gear. Once they learn how to begin, they will experience the satisfaction of discovering that they have something to say that expresses their own thoughts and feelings.

WHAT'S ON YOUR MIND?

■ **READING**

Peter Elbow, from Writing with Power *(p. 38)*

■ **PRACTICE 3.1   OPEN-ENDED WRITING (P. 39)**

This practice works well in conjunction with Practice 2.1: "Experimenting in Writing." If your students have had no experience with freewriting (unfocused writing) or open-ended writing, you might consider incorporating this kind of practice into a number of your class sessions. Students should know how to use such focused and unfocused writing as a part of their composing process, to help them start on a topic, develop it, or unblock themselves at difficult points.

The purpose of this practice is to introduce open-ended writing as a means of expression. In writing about "anything at all," many students will be surprised at what they discover. If your students will be using this writing for further development in other chapters, you might ask them to do more open-ended writing as homework. This will give them more than one choice of focus or allow them to develop their original focus a bit more.

FREE ASSOCIATION

■ READING

W. H. Gass, from On Being Blue *(p. 39)*

Play with this text in class, seeing if, collectively, the group can "get" every item listed—that is, understand its reference, explaining what, for example, blue laws and blue movies are. You need not know all the answers yourself. This is your chance to admit that you don't know everything and for class members to show that they know something. (The German phrase is puzzling; literally "in the blue into," it means something like "at random.") In playing with these "blue" terms, try to bring out the different levels of blueness, literal and figurative, that they incorporate. (This will be a good place to discuss those basic rhetorical terms themselves.) This whole exercise is a game designed to heighten the student's awareness of language.

■ PRACTICE 3.2   ON BEING _____ (P. 40)

This is probably better done at home, individually, than in a group. The student may wish to look at a dictionary for inspiration and should feel free to ask other people to help with free association of things in the chosen color. Remind your students that they are not being asked to simply call things a certain color but to find things that are already so called in language (red-eye, yellowbelly, blackfeet). The idea is to take some time listing, exploring, and thinking.

SPEAKING IMAGES

■ READING   THREE IMAGES

Edvard Munch, The Cry *(p. 42)*
Vincent Van Gogh, A Pair of Shoes *(p. 43)*
Smiling Figure, *Mexico (p. 44)*

■ PRACTICE 3.3   SELF-EXPRESSION THROUGH ART (P. 45)

Point out that this section is titled "Speaking Images" and the students' job is to give one of these images a voice. You may want to use one image in class as a group exercise to illustrate various ways of using each picture as a vehicle for self-expression. You could, for instance, divide into four groups and ask each group to produce a collective reading of the first picture—one group using the pronoun *I*, another using *you*, another *he*, and the last *she*. If you have more groups, you can use alternatives to the present tense as well. Four pronouns and two tenses will give you eight combinations if you need them.

A major point to emphasize is that the picture should not be the limit or boundary of what is said; it is just the point of departure, a way of establishing a mood that can be expanded out of the writer's own repertory of thoughts and feelings. For example, with respect to the first picture, by Edvard Munch (pronounced "Moonk"), the writer need not try to capture what the artist's subject is actually experiencing, but only what the person *might* be experiencing that could account for such an expression. Even better, what does the picture lead students to think and feel themselves?

Unlike Munch's *The Cry* or *Smiling Figure*, Mexico, Van Gogh's *A Pair of Shoes* does not call for the student to assume the image as a mask but to associate it with life experience and feelings. Perhaps traversing the road of experience itself will be the starting point for some student, while a suggestion of homelessness or a circus clown or growing old will be the one for another. Whatever the starting point, the writer should try to express the image's voice.

The third image—*Smiling Figure*, Mexico—is a work of the Teotihuacán peoples from the ancient city of that name in the central highlands. But neither you nor your students should approach this image with the knowledge of art historians. Instead, let your class try exploring the blend of expressive personality behind the mask-like uniformity. The raised open hand suggests a gesture of greeting. The apparent contest of warmth and formality might inspire some students to think about times they have felt forced to smile under certain circumstances or the way our feelings are sometimes constrained by convention.

Everything is talking if we just listen. If these images could speak, what would they say? With an assignment like this, we teachers need to curb our tendency to suggest that there is a right answer. The point of the exercise is to get students' creative juices flowing.

TOOLS AND TOTEMS

■ READING

Julia Child, On the Wearever No-Stick Aluminum Pan (p. 45)
Red Grooms, On the Umbrella (p. 46)

J. C. Herz, "Flying Toasters That You Can Play With" (p. 46)
Federico Fellini, On the Telephone (p. 48)

This is a more complex and challenging exercise than the first three. You may wish to skip it, but if your students found the other exercises obvious, they may be stimulated by this one.

QUESTIONS

1. You might ask students to volunteer reading from each of these passages to help focus on how we "hear" and characterize voice in a written text. In her passage, Julia Child comes across very much as the TV personality with which most of us are familiar: warm and somewhat bubbly. Child's voice emerges through the many adjectives she uses to describe her frying pans: "treasured," "darling," "beautiful." "I love them all, even if I don't use every one" conveys the warm and gregarious personality Child projects on her cooking shows.

    In the next brief passage Grooms may be harder for students to characterize than is Child—so discussion or writing may turn on why that is. As an ode, or poem, in praise of its subject, Grooms puts all the emphasis on a careful, even cerebral, description of this most utilitarian object. Someone may note that there is only one complete sentence in this passage (the first sentence). We have almost no evocation of a particular person in relation to this object, and this is perhaps significant in itself. After all, what could be more appropriate in describing this most generic of objects than to efface the user? Anyway, see what your students make of this question.

    Your students should have much less trouble coming up with a profile of J. C. Herz than of Red Grooms. Herz, in describing the fascination so many of us have for various rather dull computer games as "mild mental sedatives," poses here as a typical, stressed-out office worker taking a break from the pressure of the day to relax into "a complete state of flow."

    Fellini in this passage is self-justifying, lively, emotional; words like *joy, terror, charm, dullest,* and *silliest* are crucial to him. It may be interesting to see what students make of his closing paradox: how a warm and socially busy man prefers "solitude filled with voices" to the unnecessary, physical presence of other people.

    As to which text is most revealing—let that question provoke discussion. It cannot be settled.

2. Child stands as an expert—a craftsperson (or should we say "artist"?) very much in love with the tools of her trade. Grooms seems to appreciate the umbrella for intellectual reasons: a simple, yet elegant design; an inexpensive price that makes it democratically

available to all; its utilitarian, no-nonsense functionality. Herz seems to like attaching rather sophisticated meaning to the rather unsophisticated games she describes. And Fellini also seems to enjoy proposing thoughtful insights for us to ponder about an everyday experience: "communication on the telephone is more tenuous but more authentic, less real but more precise, more temporary but more spontaneous, more delicate but at the same time more intense."

3. This question will allow your students to write themselves into the conversations Child, Grooms, Herz, and Fellini begin.

4. One of the generalizations your students may make is that each writer makes their stance unique in relation to his or her object. Each has the ability to take deeply personal insights and make them understandable and interesting to us all. By way of introducing the next practice, you may point out what Ralph Waldo Emerson says in his essay "Self-Reliance" (1847): "To believe your own thought, to believe that what is true for you in your private heart is true for all men,—that is genius."

■ PRACTICE 3.4   YOUR FEELINGS ABOUT SOMETHING (P. 50)

Ideas are a lot less common than objects. In assigning this exercise, you will want to talk about how ideas are generated. Encourage your students to think about the approaches of Child, Grooms, Herz, and Fellini. One can consider the history of an object; its use; and what it allows, promises, and threatens. Above all, your students should concentrate on what the object means to them: how it affects their lives, what they think about it. Effective papers will use the writer's own experience as the basis for more general ideas about the meaning and use of the object.

4

Representing the Self
Reflection

Teaching reflective writing has two main functions. At the level of thought, it helps students learn how to express their subjectivities in objective terms, and at the level of composition, it puts a special emphasis on revision. Looking in a mirror, each of us sees our own self as an object, out there, reflected. In writing, this objectifying is not done in space but in time. We reflect by looking back at an earlier self. Some discussion of reflection as a process will help your students understand why they are being asked to write in this mode.

Have your students try to discern a typical pattern of behavior of something that happened more than once, in different circumstances. Ask them whether they keep making the same mistakes or have the same kind of learning experiences over and over. If they do, ask them to reflect on why the pattern recurs in the way that it does. If time permits, it might be a good idea to separate your students into small groups in which all members can talk about some occasion when they did something that led to their learning from a mistake or from careless or thoughtless behavior.

IMAGES

■ **READING   THREE WRITERS LOOK AT PICTURES (P. 52)**

These short readings should be gone over carefully in class. The Barthes piece is more complex on the surface, but the direction of the thought is straightforward.

Paul Auster, from Portrait of an Invisible Man *(p. 52)*

QUESTIONS

1. Students may approach the "truth" of a photograph on many levels. On the one hand, these images, seen by the son for the first time, revealed a part of his father he had never known. On the other hand, the expensive leather-bound album entitled "This Is Our Life: The Austers" was blank inside. So is the truth the father's unknown, early life or the emptiness the son feels toward the life he had with his father? The question of mounting photographs in albums brings into play the selection and presentation process itself—an attempt to create a whole out of disparate parts. See what your students think.

2. The photographs seem to hold the father's death at bay—at least for a while. Auster seems to suggest that in memory, we can create "a universe that ha[s] nothing to do with death"; that the idea of immortality is a function of memory.

3. The photographs seem to document that while his father may have been invisible or "not there" for Auster, he was there for others, at least in the past.

4. By showing him events in his father's life—particularly his social life as a young bachelor—that he had never imagined, the photographs reveal his father in a new light. They help to make visible aspects of his father's personality that in actual life were "not there."

Sharon Olds, "I Go Back to May 1937" (p. 54)

QUESTIONS

1. Most obviously, there are two kinds of innocence: the innocence of youth—untouched sexually and by worldly experience—and the innocence that contrasts with guilt—in this case, the intent not to "hurt anybody." The writer, of course, suggests that these innocent "kids" will go on to hurt their own, as well as themselves.

2. There's some violent imagery here—"the/red tiles glinting like bent/plates of blood"; the gate, "its/sword-tips black"—in contrast with the softness of "May air" and "May sunlight." The banging together of these paper doll images "at the hips like chips of flint" is a perversion of childhood play and suggests the violence of the parents' eventual sexual congress—and certainly of the speaker's assessment of it.

3. The injection of the child-grown-up into the poem—especially in lines 13ff., with their litany of the unpleasantness that is to come (that has, in fact, taken place)—makes this a painful reflection,

especially with its contrast of the last moment of her parents' innocence and her assessment of what happened afterward, all of which she must accept as the price paid for her coming into being.

Roland Barthes, "Looking for My Mother" (p. 55)

QUESTIONS

1. Perhaps the finality of his mother's death motivates Barthes to seek the signs of her mature personality in the child's image.

2. It is a paradox because assertiveness and gentleness are usually considered opposing qualities. But she was persistent in her gentleness—strongly gentle.

3. A just image goes beyond the things represented to reveal the truth behind them: accuracy plus justice. Barthes is playing on the realistic novelist's search for the *mot juste*, the "exactly right word" (Flaubert). He wants more than exactness; he wants justice in his *justesse*. And he finds it in this one picture.

■ PRACTICE 4.1   REFLECTING ON A PHOTOGRAPH (P. 56)

In this practice, students are asked to write for a reader who will not have the photograph they are writing about. This is not an exercise in description; the photograph is meant to be a stimulus to reflection rather than an object to be described. Still, the students' reflections will be more productive if they have some idea how to "read" a picture, as indicated in the following reflective report by N. R. C. on her teaching of this practice:

> Students are curious about photos used by others. My students read their essays to the class and then showed the photograph to others. This was a much-enjoyed assignment. The problem for these student writers was organizing their essays. Some started with a reading of the picture (what was there for them) and continued with a reflection on the people in the picture and/or the situation surrounding the taking of the picture. The least successful papers (and there weren't many) came from those who had difficulty reading the photo; they overlooked such things as the stance of the subject, or the closeness or distance of one or more subjects from one another. In conferences on revision, I helped students with such reading, and though their revisions were successful in the sense of organization and expansion of description and reflection, I regretted having to manipulate, or influence, what they might see themselves. What I should have done in class was go over a photograph with them. They hadn't had enough experience in reading visual texts.

TELLING STORIES

■ READING

Peter Balakian, "Words for My Grandmother" (p. 57)

QUESTIONS

1. Near the end of paragraph 7 and in paragraph 8, the words "*hokee hankisd*," in both their sound and meaning, draw the writer down deeply into memories of his grandmother, revealing words she had said to him as a child and his understanding that she was still available to him even in death through a "*Hokee kaloust*: coming of the spirit."

2. After choosing to spend the weekend with his girlfriend in Cambridge rather than attend a family memorial for his grandmother, Balakian feels guilty and impelled to create his own memorial in words.

3. Balakian's poem not only brings to mind memories he didn't know he had but also suggests a deep Armenian heritage stored in "the historical unconscious," over which his grandmother was a protective spirit.

■ PRACTICE 4.2   YOUR TURN (P. 61)

Students should need little prompting for this practice. You might want to have them write a draft of their story, then read the stories to each other in small groups. With feedback from their listeners ("I would like to hear more about that"; "This part of your story was confusing—what did you mean when you said . . . ?"), the students could then practice revising their stories.

SCHOOL DAYS

■ READING

Russell Baker, from Growing Up *(p. 61)*

QUESTIONS

1. In paragraph 1, Baker reflects on the period of time he had been interested in being a writer—a period during which he had "been

bored with everything associated with English courses." In paragraph 2, he reflects on the very beginning of his third-year English class and his anticipation at that time of "another grim year," given Mr. Fleagle's reputation.

2. Baker shows us what he was like at age sixteen, keeping the reader over his shoulder as he narrates chronologically. By allowing the reader to experience his views and his surprise as he did, the reader participates in Baker's education—and his growing up.

3. The process of memory—the first step in reflective writing— is presented in paragraphs 7 and 8. The rewards of such writing appear in paragraph 8—"it was a moment I wanted to recapture and hold for myself. I wanted to relive the pleasure of an evening at New Street." The result of his writing—the effect of his words on others—is presented in paragraph 11, where he finds himself successful in making others see that moment in the past as he did.

■ **PRACTICE 4.3   REFLECTION ON YOUR SCHOOL DAYS (P. 64)**

Students usually have no difficulty recalling past events of their school days, so the first draft, expressing their thoughts about the event and the particulars of the experience, should pose few problems. Reflecting on the events may be more difficult, especially for the writer for whom the event is still charged with emotion (e.g., the paper on receiving a poor grade, with the reflection amounting to "Teachers should not be unfair graders"). Here, the instructor should help with comments and questions that will help the student objectify the experience. Because these papers are usually very interesting, you should plan to have students read them in class. And because of the students' interest in the topic, such papers are prime candidates for revision. Furthermore, you can count on a lively discussion of pedagogical practices and philosophies of education arising from the students' reactions to one another's experiences.

OTHER WAYS OF SEEING

■ **READING**

Brent Staples, "Just Walk On By: A Black Man Ponders His Power to Alter Public Space" (p. 65)

QUESTIONS

1. Here are the various shifts in time, paragraph by paragraph:

    1. what happened more than a decade ago
    2. shift to reflection on that event
    3. shift to past events
    4. shift to present situation
    5. shift to reflection
    6. shift to reflection on present
    7. shift to past events (boyhood)
    8. shift to reflection on events
    9. shift to past events and their effect
    10. shift to recent past events as reporter
    11. shift to recent past events as reporter continued
    12. shift to reflection
    13. shift to present events
    14. shift to present events

2. Podhoretz's terror and nervousness in reference to blacks in his 1963 essay on the black man's "firm place in New York mugging literature" and on black men's "paranoid touchiness" provides a point of view for Staples to work with (and in fact against). Staples shows in his essay that such "touchiness" does not result from paranoia but is induced by society's perception of black men—a position amply demonstrated by Podhoretz. Perhaps it is he who may be considered paranoid.

3. Staples's reflection on a black man's "power to alter public space" gets to the heart of racism and white fear of the big black man. Staples shows how one kind of paranoia can breed another. Though Staples's rage may be under control, it manifests itself in the form of irony, as in the opening of the essay: "My first victim was a woman." He himself has become victimized.

■ **PRACTICE 4.4   A SELF-DEFINING EXPERIENCE OR TWO (P. 69)**

You may want to tie this practice to the class work we suggested at the beginning of this chapter on perceiving patterns in personal behavior. In any event, the key to selecting an event about which to write is that it must have led to a real change in the way the student perceived him- or herself and the way he or she acted after that change in perception.

REFLECTION AS REVISION

■ READING

Joan Swift, "The Line Up" and Its Drafts (p. 70)

A word about how to read these early versions of the poem may be in order, since some students may be tempted to skip lines crossed-out in the draft. They should, of course, read everything, and give some thought both to why the poet makes the particular changes she makes and to how the poem as a whole evolves into its final version.

QUESTIONS

1. As she drops the particular details of crime and criminals, she changes her focus to accused and accuser. By generalizing to this level, Swift humanizes her concern.

2. Both changes suggest the possibilities of escape or redemption, which the poet then opposes with the inevitability of real world punishment or the confines of accountability.

3. Just as Swift allows significant time between drafts, she returns to her subject each time with a refreshed point of view and a willingness to rethink what she is trying to say. A willingness to unsettle what has been written and to take the poem in a new direction is evidenced in reading these multiple drafts. What other "rules" of revision will your students discover?

■ PRACTICE 4.5   REVISING YOUR OWN WRITING (P. 75)

The "rules" of revision from question 3 would be a good place to start this practice, particularly if some time has passed since the students wrote their draft. This practice also works well in conjunction with the section on revision in chapter 2.

Writing the Self: Two Projects

■ **READING**

Louise De Salvo, from "A Portrait of the Puttana *as a Middle-Aged Woolf Scholar"* (p. 76)

QUESTIONS

1. Although the writer notes specific times in the past ("It is 1957. I am fourteen years old"; "Autumn, 1963. I am a senior at Douglass College"), she writes both in the present tense and the present perfect tense—"I have studied"—to include time previous. Again, in paragraph 9, she contrasts the present of that time—"She is talking"—with time gone before—"I have never. . . ." Both shifts emphasize the importance of her experience. In paragraph 10, she switches to the simple present indicative mood ("I learn," "I observe") to summarize the effects of her experience. You could spend much time with your class looking at how De Salvo locates her reflection in time, paragraph by paragraph, or look closely at just a few to exemplify this aspect of reflective writing.

2. By using the present in the past, she gives a sense of immediacy to her experiences, as if she wants the reader to experience them with her. Her textual breaks between paragraphs 2 and 3, 6 and 7, 10 and 11, 12 and 13, 14 and 15, 18 and 19, and 20 and 21 indicate larger shifts in time, setting out particular moments from the past.

■ **PROJECT 1: GETTING IT TOGETHER**

Aspects of My Self: A Collage (p. 81)

In introducing this project, it might be helpful to show what a visual collage looks like and relate it to the juxtapositioning of events in De Salvo's narrative. Lists and patterns discovered in the earlier practices in this chapter may be a good starting point for this paper.

■ **PROJECT 2: TAKING IT FURTHER**

Look Who's Talking: Cyber-Chat Selves (p. 81)

Since many young college students today are familiar with online chats, you may have some cyberspace aficionados who will really appreciate this project. Since few faculty in higher education are into this mode of recreation/communication, you may find yourself (assuming you are one of those cyber Luddites) at a distinct disadvantage. Whatever research or personal experience your students bring to this project, their focus should be on the self. If you're more curious or adventurous, an hour or two in an online chat room will give you a taste of the malleability of the self in cyberspace, or Turkle's *Life on the Screen* can give you a scholarly introduction to this subject (see an excerpt of her work in chapter 11, project 3: "Virtual Relationships"). The point here is to take some identity role—a self that the student relates to (such as athlete or music lover)—and then see how the role or self changes in cyberspace.

PART THREE

Writing and Knowledge

We believe it is important to help students understand how knowledge is constructed in an ongoing process of interpretation, and the part writing plays in that process. To that end, we distinguish "empirical data—information gained through the sensory experience of things"—and knowledge itself, which is constructed by interpreting sensory experience and interpreting the interpretation. What the writing students do in class is part of the conversation that goes on in the community of higher education, made up as it is of many specialized conversations between and among scholars in different fields. That conversation in turn is part of the culture at large. If students see their reading, writing, and interpretation as the way to enter that conversation, then they will see that work is not only critical but central to the learning project.

5

Telling What Happened or Happens
Narration

We suggest you discuss the introduction one paragraph at a time, to make sure that the concepts of scale (or level of detail), emotional effect, and point of view are understood. Make the point that narrative is used by writers of fiction and by writers of history and journalism; it is not just a "creative" kind of writing but a basic part of every writer's activity. To prepare students for reading and discussing the five passages, remind them to try to keep the writer in mind. You might suggest that they pause after every sentence and ask, "Now why did the writer do it that way? Why use that level of detail or that point of view? What effect is the writer trying to have on the reader?" Here are our thoughts about the questions that follow each reading.

PERSPECTIVES ON STORY

■ **READINGS**

EXAMPLE 1 *Louise Erdrich, "Cousin Mary" (from* The Beet Queen*) (p. 89)*

QUESTIONS

1. This is first-person narration of simple—one might say, prosaic— events. The interest is in the narrator's opinion and interpretation of those events.

2. At the beginning of the first paragraph, one might simply feel sorry for Cousin Mary, who arrives with nothing. But the narrator's

comment, "I was too old to be carried," sets up a tension between the narrator and her cousin. And the "lies" complicate the tension. Sita's feeling of unfair treatment is further developed in the second paragraph. Note the concise descriptive language—"crammed"; "legs dangling out"—which works to engage the reader's sympathy (and amuse the reader as well).

EXAMPLE 2 Richard Wright, "Going Underground" (from "The Man Who Lived Underground") (p. 89)

QUESTIONS

1. This question calls for a basic response to the text as a whole followed by a closer consideration of Wright's method of narrative manipulation. Students may very well have complex reactions to this underground man. On the one hand, they may sympathize with a hunted fugitive; on the other hand, they may wonder why he is being pursued by the police and whether he is a dangerous criminal or victim of some kind. Guide the students to make careful observations and distinctions about their own emotional response as the narrative unfolds, and to attribute those feelings to the ways Wright involves the reader in the protagonist's plight.

2. In both pieces, we see from the protagonist's point of view, but Erdrich's narration is in the first person while Wright's narration is through an omniscient observer ("I've got to hide, he told himself"). In both cases, we have to surmise the background of the circumstances to which we see the protagonists react. Though they go about it quite differently, both writers immerse us in a tense experience as it unfolds. Wright uses stronger words to convey the man's plight ("terror," "Frenziedly," etc.) than does Erdrich because the stakes in the situation seem much higher and the character more desperate.

EXAMPLE 3 Clyde A. Milner II, "The Long Walk on the White Road" (p. 91)

QUESTIONS

1. Milner may have chosen 1868 as the most significant turning point in the history of Anglo-American–Diné (Navajo) relations—the year the U.S. government signed a peace treaty that allowed the Diné to leave Bosque Redondo and return to their native homeland. By recounting their forced relocation to Bosque Redondo and their desperate conditions there, Milner sets the stage for the "remarkable story" of the Diné's return home.

2. Although he writes "objectively" as a historical scholar, Milner does not hesitate to characterize events in powerful language. Thus, he recalls the infamous military campaign at Sand Creek in 1864 as a "slaughter" and General Carleton's instructions to Colonel Kit Carson to "invade first the lands of the Apaches and then those of the Navajos." With little prompting, your students should be able to find other emotionally laden language within this passage.

EXAMPLE 4 *Jamaica Kincaid, "The Tourist's Arrival"*
(from A Small Place*) (p. 93)*

QUESTIONS

1. You are arriving (with the writer) in Antigua as a white American or European tourist. Such a point of view allows Kincaid to focus on differences in culture seen through the eyes of a person intent on pleasure.

2. The double level of irony is present here, and thus the paragraph is shaped by how you the tourist are likely to respond, and the writer's knowledge of what the facts of Antiguan life are. For example, the dreadful Antiguan roads being read as "a marvelous change" from splendid American highways suggests that you the tourist do not want to admit poverty and corruption into your holiday plans.

EXAMPLE 5 *James Joyce, "The End of Molly's Soliloquy"*
(from Ulysses*) (p. 95)*

QUESTIONS

1. This question works well with small groups, where results can be recorded after the group agrees on what has been narrated. The difficulty of the passage should make this interesting. Suggest that each group begin by having one member read the passage aloud.

2. Reading aloud works best in groups, where a reader can be chosen after discussions of tone and the effect of transforming stream-of-consciousness into "grammatically correct sentences."

■ PRACTICE 5.1 PLAYING WITH PERSPECTIVE AND LEVEL OF DETAIL (P. 97)

1. This should be an interesting challenge and, since the Erdrich piece is not long, you could have your students try this in class.

2a. The requirement here is simply to tell what happened—to report the events as objectively as possible.

2b. One of the biggest differences should be the loss of tension in an after-the-events, just-the- facts report. The issue here too is the change in time from what was happening to what happened. Consideration of Wright's rhetorical devices and descriptive language, such as his use of active verbs, should be given attention.

3. You may find that students have an easier time creating chronologies or lists of events than they do organizing that material into a coherent, dispassionate narrative. Remind them that Milner did not begin chronologically at the beginning but used a turning point (see example 3, question 1, above) to order his account.

4. This rewrite can work in either a first person (like Erdrich's) or an omniscient third person (like Wright's) form of narration. Students should enjoy finding the language to intensify or jazz up the story.

5. This assignment requires students to translate an emotional narrative into an unemotional one. Although this assignment is "creative," it runs counter to most such assignments in that students are asked to create something closer to standard academic prose than to literature—the kind of academic prose we usually call "objective." The purpose of such assignments is to persuade students that all writing is creative, and that there is an art to concealing art.

PATTERNING EVENTS

■ READING

Naguib Mahfouz, "Half a Day" (p. 98)

QUESTIONS

1. In addition to "factory" and "fortress," "prison," "orphanage," even "life" itself might come to mind.

2. See what these hierarchies and patterns suggest to your students. One of us recalled the ordering of a high school marching band.

3. It might be interesting to pose this question after the students read the story through once, then have them reread the story looking for points that encompass in a moment or a gesture a lifetime of experience. On rereading, the first sentences of paragraph 8 ("I took a few steps, then stopped and looked but saw nothing"), paragraph 13 ("We submitted to the facts, and this submission brought a sort of contentment"), paragraph 14 ("As our path revealed itself to us, however, we did not find it as totally sweet and unclouded as we had presumed"), paragraph 15 ("In addition, the time for changing one's mind was over and gone and there was no question of ever returning

to the paradise of home"), and paragraph 16 ("The bell rang announcing the passing of the day and the end of work") suggest moments when the child's time passes into the adult's time. And, of course, in paragraph 19, we learn how the exterior landscape has changed to reflect the passage of time, and with that passage the boy has become an old man. Once the students realize that the young boy's first day of school is a metaphor for his life, the phrase "half a day" should make sense.

▪ PRACTICE 5.2 FINDING A PATTERN (P. 102)

The key to this practice may be for students *not* to jump to the first metaphor that comes to mind ("high school was like prison") but rather to think about (and list) some significant events in their education first. If they can find an apt metaphor from the pattern of events they discover, they will probably find it easier and more effective to fashion a narrative around those events. If they leap to the first (and easiest) metaphor that comes to mind, they may be tempted to force the eventual list of events into that figure or find themselves with only one or two events to narrate.

ORGANIZING A LIFETIME

▪ READING

A File on Stephen Crane (p. 102)

▪ PRACTICE 5.3 WRITING STEPHEN CRANE'S LIFE (P. 109)

The challenge to the student in this assignment lies in the comprehension of the material, the necessity to form some point of view, and the choice of specific material that best illustrates that point of view. Some approaches to the material might include

- a consideration of the interaction between Crane's desire for adventure and his literary production;

- the sort of education that prepared Crane for his career (his desire to learn by living life rather than by studying it);

- an analysis of the subject matter that interested Crane: common people, such as slum dwellers like Maggie; regular soldiers; war itself.

While there is plenty of material here from which to construct a narrative of Crane's life, you might consider assigning research into further biographical material or into Crane's fiction, poetry, or journalism. In chapter 8 of this text, you will find an article by Crane, "The Last of the Mohicans." R. W. Stallman's *Stephen Crane* (rev. ed., New York: George Braziller, 1973) is a biography that also contains checklists of "Writings by Stephen Crane," "Writings on Stephen Crane," and "Related Background Writings." Stallman's *Stephen Crane: A Critical Bibliography* (Ames: Iowa State University Press, 1972) has more information.

INTERVIEW TIME

■ READING

> *Jonathan Kozol, "An Interview with Gizelle Luke and Children of the South Bronx" (p. 110)*

■ PRACTICE 5.4   REPORTING FROM INTERVIEWS (P. 115)

You will probably want to go over the three suggestions for this practice in some detail and perhaps supplement them with your own experience or insights. Kozol's narrative treatment of his interview is an excellent example of providing a context for and dramatizing what is being reported. His listening skills and deft use of the children's comments to develop his subject are also worth emulating.

WHAT IS A "GOOD STORY"?

■ READING

> *Grace Paley, "A Conversation with My Father" (p. 116)*

QUESTIONS

1. The father and daughter seem to be arguing over both how to write a story and the nature of life.

2. Based on his tragic view of life, the father insists that a story should be told with a realistic attention to detail and a linear unfolding of

plot, like the great nineteenth-century short-story writers he admires—de Maupassant, Chekhov, and Turgenev.

3. By beginning the story with a description of the father's deathbed, Paley frames the work and style of creative fiction within the context of some possible (or impossible) ultimate meaning.

4. The daughter does not believe in imposing a predetermined tragic view of life on her characters but allows the characters to live on the page and seek out their own destiny.

■ PRACTICE 5.5   WAYS OF TELLING A "GOOD STORY" (P. 121)

1. The students may want to take the dialogue immediately after the first version and write those details into the story.

2. You could have students choose which ending to add or practice both alternative endings, paying careful attention to the choice of words each style and view of life calls for.

3. As suggested in the prompt, this practice requires imaginatively inhabiting what little is known of the son, then rewriting the story from what we imagine would be his point of view.

4. It might be a good idea to assign this practice after the students have had a chance to work through at least one of the first three prompts. Once each student has completed his or her analysis, you could have them work in small groups to come up with their criteria for "a good story."

6

Reading the Seen
Description

The point of teaching descriptive writing is to emphasize the importance of viewpoint. It is a point of view that literally enables one to see. Seeing is not just looking; it is the selection and organization of things in the visual field. In teaching this section, you should admit that one seldom writes a whole essay in the descriptive mode. Practice in description is designed to improve the writer's skill at selecting and organizing detail. Facing the difficulties of translation from the visual to verbal is excellent exercise in composition.

You might also point out to students how their need to produce written versions of visual material will actually affect what they see. In this form of writing, composition reaches out from the necessary order of the written word (grammar, syntax, diction) to help organize the perceived world.

DESCRIBING A PLACE

■ **READING**

> *Marilynne Robinson, "A Kitchen" (from* Housekeeping*) (p. 124)*
>
> *Alex Kotlowitz, "The Hearing Room" (from* There Are No Children Here*) (p. 124)*
>
> *Kate Simon, "A Street" (from* Bronx Primitive*) (p. 125)*
>
> *Edward O. Wilson, "The Storm" (from* "Storm over the Amazon"*) (p. 125)*

In discussing this group, use the questions posed in the introduction to the selections. The four pieces were chosen because they present differing attitudes toward the places described. Both the Robinson and the Simon pieces describe less-than-attractive locales, but there is more dismay in Robinson, while Simon finally recalls some redeeming aspect of her childhood scene: a tree which "showered . . . [her], and only [her], with a million white blossoms." Kotlowitz's description is as spare as the small interrogation room he describes. LaJoe, about to be interrogated by a team of lawyers?, seems vaguely bemused. Wilson, on the other hand, stands in wonder before the rain forest he is observing at night, illuminated by a powerful storm.

The main point of reading and discussing these passages is to see how each writer has organized the text, so as to prepare students to write their own descriptions. Discussion can, for example, answer the basic question Where do I start? Robinson starts by flooding her kitchen with light, then showing what the light exposes from the first person view of Ruthie, the narrator, who offers a bit of commentary. Robinson's description is visually oriented and slightly distanced; Kotlowitz has a visually empty scene to describe and uses the few details he mentions to set an emotional tone for the character about to be questioned. Simon runs her eye up and down the street of her childhood, starting from her own building, while Wilson must begin with the challenge of conveying a scene so dark it is impossible to see anything in it.

■ PRACTICE 6.1   MAKING AND CHANGING AN IMPRESSION (P. 126)

1. Note that this is a two-part assignment. Unless a student has a powerful visual memory, she should probably try writing her description at the scene itself. (It's up to you whether you want to allow students to work from photographs, but if you do, understand that the photograph itself has already predetermined a composition and point of view.) First students should jot down observations and explore the details of the scene; then they should try drafting a description.

2. The second part of this assignment asks the student to consider the impression his or her description makes, and then to revise the composition to create the opposite impression. A good discussion of the reading will make the results of this practice much better than they would be without it.

CHANGING PLACES

■ READING

Nikki Giovanni, from "400 Mulvaney Street" (p. 127)

■ **PRACTICE 6.2   A PLACE WITH A HISTORY (P. 132)**

These reading and practice assignments are closely related. You should probably assign the directions for the practice when you assign the reading, and then assign the practice for the next class. The directions for the practice suggest what to look for in Giovanni's text, which is meant to serve as a model for this assignment.

Giovanni provides a reflective description of the places and people of the neighborhood she grew up in, and contrasts this neighborhood in a part of Knoxville-now-gone with the neighborhood her grandmother moved to in Knoxville present—and a house lacking the family history that made the old house a special and loved place. The many student writers who have themselves experienced moving from one place to another or who have gone back to a place after a much-loved family member has died, as Giovanni does here, will have little difficulty with this assignment.

In discussing Giovanni's text, ask students to look at the specific descriptions Giovanni gives. What does she describe? Who does she describe? How does she describe? There's enough variety in the text to provide examples for various ways of describing.

INTERPRETING A SCENE

■ **READING**

A Reading of Hogarth's "Noon" (p. 133)

■ **PRACTICE 6.3   YOUR READING OF A HOGARTH STREET SCENE (P. 135)**

The real title of Hogarth's engraving is "The Enraged Musician." We decided to omit the title from the text so as not to force "one right reading" of the picture. There are other possibilities for organizing and discussing this visual text. One group of students came up with these suggestions in class discussion:

1. kinds of facial expressions represented
2. noise, sound, and music
3. a theme of poverty and people at once crowded but in isolation
4. social-class divisions
5. religious and other symbols
6. modes of amusement

This print . . . depicts the rage and frustration of an effete violinist, probably a foreigner and a court musician, at the occupational noises and common musical sounds of the London populace, their children, and their animals.

The musician stares out his window with his hands over his ears; his violin, music sheets, ink and quill surround him. A playbill outside his window announces "The Sixty Second Day . . . Comedians . . . the [Theat]re Royal . . . Beggars Opera . . . Macheath by Mr. Walker. Polly . . . by Miss Fenton. Peachum by Hippisley . . . Vivat Rex." A parrot squawks at the musician from a lamp post. Below, a ragged, pregnant woman with a crying child sings a vaguely autobiographical ballad, "The Ladies Fall." In front of her a little girl with a noisemaker drops her ball as her eyes bulge in interest at seeing a boy companion urinate down a coal hole. A writing slab is tied to the boy's belt. Both children have constructed a bird trap and have planted twigs beside it. Directly below the violinist a street musician plays an oboe.

In the center of the scene a comely milkmaid plies her trade. In front of her a little figure dressed as a soldier with a wooden sword bangs mechanically on a drum. Beside him a man sharpens a meat cleaver on a grindstone; a dog barks at him. In the background an Irish laborer (his turned-up beehive cap reveals his nationality) lays pavement, a dustman rings his bell and shouts out, a blacksmith blows a horn, and a fish seller cries out his call. Across from the musician, "John Long Pewterer" plies his noisy trade. On his roof, a sweep calls to someone, and two cats fight. A flag flies from the church to mark a holiday, suggesting more noise from the church bells.

—Sean Shesgreen, ed., *Engraving by Hogarth* (New York: Dover, 1973)

READING THE IMAGE OF CELEBRITY

■ READING

Graham McCann, from Marilyn Monroe *(p. 137)*

■ PRACTICE 6.4   READING A CELEBRITY'S IMAGE (P. 138)

Careful analysis and discussion of McCann's text will be helpful when students proceed to write their own. McCann starts with a "typical" photograph and analyzes it, asking questions about it. He then describes it and interprets Monroe's look. Note how aware he is of the dialogue between the object and the spectator, with emphasis on the desires of the viewer. This descriptive exercise can give students some experience in cultural criticism as they analyze and describe not simply the face of a celebrity but his or her packaging and its attendant effect.

An interesting variation on this practice would be to have students break up into small groups one day and decide on a single celebrity to describe, then in the next class listen to the different ways the same person can be described.

■ PRACTICE 6.5   READING THE IMAGE OF SOMEONE YOU KNOW WELL (P. 139)

If you assigned Practice 4.1, "Reflecting on a Photograph," ask your students to consider using the same photograph for this descriptive practice unless they have another more interesting one in mind. If you've carefully discussed McCann's treatment of the Monroe image, your students should feel much more secure in reading whatever photo they choose to describe.

7

Connecting Ideas and Things
Classification

This long introductory section should be assigned and studied, to ensure that your class understands the nature and function of classification. You might combine it with the short reading from Vance Packard, to make one day's assignment and discussion. One way to start a discussion would be to put on the blackboard a brief quotation from the introduction—"Those who write, rank"—and ask for comments or explication. This statement points to both the power and the nature of writing.

CATEGORIES

■ READING

Vance Packard, from A Nation of Strangers *(p. 142)*

QUESTIONS

1. The businessman sees his community as simply divided between "commuters" and "locals." Packard separates the community into "three major groups": the locals, the Darien people, and the transients.

2. The three species are each distinguished by the length of time they have lived in Darien.

3. Those who make their living in Darien provide services for the other two groups. (Though Packard does not specify this, it is likely that these two groups commute to New York City to make their living.)

4. To "dominate the town socially" implies that the Darien people
    have the largest incomes, and as a result, their needs determine the
    nature of the services provided by locals; it further implies that the
    wives of the Darien people would lead social and volunteer groups,
    thus determining who was socially acceptable and who was not.
    The businessman's statement suggests that the locals are seen only
    as those who serve the Darien people and not as social equals.
    The transferee's wife's statement reflects her ostracism by the social
    forces (e.g., country clubs, social and volunteer organizations)
    dominated by the Darien people.

5. We have suggested that the Darien people dominate because of
    their monetary power. We might want to know what percentage of
    them are commuters and what percentage are professionals (i.e.,
    doctors and lawyers) practicing in the Darien area. We might also
    ask if ethnic or racial background and religious persuasion are
    important. We might want to know how the town is divided
    geographically; that is, whether the Darien people live in specific
    neighborhoods from which they try to exclude people they
    consider undesirable.

■ **PRACTICE 7.1   SOCIAL CATEGORIES IN AN INSTITUTION (P. 143)**

This practice works well as an in-class exercise. Students can work on the
practice in small groups, and then the class can come together to compare
the proposed classification systems for consistency of dividing principle,
exclusiveness of the classes, and completeness of the system. Since students
tend to think in binary categories, problems of exclusiveness and completeness are bound to arise. You can encourage revisionary thinking by questioning the exclusiveness of proposed classes and by mentioning groups of
people who have been left out (members of the custodial staff, campus visitors, and children in the day-care center are often left out). And, of course,
introducing the needs of actual people such as incoming students can also
lead to revision of the classificatory system.

TYPES

■ **READING**

*Monica M. Moore, "Rejection Signaling" (from "Nonverbal Courtship
Patterns in Women") (p. 144)*

Your students may find it interesting (and enlightening) to discuss this reading, and perhaps can even add some behaviors they've observed that nonverbally signal rejection. You should emphasize the importance of careful, sometimes prolonged observation, followed by an attempt to classify what has been observed.

■ PRACTICE 7.2   SOCIAL TYPES IN A PARTICULAR PLACE (P. 145)

Observation is key to this assignment. It simply does not work as well if students rely solely on their memories or on their preconceptions. Of course, to prepare for the observation, students will have to use their memories and preconceptions to figure out the kinds of data that are likely to be important. But they must also prepare to be surprised—to see and record data whose importance they had not anticipated. Before sending the students forth to observe, you should discuss how observations are made and recorded. We also suggest that you require students to submit their recorded observations along with the paper they develop from them.

FROM ABSTRACT TO CONCRETE

■ READING

Bertrand Russell, from Power *(p. 146)*

This excerpt repays careful study. While students should definitely be asked to do the first question, we suggest that you choose either the second or the third question as a follow-up.

QUESTIONS

1. An upside-down tree diagram works much better here than an outline. In working out the diagram, students sometimes discover problems with Russell's system. For example, in the "manner of influence" branch of his system, education and party politics are cited as instances of "influence by reward and punishment." However, in the "type of organization" branch of the system, education and party politics appear as examples of organizations that work by influencing opinion rather than by reward and punishment. It is worth considering why education and party politics are problems for Russell's system. In our opinion, Russell is primarily working top-down; perhaps that is one reason why the problem with education and party politics occurs.

2. In classifying "the manner of influencing individuals," Russell implicitly uses a mind-body distinction—a distinction that makes "habit" a problem. If habit is understood as a predisposition, then it would seem to belong with opinion on the mental side of the mind-body distinction. However, since habitual action does not depend on a "mental intermediary," it seems to belong on the body side of the distinction along with other effects produced by "direct physical power over [an individual's] body." Yet Russell seems unwilling to put habit in that body category (Class A), perhaps because being drilled is not as physically coercive as being "imprisoned or killed." It's possible to protect the logic of Russell's system by putting habit either into the reward and punishment class (Class B) or into the other branch of his system—the "type of organization" branch. However, it is also possible to use Russell's remarks on habit to question and revise his system, including his initial definition of *power*. By using the word "intended," Russell's definition implies that individual subjects first exist and then, secondarily, either wield or yield to power. Foucault's take on power is quite different. In deciding whether to protect or to question Russell's logic, you should allow yourself to be influenced by your students' responses to this question.

3. Like question 2, this question invites students to think critically about Russell's definition and taxonomy of power. For example, one kind of power that seems to be missing from Russell's taxonomy is the kind of reciprocal influence that characterizes dialogue—and dialogical teaching. Another is resistance, a form of power that was not entirely absent during the period of Hitler's rise.

■ PRACTICE 7.3   POWER IN AN INSTITUTION YOU KNOW (P. 148)

Although students tend to be quite interested in—and sensitive about—power, you will need to take care to prevent them from using this practice merely to gripe about unfair treatment by X. In-depth discussion of the Russell excerpt helps; so too does in-class consideration of the classification systems that one or two students are planning to use.

■ PRACTICE 7.4   FORMS OF _____ (P. 149)

In preparation for this practice, you may want to take an abstraction and work it out in class, following Russell's lead. In form, the Russell excerpt moves from abstract to concrete. Since you and the class will be engaging in a thought experiment, your way of working will necessarily be less linear and more dialectical in form than Russell's presentation. Indeed, you should use this occasion not only to point out the difference between process and product but also to show students how to move back and forth between their general ideas and specific experiences when they are defining and classifying.

THE TYPE AND THE INDIVIDUAL

■ READING

Judith Ortiz Cofer, "The Story of My Body" (p. 150)

QUESTIONS

1. For each category, Cofer has an experience growing up that crystallizes a sharp difference between the way she feels or thinks about herself and the way she realizes others see her. Cofer's story is largely about her resistance to the many stereotypical ways others see her. Although at times the judgments others make based on these categories are implacable, Cofer seems to invite us to see the categories as more interpretable than final. See what your students think of the malleability of these categories.

2. Cofer suggests that her skin color, size, and appearance were variables because as she grew older, both the facts (her height and weight) and the interpretation (her own self-image and the ways others perceived her) varied in different contexts. As she matures, her body changes: it matters and it has meaning. The only constants she felt in her life were her "brains" and her "talent in writing." If anything about her body remains invariable, it might be that she never acquiesces to that material category as entirely defining her own self-image.

3. Growing up, Cofer seems mostly to try to avoid being a victim of stereotyping once she realizes how powerfully negative those categorical judgments can be. For instance, she writes that after her parents transferred her to St. Joseph's High School (par. 16), she "found several good friends there—other girls who took their studies seriously." But even avoidance cannot entirely eliminate the occasional pain she felt when others ridiculed her ethnicity (for instance, when Ted broke off a date because of his father's prejudice [par. 17]. In college, Cofer points out that her stereotypically exotic looks were suddenly in demand and led to an active social life. As an adult, however, she bases the criteria for her own self-worth on her

constants—"brains" and "talent in writing"—and the opinions of those who respect her as an "individual person."

4. Both Cofer and Staples, on one level, seem to accept both the injustice and the inevitability of stereotypes, but rather than acquiesce to those perceptions, they seek to either avoid or subvert them. See what your students think of the similarities and differences in the ways Cofer and Staples cope.

■ PRACTICE 7.5   RESISTING STEREOTYPES (P. 159)

Using Cofer and Staples (chapter 4, reading and Practice 4.4) and the introduction to this practice, spend some time working with your students to focus on a stereotype and the ways to write about it effectively (demonstration/showing, revealing, resisting, avoiding, etc.). Rather than simply condemning the act of stereotyping, it might be helpful to point out, as both Cofer and Staples do, that perceiving people and things categorically is very human. The danger, of course, is not guarding against the prejudgments that those categories can impose.

8

Taking Things Apart
Analysis

Analyze is such a critical word—not only in many writing and exam assign-ments but in the overall project of higher education—that it is worth spend-ing a few minutes explaining what we mean by analysis, what we do when we analyze, its strengths, and its limits. As the introduction indicates, this chapter stresses the analysis of texts—written and visual—and you should emphasize the importance of this skill in all the humanities and social sci-ences, as well as in life. You may want to use William Wordsworth's lines from his poem "The Tables Turned,"

> Our middling intellect
> Mis-shapes the beauteous forms of things:—
> We murder to dissect

to consider not only what is gained but what may be lost through analysis.

LIKENESS AND DIFFERENCE

■ READING

Stephen Crane, "The Last of the Mohicans" (p. 162)

■ PRACTICE 8.1   ANALYZING A COMPARISON (P. 164)

In the first two paragraphs, Crane sets up the sources to be contrasted: the oral history of the nonliterary inhabitants of Sullivan County, and the popu-lar literary version of their history written by James Fenimore Cooper—specifically, his novel *The Last of the Mohicans*. In paragraph 3, Crane cites that there is no comparison between Sullivan County's "hero" and Cooper's, and that pathos lies in the contrast between the two. In paragraphs 4 and 5, Cooper's literary last Mohican is presented. Paragraph 4 consists of a cumulative sentence extolling the qualities of Uncas (an acerbic paraphrase from Cooper), and these qualities are further reinforced by a direct quotation from Cooper's work. In paragraph 6, Crane drives home the contrast by using a reportorial tone in presenting the real last Mohican, and his tone and description serve to deflate the swollen literary hyperbole of paragraph 5.

MAKING COMPARISONS

■ READING

> *Pieter Brueghel*, The Fall of Icarus *(p. 167)*
> *W. H. Auden, "Musée des Beaux Arts" (p. 166)*
> *William Carlos Williams, "Landscape with the Fall of Icarus" (p. 166)*

■ PRACTICE 8.2   TWO POETS AND A PAINTING (P. 168)

This is a formal comparison and contrast assignment. The instructions are very specific and elaborate. We recommend that you go over them carefully with your class and discuss the poems with your students before they undertake to write.

You may find this report on a discussion of the poems helpful in preparing your own:

> By way of illustrating how to compare and contrast things which are at once different and resemble one another, we turned to the two poems on Brueghel's *The Fall of Icarus*. First I asked if anyone knew the story of Daedalus and Icarus, and we were able to piece the myth together from students' partial recollections. The two poems were read aloud. I asked the class which poem they preferred, and they agreed that they preferred the Williams poem because it is more "poetic." Auden's poem, they felt, developed an argument and imposed a judgment, while Williams left more to the reader.
>
> In one column of their paper, students were asked to write down similarities between the two poems, and in another column, to list the differences. They seemed genuinely interested in the task; the class enjoys working with literature, and they seem to expect a certain amount of reading and interpretation in an "English class."
>
> The first student to speak observed that "Landscape with the Fall of Icarus" could more easily be compared with the second stanza of "Musée des Beaux Arts" in that the first part of Auden's poem has little to do with either the legend or the painting. The class agreed and expanded on this observation. Auden

uses the picture only as an example to support his larger thesis that "the Old Masters" understood suffering and the human position; Brueghel is just one of a number of "Old Masters." Someone else said that Auden's language is much more "powerful," in the use of such words as *suffering, torturer,* and *failure.* Another student argued that Auden's powerful language runs counter to his purpose of contrasting Icarus's drowning with everyone else's "apathy," and that Williams is more "powerful" overall because he paints a pretty picture of the landscape and then uses the word *drowning* as the final word of the poem so that it comes as a shock.

Yet another student supported this claim. She said that while Auden assumes that the reader knows the legend, Williams tells the story. Further, Williams uses words with positive connotations, such as *spring, pageantry, awake,* and *tingling,* while Auden uses negative language. This, she said, contributes to the force of the final lines of Williams's narrative because the reader is not prepared for the drowning.

As the discussion continued, someone said that Williams doesn't really place a judgment on those "concerned with themselves," but Auden "thinks that there is something deeply wrong with the fact that while some people suffer others can just continue to live normal, undisturbed lives." Still another student disagreed. He argued that the two poets pass the same judgment, but Williams expects the reader to draw the conclusion that Auden states more explicitly.

I asked two questions: (1) To which form of discourse is each of the poems most similar? and (2) Given our discussion, what are possible theses for a paper comparing the two poems? To the first question, students replied that Auden's poem is "argumentation" and Williams's poem is "description" and "narration." Finally, someone suggested that a thesis that would cover all our observations is: "Although Williams and Auden appear to treat a single subject, they do so very differently." We clarified this thesis somewhat.

This was a most successful meeting. The class enjoys working with poetry, and the discussion served as a good introduction to "synthesis" inasmuch as the exercise provides an opportunity to "compare and contrast" two things that resemble one another but turn out to be significantly different. I found this exercise a natural way to introduce the idea of formulating a thesis.

COMPARATIVE THINKING

▪ READING

Mark Edmundson, "My First Intellectual: An Ex-Jock Remembers the Teacher Who Changed His Life" (p. 170)

QUESTIONS

1. Edmundson uses Meyers to exemplify an alternative to the "us vs. them" approach to education and, more broadly, to life itself.

O'Mara represents traditional authority and structure and is associated with Nixon, General Westmoreland, and McNamara in their prosecution of the Vietnam War—a raging issue at the time. The students, too, thought in similar oppositions (and were, interestingly, mostly in favor of the war) and were therefore defiantly resisting all attempts to learn. Meyers suggested the possibility of another path to Edmundson, one that is necessary whenever practices become institutionalized and therefore stifling—the path of resistance and subversion: "'Whatever it is,' chants Groucho from the wings, 'I'm against it'" (par. 40).

2. Here's a partial list of some of the points of comparison and contrast your students may find:

    1. "powers of comprehension" on Medford as a school (par. 6–7)
    2. schools and factories (par. 9)
    3. Susan and Joseph (pars. 11–13)
    4. Meyer's *modus operandi* vs. other teachers (par. 15)
    5. the "Elect" and "the terminally Lost" (par. 19)
    6. "prisons, hospitals, and schools" (par. 21)
    7. holding class indoors and outdoors (pars. 26–27)
    8. Dan O'Mara and Doug Meyers (par. 29)
    9. us vs. them (par. 29)
    10. vision of a renovated Medford H.S. and the actual Medford H.S. (par. 31)

3. Edmundson suggests that teaching on some level is about breaking down habitual ways of thinking. "[Meyers] got what he wanted out of Medford High, which was a chance to affront his spiritual enemies, though with some generosity, and to make younger people care about the sorts of things he cared about, to pull them out of their parents' orbit and into his. All good teaching entails some kidnaping; there's a touch of malice involved" (par. 35). See if your students agree with this subversive, Socratic model.

■ **PRACTICE 8.3   SCHOOLING—TAKE TWO (P. 182)**

It's probably worth spending some time brainstorming the different aspects (or categories) that go into good teaching ("content, style, motive, practice, location, timing, and effect") with the class as a whole or encourage students to do this in small groups. Though your students' profiles are unlikely to be as long as Edmundson's, they will need to probe beneath a surface response ("My Favorite Teacher") and try to connect their teacher's characteristics to what they learned about their own potential.

TESTING A GENERALIZATION

■ READING

Robert Scholes, "On Video Texts" (from Protocols of Reading*) (p. 182)*

QUESTIONS

1. One of the pleasures of watching the beer commercial is successfully "getting it"—that is, understanding it, or, as Scholes would say, constructing the myth of America from the video text and the shared cultural assumptions on which it is based: "Our pleasure in the narrative is to some extent a constructive pleasure" (par. 4). Scholes traces and decodes the different elements that go into this myth, including the beliefs in meritocracy, social justice, and racial harmony, and, ultimately, the belief (and the pleasurable reassurance) that the system works—that America works.

2. Your students should have no trouble "reading" or "decoding" any number of different commercials. If you plan on making Practice 8.4 a key assignment in this chapter on analysis, we suggest that you tape a few interesting commercials on a VCR. You can then play them in class and encourage your students to analyze them in small groups in writing-to-learn exercises, beginning with annotated story boards that probe the video text as deeply as Scholes does.

3. We've already mentioned a few "beloved icons" above in response to question 1: meritocracy, social justice, and racial harmony, to which we could add individualism and the great American success story. Scholes suggests that we critically examine them as a way to take them "seriously," and not simply consume them as part of the daily wash of media images produced in campaigns of "massive manipulation and disinformation" (par. 8).

4. You might try teasing this meaning out with your students in your own "dialectical search for truth." As we suggest in the introduction to this chapter, in "a dialectical analysis, you examine the parts of something specific like an advertisement . . . in order to figure out the extent to which it can be understood in terms of something bigger." (8-2).

■ PRACTICE 8.4   ANALYZING A VIDEO TEXT (P. 187)

If you take our suggestion for in-class writing in response to question 2 (above), your students should have a clear idea of how to get started with this assignment. Be sure that they thoroughly "read" the commercial before they begin to interpret it. Since most TV commercials are quite brief, they need to consider every image and character, dialogue, music, and narrative voice-overs. Their interpretations should strive to make conscious (i.e., explicit) as many of the underlying cultural assumptions as possible, even though advertisers and the creative people who produce commercials for them often try to submerge (or make implicit or unconscious) those deeper meanings.

DEVELOPING A GENERALIZATION

■ READING

Douglas Kellner, "Advertising Images" (from Media Culture*) (p. 188)*

Note: In today's world, publishers have difficulty obtaining permission to reproduce advertisements for tobacco products; thus, we have not printed the illustrations that accompanied Kellner's text. Ask your students to bring in recent Marlboro and Virginia Slims ads to see how well they fit Kellner's discussion of ads from the 1980s.

QUESTIONS

1. In the first paragraph, Kellner claims that ads, both in their form and content, work like myths in contemporary culture to "resolve social contradictions, provide models of identity, and celebrate the existing social order." In other words, commercial ads are intended to and in fact do influence people's behavior by suggesting ways of looking and living.

2. Cigarette ads are designed by corporations to "associate their product with positive and desirable images and gender models" in order to induce consumers to purchase cigarettes.

    Marlboro ads/iconic cowboy image = textual system

    "nature, the cowboy, horses, and the cigarette" = masculinity, power images and text change in response to prevailing attitudes:

    1980s emphasis on nature to counteract negative ideas about smoking.

    Virginia Slims ads = "socially desirable traits" that appeal to women

    historical vignette/contrasting image of a "modern" woman

    modernity = "social progress" and "slimness" = "ideal type of femininity"

    advertising rhetoric → marked increase in cancers and eating disorders.

    1980s Virginia Slims ads were "highly antipatriarchal," responding to changing social attitudes

In general, cigarette ads are "symbolic constructs" created to "cover over and camouflage contradictions" between the message and the facts. It is important for consumers to be critically literate and to learn how to read such advertisements so they can both understand how they are manipulated by the media and resist such control.

3. With a good outline, your students should be able to compose a one-paragraph summary without too much difficulty. You may want to go over these carefully, not only to make sure that your students fully understand Kellner's argument but to emphasize the importance of summaries to analysis and argument.

4. As indicated at the end of the outline above (question 2), critical literacy enables consumers to accurately read and resist advertising when necessary.

5. With the detailed analysis Kellner provides and the continuity in both Marlboro and Virginia Slims campaigns, it should not be hard for your students to decode these corporate messages. It may be interesting for them to read recent ads in light of prevailing attitudes, and compare those changes over the last decade.

■ **PRACTICE 8.5   ANALYZING IMAGES OF WOMEN IN ADVERTISING (P. 194)**

We have tried to choose ads that are representative of their period. You will see that some things change, but some things remain the same in the eighty-seven-year span of American advertising presented here. Here are some notes on each ad.

1913 Shredded Wheat (p. 195)

Reflected in this ad is the influence of the women's suffrage movement, which was very active in 1913. However, not many states had approved women's right to vote, and until the Nineteenth Amendment was ratified in 1920, women suffragists engaged in a hard-fought struggle. The ad stresses that it is desirable to be emancipated. Emancipation means that a woman can vote, and moreover, in serving Shredded Wheat to her family for breakfast, she is freed from "kitchen worry and household care." She need have no guilt about serving prepared food because "Every biscuit is a vote for health, happiness and domestic freedom—a vote for pure food, for clean living and clean thinking." These are all states to be devoutly desired—unless one asks how much "domestic freedom" a little biscuit can hold.

1922 Resinol Soap (p. 196)

To be a bride is a state desired by all women, and one they fantasize about, as the picture makes clear. But the ad implies that while "beauty of feature, becoming dress, graceful bearing, and keen wit" are desirable attributes for those who hope to become brides, they are not enough. The foremost attribute is "a clear pleasing complexion." It should be noted that "right living" is also necessary for achieving this transformation (see Shredded Wheat).

1934 Lux Soap (p. 197)

In the 1930s, Hollywood stars possessed all that was enviable, and their perfect features frequently shone out of ads during the 1930s and into the 1940s. Remind students that this was the big era of fan clubs and the glory days of the star system at all Hollywood studios. Lux ads always featured stars, and here, Irene Dunne's tea-rose complexion has given her the power to "break hearts." If you use it, you too can win "admiration . . . romance" and "have the Charm men can't resist." The sense of active competition implied in the Resinol ad is more overt here. To have only an "average" complexion makes you a loser.

1942 General Electric (p. 198)

This ad appeared in the second year of U.S. involvement in World War II, when the government realized that the war was going to last for a while. Many ads in the 1940s featured women at work, temporarily filling "a man's job" but managing to stay lovely and desirable by using the right hand cream, shampoo, etc. This ad is representative of those praising mothers who stayed at home and took care of their children as they waited loyally for their men to return. GE is telling them they do an important job and that they shouldn't feel guilty about it. Such women are entrusted with the responsibility of keeping "dreams alive": a noble, genteel, and truly feminine thing to do. The drawing presents the purity of motherhood unsullied by any taint of the workplace. The message to married servicemen overseas was that a faithful wife was waiting in a snug little cottage for her man to return. Her dreams, of course, will be cheerful ones because GE promises things her little brain can't even imagine (What woman in 1942 could ever have imagined a four-cycle washing machine?). There is a patronizing tone to this ad, although most people would not have read it as such in 1942. Indeed, its message was one most Americans deeply believed in.

1954 Listerine (p. 199)

As we all know, bad breath is intolerable, and people with this noxious condition are socially doomed. In the 1950s, a girl had to be sweet (and not just in her mouth) to win the boys. Note the first paragraph of the text: Life for a girl is a win-or-lose situation. If you're sweet and adorable, you'll get "good times, good friends . . . gaiety . . . laughter and love and marriage." If you have bad breath, you will not be "sweet and adorable" and you'll get boredom and loneliness. Obviously, the girl in the picture uses mouthwash regularly. The big toothy smile and the gaiety symbolized by the record player confirm her sweetness. She's also fashionably dressed—she's a winner.

1966 Cosmopolitan (p. 200)

The Cosmo girl invites a comparison with the 1930s and 1940s ads. How far has she come from those days? She doesn't say that *she* is brainy but that some of "the best-looking girls" she knows are—because "they work at it." We can only assume that she wishes to be included in the "brightest" category, but the pose she strikes raises some questions. We are sure that she's worked hard at being good-looking, and the expanse of thigh, the peekaboo dress, and the little pout assert her sexuality. This ad is representative of the 1960s, when the so-called sexual revolution (which made it okay for women to say they enjoyed sex) was just beginning. At the same time, the feminist movement was beginning to assert the equality of women's brains as well. In this ad, Cosmo tries to play it both ways, but the use of "girl" instead of "woman" suggests that woman (girl) as sex object still predominates. So in the end, it's most desirable to be good-looking—the brains are a little bonus.

1977 Redbook (p. 201)

In the 1970s, women were becoming liberated and entering the job market in record numbers (many, of course, out of economic necessity rather than liberation). The ads of the 1970s frequently stressed the ability of a woman to do a man's job (somewhat like the 1940s, but in the 1970s, the job was a permanent rather than a temporary one). The picture suggests a woman in a man's world, of which she is in control. Note the business suit, the attaché case, the helicopter (there seem to have been no other passengers). She has landed on top of New York—even the phallic spire of the Empire State Building is below her. Yet the text of the ad, while asserting her power quite stridently, is also stressing femininity (it's okay if you want to stay home) and the fact that women now have choices. *Redbook*, of course, wants to appeal to both young career women and young housewives. To be over thirty-five is *not* a desirable thing.

1987 Charlie (p. 202)

To be "Charlie" is to be sexy and successful. We are meant to read the long hair and long legs of this Charlie girl as being sexy, and sexy is the love pat she's giving her companion's business-suited rump. She, too, is dressed for business, and the attaché case she carries reinforces that image. The drama of the scarf across her body catches your eye, and it pulls your gaze diagonally across her body. Her jacket has a stylish, businesslike cut, but its black-and-white checked pattern contrasts with the man's subdued business suit. The fact that she dresses distinctively (no soft little pin-striped suit from Brooks Brothers for her) is a sign of her success in the business world. The fact that she is as tall as—or even a shade taller than—the man also asserts her power. The name "Charlie" is short for either Charlotte or Charles, more commonly the latter. It would seem, then, that to be "very Charlie" is to be one of the boys, rather than your own woman.

1993 Bisou Bisou (p. 203)

This ad for Bisou Bisou (which means "Kiss Kiss" in familiar French) Nouvelle Couture is one of a series featuring women in various roles. The message here seems to be that maternity is both erotic and fashionable. This couture is a far cry from the wholesome cottony flaps-and-buttons stuff designed for nursing mothers. As a picture of pure pleasure, the photograph is evocative enough, but the words "A kiss is *not* just a kiss" further complicate the erotic message, since they refer to the song "As Time Goes By" (in which a kiss is just a kiss). The song was featured in that highly romantic movie *Casablanca* and is about lovers' clichés (and their durability). However, the ad, while intertextually co-opting romance, rejects the song's world-weary tone and asks you to rethink not just the meaning of a kiss but the kinds of lovers who kiss. Further, this kiss is not just a kiss because the lover/baby is being nurtured by the kiss. (Dare we say that the lover here feeds off the beloved? Or is it nicer to say that some lovers *can* live on love?) Where the usual representations of mother and child call up icons of the (original) Madonna, this ad tells you that motherhood can be sexy when you wear Bisou Bisou. (We should also note that the *New York Times* Style section has shown a similar ad under the heading "Fashion: Babies as Accessories." In 1993, according to the *Times*, infants are appearing not only in fashion ads and layouts but also on runways.)

1999 Calvin Klein Jeans Billboard (Kate Moss) (p. 204)

The parted lips, the open blouse, knees bent, legs spread, her upper body partially raised on her elbows, jammed into a narrow horizontal space: here is a young woman in an uncomfortable and vulnerable position. Her look is sidelong, not a come-on look but rather a what-are-you-going-to-do-to-me look. This is a different take on the most common jeans ads, which frequently present a rear shot of a jeans-clad woman, hands on hips, and butt in the in-your-face position. Sometimes she's perched on a stool, legs apart, for a crotch shot. She stares right at you, and appears charged with sexual energy. Jeans *are* sexy (on the right sort of young bodies), but they also bring with them the healthy, fresh-air heritage of the American West with its cowboys and its big skies. Not these Calvin Klein jeans. Though their styling quotes from their denim ancestry, these jeans are made of a shiny, fragile fabric, and they've been mated with shiny spike-heeled shoes, totally unsuitable for ranch life. What we have here is a late manifestation of Calvin Klein's series of Gen-X, heroin-chic ads featuring pale waifs (Kate Moss et al.) sometimes with a bunch of skinny sullen males, all of them gazing resentfully at the camera, as if summoned for a police lineup. This ad presents an inversion of the American West approach, in which the woman appears as victim, confined in a dark place. This is the transformation promised to the wearer of these Calvin Klein jeans.

Writing and Knowledge: Two Projects

■ **READING**

Toni Cade Bambara, "The Education of a Storyteller" (from Deep Sightings and Rescue Missions*) (p. 205)*

QUESTIONS

1. Miss Dorothy implies here that knowledge is communal as well as cultural—that it's neither possible nor desirable to know something exclusively, unconnected to the world in which all knowledge is constructed.

2. The different modes of writing are hardly ever used exclusively, but the following appear to predominate in the paragraphs indicated: pars. 1–6, reflection; pars. 7–20, reflection/narration; par. 20, analysis; pars. 21–24 narration; par. 25, description/analysis/reflection; pars. 26–32, reflection; pars. 33–36, classification; pars. 37–40, narration; par. 42, analysis; pars. 43–51, narration; par. 52, reflection. As an account of growing up, reflection/narration/description are central to the storytelling, but the story is itself a way of analyzing the role of knowledge and education in the African American community that fashioned the storyteller.

3. Bambara includes many different kinds of education: family, community, school, and street. Some of these—like art, literature, and politics—cross over from one site to another. Since Grandma Dorothy is the central elder in Bambara's story, we may assume that she privileges her knowledge and insight above the others.

■ **PROJECT 1: GETTING IT TOGETHER**

Ways of Learning (p. 211)

Hopefully, your students' reflection on the writing practices for part 3, "Writing and Knowledge," will suggest different ways they came to know different things. If not, some prewriting on a few key learning experiences in the home, school, place of worship, or the street may bring some differences to mind. Once they have a focus on the differences and similarities about which they want to write, remind them of the variety of techniques (reflection, narration, description, classification, and analysis) that Bambara uses in her story. If they are doing a straightforward comparison and contrast, you may also want to review the different ways they can organize that kind of essay.

■ PROJECT 2: TAKING IT FURTHER

Reading On- and Off-Line: Text and Hypertext (p. 211)

You may want to put the Landow, Birkert, and Lanham books (or excerpts) on reserve in your school library to facilitate your students' research. If you assign this project to the entire class and you have access to a computer lab, you may also want to have them read the online introductions and Lindenberger's *Dogstory* in lab sessions. They could then compare notes via chats or discussion forums on the different experiences of text and electronic media. It's probably a good idea to speak to your class beforehand on the importance of self-observation as they experience each of these media and ways of reading. Along these lines, a reading journal of their observations and experiences will help them track and reconstruct their impressions when it's time to draft their analyses.

PART FOUR

Writing and Power

Using the marriage script as an example, it may be worth reminding students of how much our system of law is based on language, and the power it can confer or enact. Beyond the legal system, per se, much of our political life is dominated by persuasive rhetoric in the form of speeches. And, of course, candidates for political office are now also marketed as commodities through advertising.

A discussion of Frederick Douglass and his 1845 *Narrative* can serve to exemplify the power of literacy. Its importance can be seen both in how far slave owners went to prevent their slaves from learning to read and write and the extent to which Douglass went in order to do so. Language was a key for Douglass to break the bonds of enslavement in his mind. Eventually, his oratorical and literary skills would make him the most influential nineteenth-century African American advocate for civil rights.

Guiding and Moving Readers
Direction and Persuasion

The distinction between "*show*[ing] the reader how to do something" through direction and "*convinc*[ing] an audience" of something through persuasion is an important one, and you should emphasize how these two are similar and how they differ.

WRITING DIRECTIONS

The main thing that must be emphasized here is the need for the writer to *imagine the reader*. You will want to repeat this emphasis with every practice. Directive discourse depends on the writer seeing things from the reader's point of view. Discussion of the pie/pastry recipe will make it clear to those who bake how inadequate the directions are for those who have never baked.

■ READING

Craig Claiborne, "Basic Pie Pastry" (from The New York Times Cookbook) *(p. 218)*

Marion Cunningham, from "Basic Master Recipe: American Apple Pie" (from The Fannie Farmer Baking Book) *(p. 220)*

QUESTIONS

1. Claiborne does not give the reader as much basic information as Cunningham, and his instructions are therefore more difficult to follow without extra knowledge.

2. Cunningham makes clear that her directions are suitable for beginners. Although Claiborne's recipe doesn't say so, it appears that he assumes his readers have some experience.

■ PRACTICE 9.1   HOW TO MAKE OR DO SOMETHING (P. 221)

Students generally have few problems coming up with a topic. Even those who feel they don't know how to do anything "special" can produce successful papers on "How to Parallel-Park a Car" or "How to Catch a Ball."

In testing one another's directions, students should look for undefined terminology and proper sequence. Directive writing tests syntactical skills, and unclear or confusing sentences should be pointed out. Certain types of directions can be tested in class as well, with one student trying to follow another's directions.

WRITING DIRECTIONS FOR UNNATURALLY DIFFICULT EVERYDAY ACTS

■ READING

Tibor Kalman and Lulu Kalman, "Problem: How to Open a CD Box" (p. 222)

QUESTIONS

1. Although the Kalmans write tongue in cheek, their directions are clear and accurate.

2. They identify with their audience and assume that anyone who has ever tried to break into a CD jewel case has been as frustrated as they have been. Their forewarned-is-forearmed approach may be taken as a form of encouragement. Besides providing some help in accomplishing this arduous task, we may assume that the Kalmans also intended to point out how absurdly, and therefore poorly, packaged CDs are.

3. We may infer that the Kalmans believe that CD manufacturers are cavalierly indifferent to the plight of their customers, or else they would have invented a more user-friendly package by now.

■ PRACTICE 9.2   HELPING OTHERS COPE (P. 223)

The key to this practice is choosing a simple, common task that is irksomely difficult. If the audience is very familiar with the activity and shares the writer's annoyance at the challenge, then a camaraderie may be assumed at the outset. This does not relieve the writer of the need to create complete and accurate directions, but it does give her the latitude to emphasize the humorous or absurd side of the experience.

GUIDING CONDUCT

■ **READING   DIRECTION THROUGH THE AGES**

Andreas Capellanus, from The Art of Courtly Love *(1174–86) (p. 224)*

Dr. John Gregory, from A Father's Legacy to His Daughters *(1774) (p. 225)*

Constance Cary Harrison, from The Well-Bred Girl in Society *(1898) (p. 226)*

Letitia Baldrige, from Amy Vanderbilt's Everyday Etiquette *(1978) (p. 227)*

Ellen Fein and Sherrie Schneider, "Rule #20: Be Honest but Mysterious," from The Rules: Time-Tested Secrets for Capturing the Heart of Mr. Right *(1995) (p. 228)*

QUESTIONS

1. To come up with subtitles, students have to posit some kind of topical unity or coherent purpose for each excerpt. They are likely to have problems relating each excerpt's specifics to some more general issue or abstract idea. Word choice also poses problems, since students not only have to negotiate the gap between their terms and those of the writer but also have to decide which terms in the excerpt are key. You can address these problems—and get discussions going—by putting suggested subtitles on the board and evaluating their appropriateness. Here is one possible set of subtitles for the excerpts: The Art of Retaining Love, The Art of Delicate Conversation, The Art of Visible Innocence, and How to Be a Well-Mannered Date.

2. We think that excerpt four is most like our description of basic directive writing; that the purpose of excerpt two and the style of excerpt three make them least like basic directive writing; and that excerpt two's emphasis on abstract ideals makes it verge on being nondirective.

3. This question should provoke debate on what it means to "attend" to the reader. Although each writer attends to the reader, they do so in different ways. Capellanus, Harrison, and Fein and Schneider clearly imagine their readers as actual performers or actors; not so Gregory, who seems more concerned with his daughters' morale. Baldrige certainly informs her readers, but her step-by-step approach suggests a rather mechanical image of their possibilities.

4.   It might be better to focus on the Gregory, Harrison, and Fein and Schneider excerpts than those of Capellanus and Baldridge. The latter concern a mature love affair and a first date, respectively, which is a difficult comparison/contrast at best. Interestingly, both show some "courtliness" in the advice given to the male. For women, one of the important differences is the extent to which the woman is revealed as a free agent in Fein and Schneider—without the protective, smothering social context that we see in Gregory and Harrison.

5.   This question invites students to consider these excerpts as sociocultural documents that can tell us something about the history and structure of relations between the sexes, of class positions, and of producing a self.

■ PRACTICE 9.3   HOW TO CONDUCT YOURSELF (P. 230)

Although students often give each other advice in private, they may be uncomfortable about going public with what they know. You can ease their way into this assignment by asking them to help you imagine—and understand—what it's like to be a new student on campus. As the class constructs a general image of the newcomer, you'll want to encourage them to imagine specific situations that are likely to pose problems for that newcomer and to think about what the newcomer needs in order to deal with those situations. Would insider information help? What about a set of rules to follow? Is morale boosting important? If so, is sympathy likely to be more or less encouraging than humor or irony? Imagining a reader different from oneself or the teacher is crucial to the success of this assignment.

PERSUASION

First of all, we certainly do not wish to advocate lying, misrepresenting, deceiving, or any other form of unethical behavior, but no citizen can afford to be unaware of the workings of persuasion. This sort of discourse must be studied, and there is no way to understand it fully without using it in the game-like situations we have devised here. Good causes need persuasive presentation. Our legal system is based on an adversary structure, wherein different persuasive discourses contend for the opinions of judges and juries. We even persuade ourselves frequently against our better judgment. To hide from persuasion is to become the victim of it. By all means, make your ethical position clear to your students, and choose the assignments here that you find most congenial, but do not pass over this without giving the techniques of persuasion some attention. Since the days of Socrates and the Sophists, the moral issues involved in persuasive discourse have been argued. Certainly, today, many teachers will have some questions about the ethical propriety of teaching persuasive discourse. This being the case, we wanted to make our own position on these issues clear.

PERSUADING THROUGH ADVERTISING

■ READING

Fly-Tox Advertisement, 1926 (p. 231)

QUESTIONS

1. The picture of the living room and the text suggest an audience of middle- to upper-class families who live in (or desire to live in) "finely appointed homes." The reference to the Mellon Institute suggests that such an audience is educated enough to believe in progress through science. And, certainly, this is an audience who wants the best for their children.

2. The ad works on the anxieties of both the housewife and the parent. The standards are "good housekeeping" on the one hand and the prevention of suffering in little children on the other. The reader is encouraged to feel revulsion and hatred for insects and pride in a well-kept, "finely appointed" home.

3. The passage's descriptions of the fly and the mosquito are the most useful here. The "assassin" insect is contrasted with the "devoted" parent who proves devotion by paying for Fly-Tox. We learn nothing about the composition of the product. Can it really be so deadly and be as "harmless to humans" as it claims? Sizes and prices are the most accurately given information.

4. The main image shows a delicate child about to eat a fly-infected sandwich. The love of children and desire to protect them is the basis for this image. Another shows a well-appointed home, appealing to pride and/or envy. The determined woman is meant as a model for others. The product is shown so it may be recognized.

■ PRACTICE 9.4   THE GHASTLY RESORT HOTEL (P. 234)

The game here is to remain faithful to the denotative level while producing copy that connotes pleasure to the reader. Students really enjoy this assignment, even though they find the transformation of the twelve ghastly features very challenging. Working out the possibilities for one of the ghastly features in class is a good idea. For example, what about those barracudas? One student's solution was this: "You'll be astounded when you find yourself swimming amongst our beautiful and world-famous sea life! Some people have even gone out and fed these magnificent fish!"

You should also stress the organization of the twelve features. For example, one paragraph might be devoted to the features of the hotel; a second paragraph might describe waterfront activities; a third, nightlife; and so on. To aid in this organization, you should suggest that students have a specific audience in mind, such as honeymooners, adventure lovers, those who enjoy the unexpected, or those who appreciate unspoiled primitive cultures.

Alternative approach: If you have used this assignment before and are tired of reading about this hotel, have your students make up alternative ghastly places. They can work in groups, devising lists of unattractive features for restaurants, summer camps, colleges, and so on. The groups can then swap these lists and write up attractive copy. Each originating group can critique the papers of the group they've swapped with.

CHANGING THE PERSUASIVE PATTERN

■ READING

The Marlboro Man, 1954 (p. 235)

As this fifth edition of *Practice* was going to press, we discovered that, in general, publishers could no longer get permission from tobacco companies for the use of their advertising. We decided to keep this practice nonetheless. Students are certainly familiar with all those Marlboro cowboys, and they can be substituted. If you have a previous edition of *Practice*, you will find the original ad in the second, third, and fourth editions. Here's our reading of the Marlboro Man from the previous Instructor's Manual.

Though the intended appeal of this advertisement is pretty obvious, you should spend some time discussing it in class to make sure students see all of its "virile" qualities. Besides the anchor tattoo (military), note the butch haircut, the cigarette dangling out of the side of his mouth, the tank undershirt revealing muscles and hairy chest, the whistle (authority), the square jaw (tough), the slightly furrowed brow (serious), and the squint-eyed (penetrating, perhaps threatening) gaze.

■ PRACTICE 9.5 REACHING A DIFFERENT AUDIENCE (P. 236)

Encourage students to name some current products undergoing a "gender" change, such as male underwear (briefs and tank tops) transformed by Calvin Klein for trendy young women; cosmetics created for men; or whiskey being promoted in ads featuring women. Students may also recall the "urban cowboy" craze and the selling of boots and Stetsons to an urban audience. To get them started, ask your students how they might sell chewing tobacco to a New York stockbroker of either sex.

Students usually have no difficulty creating ads, but this assignment requires a special leap of imagination. If your students seem bereft of ideas, have them work in groups to come up with a product, an audience, and possible campaign strategies (this is how it's done on Madison Avenue). Each member of a group can submit an ad, and these can be exchanged and critiqued within each group.

GETTING A JOB

■ READING

The Job Letter and Résumé (p. 237)

■ PRACTICE 9.6 THE JOB LETTER AND RÉSUMÉ (P. 237)

As suggested in the text, students may want to furnish their own job descriptions or advertisements for this assignment. Your career-minded students will take this assignment very seriously and will probably do quite well with it. If your students are interested, you might consider bringing a personnel director into class to discuss what he or she looks for in a letter of application. If your school has a placement office, you might send some students over to find out what advice and information is available there.

10

Reasoning with Readers
Argumentation

Learning to argue well takes time and lots of practice. To get your students started, this introduction differentiates argument from both persuasion and outbursts of anger. In so doing, it also introduces three basic terms for discussing argument: *thesis, evidence,* and *reasons.* Establishing a shared vocabulary for analyzing and evaluating arguments is a must. If you prefer another vocabulary to ours, then now is the time to introduce it. For example, if you're planning to devote a substantial part of your course to argumentation, then you might want to use Stephen Toulmin's six terms (*argument, claims, evidence, warrant, backing,* and *qualification*) rather than our three. The point is to decide on a terminology and use it relatively consistently. We recommend that you assign one of this chapter's readings along with the introduction and that you use it to clarify and complicate our introductory remarks. Gould's essay, "Integrity and Mr. Rifkin," works well with our introduction, not only because it differentiates reasoned argument from propaganda but also because it discusses a number of logical fallacies.

WHAT'S THE ARGUMENT?

■ READING

QUESTIONS

1. Here are some sentences from each letter that suggest the writer's thesis.

    Anthony: "If you accept the theory [of innate differences, such as women = love; men = wisdom,] . . . you may give up all talk of a change for woman [par. 5]." The attraction and thus the differences between the sexes comes from "the *knowledge* of the *difference of sex* . . . . it is simply the answering of the highest and holiest function of the physical organism, that is that of reproduction [par. 8]."

    Margulis: "The urgency to mate persists in all people as in all other mammals because of the evolutionary drive to continue the species; the inborn imperative for genes to reproduce and hormonal differences that evolved over millions of years [par. 2] . . . . But since the great gender differences are of relative number, rather than fixed type, generalizations are dangerous and the overgeneralizations (women = love; men = wisdom) are wicked [par. 4]."

    Patterson: "Biblical directives to men and women are based upon their equality . . . . However, from the moment of creation, differences are evident in how men and women are to function in the world [par. 5] . . . . [F]or a woman who chooses to marry, happiness and productivity will come from willingly submitting herself to the servant leadership of her husband, thereby coming under his provision and protection, and willingly making herself available to conceive and nurture offspring if God so blesses [par. 7]."

    Pollitt: "How I wish you could see the way the women's movement you helped to start has transformed our society—for the better [par. 1]. . . . [But] women are still the second sex—on the receiving end of a great deal of sexual violence, discrimination and cultural misogyny [par. 4] . . . . [W]e are in the middle of a stalled revolution, in which women's demands for equality at work and home, for social respect have come up against some rather resistant features of American life, from the lack of reliable high-quality child care to men who don't do their fair share at home [par. 6]."

2. Each writer attempts to account for or describe the differences, and place those differences in some broader ideological context (religious, biological, political, social). Anthony suggests that it is our conditioned perceptions of sexual difference that drive the relations of the sexes, ultimately based on the physical need to reproduce. Margulis is more inclined to situate those differences in biology, but claims they "are of relative number, rather than fixed type" and thus defy "overgeneralizations." Patterson seems intent on establishing a divinely ordered equality between men and women in order to justify a divinely

ordered difference or inequality in the roles married men and women should play. And finally, Pollitt writes that "No one would deny that biological differences exist between the sexes, although it's not so easy to pin them down or explain why they matter [par. 5]."

3. This question should lead to some lively discussion. You may want your class to do some writing *before* they begin talking this over, so that strong feelings and opinions do not come to predominate over reasoned arguments.

4. Cohen's role as a journalist is to provide a context both for Stanton's letter and for the request made by the *New York Times* to Margulis, Patterson, and Pollitt to respond to her letter on the occasion on the 150th anniversary of the Seneca Falls Convention. It will be interesting for your students to try to "read" her stance on the issues behind the pose of journalistic objectivity.

■ PRACTICE 10.1   IDENTIFYING ISSUES AND POSITIONS (P. 254)

a. Before assigning this practice, it is probably a good idea to review the basic tenets of argumentation (from the introduction), to discuss what goes into a true summary (as opposed to an interpretative or evaluative summary), and to characterize Cohen's journalistic style of reporting. The challenge here will be for students to report on each of these positions without criticizing them.

b. This practice will allow students to express their thoughts and feelings rather than simply summarize someone else's. If your class has already done 10.1a, they will have a good grasp of each writer's arguments, and should be able to respond more effectively, whether they are for or against. You should emphasize that their response be in the form of a letter.

POWERFUL APPEALS

■ READING

Woodrow Wilson, "An Address to the Senate," July 10, 1919 (p. 256)

■ PRACTICE 10.2   BUT IS IT REASONABLE? (P. 263)

In creating the outline, you might want to work through the speech paragraph by paragraph, identifying topic sentences, words, or phrases that convey the main ideas. As you're doing this, ask your students to consider which type(s) of rhetorical appeal (ethical, emotional, or logical) are being made.

Of course as president of the United States, Wilson stood with considerable persuasive stature invested in his person, but he presents himself here quite modestly. Rather than drawing attention to his accomplishments, sacrifices, or character, he extols all three of those in the American soldier, presented as a representative type of the American people themselves. Wilson most directly appeals on an ethical basis when he suggests that the treaty is a moral imperative made indisputable by the sacrifices of so many Americans.

Wilson goes to considerable lengths to evoke emotions in his audience. Paragraph 3 sets the stage for the arrival of the American forces by emphasizing how desperate the Europeans were. Wilson evokes the "sombre foreboding of disaster" that prevailed, and the "vigour," "confidence," and "indomitable air" that accompanied the Americans. He then connects those qualities in paragraph 4 to the fact that they "were free men under arms, not forgetting their ideals of duty in the midst of tasks of violence." Paragraph 6 then establishes the duty the president felt in negotiating the treaty (and, by implication, the duty of the Senate to ratify it) to the soldier's battlefield "triumph of freedom and of right."

Your students will have a much harder time following the logic of Wilson's argument than his relatively straightforward emotional appeal. But if they've worked through the outline, they should be able to analyze Wilson's internationalist argument for the responsibilities of American power on the world stage. After students have completed their analyses and have cast their votes as Senators it might be interesting to discuss the ultimate outcome of the treaty (it was never ratified). Some additional historical research will bring to light the reasons the Senate refused to accept Wilson's arguments.

CLAIMS AND EVIDENCE

■ READING

Gregory Mantsios, from "Class in America: Myths and Realities"
(p. 264)

Students will have little difficulty understanding this piece, in part because of its myth versus reality structure. Using this structural opposition, you might begin discussion by asking how Mantsios gets from his list of myths to his first "reality." Of course, he gets there through numbers—and you should follow suit by asking the class to look closely at what numbers he uses and how he uses them. Note especially what he chooses to report in terms of percentages, in terms of proportions, and in terms of absolute numbers. For example, if the homeless figure were given as a percentage of the entire population, would it have the same rhetorical effect as the number "three million"? Similarly, if "the wealthiest 15 percent" were given as an absolute number, would it change our response to the fact that they hold "75 percent of the total household wealth"? The point of exploring such questions is not to indict Mantsios, nor is it to suggest that numbers lie. The point is to demonstrate that numbers don't speak for themselves; they must be coded in some way and thereby made meaningful. Mantsios makes choices from the available data; codes the choices he makes in various ways; and then makes a claim about reality. Furthermore, he has reasons—and we think they are good reasons—for making the connections he does not only between his claims and the numbers but also between his claims and his thesis that "class can predict chances for both survival and success."

QUESTIONS

1. Americans don't object to the term *middle class*, probably because, as Mantsios points out, it has become such a part of the political lexicon and is meant to cover a very broad constituency. One reason the attendant terms *upper class* and *lower class* aren't in the American lexicon is that such terms are usually associated with monarchies or other nondemocratic countries. Since most Americans believe that social position is largely determined by wealth rather than birth (except for the wealthy who consider themselves "wellborn"), we designate as our social categories the rich, the middle class, and the poor. These economically based terms contribute to the perpetuation of the myth of success being possible for one and all.

2. In paragraph 14, Mantsios sets out census material that shows how unequal the distribution of wealth is in the United States, with "the wealthiest 15 percent" holding "nearly 75 percent of the total household wealth," and another 15 percent living below poverty level. Such a sharp contrast makes it "difficult to argue we live in a classless society" (par. 15).

3. The "realities" Mantsios sets out (especially 1 and 2) use statistics to show how radical the economic differences are and how movement among classes tends to be downward, not upward. Statistics can be manipulated to some degree. Mantsios has drawn on a variety of statistical information (see his sources for reality 4, for example). Here, he has emphasized the problem of physical and mental health to highlight the basic problem of survival. He might have emphasized educational levels in various classes, or types of employment, or housing.

■ **PRACTICE 10.3   WHAT'S TRUE NOW? (P. 270)**

ARGUING ABOUT THE VALUE OF INEQUALITY

■ **READING**

George Will, "Healthy Inequality," from Newsweek, *October 28, 1996 (p. 272)*

QUESTIONS

1. Will expresses his thesis in paragraph 10, after he develops his historical-statistical argument: "Information technologies also are producing additional inequality, as those people who are talented at using information technologies reap rewards that are, in turn, incentives for other people to invest time and money in increasing their inventories of talents. Thus does society progress to higher levels of sophistication."

2. See what your students think of these two analogies. We think the comparison of economists to pastors is a bit of a stretch, while the analogy of information technology to the introduction of steam and electricity in the industrial revolution captures the sense of epochal change that underlies Will's argument.

3. Will seems to value progress, as he defines it, more than anything else, and cites temporary and/or necessary inequality in the pursuit of progress as its price. Will's argument is really a variation on Andrew Carnegie's "law of competition" (which he discusses in his essay "Wealth"). He values progress because it allows individuals to pursue their own self-interest and to maximize their opportunities for excellence.

■ **READING**

Isabel V. Sawhill, "Still the Land of Opportunity?" (from The Public Interest, *Spring 1999) (p. 275)*

QUESTIONS

1. Beginning in paragraph 7, Sawhill describes three different types of society, of which she claims the United States is a blend: a meritocracy, a "fortune-cookie society," and a "class-stratified" society. Thus, she suggests, individual talent and drive, luck, and family and class origins each describes a set of rules that govern how income is ultimately distributed.

2. Debates about income inequality, she argues in paragraph 5, always come down to how much inequality is necessary for maximum opportunity—an issue that is usually impossible to resolve.

3. Sawhill seems to accept the basic tenets of American society as a meritocracy, but would like to do more to improve the fairness of opportunity, especially in the area of education.

■ **PRACTICE 10.4   TAKING A POSITION (P. 281)**

Besides working through the questions following Will's and Sawhill's essays, it might be worth a few minutes in introducing this practice to go over the formal elements of argument and discuss how those writers organized their essays. Even if students decide to write a paper putting forth their own position, point out that they should use Will and Sawhill for support or counterargument. Of course, if they expand their research to the online sites that are mentioned, they may find additional materials to help them take a position on this issue.

ARGUING ABOUT SCHOOL CHOICE

■ **READING**

John E. Chubb and Terry M. Moe, "Choice Is *a Panacea" (1990) (p. 282)*

QUESTIONS

1. By "indirect control," Chubb and Moe mean that parents would gravitate toward the most effective schools, thus increasing their funding. Schools would be organized by the teaching and managing professionals in the schools themselves, not by bureaucratic educators imposing policies and procedures from outside and top down.

2. Let students work in small groups, perhaps assigning them specific clusters of paragraphs between 29 and 50; then create lists of the key elements of the pro-choice argument. From that list, students could write brief responses to one or two that provoke strong agreement or disagreement.

3. True reform, according to Chubb and Moe, requires dismantling the institutions of bureaucratic central control in order to foster changes

developed at the local level. Thus "public authority" is enlisted to create a system beyond bureaucratic control.

4. Of course, the greatest challenge is the one addressed in response to question 3: to expect those who now control schools (politicians, education bureaucrats, and union leaders) to willingly divest themselves of that power.

■ **READING**

Nancy Kanode, "Private School Vouchers: Bad for America" (p. 294)

Questions

1. Kanode argues that the school choice movement—promoted largely by educational reformers on the one hand and religious partisans on the other—"may, unwittingly, ruin our public educational system, create bigger chasms in race, religion, and caste, and most importantly, violate our Constitution" (par. 1). Here are her main points:

   1. "changing demographics rather than a declining educational system" are responsible for falling SAT scores (par. 4);

   2. parents and home environment have more to do with poor school performance and should be addressed directly through social services (par. 5);

   3. large numbers of private religious schools, especially in the South, rather than springing up out of widespread public dissatisfaction with public schools, actually originated out of racial disharmony and an attempt in the 1960s to avoid integration (par. 6);

   4. choice is illusory, since most (85%) of the private schools are religious in nature (pars. 7–8);

   5. choice is really choice for the private school administrators who will be able to discriminate and thus exclude large numbers of students, particularly underachieving students (par. 9);

   6. choice will lead to the re-segregation of American society, along not only racial but class and religious lines as well, and a corresponding decrease in diversity and appreciation for diverse points of view (pars. 9–10);

   7. taxpayers will in some cases be forced to subsidize the very schools that are excluding their children, leading to "a caste system" (par. 11); and "exclusivism" (par. 12);

8. the "educational voucher plan draws upon public funds to support religious education, a direct violation of our Constitution and most state constitutions" (par. 15);

9. schools will not necessarily be improved by competition alone; some improvements can only occur in large, centralized systems (par. 17);

10. negative comparisons of U.S. test results with other countries don't usually take into account the fact that those systems weed out vocational students, leaving better academically able students (par. 18);

11. there is no "double taxation" under the present system, since "private school tuition is not a tax" (par. 19).

2. Kanode suggests that competition alone does not guarantee better schools and that some improvements can only occur in large, centralized systems (par. 17).

3. Kanode seems to be arguing for a diverse, secular, and democratically controlled public school system that will continue the tradition of education espoused by John Dewey.

■ **PRACTICE 10.5   A POLICY MEMO (P. 303)**

The "policy memo" format of this assignment will allow your students to focus on the elements of their arguments in the most direct ways. The issues and contending constituencies have been defined, and the challenge will be to take a position, argue for it as effectively as possible, and then take into account the strong opposition (counterargument) to that position and address those concerns as well without alienating those voters. Both readings for this section provide a wealth of information and much more can be found online. Time permitting, you might want to plan a culminating activity in which the class organizes candidate debates among two or more students, each of whom is supported and coached by "policy teams."

Writing and Power: Two Projects

■ **READING**

Jane Shattuc, from "The 'Oprahfication' of America? Identity Politics and the Public Sphere Debate" (p. 305)

QUESTIONS

1. Students should approach this outline paragraph by paragraph, identifying claims and support, counterarguments and refutations.

2. Shattuc expresses her objections to the broad "generic or psychosociological" labeling of *Oprah* and shows like it in the last sentence of paragraph 19: "It is not understanding social identity but creating identification with the participants that is paramount for the narratives of commercial television."

3. Shattuc sounds as if she is an academic feminist cultural critic. See what your students think of her evenhandedness in her critique of *Oprah*.

■ **PROJECT 1: GETTING IT TOGETHER**

Ways of Appealing (p. 316)

The first of these projects will give your students a chance to consider Aristotle's ethical, emotional, and logical elements of appeal in contemporary materials or reportage. The second asks them to consider different ways that identity politics affects experience, which in turn can be used as the basis for writing. In their response to Shattuc, your students will also have to adopt one of those writer's points of view, not so much in terms of the style but in terms of the political stance.

■ **PROJECT 2: TAKING IT FURTHER**

Online Politics and Public Opinion (p. 317)

This project could be done collaboratively, with students in small groups, each investigating one or two Internet discussion forums or Web sites, and then reporting back to the group and sharing their analysis before writing their papers. If they do this project after working through the texts in this chapter and the first part of project 1, they could also begin to draw some conclusions about the three different media (text, TV, Internet) and the kinds of persuasive appeals that occur in each.

PART FIVE

Writing with Personality, Knowledge, and Power

The process of writing discussed here is worth treating at length. Most amateur writers do not revise enough and are unskilled at refining their topics and starting over. They seldom reconsider their data in the light of the thesis they are developing. This is a good place to stop and review the whole process with your class.

As you examine the directions for the practices with your students, you may wish to discuss the techniques of critical reading: how to take notes or how to underline, annotate, and otherwise mark up a text so as to facilitate retrieving information from it. Here your own experience as a serious reader of texts can be drawn upon for methods and examples. The point is to help students move from being passive consumers of texts to being active readers with a viewpoint of their own. They should not just be reading but reading for something, looking for confirmation or qualification of a tentative thesis about what they are reading. If you can get them to read this way, they will discover that they will remember their reading better and that it is more fun.

11

Putting It Together
Synthesis

PROJECT 1: HOW SHOULD PHOTOGRAPHS BE "READ"? (p. 322)

We think this is one of the strongest assignments—but we must caution you about it. It will work only if you can give it sufficient class time so that students begin thinking seriously about interpreting photographs. You may need from 3 to 5 class hours before they will be ready to write, and all the preliminary visual and verbal material should be discussed. We recommend that you work through the preliminary material up to "Three Photographs in Context," allowing students to read each piece and study each picture in class, with a discussion to follow their reading. The material on the three photographs by Doisneau, Parks, and Arnold can be studied at home—before class discussion—since it involves more reading than you may wish to do during class. We have given a lot of thought to the order in which we present this material. Reading through it in class and discussing one thing at a time is the best way to get the most out of our arrangement, and it will prepare students to write the best papers they can.

To start this exercise properly, get your students to jot down their readings of the picture the minute you draw their attention to it.

■ READING 1

Jean Mohr, "A Photo and Some Reactions," from Another Way of Telling *(p. 323)*

QUESTIONS

1. This is clearly a question for group discussion. It can be done either with the whole class or in small groups. Ideally, everyone's response

should be heard, and the group should select the most interesting response for further discussion.

2. One thing that should emerge from this discussion is that there are different ways of being "good," and that correctness and imagination both play their parts.

Allan Sekula, from "On the Invention of Photographic Meaning"
(p. 325)

This is a short selection, but it is vital to the success of this entire assignment. Sekula offers a basic polarity that will help students see more clearly the problem of reading photographs. As he indicates, this simple division is an oversimplification, but it is an excellent place to start thinking about how we react to photos.

Questions

1. The "own words" part of this is important. We suggest having all your students jot down their summaries before you start discussing the passage.

2. Sekula is talking abut two ways of seeing, or reading, photographs; but certain pictures, as we shall see, lend themselves more easily to one or the other way of seeing.

3. This is a very open-ended question. Your students may well have some very interesting things to say about photographs, and this is the place to let them express their ideas.

John Berger Reads a Photograph (from Another Way of Telling*)*
(p. 326)

We mean this to be a good example of reading, in that it pays a lot of attention to the detail of the picture, brings in historical background knowledge, and enters the lives of the people pictured through a process of imaginative sympathy. Both of the questions are designed to let students express themselves. You may find that they resent Berger's bringing his knowledge of history to bear on the picture. Many students seem to resent all knowledge of history these days. If they feel that way, let them express those feelings so that the whole class can examine them. (This could be the most important thing you do all year.) From our perspective, Berger combines Sekula's two approaches—and we think this is a good thing—but he clearly privileges the historical. In any case, class discussion should set up the reading of the next passage from Berger.

John Berger on the Use of Photography (from About Looking*) (p. 328)*

QUESTIONS

1. Berger certainly has a political agenda. He opposes the class structure of society because he believes that it is the cause of much human suffering. Neither you nor your students need endorse this view, but you should note it in discussing question 1 and paragraph 2. We suggest that you draw students' attention to paragraph 4, to explain why Berger felt it necessary to bring history into his earlier discussion of the Hungarian photograph.

2. Berger's private/public distinction is not the same as Sekula's document/symbol distinction, in our view. For him, the private photo is always connected to some personal history, but the public photo has a way of getting disconnected. Such disconnected photos can, of course, then be read—and probably will be read—in what Sekula would call a symbolic way. So Berger and Sekula can be connected, even though they are not saying exactly the same things.

■ READING 2   THREE PHOTOGRAPHS IN CONTEXT (P. 329)

Gisèle Freund on Doisneau's Photograph (from Photography and Society*) (p. 329)*

From an Interview with Robert Doisneau (in Dialogue with Photography*) (p. 330)*

From an Interview with Gordon Parks (in The Photographs of Gordon Parks*) (p. 333)*

Martin Bush on Gordon Parks (in The Photographs of Gordon Parks*) (p. 337)*

Eve Arnold on Her Work (from The Unretouched Woman*) (p. 338)*

From an Interview with Eve Arnold (in Master Photographers*) (p. 339)*

QUESTIONS

1. Doisneau's title may be considered documentary, if one reads the picture as a typical scene in a Parisian café. On the other hand, Parks's title, "American Gothic," has a political point to make, and is, as some students may realize, taken from Grant Woods's well-known painting of a white farmer with pitchfork and his wife standing in front of an American-gothic style farmhouse. Arnold's title is documentary.

2. Our first impression is that the Doisneau photo is more of a document than is the Parks photo, yet the Doisneau can be read as an "equivalent," or a symbolic picture for the reader's mind to develop. We should keep in mind Doisneau's belief that photography is a "subjective document." Parks's photo, in comparison with the other two, looks posed, as indeed it was, and the black woman, the broom, and the flag resonate symbolically. The "casual" quality of Dietrich's pose in Arnold's photo suggests photography as reportage, to use Sekula's words. Of course, the photo can be read as an expression of Arnold's desire to capture the "unretouched woman" at work.

3. Some students may really want this information, and others may resent it. If your class splits this way, try to use the occasion to explore why students feel one way or the other about interpretation. Is it because they have some personal tendency toward the symbolic or the historical? This should be an open-ended discussion.

4. There is no right answer to this question. The point is to get students to understand the sources of their preferences. Is it subject matter, style, personal associations—or something else?

5. The broadest of questions, this is really just a way of making sure that students are ready to begin the writing assignment. By now they should have some sense of the complex possibilities of reading photographs, and should see a real problem there, which requires some thought in order to produce a synthesis.

■ PRACTICE 11.1   WRITING ABOUT PHOTOGRAPHS (P. 343)

You may wish to discuss some of these photographs in class either before your students write their papers or while they are writing them, but neither you nor they should feel obliged to "cover" all of them. This collection is meant as a resource, not a chore. We have included some photos that are pretty clearly symbolic, others that are pretty clearly documents, and some that are mixed. In particular, we have tried to find pictures that will stimulate students' thinking and provide them with things to say. Following are a few comments about each photograph.

■ THREE MORE PHOTOGRAPHS BY DOISNEAU, PARKS, AND ARNOLD

Robert Doisneau, Sidelong Glance *(p. 344)*

This is certainly a provocative document of the male gaze homing in on the desired object. How one interprets the woman's gaze—does something capture her attention, or has she deliberately averted her eyes?—is worth consideration.

Gordon Parks, Muslim School Children *(p. 345)*

A document, but with symbolic weight, especially in the gaze of the smallest boy (in "manly" dress), looking so far up to the male authority figure.

Eve Arnold, A Literacy Teacher in Abu Dhabi *(p. 346)*

We may categorize this picture as photojournalism, showing us a teacher at work. But to Western eyes, the exotic dress and especially the mask carry great symbolic weight. A binary tension of concealing (the woman) and revealing (the teacher) is at work here.

■ THREE PICTURES FROM THE VIETNAM WAR PERIOD

Associated Press, A Paratrooper Works to Save the Life of a Buddy *(p. 347)*

This is reportage—a typical moment in battle—but the picture also makes a statement about the erasure of racial difference.

John Paul Filo, Student Killed by National Guardsmen, Kent State University, May 4, 1970 *(p. 348)*

The girl (she was just fourteen) is caught forever in her scream in a picture that became "an emblem of the . . . antiwar movement" (Vicki Goldberg, *The Power of Photography*). As reportage, the picture displays the contrast between the girl's discovery of death and the other spectators' sudden awareness (and unawareness) that the ammunition used by the National Guard against these student demonstrators was live.

Huynh Cong (Nick) Ut, Children Fleeing a Napalm Strike *(p. 349)*

Here reportage captures the pain and terror of burned children, the boy's face frozen into a timeless mask of tragedy, the naked girl in the center a screaming crucifix. The soldiers, fully uniformed and armed, walk behind them, seeming almost unconcerned. As Vicki Goldberg points out, this photograph spoke for the helpless suffering of the Vietnam War.

■ A PICTURE ALBUM

André Kertész, Elizabeth and I *(p. 350)*

This is closer to surrealism rather than to document, and invites students to speculate on the relationship between Elizabeth and I.

Dorothea Lange, Drought Refugees Hoping for Cotton Work *(p. 351)*

A document of the 1930s. The eyes are especially important in this one.

Unknown, As U.S. Seventh Army Troops Advance, a German Woman Surveys the Wreckage of Her Home in Bensheim, Germany (p. 352)

Students may make any number of observations on this photograph: the power of the young, armed soldier and the powerlessness of the old woman; the devastation of war; the mixed emotions that attended the liberation of Europe.

Abbey Rowe, A Birthday Party for David Eisenhower, Grandson of President Eisenhower. In Attendance Were Movie and Television Stars Roy Rogers and Dale Evans (p. 353)

In an era often identified with complacency, this photograph is almost a set piece (and a highly staged one at that) of an adult view of a happy childhood (but was it really?). Note the Wild West motif in the toys on the table, and the presence of those icons of the happy West, Roy Rogers and Dale Evans. And see if you can spot the lone Indian with drawn bow among all the cowboys.

Garry Winogrand, World's Fair, New York City (p. 354)

Here we see three animated conversations on one park bench. The dynamic energy of these conversationalists, seen compositionally along a slight diagonal, is mirrored above in the pedestrians walking the fairgrounds in the distant background.

Automatic Reconnaissance Camera, Mirage Jet (p. 355)

While this photo exemplifies truly objective photography, it is certainly a highly expressive picture of technology terrifying humankind. Or as *Life* magazine put it: "The shadow is like that of a hawk over a barnyard. An Israeli Mirage flashes over Egyptian soldiers lying in the desert during the Six-Day War."

W. Eugene Smith, Tomoko in the Bath *(p. 356)*

This is a historical document that figured in a legal case against the company whose pollution of the waters where Tomoko's people fished caused the mercury poisoning that led to her deformed birth—and other such births. But it is also in the iconographic tradition of the Pietà, of Mary holding the body of her crucified son. Tomoko is a daughter not a son, of course, but the picture symbolizes a mother's love and sorrow for all children hurt by the world. It is a powerful example of how a photograph can be a document and a symbol at the same time.

Charles Martin, Window Dressing *(p. 357)*

A (postmodern?) cultural document of complexity and expressiveness. Who's inside and who's outside? Who's the reflector and who's the reflected?

Dayna Smith, Woman Comforted by Relatives and Friends at Husband's Funeral, *Izbica, Kosovo (p. 358)*

The poignancy of this woman's grief is palpable as are the hands holding and reaching to comfort her. What do the expressions of the two women behind her suggest?

PROJECT 2: THE AMERICAN FRONTIER AND AMERICAN CULTURE (p. 359)

■ READING 1

Frederick Jackson Turner, from "The Significance of the Frontier in American History" (p. 359)

QUESTIONS

1. The last two sentences of paragraph 1 articulate Turner's overall thesis. In paragraph 2, he begins to make his case that "a recurrence of the process of evolution in each western area" that was developed created a return "to primitive conditions on a continually advancing frontier." The resulting effects on "social development . . . furnish the forces dominating American character."

2. Turner argues that rather than view the frontier in terms of the clashes of European colonial powers with each other and Native Americans, we should focus more attention on the challenges the Europeans faced in settling the frontiers as they advanced west. Beginning in paragraph 6, Turner sketches the history of that advancing frontier and its effect on the formation of American character and institutions.

3. Turner argues that in the unique struggle that was the confrontation with the wilderness, the European settler was transformed into an American. We may infer that the qualities needed to survive on the outskirts of civilization—especially individualism, self-reliance, and independence—are at the core of the American character, as Turner generalizes it from his thesis.

4. You may want to remind your students of the difference between a true summary and an evaluative or interpretive summary here. In this case, a true summary is called for, one which accurately reflects Turner's thesis and the development of his ideas.

■ READING 2

Richard Slotkin, "Buffalo Bill's Wild West" (from Gunfighter Nation: The Myth of the Frontier in Twentieth-Century America*) (p. 364)*

QUESTIONS

1. Both Turner and Buffalo Bill Cody had an essentially mythic view of the past. Turner applied the logic of the academic historian to de-

scribe the line of evolution, as he saw it, from one epoch to another. Cody had a showman's flair for designing spectacles, loosely based on historical events, whose power was derived from authenticating details (costumes, even actual participants) engaged in a fictive and accessible narrative. See what similarities and differences your students find.

2. After they trace Buffalo Bill's "construction of himself as a hero," your class should have some fun thinking of contemporary counterparts. Arnold Schwarzenegger might come to mind as a person whose early life as a bodybuilder was a blend of real athleticism and showmanship (as Mr. Universe). He then parlayed that experience into his very successful career as an action-movie star and real-estate businessman. See if your students can think of other "self-invented" celebrities who have achieved iconic cultural status. Madonna?

3. This question, like all of those requiring summaries, demands a careful rereading of Slotkin's account, and an accurate presentation of Buffalo Bill's version of the frontier.

■ READING 3

Edward L. Wheeler, from Deadwood Dick, the Prince of the Road; or, The Black Rider of the Black Hills *(p. 375)*

QUESTIONS

1. Try breaking up your class into small groups, with each group deciding on a recorder. Then have the groups come up with lists of characteristics from these two chapters. Once the lists are created, they can relate some of those characteristics to present-day popular characters. When the small groups compare notes, it will be interesting to see if any contemporary characters are agreed upon.

2. Perhaps one lesson is that frontier justice is swift and decisive and relies on individuals for its execution. On the other hand, there's a suggestion at the end of chapter 3 that Harry Redburn has been goaded by Ned Harris into taking on much more than he bargained for.

■ READING 4

Stephen Crane, "The Blue Hotel" (p. 386)

QUESTIONS

1. From paragraph 4 through paragraph 98, the Swede is obsessed with fear. In paragraph 90, the Easterner explains that the Swede's fear is

probably inspired by "reading dime novels." Beginning in paragraph 98, when he enters the room "laughing bravely," the Swede's actions are characterized by an exaggerated and false bravado. With just these few observations, your class should be able to consider Crane's story as a "study in fear."

2. Crane strives throughout "The Blue Hotel" to debunk the stereotypes of the western dime novel, and his characterization of the gambler and his middle-class home life are consistent with that effort. Note paragraph 126 in chapter 3 of "Deadwood Dick" for Wheeler's description of the gambler.

3. The Swede, having found his false courage, "insist[s] on another game of High-Five" (par. 120) and then accuses Johnnie of cheating (par. 122), culminating in a free-for-all (par. 124). The Swede insists he saw the cheating; the Easterner (who later admits he also saw the cheating [par. 265]) tries to calm things down (par. 130) but to no avail.

4. Crane suggests that the misperceptions and expectations fostered by Western novels lead to wildly inappropriate behavior based on such fictive models. The West, as Crane sees it, is a very different place—a real place, and not the hackneyed theater of Wild West shows.

■ READING 5

Patricia Nelson Limerick, "Travels in Frontierland" (p. 411)

QUESTIONS

1. Of course the Internet is sometimes imagined as a new frontier, as is genetic engineering and biomedical technology in general. Space, especially deep space, is still often figured as an unexplored frontier.

2. See what your students think of Frontierland, especially those who have experienced it firsthand. You might want to connect this Disney exhibit and the Wild West show to the whole subject of docudramas and their entertainment versus educational value. Do movies like *JFK* or *The Patriot* attain higher poetic truths as they manipulate and distort historical facts or are they created for commercial purposes, to attract and entertain as large an audience as possible? Are these two purposes strictly exclusive?

■ PRACTICE 11.2   THE FRONTIER AS AMERICAN MYTHOLOGY (P. 417)

PROJECT 3: VIRTUAL RELATIONSHIPS (P. 418)

■ **READING 1   A COLLECTION OF QUOTATIONS ON ONLINE COMMUNICATIONS AND RELATIONS (P. 418)**

Howard Rheingold, from The Virtual Community *(p. 418)*

Sven Birkerts, from The Gutenberg Elegies *(p. 419)*

Deborah Tannen, from "The Gender Gap in Cyberspace" (p. 419)

Charles Moran, "Notes Towards a Rhetoric of E-Mail" (p. 420)

Michael Spooner and Kathleen Yancy, "Postings on a Genre of E-Mail" (p. 420)

Laurie Anderson, from "Dazed and Bemused" (p. 421)

Steven Johnson, from Interface Culture *(p. 421)*

QUESTIONS

1. This, of course, is a very open and general question to get a discussion going.

2. Rheingold notes that we usually find friends from among those who share our values and interests, and since the Internet organizes communities along just those lines, it facilitates locating like-minded people. Anderson seemed to be operating under the same assumption, but found that her interlocutor with a common interest in music and sand was only four years old.

3. Birkerts argues that although online communication appears to offer connections, it cannot deliver the embrace we all long for—to be "known and valued not abstractly but in presence" (par. 3). Tannen seems to argue to the contrary that physical presence inhibits real communication and that many people, especially men, can express their feelings more completely through the screen of cyberspace.

4. Again, this is a personal experience and value question that should invoke some interesting discussion. There is no right or wrong answer here; let multiple viewpoints flourish.

5. Your students, most of whom will probably be somewhat if not very familiar with e-mail, might want to brainstorm on the statement "E-mail style is conversational," then go back to Spooner and Yancy and Johnson and compare what they've said to those writers.

■ **READING 2**

Sherry Turkle, from Life on the Screen: Identity in the Age of the Internet *(1995) (p. 422)*

QUESTIONS

1. Turkle describes the computer in paragraph 2 as a tool, a mirror, and a looking glass. With these images in mind, students can begin to think about how they most often use and think about the computer.

2. This question should open up the larger issue of whether the Internet is a qualitatively different medium from print or video or face-to-face experience, or whether that purported uniqueness is part of its growth and commercialization.

3. Turkle goes on in paragraph 4 to talk about the fluid possibilities and "fundamental shifts in the way we create and experience human identity," and in paragraph 7 she connects "multiple identities" to "postmodern times." This is one area where students may be quite open to theorizing their own experience or hearing you do so.

4. You might want to remind your students of the practice of focused freewriting and then let them go. If you have access to a computer lab, perhaps they could send their freewriting to you or each other as e-mails.

■ **READING 3**

John Suler, from "E-Mail Communications and Relationships," in The Psychology of Cyperspace *(p. 426)*

QUESTIONS

1. Suler makes an interesting point when he reminds us that few people have moved to accessorize their telephone conversations with video, apparently preferring only the auditory communication. E-mail, as a purely textual medium for the most part, affords a reflective filter that is unavailable in auditory, visual, or face-to-face encounters. See what your students think.

2. "TextTalk," "No Face-to-Face Cues," and "Adjustable Conversing Speed" all seem quite essential to the intimacy of online relationships, as does "Anonymity" for many people. Your students will probably have their own experience to draw on in determining which of these is the most important.

3. Suler points out that e-mail is largely favored by those who either like to write or are at least minimally competent at it. Different

expressive styles and different levels of ability can impede effective communication and the development of online relationships.

4. E-mail relationships become more real when the participants reveal more and more of their "ACTUAL identity [, which] is taken as a sign of intimacy and commitment," (par. 16) and eventually move "OUT of cyberspace and into the face-to-face encounter" (par. 19).

■ READING 4

Meghan Daum, "Virtual Love" (The New Yorker, Aug. 25/Sept. 1, 1997) (p. 432)

QUESTIONS

1. With the exception of the relatively early phone call, their relationship develops from hesitant, online overtures to full-blown all-night online sessions. As Suler predicts, Daum and Pete eventually decide to test their apparent virtual intimacy with face-to-face meetings, but their relationship never survives the real world.

2. Daum seems a little defensive at first, wearing her urban irony and wit as a mask of sophistication (par. 6) to protect her from her own deep desire ("I wanted unfettered affection, soul-mating, true romance" [par. 16]). See what your students think of her as she relates her encounters with Pete, both real and virtual.

3. In paragraph 12, Daum admits that she finds e-mail "more authentic than much of what I experienced in the daylight realm of living beings," because she and Pete are able to let down their guards.

4. This is a purely speculative question, so see what your students make of it. Might her correspondence, like her face-to-face meetings with Pete, have been at odds with her idealized e-mail with PFSlider?

■ READING 5

Sylvia Brownrigg, from The Metaphysical Touch *(p. 441)*

QUESTIONS

1. This question will give your students a chance to practice a kind of textual criticism, using Suler's framework to "read" Sylvia's character through her e-mail style. Sylvia seems literate, witty, and quick to elaborate and extend a line of thought with Hamlet and to identify with him (par. 9).

2. Hamlet seems self-deprecating but also anxious to pick up on Sylvia's threads and weave them into impressive ripostes.

3. We have all been children, of course, and conveying our experiences from that phase of our life (or relating to fictional accounts of childhood) provides a context for sharing certain intimacies. Children are also relatively "safe" ways to signal romantic interest and suitability, as well as attitudes toward commitment.

4. At every point when either Sylvia or Hamlet tests the other about continuing a thread ("I don't want to pry" [par. 22]; "Yours clearly fishing for more curiosity on your part but not wanting to assume you want to hear the whole damn thing" [par. 23]), each jumps at the chance to hear and say more ("No, no, pry away" [par. 23]; "OK, I'm biting, I'm biting" [par. 24]). Chances are good they will continue to deepen their exchanges and reveal more and more of their actual identities, perhaps eventually moving to a face-to-face or off-line relationship. Is any relationship, real or virtual, "likely to last for a long time?" Who knows? Beyond guessing, try to get your students to give sound textual reasons to support whatever position they take.

▪ PRACTICE 11.3   THE VALUE OF VIRTUAL RELATIONSHIPS (P. 446)

This is a topic about which many students are likely to have strong opinions and extensive experience, so it's important for you to stress that they are not being asked to argue for or against virtual relationships. You might ask them to review their writings on reflection and analysis. Beyond that, feel free to structure this project with additional research—either interviews, online transcripts, or both—which will most likely deepen both the students' reflections and their analyses.